ELEMENTS OF

Writing

REVISED EDITION

Third Course

James L. Kinneavy

John E. Warriner

HOLT, RINEHART AND **WINSTON**
Harcourt Brace & Company

Austin • New York • Orlando • Atlanta • San Francisco
Boston • Dallas • Toronto • London

Critical Readers

Grateful acknowledgment is made to the following critical readers who reviewed pre-publication materials for this book:

John Algeo
University of Georgia
Athens, Georgia

Anthony Buckley
East Texas State
    University
Commerce, Texas

David England
Louisiana State
    University
Baton Rouge, Louisiana

Elaine A. Espindle
Peabody Veterans Memorial
    High School
Peabody, Massachusetts

Eileen T. Lundy
The University of Texas
    at San Antonio
San Antonio, Texas

Mary McFarland-McPherson
Chicago Public Schools
Chicago, Illinois

Jamye Merritt
Stratford High School
Nashville, Tennessee

Linda E. Sanders
Jenks High School
Tulsa, Oklahoma

Phillip Sipiora
University of
    South Florida
Tampa, Florida

Staff Credits

Associate Director: Mescal K. Evler
Executive Editors: Kristine E. Marshall, Robert R. Hoyt
Editorial Staff: Managing Editor, Steve Welch; *Editors,* Cheryl Christian, A. Maria Hong, Kathryn Rogers Johnson, Karen Kolar, Christy McBride, Laura Cottam Sajbel, Patricia Saunders, Michael L. Smith, Amy Strong, Suzanne Thompson, Katie Vignery; *Copyeditors,* Michael Neibergall, Copyediting Supervisor; Katherine E. Hoyt; Carrie Laing Pickett; Joseph S. Schofield IV; Barbara Sutherland; *Editorial Coordinators,* Amanda F. Beard, Senior Editorial Coordinator; Rebecca Bennett; Susan Grafton Alexander; Wendy Langabeer; Marie Hoffman Price; *Support,* Ruth Hooker, Senior Word Processor; Christina Barnes; Kelly Keeley; Margaret Sanchez; Raquel Sosa; Pat Stover
Permissions: Catherine J. Paré, Janet Harrington
Production: Pre-press, Beth Prevelige, Simira Davis; *Manufacturing,* Michael Roche
Design: Dick Metzger, Art Director; Lori Male, Designer
Photo Research: Peggy Cooper, Photo Research Manager; Karen Grandfield, Kristine Hook, Sam Dudgeon, Victoria Smith, Photo Research Team

James L. Kinneavy, the Jane and Roland Blumberg Centennial Professor of English at The University of Texas at Austin, directed the development and writing of the composition strand in the program. He is the author of *A Theory of Discourse* and coauthor of *Writing in the Liberal Arts Tradition.* Professor Kinneavy is a leader in the field of rhetoric and composition and a respected educator whose teaching experience spans all levels—elementary, secondary, and college. He has continually been concerned with teaching writing to high school students.

John E. Warriner developed the organizational structure for the Handbook of Grammar, Usage, and Mechanics in the book. He coauthored the *English Workshop* series, was general editor of the *Composition: Models and Exercises* series, and editor of *Short Stories: Characters in Conflict.* He taught English for thirty-two years in junior and senior high school and college.

Writers and Editors

Ellen Ashdown has a Ph.D. in English from the University of Florida. She has taught composition and literature at the college level. She is a professional writer of educational materials and has published articles and reviews on education and art.

Norbert Elliot has a Ph.D. in English from the University of Tennessee. A director of the writing program at New Jersey Institute of Technology, he is a specialist in test development and writing assessment.

Phyllis Goldenberg has an A.B. in English from the University of Chicago. She has been a writer and editor of educational materials in literature, grammar, composition, and critical thinking for over thirty-five years.

Alice M. Sohn has a Ph.D. in English Education from Florida State University. She has taught English in middle school, secondary school, and college. She has been a writer and editor of educational materials in language arts for seventeen years.

Patricia Street was an honors major in English Expression at Brown University. A professional writer for thirty years and a writer/editor of educational materials in language arts for ten years, she is currently compiling a reference book for writers.

Glenda A. Zumwalt has an Ed.D. in Teaching Composition and Rhetoric from East Texas State University. She teaches composition at Southeastern Oklahoma State University. She is a writer of educational materials in composition and literature.

Acknowledgments

We wish to thank the following teachers who participated in field testing of pre-publication materials for this series:

Susan Almand-Myers
Meadow Park
   Intermediate School
Beaverton, Oregon

Theresa L. Bagwell
Naylor Middle School
Tucson, Arizona

Ruth Bird
Freeport High School
Sarver, Pennsylvania

Joan M. Brooks
Central Junior High
   School
Guymon, Oklahoma

Candice C. Bush
J. D. Smith Junior High
   School
N. Las Vegas, Nevada

Mary Jane Childs
Moore West Junior High
   School
Oklahoma City,
   Oklahoma

Brian Christensen
Valley High School
West Des Moines, Iowa

Lenise Christopher
Western High School
Las Vegas, Nevada

Mary Ann Crawford
Ruskin Senior High
   School
Kansas City, Missouri

Linda Dancy
Greenwood Lakes
   Middle School
Lake Mary, Florida

Elaine A. Espindle
Peabody Veterans
   Memorial High School
Peabody, Massachusetts

Joan Justice
North Middle School
O'Fallon, Missouri

Beverly Kahwaty
Pueblo High School
Tucson, Arizona

Lamont Leon
Van Buren Junior High
   School
Tampa, Florida

Susan Lusch
Fort Zumwalt South High
   School
St. Peters, Missouri

Michele K. Lyall
Rhodes Junior High
   School
Mesa, Arizona

Belinda Manard
McKinley Senior High
   School
Canton, Ohio

Nathan Masterson
Peabody Veterans
   Memorial High School
Peabody, Massachusetts

Marianne Mayer
Swope Middle School
Reno, Nevada

Penne Parker
Greenwood Lakes Middle
   School
Lake Mary, Florida

Amy Ribble
Gretna Junior-Senior High
   School
Gretna, Nebraska

Kathleen R. St. Clair
Western High School
Las Vegas, Nevada

Carla Sankovich
Billinghurst Middle
   School
Reno, Nevada

Sheila Shaffer
Cholla Middle School
Phoenix, Arizona

Joann Smith
Lehman Junior High
   School
Canton, Ohio

Margie Stevens
Raytown Middle School
Raytown, Missouri

Mary Webster
Central Junior High
   School
Guymon, Oklahoma

Susan M. Yentz
Oviedo High School
Oviedo, Florida

We wish to thank the following teachers who contributed student papers for the revised edition of *Elements of Writing, Third Course.*

Patricia Attri
Bret Harte Junior High
   School
Oakland, California

Naomi Dominguez-Peyton
Hallandale High School
Hallandale, Florida

Lorraine Dyson
Don Lugo High School
Chino, California

Contents in Brief

PART ONE
WRITING

INTRODUCTION TO WRITING   *Hidden Agents* 2

WRITING HANDBOOK
1 Writing and Thinking 14
2 Understanding Paragraph Structure 62
3 Understanding Composition Structure 104

AIMS FOR WRITING
4 Expressive Writing: Narration 132
5 Using Description 166
6 Creative Writing: Narration 202
7 Writing to Inform: Exposition 248
8 Writing to Persuade 284
9 Writing About Literature: Exposition 322
10 Writing a Research Paper: Exposition 362

LANGUAGE AND STYLE
11 Writing Complete Sentences 406
12 Writing Effective Sentences 421
13 English: Origins and Uses 441

PART TWO
HANDBOOK

GRAMMAR
14 The Parts of Speech 464
15 The Parts of a Sentence 500
16 The Phrase 531
17 The Clause 562

USAGE
18 Agreement 587
19 Using Verbs Correctly 616
20 Using Pronouns Correctly 648
21 Using Modifiers Correctly 673
22 A Glossary of Usage 695

MECHANICS
23 Capital Letters 717
24 End Marks and Commas 739
25 Semicolons and Colons 768
26 Italics and Quotation Marks 787
27 Apostrophes 805
28 Hyphens, Dashes, Parentheses 824
29 Spelling 836

30 Correcting Common Errors 864

PART THREE
RESOURCES

31 Speaking 896
32 Listening and Viewing 908
33 The Library/Media Center 918
34 The Dictionary 925
35 Vocabulary 929
36 Letters and Forms 937
37 Reading, Studying, and Test Taking 946

Table of Contents

PART ONE **WRITING**

Hidden Agents

An Introduction to Writing by James L. Kinneavy 2

WRITING HANDBOOK

CHAPTER 1 WRITING AND THINKING 14

Reading About One Writer's Process 16

from *Report—From part one*
Gwendolyn Brooks

Aim—the "Why" of Writing 20

Process—the "How" of Writing 20

PREWRITING 22
Finding Ideas for Writing 22
Considering Purpose and Audience 36
Critical Thinking Analyzing Your Audience 38
Arranging Ideas 40
Critical Thinking Arranging Information 40
   Using Charts 43

WRITING A FIRST DRAFT 45
Critical Thinking Synthesizing Ideas 46

EVALUATING AND REVISING 49
   Evaluating 49
   Revising 51

PROOFREADING AND PUBLISHING 56
Critical Thinking Reflecting on Your Writing 58

MAKING CONNECTIONS 61
   DESKTOP PUBLISHING

▶ CHAPTER **2** **UNDERSTANDING PARAGRAPH STRUCTURE** 62

Reading a Model of Paragraph Variety 64
from *Barrio Boy*
Ernesto Galarza

What Makes a Paragraph 68
The Main Idea 68
The Topic Sentence 69
Supporting Sentences 71
  Sensory Details 71
  Facts and Statistics 72
  Examples 73
The Clincher Sentence 75
Unity 76
Coherence 79
  Order of Ideas 79
  Connections Between Ideas 83
Strategies of Development 89
  Description 90
  Narration 91
  Classification 94
  Evaluation 97

MAKING CONNECTIONS 99
  WRITING PARAGRAPHS FOR
    DIFFERENT PURPOSES 99
  Writing a Paragraph to
    Express Yourself 99
  Writing a Paragraph to
    Inform 100
  Writing a Paragraph to
    Persuade 101
  Writing a Paragraph
    That Is Creative 102

▶ CHAPTER **3** **UNDERSTANDING COMPOSITION STRUCTURE** 104

Reading a Model of Composition Form 106
"Left Face"
Vincent Bozzi

What Makes a Composition 110

The Thesis Statement 111
Hints for Writing and Using a Thesis Statement 111
Early Plans and Formal Outlines 115
The Early Plan 115
The Formal Outline 116
A Writer's Model 117
The Introduction 120
Techniques for Writing Introductions 120
The Body 124
Unity 124
Coherence 124
The Conclusion 126
Techniques for Writing Conclusions 126

MAKING CONNECTIONS 130
Writing an Informative Essay

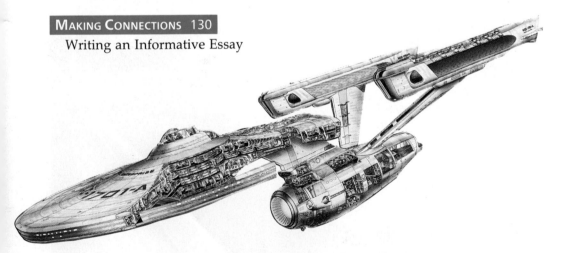

Starship Enterprise, David Kimble (1986). Star Trek © 1996 Paramount Pictures. All rights reserved.

▶ CHAPTER 4   EXPRESSIVE WRITING: NARRATION   132

Reading a Model of Expressive Writing   134

from *The Blue Jay's Dance*
"Skunk Dreams," Louise Erdrich

Writing a Personal Narrative   139

PREWRITING   139
Choosing a Topic   139
Critical Thinking   Evaluating Topics for Your Personal Narrative   141
Thinking About Purpose, Audience, and Tone   143
Usage Hint   Using Personal Pronouns   144
Gathering and Organizing Details   145
    Gathering Details   145
    Organizing Details   149
    Reflecting on the Meaning of the Experience   150

WRITING YOUR FIRST DRAFT   151
    The Structure of a Personal Narrative   151
    The Basic Elements of a Personal Narrative   151
    A Newspaper Article   152
    "Tale of the Rodent," Roger Starr
    A Simple Framework for a Personal Narrative   154
    A Writer's Model   154

EVALUATING AND REVISING   157

PROOFREADING AND PUBLISHING   159
    A Student Model   160
    "A New Beginning," Jahtzael Ochoa

WRITING WORKSHOP   161
    JOURNALS   Writing a Personal Journal Entry

MAKING CONNECTIONS   163
    NARRATIVES ACROSS THE CURRICULUM
    History • from "The Woods Were Tossing
    With Jewels," Marie St. John   163
    NARRATIVES IN LITERATURE   Poetry   165
    "The Runaway," Robert Frost

Reading a Model of Description 168
from *An American Childhood*
"Streetcars on Penn Avenue," Annie Dillard

Describing a Mechanism 172

PREWRITING 172
Finding a Focus 172
  Choosing a Mechanism to Describe 172
  Identifying Your Purpose 173
  Thinking About Audience and Tone 173
Planning Your Description 177
  Using Two Types of Descriptive
    Details 177
  Using Comparisons 179
  Collecting Descriptive Details 179
  Organizing Details 182
Critical Thinking Evaluating Details 183
  Using Graphics 185

WRITING YOUR FIRST DRAFT 186
  The Basic Elements of Objective Description 186
  An Article in a Book 186
  "Light Bulb," Michael Folsom and Marcia Folsom
  A Writer's Model 188

EVALUATING AND REVISING 191
Grammar Hint Using Precise Words 191

PROOFREADING AND PUBLISHING 194
  A Student Model 195
  "The Bicycle," Alfredo Anica

WRITING WORKSHOP 196
  SUBJECTIVE DESCRIPTION • from *An American Childhood*, Annie Dillard
  • Writing a Subjective Description

MAKING CONNECTIONS 199
  DESCRIPTION AND MASS MEDIA Writing a Classified Ad 199
  CREATIVE WRITING Free Verse • "Without Title," Diane Glancy 200

CHAPTER 6 CREATIVE WRITING: NARRATION 202

Reading a Short Story 204
"The Happy Man's Shirt"
Italo Calvino

Writing a Short Story 209

PREWRITING 209
Thinking of Story Ideas 209
Planning Your Story 211
Thinking About Purpose, Audience, and Tone 211
Choosing a Point of View 213
Thinking About Characters and Setting 215
Developing the Plot 217
Creating a Story Map 218

WRITING YOUR FIRST DRAFT 220
The Basic Elements of Stories 220
Looking at a Short Story 221
A Short Story 222
"The Six Rows of Pompons," Toshio Mori
A Basic Framework for a Short Story 229
A Writer's Model 230

EVALUATING AND REVISING 233
Critical Thinking Evaluating Dialogue 235

PROOFREADING AND PUBLISHING 239
Mechanics Hint Punctuating Dialogue 239
A Student Model 241
from "Spearhead Days," Abigail Smigel

WRITING WORKSHOP 242
A NEWS STORY • "Flood Is Called Right Tonic for Grand Canyon,"
The New York Times • Writing a News Story

MAKING CONNECTIONS 245
A HUMOROUS SKIT 245
A BIOGRAPHICAL SKETCH 246

CHAPTER 7 WRITING TO INFORM: EXPOSITION 248

Reading a Model of a "How-to" Explanation 250
from "The Lobster-Quadrille"
Lewis Carroll

Writing a Process Paper 255

PREWRITING 255
Choosing a "How-to" Process
to Explain 255
Thinking About Purpose, Audience,
and Tone 258
Gathering Your Information 260
Critical Thinking Arranging Details 261

WRITING YOUR FIRST DRAFT 264
The Basic Elements of "How-to"
Process Papers 264
A Magazine Article 264
"How to Shoot Your Own Video,"
David Hajdu
A Basic Framework for a "How-to"
Process Paper 270
A Writer's Model 270

EVALUATING AND REVISING 273
Grammar Hint Using Varied Sentences 274

PROOFREADING AND PUBLISHING 276
A Student Model 277
"How to Turn Trash into Cash," Chris McDowell

WRITING WORKSHOP 278
THE CAUSE-AND-EFFECT ESSAY • from "The Secret World of Pandas,"
Byron Preiss and Gao Xueyu • Writing a Cause-and-Effect Essay

MAKING CONNECTIONS 281
WRITING ACROSS THE CURRICULUM Science 281
SPEAKING AND LISTENING The "How-to" Video 282

CHAPTER 8 WRITING TO PERSUADE 284

Reading a Model of Persuasion 286
from *The Piano Lesson*
August Wilson

Writing a Persuasive Essay 291
PREWRITING 291
Choosing a Topic 291
Thinking About Purpose, Audience, and Tone 295
Supporting Your Opinion 297
    Logical Appeals 297
    Emotional Appeals 298
Critical Thinking Evaluating Your Reasoning 299

WRITING YOUR FIRST DRAFT 303
    The Basic Elements of Persuasive Essays 303
    A Magazine Editorial 304
    "Calling Arthur Murray," E. M. Swift
    A Simple Framework for a Persuasive Essay 306
    A Writer's Model 307

EVALUATING AND REVISING 310
Usage Hint Using Active Voice 313

PROOFREADING AND PUBLISHING 314
    A Student Model 315
    from "Discipline by Suspension," Sara Schille

WRITING WORKSHOP 316
    A LETTER TO THE EDITOR

MAKING CONNECTIONS 318
    SPEAKING AND LISTENING Advertising
    and Persuasion 318
    PERSUASION ACROSS THE CURRICULUM
    Social Studies 320
    A Speech Before Congress 321
    "A Great American Symbol," Richard Durbin

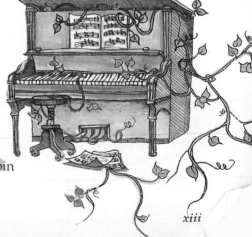

CHAPTER 9 WRITING ABOUT LITERATURE: EXPOSITION 322

Reading a Critical Review 324
"Dark Side of the Moon"
Owen Gleiberman

Writing a Literary Analysis 330

Reading and Responding to Stories 330
Responding to Stories 330
A Short Story 330
"A Man Who Had No Eyes," MacKinlay Kantor
Understanding the Basic Elements of Stories 334
Critical Thinking Analyzing a Short Story 336

PREWRITING 338
Structuring Your Literary Analysis 338
Developing Your Literary Analysis 340
Reading Stories Closely 340
Choosing Story Elements for Analysis 342
Identifying Your Main Idea 342
Thinking About Audience, Purpose, and Tone 343
Collecting and Organizing Details 344

WRITING YOUR FIRST DRAFT 346
A Writer's Model 346
A Simple Framework for a Literary Analysis 348

EVALUATING AND REVISING 350

PROOFREADING AND PUBLISHING 353
Mechanics Hint Using Quotation Marks 353
A Student Model 355
"Studies in Contrast," Yolanda Doss

WRITING WORKSHOP 356
A DEFINITION Writing a Definition

MAKING CONNECTIONS 359
WRITING ACROSS THE CURRICULUM Creative Writing 359
INFORMING THROUGH EVALUATION Writing a Review • "Stand
and Deliver," Roger Ebert 359

► CHAPTER 10 WRITING A RESEARCH PAPER: EXPOSITION 362

Reading a Model of Reporting 364
from "The Cold Facts About Human Survival," Richard Wolkomir

Writing a Research Paper 369

PREWRITING 369
Finding a Topic for Your Report 369
  Identifying a General Subject for Your Research 369
  Limiting Your Subject to a Specific Topic 370
  Selecting a Suitable Topic 371
  Thinking About Purpose, Audience, and Tone 372
  Developing Research Questions 374
Finding and Evaluating Sources of Information 376
  Locating Sources of Information 376
  Evaluating Sources of Information 377
  Preparing Source Cards 378
Mechanics Hint Punctuating Titles 381
Planning, Recording, and Organizing Information 383
  Preparing an Early Plan 383
  Taking Notes 383
  Preparing an Outline 386

WRITING YOUR FIRST DRAFT 388
  Combining the Basic Elements of a Report 388
Critical Thinking Synthesizing Ideas and Information **388**
  Giving Credit to Your Sources 390
  A Writer's Model 392

EVALUATING AND REVISING 397

PROOFREADING AND PUBLISHING 400
  A Student Model from "The Mysteries of the Anasazi," Emily Courtney

WRITING WORKSHOP 402
  THE I-SEARCH REPORT Writing an I-Search Paper

MAKING CONNECTIONS 404
  INFORMING THROUGH EVALUATION Writing a Book Report **404**
  SPEAKING AND LISTENING Research and Nonprint Media **405**

CHAPTER 11 WRITING COMPLETE SENTENCES   406

Sentence Fragments 406

Phrase Fragments 409
  Verbal Phrases 409
  Appositive Phrases 410
  Prepositional Phrases 410
Subordinate Clause Fragments 411

Run-on Sentences 415

Revising Run-on Sentences 416

> MAKING CONNECTIONS 419
>
> SENTENCES IN POETRY 419
> "The Time We Climbed Snake Mountain,"
> Leslie Marmon Silko

CHAPTER 12 WRITING EFFECTIVE SENTENCES   421

Combining Sentences 421

Inserting Words 422
Inserting Groups of Words 424
  Prepositional Phrases 424
  Participial Phrases 424
  Appositive Phrases 425
Using Compound Subjects and Verbs 426
Usage Hint Checking for Subject-Verb Agreement 427
Creating a Compound Sentence 428
Creating a Complex Sentence 430
  Adjective Clauses 430
  Adverb Clauses 430
  Noun Clauses 430

Improving Sentence Style 432

Using Parallel Structure 432
Revising Stringy Sentences 433
Revising Wordy Sentences 435
Varying Sentence Beginnings 436

MAKING CONNECTIONS 440

SENTENCE CRAFT 440
from "Marigolds,"
Eugenia W. Collier

▶ CHAPTER **13** ENGLISH: ORIGINS AND USES   441

From Yesterday to Tomorrow 441

The Beginnings of English 442
Old English 443
Middle English 443
The Birth of Modern English 444
  London Sets the Standard 444
  English Travels Abroad 445
American English 446
English: The Twentieth Century and Beyond 447
  Vocabulary Growth 447
  World Use 447

The Varieties of English 448

Dialects of American English 448
  Regional Dialects 448
  Ethnic Dialects 449
Standard American English 449
Standard English—Formal to Informal 451
Uses of Informal English 452
  Colloquialisms 452
Looking at Language Where Do Colloquialisms Come From? **453**
  Slang 453

Worlds of Meaning 455

Idioms 455
Jargon 456
Denotation and Connotation 456
Loaded Words 457
Euphemisms 458
Tired Words 459
Clichés 460

MAKING CONNECTIONS 461
  WRITE AN ADVERTISEMENT 461

PART TWO **HANDBOOK**

▶ CHAPTER **14** **THE PARTS OF SPEECH** 464

The Work That Words Do

DIAGNOSTIC TEST Identifying Parts of Speech 464

The Noun 465
Common and Proper Nouns 465
Concrete and Abstract Nouns 466
Compound Nouns 467

The Pronoun 469
Antecedents 469
Personal Pronouns 470
Other Commonly Used Pronouns 471

The Adjective 472
Pronoun or Adjective? 473
Nouns Used as Adjectives 473
Articles 474
Adjectives in Sentences 474
Writing Application Using Adjectives to Make Your Writing Exact 476

The Verb 477
Action Verbs 477
Transitive and Intransitive Verbs 478
Picture This 479
Linking Verbs 480
Verb Phrases 482

The Adverb 485
Adverbs Modifying Verbs 485
Adverbs Modifying Adjectives 486
Adverbs Modifying Other Adverbs 488
Forms of Adverbs 488

The Preposition 491

The Conjunction 493

The Interjection 495

Determining Parts of Speech 496

Review 498

POSTTEST 1 Identifying Parts of Speech **498**

POSTTEST 2 Writing Sentences Using the Same Words as Different Parts of Speech **498**

SUMMARY OF PARTS OF SPEECH 499

▶ CHAPTER 15 THE PARTS OF A SENTENCE 500

Subject, Predicate, Complement

DIAGNOSTIC TEST A. Identifying the Parts of Sentences 500
B. Identifying and Punctuating the Kinds of Sentences 501

The Sentence 501

Subject and Predicate 502
The Simple Subject 504
The Simple Predicate 505
Finding the Subject 508
Sentences That Ask Questions 510
Sentences Beginning with *There* 511
Picture This 512
The Understood Subject 513
Compound Subjects 514
Compound Verbs 515

Complements 517
The Subject Complement 519
Writing Application Using Linking Verbs to Express Sensory Details 521
Objects 522

Classifying Sentences by Purpose 527

Review 529

POSTTEST 1   A. Identifying the Parts of a Sentence **529**
              B. Identifying and Punctuating the Kinds of Sentences **530**

POSTTEST 2   Writing Sentences **530**

CHAPTER **16** THE PHRASE **531**

Prepositional, Verbal, and Appositive Phrases

DIAGNOSTIC TEST   A. Identifying and Classifying Prepositional Phrases **531**
                  B. Identifying Verbals and Appositives **532**

Prepositional Phrases 533
The Adjective Phrase 535
The Adverb Phrase 537
Writing Application Using Prepositional
   Phrases to Add Detail to Your Writing 540

Verbals and Verbal Phrases 541
The Participle 541
The Participial Phrase 544
The Gerund 546
The Gerund Phrase 548
The Infinitive 550
The Infinitive Phrase 551
The Infinitive with *to* Omitted 552
Picture This 555

Appositives and Appositive Phrases 556

Review 559

POSTTEST 1   A. Identifying and Classifying
                 Prepositional Phrases **559**
             B. Identifying Verbals and Appositives **560**

POSTTEST 2   Writing Sentences with Phrases **561**

CHAPTER 17 THE CLAUSE 562

Independent and Subordinate Clauses

DIAGNOSTIC TEST A. Identifying and Classifying Clauses 562
                B. Identifying and Classifying Subordinate Clauses 563
                C. Classifying Sentences According to Structure 564

Kinds of Clauses 564

Uses of Subordinate Clauses 567
The Adjective Clause 567
Relative Pronouns 567
The Adverb Clause 570
Subordinating Conjunctions 571
Picture This 574
The Noun Clause 574

Sentences Classified According to Structure 577
Writing Application Using a Variety of Sentence Structures in Writing 580

Review 584

POSTTEST 1 A. Identifying and Classifying Subordinate Clauses 584
            B. Classifying Sentences According to Structure 585
POSTTEST 2 Writing a Variety of Sentence Structures 586

► CHAPTER **18** **AGREEMENT**   587

Subject and Verb, Pronoun and Antecedent

DIAGNOSTIC TEST A. Correcting Errors in Subject-Verb and
   Pronoun-Antecedent Agreement **587**
B. Identifying and Correcting Errors in Subject-Verb
   and Pronoun-Antecedent Agreement **588**

Number 589

Agreement of Subject and Verb 590
Writing Application Using Correct Subject-Verb Agreement 596
The Compound Subject 597
Other Problems in Agreement 602

Agreement of Pronoun and Antecedent 608
Picture This 611

Review 613

POSTTEST A. Proofreading Sentences for Subject-Verb and
   Pronoun-Antecedent Agreement **613**
B. Proofreading a Paragraph for Subject-Verb and
   Pronoun-Antecedent Agreement **614**

► CHAPTER **19** **USING VERBS CORRECTLY**   616

Principal Parts, Tense, Voice

DIAGNOSTIC TEST A. Using the Past and Past Participle Forms of Irregular
   Verbs **616**
B. Revising Verb Tense or Voice **617**
C. Identifying Errors in the Use of *Lie* and *Lay*, *Sit* and *Set*, and
   Rise and *Raise* **617**

The Principal Parts of Verbs 618
Regular Verbs 618
Irregular Verbs 620

Tense 629
Consistency of Tense 631
Writing Application Using Verb Tense to Make Instructions Clear **631**

Active and Passive Voice 633
Using the Passive Voice 635
Picture This 637

Special Problems with Verbs 637
Lie and *Lay* 637
Sit and *Set* 639
Rise and *Raise* 641

Review 646

POSTTEST Proofreading Paragraphs for Correct Verb Forms **646**

► CHAPTER **20** USING PRONOUNS CORRECTLY   648

Nominative and Objective Uses

DIAGNOSTIC TEST A. Identifying Correct Forms of Pronouns **648**
B. Proofreading a Paragraph for Correct Pronoun Forms **649**

Case 649
The Case Forms of Personal Pronouns 650
The Nominative Case 651
The Objective Case 654

Special Pronoun Problems 662
Who and *Whom* 662
Picture This 664
The Pronoun in an Incomplete Construction 668
Inexact Pronoun Reference 669

Review 671

POSTTEST A. Correcting Pronoun Forms **671**
B Proofreading a Paragraph for Correct Pronoun Forms **672**

CHAPTER 21 USING MODIFIERS CORRECTLY 673

Comparison and Placement

DIAGNOSTIC TEST A. Correcting Forms of Modifiers 673
               B. Correcting Dangling and Misplaced Modifiers 674

Comparison of Modifiers 675
Regular Comparison 675
Irregular Comparison 677
Use of Comparative and Superlative Forms 680
Writing Application Using Comparative and Superlative Forms
  of Modifiers 684

Dangling Modifiers 686
Correcting Dangling Modifiers 687

Misplaced Modifiers 689
Misplaced Clause Modifiers 690

Review 693

POSTTEST A. Revising Sentences by Correcting Modifiers 693
         B. Using Modifiers Correctly in a Paragraph 694

▶ **CHAPTER 22** **A GLOSSARY OF USAGE** 695

Common Usage Problems

DIAGNOSTIC TEST A. Solving Common Usage Problems **695**
B. Proofreading a Paragraph for Standard Usage **696**
Picture This **707**

The Double Negative 711
Writing Application Using Formal Standard English in a Business Letter **713**

Review 716
POSTTEST Revising a Passage by Correcting Errors in Standard Usage **716**

▶ **CHAPTER 23** **CAPITAL LETTERS** 717

The Rules for Capitalization

DIAGNOSTIC TEST A. Correcting Sentences by Capitalizing Words **717**
B. Proofreading a Paragraph for Correct Capitalization **718**
Picture This **724**
Writing Application Using Capital Letters Correctly **734**

Review 735
POSTTEST A. Correcting Sentences That Contain Errors in Capitalization **735**
B. Correcting Capitalization Errors in a Paragraph **736**

▶ **CHAPTER 24 PUNCTUATION**   739

End Marks and Commas

DIAGNOSTIC TEST A. Correcting Sentences by Adding End Marks and
                     Commas **739**
                 B. Proofreading a Paragraph for End Marks and
                     Commas **740**

End Marks 741
Picture This 745

Commas 745
Writing Application · Using Commas to Give Clear Directions **765**

Review 766

POSTTEST Correcting Sentences by Adding End Marks and Commas **766**

▶ **CHAPTER 25 PUNCTUATION**   768

Semicolons and Colons

DIAGNOSTIC TEST A. Correcting Sentences by Using Semicolons and
                     Colons **768**
                 B. Proofreading for Correct Use of Semicolons and
                     Colons **769**

Semicolons 770

Colons 779
Writing Application Using Colons in a Business Letter **782**

Review 784

POSTTEST A. Correcting Sentences by Adding Semicolons and Colons **784**
          B. Proofreading a Letter for Correct Use of Semicolons and
              Colons **785**

Italics and Quotation Marks

DIAGNOSTIC TEST A. Correcting Sentences by Adding Underlining (Italics) and Quotation Marks **787**

B. Punctuating Dialogue by Adding Quotation Marks **788**

Italics 789
Picture This 791

Quotation Marks 792
Writing Application Using Quotation Marks in a Dialogue **796**

Review 802

POSTTEST A. Correcting Sentences by Adding Underlining (Italics) and Quotation Marks **802**

B. Correcting Paragraphs of Dialogue by Adding Underlining (Italics) and Quotation Marks **803**

► **CHAPTER 27 PUNCTUATION** 805

Apostrophes

DIAGNOSTIC TEST A. Correcting Sentences by Using Apostrophes
Correctly **805**
B. Proofreading a Paragraph for Correct Use of
Apostrophes **806**

Possessive Case 807
Writing Application Using Apostrophes to Make Nouns Possessive **815**
Picture This 817

Contractions 818

Plurals 820

Review 822

POSTTEST Revising Sentences in a Letter by Using Apostrophes Correctly **822**

► **CHAPTER 28 PUNCTUATION** 824

Hyphens, Dashes, Parentheses

DIAGNOSTIC TEST A. Using Hyphens, Dashes, and Parentheses Correctly **824**
B. Adding Hyphens, Dashes, and Parentheses **825**

Hyphens 826

Dashes 829

Parentheses 831
Picture This 833

Review 834

POSTTEST A. Identifying Appropriate Uses of Hyphens, Dashes, and
Parentheses **834**
B. Using Hyphens, Dashes, and Parentheses **835**

▶ CHAPTER **29** **S**PELLING   836

Improving Your Spelling

Good Spelling Habits 836

Spelling Rules 839
  ie and *ei* 839
  –cede, *–ceed*, and *–sede* 839
Adding Prefixes 840
Adding Suffixes 840
  Doubling Final Consonants 843
Forming Plurals of Nouns 844
  Compound Nouns 846
  Latin and Greek Loan Words 847
  Numerals, Letters, Symbols, and Words Used as Words 847
Spelling Numbers 849

Words Often Confused 850
  75 Commonly Misspelled Words 860
  300 Spelling Words 861

▶ CHAPTER **30** **C**ORRECTING **C**OMMON **E**RRORS   864

Key Language Skills Review

Grammar and Usage 865
Grammar and Usage Test: Section 1 878
Grammar and Usage Test: Section 2 880

Mechanics 882
Mechanics Test: Section 1 890
Mechanics Test: Section 2 892

PART THREE RESOURCES

▶ **CHAPTER 31 SPEAKING**   896

Skills and Strategies
The Communication Cycle 896
Nonverbal Communication 897

Speaking Informally 897
Impromptu Speaking 897
Communicating Effectively 898
Speaking on the Telephone • Giving Instructions or
Directions • Making Social Introductions

Speaking Formally 898
Preparing a Speech 898
Selecting a Topic 899
Analyzing Your Audience 899
Organizing Speech Notes and Materials 900
Speaking Expressively 900
Giving Your Speech 901
Special Types of Formal Speaking Situations 901
Making Announcements 901
Making an Introduction to a Presentation 902

Group Discussions 902
Establishing a Purpose 902
Assigning Roles for a Discussion 902
Using Parliamentary Procedure 903

Oral Interpretation 904
Adapting Material 904
Presenting an Oral Interpretation 904

Review 905

Strategies for Listening and Viewing

Listening with a Purpose 908

Listening for Information 909
Listening for Details 909
Listening to Instructions 909
Listening and Responding 909
Using the LQ2R Method 910
Conducting an Interview 910

Critical Listening 911
Taking Lecture Notes 912
   Paraphrasing • Summarizing

Advertising and Mass Media 913

Critical Viewing 914
The Sights and Sounds of TV 915
   Setting • Dialogue and Sound Effects
Television Versus Reality 916

Review 916

▶ **CHAPTER 33 THE LIBRARY/MEDIA CENTER** 918

Finding and Using Information

Classifying and Arranging Information 918
Online Catalog and Card Catalog 919

Using Reference Materials 921
The *Readers' Guide* 921
Special Information Sources 921
Electronic Information Sources 922
Reference Sources 923

Review 924

▶ **CHAPTER 34 THE DICTIONARY** 925

Types and Contents

Types of Dictionaries 925
A Sample Entry 926

Review 927

▶ CHAPTER 35 VOCABULARY 929

Learning and Using New Words
Add to Your Word Bank 929

Using Context Clues 930
Determining Meanings from the General Context 931
Choosing the Right Word 931

Using Word Parts 931
Roots 932
Prefixes 933
Suffixes 934

Review 935

▶ CHAPTER 36 LETTERS AND FORMS 937

Style and Contents
The Appearance of a Business Letter 937

Writing Business Letters 938
The Parts of a Business Letter 938
Types of Business Letters 940
   Request or Order Letters • Complaint or Adjustment Letters
   • Appreciation or Commendation Letters

Writing Informal or Personal Letters 942
   Thank-you Letters • Invitations • Letters of Regret

Addressing an Envelope 943

Completing Printed Forms 943

Review 944

► CHAPTER 37 **READING, STUDYING, AND TEST TAKING**   946

Using Skills and Strategies

Planning a Study Routine 946

Strengthening Reading and Study Skills 947
Reading and Understanding 947
Writing to Learn 947
  Using Word-Processing Tools for Writing 948
  Using the SQ3R Reading Method 949
Interpreting and Analyzing What You Read 950
  Stated Main Idea • Implied Main Idea
  Reading to Find Relationships Among Details 950
  Reading Passage and Sample Analysis 951
Applying Reasoning Skills to Your Reading 952
Reading Graphics and Illustrations 953
Applying Study and Reading Strategies 955
   Taking Notes • Classifying • Organizing Information Visually • Outlining
   • Paraphrasing • Summarizing • Memorizing

Improving Test-Taking Skills 962
Preparing for Different Kinds of Tests 962
Objective Tests 963
   Taking Different Kinds of Objective Tests 964
   Multiple-Choice Questions • True/False Questions • Matching Questions
   • Reasoning or Logic Questions • Analogy Questions • Short-Answer
   Questions
Essay Tests 970
   Taking Essay Tests 970

Review 973

APPENDIX: DIAGRAMING SENTENCES 978

GLOSSARY OF TERMS 994

GLOSSARY 1005

INDEX 1011

ACKNOWLEDGMENTS 1036

PHOTO CREDITS 1040

ILLUSTRATION CREDITS 1042

Fiction

Ron Arias, "El Mago"
Toni Cade Bambara, "Raymond's Run"
Pearl S. Buck, "The Old Demon"
Italo Calvino, "The Happy Man's Shirt"
Lewis Carroll, "The Lobster-Quadrille," *Alice's Adventures in Wonderland*
Walter Van Tilburg Clark, "The Portable Phonograph"
Eugenia W. Collier, "Marigolds"
Robert Cormier, "The Moustache"
Roald Dahl, "Poison"
Daphne du Maurier, "The Birds"
Ernesto Galarza, *Barrio Boy*
MacKinlay Kantor, "A Man Who Had No Eyes"
Andrea Lee, "Mother"
Ursula K. Le Guin, *Always Coming Home*
Sinclair Lewis, *Babbitt*
Jack London, "To Build a Fire"
Anne McCaffrey, *Nerilka's Story*
Toshio Mori, "The Six Rows of Pompons"
Helen Norris, "The Singing Well"
Edwin Way Teale, "The Death of a Tree"

Nonfiction

Muriel Beadle, *The Cat: History, Biology, and Behavior*
Jane Bosveld, "Apocalypse, How?" *Omni*
Vincent Bozzi, "Left Face," *Omni*
Gwendolyn Brooks, *Report—From part one*
Daniel Cohen, *The Encyclopedia of Monsters*, "The Victims," *Masters of Horror*
Richard Corliss, "Saints in the Neighborhood," *Time*
"Dialogue on Film: Bill Moyers," *American Film*
Annie Dillard, "Living Like Weasels";
    "Streetcars on Penn Avenue," *An American Childhood; The Writing Life*
Marjory Stoneman Douglas, *The Everglades: River of Grass*
Richard Durbin, "A Great American Symbol," *Harper's Magazine*
Gerald Durrell, *How to Shoot an Amateur Naturalist*
Roger Ebert, "Stand and Deliver," *Roger Ebert's Movie Home Companion, 1990 Edition*
Paul and Anne Ehrlich, *Extinction*
Ralph Ellison, *Writers at Work*
Christine El Mahdy, *Mummies, Myth and Magic*
Cesare Emiliani, L. B. Knight, and Mark Handwerker, "Cold and Warm Fronts," *Earth Science*
Louise Erdrich, "Skunk Dreams," *The Blue Jay's Dance*
Kai Erikson, *Everything in Its Path*
David Feldman, *Imponderables*

Jack Fincher, "I felt freedom in my bones," *Smithsonian*
"Flood Is Called Right Tonic for Grand Canyon," *The New York Times*
Michael Folsom and Marcia Folsom, *The Macmillan Book of How Things Work*
Ian Frazier, "Canal Street," *The New Yorker*
Owen Gleiberman, "Dark Side of the Moon," *Entertainment Weekly*
Tom Gliatto, "Sense and Sensibility," *People Weekly*
Bob Greene, *Rebound*
"Guiltless Snacks," *The Saturday Evening Post*
David Hajdu, "How to Shoot Your Own Video," *Seventeen*
Jesse Kornbluth, *Airborne Again!*
David Macaulay, *The Way Things Work*
Scott Martin, "Are Road Bikes Dead?" *Bicycling*
Peter Flagg Maxson, "Mushrooming Meters," *Austin American-Statesman*
Annetta Miller, "Work and What It's Worth," *Newsweek*
Martina Navratilova with George Vecsey, *Martina*
Charles Panati, *Panati's Browser's Book of Beginnings*
Byron Preiss and Gao Xueyu, "The Secret World of Pandas," *Life*
Marie St. John, "The Woods Were Tossing With Jewels," *American Heritage*
Roger Starr, "Tale of the Rodent," *The New York Times*
Donald and Lillian Stokes, *The Bird Feeder Book*
E. M. Swift, "Calling Arthur Murray," *Sports Illustrated*
Geoffrey C. Ward, with Ken Burns and Ric Burns, *The Civil War: An Illustrated History*
Lawrence R. White, "Camera," *The World Book Multimedia Encyclopedia™*
Richard Wolkomir, "The Cold Facts About Human Survival," *National Wildlife Magazine*
Howard Wornom, "For Goodness Sake?" *Omni*
William Zinsser, "Trust Your Material," *On Writing Well*

Poetry

Robert Frost, "The Runaway"
Diane Glancy, "Without Title"
Pat Mora, "Bribe"
Dorothy Parker, "One Perfect Rose"
Leslie Marmon Silko, "The Time We Climbed Snake Mountain"
William Stafford, "fifteen"

Drama

August Wilson, *The Piano Lesson*

PART ONE

ADMIT ONE

253002

253002

INDIANA TICKET

WRITING

Introduction to Writing
Hidden Agents

Writing Handbook
1 Writing and Thinking
2 Understanding Paragraph Structure
3 Understanding Composition Structure

Aims for Writing
4 Expressive Writing: Narration
5 Using Description
6 Creative Writing: Narration
7 Writing to Inform: Exposition
8 Writing to Persuade
9 Writing About Literature: Exposition
10 Writing a Research Paper: Exposition

Language and Style
11 Writing Complete Sentences
12 Writing Effective Sentences
13 English: Origins and Uses

HIDDEN AGENTS

James L. Kinneavy

Imagine a planet that has **hidden agents** who are able to keep all enemy airplanes on the ground during a war. These same hidden agents can block touchdown passes in football games, build smart cars that make decisions for their drivers, and sway vast numbers of voters in an election. They can even make 110 million people laugh at the same time.

This strange planet is not imaginary at all. It is our earth. Hidden agents are everywhere on earth, and they have tremendous power.

Do you know who these hidden agents are? Do you know what their power is?

Who Are These Agents?

The agents are the writers, planners, and communicators who deal with the world's complicated problems. They're the power behind the scenes in war and politics, football games and automobile manufacturing, space exploration, business, science, and the arts.

You may know the names of the winning generals and the star quarterbacks, but you probably can't name the hidden agents who planned the troop movements or drew the game plays. You may know the names of the space shuttle astronauts and the winners of the Indianapolis 500 for the past ten years. But you probably don't know who designs the Indy cars or the space shuttle's computer systems. If asked, you probably couldn't say who writes the scripts of your favorite sitcoms or the million-dollar-a-minute ads for the Super Bowl. But their writing is part of your life.

Not all these agents are hidden. Some are public figures, visible in politics, industry, and entertainment. You can name many of them and identify exactly what they do. They're the people giving the speeches, directing the latest blockbuster movies, and hosting the late-night talk shows.

Hidden or visible, writers, planners, and communicators are powerful agents who help shape our complicated civilization.

What Is Their Power?

Whether they're behind the scenes or out in front, all writers and planners have one thing in common: the power of communication. When *writers* communicate, they have something to say (a *subject*), someone to say it to (an *audience*), and a way to say it (a *language*). You can think of these elements as a communication triangle with language—both written and spoken—at its very center.

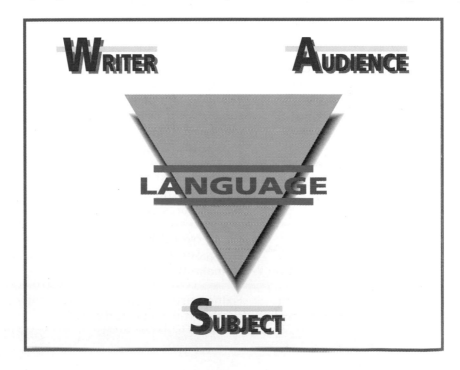

How Do They Communicate?

The Writing Process

The power of communication comes from being able to convey ideas well. Writers do this with words. Good writers know that there is a general process they can use to develop their ideas and communicate them clearly in written language. It's called the *writing process.* Not all writers go through this process in exactly the same way, but they usually work through a series of stages or steps.

Prewriting	Thinking and planning; choosing a subject, purpose, and audience; collecting ideas and details; making a plan for presenting ideas and details
Writing	Writing a first draft—putting ideas into sentences and paragraphs; following a plan for presenting ideas
Evaluating and Revising	Going over the draft to decide what works and what doesn't; making changes to make the draft better
Proofreading and Publishing	Fixing mistakes; making a final copy and sharing it with an audience

Why Do They Communicate?

The Aims of Writing

Writers always have a reason for dealing with words. They have an *aim,* a purpose, something they want to accomplish. All writing has one of these four basic aims or some combination of them: to inform, to persuade, to express oneself, to be creative.

To Inform	Some writers want to give facts and other kinds of information or explain something to their readers.
To Persuade	Sometimes writers want to persuade other people to change their minds about something or to act in a certain way.
To Express Themselves	Sometimes writers simply want to express their own feelings and thoughts.
To Be Creative	Some writers create stories, poems, songs, and plays.

Next you'll read four different models—one to illustrate each aim. All four models, each by a different writer, have the same topic—a motorcycle accident. As you read, think about how differently each writer handles the topic.

INFORMATIVE WRITING

Accident victim disappears

The victim of an apparently serious motorcycle accident near the Seventeenth Street Bridge rode off on his motorcycle yesterday before help could be summoned, according to John Horn, who was at the scene of the accident.

Horn, a sophomore at Marshall High School, was walking south of the bridge at 4:00 P.M. yesterday when he discovered a motorcycle lying on its side with the engine running. Nearby he found a man who appeared to be just regaining consciousness. Horn said that he thought the victim was in his mid-twenties. He had black hair and green eyes

and was not wearing a protective helmet.

"I think he must have flipped over the bridge rail," Horn said.

Horn described the man as very pale and said that he had blood on one of his hands. Horn helped the victim walk to his motorcycle. The victim thanked him, got on his cycle, and rode away. Police are concerned that the man may have suffered a serious head injury, but no one fitting his description has been treated recently at the local hospital.

READER'S RESPONSE

1. Does this article answer all your questions about the accident? What else would you like to know?
2. Does the article give only facts about the accident, or does it give the writer's opinions and feelings about the accident? Explain.

I keep thinking about finding that guy at the bridge yesterday. I guess I really should say findin... the motorcycle because the truth... the mos...

I keep thinking about finding that guy at the bridge yesterday. I guess I really should say finding the motorcycle because the truth is the motorcycle was the most important thing to me.

There it was—just lying on its side, still running. I wanted to get on it and ride away. I didn't even think at first about how somebody might be hurt. Or even wonder how it got there. I just thought of it as a kind of gift—as if by magic someone had put it there for me to find. For a little while I really felt that I could ride away and it would be mine. It was a terrific feeling! I guess that's why it took me longer than it should have to remember the machine belonged to somebody.

I found the guy in the grass. He looked terrible—like he'd been unconscious and was just coming to. I helped him get up and walk to his motorcycle. He thanked me, said I was a good man or something. And then he rode off.

I wonder if maybe he'd hurt his head. He wasn't wearing a helmet and he sure looked weird. I guess I'll never know.

READER'S RESPONSE

1. Who is the "I" in this journal entry? Is the entry mostly about the motorcycle accident or about the writer's thoughts and feelings?
2. Suppose you'd found the motorcycle. How would you have felt? What do you think you would have done?

PERSUASIVE WRITING

Dear Editor:

The events surrounding the motorcycle accident near the Seventeenth Street Bridge last week serve to point out the importance of enforcing this state's helmet law.

All motorcyclists and passengers are required to wear helmets that meet federal D.O.T. (Department of Transportation) standards. Cyclists without helmets can be ticketed by police for a traffic violation.

In last week's accident, the cyclist was indeed very lucky. Statistics show that serious, permanent injury and even death are more than four times greater when motorcyclists are not wearing helmets.

If you own or ride a motorcycle, we urge you to buy a helmet that meets the D.O.T. standards and wear it whenever you ride. Only you can protect your own life.

We also urge the police to strictly enforce this state's helmet law. If more tickets are handed out, perhaps there will be fewer serious injuries and deaths.

Sincerely yours,

Helen Kwong

Helen Kwong, Chair
Safety First Committee

READER'S RESPONSE

1. Would you ride a motorcycle without wearing a helmet? Why or why not?
2. Did this letter convince you or change your mind? If it did, what reasons or facts persuaded you?

CREATIVE WRITING

fifteen

by William Stafford

South of the Bridge on Seventeenth
I found back of the willows one summer
day a motorcycle with engine running
as it lay on its side, ticking over
slowly in the high grass. I was fifteen.

I admired all that pulsing gleam, the
shiny flanks, the demure headlights
fringed where it lay; I led it gently
to the road and stood with that
companion, ready and friendly. I was fifteen.

We could find the end of a road, meet
the sky out on Seventeenth. I thought about
hills, and patting the handle got back a
confident opinion. On the bridge we indulged
a forward feeling, a tremble. I was fifteen.

Thinking, back farther in the grass I found
the owner, just coming to, where he had flipped
over the rail. He had blood on his hand, was pale—
I helped him walk to his machine. He ran his hand
over it, called me a good man, roared away.

I stood there, fifteen.

READER'S RESPONSE

1. How do you suppose the fifteen-year-old feels as the cyclist rides away? Did you ever feel this way?
2. Do you enjoy reading poems like this? Or did you prefer the newspaper article? Explain.

Writing and Thinking Activities

1. Get together with two or three classmates to discuss the following questions.
   a. Which model convinces readers to do something? How?
   b. Which one gives the most details, facts, and information about the accident?
   c. Which one uses words in a special way—different from the way we usually talk or write?
   d. Which model is mostly about the writer's thoughts and feelings?
2. How do you communicate? Track your communication during a typical day. Jot down all your uses of language—writing, reading, speaking, and listening. How much of your communication is informative, persuasive, self-expressive, or creative? With two or three other students, discuss what you discover about your own communication patterns.
3. Bring a copy of a magazine or your daily newspaper to class. With two or three other students, find examples of these four types of writing: information, persuasion, self-expression, and creative writing. Which type of writing is most common? Do all of the magazines and newspapers seem to have the same amount of the four kinds of writing?
4. What do you think of when someone mentions creative writing? Short stories? novels? poems? plays? What about other kinds of writing, such as speeches, editorials, letters to the editor, or journal entries? Can these also be creative? In what way? Try to think of other kinds of writing which you would call original or creative.

"You see things vacationing on a motorcycle in a way that is completely different from any other.... You're completely in contact with it all. You're _in_ the scene, not just watching it anymore, and the sense of presence is overwhelming."

Robert M. Pirsig
Zen and the Art of Motorcycle Maintenance

1 WRITING AND THINKING

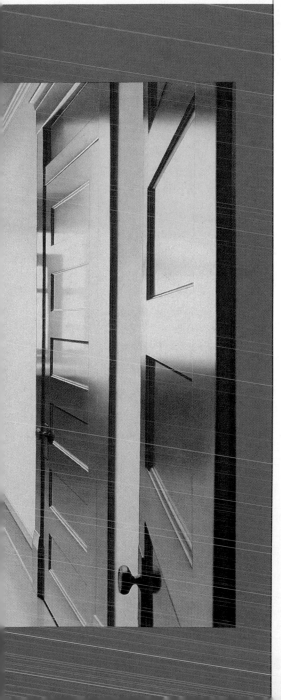

Looking at the Process

Good writing is more than just putting words down on paper. It's a **process** of thinking, researching, arranging, and analyzing.

Writing and You.   Why do you write? Where do you get your ideas? Do the words come easily, or do you need things to be just right before words begin to flow onto the page? Every writer—even you—will answer these questions differently. You might even answer the same question differently depending upon what you're writing at the time. Do you find it easier to write just for yourself?

As You Read.   Well-known poet Gwendolyn Brooks has her own unique answers about writing. As you read the following interview between the poet and Paul M. Angle, notice her ideas about all the activities that her writing involves—including thinking.

Billy Morrow Jackson, *Reading* (1979–1980). Collection of Wichita Art Museum, through the cooperation of Jane Haslem Gallery, Washington, D.C. Photo by Henry Nelson, courtesy of University of Illinois Press, Urbana & Chicago, publishers of *Billy Morrow Jackson: Interpretations of Time and Light* by Howard E. Wooden, © 1990.

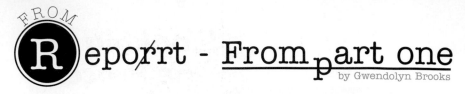

Reporrt - From part one

by Gwendolyn Brooks

ANGLE: Was it always your ambition from childhood to write, or was it a compelling necessity rather than an ambition?

BROOKS: It was a necessity. *Ambition* doesn't seem a proper word to describe what I felt as I grew up and continued to write. I enjoyed it very much, and I was convinced that it would be good to "enchant" others with these products of MY MIND. Once, I considered *burying* my precious manuscripts in the back yard so that in the future—at some time in the hundreds of years to come—they would be discovered and loved.

ANGLE: You wrote because you wanted to.

BROOKS: Yes.

ANGLE: And you still write because you want to?

BROOKS: Yes, I still write because I want to, but there is a difference now. Recently, I confided to friends how much more fun writing was in those years of my youth, when I had no publishing prospects. I was free. If things were not "right," what difference did it make? But now, when I have pretty good prospects of having what I write published, I'm very concerned. I want to be sure that everything is good, and this imposes a constraint.

ANGLE: Do you find writing hard work?

BROOKS: Yes. It is hard work. It gets harder all the time.

> ...I was convinced that it would be good to "enchant" others with these products of MY MIND.

ANGLE: Partly because of the compulsion you have to come as close to perfection as you think you're capable of coming?

BROOKS: That's true.

ANGLE: Now let me ask you another question. It is said that during much of his career Marcel Proust wrote in a windowless, sound-proof room, shutting himself off from not only intrusion, but also from humanity insofar as it was possible for him to do so. Could you write under such circumstances? Or would you want to write under such circumstances?

BROOKS: Yes, I would enjoy it. That's one of my problems—finding extended privacy. I'm thinking now of going away at the end of summer—*some* summer—to a hotel in which I would have just such a situation. I would stay in my room, and have my meals delivered; and I would write, write, write.

ANGLE: That sounds pretty good. But in fact you do have to write in an environment. You cannot, month in and month out, exclude the surroundings in which you live.

BROOKS: No. I cannot.

ANGLE: Now, do you find that environment—and let's use the term in a broad sense—encouraging, thwarting or of no significance?

BROOKS: You say do I find the environment encouraging, thwarting or . . .

ANGLE: Of no significance—having no effect upon the creative process.

BROOKS: You don't have noise in mind, do you?

ANGLE: No, something else.

BROOKS: Then I have to say that I find I am not disturbed by my environment. In my twenties when I wrote a good deal of my better-known poetry I lived on 63rd Street—at 623 East 63rd Street—and there was a good deal of life in the raw all about me. You might feel that this would be disturbing, but it was not. It contributed to my writing progress. I wrote about what I saw and heard in the street.

READER'S RESPONSE

1. Do Gwendolyn Brooks's comments about why she writes remind you of anything about yourself? What similarities or differences are there between you and Brooks?
2. Brooks says that writing is "hard work" and that it "gets harder all the time." Do you agree with her? Why?
3. At the end of the excerpt, Brooks talks about living on a city street. She says this busy location "contributed to my writing progress. I wrote about what I saw and heard in the street." What about you? Does a busy environment disturb or stimulate your writing? Do you ever write about what you see and hear around you?

LOOKING AHEAD

This chapter shows you a general approach or process that you can apply to all types of writing. As you work through the chapter, remember that

- writing and thinking are related
- the writing process is flexible: you can adapt it to your own writing style
- like other writers, you write for one of four basic purposes

"I always enjoyed reading when I was a child. Pretty soon, I suppose, it occurred to me that it might be wonderful if I could create something, too."

Gwendolyn Brooks

Aim—The "Why" of Writing

People write for the same reason they talk. They have something to say, somebody to say it to, and some purpose for saying it. But that's the general *why*. What are the more specific *why*'s, or purposes, people have for writing?

You might think there are hundreds, even thousands, of purposes. But there are really only a few.

WHY PEOPLE WRITE	
To express themselves	To get to know themselves; to find meaning in their own lives
To share information	To give other people information that they need or want; to share some special knowledge
To persuade	To convince other people to do something or believe something
To create literature	To be creative, to say something in a unique way

Process—The "How" of Writing

Everything that you say or write has one of the four purposes you've just read about. Sometimes a single piece of your writing has more than one of these purposes. You may want to share information as well as to persuade, to express yourself as well as to create literature.

But as you probably know, writing isn't something that just happens. Good writing is the result of a whole process or series of stages. And thinking is an important part of the process. In fact, in the first stage, prewriting, you do much more thinking than writing. Later in the process, you may focus more on writing than on thinking. That's why you'll find that different parts of this chapter sometimes focus more on one activity than on the other.

The diagram below shows the stages that usually take place during the writing process. As the diagram shows, at any point in the process, you can go back to an earlier stage or even start all over again.

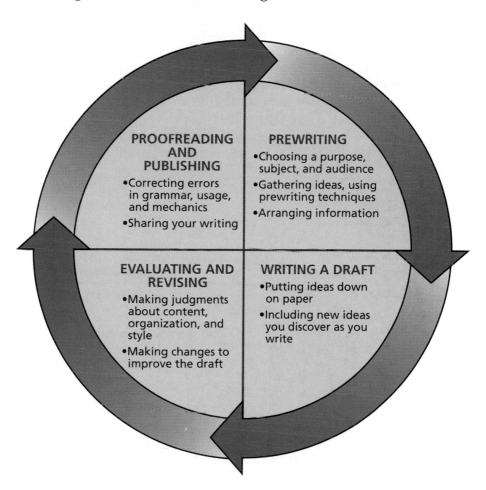

For example, suppose your state legislature is on the brink of passing a law that students with poor attendance can't get a learner's driving permit. You think the law would be unfair, so you begin writing a letter to your local newspaper. As you write, however, you realize that you don't know enough about the proposed law. You do more prewriting by reading a newspaper article or two about it. With this new information, you return to writing your first draft.

 *Prewriting*

Finding Ideas for Writing

Someone once said, "There's nothing new under the sun." And that's certainly true about prewriting to gather information. As long as people have been writing, they've been spending time thinking up ideas. When you write, you may not realize that this process is going on. It may seem that the writing just happens (or just doesn't happen). The techniques in this section will help you think up ideas and make writing an easier job.

PREWRITING TECHNIQUES		
Writer's Journal	Recording personal experiences and observations	Page 23
Freewriting	Writing for a few minutes about whatever comes into your mind	Page 24
Brainstorming	Listing ideas as quickly as they come	Page 25
Clustering	Using circles and lines to show connections between ideas	Page 27
Asking Questions	Using the reporter's *5W-How?* questions	Page 29
Using Your Five Senses	Observing details of sight, hearing, smell, taste, touch	Page 30
Reading with a Focus	Reading to find specific information	Page 31
Listening with a Focus	Listening to find specific information	Page 32
Asking "What if?" Questions	Imagining what would happen if one thing changed	Page 33
Visualizing	Making mental images of something	Page 34

Although the prewriting techniques are presented separately, you'll often use more than one technique at a time. Also, you'll find that different writing situations may suggest using certain techniques. For instance, if you're writing posters to raise money for the animal shelter, you might ask the *5W-How?* questions to think of basic information for the posters. But if you're writing a science fiction story, *visualizing* might help you discover ideas for the opening scene.

Writer's Journal

If you don't have one now, start keeping a ***writer's journal***. Use your journal to record experiences and observations, feelings and opinions, brilliant ideas and questions. You can also use your journal to collect poems, songs, quotations, newspaper articles, or cartoons. Soon your journal will be a sourcebook full of ideas for you to write about.

Here are some suggestions for getting started.

1. Use a blank book, a special notebook, or a file folder.
2. Get in the habit of writing daily, and date your entries. Some people like to write every day at a certain time—maybe at night while listening to music. Others keep their journals handy and write whenever inspiration strikes.
3. Neatness definitely doesn't count, and you don't have to worry about grammar and punctuation.
4. Use your imagination. Write down dreams and daydreams. Try creating songs, poems, story ideas.
5. If you include something you like (a quotation, article, song lyric), tell why you like it.

 COMPUTER NOTE: Consider storing your observations, prewriting notes, and drafts in separate files on a floppy disk.

E X E R C I S E 1 ▶   **Keeping a Writer's Journal**

People who've explored new continents, trekked across the prairies, and even traveled to the moon have kept journals. You weren't part of these dramatic events, but your experiences and observations are important, too. If you haven't already started a journal, begin right now. Think of what happened yesterday, and write your first journal entry.

Freewriting

When you *freewrite,* you write whatever pops into your head.

1. Set a timer for three to five minutes, and keep writing until the timer goes off.
2. Start with a word or topic that's important to you. Write whatever the word or topic makes you think about or remember. Don't worry about complete sentences or proper punctuation. Just let your hand put down on paper what's in your head.
3. If you can't think of anything new to write, copy the same word or phrase until something comes to mind.

You can also focus on one word or phrase from your original freewriting and use it to start freewriting again. This is called *focused freewriting* or *looping,* because you make a loop between freewritings.

Here's a sample of a few minutes of freewriting based on the word *freedom.*

HERE'S HOW

Freedom. Freedom. Freedom—feeling free. Statue of Liberty I saw last year. Freedom. Feeling free on warm spring day when coats come off. Bell ringing at 3:15. Being outside in the sun and wind. Not everyone's so free. What about animals in cages at zoos? What about animals in cages? What about whales that swim around in small tanks? Do we have a right to do that to animals? IS FREEDOM ONLY FOR HUMANS?

E X E R C I S E 2 ▶ **Using Freewriting**

What's your favorite quotation? Write it down on your paper. Then freewrite about the quotation for three or four minutes, just putting down whatever comes into your mind about it. You may want to use this quotation from baseball great Yogi Berra: "The game isn't over till it's over."

Brainstorming

Brainstorming is a way of coming up with ideas by using free association. You can brainstorm alone, with a partner, or in a group. Here's how it works.

1. Write down a subject—any subject—at the top of a sheet of paper (or on the chalkboard).
2. List every idea about the subject that comes to your mind. (In a group brainstorming session, one person should record all of the ideas.)
3. Don't stop to evaluate (judge) any of the ideas—you can do that later.
4. Keep going until you run out of ideas.

Here are brainstorming notes that you might make on the subject of *mummies*. Notice there are some silly ideas that you could discard later.

HERE'S HOW

Mummies	
mummies	peat bog mummies
daddies	movie mummies
Egyptian mummies	Boris Karloff
famous mummies	horror movies—mummies
pyramids	trailing bandages
pharaoh mummies	mummies—how preserved
King Tut	mummies—why
graves	religion
grave robberies	afterlife

EXERCISE 3   **Using Brainstorming**

Coming up with ideas is easier when there's more than one person. With a partner or in a small group, brainstorm to find and list ideas about one of the topics listed below. Or use a topic of your own.

1. computers
2. Vietnam Veterans Memorial
3. inventions
4. advertising
5. dieting
6. study habits

Clustering

Clustering is sometimes called *webbing* or *making connections*. Like brainstorming, it is useful for thinking of topics or gathering information. When you use clustering, you break a large subject into its smaller parts, just as you do when you brainstorm. (You can also organize ideas with a *tree diagram*, showing your main subject as the trunk and supporting details as the branches and twigs.)

1. Begin by writing a subject in the center of your paper. Circle the subject.
2. In the space around the subject, write whatever related ideas (single words or phrases) occur to you. Circle these new ideas, and draw lines connecting the new ideas with the original subject.
3. Don't hesitate to let your mind wander. New ideas may make you think of other related ideas. Keep drawing circles and lines to show the connections.

A cluster diagram doesn't always make complete sense to someone looking at it, but the writer always understands the connections. The following diagram shows a cluster diagram that you might make to find a topic related to photography as a hobby.

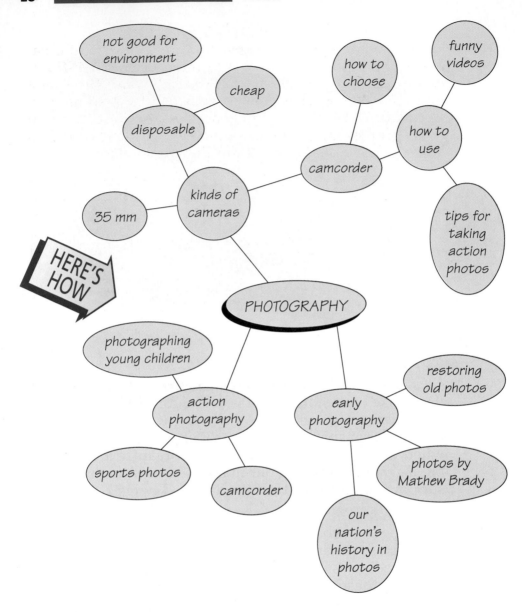

EXERCISE 4 ▶ **Using Clustering**

Using one of the topic ideas you *didn't* use in Exercise 3 (page 26), create a cluster diagram. If you want, you may instead create a cluster for a topic of your own. Be sure to follow the hints about how to cluster.

Asking Questions

Have you thought about how reporters collect information for their news stories? They often use the *5W-How? questions: Who? What? Where? When? Why? How?* Not every question applies to every topic, and sometimes you can think of more than one good question for a question word. For example, here are some questions that you might ask to find out about the Cuban Revolution.

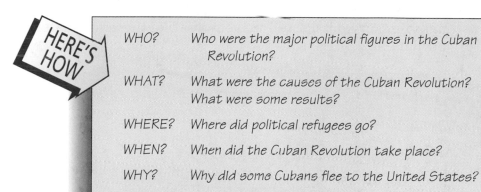

HERE'S HOW

WHO?	Who were the major political figures in the Cuban Revolution?
WHAT?	What were the causes of the Cuban Revolution? What were some results?
WHERE?	Where did political refugees go?
WHEN?	When did the Cuban Revolution take place?
WHY?	Why did some Cubans flee to the United States?
HOW?	How did the revolution affect life in Cuba?

E X E R C I S E 5 ▶ **Asking the *5W-How?* Questions**

You're writing a school newspaper article about recycling in your community. Make a list of *5W-How?* questions that will help you gather ideas for the article.

Using Your Five Senses

Have you ever heard the expression "I won't believe it till I see it"? Most people rely mainly on their sense of sight. But every second you're awake, your brain is taking in information through all five senses: sight, hearing, smell, taste, and touch. If you stop to focus on all the sensory details around you, you'll have an endless supply of specific details for your writing. Suppose you spent a day at a Chinese New Year's festival. You might observe many sensory details and make notes like these for a later journal entry.

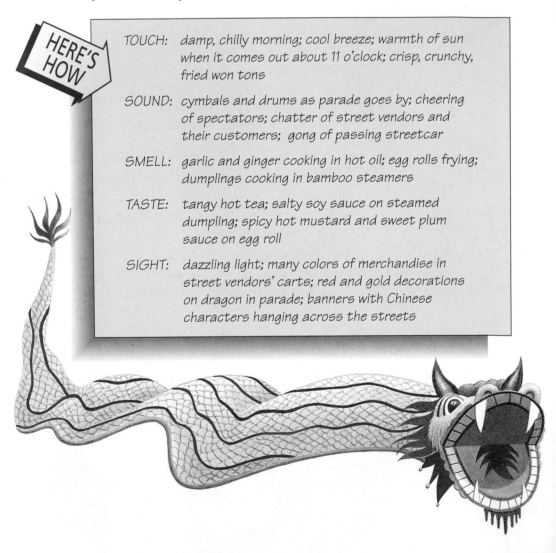

HERE'S HOW

TOUCH: damp, chilly morning; cool breeze; warmth of sun when it comes out about 11 o'clock; crisp, crunchy, fried won tons

SOUND: cymbals and drums as parade goes by; cheering of spectators; chatter of street vendors and their customers; gong of passing streetcar

SMELL: garlic and ginger cooking in hot oil; egg rolls frying; dumplings cooking in bamboo steamers

TASTE: tangy hot tea; salty soy sauce on steamed dumpling; spicy hot mustard and sweet plum sauce on egg roll

SIGHT: dazzling light; many colors of merchandise in street vendors' carts; red and gold decorations on dragon in parade; banners with Chinese characters hanging across the streets

EXERCISE 6 ▶ **Using Your Five Senses**

Even the most common places around you overflow with sensory details—if you just stop to notice them. Choose one of the following places and write down all the sensory details you can think of about it. To use all your senses, you might want to divide your paper into five columns—one column for each sense.

1. a video game arcade
2. a baseball game
3. the school cafeteria
4. inside a bus (subway)
5. a busy kitchen—at home or at a fast-food restaurant
6. outside late at night
7. outside in a storm
8. a supermarket (or other store)
9. your street at dawn
10. a classroom during the "big test"

Reading with a Focus

Sometimes you'll write about something you haven't experienced or can't observe. In this case, getting ideas for writing might mean reading books, newspapers, or magazines. Reading to find specific information is very different from reading for pleasure or just browsing through a book. When you read to find information, you look for main ideas and supporting details. Keep these suggestions in mind.

1. Don't read everything. Use the index, check the table of contents, and look for chapter headings and subheadings. Skim, or glance through, the material, searching only for information about your topic.
2. When you find relevant information, slow down. Read carefully for main ideas. You'll want to take notes on specific details as well as main ideas.

EXERCISE 7 ▶ **Reading with a Focus**

What famous person do you admire? A celebrity—a singer, songwriter, actor, or athlete? a politician? a scientist? Find a book or article about that person and read it for answers to the following questions. Jot down notes and share your information with a small group.

1. What is the person's background? When was he or she born? Where did the person grow up?
2. How did the person get started in his or her career?
3. What problems or obstacles did the person have to overcome?
4. What is the person most famous for?

Listening with a Focus

Reading isn't the only way to get beyond what you can experience and observe. You can also gather ideas for writing by listening to radio and television programs, audio tapes, and experts in personal or telephone interviews. Whenever you're going to gather information by listening, it helps to prepare in advance. Try using these suggestions.

1. Write down your topic.
2. Brainstorm what you already know about the topic, or refer to your notes if you've already done some research.
3. Write down what you want to know. This list of questions should help guide and focus your listening.
4. Listen carefully with your questions in front of you. Take careful notes, and don't let your mind wander.

☞ REFERENCE NOTE: For information on interviewing, see pages 910–911.

EXERCISE 8 ▶ **Listening for Specific Information**

Listen to a radio or TV news program—either national or local news. What national or local news story strikes you as being most important and dramatic? As you listen, jot down answers to the following questions. You and your classmates might want to swap ideas about what stories caught your attention.

1. What is the news story about?
2. What happened? Where and when did it happen?
3. Who was involved?

Asking "What if?" Questions

What if there were no fast-food restaurants? What if pigs could fly? Asking *"What if?" questions* is a creative thinking technique that can help you gather ideas for writing. It's really an exercise in cause-and-effect thinking. If one thing changes (cause), what will happen (effect)? Asking questions like these can help you discover topics and details.

1. *What if I could change one thing in the past?* (What if there were only one language in the whole world? What if schools had never been invented?)
2. *What if something we take for granted were totally different?* (What if the sun never shone and it was always night on earth? What if there were no gravity on earth?)
3. *What if I could make one change in the way an object or situation is now?* (What if cars weren't allowed in cities? What if there were no such thing as television?)

You can also ask "What if?" questions about a specific topic. For example, these questions might help you discover ideas about the topic "how to get more Americans to vote."

- <u>*What if*</u> *everyone who didn't vote had to pay a fine?*

- <u>*What if*</u> *people who did vote in every election were rewarded in some way—say, with a credit on their income tax?*

- <u>*What if*</u> *everybody over eighteen were mailed a ballot and the only way you could vote was by mail?*

E X E R C I S E **9** ▶   **Asking "What if?" Questions**

Working with a partner or a small group, write at least five "What if?" questions for any two of the following items. You might enjoy sharing your work with other groups.

1. the use of language
2. the invention of weapons
3. daytime schedules
4. the climate in North America
5. the use of computers

Visualizing

Visualizing means making images of something in your "mind's eye." Although the word *visualizing* comes from the same root as the word *vision*, visualizing can use all the senses. You can use visualizing to think of details for your writing. For example, visualize yourself driving a snappy red sports car down a country road at sunset. Isn't that more exciting than just thinking about cars in general?

You can also visualize the answer to a "What if?" question. For example, try to picture the situation suggested by the question "What if there were no cars?" Imagine yourself on the street outside your home—in a world without cars. As you visualize what the scene would be like, you might jot down notes like these.

HERE'S HOW

> Crowded with bicycles, like China. No more exhaust
> fumes. Bicycle traffic jams. Healthy people and
> fresh air. Riders in ponchos during heavy rain,
> splashing through huge puddles. Two riders holding
> hands—must be dating.

EXERCISE 10 ▶ **Visualizing Specific Details**

You're writing a short story for your school literary magazine or newspaper. Select two of the following story elements, and visualize specific details for your story.

EXAMPLE   *An old car—many shades of faded silver; rough and peeling like bad sunburn; needs a paint job; rusted hatchback; two-door; motorboat sounds—muffler needs replacing; gray vinyl inside—ripped on driver's side*

1. a teenager
2. a dog
3. a city street at night
4. an accident

Prewriting

Considering Purpose and Audience

When you write, you always have some *purpose* in mind. You write in many different forms, but you have one or more of these purposes.

MAIN PURPOSE	FORMS OF WRITING
To express yourself	Journal, letter, personal essay
To be creative	Short story, poem, play
To explain or inform	Science and history writing, newspaper or magazine article, biography, autobiography, travel essay
To persuade	Persuasive essay, letter to editor, advertisement, political speech

As you consider your purpose, think about your *audience* (your readers) at the same time. How will they affect what you write? The following paragraphs are from an article about African American soldiers who fought in the Civil War. Led by Robert Gould Shaw, the all-black 54th Massachusetts Regiment stormed a heavily armed fort and had many casualties. As you read, think about the article's purpose and audience.

> At 7:45, the bombardment stopped and the attack signal came. Shaw spoke to his soldiers: "Move in quick time until within a hundred yards of the fort, then, double-quick and charge!" Off they rushed into history as 1,700 Confederate riflemen—almost six times as many as Union military intelligence had said were in Fort Wagner—clambered from their shell-battered bombproofs and raced to the ramparts (only eight of them died from the Union bombardment). Confederate batteries, mostly silent during the day to save ammunition, now opened up from the harbor's other islands.

Just before battle, Sgt. Robert Simmons, one of Shaw's men, sent a prophetic note to the members of his family, who only three days before had been under violent racist assault back in New York City: "God bless you all! Good-bye!" Despite a moat, some wire and a rifle pit, Shaw and a few of his men actually reached the parapets of the fort before being cut down by fire. The rest, less than half of the assault force, were driven back. For having carried the regimental colors despite multiple wounds, Sgt. William Carney became the first black to win the Medal of Honor. "The old flag never touched the ground, boys!" he shouted.

Jack Fincher, "I felt freedom in my bones"

The writer of the preceding article had a clear purpose: to inform a general audience of educated readers about the role of African American soldiers in the Civil War. Now suppose you're writing a newspaper article to persuade your classmates to see *Glory*, the movie about the 54th Massachusetts Regiment. Your article might begin like the following one. As you read, notice both what the writer says and how she says it.

Don't miss renting Glory, a Civil War movie about the heroics of the 54th Massachusetts Regiment. The courage these black soldiers show as they turn from former, mostly uneducated slaves into a closely knit, expert fighting unit is an inspiration. For a long time, they train without uniforms in the bitter cold and even without shoes until their feet are bleeding and raw. When they are informed they are to be paid only ten dollars a month rather than the thirteen dollars a month the white soldiers are paid, they demonstrate their pride by refusing pay at all.

In the most dramatic scene of the movie, when the 54th leads the attack on Fort Wagner, the men follow their leader to what they know is certain death. They do this for the glory of their country and for their own glory as free men. And you can share that glory by visiting your video store.

WRITING NOTE Whatever your audience or purpose, try to write in an honest, natural *voice.* Even in a formal essay, you don't want to sound stuffy or stilted. Using a natural writing voice, just like using a natural speaking voice, doesn't mean being sloppy or careless with language. But it does mean sounding like the best part of yourself.

CRITICAL THINKING

Analyzing Your Audience

You may not realize it, but you often write for many different audiences. In a journal or in prewriting notes, you write for yourself. You may write letters to friends or relatives or even to school or local newspapers. As you practice writing in school, you often write for your teachers and classmates. Later, in the workplace, you may write for your supervisor or co-workers. Good writers always adjust what they say and how they say it to fit their audiences.

Unless you're writing for yourself, audiences always expect certain things from you. For example, they expect writing that is clear and easily understood. They also expect writing that shows that you're knowledgeable about your topic. Before you write, consider these questions about your audience.

- Why is my audience reading my writing? Do they expect to be informed, amused, or persuaded?
- What does my audience already know about my topic? (Is there a way to take advantage of what they already know?)
- What does the audience want or need to know about the topic? What will interest them?
- What type of language suits my readers? Should vocabulary be simple or somewhat complex? Should sentences be long, short, or a combination of both?

 CRITICAL THINKING EXERCISE:
Writing for a Different Purpose and Audience

The following paragraph appeared in *Newsweek,* a news-magazine read mostly by adults. In a small group, discuss this question: How would you change the paragraph to persuade teenagers *not* to take part-time jobs? Then rewrite the paragraph for that audience and purpose. Share your work with another group.

> The increase in the percentage of working teens has been fueled, in part, by the expanding service-sector economy. The number of low-wage, part-time jobs grew in the 1980s, making teens a valuable commodity in the labor market. The upshot is that about 7.7 million, or about one third, of 14- to 19-year-olds worked in 1988—and they have inherited the consumerist mentality of the 1980s. In wealthy areas, teens can earn upwards of $200 a week. It's true that some teens save their earnings to pay for college, but many others do not. Laurence Steinberg, coauthor of the book "When Teenagers Work," believes youngsters are motivated more by luxurious tastes than by economic need. Working teens "are supporting their lifestyles," he says. "If you want to buy Reeboks with a pump, you have to have $125 to spend on them."
>
> Annetta Miller, "Work and What It's Worth"

Prewriting

Arranging Ideas

"Enough!" you cry. "I have enough information!" But before you start writing, you need to spend some time arranging your prewriting ideas. The following chart shows four of the most common ways of ordering, or arranging, information.

ARRANGING IDEAS		
TYPE OF ORDER	DEFINITION	EXAMPLES
Chronological	Narration: Order in which events happen in time	Story, narrative poem, explanation of a process, history, biography, drama
Spatial	Description: Order in which objects are described according to location	Descriptions (near to far, left to right, top to bottom, etc.)
Importance	Evaluation: Order in which details are given, from least to most important or the reverse	Persuasive writing, description, explanations (main idea and supporting details), evaluative writing
Logical	Classification: Order in which items and groups are related	Definitions and classifications

 REFERENCE NOTE: For more information on arranging ideas, see pages 79–83.

CRITICAL THINKING

Arranging Information

How you arrange ideas depends on your purpose, audience, and topic. Sometimes, information is arranged to be helpful to the people who will use it. Names in a telephone book, for example, are arranged in alphabetical order. Television schedules are arranged in the order the shows are broadcast. Sometimes, the subject itself suggests an order. The following passage presents General Robert E. Lee's surrender to General Ulysses S. Grant at Appomattox. The events took place over time, so the natural order is *chronological*.

> The two men shook hands. "What General Lee's feelings were, I do not know," Grant later wrote. "As he was a man of much dignity, with an impassible face . . . his feelings . . . were entirely concealed from my observation."
>
> The Federal commander did his best to ease the tension, reminding Lee that they had met once before, during the Mexican War. Lee said he had not been able to remember what Grant looked like. "Our conversation grew so pleasant that I almost forgot the object of our meeting," Grant said. Finally, "General Lee called my attention to the object."
>
> The terms Grant offered were simple and generous. Confederate officers could keep their side arms and personal possessions; officers and men who claimed to own their horses could keep them, too; and "each officer and man will be allowed to return to his home, not to be disturbed by the United States authorities."
>
> Geoffrey C. Ward, with Ken Burns and Ric Burns, *The Civil War: An Illustrated History*

CRITICAL THINKING EXERCISE:
Analyzing the Order of Details

Using the chart on page 40, decide which type of order each paragraph uses.

1.   The covered wagon had a wide drawer that would slide under the body of the wagon, handle and all, so it could be pulled out from the rear. In this deep and

roomy box were packed our camping equipment and food supplies. The camping outfit consisted of a huge tent, a folding cot apiece, folding chairs, and a table. Our outdoor cookware was of heavy black iron. One big kettle stood up on three long legs to sit over a fire. There were dutch ovens, tin cups, cutlery, and bowls. The blankets, sheets, pillows, and other bedding were rolled in a canvas and tightly strapped. This "cushion" was fitted into the body of the wagon and served as a seat for the three of us who rode in the back.

Marie St. John, "The Woods Were Tossing With Jewels"

2.   After dogs became domesticated, they developed certain traits that distinguished them from wild relatives. One such characteristic is the upturned tail, ranging from a sickle shape to a tight curl. This feature probably comes from the original stock of domestic dog, pointing to a common ancestry for all breeds. A further trait that distinguishes the dog from the wolf is its smaller teeth, which suggests that early man may have found the smaller, less toothy animals easier to tame and control. Barking, too, is an exclusive and inherent trait acquired by the domestic dog.

Charles Panati, *Panati's Browser's Book of Beginnings*

3.   As a sport, basketball was ideally suited to turn its stars into celebrities. . . . Basketball is simple to follow, and the ball is easy to see. The court is small enough so everyone in the stadium can get a fair view of the players' faces, something that can't be said about football or baseball. The ball is constantly in play and points mount up quickly, making basketball a livelier game than baseball or football. And, most important of all, basketball is the one team sport that can be dominated by one dazzlingly gifted player.

Jesse Kornbluth, *Airborne Again!*

Using Charts

Making a chart is a good way to arrange your prewriting notes, because a chart is actually a graphic aid for ordering information. The most important step in creating a chart is to decide on the headings that will cover the information.

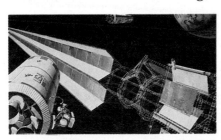

Here is a chart about scientific research that can be conducted in space. The writer wants to organize information according to two categories: branch of science and type of experiment, or study.

SCIENTIFIC RESEARCH IN SPACE	
BRANCH OF SCIENCE	TYPE OF EXPERIMENT
Biology	Experiments on how zero gravity affects the biological clocks of living things such as fish and plants
Physics	Experiments on how zero gravity affects the development or manufacture of crystals
Astronomy	Studies of the universe, using X-ray astronomy, without the distorting effects of the earth's atmosphere

A time line is a way to arrange information chronologically. The following example traces civil rights events.

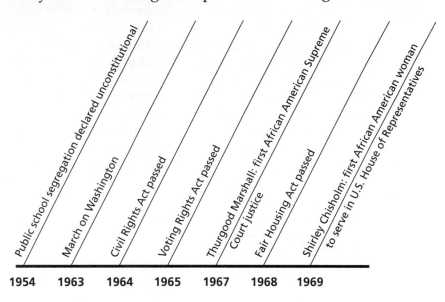

EXERCISE 11▶ **Using Charts to Organize Information**

With a partner or small group, make a chart to organize the following information about emergency treatment of bites and stings. Be sure to discuss the headings you might use, and share your chart with other groups.

animals (dogs, etc.)—wash with clean water, soap; hold under running water for several minutes; sterile bandage; call doctor for further treatment

snake bite (poisonous)—rush to doctor or emergency room; keep victim at rest; apply tourniquet between bite and heart (but not too tight)

snake bite (nonpoisonous)—treat as cut; not necessary to call doctor

bee, wasp, hornet, ant—scrape (do not pull) stinger to remove it; cold compresses or ice cube on bite; call doctor for medication if severe reaction

spider bite—ice cube over bite to reduce pain; consult doctor for medication

Writing a First Draft

You can't go on gathering information and organizing it forever. At some point, you have to say, "Stop! It's time to try some of this out." You can always go back and search for more information and rethink how to organize it. Now it's time to get a first draft on paper.

There's no single approach to turning prewriting notes into a first draft. Some writers work from very rough prewriting notes, while others work from a detailed outline. Some write quickly, trying just to get their ideas down on paper in sentences. Others shape each sentence slowly and connect ideas carefully. As you write your first draft, try these suggestions.

- Use your prewriting plans to guide your draft.
- Write freely, focusing on expressing your ideas clearly.
- Remember that writing is a way of discovering ideas. Include new ideas that you discover about your topic.
- Don't worry about catching or correcting errors in grammar, usage, and mechanics at this stage—you can do that later.

Here is the first draft of a paragraph about being an active listener. As you read, notice how the writer makes some changes even in the first draft. Also notice how the writer indicates a return to prewriting by inserting notes to be checked later. You can do the same things as you develop your own first draft.

I read somewhere the other day that it's not enough to just listen to people, you should be a listener. That means that you <u>really</u> listen to what another person is saying. In case you're interested, here are some of the things that an active listener is supposed to do. First, you should make eye contact. Eye contact means the listener is looking at you—he or she's not reading a newspaper or watching television or looking around at other people in the room. An active listener says things like [NOTE: Check brainstorming list for what listener says.] That shows he's still awake and paying attention. My sister Sara really listens, and I think that might be why she's so popular and people like her so much. Sara gives off the feeling that she really cares about you. ~~There are~~ An active listener uses nonverbal clues too. [NOTE: Find out exactly what these clues are--can't remember.]

CRITICAL THINKING

Synthesizing Ideas

Synthesis is the critical thinking skill that involves putting together parts into a unified whole. As you synthesize your prewriting material into your first draft, you must keep in mind your topic, audience, and purpose. For some writers, this is an overwhelming experience—so much so that they have a hard time getting started. There's even a name for this difficulty—writer's block.

Hagar the Horrible reprinted with special permission of King Features Syndicate, Inc.

Getting those first ideas down on paper isn't easy, and they're usually far from perfect—but that's okay. If you have a hard time beginning your first draft, try these tips.

- Force yourself to write. Get a piece of paper, and don't move until you fill one side of it.
- Make an appointment with yourself. Set aside a definite time and place, and don't get up or do anything else until you've finished the first draft (or at least a big chunk of it).
- When you've finished, reward yourself! Call a friend, watch a favorite TV program, or go outside to shoot some baskets.

CRITICAL THINKING EXERCISE:
Synthesizing Ideas into a Draft

On the next page (page 48), there are some prewriting notes on a topic you might know something about—the personal stereo. Working with a partner or small group, arrange the details. Then, use them to write the first draft of a paragraph. Feel free to add more details.

the personal stereo—one of the greatest inventions
every teenager needs one
tune out the world
tune in favorite music—always available
best kind have belt clips, play cassette tapes as
   well as radio
question of whether you can listen *and* do homework (Are you wearing one right now?)
doctors caution: hearing damage from long-term
   listening at high volume

EXERCISE 12▶   **Writing a First Draft**

Here are some prewriting notes about a great American
Indian leader, Tecumseh. Arrange the details in order,
and add to them if you like. Then, write the first draft of a
paragraph about Tecumseh.

allied himself with Britain during
   the War of 1812
fought under Chief Little Turtle
   against U.S. troops in the 1790s
a Shawnee chief, in the Ohio
   Valley, Northwest Territory
led American Indian forces in
   the invasion of Ohio for the
   British (War of 1812)
born about 1768 in Ohio
opposed the 1809 treaty in which
   chiefs of several peoples sold
   land (3 million acres) to
   U.S. government
called a brilliant leader, marvelous speaker
with his brother (who was called the Prophet)
   set out to organize all American Indians east of
   the Mississippi to reject the 1809 treaty
1811, Battle of Tippecanoe in Indiana—U.S.
   defeated American Indians in Prophet's village
finally defeated and killed at Battle of the Thames, 1813

Evaluating and Revising

Evaluating and revising are two separate steps in checking over your work, but they often occur almost at the same time.

> Evaluating—deciding on the strengths or weaknesses of the paper
>
> Revising—making the improvements

Evaluating

You may not realize it, but you evaluate all the time: the movies and television programs you see, the music you hear. And you use those evaluations to decide whether to watch the show again or buy the tape. It's much harder to evaluate your own work, though, especially your writing.

Self-Evaluation.　These techniques can help you evaluate your own writing.

Tips for Self-Evaluation

1. **Reading Carefully.** Read your paper more than once. First read for *content* (what you say), then for *organization* (how you've arranged your ideas), and then for *style* (how you've used words and sentences).

2. **Listening Carefully.** Use a different sense. Read your draft aloud and try to "hear" what you've written. Sometimes you notice things you wouldn't pick up during a silent reading.

3. **Taking Time**. Set your draft aside for a while and come back to it later. Taking time away from your work can help you become objective about it.

Peer Evaluation.　Professional writers almost always have someone else read what they've written—a friend, a family member, another writer, an editor with their publishing company. They know that someone else always has a more objective eye.

You can use that technique yourself by working with your classmates in peer-evaluation groups. A group may be as small as just you and a partner, or it may include four or five students. In a peer-evaluation group, you will have two roles—part of the time you'll be the writer whose work is being evaluated, and part of the time you'll be the evaluator of someone else's work.

PEER-EVALUATION GUIDELINES

Guidelines for the Writer

1. Make a list of questions or concerns for your classmate. What part of your paper are you worried about?
2. Keep a positive attitude. Try to make use of the evaluator's comments rather than being defensive about them. Remember that your classmate is trying to help you.

Guidelines for the Peer Evaluator

1. Remember that people like to know what they've done well. Tell your classmate what you think is particularly effective. Point out strengths as well as weaknesses.
2. Provide some encouragement—suggest something your classmate can do to improve the paper. Remember that it's discouraging to hear that something is weak without also hearing how it can be improved.
3. Look at content and organization. Don't comment on mechanical errors such as spelling or punctuation. The writer will catch those problems in proofreading.
4. Give your classmate's paper your best effort, but also be sensitive to the writer's feelings. When you spot a weakness, try asking a question about it rather than pointing it out as a problem.

Revising

By the time you and your classmates have evaluated your work, you've got a good idea about what parts of your paper need help. Now it's time to think about the evaluations. Which comments from your classmates do you think are most helpful, given your purpose and audience? Which suggested changes do you want to make? Once you've decided, you can begin revising—making the actual changes in your paper.

The important thing is not to take a shortcut and skip the revising stage. If you write in longhand or use a typewriter, write or type your paper over again. Make handwritten corrections on your paper, perhaps using a different color ink, and then write or type a new copy. You can indicate any changes by using the revising and proofreading symbols on page 60. If you have a word processor, you'll find revising easier. You can change your draft on the screen and print out a new copy. (See pages 948–949 on using a word processor.)

Revision involves looking at content, organization, and style. *Content* is what you have to say about your topic. *Organization* is the order in which ideas and details are presented. *Style* involves word choice and meaning—how you express your ideas about your topic. When you revise, use the following techniques to make changes.

REVISING	
TECHNIQUE	EXAMPLE
1. *Add.* Add new information and details to help your audience understand your main idea. Add words, phrases, sentences, whole paragraphs.	(⌃ a Native American people⌃) The Mayas ⌃ wrote in hieroglyphics and used extremely accurate calendars.
2. *Cut.* Take out information, details, examples, or words that will distract your audience. Cut repetition, wordiness, and details unrelated to your main idea.	The Mayas' civilization flourished until it fell to Spanish conquistadors about ~~the year~~ A.D. 1600.
3. *Replace.* Take out weak words, clichés, awkward-sounding sentences, unnecessary information or details. Replace with more precise words, more relevant details, and more vivid comparisons.	*The Living Maya* is a book by Jeffrey Foxx with ⌃detailed, ~~really very~~ beautiful color photographs of Mayas today in ⌃Central ~~various~~ ⌃America and Mexico. ~~parts of the world.~~
4. *Reorder.* Move information, details, examples, or paragraphs for variety and an order that makes sense.	If you are at all interested in photography, you will enjoy reading this book, or (in native American traditions,) about the Mayas.

Here's the paragraph on active listening (page 45), revised by using the four revision techniques. To understand the changes, you may want to refer to the chart of revising and proofreading symbols on page 60. Notice how the writer has answered the notes in the first draft.

HERE'S HOW

I read ~~somewhere the other day~~ that it's not enough to just listen to people: you should be an active listener. That means that you really listen to what another person is saying, ~~In case you're interested,~~ here are some of the things that an active listener ~~is supposed to do~~. **should** First, you should make eye contact. ~~Eye contact means the listener~~ **This means that you should look into the speaker's eyes as you listen. You don't read** ~~is looking at you--he or she's not reading~~ a newspaper or watching television or looking around at other people in the room. An active listener ~~says things like~~ **also responds with** "Yes," "Uh-huh," or "Really?" every once in a while. ~~That shows~~ that **Do this to show you are interested** ~~he or she's still awake~~ and paying attention. My sister Sara really listens, and I think that might be why she's so popular. Sara gives off the feeling that she really cares about ~~you~~. **people** ~~There are~~ nonverbal clues, too. ~~Nonverbal~~ **finally, an active listener uses** **them** ~~means body language, an active listener~~ might nod, leans **You and** forward, ~~as if what they're listening to~~ is really important. **to show that what the speaker's saying** **to you.**

Trying to judge and improve everything in your paper at once can be tricky. For that reason, most writers and editors look at only one aspect at a time. As you evaluate and revise, plan to read through your paper at least three times. Focus each time on one important aspect: content, organization, or style. By concentrating on each aspect separately, you won't be so distracted by all the things you've noticed. Just direct your energy to fixing one thing at a time.

You'll learn more about evaluating and revising specific kinds of writing in later chapters in this book. Following are some general guidelines that apply to all types of writing.

GUIDELINES FOR EVALUATING AND REVISING

EVALUATION GUIDE	REVISION TECHNIQUE
CONTENT	
1 Is the writing interesting?	**Add** examples, an anecdote (brief story), dialogue, and additional details. **Cut** repetitious or boring details.
2 Does the writing do what the writer wanted it to?	**Add** details that inform or explain, express feelings, create pictures, or persuade.
3 Are there enough details?	**Add** more details, facts, or examples to support ideas about the topic.
4 Are there unrelated ideas or details that distract the reader?	**Cut** irrelevant or distracting information.
5 Are unfamiliar terms explained or defined?	**Add** definitions or other explanations of unfamiliar terms. **Replace** unknown or hard terms with familiar ones.
ORGANIZATION	
6 Are ideas and details arranged in the best possible order?	**Reorder** ideas and details to make the meaning clear.
7 Are the connections between ideas and sentences clear?	**Add** transitional words to link ideas: **first**, **since**, or **then**.
STYLE	
8 Is the meaning clear?	**Replace** vague or unclear wording. Use words and phrases that are precise and easy to understand.
9 Does the writing contain clichés or tired phrases?	**Cut** or **replace** with specific details and fresh comparisons.
10 Does the language fit the audience and purpose?	**Replace** formal words with less formal ones to create an informal tone, or feeling. To create a more formal tone, **replace** slang and contractions.
11 Do sentences read smoothly?	**Reorder** to vary sentence beginnings and structure.

| **E X E R C I S E 13**▶ | **Evaluating and Revising a Paragraph** |

Working with a partner, evaluate and revise the following first draft of a paragraph. You'll notice some grammatical errors in the draft. For this activity, focus on the draft's content, organization, and style. Be sure to refer to the Guidelines for Evaluating and Revising on page 54. You might want to compare your revised version with another pair's work.

Girls who play sports were once called tomboys, that word just isn't used any more. And tomboys weren't a good thing to be, either, most people thought. Nowadays, girls participate in sports as much as boys or almost as much as boys do, they are encouraged by their parents to do so. This is called gender equality in sports. A national survey reported that the number of girls participating in high school sports has been steadily increasing every year while the number of boys remains about the same. The most popular sport for high school girls is basketball, track and field, volleyball, softball, soccer, tennis, and cross-country in that order. Playing sports increases girl's self-esteem and there are health benefits, too. Studies have show that sports helps protect girls from obesity and from getting breast cancer, too. So why do the numbers of girls participating in high school sports drop? Almost a third of high school freshman girls play some sport; fewer than 20 percent of female seniors do.

Proofreading and Publishing

One modern artist, as the story goes, sometimes sneaks into exhibits of his own paintings with a small paint box. When no one's looking, he makes small adjustments to the "finished" paintings. At this point in the writing process, it's also time for you to do your final touching up—also called *proofreading*.

Proofreading. When you proofread, you carefully reread your revised draft to correct mistakes in grammar, usage, and mechanics (spelling, capitalization, and punctuation). Unfortunately, you're so familiar with what you *meant* to say that it's easy to skip over mistakes. Allow enough time to put your writing away for a while. A little distance will help you see mistakes.

When you proofread, slow down and read each word carefully. These techniques can help make proofreading easier. Different techniques work better for different people, so use the ones that work best for you.

1. Focus on one line at a time. Use a sheet of paper to cover all the lines below the one you are proofreading. Some writers proofread backward—beginning with the bottom line and moving to the top. Some writers also proofread by reading from right to left.
2. Try peer proofreading. Exchange papers with a classmate or two and check each other's papers for errors.
3. When you're not sure if something's right, look it up. Use a college dictionary for spelling and a handbook like the one found in this book for grammar, usage, and mechanics.
4. Indicate any changes by using the revising and proofreading symbols on page 60.

The following guidelines apply to almost all the writing you will do for school. Before you proofread, review these guidelines to remind yourself of the kinds of errors you are looking for.

GUIDELINES FOR PROOFREADING

1. Is every sentence a complete sentence, not a fragment or run-on? (See pages 406–418.)
2. Does every sentence end with the appropriate end punctuation mark? Are other punctuation marks used correctly? (See pages 739–831.)
3. Does every sentence begin with a capital letter? Are all proper nouns and appropriate proper adjectives capitalized? (See pages 717–738.)
4. Does every verb agree in number with its subject? (See pages 589–608.)
5. Are verb forms and tenses used correctly? (See pages 616–647.)
6. Are subject and object forms of personal pronouns used correctly? (See pages 649–670.)
7. Does every pronoun agree with its antecedent in number and in gender? Are pronoun references clear? (See pages 608–613.)
8. Are frequently confused words (such as *lie* and *lay*) used correctly? (See pages 637–641.)
9. Are all words spelled correctly? Are the plural forms of nouns correct? (See pages 836–863.)
10. Is the paper neat and in correct manuscript form? (See page 59.)

EXERCISE 14 ▶ **Proofreading a Paragraph**

Proofread the following paragraph for mistakes in grammar, usage, and mechanics. You should find ten mistakes. Refer to the handbook at the back of the book and to a dictionary to correct these errors.

My sister Junie and her friend Rosa have just recorded a song they wrote about a year ago. Its a song about scuba diving. They wrote this song after they tooked a scuba diving class last summer. the class met twice a week for six weeks. For the first five weeks Junie and Rosa learned how to scuba in a swimming pool Before the class ended, everyone went diveing in the ocean. Mr.

Morrison, the person who teached the class, had a boat big enough for all them students. So there song is called "Mr. Morrison, You Showed Us the World Under Water." I dont think it'll be a big hit.

Publishing. Deciding on an audience earlier in the writing process meant you were planning to share your paper with others. Now is the time to do that. Besides turning in your writing to your teacher, here are some other ways to share your writing.

- Enter a writing contest. Some contests have prizes or certificates. Ask your teacher or counselor for information about writing contests.
- Make a class anthology. Each student might contribute one piece of writing, a drawing, or a favorite cartoon. Donate your class anthology to your school library or to the children's floor in a hospital.
- Post book and movie reviews written by students on a school bulletin board or in the library.

CRITICAL THINKING

Reflecting on Your Writing

It is always possible to learn something from your own writing process. You may learn more about how you write, about a topic, or even about yourself. A good way to discover what you have learned is to reflect on your writing and to write about those reflections.

One place to keep those reflections is in your portfolio. A **portfolio** is a collection of your writing that is designed to show how you grow and change as a writer. Every piece of writing in the portfolio should be dated so that both you and your teacher can trace your progress.

Sometimes your teacher will require you to put certain papers in your portfolio, but at other times you will probably choose what to include. To make those choices, you need to think critically about your writing, and you need to reflect on your objectives and on your growth as a writer.

CRITICAL THINKING EXERCISE:
Reflecting on Your Writing

Try to recall the writing you have done over the past few weeks or months. If you have some of those papers, reread them. Reflect on your writing by answering the following questions. Then, date your paper and add it to your portfolio.

1. What part of the writing process seems to be easiest for you? finding a topic? proofreading? Why?
2. What have you learned about your writing process from these assignments?

Whenever someone else reads your paper, its appearance is important. These guidelines will help improve the appearance of your paper.

GUIDELINES FOR MANUSCRIPT FORM

1. Use only one side of a sheet of paper.
2. Write in blue or black ink, or type.
3. If you write by hand, don't skip lines. If you type, double-space the lines.
4. Leave margins of about one inch at the top, sides, and bottom of a page.
5. Indent the first line of each paragraph.
6. Number all pages except the first page. Place the number in the upper right-hand corner.
7. All pages should be neat and clean. You may make a few corrections with correction fluid.
8. Follow your teacher's instructions for placing your name, the date, your class, and the title of your paper.

EXERCISE 15 ▶ **Publishing Your Writing**

With your classmates, compile a list of ideas for publishing your writing. Consider writing contests or magazines or newspapers that publish student writing, or discuss sharing a classroom anthology with other classes.

SYMBOLS FOR REVISING AND PROOFREADING

SYMBOL	EXAMPLE	MEANING OF SYMBOL
≡	Fifty-first street	Capitalize a lowercase letter.
/	Jerry's Aunt	Lowercase a capital letter.
^	differant (e)	Change a letter.
^	the capital Ohio (of)	Insert a missing word, letter, or punctuation mark.
	beside the ~~river~~ (lake)	Replace a word.
	Where's the ~~the~~ key?	Leave out a word, letter, or punctuation mark.
	an invisibile guest	Leave out and close up.
	a close friend ship	Close up space.
	thier	Change the order of letters.
(tr)	Avoid having too many corrections of your paper on the final version.	Transfer the circled words. (Write (tr) in nearby margin.)
¶	¶ "Hi," he smiled.	Begin a new paragraph.
⊙	Stay well⊙	Add a period.
^	Of course you may be wrong.	Add a comma.
#	icehockey	Add a space.
(:)	one of the following(:)	Add a colon.
^	Maria Simmons, M.D. Jim Fiorello, Ph.D.	Add a semicolon.
=	a great=grandmother	Add a hyphen.
^	Pauls car	Add an apostrophe.
(stet)	On the fifteenth of ~~July~~	Keep the crossed-out material. (Write *stet* in nearby margin.)

MAKING CONNECTIONS

DESKTOP PUBLISHING

Imagine a report on plain paper that includes a well-written description of tigers—what they look like, where they live, and what they eat. Now, imagine a booklet with color photos of leaping tigers and a map showing countries where they're found. Which would you rather read, the report or the booklet?

If you're like most people, you'd probably reach for the booklet first. Both the report and the booklet may have the same information about tigers, but the booklet's presentation looks more polished and interesting.

Of course, the plain report is easier to create. One way to make the booklet is to type the text, clip out or copy the illustrations, cut everything to fit in the space available, and then arrange and paste it all down—a lot of hard work.

With a computer, though, and a special class of computer programs called *desktop publishing software*, a writer can put away the scissors and glue and electronically design documents in a fraction of the time it might otherwise take to create them.

With desktop publishing software, a writer can

- add pictures, maps, tables, and graphs to a document
- use different type styles for headlines and subheads
- arrange the text of a document in several-column pages as in newspapers or magazines
- create boxes or borders to set off interesting quotations that will catch a reader's eye

If you have a desktop publishing program at school or at home, take one of the papers you've written recently, and change it into a booklet or magazine article with illustrations and headlines. If you don't have access to such software, do some research to find out what desktop publishing programs are available, what they do, and how much they cost. Then, prepare an oral report.

2 UNDERSTANDING PARAGRAPH STRUCTURE

Looking at the Parts

Think about paragraphs for a minute. They must be important. Every magazine, newspaper, letter, or book you pick up has them. You even write them yourself. And you're reading one right now.

Writing and You. Like you, paragraphs are individuals. Some are long; others are short. Sometimes they stand alone. But usually they are an important **part** of a crowd, working with others to bring a thought together. You might think of a paragraph as a link in a chain— separating, yet connecting, ideas. What else have you observed about paragraphs?

As You Read. As you read the following selection, notice how Ernesto Galarza links his ideas to show us how going to school in California started his "Americanization."

from Barrio Boy
by Ernesto Galarza

At Lincoln, making us into Americans did not mean scrubbing away what made us originally foreign. The teachers called us as our parents did, or as close as they could pronounce our names in Spanish or Japanese. No one was ever scolded or punished for speaking in his native tongue on the playground. Matti told the class about his mother's down quilt, which she had made in Italy with the fine feathers of a thousand geese. Encarnación acted out how boys learned to fish in the Philippines. I astounded the third grade with the story of my travels on a stagecoach, which nobody else in the class had seen except in the museum at Sutter's Fort. After a visit to the Crocker Art Gallery and its collection of heroic paintings of the golden age of California, someone showed a silk scroll with a Chinese painting. Miss Hopley herself had a way of expressing wonder over these matters before a class, her eyes wide open until they popped slightly. It was easy for me to feel that becoming a proud American, as she said we should, did not mean feeling ashamed of being a Mexican.

"... making us into Americans did not mean scrubbing away what made us originally foreign."

The Americanization of Mexican me was no smooth matter. I had to fight one lout who made fun of my travels on the *diligencia* and my barbaric translation of the word into "diligence." He doubled up with laughter over the word until I straightened him out with a kick. In class I made points explaining that in Mexico roosters said "qui-qui-ri-qui" and not "cock-a-doodle-doo," but after school I had to put up with the taunts of a big Yugoslav who said Mexican roosters were crazy.

But it was Homer who gave me the most lasting lesson for a future American.

Homer was a chunky Irishman who dressed as if every day was Sunday. He slicked his hair between a crew cut and a pompadour. And Homer was smart, as he clearly showed when he and I ran for president of the third grade.

Everyone understood that this was to be a demonstration of how the American people vote for president. In an election, the teacher explained, the candidates could be generous and vote for each other. We cast our ballots in a shoe box and Homer won by two votes. I polled my supporters and came to the conclusion that I had voted for Homer and so had he. After class he didn't deny it, reminding me of what the teacher had said—we could vote for each other but didn't have to.

READER'S RESPONSE

1. What do you think about Galarza's school? Is it the kind of school you'd want to attend? Why?
2. Beginning an education is usually a memorable experience—whether you're starting first grade or transferring to a new school later on. What beginning do you remember? In your journal, write a brief entry describing your experience.

WRITER'S CRAFT

3. What main idea is Galarza trying to convey in these paragraphs?
4. Notice how Galarza uses a variety of paragraphs—some long, some short. Why do you think he does this?

LOOKING AHEAD

In this chapter, you'll study the form and structure of paragraphs. Keep in mind that

- most paragraphs are part of a longer piece of writing
- a main idea may be supported with sensory details, facts or statistics, or examples
- most paragraphs have a main idea
- there are four basic strategies for developing paragraphs

What Makes a Paragraph

The Main Idea

Most paragraphs, and certainly those that stand alone, are organized around one main idea. Together, the sentences in the paragraph make that main idea clear. If the paragraph is part of a longer piece of writing, the surrounding paragraphs help you understand the main idea.

Read the following paragraph from the chapter's opening selection (page 64). What is its main idea?

> At Lincoln, making us into Americans did not mean scrubbing away what made us originally foreign. The teachers called us as our parents did, or as close as they could pronounce our names in Spanish or Japanese. No one was ever scolded or punished for speaking in his native tongue on the playground. Matti told the class about his mother's down quilt, which she had made in Italy with the fine feathers of a thousand geese. Encarnación acted out how boys learned to fish in the Philippines. I astounded the third grade with the story of my travels on a stage-coach, which nobody else in the class had seen except in the museum at Sutter's Fort. After a visit to the Crocker Art Gallery and its collection of heroic paintings of the golden age of California, someone showed a silk scroll with a Chinese painting. Miss Hopley herself had a way of expressing wonder over these matters before a class, her eyes wide open until they popped slightly. It was easy for me to feel that becoming a proud American, as she said we should, did not mean feeling ashamed of being a Mexican.
>
> Ernesto Galarza, *Barrio Boy*

The main idea in this paragraph is stated in its first sentence. All the other sentences give more specific information to support that idea. By looking at the longer passage (pages 64–66), you'll see that the other paragraphs also address this main idea. They point out that other students played a part in the process of becoming American, too.

The Topic Sentence

You'll often express the main idea of a paragraph in a single sentence, called the *topic sentence.*

Location of a Topic Sentence. Although a topic sentence can occur at any place in the paragraph, it often appears as the first or second sentence. In the first paragraph about the students at Lincoln school (page 64), for example, the first sentence is a topic sentence.

A topic sentence at the beginning of a paragraph helps a reader know what to expect in the rest of the paragraph. However, to create surprise or to summarize ideas, you may want to place a topic sentence at or near the end of the paragraph.

As you read the following paragraph, look to see how the writer draws all the details together with a topic sentence at the very end.

> In the summer, hosts of big red-and-yellow grasshoppers, with heads shaped like horses, will descend and eat holes in all the softer leaves. Walking sticks fly like boomerangs. Shining brown leaf-shaped palmetto bugs scurry like cockroaches. Spiders like tiny crabs hang in stout webs. The birds snap at small moths and butterflies of every kind. A blue racer, the snake that moves across the cleared sand like a whiplash, will with one flick destroy the smooth, careful cup of the ant lion in the hot sand. The whole world of the pines and of the rocks hums and glistens and stings with life.
>
> Marjory Stoneman Douglas,
> *The Everglades: River of Grass*

Importance of a Topic Sentence. Many paragraphs you read won't have a topic sentence. In fact, some of them, especially those that relate a sequence of events or actions, won't even seem to have a single main idea. But that doesn't mean topic sentences aren't useful. Topic sentences at the beginning of a paragraph help you when you're reading. They let you know what to expect in the rest of the paragraph. They also help you focus your paragraph when you're writing. Whether you're writing a paragraph or reading one, the topic sentence can also help you by suggesting the order of details in the paragraph—order by comparison and contrast or by cause and effect, for example.

EXERCISE 1 ▶ **Identifying Main Ideas and Topic Sentences**

Each of the following paragraphs develops a main idea. State the main idea of each paragraph and, if there is a topic sentence, identify it. If there is no topic sentence, you may find it a little harder to say what the main idea is.

1.   In my country, sports were one way to show national pride, one of the few safe ways. You could cheer for a Czech hockey team or soccer team, even against the Soviet Union. It was a tradition going back to the nineteenth century when people formed sports clubs like Sokol, to compete in gymnastics. It was the only way you could say to the Hapsburgs, "Look, we're still Czechs, even if we now belong to the Austro-Hungarian Empire."

Martina Navratilova with George Vecsey, *Martina*

2.   Throughout the Western United States, you can buy postcards with a photograph of the fabulous jackalope. Stuffed specimens of this creature can sometimes be found on display, usually in bars. The jackalope is said to be a rare, nearly extinct antlered species of rabbit. Up close, the jackalope looks like a stuffed rabbit with a pair of horns or antlers stuck onto it. And, of course, that is exactly what it is.

Daniel Cohen, *The Encyclopedia of Monsters*

Fabulous Jackalope

Supporting Sentences

The topic sentence of a paragraph states a general idea. To make that idea clear and interesting to the reader, you have to elaborate on it, or develop it in great detail. Other sentences in the paragraph give specific details or information to support the main idea of the paragraph. Depending on the subject you're writing about, you might support your main idea with sensory details, facts or statistics, or examples.

WRITING NOTE

With or without a topic sentence, a paragraph needs specific bits of information to support the main idea.

Sensory Details

Sensory details are precise bits of information that you observe, or collect, through any of your five senses— sight, sound, smell, touch, taste. You might include a detail about the color of something, how it sounds when it moves, or what it feels like when you touch it.

In the following paragraph, the writer uses details of sight, sound, and smell to elaborate on a description of her childhood home in the morning.

Sight	In the summer my mother got up just after sunrise, so that when she called Matthew and me for breakfast, the house was filled with sounds and smells of her
Smell	industrious mornings. Odors of frying scrapple or codfish cakes drifted up the back stairs, mingling sometimes with the
Smell	sharp scent of mustard greens she was cooking for dinner that night. Up the laundry
Smell/Sight	chute from the cellar floated whiffs of
Sound	steamy air and the churning sound of the washing machine. From the dining room, where she liked to sit ironing and chatting
Smell	on the telephone, came the fragrance of

Sound

Sight

Sound

hot clean clothes and the sound of her voice: cheerful, resonant, reverberating a little weirdly through the high-ceilinged rooms, as if she were sitting happily at the bottom of a well.

Andrea Lee, "Mother"

Facts and Statistics

Another way to support a main idea with specific information is to use facts or statistics. A *fact* is something that can be proven true by concrete information: General Lee surrendered to General Grant in the front parlor of the Wilmer McLean house. A *statistic* is a fact that is based on numbers: During the Civil War, the South lost about 260,000 soldiers, and the North lost about 360,000.

In the following paragraph about movie theaters, facts and statistics support and prove the main idea that concession sales are big moneymakers. In case you're wondering about the word *Rialto,* it is a name for a theater district. The writer uses it to mean theaters in general.

Statistic

Fact

Statistic

Statistic

Fact

Let's look at how concession sales affect the bottom line of the Rialto. In large cities, about 15–20 percent of all customers will stop at the concession stand (in smaller towns, even more customers eat), and the theater owner figures to gross about 75 cents for every customer who walks through the turnstile, meaning that the average purchase is over $3. The key to making money in the concession area is maintaining a high profit margin, and the

Statistics

items sold do a terrific job. The average profit margin on candy—77 percent; on popcorn—86 percent; on soft drinks—a whopping 90 percent. For every dollar spent at the concession counter, the theater operator nets over 85 cents.

David Feldman, *Imponderables*

Examples

You can also use one or more examples to support a main idea. *Examples* are specific instances, or illustrations, of a general idea. A cow is an example of an animal; your test score of 67 is an example of what can happen if you don't study. The following paragraph uses specific examples of bird behavior to show how bathing varies among birds.

Main Idea

Example 1

Example 2

Example 3

Example 4

Bathing behavior varies from species to species. Many birds stand in shallow water and, through a complex series of movements—rolling their head and body and fluttering their wings—get water trapped in featherless areas next to their body and then press the water out through their feathers. Some aerial birds, like swallows, may dive into water and immediately fly up. Still others may jump into water and be briefly submerged before getting out. Some birds bathe in rain or drizzle, in dew on grass, or among wet leaves. Take time to watch bathing behavior; it is fascinating.

Donald and Lillian Stokes,
The Bird Feeder Book

EXERCISE 2 ▶ **Collecting Supporting Details**

Three general ideas you could write about are listed below. With each idea, a type of support—examples, facts and statistics, and sensory details—is suggested. Think up at least two details to support each main idea. You may have to do a little research (reading or talking to knowledgeable people) to find support, especially facts or statistics.

EXAMPLE **1.** Shakespeare's audience loved puns, and he included several in *Romeo and Juliet.* (examples)

1. *When Mercutio is dying, he says, "Ask for / me tomorrow and you shall find me a grave / man." The pun is on the word* grave, *which means "serious" as well as "burial place." Romeo creates a pun with* soles *and* soul *in the following lines: "You have dancing shoes / With nimble soles; I have a soul of lead / So stakes me to the ground I cannot move."*

1. Physical education classes develop skills that you'll use throughout your life. (examples)

2. Ponce de León, the Spanish explorer, led an expedition to what is now Florida. (facts and statistics)

3. On a rainy, cold afternoon, nothing could be better than going to see a movie. (sensory details)

The Clincher Sentence

Sometimes, especially in long paragraphs, you may want to end with a sentence that restates or summarizes the main idea. This concluding sentence is called a *clincher sentence* because it pulls all the details together. The following paragraph uses a clincher to restate the idea that Michael Jordan is still the "best player in basketball."

> Coming into New Jersey to play the Nets, the Bulls had won five games and lost only two since Jordan's return. Any doubts anyone might have had about his potential to reclaim his standing as the best player in basketball had been effectively removed three days after he hit the winning shot in Atlanta, when the Bulls traveled to New York to play the Knicks in Madison Square Garden. Jordan's performance that night—55 points, 21-for-37 shooting from the field, 10-of-11 free throws, all of this in only 38 minutes on the court—could not have taken place in a better setting for him (the New York and national media were on hand in force), and could not have come at a better time (the game was nationally telecast, to an audience that had been reading the stories about Jordan's struggles, had been seeing the TV coverage of his missed shots and missteps). Since that night he had scored 23 points in a win over the Boston Celtics, then only 12 points on 5-for-19 shooting against the Philadelphia 76ers. But the evening in New York had defined the possibilities inherent in his comeback; now the world was clamoring to watch every shot he took, and tickets to Bulls games, always extremely difficult to get, were just about impossible to buy at any price. <u>No one wanted to miss the next night when Jordan might explode.</u>

Bob Greene, *Rebound*

Unity

When something has *unity,* all of its parts work together as a unit—as one. A paragraph has unity when all the sentences work together as a unit to express or support one main idea. Sentences can work as a unit in one of three ways: (1) by supporting a main idea that is stated in a topic sentence, (2) by supporting a main idea that is implied (understood without being directly expressed), or (3) by expressing a related series of actions.

All Sentences Relate to the Main Idea Stated in the Topic Sentence. In the following paragraph, the topic sentence tells us the main idea—whales are physical wonders. Look at each of the supporting sentences to see how each includes a detail related to physical wonder.

Topic Sentence	Whales not only have fascinating behavior but are physical wonders as well.
Detail	The Blue Whale is the largest animal that has ever graced our planet. Such giant herbivorous dinosaurs as the brontosaurus weighed up to fifty tons. A Blue Whale weighs that much long before it reaches puberty; full grown they weigh a hundred and fifty tons, as much as three brontosauri!
Detail	
Detail	Blue Whales grow to more than a hundred feet—longer than any other animals.
Detail	When such a whale is vertical in the water with its tail at the surface, its nose is deep enough to be subjected to the weight of three atmospheres.
Detail	It is possible that they dive deep enough, more than a mile, to be subjected to more than two hundred times the atmospheric pressure experienced by people on land at sea level.

Paul and Anne Ehrlich, Extinction

All Sentences Relate to an Implied Main Idea. The following paragraph doesn't have a topic sentence. But each sentence helps support an implied main idea—when he opens his eyes, the man sees the results of the birds' attack.

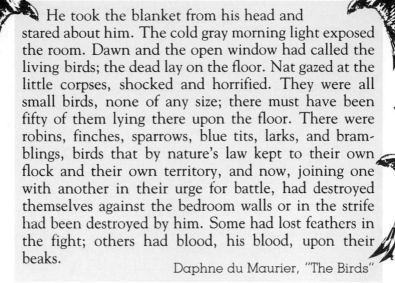

He took the blanket from his head and stared about him. The cold gray morning light exposed the room. Dawn and the open window had called the living birds; the dead lay on the floor. Nat gazed at the little corpses, shocked and horrified. They were all small birds, none of any size; there must have been fifty of them lying there upon the floor. There were robins, finches, sparrows, blue tits, larks, and bramblings, birds that by nature's law kept to their own flock and their own territory, and now, joining one with another in their urge for battle, had destroyed themselves against the bedroom walls or in the strife had been destroyed by him. Some had lost feathers in the fight; others had blood, his blood, upon their beaks.

Daphne du Maurier, "The Birds"

All Sentences Relate to a Sequence of Events. In the following paragraph, the narrator is trying to save Harry, who fears a deadly snake has slithered into his bed. The paragraph doesn't actually have a main idea. But each action detail is part of a sequence that begins when the narrator leaves the room and ends as he stands beside the bed wondering what to do.

Like all narrative paragraphs, this paragraph is actually a cause-and-effect paragraph. What one character does (cause) results in the next action (effect).

I went softly out of the room in my stocking feet and fetched a small sharp knife from the kitchen. I put it in my trouser pocket, ready to use instantly in case something went wrong while we were still thinking out a plan. If Harry coughed or moved or did something to frighten the krait and got bitten, I was going to be ready to cut the bitten place and try to suck the venom out. I came back to the bedroom and Harry was still lying there very quiet and sweating all over his face. His eyes followed me as I moved across the room to his bed, and I could see he was wondering what I'd been up to. I stood beside him, trying to think of the best thing to do.

Roald Dahl, "Poison"

EXERCISE 3 ▶   **Identifying Sentences That Destroy Unity**

Find the sentences that destroy unity in the following paragraphs. Remember: To have unity, all details in a paragraph must be related to the main idea or the sequence of actions.

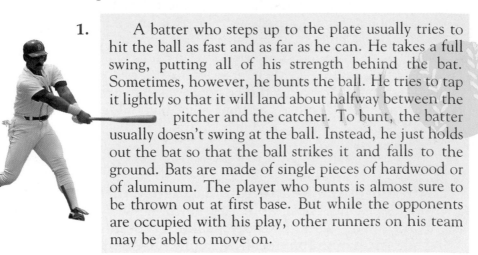

1.   A batter who steps up to the plate usually tries to hit the ball as fast and as far as he can. He takes a full swing, putting all of his strength behind the bat. Sometimes, however, he bunts the ball. He tries to tap it lightly so that it will land about halfway between the pitcher and the catcher. To bunt, the batter usually doesn't swing at the ball. Instead, he just holds out the bat so that the ball strikes it and falls to the ground. Bats are made of single pieces of hardwood or of aluminum. The player who bunts is almost sure to be thrown out at first base. But while the opponents are occupied with his play, other runners on his team may be able to move on.

2.   The women's rights movement began at the Seneca Falls Convention in New York in 1848. At that time, Elizabeth Cady Stanton introduced a resolution demanding suffrage, or the right to vote, for women. In 1869, Stanton and Susan B. Anthony formed a national organization to seek voting rights for women. In 1872, Anthony was arrested for breaking the law by voting in a presidential election, but by 1896, four states had given women the right to vote. In 1912, women's suffrage at last became an issue in a presidential campaign. Two years later, a suffrage petition signed by 404,000 women was presented to Congress. President Woodrow Wilson, responding to pressure by women's groups, endorsed a new amendment. Black males were granted the right to vote after the Civil War by the Fourteenth and Fifteenth Amendments. Finally, in 1919, the Nineteenth Amendment, giving women the right to vote, was passed by Congress.

Coherence

If you've ever read a paragraph that didn't make any sense to you, it probably didn't have *coherence.* In other words, it wasn't easy for you to see how all the ideas in the paragraph fit together, how they were arranged and connected. You can create coherence by paying attention to two things: (1) the order in which you arrange your ideas, and (2) the connections you make between ideas.

Order of Ideas

How you arrange, or order, ideas in your paragraph can help your readers to follow them. Often, the subject you're writing about will suggest the order of ideas.

Chronological Order.   *Chrono–* means "time." If you are writing about a series of actions or events in time, it makes sense to arrange them according to the time they happened. Chronological order works because it often shows a cause-and-effect sequence. One action (cause) results in another action (effect), and so on. This order is especially useful when you are explaining a process or telling a story. In the following example, the writer uses chronological order to arrange the actions between an old woman and a wounded young man.

> So she went back to the young man. He was lying as she had left him, propped against the dike, panting and very pale. He had opened his coat, and he had a little bag from which he was taking out strips of cloth and a bottle of something. And again he spoke, and again she understood nothing. Then he made signs, and she saw it was water he wanted, so she took up a broken pot from one of many blown about the street, and, going up the dike, she filled it with river water and brought it down again and washed his wound, and she tore off the strips he made from the rolls of bandaging. He knew how to put the cloth over the gaping wound and he made signs to her and she followed these signs. All the time he was trying to tell her something, but she could understand nothing.
>
> Pearl S. Buck, "The Old Demon"

Spatial Order.   Look at this term closely and you'll get a clue to its meaning. Spatial order is arrangement by ordering details according to how they are spaced—nearest to farthest, left to right, or any other reasonable arrangement. It's especially useful in descriptions because it helps the reader picture how details fit together. In the following example, spatial order helps us "see" the city from outside to inside.

Outside the city

Within the city

Within a house in the city

> Sai was walled, with a guarded gate of great size and beauty; outside the walls were innumerable barns, stables, shops, and barrack-houses, and inside them the streets were straight and wide like those of South City but still wider and longer. The street that led in from the gate ended in a huge building, window above window above window, and the barrack-houses and family houses were all higher and solider and finer than those of South City. Terter House in Sai had its own wall around its gardens, of polished black stone; its roof was of carved cedar, with decks and walkways on it; and down inside it the rooms seemed endless, apartments and divisions and screened-off corners and nooks and angles, all without windows yet bright, and warm as the silky nest of the wood rat inside her many-tunnelled tall house. The rooms deepest inside were the women's quarters.
>
> Ursula K. Le Guin,
> *Always Coming Home*

Order of Importance.   Sometimes one detail or piece of supporting information is more important than another. Then you may want to arrange your ideas by order of importance. Don't forget that readers usually pay more attention to what they read first or what they read last. The writer of the following paragraph begins with the least serious problem—restrictions on watering lawns and washing cars. The paragraph ends with the most serious problem—the threat of fire.

The two-year-long drought is causing serious problems in my hometown. For several months we have lived with severe limits on using water. We can water lawns or wash cars only from midnight to 4:00 A.M. Recently, restrictions have become even more severe. Our water use is regulated, so we must monitor how much water we use to wash laundry or dishes and bathe. Water quality has also become a problem. The water now has a sour odor, and most people do not feel safe drinking it. But the worst problem we are facing is the threat of serious fires. Three homes recently burned to the ground when a small grass fire grew out of control. Carelessness with fire, or lightning during a thunderstorm, could set our whole town ablaze.

Logical Order. Something that is logical makes sense. Sometimes in writing it makes sense to group or arrange ideas together to show how they are related. This grouping helps to make relationships clear. You will find this type of order especially useful in definitions and classifications. The writer of the following paragraph, for example, uses logical order to arrange a group of examples in discussing different kinds of cats.

Cats vary as much within their species as people do within theirs. Some cats are so dull-witted from birth that never in their lives do they learn that a door which is ajar can be nudged farther open. Other cats can open shut doors and get the lids off garbage cans as easily as if they had two hands with opposable thumbs. Some cats are born with unshakably equable dispositions and others are so high-strung they go all to pieces when a doorbell rings. The kind of household a cat lives in also affects its temperament. Like human infants, cats do better in orderly and predictable environments. Disorganized and excitable families can produce cats with ulcers.

Muriel Beadle, *The Cat: History, Biology, and Behavior*

| EXERCISE 4 ▶ | **Choosing an Order of Ideas** |

For each of the following topics, decide which order of ideas would make the most sense to you: *chronological order, spatial order, order of importance,* or *logical order.* For some topics, you might think more than one type of order would work.

1. four characteristics of a good quarterback
2. choosing an after-school job
3. the perfect room for a teenager
4. kinds of weight-loss diets
5. the right way to study for a test

| EXERCISE 5 ▶ | **Identifying Order of Ideas** |

One of the following paragraphs uses an order of ideas that makes sense, but one doesn't. Which paragraph is it? Rewrite the paragraph, rearranging the sentences into an easily understood order. Then decide which order of ideas is used in the other paragraph.

1.   The naturalist Paul Rezendes has this advice for seeing nature and the great outdoors: Don't rush. Walk rather than drive a car or take a tour bus. Also try to spend some time alone. You notice new things when you aren't distracted by other people. Most important, he says, is to take your time. Take a pad and draw sketches or keep a journal, but don't take a camera. Rezendes says a camera makes you think you're capturing the place on film, when what you really need to do is to capture it in your mind.

2.   On the Fourth of July, we thought we'd make a real holiday of it. We took the first train into Boston. We stopped first at the *Constitution,* the first American naval ship. Then we walked to historic Old North Church. We bought a take-out dinner. After a quick lunch, we took a bus to see the aircraft carrier *John F. Kennedy.* At seven o'clock we ate our picnic,

> stretched out on a blanket beside the Charles River, waiting for the concert. By the time we finished our tour, it was almost five o'clock. After enjoying the *1812 Overture* and the fireworks show, we made the long trip home.

Connections Between Ideas

Besides putting ideas in an order that makes sense, you need to show how they are connected. You can show connections by

1. making *direct references* to something else in the paragraph, or
2. using words that make a *transition,* or bridge, from one idea to another

☞ REFERENCE NOTE: Direct references and transitional words and phrases can make connections between paragraphs as well as within paragraphs. See page 124.

Direct References. Direct references link ideas by referring to a noun or pronoun that you've used earlier. You can make that reference in several ways:

1. Use a noun or pronoun that refers to a noun used earlier.
2. Repeat a word used earlier.
3. Use a word or phrase that means the same thing as one used earlier.

The following paragraph uses several direct references to make connections between ideas. Each reference is coded with the numbers above to show you what type of reference it is.

> At the man's heels trotted a dog, a big native husky[3], the proper wolf dog[3], gray-coated and without any visible or temperamental difference from its[1] brother, the wild wolf[2]. The animal[3] was depressed by the tremendous cold. It[1] knew that it was no time for traveling. Its[1] instinct told it[1] a truer tale than was told to the man[2] by the man's[2] judgment. In reality, it was not merely colder than fifty below zero; it was

colder than sixty below, than seventy below. It was seventy-five below zero[2]. Since the freezing point is thirty-two above zero[2], it meant that one hundred and seven degrees of frost obtained. The dog[2] did not know anything about thermometers. Possibly in its[1] brain there was no sharp consciousness of a condition of very cold such as was in the man's[2] brain[2]. But the brute[3] had its instinct. It[1] experienced a vague but menacing apprehension that subdued it[1] and made it[1] slink along at the man's[2] heels, and that made it[1] question eagerly every unwonted movement of the man[2], as if expecting him[1] to go into camp or to seek shelter somewhere and build a fire. The dog[2] had learned fire[2], and it[1] wanted fire[2], or else to burrow under the snow and cuddle its[1] warmth away from the air.

Jack London, "To Build a Fire"

Transitional Words and Phrases. *Trans–* means "across" or "over." A transition in writing—whether it's a word, a phrase, or even a sentence—reaches *across* or *over*, connecting one idea to another. When you use transitions, you not only connect ideas, but also show *how* they are connected. Transitional words and phrases include conjunctions and prepositions that show chronological or spatial order. As you refer to the following chart, notice that certain transitions are also related to certain types of writing.

TRANSITIONAL WORDS AND PHRASES

Comparing Ideas/Classification and Definition

also	another	similarly
and	moreover	too

Contrasting Ideas/Classification and Definition

although	in spite of	on the other hand
but	instead	still
however	nevertheless	yet

Showing Cause and Effect/Narration

as a result	for	so that
because	since	therefore
consequently	so	

Showing Time/Narration

after	eventually	next
at last	finally	then
at once	first	thereafter
before	meanwhile	when

Showing Place/Description

above	beyond	into
across	down	next
around	here	over
before	in	there
behind	inside	under

Showing Importance/Evaluation

first	mainly	then
last	more important	to begin with

The following paragraph uses transitional words and phrases, which are underlined, to make connections in time and place.

> With nervous hands he lowered the piece of canvas which served as his door, <u>and</u> pegged it at the bottom. <u>Then</u> quickly <u>and</u> quietly, looking at the piece of canvas frequently, he slipped the records into the case, snapped the lid shut, <u>and</u> carried the phonograph to his couch. <u>There</u>, pausing often to stare at the canvas <u>and</u> listen, he dug earth from the wall <u>and</u> disclosed a piece of board. <u>Behind</u> this there was a deep hole in the wall, <u>into</u> which he put the phonograph. <u>After</u> a moment's consideration, he went <u>over</u> <u>and</u> reached <u>down</u> for his bundle of books and inserted it <u>also</u>. <u>Then</u>, guardedly, he once more sealed up the hole with the board <u>and</u> the earth. He <u>also</u> changed his blankets, and the grass-stuffed sack which served as a pillow, <u>so that</u> he could lie facing the entrance. <u>After</u> carefully placing two more blocks of peat on the fire, he stood for a long time watching the stretched canvas, <u>but</u> it seemed to billow naturally with the first gusts of a lowering wind. <u>At last</u> he prayed, <u>and</u> got in <u>under</u> his blankets, <u>and</u> closed his smoke-smarting eyes. <u>On the inside</u> of the bed, <u>next to</u> the wall, he could feel with his hand, the comfortable piece of lead pipe.
>
> Walter Van Tilburg Clark,
> "The Portable Phonograph"

WRITING NOTE   If you used transitional words and phrases (with the exception of *and* and *but*) in every sentence, your writing might sound artificial. Since direct references are more natural, feel free to use them frequently in your writing. Your readers will appreciate it.

EXERCISE 6 ▶ **Identifying Direct References and Transitions**

The following paragraph uses both direct references and transitional words and phrases to connect ideas. Make two lists: one list of direct reference words and one list of transitions you find in the paragraph. [Hint: there are at least fourteen direct reference words and six transitions.]

EXAMPLE   My father started high school in Frederick, Maryland. When he was a junior, his family moved and he finished high school in Baltimore.

Direct References	*Transitions*
he	*in*
his	*When*
he	*and*
high school	*in*

At Waterford Crystal in Ireland, each piece of crystal is still handmade. First, the glass-blowers dip long pipes into a 1,200-degree furnace. In the furnace, their pipes collect fiery lumps of molten crystal.

Then they blow the hot lumps of crystal into "blank" cups, vases, and bowls of various sizes and shapes. Each piece must be thin and clear, yet thick enough to be engraved later. After the blank glass has cooled, the "masters" take over. They use dime-sized diamond wheels to engrave the glass in one of Waterford's beautiful patterns. A typical Waterford glass takes about eight hours to make. To create a large, expensive piece, experienced engravers may take several weeks and go through a number of blank pieces of glass.

| EXERCISE 7 ▶ | **Using Transitions** |

The following paragraph isn't completely clear. Revise it by adding transitions to make the connections it needs. Feel free to rewrite or combine sentences, too.

Jason decided to hike across Glacier National Park. He decided this at a young age. He never actually did much hiking. On his eighteenth birthday, he and a friend made plans to explore Glacier National Park on foot. Jason researched the history and terrain of the park. He wrote to the park. He received a package full of information and maps. He found out that much of the park, which is in the northern Rockies, is very rugged and isolated. He bought clothing and packed provisions for wilderness living. He arrived at the park and talked to the park rangers. They told Jason the best trails to follow. They gave him safety tips.

Strategies of Development

Earlier in this chapter you looked at the need to elaborate on, or support, a main idea. Then you looked at some ways of arranging the supporting details so that they make sense. Now you're going to look at some strategies for developing your main ideas: description, narration, classification, and evaluation. These four strategies of development are basically different ways of looking at a topic or subject.

STRATEGIES OF DEVELOPMENT	
Description	Looking at individual features of a particular subject
Narration	Looking at changes in the subject over a period of time
Classification	Looking at a subject in relation to other subjects
Evaluation	Looking at the value of the subject (judging)

You can use these strategies in single paragraphs and in longer pieces of writing. You may write a letter to a television station, for example, evaluating the quality of a new show. Or you may write in your journal, narrating the excitement at the basketball playoffs. You'll also use these strategies in school. For example, in science you may write a paragraph explaining the process of cell division (narration) or a paragraph describing the trees in your neighborhood (description). In a job, you may be asked to write a report comparing your product to that of a competitor's (classification). Or you may have to write a recommendation for an employee (evaluation).

WRITING NOTE   In your reading, you'll find that most paragraphs and longer pieces of writing combine more than one strategy of development. For example, description and narration are often combined.

Description

What does a black widow spider look like? How will I know which building is the Empire State Building?

When you want to tell what something is like or what it looks like, you need to consider its particular features. You need to use description. In a description, you'll use sensory details as support, and you'll often use spatial order. Notice how the writer of the following paragraph uses details and spatial order to describe a room.

The room displayed a modest and pleasant color-scheme, after one of the best standard designs of the decorator who "did the interiors" for most of the speculative-builders' houses in Zenith. The walls were gray, the woodwork white, the rug a serene blue, and very much like mahogany was the furniture—the bureau with its great clear mirror, Mrs. Babbitt's dressing-table with toilet-articles of almost solid silver, the plain twin beds, between them a small table holding a standard electric bedside lamp, a glass for water, and a standard bedside book with colored illustrations—what particular book it was cannot be ascertained, since no one had ever opened it. The mattresses were firm but not hard, triumphant modern mattresses which had cost a great deal of money; the hot-water radiator was of exactly the proper scientific surface for the cubic contents of the room. . . . It was a masterpiece among bedrooms, right out of Cheerful Modern Houses for Medium Incomes. Only it had nothing to do with the Babbitts, nor with anyone else. . . . It had the air of being a very good room in a very good hotel. One expected the chambermaid to come in and make it ready for people who would stay but one night, go without looking back, and never think of it again.

Sinclair Lewis, *Babbitt*

EXERCISE 8 ▶ **Using Description as a Strategy**

How would you describe your room, a cockroach, a snazzy car? Choose one of the following subjects, and list the features that will help describe it—something you can see, hear, smell, taste, or feel. To think of features, you may want to use a technique such as observing or brainstorming. (See pages 25–30.)

1. the messiest room you've ever seen
2. a professional athlete who has just won a game
3. an animal or insect that you think is disgusting
4. your school the day before summer vacation

 COMPUTER NOTE: Use your word-processing program's outline function to create and organize a list of sensory details.

Narration

What happened when Ebenezer Scrooge met the Ghost of Christmas Past? How did the Egyptians build the pyramids? What caused the American Revolution?

To answer these questions, you have to describe changes over time—using narration. Since narration involves events or actions in time, you'll usually arrange your ideas in chronological order. You may use narration to tell a story (what happened to Scrooge), to explain a process (how they built pyramids), or to explain causes and effects (causes of the American Revolution).

Telling a Story.   You can develop a narrative paragraph by telling a story. The story may be true or imaginary (fiction). In the following paragraph, the writer tells a story to explain how a place came to be called ape canyon.

Near Mount Saint Helens in the state of Washington there is a place known locally as "ape canyon." There, so the story goes, a group of miners was attacked by a party of seven-foot apes. Earlier in the day, a miner had shot one of the "giant apes," and in the evening a gang of them bombarded the miners' windowless cabin with rocks and boulders. The miners crouched inside the cabin for hours while rocks rained down on them. When the attack was over, the miners fled down the mountain and back to town. They returned to the canyon with a bunch of well-armed friends, but the apes had departed, leaving behind only their giant footprints and a badly battered cabin. The giant apes of Mount Saint Helens, if they were ever more than a tall tale, are doubtless extinct today because of the eruption of the Mount Saint Helens volcano. In 1982 a retired logger named Rant Mullens claimed he and a friend started the Mount Saint Helens story by rolling rocks down on the miner's cabin, as a joke.

Daniel Cohen,
The Encyclopedia of Monsters

Explaining a Process.   When you need to tell how something works or how to do something, you're explaining a process. In explaining a process, you look at your subject as it changes over time. Again, you use narration. In the following paragraph, the writer explains how to find the source of honey.

To find a honey tree, first catch a bee. Catch a bee when its legs are heavy with pollen; then it is ready for home. It is simple enough to catch a bee on a flower: hold a cup or glass above the bee, and when it flies up, cap the cup with a piece of cardboard. Carry the bee to a nearby open spot—best an elevated one—release it, and watch where it goes. Keep your eyes on it as long as you can see it, and hie you to that last known place. Wait there until you see another bee; catch it, release it, and watch. Bee after bee will lead toward the honey tree, until you see the final bee enter the tree.

Annie Dillard, *The Writing Life*

Explaining Cause and Effect.   When you want to explain what caused something or the effects of something, you need to look at the way things have changed over the course of time. This is another time you use narration. The following paragraph looks at the violent effects of the collapse of a dam.

At one minute before 8:00, the dam simply collapsed. There is little evidence that water came over the top of the dam, although that remains one of the obvious possibilities. It is a good deal more likely that the whole structure became saturated with moisture, dissolved into something resembling wet paste, and just slumped over on its foundation of silt and sludge. In any event, the entire lake of black water, all 132 million gallons of it, roared through the breach in a matter of seconds. It was already more than water, full of coal dust and other solids, and as it broke through the dam and landed on the banks of refuse below, it scraped up thousands of tons of other materials, the whole being fused into a liquid substance that one engineer simply called a "mud wave" and one witness described as "rolling lava." The wave set off a series of explosions as it drove a channel through the smoldering trough of slag, raising mushroom-shaped clouds high into the air and throwing great spatters of mud three hundred feet up to the haul road where a few men were returning from the mines. The rock and debris dislodged by those explosions were absorbed into the mass too. By now, there were something like a million tons of solid waste caught up in the flow.

Kai Erikson, *Everything in Its Path*

EXERCISE 9 ▶ **Using Narration as a Strategy**

What happened first? What happened next? Did one thing cause another? Follow the instructions for using narration to develop the items given below.

1. Select one of the following subjects and list at least four actions that took place.
   a. the time I was locked out of the house (make up the actions)
   b. how Washington crossed the Delaware (check an encyclopedia or history book)

2. Select one of the following subjects and list at least four steps in the process.
   c. how to make a copy of an audiocassette (if you don't know how, ask someone)
   d. how to make a good salad (if you don't know how, now's the time to learn)
3. Select one of the following subjects and list at least three causes or effects.
   e. getting a lower grade than you expected at the end of a grading period (identify the causes)
   f. air pollution (list the effects; you may need to check some newspapers or magazines or talk to someone interested in the environment)

EXERCISE 10 ▶   **Speaking and Listening: Explaining a Process**

Think about a process you can explain clearly, something you know how to do well or have read about. Jot down notes about the process and explain the steps in order to the class or a small group. Exchange ideas with your classmates: What's new to you? What would you like to try out?

Classification

Which states are increasing in population? What is a youth hostel? What are the differences in the reasons for building the Great Wall of China and the Berlin Wall? (The Berlin Wall, of course, has now come down. Why does the Great Wall of China still stand?)

To answer any of these questions, you need to look at a subject as it relates to other subjects in a group. You need to *classify.* When you classify, you may divide a subject into its parts (the fifty states), define it (youth hostel), or compare and contrast it with something else (the Great Wall and the Berlin Wall).

Dividing.   Sometimes you need to look at the parts of a subject in order to explain it. For example, to explain the Bill of Rights of the Constitution, you may have to divide it into its parts—the ten rights it guarantees. To discuss recreational sports, you may have to divide this subject into team sports, individual sports, and sports where you need a partner. The following paragraph uses the strategy of dividing in order to explain the human muscular system.

Our muscles represent about 40 percent of the weight of our bodies, but they are not all alike. We actually have three different types of muscles. One type of muscle, the cardiac muscle, is present only in the heart. The cells of the cardiac muscle form long rows of fibers. Unlike other muscle tissue, cardiac muscles contract independently. Another type of muscle, the smooth muscle, is present in the walls of internal organs, our arteries, and our veins. Since we can't control our smooth muscles, they are called involuntary muscles. The third type of muscle, the striated muscle, is called a voluntary muscle. Striated muscles are voluntary because we can control them, and they are attached to our legs, arms, back, and torso.

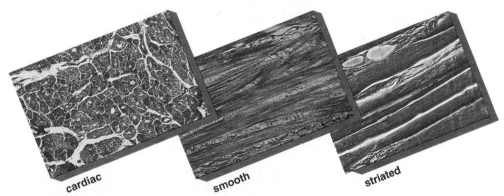

cardiac   smooth   striated

Defining.   When you define a subject, you first identify the large class or group it belongs to. Then you tell what makes the subject unique, or different, from other members of that group. In the paragraph above, the large group—muscles—was explained by dividing it into types. Then each type of muscle—cardiac, smooth, and striated—was explained by defining. In the following paragraph, the first sentence defines *mummy,* and the other sentences give examples to further define, or explain, what a mummy is.

Definition

Example

Example

Example

A mummy is the preserved body of a human being or an animal, by any means, either deliberate or accidental. Mummies survive from many ancient cultures, some preserved in a wet state, others dry. The bog bodies of northern Europe, such as the 2,000-year-old Lindow Man, found in Cheshire, England, in 1984, belonged to people who had either fallen, or been thrown, into wet, marshy places. The exclusion of oxygen and acidity in the peat of the bog effectively preserved their bodies. Most mummies, though, were preserved by being dried, or desiccated. Many civilizations, including the Egyptian, Chinese and some South American cultures, tried to achieve this artificially.

Christine El Mahdy, *Mummies, Myth and Magic*

Comparing and Contrasting.

Comparing and contrasting are closely related to dividing and defining. For example, when the writer divided the subject of muscles into three types, she also looked at the differences (contrasts) among them. You can look at subjects by comparing them (telling how they are alike), contrasting them (telling how they are different), or by both comparing and contrasting them. The following paragraph contrasts places used to film a nature series.

Contrast 1

Contrast 2

Contrast 3

The fascinating thing about shooting this series was the contrast. One minute you would be filming in snow and the next minute sweating in the heat of a tropical forest. One minute paddling a canoe down an English river, the next minute paddling a canoe over a tropical reef. So in this case we had a contrast, for we left the giant cactus forests of Arizona and flew down to the rolling grasslands of southern Africa. . . .

Gerald Durrell, *How to Shoot an Amateur Naturalist*

| EXERCISE 11 | **Using Classification as a Strategy** |

What is it? How can it be divided into distinct parts? How are items in a group alike or different? Follow the directions telling which classification strategy to use to develop each main idea given below.

Main Idea	**Classification Strategy**
1. Whatever your taste, there is a type of music that will appeal to you.	Look at the subject of music by dividing it into types; then, list details for each type to support this main idea.
2. A cat's behavior is not a simple thing.	Look at the subject of cat behavior by defining it: identify the larger group to which cat behavior belongs, then list some features that make it different from other behaviors.
3. People who like ice-skating will probably enjoy roller-skating on single-blade skates.	Look at the subjects by comparing and contrasting them; then, list likenesses and differences. (If you don't think you know enough about skating, do some research or choose two other sports.)

Evaluation

Should our school continue to publish the names of honor roll students? Is Steven Spielberg's latest movie worth going to see?

When you *evaluate* a subject, you attempt to determine its value. You make a judgment about it. Sometimes your purpose in evaluating a subject is to inform other people. At other times, your purpose may be to persuade them to think or act differently. Once you tell your readers what your evaluation is, you also need to support your ideas. The following paragraph is an excerpt that evaluates the documentary *Anne Frank Remembered*.

Evaluation

> One tonic effect of Jon Blair's documentary *Anne Frank Remembered* is to restore the human scale to an immense atrocity. . . . The film's secret star is Miep Gies, a Gentile who worked for Otto's company. Today she looks like a stoic

Support

> maiden aunt; kids at a family dinner would peg her as a stodge. But that is because Hollywood teaches us to look for shining ideals in a pretty face. Gies has the plain

Support

> face of true-life heroism. Each day for two years she took food, magazines, and news of the war to the Franks. She persuaded them to accept Fritz Pfeffer as a boarder. When the family was seized, she boldly con-

Support

> fronted the Nazis. She also saved Anne's diary. Today Gies is still doing good. In the film she meets Pfeffer's son and assures him

Support

> that his father, vilified to the world in Anne's diary [where he is called Albert Dussel], was a "lovely, lovely man." Their handshake is a heartbreaker.
>
> Richard Corliss, "Saints in the Neighborhood"

EXERCISE 12 ▶ Using Evaluation as a Strategy

What do you think about it? Why do you think that? Evaluate each of the following broad subjects. Then list two or three reasons you could use to support your judgment.

EXAMPLE **1.** our town's St. Patrick's Day Parade
1. *Evaluation: It's a good parade for a small town.*
Reasons: (1) In last year's parade there were two floats with motorized movement.
(2) Last year's parade had marching bands from as far as fifty miles away.
(3) The parade always draws a crowd of four or five thousand people.

1. a movie you've recently seen
2. a magazine or book you've read recently
3. a sport or musical event at your school

MAKING CONNECTIONS

WRITING PARAGRAPHS FOR DIFFERENT PURPOSES

Writing a Paragraph to Express Yourself

When you think about something in your life, do you ever try writing about it? Sometimes writing just for yourself helps you learn more about yourself and your own life.

A diary or writer's notebook is a good place to write an expressive paragraph. But any sheet of paper will do. Use one of the following sentences as a starter, and write a paragraph expressing your thoughts or feelings.

Starter Sentences for Expressive Writing
The happiest time in my life was ____.
The person who has influenced me most is ____.
When I think about the future, I wonder ____.
When I think about ____, I get angry.
When I think about ____, I feel happy.

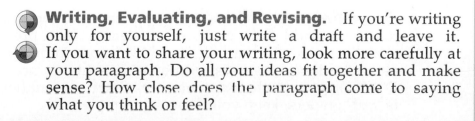

Prewriting. Your topic might be one about which you have a jumble of thoughts or feelings. If so, try to collect as many of these thoughts and feelings as you can. Then sort them out to bring them into focus—perhaps by listing or clustering. Or, you might be exploring a topic—to see what you know, think, or feel about it. Brainstorming, asking yourself questions, and reviewing old journal entries are good for this kind of prewriting. (See pages 22–35 for a review of prewriting techniques.)

Writing, Evaluating, and Revising. If you're writing only for yourself, just write a draft and leave it. If you want to share your writing, look more carefully at your paragraph. Do all your ideas fit together and make sense? How close does the paragraph come to saying what you think or feel?

Proofreading and Publishing. Make your paragraph presentable by correcting errors in usage or mechanics. Your class might publish all the expressive paragraphs in a booklet.

Writing a Paragraph to Inform

We all need information at times. When you write to inform, you try to give clear, useful information to your readers. The chart below contains some information about how hard worker bees work. Use this information to write an informative paragraph. Begin with the topic sentence below. Then use the statistics in the chart to write two or three supporting sentences. (You can also research more statistics about bees if you'd like.) Finally, write a clincher sentence (page 75). Think of your audience as sixth-graders who would be interested in more information about bees. For this paragraph, you might consider using narration as a strategy of development (pages 91–93).

Bees stay busy!

Average bee colony	50,000 worker bees
Average life span of worker bee (summer)	6 weeks
Number of flowers workers visit to make 1 lb. of honey	20–29 million
Honey produced by average worker bee in its lifetime	$\frac{1}{10}$ lb.

Topic Sentence: If you think you work hard, imagine the life of a worker bee.

 Prewriting and Writing. Start with your topic sentence and add two or three sentences that present statistics from the chart. If you have more information about hard-working bees, add another sentence or two. Don't forget a clincher sentence, too. Since your audience is sixth-graders, keep your language simple.

Evaluating and Revising. Does your paragraph make sense? Will sixth-graders understand it? Is there a better way to organize your information? Does your last sentence really clinch your ideas? Depending on your answers to these questions, you might decide to explain any hard words, change the order of sentences, or rewrite your last sentence.

Proofreading and Publishing. Correct any errors in usage or mechanics that might get in your reader's way. Share your writing with a younger brother or sister or with some younger students you know.

Writing a Paragraph to Persuade

Your town boasts a beautiful park. People go there to picnic, relax, and play games—and it's the only park in town. But the mayor is considering selling the park to a large manufacturer. The manufacturer plans to replace the park with a factory that will provide 250 new jobs. Many people in the town are out of work.

Write a paragraph in which you try to persuade the mayor either to save the park or to sell it to the manufacturer. When you organize this paragraph, you'll use the strategy of evaluation that you read about on page 97. If you want, use one of the following topic sentences.

Topic Sentences:

Central Park is an important part of community life in our city, and it should not be destroyed.

For the people in our city, new jobs are much more important than trees and tennis courts.

Prewriting. Think of information that might convince the mayor to do what you want. List two or three convincing reasons and information that supports them.

Writing, Evaluating, and Revising. After you write your draft, look at the reasons you've given the mayor. Do you have enough reasons? Are they important enough to convince someone who doesn't agree with you? Revise your paragraph to improve it.

Proofreading and Publishing. Correct any errors in usage and mechanics—if your paragraph did reach the mayor, you wouldn't want any mistakes in it. To see whether someone else can be convinced, share your paragraph with a parent or other adult.

Writing a Paragraph That Is Creative

What makes Monet's painting of apple trees (page 103) different from an ordinary photograph of apple trees? What makes a great piece of music—whether it's by Mozart or by a rock group—different from the tunes we hum when we're alone? Part of the difference is creativity—the urge to create something different, something out of the ordinary. Most stories and poems are attempts to be creative—to use language to make something new and special. For example, poet Ted Kooser describes the snowy winter night as a sleeping animal with "diamonds in his fur." Be as creative as Monet and Kooser. Write a paragraph describing a scene that is familiar to you, but describe it in a new and different way.

Prewriting. Picture the scene in your mind, and jot down the details that seem striking to you—colors, sounds, smells. Now, think about a creative way to share those details with others. To what can you compare the colors? the sounds? the smells? What parts of the scene

can you stress? For example, you might focus on the knot on a tree, the pothole in a street, or the weed growing in the middle of an asphalt parking lot.

 Writing, Evaluating, and Revising. Write a draft of your paragraph, trying to create an unusual "picture" of the scene. Then, exchange your paragraph with a classmate. Does your reader "see" the scene as you tried to create it? If not, revise to add or change details.

Proofreading and Publishing. Correct any errors in usage or mechanics, and share your paragraph with some classmates, perhaps by reading it aloud in a small group. You may also compile a class booklet of paragraphs.

 Reflecting on Your Writing

If you plan to include any of these paragraphs (expressive, informative, persuasive, or creative) in your **portfolio,** use these questions to write your reflections:

- How did you decide whether to state your main idea in a topic sentence?
- Did you feel that writing just one paragraph was effective, or did you feel you needed to write more?
- Which kind of paragraph seemed easiest to write— expressive, informative, persuasive, or creative? Which did you enjoy most?

---

3 UNDERSTANDING COMPOSITION STRUCTURE

Looking at the Whole

If you looked at just one cabin on a ship, you'd never be able to tell what the whole ship looks like. A composition works the same way. It has pieces—words, sentences, paragraphs. But you have to put them together to make a **whole** composition.

Writing and You. You read compositions often. Magazine and newspaper articles tell about special events and people. Textbooks explain history, science, and literature. Can you think of other kinds of compositions?

As You Read. As you read the following article, notice how Vincent Bozzi uses the elements of composition form to tell some unusual ideas about faces.

Left Face

←

by Vincent Bozzi

Debating whether to give your child music lessons? Rather than checking his finger dexterity, perhaps you should determine whether your youngster is left- or right-faced. "With rare exceptions, all talented musical performers—singers, instrumentalists, jazz artists, composers, conductors, and even country music artists—are left-faced," says psychologist Karl Smith, professor emeritus at the University of Wisconsin-Madison.

Just as most of us are either left- or right-handed, most people have a more dominant, flexible facial side that steers the production of speech. "And unlike handedness," says Smith, "which isn't determined until at least age two or three, facedness is decided before birth."

"With rare exceptions, all talented musical performers . . . are left-faced. . . ."

Clockwise from top left: Ludwig van Beethoven (composer), Zubin Mehta (conductor) Beverly Sills (opera singer), Aretha Franklin ("the Queen of Soul"), and Reba McEntire (country singer).

Most of the great composers, including Beethoven, Brahms, Schubert, Tchaikovsky, and Liszt, were left-faced, in some cases so dramatically "as to almost distort their faces." And fully 98 percent of the opera singers who've performed at the Met in the last 50 years have been left-faced, Smith says.

Smith speculates that facedness reflects a link to the dominant side of the brain and that left-faced people are better able to tap into the right side of the brain. "There are varied claims and reports that one of the specializations of the right brain hemisphere is in musical performance, while the left hemisphere is specialized for cognitive processes and language," says Smith.

But right-facers need not despair. They may not make beautiful music, but most mathematicians and scientists are right-faced. And while left-facers have better control of vowels, right-facers have a better handle on consonants, giving them an edge in speech. "Most great orators, and every president except Bush, have been right-faced," Smith says.

To determine whether you are one of the 12 percent of Americans who are left-faced, look in the mirror and note which side of your face is larger, more muscular, more flexible, has deeper dimples and a higher eyebrow. If you're right-faced, chances are those childhood piano-lesson memories aren't too pleasant. "But if you have a left-faced child who has an unusual interest in music at two to five years of age," advises Smith, "you'd be crazy not to enroll him in music lessons."

"As a beauty I'm not a great star,

There are others more handsome by far,

But my face, I don't mind it,

Because I'm behind it —

'Tis the folks in the front that I jar."

Anthony Henderson Euwer

READER'S RESPONSE

1. Do you know without looking whether you're right- or left-faced? When you look, can you see a sharp difference? Can your friends see one?
2. What do you think of Karl Smith's theory? Does it help to explain your musical talent—or its absence?

WRITER'S CRAFT

3. Bozzi refers to famous people in his article. How do these examples help him support his main idea?
4. At the end of the article, Bozzi tells you to see if you're right- or left-faced. Is this a good conclusion for his article? Did you feel like looking in the mirror?

LOOKING AHEAD

In this chapter, you'll study the parts of a composition. You'll learn that

- most compositions have a thesis statement
- most have a good introduction that attracts the reader's attention
- each paragraph in the body is unified and clearly connected to the surrounding paragraphs
- most compositions have a strong conclusion that leaves readers with a sense of completeness

What Makes a Composition

You'll use the composition form both in and out of school. In school, you'll use it to write compositions, or *essays*, both for assigned papers and for tests. Outside of school, you'll use the same principles of form in other kinds of writing. One day, for example, you might find that perfect job and have to use the composition form to write a letter to apply for it. Then, after you *get* that perfect job, you'll discover that you have to use the same form to write business memos and reports.

In other chapters, you'll learn how to use the composition form when writing persuasive essays and research papers, when writing about literature, or when explaining a process. In this chapter, you'll learn some basic principles of composition form.

In this book, or the author show

Memo

To: Marketing Department
Re: Purchasing Policy

The Thesis Statement

If you've ever wanted to tell a rambling speaker to get to the point, you can easily understand the importance of a thesis statement. A *thesis statement* is a sentence or two that announces your limited topic and your main, or unifying, idea about it. A thesis statement works in a composition like a topic sentence works in a paragraph.

Some thesis statements simply identify what the writer is going to write about: "There are several qualifications for the Young American Medal for Bravery." Other thesis statements identify an idea that the writer is actually trying to prove to the reader. For example, later in this chapter, you'll read this thesis statement: "While it's true that the brain's two sides have different functions, they work together, not in conflict." Most of the thesis statements you'll see in this chapter are of this type: they identify a point the writer wants to prove or discuss.

Hints for Writing and Using a Thesis Statement

1. **Develop your thesis statement from the information you've gathered.** A thesis statement comes *out of* your prewriting material. Review your facts and details, and begin thinking about how they fit together. *What main, or unifying, idea do you see?*
2. **Check your thesis statement for both a limited topic and your main idea about it.** Remember the two parts. The question your thesis statement must answer is not just *What's my topic?* but also *What about the topic?* You might try underlining your topic and circling your main idea. Notice, for example, this thesis statement: "While it's true that the brain's two sides have different functions, they work together, not in conflict." Here the writer's limited topic is the two sides of the brain. His main idea is that the two sides work together, not in conflict.
3. **Be clear and specific.** Suppose the writer had written, "The brain has two sides that work in a very interesting way." This thesis statement is not only boring—it's fuzzy. Check your thesis statements for vague words like *interesting* and *important*. Then sharpen your language and present a definite, focused idea.

4. **Rewrite your thesis statement if necessary.** You may have to try out more than one statement to find the one that works best. Remember, your thesis is never carved in stone. You can revise it if you get new ideas while working with your information.

5. **Use your thesis statement as you outline, draft, and revise.** In every stage of your writing, your thesis statement is a good checkpoint. You can test ideas and details against your main idea. You can then cut the ones that don't support, illustrate, or explain the main point.

WRITING NOTE

Look at some thesis statements in essays by professional writers. They probably seem different from the ones you write—more lively, maybe. With practice, you can learn to write thesis statements that pack a real punch.

When you're planning your composition, you'll probably want to work with a thesis statement that is direct and straightforward. But your readers may not need this thesis word for word. When you begin to draft your introduction, you may find that you need to change the wording so that the thesis statement sounds smooth and interesting.

Here's an example of how a final thesis statement can be different from one used in prewriting or planning.

In an article about the sense of smell, the poet Diane Ackerman might have had something like this in mind as a thesis statement: "Smell is a powerful, emotional sense for two reasons: (1) humans' sense of smell is very precise and (2) odor molecules go directly to the brain."

This thesis would be a clear starting point for her writing. But in her finished essay, Ackerman used this short, attention-getting thesis statement instead. Notice that while this statement announces the topic, it only hints at what the main idea is.

Nothing is more memorable than a smell.

EXERCISE 1 ▶ **Analyzing Thesis Statements**

What are the two parts in the following thesis statements? For each, identify the writer's limited topic and main idea.

EXAMPLE   **1.** Our right to free speech was assaulted in two highly publicized cases this year. (Howard Wornom, "For Goodness Sake?")

     1. *Limited topic: free speech*
          Main idea: violated in two instances

1. For years U.S. business has grumbled about the quality of the nation's high school graduates. (Susan Tifft, "Our Student-Back Guarantee")

2. In San Gabriel, Calif., Wu Li-Hsia has been using acupuncture to treat a school of sick goldfish for listlessness, poor appetite and red splotches. (Bruce Ingersoll, "Acupuncturists Find A Fervent Following Among the Pet Set")

3. Somewhere out there is an asteroid or comet that's on a collision course with planet Earth. (Jane Bosveld, "Apocalypse, How?")

4. Despite its long and colorful history, salt is a relatively recent addition to the human diet. (Jane Brody, *Jane Brody's Nutrition Book*)

5. When the Boston Celtics arrived in New York yesterday, Larry Bird was not with them. ("Back Rest Scheduled For Bird," *The New York Times*)

EXERCISE 2 ▶   **Writing a Thesis Statement**

Working in a small group, write a thesis statement for each limited topic and list of details below. Ask yourself: What main idea do I get from the details? What statement will prepare my readers for this information?

1. Limited topic: the snack temptation
   Ideas and details:
     everybody gets cravings between meals
     question is *what* to eat
       whole grains, fruits, vegetables: bagel, baked potato, banana and yogurt shake
       crunchy cookie cravings: try breadsticks, pretzel sticks, popcorn, frozen grapes, carrots
     avoid high-fat, high-calorie, high-salt foods
     snacking can be a good "binge control"
       not always time for full meal—snacks give some nutrients
       be prepared—have something on hand besides potato chips
       younger, smaller people need to eat more often

2. Limited topic: how to control spending sprees
   Ideas and details:
     set up budgets: for clothes, entertainment, so on
     appoint a "budget manager"—possibly a parent
     get away from places of high temptation: shopping malls, bowling alleys, skating rinks, video game arcades
     get a part-time job

Early Plans and Formal Outlines

Now that you have a thesis statement, you're ready to plan—to group and order information. You're ready to organize a set of items into a map of your paper from beginning to end. That way, when you're writing, you'll be less likely to skip around, come to a dead end, include details you don't need, or leave out ones you do.

Writing a whole composition is much like writing a paragraph. They both require planning. But a composition—which usually involves more information than a single paragraph—requires more and different planning.

The Early Plan

An *early plan,* sometimes called an informal or rough outline, doesn't have a set form. You simply sort your ideas or facts into groups and arrange the groups in order.

Grouping.   To sort your information into groups, ask yourself: *Which items belong together? What do they have in common? Which items don't fit anywhere?* (You can put these into a separate list. You may find a spot for them later on.) Then group the items, and give each group a heading that shows how the items in it are related.

Ordering.   Next, order, or arrange, your information in a way that will make sense to your readers. Some compositions will suggest a natural order. To explain a step-by-step process like tie-dyeing, you'll use *chronological (time) order*. To describe a favorite place, you may use *spatial order*. To argue that record labeling is unnecessary, you may use *order of importance:* from most important reason to least, or vice versa. To write a composition on how some students support school causes while others do nothing, you may even use *classification*.

But at other times, you just have to decide what makes sense for your material. More than one order may be possible. The test is whether readers can follow your thoughts and facts easily. Ask this question: *Is the purpose and the order of each grouping of details understandable?*

The writer of the composition on the two sides of the brain (page 117) decided that readers should understand brain structure first. He also decided to discuss each hemisphere before talking about how they cooperate. But the right and left sides could be explained in either order.

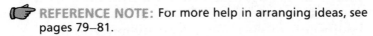 **REFERENCE NOTE:** For more help in arranging ideas, see pages 79–81.

The Formal Outline

A *formal outline* is a highly structured, clearly labeled writing plan. It has a set pattern, using letters and numbers to label main headings and subheadings. An outline can use either topics (words and phrases) or complete sentences for each item.

 **REFERENCE NOTE:** For more information on formal outlines, see pages 386–387.

Here is a portion of a topic outline that goes with the essay "Two Brains or One?" on pages 117–119. You may want to compare the outline with the actual composition.

Title: Two Brains or One?
Thesis statement: While it's true that the brain's two sides have different functions, they work together, not in conflict.

I. Structure of brain
   A. Cerebrum: two hemispheres
   B. Nerve connection (corpus callosum)
   C. Specialization

II. Left hemisphere
   A. Language (symbols)
   B. Analysis
   C. Sequence
     1. Counting
     2. Marking time
     3. Steps
     4. Logical statement

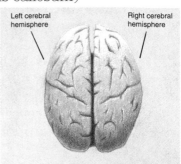

Left cerebral hemisphere

Right cerebral hemisphere

A formal outline like this one may not be required for every essay, but it's often useful. First, it forces you to think about how all your material fits together. Second, a formal outline can help some readers—it's a sort of table of contents that also summarizes. Business reports, for example, often include formal outlines.

EXERCISE 3 ▶	**Making an Early Plan or a Formal Outline**

Working with a partner, write a thesis statement from the following notes. Then prepare an early plan or a formal outline for a composition on this topic. Feel free to make up details that would make your plan or outline more interesting.

Why I Like Elena

found a wallet with $100 in it—took it to the police
has been my best friend since second grade
does everything with me—studying, ice skating, shopping
gave circus tickets she won to children who had never
    seen a circus
refused to let one of our friends copy our math homework
gives back change if a clerk gives her too much
belongs to a club that does community service work
likes visiting elderly in nursing home
listens to my problems
worries about elderly who have no one to visit them
helped me feel better when I lost a school election
took an abandoned kitten to the vet and found a
    home for it

A WRITER'S MODEL

The writer who created the formal outline on page 116 wrote the following composition. Do you see how the writer used the outline as a guide for the second and third paragraphs? What do you think the rest of his outline looked like?

Two Brains or One?

INTRODUCTION   If you're right-brained, you're creative and emotional. If you're left-brained, you're logical and steady. Perhaps you've heard this popular explanation of the "two-sided" human brain—and haven't liked it. Are there only two kinds of people in the world? Are we really ruled by one

Thesis statement

side of our gray matter? No. While it's true that the brain's two sides have different functions, they work together, not in conflict.

**BODY
Main topic:
Brain structure**

It's a fact that the human brain is split in two. The cerebrum, the brain's large upper part, has two separate sides, called hemispheres. A band of nerve fibers (the corpus callosum) connects them and is constantly passing information back and forth. What scientists have learned is that the brain's two hemispheres are specialized, with each side being better at different mental work.

**Main topic:
Left hemisphere**

The left hemisphere, for example, allows us to speak and is better at all language skills. It is good with anything symbolic, like words and numbers. Also, when you are analyzing something—breaking it into parts to understand it—you are mostly using your left brain. Counting, marking time, planning step by step, and making logical statements are typical functions. The left brain likes to go in sequence.

**Main topic:
Right hemisphere**

The right hemisphere, on the other hand, is more visual and is good at taking in patterns. Combining is its strength. Typical functions are recognizing musical melodies, seeing relationships, and thinking in metaphors (comparisons). The right brain can work like the "flash" of intuition: it sees things whole, all at once.

**Main topic:
Relation of sides**

(Note: This topic is covered in three paragraphs, because the writer has several examples.)

The two sides of the brain, however, are not in conflict. Through research, psychologists know that no one uses only a single side of the brain. People may strongly favor one side, but one hemisphere doesn't "dominate"—control—the other. Painters and musicians are not necessarily illogical and scatterbrained. People good at math and grammar don't automatically have dull imaginations.

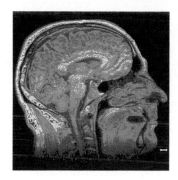

Instead, both hemispheres are needed for most mental acts. For example, people do have sudden creative breakthroughs, but first they lay some groundwork of step-by-step thinking. And logical analysis is a dead end until people draw conclusions—organize the details into a meaning. Besides this, scientists explain that language isn't "in" the left brain and music or shapes "in" the right.

When people read poetry or stories, both sides show electrical activity because literature involves images, feelings, and metaphors. When people listen to music, they hear melody with the right brain, but they use the left brain to focus on arrangement, instruments, and so on.

CONCLUSION

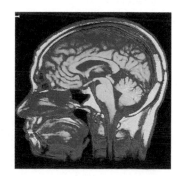

The two hemispheres of the brain have different styles of thinking, but they are partners. And while your brain may seem to be more talented at one style, it uses the other one too. Just because you can't carry a tune doesn't mean you can't be creative in other ways. Just because you struggle with algebra doesn't mean you can't be logical about decisions. If you want to apply the split-brain theory to yourself, use it to expand your mental power. Don't let it pigeonhole your personality!

The Neighborhood reprinted with special permission of King Features Syndicate, Inc.

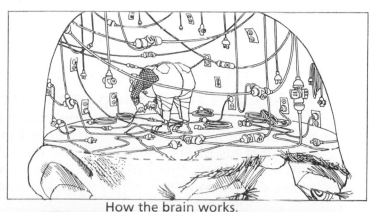

How the brain works.

The Introduction

Suppose the writer of "Two Brains or One?" had started this way: "In this essay, I will discuss the two sides of the brain." Would you have started snoring? It's likely. What the *introduction* ought to do is catch the reader's attention, set the tone, and present the thesis statement.

Catching the Readers' Interest. The *introduction* of a composition should make readers want to hear more. Writers use a variety of techniques. For example, the writer of the composition about the brain begins by making statements that will interest most readers. He intends, however, to contradict these statements. Readers don't know that at first, so the thesis statement provides them with an interesting surprise. The writer also asks questions that make readers think and wonder. But the audience gets another surprise when he answers his questions "No."

Setting the Tone. As you attract the reader's attention, you also set the composition's *tone*—the feeling you convey about your topic. An introduction should let the audience know what your attitude is toward your topic and how you want *them* to feel about it.

The writer of the composition on pages 117–119, for example, creates an effective informal tone by speaking directly to readers: "If you're right-brained. . . ." His introduction shows that he takes his topic seriously, but it also draws readers into the subject personally—because that's the way he's approaching it.

Presenting the Thesis. Finally—to let readers know exactly where you (and they) are headed—you'll want to include your *thesis statement* in your introduction. Often the thesis statement is the introduction's last sentence, its clincher, but not always.

Techniques for Writing Introductions

The writer of the composition about the brain tries to get your attention by beginning with a question that seems to contradict his thesis. But what if you don't want to begin this way? What other methods can you use to get your readers' attention? You might try one of the following:

1. **Begin with an anecdote or example.** An example or anecdote (a short, interesting, or humorous incident) draws readers into your essay with concrete, vivid details. These details not only spark interest but can introduce important aspects of your topic.

> It's five o'clock and you're hungry. A bag of chips sits on the counter. There's nothing in the refrigerator but a few wilted carrot sticks and limp stalks of celery. Temptation strikes.
>
> The problem with snacking is not when you snack or even that you snack in the first place—but what you choose to eat.
>
> "Guiltless Snacks," *The Saturday Evening Post*

2. **Begin by stating a startling fact or by adopting an unusual position.** Surprising facts or an unexpected opinion can give readers a jolt and make them curious.

> Those prone to nightmares or panic attacks may not want to read this. It's the ultimate cosmic horror story: Somewhere out there is an asteroid or comet that's on a collision course with planet Earth. Someday it will fulfill its destiny, careening through our atmosphere and dealing a devastating blow. We may never even know what hit us.
>
> Jane Bosveld, "Apocalypse, How?"

3. **Use an appropriate quotation.** Don't hesitate to use someone else's words if those words are interesting and make a point important to your topic. You can quote experts, authors, or someone mentioned in your composition.

> George Orwell's novel *1984* opens with "It was a bright cold day in April and the clocks were striking thirteen," implying something is terribly wrong with the world.
>
> Far too many Americans believe that the censorship described in *1984* could not exist under the vigilant eye of the First Amendment. But it does happen. Our right to free speech was assaulted in two highly publicized cases this year.
>
> Howard Wornom, "For Goodness Sake?"

4. **Start with background information.** Sometimes setting the scene is a good way to begin. Background details may help readers understand your thesis, or remind them what they know about your topic, or simply build interest.

> Bill Moyers acquired his love of conversation as a boy in Marshall, Texas, a half-century ago. Although he would grow up to become a broadcast journalist of the first rank with ground-breaking PBS series like *Bill Moyers' Journal* and *A Walk Through the 20th Century*, it's Moyers' love of conversation that has been his greatest gift to the medium.
>
> "Dialogue on Film:
Bill Moyers,"
American Film

5. **Begin with a simple statement of your thesis.** Every introduction doesn't have to be surprising or unusual. You can just state your thesis plainly— which immediately focuses attention on your main idea.

> If you have a monster or a villain, you must also have a victim. The victim in the horror film is almost always a woman. It isn't that the monsters don't kill men. They wipe out scores of males. A really good monster can stomp out a whole village. But in the end, it always comes down to the scene where the monster or villain menaces the girl.
>
> Daniel Cohen, "The Victims"

WRITING NOTE How long should an introduction be? There's no set number of paragraphs. In essays by professional writers, you'll see that writers use one, two, or even more paragraphs, depending on their opening techniques and content. But a single paragraph is usually enough for a brief composition. No matter how interesting it is, few readers have patience with an introduction that is as long as, or longer than, the body of the composition.

EXERCISE 4   **Analyzing an Introduction**

The writer Vincent Bozzi uses more than one method to capture readers' attention in "Left Face" (page 106). Reread his introduction, and answer the following questions.

1. What methods does Bozzi use in his introduction?
2. How well do you think his methods work?
3. How would you describe the tone, or the writer's attitude, in Bozzi's introduction? What words and details show you his attitude toward his topic?
4. Write a new introduction to "Left Face" using one of the methods you studied on pages 120–123.

The Body

The *body* states and develops the composition's main points. When writing the body of your composition, you're building a whole out of parts. Your goal is to draft sentences and paragraphs that give support to the main idea expressed in your thesis. That's why your writing focus now shifts to unity and coherence (connections).

Unity

Unity means "oneness." All the parts fit together. In an essay, unity means that all the paragraphs work together to support *one* main idea—the thesis. Each body paragraph in an essay has its own main idea that must relate to or support the essay's thesis.

Coherence

You know when you've read an essay that *flows*. One sentence leads easily to another, one paragraph to the next. Somehow you are pulled smoothly through the writing from beginning to end. Essays like this have *coherence:* The ideas are connected in a way that makes them easy to follow. You can achieve coherence by arranging your ideas in an order that makes sense to readers and by making sure readers can see how ideas are connected.

Direct References.   One way to link ideas is to make *direct references* to something you've mentioned earlier. You can

1. use pronouns (*he, they, this*) to refer to nouns or ideas
2. repeat key words
3. use synonyms or slight rephrasings of previous words and ideas

Transitional Expressions.   Another way to connect ideas within and between paragraphs is to use *transitional expressions*—words and phrases that show readers how ideas and details fit together, how they are related. (The transitions you learned about in Chapter 2, Understanding Paragraph Structure, are the same ones you'll use when you write a composition.)

REFERENCE NOTE: See pages 83–86 for more information about direct references and transitions.

| EXERCISE 5 ▶ | **Analyzing Coherence** |

Working with two or three classmates, identify transitions and direct references in the following passage. Use the information about transitions and direct references on page 124 as you do this activity. Be prepared to explain what you find: What relationship does a transition show? What key words are repeated? What words or ideas do pronouns refer to? How are the two paragraphs connected to one another?

Jane Austen once compared her very particular genius for comedy to scrimshaw. Her novels, she wrote, are "the little bit (two inches wide) of ivory on which I work with so fine a brush." But as *Clueless, Persuasion,* and now *Sense and Sensibility* happily demonstrate, you can blow up her stories as big as a movie screen, and they still enthrall.

Sense, published in 1811, is the tale of two yin-and-yangy sisters. Passionate Marianne Dashwood (Kate Winslet) sings and plays the pianoforte with deep feeling. The ever-prudent Elinor (Emma Thompson) doesn't care to sing at all. Both have reached marrying age, and though the Dashwoods possess neither dowry nor barouche, suitors keep dropping in.

Tom Gliatto, "Sense and Sensibility"

The Conclusion

Most readers don't like to be left hanging or to feel that they've been abruptly dismissed. A composition without a clear conclusion can leave readers feeling dissatisfied. A *conclusion* doesn't have to have fireworks, any more than an introduction does, but it does have to give the composition a sense of completeness, of "being over."

Although some compositions—like news stories—don't have conclusions, most compositions do. To achieve that sense of completion, the conclusion must bring readers back to your main idea.

Techniques for Writing Conclusions

1. **Restate your main idea.** The most direct conclusion is a restatement of your thesis *in different words*. Find a new wording. Here the author repeats her thesis that the earth will be struck by an asteroid or comet.

> In the end, the vastness of space, which seems so peaceful by earthly standards, may be so only for what amounts to a cosmic moment. Sooner or later, the moment will end and we may see a faint light coming toward us, casting a shadow on the face of civilization.
>
> Jane Bosveld, "Apocalypse, How?"

COMPUTER NOTE: Your word-processing program's built-in thesaurus can help you find synonyms and related words to use in restating your thesis.

---

2. **Summarize your major points.** You can emphasize the major points you've made by summarizing them for your reader.

> Trust your material—it's stronger than you think. But it's only as strong as the structure you build for it and the control you maintain over it from the first sentence to the last.
>
> William Zinsser, "Trust Your Material"

3. **Close with a final idea or example.** Sometimes a final example allows you to reinforce or pull together your main points.

> *Sense and Sensibility* takes some getting used to. Written by Thompson and directed by Ang Lee, . . . much of it has a bland, picture-postcard cheeriness, and some of the supporting characters are discordantly boisterous, like tubas suddenly going *wamp-wamp* during a string quartet. But the main characters are perfect, delightfully silly one moment, heartbreaking the next. It's hard to say whether it's more satisfying to watch Thompson slowly uncorseting her emotions or Winslet learning to rein them in.
>
> Tom Gliatto, "Sense and Sensibility"

"I don't wait to be struck by lightning and don't need certain slants of light in order to write."

Toni Morrison

4. **End with a comment on the topic.** A final comment can take several forms: a thoughtful observation, a personal reaction, a look to the future or to larger issues. Here the writer tells what he thinks about the possibility that road bikes are disappearing.

> It's intriguing to speculate, of course, but in a way it doesn't matter which bikes thrive and which fade, as long as people keep riding something. Only if they stop will we really have cause to mourn.
>
> Scott Martin, "Are Road Bikes Dead?"

5. **Call on your readers to take action.** Especially in persuasive essays, you may want to urge readers to do something or to accept a belief. A direct appeal to your audience, though, can work in other kinds of compositions—as it does in the writer's conclusion of the essay on page 119.

> The two hemispheres of the brain have different styles of thinking, but they are partners. And while your brain may seem to be more talented at one style, it uses the other one too. Just because you can't carry a tune doesn't mean you can't be creative in other ways. Just because you struggle with algebra doesn't mean you can't be logical about decisions. If you want to apply the split-brain theory to yourself, use it to expand your mental power. Don't let it pigeonhole your personality!

6. **Refer to your introduction.** Writers often make a direct reference back to something in their introduction, so that readers feel they've come full circle. For example, the conclusion of "Left Face" (page 108) comes back to the "music lessons" of the introduction (page 106).

| E X E R C I S E **6** ▶ | **Improving a Conclusion** |

Here's a possible conclusion for a short composition on a teenager's try at saving money, but it's a weak one. Rewrite the conclusion to make it stronger. You can change it in any way you like—even start over completely. (You may also want to refer to the notes on pages 126–129.)

I've tried everything I can think of—staying away from malls, video arcades, and even friends who want to borrow money. I guess I'm always going to be a failure when it comes to controlling my spending habits.

| E X E R C I S E **7** ▶ | **Writing a Conclusion** |

Write a different conclusion for the composition about the brain (pages 117–119). [Two hints: Use the list of conclusion techniques to get ideas, and reread the whole composition before you begin.]

FRAMEWORK FOR A COMPOSITION

Introduction	■ Arouses the reader's interest
	■ Sets the tone
	■ Presents the thesis statement
Body	■ States the main points
	■ Provides support for the main points
Conclusion	■ Reinforces the main idea
	■ Leaves reader with a final impression and a sense of completeness

MAKING CONNECTIONS

Writing an Informative Essay

By now you know that we write for different purposes—to express our feelings, to be creative, to persuade others, or to explain or inform. You can adapt the composition form in this chapter to achieve any of those purposes. For this assignment, you'll use the form to inform readers about women in the U.S. Army.

Study the facts in the chart below, and use them to write an informative composition for a high school audience.

WOMEN IN THE U.S. ARMY TODAY

1. Women are eligible to serve in all Army positions except those that involve direct ground combat.
2. Women in the Army may support ground combat troops by serving in a variety of important roles—as intelligence officers, pilots, or engineers, for example.
3. Some military men think women cannot take the pressure of combat and are not physically strong enough.
4. Others believe that women are perfectly fit. These men would be proud to serve with women in direct ground combat.
5. Some women in the Army resent the restrictions placed on them.
6. Other women do not want to serve in ground combat.
7. Women join the armed forces for the same reasons men do: patriotism, job training, money for college, travel.
8. Many women volunteered to serve in the Persian Gulf Conflict.

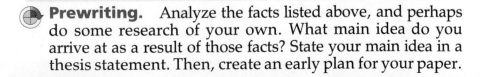 **Prewriting.** Analyze the facts listed above, and perhaps do some research of your own. What main idea do you arrive at as a result of those facts? State your main idea in a thesis statement. Then, create an early plan for your paper.

Writing. As you draft your composition, think about how you can best capture your readers' attention. Perhaps you'll want to use one of the methods suggested on pages 120–123. As you draft the body paragraphs of your composition, remember that each paragraph should make a point that relates clearly to your thesis. In turn, everything within a paragraph should relate to the paragraph's point. To give your composition a sense of completeness, consider using one of the techniques on pages 126–129 to write a conclusion.

Evaluating and Revising. Now it's time to consider how to improve your draft. You may want to share it with one or two other students and ask them for feedback. Here are some questions you might ask:

1. Does my introduction capture your attention?
2. Is my thesis statement clear?
3. Does each body paragraph support the thesis?
4. Is each body paragraph clearly connected to the paragraph before and after it?
5. Does my conclusion convey a sense of completeness?

Proofreading and Publishing. Now that you've revised your composition, it's time to focus on correcting errors in grammar, usage, and mechanics. Once you have a clean, corrected copy, share your paper with an audience. You and your classmates might simply post your compositions on the bulletin board, send them to the school paper, or read them to another class.

 Reflecting on Your Writing

Date your answers to these questions, and then add them to your **portfolio.**

- Did your main idea change as you worked on your paper? How?
- Did you make an early plan? How did it help, or how could it have helped?
- What was the most difficult part of this assignment?

---

4 EXPRESSIVE WRITING: NARRATION

Discovering Yourself

Deep within you are feelings, thoughts, hopes, and dreams you have yet to discover. Exploring these emotions can help **you discover** who you are and how you feel about many things.

Writing and You.   We often write to examine our feelings about ourselves and our experiences. If we want to keep those feelings private, we jot them down in a journal or diary. Like the dancers on these pages, at other times we make our feelings public—sharing them with others in an essay. How do you think this can help us gain a better understanding of ourselves?

As You Read.   In the following selection, Louise Erdrich explores a rare experience and her feelings about it. What does she think she gained from this encounter? Why is she sharing it with us?

FROM *THE BLUE JAY'S DANCE*

Skunk Dreams

BY LOUISE ERDRICH

When I was fourteen, I slept alone on a North Dakota football field under cold stars on an early September night. Fall progresses swiftly in the Red River Valley, and I happened to hit a night when frost formed in the grass. A skunk trailed a plume of steam across the forty-yard line near moonrise. I tucked the top of my sleeping bag over my head and was just dozing off when the skunk walked onto me with simple authority.

Its ripe odor must have dissipated in the heavy summer grass and ditch weeds, because it didn't smell all that bad, or perhaps it was just that I took shallow breaths in numb surprise. I felt him, her, whatever, pause on the side of my hip and turn around twice before evidently deciding I was a good place to sleep. At the back of my knees, on the quilting of my sleeping bag, it trod out a spot for itself and then, with a serene little groan, curled up and lay perfectly still. That made two of us. I was wildly awake, trying to forget the sharpness and number of skunk teeth, trying not to think of the high percentage of skunks with rabies, or the reason that on camping trips my father always kept a hatchet underneath his pillow.

Inside the bag, I felt as if I might smother. Carefully, making only the slightest of rustles, I drew the bag away from my face and took a deep breath of the night air, enriched with skunk, but clear and watery and cold. It wasn't so bad, and the skunk didn't stir at all, so I watched the moon—caught that night in an envelope of silk, a mist—pass over my sleeping field of

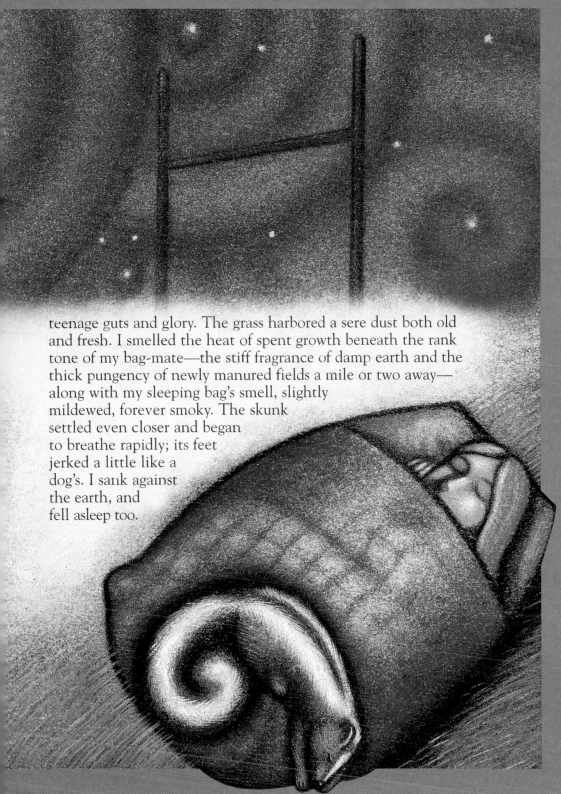

teenage guts and glory. The grass harbored a sere dust both old and fresh. I smelled the heat of spent growth beneath the rank tone of my bag-mate—the stiff fragrance of damp earth and the thick pungency of newly manured fields a mile or two away— along with my sleeping bag's smell, slightly mildewed, forever smoky. The skunk settled even closer and began to breathe rapidly; its feet jerked a little like a dog's. I sank against the earth, and fell asleep too.

" . . . I may be

a woman

who has

dreamed herself

a skunk,

Of what easily tipped cans, what molten sludge, what dogs in yards on chains, what leftover macaroni casseroles, what cellar holes, crawl spaces, burrows taken from meek woodchucks, of what miracles of garbage did my skunk dream? Or did it, since we can't be sure, dream the plot of *Moby-Dick,* how to properly age Parmesan, or how to restore the brick-walled tumbledown creamery that was its home? We don't know about the dreams of any other biota, and even much about our own. If dreams are an actual dimension, as some assert, then the usual rules of life by which we abide do not apply. In that place, skunks may certainly dream themselves into the vests of stockbrokers. Perhaps that night the skunk and I dreamed each

or **a skunk**

still dreaming

that she is

a woman. . . ."

other's thoughts or are still dreaming them. To paraphrase the problem of the Taoist philosopher Chuang Tzu, I may be a woman who has dreamed herself a skunk, or a skunk still dreaming that she is a woman. . . .

I woke at dawn, stunned into that sprayed state of being. The dog that had approached me was rolling in the grass, half addled, sprayed too. My skunk was gone. I abandoned my sleeping bag and started home. Up Eighth Street, past the tiny blue and pink houses, past my grade school, past all the addresses where I baby-sat, I walked in my own strange wind. The streets were wide and empty; I met no one—not a dog, not a squirrel, not even an early robin. Perhaps they had all scattered before me, blocks away. I had gone out to sleep on the football field because I was afflicted with a sadness I had to dramatize. Mood swings had begun, hormones, feverish and raw. They were nothing to me now. My emotions had seemed vast, dark, and sickeningly private. But they were minor, mere wisps, compared to skunk.

READER'S RESPONSE

1. Louise Erdrich recalls a time when she was sad. She describes how a particular experience changed how she felt. Can you think of a time when a person or an event altered your mood?
2. What images in Erdrich's description make a strong impression on you? How would you react if you were in her situation?

WRITER'S CRAFT

3. What are some of the details that Erdrich uses to re-create her stressful situation? What sensory details does she include? How does she personify the skunk?
4. The skunk is an uninvited "guest." How does Erdrich feel about this intrusion? What are her feelings toward the skunk at the end of the narrative?

Ways to Express Yourself

Personal expression can occur in different forms and different places: letters to friends, magazine articles, or newspaper columns. A piece of writing is considered personal expression when the writing emphasizes what the writer experiences, feels, and thinks. Here are examples of ways that you can develop an expressive message.

- in a letter to a friend, writing about an event that was especially important to you
- in your journal, writing about autobiographical events
- in an essay for English class, describing a place that means a great deal to you
- in your journal, describing a person who holds a special place in your heart
- in a magazine article, defining the word *loyalty* and explaining what it means to you
- in an essay for history class, comparing your reactions to two similar historical events and explaining why you felt as you did
- in a personal narrative, evaluating the influence another person has had on your life
- in a company newsletter, discussing the value an activity or hobby has for you

LOOKING AHEAD

In the main assignment in this chapter, you'll use narration to write about a personal experience. Keep in mind that an effective personal narrative

- usually tells about events in the order they happened
- uses details about the experience, including sensory details
- shows the meaning of the experience to the writer

Writing a Personal Narrative

Prewriting

Choosing a Topic

What has been your greatest achievement? When was the last time you were angry? or disappointed? What was the best day of your life? How about the worst?

When you write a personal narrative, you write about important, memorable events that have happened to you. Everyone has had experiences worth telling about. You may remember, for example, the time no one showed up for your birthday party. Or perhaps you'll never forget the time you fell down playing basketball and broke your ankle. When you're choosing a topic for your personal narrative, think about these three questions:

- **How important was the experience to you?** It doesn't have to be earthshaking or important to others—it just has to have meaning for you.
- **How well do you remember the experience?** No one remembers every detail about an experience, of course, and there are ways you can jog your memory. But begin with an experience that's still sharp in your memory.
- **Are you willing to share the experience?** A personal narrative is written to be shared with readers, so choose a topic that isn't private.

$\boxed{\text{E X E R C I S E } \mathbf{1}}\blacktriangleright$ **Freewriting to Explore Topics**

Choose one of the following topics or make up one of your own, and freewrite about it for ten minutes. Remember just to keep your pen moving to record your thoughts—don't worry about spelling, punctuation, or organization. (For more help with freewriting, see pages 24–25.)

1. an argument
2. a day I'll never forget
3. a disappointment
4. a good friend
5. a special family time

PART 1:
Exploring Possible Topics

What experience has been important to you? Why? Think of two possible topics to write about, either ones you discovered in freewriting or other ones. Then, write them down ("a disappointing birthday"; "the day I won the race") and share them with one or two classmates. Which topic seems more suitable for a personal narrative?

Kudzu by Marlette. By permission of Marlette and Creators Syndicate.

CRITICAL THINKING

Evaluating Topics for Your Personal Narrative

Evaluating means judging something on the basis of certain guidelines, or criteria. When you evaluate a movie or a computer game, for example, the guidelines you use probably have to do with entertainment value. How entertaining is the movie or the game? When you evaluate the topic of your personal narrative, your guidelines have to do with the importance of the experience, your memories of it, and your willingness to share it.

Suppose you've thought about two possible topics. One is an experience when you were ten years old and couldn't have Thanksgiving dinner with your family because you had the measles. Later you found that your family waited until you were well so everyone could celebrate together. Another topic might be a day you spent at the beach with your family and friends last year. Here's the way you might evaluate these topics.

- I couldn't believe that my family would save Thanksgiving dinner for me. We all had a good time. And I realized that my parents, even though they always make me clean up my room and do my homework, aren't so bad after all. I had a good time at the beach, too, but I guess nothing special really happened there.
- I remember a lot about that Thanksgiving, especially how good the turkey tasted and how we all laughed together. The beach I remember pretty well, too, but nothing really stands out in my mind.
- I can share both these experiences. I've already told some of my friends about that Thanksgiving.

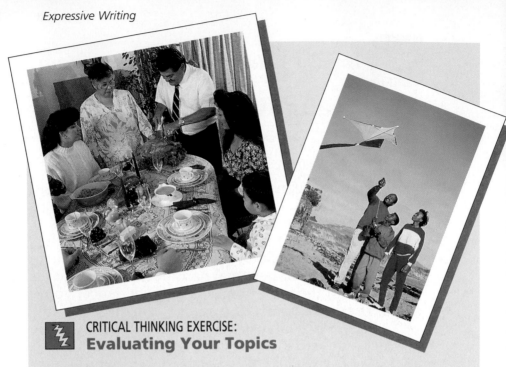

 CRITICAL THINKING EXERCISE:
Evaluating Your Topics

In Writing Assignment, Part 1 (page 140), you thought about possible topics for your personal narrative. How suitable are the experiences you've chosen? Evaluate your topics by answering the following questions:

1. Which experience was more important to you? What happened that made it important?
2. Which experience do you remember better? What do you remember most about it? least?
3. Which experience are you more willing to share with others?
4. Based on this evaluation, which experience would you choose to write about?

WRITING ASSIGNMENT

PART 2:
Choosing a Topic

Using your work from the Critical Thinking Exercise on this page, choose one topic to write about in your personal narrative. Then, write a single sentence that tells what experience you'll explore in your paper.

Prewriting

Thinking About Purpose, Audience, and Tone

What's the purpose for writing your narrative? Who will read it? Do you want it to sound friendly and informal or serious and formal? Thinking about your purpose, audience, and tone will result in a more effective narrative.

Purpose. The purpose of a personal narrative is to express yourself. You do this by telling about important events that happened to you and by exploring your thoughts and feelings about the events. In this way, you learn something about yourself. Your purpose affects what you write. You want your readers to share your experience, so you make it seem real by using specific details to describe it. You also want your readers to understand how you felt and what you thought, so you include details to suggest thoughts and feelings.

Audience. Who is the audience for your personal narrative? Besides you, your teacher will probably read it. Will you also share it with your classmates? a friend? your parents? an adult you trust? Will it reach a wider audience? Ask yourself what your readers will need to know about your topic. For example, suppose your narrative is about the disastrous experience at your first piano recital. If you're writing for readers who weren't there—your teacher and classmates—they probably need some background: what goes on at a recital, where and when yours was held, and who was in the audience.

Tone. Since you're writing to express yourself, your tone should be friendly and informal, as though you were having a conversation with your readers. You want to sound like *you*, so you should use the language of your everyday speech. To close the distance between you and your readers, you should also write from the *first-person point of view*. That means that you speak directly to your readers, using first-person pronouns—*I*, *me*, and *our*.

USAGE HINT

Using Personal Pronouns

Writers of personal narratives use first-person pronouns to refer to themselves. These pronouns have different forms according to their use in sentences. Use the forms *I* and *we* when the pronoun is a subject or predicate nominative. Use the forms *me* and *us* when the pronoun is an object in the sentence.

EXAMPLES   *Subject:* *I* was determined not to feel defeated.
          Predicate Nominative: If there was one person
            who usually gave up, it was *I*.
          Object: The baby's screams startled *me*.

Because of the informal tone of personal narratives, writers sometimes use *me* or *us* for personal pronouns that are predicate nominatives:

If there was one person who usually gave up, it was *me*.

 REFERENCE NOTE: For more information on personal pronouns, see page 470.

PART 3:
Analyzing Purpose, Audience, and Tone

In Writing Assignment, Part 2 (page 142), you chose a topic for your personal narrative. Get together with two or three classmates, and use these directions to think about your narrative's purpose, audience, and tone.

1. Tell your classmates which topic you've chosen and what you felt and thought about the experience.
2. Ask your classmates to tell you two things they need to know about your topic.
3. Write down two or three sentences about the experience. Do the sentences sound as friendly and informal as you do when you speak?

Prewriting

Gathering and Organizing Details

Now is the time to gather and organize details about the experience and its meaning to you. Details for a personal-experience narrative are different from details you use in other types of writing. For a research report, you can read or watch videotapes. Details for a personal narrative, however, must be recalled from your past.

Gathering Details

Recalling Details. Memories can be tricky things. Some people can vividly recall a specific instant (a moment of panic the first time you tried to swim), but they can't remember events that led up to the moment. As you think about your topic, you may find holes in your memory. How do you fill in the gap? One approach is to use a technique like brainstorming or freewriting. (For more help with these techniques, see pages 22–35.) Another is to talk with friends and relatives who remember the experience. As you gather details, think about events, people, places, and your thoughts and feelings.

Calvin & Hobbes copyright 1989 Watterson. Distributed by Universal Press Syndicate. Reprinted with permission. All rights reserved.

Details About Events.   What exactly happened? What major events make up the experience you're writing about? For example, a narrative about a disappointing birthday when you were eight years old might include these events: (1) planning and preparing for the party, (2) waiting for the guests to appear, (3) crying in the bedroom when no one appears, and (4) finding the invitations that you, in your excitement, forgot to deliver.

What are the important details about each event? These are the small actions that you and others do. As part of planning the birthday party, you might have drawn funny pictures on each invitation, made decorations out of construction paper, and helped to get the food and games ready. Try to recall several details about each event.

Details About People. You are the most important person in your personal narrative, but your experience probably involved other people as well. What did they look like, sound like? What did they do or say that's important? Draw on your visual memory for details about how people looked, but remember that you also have a memory for details of sound, touch, taste, and smell.

When you think about a disastrous baby-sitting experience, for example, you might recall the *sight* of the baby as she turned a bowl of strained apricots upside down on her head, but you might also remember the clean powdery *smell* of the baby after her bath, her gurgling *sounds* as she laughed, and the soft *touch* of her skin. If an animal plays an important part in your personal narrative, use sensory details to describe it, too.

WRITING NOTE

Using *dialogue,* the words that people say, helps to make both people and experiences seem real.

As you recall details about the people in your narrative, think about what they said. Later, when you write dialogue, remember that not everyone sounds alike. An eight-year-old uses different words and sentence structure from a thirteen-year-old. And when you're speaking, you use shorter sentences and are often interrupted by another person before you complete a sentence. Try to make dialogue sound as natural and real as possible. (For more help with dialogue, see pages 221, 235–236.)

Details About Places. Where do the events in your experience happen? The places don't have to be exciting or glamorous. But important details from all the senses make the place seem real to readers. If your personal narrative is about winning a neighborhood race, recall the *sight* of the bright fall morning or the *smell* of the cool air.

Details About Thoughts and Feelings. What did you think and feel about your experience? What did other people think and feel? You can tell your thoughts and feelings directly ("I was proud"), but you can also share them through details of action and dialogue. In your narrative about winning a race, you might recall details like these: *got a prize; "Good job!"; father hugged me.*

As you recall details about the important parts of your experience, make a chart to keep a record of them. Your chart might look like the one on the following page.

COMPUTER NOTE: Create tables within your word processing program, and use them to organize your prewriting notes.

HERE'S HOW

Topic: A disastrous baby-sitting experience

	Who or What?	Details
Events	1. Feeding baby	spooning strained apricots into baby that she spit out; baby knocking food off spoon onto herself; baby dumping bowl of apricots on her head
	2. Bathing baby	baby throwing wet toys on floor; splashing water all over me and bathroom
People	Me	arriving in clean jeans and T-shirt, leaving as a wet, wrinkled mess; sound of my voice begging, "<u>Please</u>, stop throwing food."
	Baby	the sound of her screaming; the sticky feel of apricots in her hair
Places	Living room	toys and diapers scattered everywhere; sound of my favorite TV program I can't watch
	Kitchen	good smell of breakfast lingering in air; spotless look of kitchen; gobs of apricots drying on floor
	Baby's room	squeaking of playpen as baby jumps up and down
Thoughts and feelings	Thoughts about depending on Mom; feeling of helplessness	feeling like saying "Help! Mom!"; looking at toys all over; thinking about dried food all over kitchen and baby; remembering my favorite TV program
	Feeling of accomplishment	putting phone down firmly when I decided not to call Mom; dragging weary body off couch and getting to work; looking at now spotless kitchen

To recall details about your experience

- use methods like freewriting and brainstorming (see pages 24–26)
- talk to people who shared the experience
- close your eyes and try to remember the experience, jotting down details as you recall them

---

EXERCISE 2 ▶ **Speaking and Listening: Revealing Details**

Working with two or three classmates, create a skit about one of the following situations. Think about the conversation that might take place between the characters involved. Be certain that the conversation reveals their thoughts and feelings about the situation. When your group is ready, present your skit to your classmates.

1. Identical twins or triplets, separated since birth, meet for the first time at a bus stop.
2. Three students working on a paper together lose it the night before it's due. They try to explain this to their teacher.
3. Three or four students who are baby-sitting for a two-year-old and a three-year-old find themselves locked out of the house by the children.

Organizing Details

Most narratives begin with the background information that readers need to understand the writer's experience. Then they follow *chronological order.* That means that you tell about the events or actions in the order they happened. You discuss the first event first, then the second event, and so on. To help your readers follow this order, you can use transitions such as *at first, to begin, then, later, after that, at last,* and *finally.*

☞ REFERENCE NOTE: For more help with chronological order and transitions, see pages 79, 83–86.

Reflecting on the Meaning of the Experience

The experience you chose as the topic for your narrative was important to you in some way—it had some meaning for you. You can reflect on its meaning by asking yourself questions like these:

- What was I like at the start of the experience?
- How did the experience cause me to change or see things differently?
- What did I learn about myself or others from the experience?
- How did I feel as a result of this experience?

In your personal narrative, you want your readers to understand this meaning. You may not yet understand it yourself, but one goal in writing your narrative is to explore what the experience meant to you. You can convey this meaning by including details and dialogue that show your thoughts and feelings about the experience. You can also write a conclusion in which you discuss the effect of the experience on you or its meaning to you.

"The idea is to get the pencil moving quickly."

Bernard Malamud

| WRITING ASSIGNMENT | PART 4:
Gathering and Organizing Details |

Now's the time to collect the raw material for your narrative. First, make a chart like the one on page 148 with columns labeled *Events, People, Places,* and *Thoughts and Feelings.* Jot down details you recall about these parts of the experience. Next, look at your list of events and number them in the order they happened. Finally, at the bottom of your chart, write a single sentence that explains why this experience was important to you. Save your work to use later when you write your draft.

Writing Your First Draft

The Structure of a Personal Narrative

Most personal narratives have three parts:

- an *introduction* that captures the reader's interest and gives important background information
- a *body* that tells about important events in the order they happened, describes people and places, and gives the writer's thoughts and emotions
- a *conclusion* in which the writer explains the meaning of the experience

The Basic Elements of a Personal Narrative

After you've gathered and organized your ideas, think about how to bring them together in an effective personal narrative—one in which you explore and share the meaning of a personal experience.

Keep in mind that a personal-experience narrative

- is about an experience that happened to you
- describes important events, people, and places that were part of the experience
- includes details that show your thoughts and feelings about your experience
- uses specific sensory details
- explains what the experience meant to you

Writers vary in the way they use these elements. In the following narrative, Roger Starr describes an experience he had in New York City. As you read, ask yourself how the author has used the elements of the personal narrative.

A NEWSPAPER ARTICLE

Tale of the Rodent
by Roger Starr

INTRODUCTION
Background
information

Sensory details
about the
rodent

EVENT 1

Sensory details
about the
rodent

Thoughts and
feelings

Sensory
details

EVENT 2

Details about
the rodent

EVENT 3

The startled movement of a young woman in one corner of the bus shelter indicated that something was wrong. She moved again, a gesture of discomfort, even fear. Then I saw what troubled her: an infant rodent—perhaps mouse, perhaps rat—a small band of brown cotton, with a toothpick for a tail. It had somehow crossed Seventh Avenue, climbed the curb and was moving through the shelter and across the sidewalk.

I say moving rather than running because the creature was too compact to reveal legs. Its speed was so erratic, and its direction so changeable, that it could have been a battery-driven toy riding on a hidden eccentric wheel. Another woman gasped at the sight of the little thing, children pointed, men went out of their way to avoid it.

To me it seemed more incongruous than scary, not merely outnumbered by people but intimidated by the hardness of the world into which it had suddenly emerged. From where? In what soft place on the other side of this busiest highway had its mother gnawed a nest in a fortress of brick and concrete, glass and steel?

Between the legs of pedestrians, the animal darted to the door of a candy store. Its feeding instincts were sound, although it could not poke through the slit between the bottom of the glass door and the sill. The instinct that had taken it to that store made its adult role obvious. It abandoned the candy store for the adjacent entrance to a large office building.

EVENT 4

EVENT 5

Thoughts and feelings

Details about the rodent

EVENT 6

Thoughts and feelings

EVENT 7

Sensory details about the rodent

EVENT 8

CONCLUSION
Meaning of the experience

The superintendent, a bundle of keys hanging from his belt, was standing at the door. Rodent and superintendent vanished into the lobby, only to emerge moments later, animal first.

The superintendent kicked at it, driving the animal back to the sidewalk. Then he looked at me almost regretfully. Whatever the rodent might sometime become, the keeper of the keys knew it was not yet a fair match for the guardian of an office building.

The superintendent's kick must have hurt the animal; its movements became even more erratic than before. But to my astonishment, it crossed the curb and darted into the street, the traffic light in its favor. Unthinkingly wishing it safe passage, I saw it disappear beneath each passing car, then emerge again and move erratically onward.

The game—if game it was—was not to last. The light changed, releasing a torrent of cars across 44th street, and when they had gone, the animal was left motionless on the pavement. No blood, no gore, just a tiny dead thing, hardly bigger than a large beetle, in the middle of the avenue, invisible to any passing motorist. Moments later my bus came and took me home to my apartment house.

I felt I had witnessed something small, but supremely serious.

The New York Times

EXERCISE 3 ▶ **Analyzing the Organization of a Personal Narrative**

After you read Roger Starr's narrative (pages 152–153), meet with two or three classmates to discuss the following questions.

1. Have you ever had a similar experience in which you realized that something that seemed small was really very serious? If so, tell about the experience.
2. Do you think Roger Starr successfully shares a personal experience and its meaning with you? Does he make the experience seem real? How?
3. In what order are most of the events organized? What transitions does Starr use to help readers follow the order?
4. What are some examples of sensory details that Starr uses to describe the rodent? To what sense do most of these details appeal?
5. What thoughts or feelings does Starr have about the rodent? What thoughts and feelings does he show that the superintendent has?
6. Why does Starr think the experience is important?

A Simple Framework for a Personal Narrative

Roger Starr's essay shows you one way of writing a personal narrative. But Starr has had a great deal of practice writing—in fact, he makes his living that way. It's often helpful to follow a simpler model. The following model, although less complex, has the same basic structure and purpose as Starr's.

A WRITER'S MODEL

My Mother's Shoes

INTRODUCTION
Background
Thoughts and feelings

    For weeks I begged my mother to buy me the white leather running shoes in the window at Delphine's Shoe Emporium. I wanted those shoes more than anything else in the world, but my

EVENT 1

mom said they were too expensive. Finally, after I refused to go to Jennie's party in my old shoes, she gave in and bought me the running shoes.

EVENT 2

The next week my school had its Open House. My whole family went and, as usual, my mother wore her ugly beige shoes. "Those shoes look

Sensory details
Thoughts and feelings

terrible," I said. "Why do you always have to wear them?" She didn't answer me. She just picked up my little sister, Elizabeth, and headed for the car.

EVENT 3
Sensory details
Thoughts and feelings

Open House went okay, except that I was sure everyone was looking at the scuffed toes and floppy heels of my mother's shoes. "Why can't I have a mother who has taste?" I wondered. On the way home I asked her again why she didn't

Details

get rid of those shoes. "They embarrass me," I added.

EVENT 4

When we got home, my mother and father immediately went to the kitchen to start dinner, and I took Elizabeth into my room. I could hear Dad's low voice, but I knew that it was Mom who was rattling pots and pans, opening and closing

Sensory details

the refrigerator. Soon I could smell chicken frying, but I couldn't hear Mom singing. She

Thoughts and feelings

always sings in the kitchen, and I was beginning to wonder if I'd really hurt her feelings. Then I heard a knock on my door. Elizabeth toddled

EVENT 5

over to open it, and Dad came in.

"Alice," he said, "don't you think your mother

Thoughts and feelings

is sick of those shoes? Don't you think she knows they're ugly? How do you expect her to buy shoes for herself when you demand shoes that cost

three or four times what they ought to cost? We don't have that kind of money."

CONCLUSION
Meaning of the experience

He said a lot more, too, but he didn't need to. I realized that some things are just too much to ask.

You may find it helpful to model your essay after "My Mother's Shoes." It follows the general framework given below.

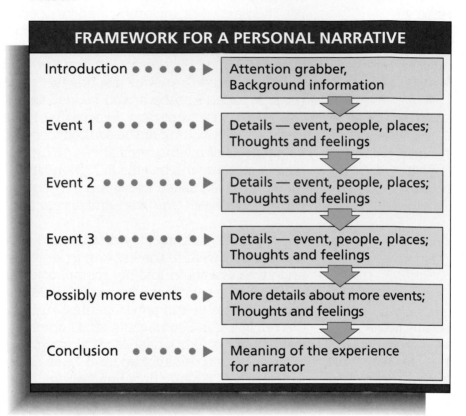

FRAMEWORK FOR A PERSONAL NARRATIVE

Introduction ● ● ● ● ● ▶ | Attention grabber, Background information

Event 1 ● ● ● ● ● ● ● ▶ | Details — event, people, places; Thoughts and feelings

Event 2 ● ● ● ● ● ● ● ▶ | Details — event, people, places; Thoughts and feelings

Event 3 ● ● ● ● ● ● ● ▶ | Details — event, people, places; Thoughts and feelings

Possibly more events ● ▶ | More details about more events; Thoughts and feelings

Conclusion ● ● ● ● ● ▶ | Meaning of the experience for narrator

WRITING ASSIGNMENT

PART 5:
Writing Your First Draft

You've done all your planning—now it's time to write. Keeping the framework on this page in mind, write a draft of your personal narrative. Be sure to use the chart you developed in Writing Assignment, Part 4 (page 150) and any other prewriting notes.

Evaluating and Revising

This chart will help you evaluate and revise your personal narrative. First, ask yourself a question in the left-hand column below. Then, if you find a weakness in your narrative, use the revision technique suggested in the right-hand column.

EVALUATING AND REVISING PERSONAL NARRATIVES

EVALUATION GUIDE	REVISION TECHNIQUE
1 Is the tone friendly and informal? Does the writer use the first-person viewpoint?	**Replace** third-person pronouns with first-person pronouns. **Replace** stiff-sounding words with words that sound like ordinary speech.
2 Has the writer provided enough background information?	**Add** details that help readers understand the experience.
3 Has the writer used details that make events, people, and places seem real?	**Add** details that appeal to all of the five senses.
4 Has the writer included details about thoughts and feelings?	**Add** details about the important thoughts and feelings of people in the narrative.
5 Has the writer discussed the meaning of the experience?	**Add** a few sentences to the conclusion about the importance of the experience.
6 Is the order of events clear to the reader?	**Reorder** the events in the order they happened. **Add** transitions like *at first, then,* and *after that* to show the order.

EXERCISE 4 ▶   **Analyzing a Writer's Revisions**

Study the following revisions of the first paragraph of the personal narrative on pages 154–155. Then, answer the questions that follow.

For weeks I begged my mother to buy
(white leather running)
me the ⌐shoes in the window at Delphine's   **add**

Shoe Emporium. I wanted those shoes

more than anything else in the world, but
(they were too expensive)
my mom said ~~no. It was with great~~   **replace/cut**

~~anticipation that I thought about them.~~   **cut**

Finally, she gave in and bought me the   **reorder**
running
shoes. ~~That was~~ after I refused to go to   **add/cut**

(Jennie's party in my old shoes.)   **replace**

1. Why did the writer add *white leather running* to *shoes* in the first sentence? How does this change help you share the writer's experience?
2. In the second sentence, why is *my mom said they were too expensive* a better choice than *my mom said no*? How does the new sentence relate to the meaning that the writer discusses in the conclusion?
3. Why did the writer delete the third sentence? [Hint: Review page 143].
4. Why did the writer delete two words and move the rest of the last sentence? [Hint: What happens first?]

WRITING ASSIGNMENT   PART 6:
Evaluating and Revising Your Personal Narrative

Using the chart on page 157, decide what to improve in your narrative. Then, exchange papers with another student and evaluate each other's work. When you get your paper back, consider your partner's suggestions as well as your own evaluation of your narrative. Then revise your personal narrative to improve it.

Proofreading and Publishing

Proofread your personal narrative carefully for errors in mechanics, grammar, and usage. Then, publish your narrative by sharing it with a wider audience. Here are two ways you can do that.

- Turn yourself into a storyteller, and share your story aloud. Memorize the plot, but don't worry about exact wording. Practice telling your story with appropriate tones, expressions, and gestures, and then tell it to your classmates.
- Plan a drama day. You and your classmates can write scripts based on the narratives and present them as one-act plays.

WRITING ASSIGNMENT

PART 7:
Proofreading and Publishing Your Narrative

"To err is human," said Alexander Pope. But eliminate as many errors as possible from your narrative. Proofread it carefully and correct the errors. Then, publish your personal narrative in one of the ways suggested above or in another way of your choice.

 Reflecting on Your Writing

You may like your personal narrative enough that you'll decide to add it to your **portfolio.** If you do, make sure to date the paper and to include a written response to each of the following questions:

- What narrative topics did you think about and then decide not to use? Why?
- Do you find it difficult or easy to write from the first-person point of view? Why?
- What technique did you use to recall details about this event? Was the technique effective?

A STUDENT MODEL

Writing personal narratives may stir up memories. Jahtzael Ochoa, a student at Hallandale High School in Hallandale, Florida, recalls the time when he could not speak English. To write about an important event, his advice is to "put your ideas together" and "always tell the truth."

A New Beginning
by Jahtzael Ochoa

I can clearly remember that morning when I entered that third-grade class where everyone was speaking a language I didn't understand. I was seven years old, a short Spanish kid who didn't speak English. I had been in this country for one month and three days; I knew how to say a few words, but I thought I may say them wrong and the kids would laugh at me.

At the end of the first day, I didn't know anyone, but when I got home, I told myself, "I'm going to learn English no matter what it takes." The second day I met some kids that knew some Spanish. They were really nice, and they taught me some basic English for emergencies. On the other hand, there were students who didn't like me, so they blamed everything that happened in the class on me. This went on for many days, but by the middle of the year, I knew how to speak a little English, and I could defend myself.

By the end of third grade, I had friends, and I knew how to defend myself with what I had learned. For two years, I kept saying to myself, "I'm going to learn English and be a good student." Coming here without knowing the language was very hard, and I hope that I never experience again what I felt those first days in the third-grade class. That experience has left me with a belief that I should never make fun of or hurt anyone who doesn't speak the language or is different in any way.

WRITING WORKSHOP

Journals

The idea of talking to yourself in print isn't new. People probably kept some form of journal or diary when they were still chiseling in stone. And since those early days people have kept more modern pen-and-paper or even word-processor journals to record unusual experiences, to note their observations about people and events, and just to explore their own thoughts and feelings. A popular use of the journal is to explore personal goals in order to learn more about yourself.

As you read the following journal entry, think about the goal the writer has set. What do you think the writer learns from the entry?

January 31, 1998

Me, one month ago: I resolve that I'm going to practice tennis at least five hours a week. I wanted to make the team. Not bad enough, I guess. Just too many days when I felt too tired to play. Then I got behind on my homework and had to spend my spare time studying. The same thing happened last year when I wanted to make the track team and told myself I'd run every day and keep in shape. It's easy to say things you want to do, but it's harder to do them, especially when they involve work or making choices. Maybe if I said to myself at first, Now, this isn't going to be easy, I'd do better. Okay. I'm not going to give up. I know it'll be hard work, but I'll try again. I'll practice tennis one hour Monday to Friday, then homework and bed by 10:00.

1. What personal goal did this writer set?
2. Why does the writer say that the goal wasn't met?
3. What does the writer learn about why the goal may not have been reached?
4. How does the writer change the goal at the end of the entry?

Writing a Personal Journal Entry

Prewriting. Think about a goal you have set for yourself. Perhaps you've decided to help out more at home, to get yourself into better shape, or to study more. Think about your experiences trying to meet the goal. What success have you had? In what ways have you fallen short of the goal? Will you continue to work for the goal, change the goal in some way, or decide to give it up?

Writing, Evaluating, and Revising. Write a first draft of your journal entry. Remember that you are "thinking aloud" for yourself. Unlike your personal narrative, there's no set form for journal entries, and they are very informal. Remember: This is for you.

Proofreading and Publishing. Writers usually don't proofread their journals unless the journals are published. And most journals aren't published during the writer's lifetime— they're published years later by someone else. As a way of publishing your entry, you might write your goal on a long strip of paper, perhaps decorating it with pictures that represent the goal. Then, hang the paper in your bedroom or someplace else where you'll see it and be reminded of your goal.

Since your journal entry is private, you may not want to add it to your **portfolio.** However, you may want to reflect on your journal entry by writing a response to the following question: What did you enjoy about writing for yourself?

MAKING CONNECTIONS

NARRATIVES ACROSS THE CURRICULUM

History

Personal narratives are one important source of knowledge about the history of this country. In the following narrative, a woman describes her family's journey through the Florida Everglades when it was still a wilderness area. As you read, look for details about the events, people, and places that were part of her experience.

from The Woods Were Tossing With Jewels
by Marie St. John

This third day out, and the days to come, found us in the unsettled wilds of Florida. Sometimes we would strike camp early enough for papa and the boys to shoot fox squirrels or quail for supper. No matter what time of day we came to a good fishing place, we would stay for the rest of the day. One such place was a white-clear stream that ran out of a spring in a vast cypress swamp. Its underwater grasses looked like green ribbons constantly unrolling, and the trees held thick sprays of wild orchids. Papa had given each of us a pole, and what with six of us fishing and the fish so plentiful, we usually had a catch in a matter of minutes. As an added treat papa sometimes would cut the heart out of a cabbage palmetto, and mama would cook it, slowly, in the black kettle. There was no shortage of these groves. Always, it seems, we were in or near a grove of cabbage palmettos.

One day I got sick and had a high fever. We were near Arcadia but still too far to drive on. So papa pitched camp and went on into town on horseback and brought a doctor back with him. We had to stay in camp for several days until I was well.

Then we drove on to a small crossroads and stopped at a hotel, a two-story frame building no larger than a big house, until I was strong enough to resume the journey.

As we drove off, Arcadia with its dirt streets and free-roaming cattle, its barns and outhouses, looked like a metropolis. We were not to see such a city again for over a year. Soon enough our eyes were bugging at the size of the oak trees that grew in clusters wherever the earth rose up from the flood plains of the creeks and rivers. These lush hammocks were green with ferns. The burly arms of the oaks were huge with fern and blooming bromeliads. Redbirds, tanagers, and painted buntings flew back and forth across the trail, leaving a child with the impression that the woods were tossing with jewels.

What could you write that might later become a source of knowledge about life today? Write about an experience you've had—a trip with your family, a weekend outing, or even a trip to the mall. Describe your experience so that you leave a record of what your life is like today.

NARRATIVES IN LITERATURE

Poetry

Poems are ideal for exploring and describing a personal experience. As you read "The Runaway" by Robert Frost, look for details that describe the runaway. What meaning do you think the experience has for the speaker in the poem?

The Runaway
by Robert Frost

Once when the snow of the year was beginning to fall,
We stopped by a mountain pasture to say, "Whose colt?"
A little Morgan had one forefoot on the wall,
The other curled at his breast. He dipped his head
And snorted at us. And then he had to bolt.
We heard the miniature thunder where he fled,
And we saw him, or thought we saw him, dim and grey,
Like a shadow against the curtain of falling flakes.
"I think the little fellow's afraid of the snow.
He isn't winter-broken. It isn't play
With the little fellow at all. He's running away.
I doubt if even his mother could tell him, 'Sakes,
It's only weather.' He'd think she didn't know!
Where is his mother? He can't be out alone."
And now he comes again with clatter of stone,
And mounts the wall again with whited eyes
And all his tail that isn't hair up straight.
He shudders his coat as if to throw off flies.
"Whoever it is that leaves him out so late,
When other creatures have gone to stall and bin,
Ought to be told to come and take him in."

Write a narrative poem of your own. Tell about something that happened to you, and make the meaning of the experience clear.

Creating Pictures and Images

Painters use oils or watercolors to create lifelike **pictures** and **images.** Writers use descriptive words—words that pop a scene or character right off the page, smack into the mind's eye.

Writing and You. A novelist may use description to "show" you what the main character looks like. A travel writer may use words that help you "see" the sands of Oahu. In a memo, an engineer may use words that help her supervisor "picture" a design for a new electronic part. The more specific a writer's language, the clearer the image. Have you ever read a description so vivid that you could close your eyes and see what you've only read about?

As You Read. As you read the following selection, pay careful attention to the word-pictures Annie Dillard draws. Notice how your mind's eye picks up the images she wants you to see.

Alexander J. Guthrie, *Roll Along to Ely* (1992). Watercolor, 22 × 30". Private Collection. Courtesy Horwitch Newman Gallery.

from An American Childhood

STREETCARS
ON PENN AVENUE

by Annie Dillard

Streetcars ran on Penn Avenue. Streetcars were orange, clangy, beloved things—loud, jerky, and old. They were powerless beasts compelled to travel stupidly with their wheels stuck in the tracks below them. Each streetcar had one central headlight, which looked fixedly down its tracks and nowhere else. The single light advertised to drivers at night that something was coming that couldn't move over. When a streetcar's tracks and wires rounded a corner, the witless streetcar had to follow. Its heavy orange body bulged out and blocked two lanes; any car trapped beside it had to cringe stopped against the curb until it passed.

Sometimes a car parked at the curb blocked a streetcar's route. Then the great beast sounded its mournful bell: it emitted a long-suffering, monotonous bong . . . bong . . . bong . . . and men and women on the sidewalk shook their heads sympathetically at the motorman inside, the motorman more inferred than seen through the windshield's bright reflections. . . .

The streetcars' overhead network of wires made of Penn Avenue a loose-roofed tunnel. The wires cut the sky into rectangles inside which you could compose various views as you walked. Here were a yellow brick apartment top and some flattened fair-weather clouds; here were green sycamore leaves in the foreground, and a faded orange rooftop advertising sign, and a yellow streetlight, and a slab of neutral sky.

Streetcars traveled with their lone trolley sticks pushed up by springs into these overhead wires. A trolley stick carried a trolley wheel; the trolley wheel rolled along the track of hot electric wire overhead as the four wheels rolled along the cold grooved track below. At night, and whenever it rained, the streetcars' trolleys sparked. They shot a radiant fistful of sparks at every crossing of wires. Sometimes a streetcar accidentally "threw the trolley." Bumping over a switch or rounding a bend, the trolley lost the wire and the spring-loaded stick flew up and banged its bare side crazily against the hot wire. Big yellow sparks came crackling into the sky and fell glowing toward the

roofs of cars. The motorman had to brake the streetcar, go around to its rear, and haul the wayward, sparking trolley stick down with a rope. This happened so often that there was a coil of rope for that purpose at the streetcar's stern, neat and cleated like a halyard on a mast.

So the big orange streetcars clanged and spat along; they stopped and started, tethered to their wires overhead and trapped in their grooves below. Every day at a hundred intersections they locked horns with cars that blocked their paths— cars driven by insensible, semiconscious people, people who had just moved to town, teenagers learning to drive, the dread Ohio drivers, people sunk in rapturous conversation.

READER'S RESPONSE

1. If you closed your eyes while someone read Annie Dillard's description to you, would you be able to picture the places and things she describes? Explain. Which of her word-pictures do you find most vivid?
2. Has a machine ever captured your imagination the way streetcars capture Annie Dillard's? In a journal entry, describe such a mechanism—perhaps one that intrigues you or that you remember fondly.

WRITER'S CRAFT

3. What words or phrases does Annie Dillard use to make you see and hear the streetcars?
4. Do you think the drawing below adds to or detracts from Annie Dillard's description? Explain.
5. What action words does Annie Dillard use to help you picture the streetcars' movements?

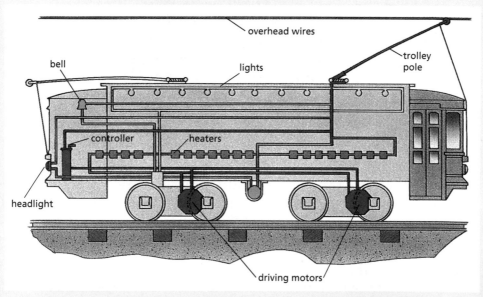

A streetcar receives power from a system of overhead wires. The trolley pole, or trolley stick, conducts electricity from the overhead wires to the controller. Current finally arrives at the driving motors, which propel the streetcar.

Uses of Description

Although the point is always to get the reader to "see," different writers may have different reasons for describing. Before you write a description, have your purpose in mind. Here are some examples of possible purposes.

- in a description of your grandmother, expressing what she means to you
- in a journal entry, describing a toy that was once especially important to you
- on a job application, describing your duties at your current job
- in a newspaper ad, describing the bookcase you made and would like to sell
- in a police report, giving an accurate description of the purse snatcher you saw at the mall
- in a science report, describing how a microwave oven works
- in a story, describing a character you've invented
- in a poem, creating a word-picture of a car

Because writers use description for a variety of purposes, descriptive writing is likely to appear almost anywhere—in advertisements, in news stories, in poems, and in technical reports, as well as in textbooks, owner's manuals, and novels. Nevertheless, all successful descriptions have one thing in common—they make the reader "see."

LOOKING AHEAD

In the main assignment in this chapter, you'll write an objective description of a mechanism. Your basic purpose will be to inform. Keep in mind that a good description

- includes factual and sensory details to help the reader picture the subject clearly
- uses precise words
- is clearly organized and easy to follow

Describing a Mechanism

Prewriting

Finding a Focus

Before you take a picture, you make sure that whatever you're aiming at is sharply in focus. The same is true as you plan your description of a mechanism. You'll also need to focus your description by thinking about your subject, purpose, and audience.

Choosing a Mechanism to Describe

The word *mechanism* may make you think of a complex machine such as a computer or a car. But simple, everyday things—a mechanical pencil, a pizza cutter, a kaleido-scope—are mechanisms too. In fact, anything whose parts work together as a unit can be thought of as a mechanism: an atom, a guitar, a soccer team.

Sometimes your subject is built into a writing assignment. In a lab report, for example, you're asked to describe the nervous system of a frog. But if you're free to choose a subject, try these suggestions.

- Think of something familiar—an object you know well.
- Choose a mechanism you can observe directly. It's easier to collect details when your subject is in front of you.
- Limit your subject to one you can describe in detail in a few paragraphs—for example, a sink rather than the plumbing system of a house.

Identifying Your Purpose

In this chapter, your purpose will be to inform. Informative writing calls for *objective* description, the kind that appears in textbooks, encyclopedia articles, and informational reports. An ***objective*** description is made up of factual details and sensory details. The number and kind of details you include depend on your purpose: Are you describing the mechanism so that the reader will be able to build it, or simply so that the reader can use it? These different purposes will result in very different descriptions.

Thinking About Audience and Tone

You will also want to identify your audience before you write. That's because your readers' level of familiarity with the mechanism determines the kinds of details you'll include. For example, most readers have probably seen a vegetable peeler more times than they want to remember. But you can help them understand why it's such a handy tool by focusing on its parts and how they work together.

   If your readers aren't familiar with the mechanism you are describing, they'll need more information about its function. For example, if they've never heard of a virtual-reality headset, you'll need to include basic information about what it's for and how it operates, as well as what it looks like. You'll also need to define unfamiliar terms, and you may have to give some background information.

   Your readers even affect the kinds of words you use. For example, if you had written the description of the streetcar at the beginning of this chapter for a group of sixth-graders, would you need to replace *monotonous* or *semiconscious* with easier words?

   The tone of objective descriptions is neutral, businesslike, and somewhat formal. Like an invisible movie camera, you report the facts without revealing your thoughts and feelings. Written from the third-person point of view, objective descriptions use the pronouns *he, she, it,* and *they*. That puts the emphasis on the subject rather than on the writer. (Occasionally, objective descriptions are written from the second-person point of view; the pronoun *you* creates a more conversational tone.) Notice the factual details and neutral tone in this objective description of a vacuum cleaner.

> Cylinder vacuum cleaners work entirely by suction. An electric motor in the cleaner drives a fan that pumps the air out of the hose. The pressure of the atmosphere pushes air into the cleaning attachment and up the hose, pulling in dust and dirt with it. The dust-laden air then passes through a dust bag, which retains the dust and dirt, before leaving the back of the cleaner. In some cleaners, this air is directed to the base of the machine to form an air cushion. The cleaner then hovers above the floor and can be moved easily.
>
> Upright models have a rotating brush that beats the dust and dirt out of a carpet before it is sucked into the dust bag.
>
> David Macaulay, *The Way Things Work*

"Hello, Emily. This is Gladys Murphy up the street. Fine, thanks . . . Say, could you go to your window and describe what's in my front yard?"

WRITING NOTE   When your purpose is to express yourself, to be creative, or to persuade, your description will be mostly *subjective*. In addition to factual and sensory details, you'll include your thoughts and feelings and, sometimes, figures of speech (pages 196–197). These details work together to create a mood or main impression. Many subjective descriptions are written from the first-person point of view: The pronouns *I*, *me*, *we*, and *us* refer to the writer (who's also the observer). That usually makes the tone less formal.

EXERCISE 1 ▶   Analyzing Subject, Purpose, Audience, and Tone

Get together with two or three classmates, and read the following description. Then, discuss these questions.

1. What is the subject of the description?
2. What do you think is the writer's purpose—to express thoughts and feelings, to persuade, to inform, or to create a literary work? How can you tell?
3. Who do you think is the intended audience? What makes you think so?
4. Is the description subjective or objective? Is the tone formal or conversational?

All cameras—those that take photographs and those that make motion pictures—use the same basic principles. Light reflects from the scene being photographed and strikes the lens of the camera. The light passes through the lens and forms an upside-down image on the film at the back of the camera. The image can be sharpened by adjusting the distance between the lens and the film. Many cameras have a focusing mechanism by which the photographer moves the lens a short distance to sharpen the image.

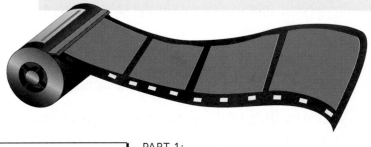

In addition, most cameras have a viewfinder, a sighting instrument that the photographer looks through to frame the subject. Most cameras also have a film advance. With this device, the photographer winds the film through the camera to put unexposed film in position to take a picture. After each picture has been taken, the film advance moves the exposed film out of the way.

The World Book Multimedia Encyclopedia™

WRITING ASSIGNMENT

PART 1:
Beginning Your Description

In this chapter, you'll write an objective description of a mechanism. Using the suggestions on page 172, choose a subject for your description. Then, focus your writing by filling out a chart for your subject like the one below.

SUBJECT:	the computer desk I made for my sister
PURPOSE:	to inform
TYPE OF DESCRIPTION:	objective
AUDIENCE:	my applied-technology teacher
TONE:	fairly formal
POINT OF VIEW:	third person

Prewriting

Planning Your Description

Before you write a description, you need to gather specific descriptive details and figure out how to arrange them. For an objective description, your specific details will be realistic ones: They will include both factual details and sensory details. Together, these two types of details make for effective description.

Using Two Types of Descriptive Details

Factual Details. Details that can be measured or checked are *factual details.* You'll use them in all kinds of descriptions, but they are especially important in scientific and technical writing. Notice the many factual details in this example.

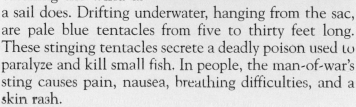

The Portuguese man-of-war, a colony of creatures, is the world's most poisonous marine animal. The only part visible on the ocean's surface is a gas-filled sac. Varying in size, this sac can be up to ten inches long. It helps keep the colony afloat; it also moves the entire colony by catching the wind as a sail does. Drifting underwater, hanging from the sac, are pale blue tentacles from five to thirty feet long. These stinging tentacles secrete a deadly poison used to paralyze and kill small fish. In people, the man-of-war's sting causes pain, nausea, breathing difficulties, and a skin rash.

Sensory Details.   Words and phrases that appeal to the senses (sight, hearing, touch, smell, and taste) are called *sensory details.* They're another resource for re-creating your subject for your reader to visualize. Although beginning writers tend mostly to use visual details, they can learn to appeal to other senses as well.

To come up with words that appeal to the senses, some writers use a thesaurus. But writers also create their own storehouses of words, called *word banks,* like the one that follows. You can do the same in your journal.

WORD BANK			
Sight Words	glossy bronze	triangular crimson	tapering bleached
Sound Words	clang screech	roar buzz	whine hum
Smell Words	fragrant stale	fresh piney	spoiled musty
Touch Words	slimy oily	icy silky	fuzzy gritty
Taste Words	bitter tangy	tart sour	salty metallic

Here are sensory details that describe a slide trombone.

SIGHT: *gleaming yellow brass tube coiled back on itself twice; cup-shaped mouthpiece; funnel-shaped bell (opening)*

SOUND: *brilliant, piercing tones, lowest when slide fully open, highest when slide closed*

TOUCH: *smooth, cool metal against fingers; gentle pressure of lips against mouthpiece; vibration of lips*

TASTE: *metallic taste of mouthpiece*

SMELL: *whiff of pungent, ammonia-like trace of brass polish*

Using Comparisons

One way to describe an unfamiliar object is by making a comparison, or analogy, to something familiar. Comparisons are useful when you are trying to help your readers visualize mechanisms and other physical objects, as well as more abstract structures. For example, the sewn-up seams of a softball can be compared to a laced shoe, and the Internet can be compared to a national road and highway system.

> A laser disc looks something like a phonograph record without grooves.
>
> Michael Folsom and Marcia Folsom,
> *The Macmillan Book of How Things Work*

EXERCISE 2 ▶ **Identifying Descriptive Details**

The photograph below shows a mechanism you're probably familiar with. What kinds of descriptive details can you identify in the photograph? What comparisons can you make? Working with a partner, label three columns on a sheet of paper: sensory details, factual details, and comparisons. Study the photograph, and then list the details you identify for each column. Exchange papers with another group, and compare your lists.

Collecting Descriptive Details

The raw material for a description of a mechanism is all around you—if you know how to find it. Just observe, read, or recall.

Observing the Subject Directly. Plant yourself in front of your subject, and spend at least ten minutes observing and taking notes. Look at it as a whole—from several different angles, if possible. Then, examine each part, and note how the parts are put together. Observe the object at rest and, if it has moving parts, in operation. Identify its most important features—size, shape, color, materials, weight, and so on. Can you compare it with another object? For example, is the tape-recording head about the size of a dime? Don't just look. Use your other senses, too. How does the leather belt smell? How does the buckle feel?

If you like to draw, try sketching the mechanism. What angle would best help your readers understand its features and function? You can make one or more drawings of the exterior (in detail or in outline) or even cutaway views to show the object's inner parts. (See page 185 for more on graphics.)

Reading About Your Subject.
You can also observe "secondhand," by reading what others have observed. Encyclopedias, magazine articles, owner's manuals, and travel essays can be mined for descriptive details. For example, you can describe how an acoustic guitar works by looking at photographs or drawings and reading an encyclopedia or magazine article.

Recalling Details.
Memories, some scientists say, aren't erased. According to this theory, you can recall memories from somewhere deep inside your brain. To describe a mechanism from memory, shut your eyes and concentrate. Call up a mental picture of it. Then, try to retrieve details other than visual ones. What sounds do you recall? What textures?

To collect descriptive details, ask yourself these questions about your subject:

- What are its most important features?
- What sensory details will help the reader picture it?
- What factual details will help the reader understand it?
- What can I compare it with?
- What details could I gather by reading about my subject?
- What details can I recall about it?

EXERCISE 3 ▶ **Collecting Descriptive Details**

Working with a partner or a small group, select one of the following subjects. Gather as many details as you can by observing, reading, or recalling. Then, get together with another group that chose the same subject. What similarities and differences are there in the details you gathered?

1. a diving board
2. a pair of scissors
3. a globe
4. a baseball
5. a kaleidoscope

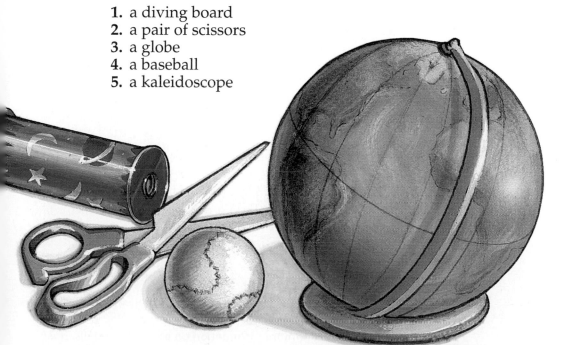

WRITING ASSIGNMENT

PART 2:
Gathering Descriptive Details

Now, try your hand at gathering details for the subject you chose in Writing Assignment, Part 1 (page 176). List as many details as you can. Save your list to use later.

Organizing Details

Nobody can look at everything at once. Because of this, part of planning a description is arranging details in an order that makes sense to your readers. The chart below shows three ways to arrange details.

ARRANGING DESCRIPTIVE DETAILS		
TYPE	DEFINITION	USE
spatial order	arranging details according to how they are located in space—top to bottom, front to back, outside to inside, clockwise, and so on	works well for describing the physical appearance of an object with no moving parts (for example, a football) or a mechanism at rest
order of importance	placing the most important details either first or last	useful when readers need to understand only some parts of an object (for example, the "on" and "play" buttons of a CD player) in detail
operating order	essentially chronological (time) order, describing the parts in the sequence in which they work	especially useful for emphasizing the function of a mechanism (for example, how a camera takes a photograph) rather than its appearance

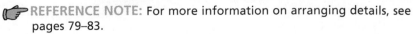

REFERENCE NOTE: For more information on arranging details, see pages 79–83.

CRITICAL THINKING

Evaluating Details

By now you have a whole list of details, probably more than you can use. How do you choose which ones to include? With practice, you develop the skill of evaluating details. That means you judge which ones will help you accomplish your purpose and which ones won't. Here are guidelines you can use when writing your description.

Include

- details that define the object by identifying its class and explaining how it differs from other members of that class (for example, "A mountain bike is an off-road bicycle with 26-inch wheels and 18 to 24 speeds.")
- details that explain the function or purpose (for example, "A parachute is a device for slowing the speed of a person or thing dropped from an aircraft.")
- details that give accurate physical measurements (for example, "The ice cube tray is 11 inches long by $4\frac{3}{8}$ inches wide by $1\frac{3}{4}$ inches deep.")

Do Not Include

- details about your thoughts and feelings (for example, "The jewelry box is special to me because my Uncle Dwayne brought it from Ghana.")
- details that give instructions for making or assembling the mechanism (for example, "For the sundial face, cut a circle 20 inches in diameter from $\frac{3}{4}$-inch plywood."). Instructions are more suitable for a process ("how-to") paper (see Chapter 7, pages 255–277). For a description, reword such details (for example, "The sundial face, made from $\frac{3}{4}$-inch plywood, measures 20 inches in diameter.").

CRITICAL THINKING EXERCISE:
Evaluating Details

Here is a list of details a writer made while observing a basketball court at a city park. Using the criteria listed on page 183, evaluate the details and make two lists. In the first list, place the details you would use for an objective description of the backboard and basket—details that define, classify, explain function, or give measurements. In the second list, place details about thoughts, feelings, or processes—how something is made or done. While it may seem that some of the details could go in either list, each actually works better in either one list or the other. After you've completed your lists, get together with two or three other students and compare the results.

flat, fan-shaped wood painted white

echoes of shouts, "Hey, Jess. Here. Got it, man!"

wood originally painted white, now scuffed and peeling

metal ring supports basket

pickup games the most fun

swoosh of the ball through the net

ring $\frac{5}{8}$ inch thick, bright orange

inside diameter of ring 18 inches

basket 10 feet above ground, parallel to floor

crunch of sneakers on gravel

grunts and groans as players rebound for the ball

net made of sturdy twine

fresh smell of spring evening, mixed with smell of sweat and asphalt

sweat glistening on foreheads of players

PART 3:
Evaluating and Arranging Details

Look over the list of details you made for Writing Assignment, Part 2 (page 182). Evaluate the details, and select the ones that you think will work best in your description. Next, decide in what order the details will make the most sense to your readers. Finally, number the details on your list in the order in which you plan to use them.

Using Graphics

Whoever said "a picture is worth a thousand words" might well have been struggling to describe a mechanism with words only. Graphics—photographs, line drawings, and computer-generated images—can greatly help your audience understand and think about your subject.

To decide whether your description would be improved with illustrations, ask yourself this: What information might my readers grasp more easily and quickly if I presented it graphically? Then, think about what kind of graphic would be most appropriate—diagram, drawing, flowchart, and so on.

As you develop your graphics, make sure text and art complement one another. Refer to graphics in your text (for example, "See the figure below"), and make sure your text explains the graphic if necessary. Do not, however, needlessly duplicate information in text and graphic.

COMPUTER NOTE: If you have access to graphics software, you can create, store, retrieve, and edit art on the computer just as you can written text.

PART 4:
Illustrating Your Description

Think about what parts of your description would be clarified with a graphic. Then, find or create illustrations, plan where they will go, and decide how to adjust your written description (eliminating some description, adding references, and so on).

Writing Your First Draft

You're making progress. You've decided what you're going to describe, collected your details, and thought about how to put them together. Now you can begin to bring everything together in a first draft.

The Basic Elements of Objective Description

As you write your first draft, remember that an objective description

- opens with an introduction that identifies and describes the mechanism
- organizes details to create a clear picture of the mechanism
- uses factual details, sensory details, and comparisons to convey the subject's appearance, function, or both
- uses the second- or third-person point of view
- has a fairly formal tone
- concludes by explaining how the parts work together

As you read this description of a light bulb, notice the kinds of details the writers have chosen to help readers picture and understand the mechanism.

AN ARTICLE IN A BOOK

Light Bulb
by Michael Folsom and Marcia Folsom

INTRODUCTION

With a light bulb, electricity seems to turn night into day.

Factual details

A metal called *tungsten* and a gas called *argon* make a light bulb work. The filament,

Sensory detail—sight

a glowing wire inside the bulb, is made of tungsten. The bulb protects the glowing tungsten filament from burning up. In the air, the metal filament would combine with oxygen and burn. But the sealed bulb is filled with argon gas, which cannot combine with tungsten to burn. So the filament glows brightly for hundreds of hours.

Factual details

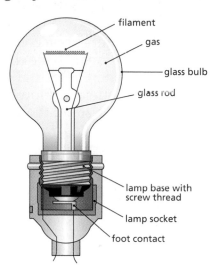

filament
gas
glass bulb
glass rod
lamp base with screw thread
lamp socket
foot contact

Function

When a light bulb is screwed into a socket and the switch is turned on, the electrical circuit is completed. Current can then flow through the filament.

Sensory details—sight and touch

Electricity makes the tungsten wire glow bright and hot. The wires that carry electricity usually allow the current to flow easily, like water through a big pipe. But if the wire is very thin, the electric power must force its way through. The thin wire resists the flow of the current.

Comparison

Comparison

This resistance is like friction, the action that makes your hands warm when you rub them together. When electricity meets resistance, its force can make a wire heat up. If the resistance is great enough, the wire becomes so hot that it begins to glow and shed light. This is called *incandescence.*

Factual details

Sensory details—sight and touch

The Macmillan Book of How Things Work

E X E R C I S E 4 ▶ **Analyzing an Objective Description**

After you read the description of a light bulb, meet with two or three classmates to discuss the following questions.

1. What point of view do the writers use? How can you tell?
2. The writers use a combination of orders to arrange details. Identify the different orders.
3. In addition to factual details, the writers use some sensory details. How do these sensory details help you understand the workings of a light bulb?
4. The writers also use comparisons. Did you find them useful? Explain.

A Writer's Model for You

The description you've just read was written by professional writers who very effectively organized details to create a picture of a light bulb. Now that you're writing your own objective description, it might be helpful to have a model more like what you might write. As you read, look for the basic elements of objective description. Also, notice that the model begins with a short introduction that defines the mechanism and ends with a conclusion that explains how the parts work together.

A WRITER'S MODEL

INTRODUCTION
Name
Function

Overview of major parts

Major part
Comparison

A peeler is a kitchen device that removes a thin layer of skin or rind from fruits and vegetables. About the size and shape of a small paring knife, it is made of steel and has three major parts: the blade, the tang, and the handle.

The blade is rounded, like a piece of tubing cut in half lengthwise. The sharpened inner edges of a lengthwise slit in the center of the blade form its two cutting edges. At its free

Factual details/ Comparison	end, the blade is tapered like the tip of a small spoon, allowing the user to dig out any small bad spots in the food. Its opposite end is
Sensory details— sight	tightly rolled inward to fit through a hole in the handle and clasp the tang.
Major part **Factual details**	The tang is a slender cylindrical rod that connects the blade to the handle. It passes through the center of the handle, which is hollow, and exits through a small round hole.
Comparison	There, it is held in place by a head like a nail-head just outside the handle and by two "ears" just inside it.
Major part **Sensory details—sight and touch**	The handle consists of a flat strip of steel bent lengthwise and curved to provide a comfortable grip. At the blade end, the edges of a slot in each end of the strip are bent parallel to the blade and welded together to form prongs.
CONCLUSION **How the parts work together**	In operation, the convex side of the blade (the side that curves outward) is scraped along the surface of the food. Depending on the direction of the scraping, one or the other
Sensory detail—touch	of the sharp edges peels the skin away, and the peeling comes up through the slit. The blade-and-tang assembly rotates up to 90 de-
Factual details	grees to adjust to uneven spots on the food's surface. The prongs on the handle keep the blade from spinning all the way around.

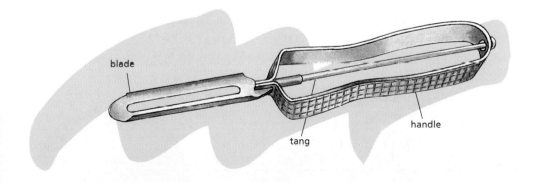

You may find it helpful to model your description on the one of the peeler. It follows the framework given below.

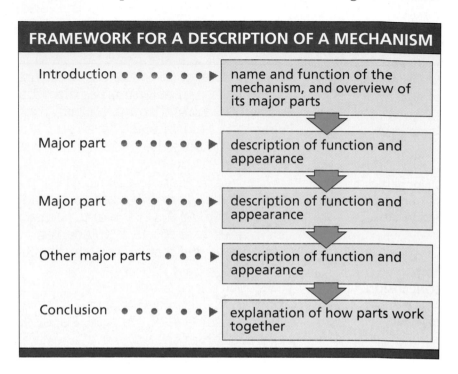

FRAMEWORK FOR A DESCRIPTION OF A MECHANISM

Introduction ● ● ● ● ● ● ▶	name and function of the mechanism, and overview of its major parts
Major part ● ● ● ● ● ● ▶	description of function and appearance
Major part ● ● ● ● ● ● ▶	description of function and appearance
Other major parts ● ● ● ▶	description of function and appearance
Conclusion ● ● ● ● ● ● ▶	explanation of how parts work together

WRITING ASSIGNMENT

PART 5:
Writing a Draft of Your Description

You've seen that you don't have to be a professional writer to create an effective description. Use your list of details from Writing Assignment, Part 3 (page 185) to write the first draft of the description that you've been working on. Also, add any graphics you created in Writing Assignment, Part 4 (page 185).

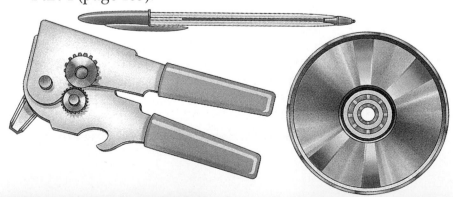

Evaluating and Revising

Evaluating. With a first draft in hand, you're ready to evaluate and revise your description. When you evaluate, you look for weaknesses in content, organization, and style, or language. What doesn't make sense? What could you describe more accurately and precisely?

GRAMMAR HINT

Using Precise Words

Use precise nouns, verbs, adjectives, and adverbs to create a sharp, clear image for your readers.

VAGUE   In a coffee maker, water goes up a spout.
         Then water goes back down through the coffee.
PRECISE In a coffee percolator, hot water streams up a cen-
         tral spout. Then the hot water percolates down
         through the ground coffee.

Precise verbs—words like *dig, clasp,* and *spin*—are almost always action verbs. Action verbs will help your reader visualize how a mechanism works; they also bring life and excitement to your writing. The essay on the light bulb, for example, uses the verbs *protects, glow, force,* and *resists.* Avoid lifeless constructions such as "There is a _____," or "One part of the mechanism is a _____."

 REFERENCE NOTE: See pages 465–467 and 472–489 for more on nouns, verbs, adjectives, and adverbs.

Revising. When you revise, you make changes to eliminate these weaknesses. Use the chart on the next page to evaluate and revise your objective description. Begin by asking yourself each question in the left-hand column. If you identify a problem, use the revision technique suggested in the right-hand column.

EVALUATING AND REVISING OBJECTIVE DESCRIPTIONS

EVALUATION GUIDE	REVISION TECHNIQUE
1 Is there a clear introduction to the function and parts of the mechanism?	**Add** a brief, clearly worded introduction.
2 Do realistic details (factual details and sensory details) and comparisons give a clear picture of the subject?	**Add** factual and sensory details, including details that appeal to senses other than sight. **Replace** unfamiliar comparisons with more familiar ones.
3 Are the details organized in such a way that the reader creates an accurate mental image?	**Reorder** details so they will make sense to the reader.
4 If your report contains graphics, have you chosen types that convey the information clearly? Are they placed effectively?	**Replace** graphics as necessary, and place them close to the text they support.
5 Does the writer leave out thoughts and feelings?	**Replace** thoughts and feelings with neutral factual and sensory details.
6 Are the tone and point of view impersonal and fairly formal?	**Replace** first-person (*I*) references with third-person references (*it* or *they*). Replace informal words with more formal language.
7 Does your description contain precise words and action verbs?	**Replace** vague, lifeless words with descriptive words and action verbs.
8 Does your description conclude with an explanation of how the parts work together?	**Add** a summary of how the mechanism's parts function as a whole.

E X E R C I S E 5 ▶ **Analyzing a Writer's Revisions**

This is the third paragraph in the description you read on pages 188–189. Study the writer's revisions, and then answer the questions that follow the paragraph.

slender cylindrical 　　　　The tang is a ~~skinny~~ rod that	replace/add
connects the blade to the handle. It　*center of the* 　passes through ⁼the handle, which is	add
exits hollow, and ~~goes out~~ through a small	replace
round hole. It is held in place there by	reorder
a head ~~that looks a lot~~ like a nailhead	cut
just outside the handle and by two	
just inside it⊙ "ears."	add

1. Why do you think the writer replaced the words *skinny* and *goes out* with the words *slender* and *exits*?
2. How does adding the word *cylindrical* improve the paragraph?
3. How does moving the word *there* to the beginning of the second sentence make the paragraph read more smoothly?
4. Why do you think the writer cut the phrase *that looks a lot*?
5. What is the effect of adding the words *just inside it* to the end of the sentence?

WRITING **ASSIGNMENT**	PART 6: **Evaluating and Revising** **Your Description**

Apply the guidelines on page 192 to your first draft. Then, exchange papers with a partner, and comment on each other's descriptions. Basing the changes on your self-evaluation and your partner's evaluation, revise your first draft.

Proofreading and Publishing

You've worked hard to create a good objective description. Now, proofread your revised version carefully for mistakes in grammar, usage, and mechanics. Then, share your writing. Here are two suggestions.

- Take turns reading aloud descriptions without naming the objects being described. Then, ask listeners to try to draw the mechanism you're describing.
- Display written descriptions, together with illustrations, on a wall or bulletin board.

WRITING ASSIGNMENT

PART 7:
Proofreading and Publishing Your Description

Put the finishing touches on your description by proofreading it carefully and correcting all errors. Then, publish or share your description.

 Reflecting on Your Writing

If you choose to add your description to your **portfolio,** date it and attach your answers to these questions:

- Was it easy to write an objective description? Why?
- How can you use description in other types of writing?
- What might you do differently the next time you write an objective description?

"...Choose the exact word, the one that flies straight to the target, rather than the diffuse word that hits other things besides the target...."

Theodore M. Bernstein,
Watch Your Language

A STUDENT MODEL

Alfredo Anica says the easiest part of writing his paper was describing the mechanism, a bicycle—"because I use it every day." Alfredo, who is a student at Don Lugo High School in Chino, California, recommends that writers of papers like this one should "choose a mechanism that you know well."

The Bicycle
by Alfredo Anica

People have invented many things to move from one place to another—for example, the car, the train, the boat, and the airplane. The bicycle is one of these, a very useful mechanism.

The bicycle helps people move faster than they do when they walk. It comes in several different sizes, like 16, 20, 24, 26, and 27 inches in height. The bicycle has a frame, two tires with rims and tubes, a seat, handlebars, two pedals, a chain, a chainwheel (also called a front sprocket), and a cluster of rear sprockets. This cluster is one of the most important parts of the bicycle.

The bicycle moves by being pedaled. This turns the front sprocket, which moves the chain. The moving chain, which fits around one of the rear sprockets, causes the whole cluster to turn, which turns the rear wheel. The bicycle moves forward. The speed depends upon the rider. You can go fast or slow. With the handlebars, you can move the front wheel in the direction you want to go.

Subjective Description

Much of what you've learned about objective description also applies to *subjective* description. When your purpose is self-expression, creativity, or persuasion, your description will be mostly subjective—you'll include your thoughts and feelings. The tone of subjective description ranges from informal to poetic; it's never stiff and formal. Subjective descriptions are often written from the *first-person point of view* (using *I, me, we,* and *us*), which helps create an informal tone. A subjective description contains

- the writer's thoughts and feelings on the subject
- factual and sensory details
- figures of speech, sometimes

  Figures of speech are words or groups of words the writer doesn't mean literally. Think of them as a spice to be sprinkled very lightly on description.

- A *simile* compares two basically unlike things, using the words *like* or *as.*

  > Weasel! I'd never seen one wild before. He was ten inches long, thin as a curve, a muscled ribbon, brown as fruitwood, soft-furred, alert.
  > Annie Dillard, "Living Like Weasels"

- A *metaphor* makes a direct comparison without using *like* or *as.* A metaphor says that something *is* something else.

  > The traffic on Canal Street never stops. It is a high-energy current jumping constantly between the poles of Brooklyn and New Jersey.
  > Ian Frazier, "Canal Street," *The New Yorker*

■ **Personification** gives human characteristics to nonhuman things.

> Sometimes one knows the drums are relaying good news, happy tidings. The beat seems brighter, higher-pitched, as if the very skins are singing with pleasure at their work. So if I fancied that the drums were weeping today, who could blame me?
>
> Anne McCaffrey, *Nerilka's Story*

As you read the following excerpt, notice how Annie Dillard expresses her thoughts and feelings about a childhood experience.

from An American Childhood
by Annie Dillard

Behind me, tall chilled windows gave out onto the narrow front yard and the street. A motion must have caught my mother's eye; she rose and moved to the windows, and Father and I followed. There we saw the young girl, the transfigured Jo Ann Sheehy, skating alone under the streetlight.

She was turning on ice skates inside the streetlight's yellow cone of light—illumined and silent. She tilted and spun. She wore a short skirt, as if Edgerton Avenue's asphalt had been the ice of an Olympic arena. She wore mittens and a red knitted cap below which her black hair lifted when she turned. Under her skates the street's packed snow shone; it illumined her from below, the cold light striking her under her chin.

I stood at the tall window, barely reaching the sill; the glass fogged before my face, so I had to keep moving or hold my breath. What was she doing out there? Was everything beautiful so bold? I expected a car to run over her at any moment: the open street was a fatal place, where I was forbidden to set foot.

1. If you closed your eyes while someone read Annie Dillard's description to you, would you be able to picture the events she describes? Why?
2. Which word-picture do you find most vivid? Why does it appeal to you?

Writing a Subjective Description

Prewriting. Choose a place that's special to you—perhaps your family's kitchen, or your own room. Focus your writing by making notes on these aspects of your topic: subject, purpose, audience, point of view, and tone. Then, list as many details about your subject as you can.

Writing, Evaluating, and Revising. Use your list of details to write a first draft of your description. Remember to include both factual and sensory details; see if you can include one or two figures of speech. As you evaluate your description, make sure that you've included your thoughts and feelings, and that tone and point of view are personal and informal.

Proofreading and Publishing. Check spelling, punctuation, and capitalization before you create your final copy. You might want to share your description with a friend or family member. To add your work to your **portfolio,** date it and write a brief reflection. Which did you enjoy writing more, an objective description or a subjective one? Why?

MAKING CONNECTIONS

DESCRIPTION AND MASS MEDIA

Writing a Classified Ad

People trying to sell things sometimes place classified advertisements in the newspaper. The purpose of the ad is to persuade someone to buy the item. A classified ad should give the object's significant details (such as size, age, condition, appearance, and price) and tell how to get in touch with the seller. Space also counts (newspapers charge per word or per line), so advertisers try to be brief.

Most classified ads are a mixture of subjective and objective description. Advertisers use realistic details to describe the item, but they usually add words that also reflect their own feelings about it. These words are meant to intrigue the reader, making the item sound more desirable than similar advertised items. In the following examples, what words show the writer's feelings?

EXAMPLES

objective

Windsurfer, 12′6″ beginner board, fully rigged with two sails, exc. cond., one owner, best offer. 555-5582.

Adorable Siamese kittens, 2 male, 2 female, pedigree, good-natured, 6 weeks, all shots, $80. Call Marty, 555-9622, nights.

subjective

Write a three-line (twenty-two characters per line) classified ad for something you might want to sell someday, such as a computer or a pair of skates. Exchange ads with your classmates. Whose ad would you respond to?

CREATIVE WRITING: FREE VERSE

Description is vital to poetry. *Free verse poems* use the rhythm of everyday speech and may or may not have rhyming lines. They also use imagery and figures of speech (pages 196–197). In this poem, what do the buffalo, shaman, and arrow represent?

Without Title
for my Father who lived without ceremony
by Diane Glancy

It's hard you know without the buffalo,
the shaman,[1] the arrow,
but my father went out each day to hunt
as though he had them.
He worked in the stockyards.
All his life he brought us meat.
No one marked his first kill,
no one sang his buffalo song.
Without a vision he had migrated to the city
and went to work in the packing house.
When he brought home his horns and hides
my mother said
get rid of them.
I remember the animal tracks of his car
out the drive in snow and mud,
the aerial on his old car waving
like a bow string.
I remember the silence of his lost power,
the red buffalo painted on his chest.
Oh, I couldn't see it
but it was there, and in the night I heard
his buffalo grunts like a snore.

---

[1] *shaman:* a priest or medicine man in some American Indian cultures

Woody Crumbo, *Sunset in Memoriam* (1946). Oil on canvas.
46.45.6. Philbrook Museum of Art, Tulsa, Oklahoma.

Try your hand at writing a free verse poem. Think of a person, place, or thing you would like to write about. It could be a friend, or a place you like to go; or it could be an experience you remember vividly or something you like to do. Jot down four or five objects that you associate with your subject (for example, if you like to paint, you might list objects such as a brush, a favorite color, and a scene you have painted). Then, write down four or five sensory details and at least one figure of speech that describe your subject.

Now, draft your poem. Try out different words and details before you choose the ones you think work best. (Look again at Glancy's poem to see how she weaves objects, sensory details, and figures of speech into her poem.) Vary line length to create emphasis. If most lines are long, for example, a short line will draw the reader's attention. If you're not sure where to break the lines, read your poem aloud (or have someone read it to you). Listen for the places where it sounds natural to end a line. Ask someone to read your poem: Does it make sense? Is the subject sharply, freshly pictured? You might illustrate your poem or copy it in an artistic script.

6 CREATIVE WRITING: NARRATION

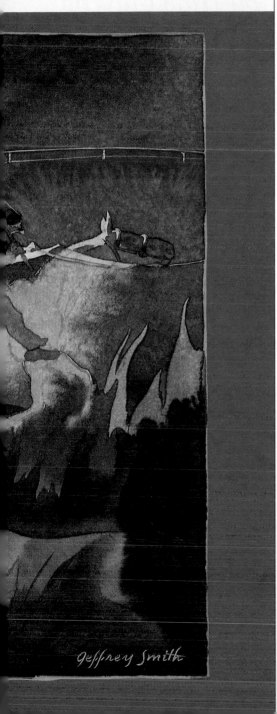

geffrey Smith

Imagining Other Worlds

Imagine having your own time machine. Would you rather zoom into the future or zap yourself backward in time? What would people look like then? What would they say? Your **imagination** can take you to a million **places.**

Writing and You.   We all love storytelling because it allows us to use our imagination. As children we never tire of the imaginary worlds of Dr. Seuss or Pinocchio. Later, we enjoy stories in books, television, and movies. We like people to tell us stories, and we love to make up our own. Have you heard or told a good story lately?

As You Read.   Most stories simply entertain us. But some also carry a message. As you read the following story, look for what it teaches about life.

Jeffrey Smith, *Redfish* (1988).

The Happy Man's Shirt

by Italo Calvino

A king had an only son that he thought the world of. But this prince was always unhappy. He would spend days on end at his window staring into space.

"What on earth do you lack?" asked the king. "What's wrong with you?"

"I don't even know myself, Father."

"Are you in love? If there's a particular girl you fancy, tell me, and I'll arrange for you to marry her, no matter whether she's the daughter of the most powerful king on earth or the poorest peasant girl alive!"

"No, Father, I'm not in love."

The king tried in every way imaginable to cheer him up, but theaters, balls, concerts, and singing were all useless, and day by day the rosy hue drained from the prince's face.

The king issued a decree, and from every corner of the earth came the most learned philosophers, doctors, and professors. The king showed them to the prince and asked for their advice. The wise men withdrew to think, then returned to the king. "Majesty, we have given the matter close thought and we have studied the stars. Here's what you must do. Look for a happy man, a man who's happy through and through, and exchange your son's shirt for his."

That same day the king sent ambassadors to all parts of the world in search of the happy man.

"Look for a happy man, a man who's happy through and through, and exchange your son's shirt for his."

A priest was taken to the king. "Are you happy?" asked the king.

"Yes, indeed, Majesty."

"Fine. How would you like to be my bishop?"

"Oh, Majesty, if only it were so!"

"Away with you! Get out of my sight! I'm seeking a man who's happy just as he is, not one who's trying to better his lot."

Thus the search resumed, and before long the king was told about a neighboring king, who everybody said was a truly happy man. He had a wife as good as she was beautiful and a whole slew of children. He had conquered all his enemies, and his country was at peace. Again hopeful, the king immediately sent ambassadors to him to ask for his shirt.

The neighboring king received the ambassadors and said, "Yes, indeed, I have everything anybody could possibly want. But at the same time I worry because I'll have to die one day and leave it all. I can't sleep at night for worrying about that!" The ambassadors thought it wiser to go home without this man's shirt.

At his wit's end, the king went hunting. He fired at a hare but only wounded it, and the hare scampered away on three legs. The king pursued it, leaving the hunting party far behind him. Out in the open field he heard a man singing a refrain. The king stopped in his tracks. "Whoever sings like that is bound to be happy!" The song led him into a vineyard, where he found a young man singing and pruning the vines.

"Good day, Majesty," said the youth. "So early and already out in the country?"

"Bless you! Would you like me to take you to the capital? You will be my friend."

"Much obliged, Majesty, but I wouldn't even consider it. I wouldn't even change places with the Pope."

"Why not? Such a fine young man like you . . ."

"No, no, I tell you. I'm content with just what I have and want nothing more."

"A happy man at last!" thought the king. "Listen, young man. Do me a favor."

"With all my heart, Majesty, if I can."

"Wait just a minute," said the king, who, unable to contain his joy any longer, ran to get his retinue. "Come with me! My son is saved! My son is saved!" And he took them to the young man. "My dear lad," he began, "I'll give you whatever you want! But give me . . . give me . . ."

"What, Majesty?"

"My son is dying! Only you can save him. Come here!"

The king grabbed him and started unbuttoning the youth's jacket. All of a sudden he stopped, and his arms fell to his sides.

The happy man wore no shirt.

translated by George Martin

READER'S RESPONSE

1. Do you think this story is only about a king and a prince, or is it about all kinds of people? Why do you think so?
2. Can you make unhappy people happy by changing their shirts? their jobs? their homes? In your journal, write a short entry about what you think would make an unhappy person happy.

WRITER'S CRAFT

3. Most stories have a conflict, or problem, that their characters have to solve. What is the conflict in this story?
4. How do you know the King really loves his son? What is the one thing the King cannot do for his son?
5. Stories are written to entertain their readers, but they may also have another purpose. What do you think this author wants readers to learn about life?

Happiness depends,
as Nature shows,
Less on exterior things
than most suppose.

WILLIAM COWPER

Ways to Write Creatively

This chapter shows how to write a story, one type of creative writing. Other types of creative writing include poems, plays, TV and movie scripts, song lyrics, and novels. Any time writers use their imagination and skill with language to make something unique and special, they are writing creatively. Here are some ways writers develop their creative writing.

- in a story, telling what happens when Martians land on Earth
- in a poem, telling what happens when a young girl takes her brother's place during a baseball game and scores the winning run
- in a story, describing what caused a disappointed look on a football coach's face
- in a song, describing the man in the moon
- in a movie about an exchange student, showing her life at home and her life at her new school
- in a poem, comparing a bat to a mouse with a human face
- in a story, showing how vanity destroys someone's life
- in a poem, judging people who are overly concerned with material things

LOOKING AHEAD

In the main assignment in this chapter, you'll use narration to write a story. Keep in mind that a good short story

- entertains the reader
- develops an interesting conflict, or problem
- includes well-developed characters, setting, and plot

Writing a Short Story

Prewriting

Thinking of Story Ideas

Free your imagination to develop a story idea. For example, in recent years, screenwriters have come up with ideas for stories like these:

- A talking piglet aspires to be a sheepdog.
- A young man fakes being a genius to win the love of Albert Einstein's niece.
- Toys come alive to defend themselves from someone determined to hurt them.

How do writers think of new ideas like these? Sometimes, they get together and brainstorm ideas that may seem silly at the time. They may also ask "What if?" questions (see pages 33–34):

- What if the earth were entirely covered with water and people lived their whole lives on boats, searching for dry land?
- What if a young girl discovers that one of her ancestors was a creature who was both woman and seal?
- What if a teenage genius who has been sheltered from the world is suddenly forced into a reform school?

WHAT IF?

Writers don't usually have a fully developed idea in mind when they write a short story. They may remember a piece of dialogue they overheard on a bus or a train or from a friend. Or they may recall their feelings about an event they witnessed, perhaps an argument between two friends. They may write about their families, their pets, their problems, their hopes and their fears. Anything that sticks in their minds may be the kernel, or seed, that a story grows from.

To help you find ideas for stories

- think about your own experiences—what you see when you walk down the street, what you observe going on all around you
- flip through a family photo album
- ask yourself "What if?" questions

   PART 1:
Developing a Story Idea

Free your imagination to form the kernel of an idea for a story. Brainstorm with classmates, ask yourself some "What if?" questions, and think back over your observations and experiences. (For more help with these prewriting techniques, see pages 22–35.) Let the idea germinate in your mind for a while.

Shoe reprinted by permission: Tribune Media Services.

Prewriting

Planning Your Story

The idea for a story doesn't spring full-blown from the mind of writers. Instead, they make a careful plan, sometimes even posting it on a bulletin board in front of them. Part of that plan is thinking about purpose, audience, and tone. Point of view, characters, setting, and plot also come into play here.

Thinking About Purpose, Audience, and Tone

Purpose. The main purpose for writing stories is always to be creative, to open up the imagination. But writers may have other purposes as well—to entertain and sometimes also to give a message to their audience. If so, they have an underlying meaning, or *theme*, in mind when they write. For instance, you may write about problems on a camping trip to entertain your readers with a wild adventure story. You might also tell the story to make a point: only fools go into the wilderness unprepared.

WRITING NOTE   A story doesn't have to be funny to be entertaining; a good mystery or science fiction story may not be humorous, but it can certainly keep readers interested. Suspense and exciting action are also ways of entertaining readers.

Audience. Who will read your story? Your audience may be young or old. It may be your classmates, your teacher, your family, some friends, or students in a younger grade. Maybe you'll publish your story in a school magazine that all these people will read.

Keep this audience in mind as you write your story. The humor that appeals to a very young audience, for example, won't appeal to students your own age. Talking animals might be appropriate for small children, but not for your classmates. Remember that you've given stories like C. S. Lewis's *The Lion, the Witch, and the Wardrobe* away to younger children, or you've put them in the back of a closet somewhere.

WRITING NOTE   It's important to keep the background and age of your audience in mind.

- Will they need definitions of any words or phrases in your story?
- Will they understand the jokes or humor your story is based on?
- Will they understand the situation and conflict?

Tone.   *Tone* simply means the writer's attitude toward the characters and events in the story. Do you feel serious, funny, or sarcastic toward your characters and events? Are you angry about something, or do you want to create an air of mystery? Decide what attitude you feel toward your characters and events, and keep that feeling in mind as you develop your story.

EXERCISE 1 ▶   **Analyzing Purpose, Audience, and Tone**

How well can you target the purpose, audience, and tone for your story? Here are some items that you might include in a story. Get together with two or three classmates. Decide which items would be suitable for a humorous story for an audience of your classmates and teacher. Tell why the items you don't choose aren't suitable for the story.

1. The Chicago fire of 1871 left 90,000 people homeless.
2. Bozo, the talking dog, was the star of the circus.
3. The jewel thieves planned the robbery well, but one of them liked the clerk so much that he gave her his telephone number and asked her out for a date.

4. A mad scientist underwent an operation to make him glow in the dark, but the surgery did just the opposite—he glowed in the daylight.
5. Thieves kidnapped a little boy but had to pay the parents to take him back because he was so wild.

Choosing a Point of View

Someone always has to tell the story. That someone is the *narrator.* If the narrator is a character in the story, the story has *first-person point of view.* This narrator speaks directly to the reader, using the pronoun *I.* If the narrator doesn't tell the story directly to the reader, then the story has *third-person point of view.*

In *third-person-omniscient point of view,* the narrator is outside the story and can understand the thoughts and feelings of *all* the characters. (The word *omniscient* means "all-knowing.") The chart below shows the differences between first-person and third-person point of view.

POINT OF VIEW		
First-person	Character in story speaks directly to reader; uses the first-person pronoun *I*	Limited to what this one character knows, feels, and thinks
Third-person, omniscient	Story told by narrator outside the story; uses third-person pronouns like *he* and *she*	Narrator can know everything other characters think and feel

Whatever point of view you choose, keep it the same throughout the story. Don't switch in midstream. Notice the difference point of view can make in this conversation.

First-person: "I saw Rita say hello to Brad in the hall."

Third-person: "When Rita said hello to Brad in the hall, he felt his heart race and his hopes rise. Maybe, he thought to himself, she would go with him to the dance."

E X E R C I S E 2 ▶   **Thinking About Point of View**

What goes through a runner's mind during a race? In the following passage, written in first-person point of view, a runner describes her feelings during a race. Get together with two or three classmates. You're all characters watching the race. Now, rewrite the passage from the third-person-omniscient point of view. [Hint: You might want to include some of Gretchen's thoughts as well.]

> And then I feel my weight coming back just behind my knees then down to my feet then into the earth and the pistol shot explodes in my blood and I am off and weightless again, flying past the other runners, my arms pumping up and down and the whole world is quiet except for the crunch as I zoom over the gravel in the track. I glance to my left and there is no one. To the right, a blurred Gretchen, who's got her chin jutting out as if it would win the race all by itself.
>
> Toni Cade Bambara, "Raymond's Run"

Thinking About Characters and Setting

Characters.   Is your main character going to be strong or weak, male or female, athletic or clumsy? What makes him or her tick? To create good, effective characters, get to know them in your own mind. Live with them for a while. Feel free to create characters from bits and pieces of people you know or have known. (Professional writers do just this all the time.) People you see in ads, on subways and buses, and just walking on the sidewalk might give you ideas for characters.

The following questions might trigger more ideas about your characters:

- What does my character look like? sound like?
- How does he or she dress? stand? move?
- What are my character's important personality characteristics? Is he or she kind? patient? angry? stubborn?
- What does he or she think and feel? What are my character's values or beliefs?
- What is his or her background? Where does he or she live? Where did my character come from?
- What are my character's dreams and aspirations?

Setting.   The *setting* is where and when the story takes place. In some stories the setting is more important than in others. It is especially important if you want to create a mood, or feeling, about the story.

Dark nights, rain, and mist usually result in a mood of mystery and suspense. And setting may be very important when the plot depends on it. In Jack London's story "To Build a Fire," for example, the main character comes into direct conflict with the frigid, barren Arctic when he is unable to light a fire for warmth and survival.

Ask yourself the following questions to get ideas about the setting for your story:

- How important is the setting to my story? Does the action depend on it?
- Do I need to use the setting to create a mood?
- What place(s) will I need to describe?
- What sights will be important? What sounds? What smells?
- Do I need to describe the time, the day, the weather, or the season?

WRITING ASSIGNMENT

PART 2:
Thinking About Characters and Setting

Who will the characters in your story be? The sheriff of a dusty, deserted town? aliens from outer space? a teenager like you? What's your setting going to be: a decaying mansion, an asteroid, perhaps even your own bedroom? Jot down your ideas, using the questions above and on page 215 to get your imagination started.

Developing the Plot

What's going to happen next in the story? How will one event cause the next? Will Superman get there in time to save Lois Lane? What happens now that Lois knows that Clark Kent is really Superman? The *plot* is what keeps readers involved so they want to find out what happens next.

The plot of a story centers on a *conflict,* or problem, that the main character faces. The conflict can be either *internal* (within the character) or *external* (between the character and someone or something else).

TYPES OF CONFLICT		
Internal	The character is struggling with a problem in his or her own personality.	Chip never wants to take advice from anyone.
External	(1) The character has a problem with another character.	Maria's mother is afraid to let her make any decisions on her own.
	(2) The character faces a conflict with nature.	Todd's grandmother is stranded in a house surrounded by flood waters.

Once you've decided on a basic conflict, or problem, plan the rest of the plot. Plot is made up of a series of events that follow each other and that cause each other to happen. Not knowing what the result of an event will be makes the reader feel suspense. Will the burglars' accidentally tripping the alarm cause the police to arrive? The suspense builds to the high point, or climax, of the story. Then the problem or conflict is resolved—the mystery ends—and the story ends.

To develop your plot, ask yourself questions like these:

- What is the basic conflict, or problem, in the story?
- What are the events in the order they happen?
- What do the characters do that cause the events to happen?
- What complications make it difficult for the characters to solve their problems? (This difficulty creates suspense.)
- What will be the climax, the highest point of suspense, of the story?
- How will you arrange the events in the plot? (Usually, you'll list the story's events in chronological order, the order in which they happen.)

PART 3:
Gathering Plot Details

What will happen in your story? What conflict will your main character face? How will the story turn out? Using the questions in the Reminder box on this page as a guide, jot down the details of your story's plot.

Creating a Story Map

You've done a great deal of thinking about your story, but until now you've been working with isolated chunks. At this stage in the process, you can use a *story map*, or plan, to pull all these chunks together. This plan shows how one writer mapped out the essential elements of a story.

HERE'S HOW

POINT OF VIEW:	*Third-Person*
CHARACTERS:	*Gina, 14; only girl in family; not very athletic* *Mark, 16; very athletic; likes to tease Gina* *Father; enjoys his family; generous and understanding*
SETTING:	*Orange grove in Florida near lake; cool weather; afternoon near Labor Day*
PLOT:	*Problem. Gina isn't very athletic, and she doesn't want to try the rope swing. Her brothers tease her for being a sissy, and she wants to show them she's not scared.* *Events.* *(1) Gina's family goes to the lake for a last fling before school begins—her brothers bring a rope swing.* *(2) The brothers have fun jumping off the tree on the rope swing.* *(3) They tease Gina.* *(4) Gina finally gets up the courage to try the rope swing.* *Outcome. Gina's brothers stop teasing her. She's pleased about overcoming her fear.*

WRITING ASSIGNMENT

PART 4:
Creating a Story Map

Get your own story fixed in your mind by developing a story map like the one above. This is a good time to share your ideas with your classmates, friends, and families. What are their reactions? It's also a good idea to post your plan where you can refer to it as you write your story. Begin by taking a sheet of paper and dividing it into the following categories: point of view, characters, setting, and plot. Then, fill out each category with your story ideas and details.

Writing Your First Draft

With all your planning done, now's the time to free your imagination to write the first draft of your story.

The Basic Elements of Stories

The true test of a good story is whether readers can put it down before it's finished. Create a good, suspenseful story through interest, characters, dialogue, and a strong ending.

Creating Interest.   A good story hooks its readers right away and then keeps them interested. Try creating immediate suspense to draw your reader in, perhaps giving just a hint of the conflict to come, as Arthur Porges does in "The Ruum": "The cruiser *Ilkor* had just gone into her interstellar overdrive beyond the orbit of Pluto when a worried officer reported to the Commander." Continue to develop interest with a fast-moving plot, well-developed characters, lifelike dialogue, and a strong ending.

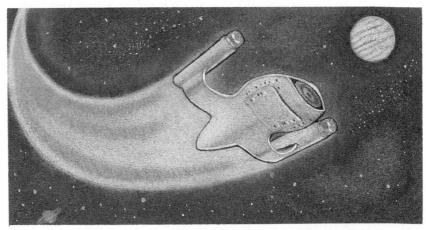

Creating Characters.   You usually get to know people through what they say, what they do, and what others say about them. Let your reader get to know your characters in those three ways also.

What the character says: "Mr. Lee, I don't have my homework. I forgot it," Jack moaned.
What the character does: Jack searched his notebook, then slowly walked up to Mr. Lee's desk.
What others say: "Jack forgot his homework again! You should've seen him squirm!" laughed Pablo.

 COMPUTER NOTE: Many computer software programs exist that make It easier to do things like keeping track of characters in a story or novel.

Creating Dialogue. "Talk," or conversation—called *dialogue* in a story—is one of the things that make people interesting. Good dialogue reveals your characters' personalities and helps move the plot along. Here are some tips for writing dialogue:

- Make the words fit the character.
- Use short sentences, phrases, contractions, and slang.
- Let your dialogue show what characters are like *and* move your story along.
- Use dialogue tags—phrases like "she shouted" or "he whispered"—to show *how* the characters speak.

Creating a Strong Ending. By the end of the story, your readers will want to have their curiosity satisfied. How do things turn out for the main character after all? Don't leave your readers hanging. Once you've solved the problem and tied up loose ends, finish quickly. Your ending can be happy, sad, or surprising—just be sure it fits logically with your story.

Looking at a Short Story

Stories vary a great deal in the way they are put together. They may begin with a description of the setting or a character, or plunge right into the middle of the action. The writer of the following story begins with a description of the main character. As you read, notice how the writer combines the elements of character, setting, plot, and dialogue to entertain his audience.

A SHORT STORY

The Six Rows of Pompons
by Toshio Mori

BEGINNING
Background

Attention
grabber
Introduction of
main characters

Introduction of
conflict

Setting

When little Nephew Tatsuo came to live with us he liked to do everything the adults were doing on the nursery, and although his little mind did not know it, everything he did was the opposite of adult conduct, unknowingly destructive and disturbing. So Uncle Hiroshi after witnessing several weeks of rampage said, "This has got to stop, this sawing the side of a barn and nailing the doors to see if it would open. But we must not whip him. We must not crush his curiosity by any means."

And when Nephew Tatsuo, who was seven and in high second grade, got used to the place and began coming out into the fields and pestering us with difficult questions as "What are the plants here for? What is water? Why are the bugs made for? What are the birds and why do the birds sing?" and so on, I said to Uncle Hiroshi, "We must do something about this. We cannot answer questions all the time and we cannot be correct all the time and so we will do harm. But something must be done about this beyond a doubt."

"Let us take him in our hands," Uncle Hiroshi said.

So Uncle Hiroshi took little Nephew Tatsuo aside, and brought him out in the fields and showed him the many rows of pompons growing. "Do you know what these are?" Uncle Hiroshi said. "These things here?"

"Yes. Very valuable," Nephew Tatsuo said. "Plants."

"Do you know when these plants grow up and flower, we eat?" Uncle Hiroshi said.

Nephew Tatsuo nodded. "Yes," he said, "I knew that."

"All right. Uncle Hiroshi will give you six rows of pompons," Uncle Hiroshi said. "You own these six rows. You take care of them. Make them grow and flower like your uncle's."

"Gee!" Nephew Tatsuo said.

"Do you want to do it?" Uncle Hiroshi said.

"Sure!" he said.

"Then jump right in and start working," Uncle Hiroshi said. "But first, let me tell you something. You cannot quit once you start. You must not let it die, you must make it grow and flower like your uncle's."

Dialogue

"All right," little Nephew Tatsuo said, "I will."

"Every day you must tend to your plants. Even after the school opens, rain or shine," Uncle Hiroshi said.

"All right," Nephew Tatsuo said. "You'll see!"

Development of characters

So the old folks once more began to work peacefully, undisturbed, and Nephew Tatsuo began to work on his plot. However, every now and then Nephew Tatsuo would run to Uncle Hiroshi with much excitement.

"Uncle Hiroshi, come!" he said. "There's bugs on my plants! Big bugs, green bugs with black dots and some brown bugs. What shall I do?"

"They're bad bugs," Uncle Hiroshi said. "Spray them."

"I have no spray," Nephew Tatsuo said excitedly.

"All right. I will spray them for you today," Uncle Hiroshi said. "Tomorrow I will get you a small hand spray. Then you must spray your own plants."

Several tall grasses shot above the pompons and Uncle Hiroshi noticed this. Also, he saw the beds beginning to fill with young weeds.

"Those grasses attract the bugs," he said. "Take them away. Keep the place clean."

MIDDLE

It took Nephew Tatsuo days to pick the weeds out of the six beds. And since the weeds were not picked cleanly, several weeks later it looked as if it was not touched at all. Uncle Hiroshi came around sometimes to feel the moisture in the soil. "Tatsuo," he said, "your plants need water. Give it plenty, it is summer. Soon it will be too late."

Nephew Tatsuo began watering his plants with the three-quarter hose.

"Don't hold the hose long in one place and short in another," Uncle Hiroshi said. "Keep it even and wash the leaves often."

In October Uncle Hiroshi's plants stood tall and straight and the buds began to appear.

Nephew Tatsuo kept at it through summer and autumn, although at times he looked wearied and indifferent. And each time Nephew Tatsuo's enthusiasm lagged Uncle Hiroshi took him over to the six rows of pompons and appeared greatly surprised.

"Gosh," he said, "your plants are coming up! It is growing rapidly; pretty soon the flowers will come."

"Do you think so?" Nephew Tatsuo said.

"Sure, can't you see it coming?" Uncle Hiroshi said. "You will have lots of flowers. When you have enough to make a bunch I will sell it for you at the flower market."

"Really?" Nephew Tatsuo said. "In the flower market?"

Uncle Hiroshi laughed. "Sure," he said. "That's where the plant business goes on, isn't it?"

One day Nephew Tatsuo wanted an awful lot to have us play catch with him with a tennis ball. It was at the time when the nursery was the busiest and even Sundays were all work.

"Nephew Tatsuo, don't you realize we are all men with responsibilities?" Uncle Hiroshi said. "Uncle Hiroshi has lots of work to do today. Now is the busiest time. You also have lots of work to do in your beds. And this should be your busiest time. Do you know whether your pompons are dry or wet?"

"No, Uncle Hiroshi," he said. "I don't quite remember."

"Then attend to it. Attend to it," Uncle Hiroshi said.

Nephew Tatsuo ran to the six rows of pompons to see if it was dry or wet. He came running back. "Uncle Hiroshi, it is still wet," he said.

"All right," Uncle Hiroshi said, "but did you see those holes in the ground with the piled-up mounds of earth?"

Development of plot

"Yes. They're gopher holes," Nephew Tatsuo said.

"Right," Uncle Hiroshi said. "Did you catch the gopher?"

"No," said Nephew Tatsuo.

"Then attend to it, attend to it right away," Uncle Hiroshi said.

One day in late October Uncle Hiroshi's pompons began to bloom. He began to cut and bunch and take them early in the morning to the flower market in Oakland. And by this time Nephew Tatsuo was anxious to see his pompons bloom. He was anxious to see how it feels to cut the flowers of his plants. And by this time Nephew Tatsuo's six beds of pompons looked like a patch of tall weeds left uncut through the summer. Very few pompon buds stood out above the tangle.

Development of plot

Few plants survived out of the six rows. In some parts of the beds where the pompons had plenty of water and freedom, the stems grew strong and tall and the buds were big and round. Then there were parts where the plants looked shriveled and the leaves were wilted and brown. The majority of the plants were dead before the cool weather arrived. Some died by dryness, some by gophers or moles, and some were dwarfed by the great big grasses which covered the pompons altogether.

When Uncle Hiroshi's pompons began to flower everywhere the older folks became worried.

Suspense

"We must do something with Tatsuo's six beds. It is worthless and his bugs are coming over to our beds," Tatsuo's father said. "Let's cut it down and burn them today."

"No," said Uncle Hiroshi. "That will be a very bad thing to do. It will kill Nephew Tatsuo. Let the plants stay."

So the six beds of Nephew Tatsuo remained intact, the grasses, the gophers, the bugs, the buds and the plants and all. Soon after, the buds began to flower and Nephew Tatsuo began to run around calling Uncle Hiroshi. He said the flowers are coming. Big ones, good ones. He wanted to know when can he cut them.

"Today," Uncle Hiroshi said. "Cut it today and I will sell it for you at the market tomorrow."

Next day at the flower market Uncle Hiroshi sold the bunch of Nephew Tatsuo's pompons for twenty-five cents. When he came home Nephew Tatsuo ran to the car.

"Did you sell it, Uncle Hiroshi?" Nephew Tatsuo said.

"Sure. Why would it not sell?" Uncle Hiroshi said. "They are healthy, carefully cultured pompons."

Climax

Nephew Tatsuo ran around excitedly. First, he went to his father. "Papa!" he said, "someone bought my pompons!" Then he ran over to my side and said, "The bunch was sold! Uncle Hiroshi sold my pompons!"

At noontime, after the lunch was over, Uncle Hiroshi handed over the quarter to Nephew Tatsuo.

"What shall I do with this money?" asked

Nephew Tatsuo, addressing all of us, with shining eyes.

"Put it in your toy bank," said Tatsuo's father.

"No," said Uncle Hiroshi. "Let him do what he wants. Let him spend and have a taste of his money."

"Do you want to spend your quarter, Nephew Tatsuo?" I said.

"Yes," he said.

"Then do anything you wish with it," Uncle Hiroshi said. "Buy anything you want. Go and have a good time. It is your money."

On the following Sunday we did not see Nephew Tatsuo all day. When he came back late in the afternoon Uncle Hiroshi said, "Nephew Tatsuo, what did you do today?"

"I went to a show, then I bought an ice cream cone and then on my way home I watched the baseball game at the school, and then I bought a popcorn from the candy man. I have five cents left," Nephew Tatsuo said.

"Good," Uncle Hiroshi said. "That shows a good spirit."

END

Uncle Hiroshi, Tatsuo's father, and I sat in the shade. It was still hot in the late afternoon that day. We sat and watched Nephew Tatsuo riding around and around the yard on his red tricycle, making a furious dust.

"Next year he will forget what he is doing this year and will become a wild animal and go on a rampage again," the father of Tatsuo said.

"Next year is not yet here," said Uncle Hiroshi.

"Do you think he will be interested to raise pompons again?" the father said.

"He enjoys praise," replied Uncle Hiroshi, "and he takes pride in good work well done. We will see."

"He is beyond a doubt the worst gardener in the country," I said. "Probably he is the worst in the world."

"Probably," said Uncle Hiroshi.

"Tomorrow he will forget how he enjoyed spending his year's income," the father of Tatsuo said.

"Let him forget," Uncle Hiroshi said. "One year is nothing. We will keep this six rows of pompon business up till he comes to his senses."

Outcome

We sat that night the whole family of us, Uncle Hiroshi, Nephew Tatsuo's father, I, Nephew Tatsuo, and the rest, at the table and ate, and talked about the year and the prospect of the flower business, about Uncle Hiroshi's pompon crop, and about Nephew Tatsuo's work and, also, his unfinished work in this world.

EXERCISE 3 ▶ **Analyzing the Organization of a Short Story**

After you read the story about Nephew Tatsuo and his pompons, answer these questions about it.

1. Did you enjoy the story? Why?
2. How does the author create interest at the beginning of the story? Does he make you curious about what will happen to Nephew Tatsuo?
3. What conflict, or problem, do the characters face?
4. What is the main setting of the story? Is it important to the development of the story? Why or why not?
5. What is the outcome of the story? Was it surprising, or did you expect it?

A Basic Framework for a Short Story

Mori's story emphasizes character and theme. Although we wonder how it will turn out, it is not a story that is full of mystery or suspense. Your story may not emphasize a serious theme, but it can be just as interesting. The following writer's model has a simple plot and a basic chronological framework. You might wish to use this story as a model for your own.

A WRITER'S MODEL

BEGINNING
Event 1

Conflict

Dialogue

Background

Event 2

Setting

MIDDLE

Conflict
Event 3
Dialogue

Inner conflict

Gina watched as her father loaded the van for the trip to the lake. He put in the skis, the life jackets, and the beach chairs. Gina was glad to see that he'd forgotten the rope swing. She hated that swing!

But Gina's relief didn't last. "Hey, Dad, where should I put this?" shouted her brother Mark, pointing to the long, knotted rope.

"Put it in the tool box. Is everybody ready?"

Gina's three other brothers, following their mother, came out of the house and jumped into the van. This trip was a Labor Day tradition. With two other families, they'd go to the lake for a day of swimming and water skiing.

Gina was really dreading this trip. Last year Gina's brothers and their friends had found a tree just off the bank of the canal leading to the lake. It towered over the other trees. They decided it was perfect for a rope swing and nailed up a few planks for a ladder. Then they took turns climbing up to a limb and jumping off.

Gina had been afraid to try the swing last year. She knew her brothers were going to torment her about it. This morning, though, the thought of that first dive in the cool water helped Gina forget the dreaded rope swing.

After skiing and swimming for most of the morning, Gina's brothers begged their dad to take them to their tree. After everyone had jumped twice, Dad turned to Gina.

"Your turn, Gina," he said.

"Oh, Dad, just skip her," Mark insisted. "She's such a baby, so scared of heights." Then he put his hand up to his forehead and pretended to faint. All the others laughed.

Gina glared at him and stepped up to the tree. He was right; she was afraid. This year the tree seemed even smaller and shakier. She

couldn't imagine pushing off the limb and actually letting go for the long drop into the water.

Suspense

Dad held his hands down to give Gina a leg up to the ladder. She started to sweat.

Dialogue

"You can do it, Sweetie," Dad whispered in Gina's ear. "Show your brothers that you can do anything they can do."

They had all made some bad jumps, but it didn't stop them from jumping. Last year Gina couldn't even make herself climb the ladder.

"This year will be different," she told herself.

Inner conflict

She hated being made fun of, especially in front of her brothers and their friends. They never stopped teasing her.

Suspense

Dad lifted Gina up, and she climbed quickly up the tree before she had time to get scared. But on the high limb, she felt dizzy. She couldn't look down, but she could hear them all laughing. She

Climax

Event 4
OUTCOME

Setting

Dialogue

heard Mark say, "Ah, she'll never do it." Those words made her grab the rope and push off.

Gina felt herself swinging high over the water, and then she let go. She plunged into the cool water. Almost immediately, she felt her toes touch the soft bottom of the canal. She had jumped in just the right spot! She heard the hooting and clapping as she swam to shore.

"Great jump, great jump!" Mark said. He reached down to help her out of the water. He even looked proud.

Gina smiled and said, "I still have one more turn left."

| WRITING ASSIGNMENT | PART 5: **Writing Your Story** |

Using your story plan and any prewriting notes, write your own short story. Remember that it doesn't have to be the polished work of a professional—the fact that you create it from your own imagination is good enough.

Evaluating and Revising

Now you can evaluate and revise the elements of your short story. Use the chart on the following page to decide about the weaknesses in your story and how to improve them. Ask yourself each question in the left-hand column. If you answer *no* to any one of the questions, use the revision technique in the right-hand column to improve your story.

EVALUATING AND REVISING SHORT STORIES

EVALUATION GUIDE	REVISION TECHNIQUE
1 Is the point of view the same throughout the story?	**Cut** statements that change the point of view. **Add** (or rewrite) sentences in the proper point of view (first-person or third-person).
2 Do the actions move the story along? Is the order of events clear?	**Add** actions that are faster paced. **Reorder** events in chronological order. **Add** words that show the order of events.
3 Is there an interesting conflict that is solved by the end of the story?	**Add** a conflict between characters or within a character. **Add** details that tie up loose ends and solve the conflict.
4 Are the characters real and interesting? Does the dialogue sound like the speech of real people?	**Add** details about what characters do, feel, say, and think. **Add** realistic dialogue.
5 Does the setting help create a mood or atmosphere? Does it compete with the conflict rather than promote it?	**Add** specific details that make the setting vivid. **Cut** details that are not central to the mood of the story or to the conflict.

CRITICAL THINKING

Evaluating Dialogue

Good dialogue makes characters and actions seem real. Evaluate your dialogue to make sure it's as lifelike as possible. Use the following questions to help you decide whether the dialogue in your story is realistic.

1. Do the characters use words and sentences that fit their ages and backgrounds? Remember that people of different ages and backgrounds use different vocabulary and sentence structure.
2. Do the characters use informal language, contractions, and phrases instead of sentences? Let them interrupt each other, repeat themselves, and use incomplete sentences. Remember that people don't speak the same way they write.
3. Does the dialogue serve a function in the story? Dialogue should move the action along or reveal what the characters are like. Don't let your characters chatter about things that aren't important to the story.
4. Is it clear who's speaking? To identify the speaker, writers often use dialogue tags, which come before or after the dialogue. The most common one is "he said" or "she said." You can also get more mileage from these tags by using vivid verbs or adverbs with them: "Oh, no!" **he exclaimed softly**; "Let's go," **she pleaded desperately**.

CRITICAL THINKING EXERCISE:
Evaluating Dialogue

A writer put the following dialogue into the first draft of a story. Get together with two or three classmates and evaluate the dialogue by answering the list of questions above. Then make suggestions for revising the dialogue. [Hint: Try reading the dialogue out loud. Does it sound the way people really talk?]

"The house looks great, honey," said Mom.

"Yes," said Dad, "the house does look great. The rec room is not a wreck anymore, I notice."

"Well," I said modestly, "it's the least I can do for your anniversary. And you must admit that for once I did not forget a single thing."

"Well, honey," said Mom, "there is one little thing."

"What is it?" I said. "I cannot think of anything."

"The thing you forgot," Dad said, "really doesn't have much to do with the house."

"No," said Mom, "it doesn't have to do with the house at all."

"The fact is," said Dad, "that today is not our anniversary. It is Friday, the day of your big chemistry test."

"My goodness," I said. "I did not know that."

EXERCISE 4 ▶ Analyzing a Writer's Revisions

It's impossible to see into a writer's mind, but try to figure out why this writer made these changes. This is the first draft of two paragraphs from the sample story on pages 230–232. Study the changes, and then answer the questions that follow. (You may want to refer to the evaluating and revising chart on page 234.)

> Dad lifted Gina up, and ~~I~~ *she* climbed   **replace**
>
> quickly up the tree before she had time to
>
> get scared. But on the high limb, she felt
>
> dizzy. ~~I~~ *She* couldn't look down, but she could   **replace**
>
> hear them all laughing. She heard Mark
>
> say, "~~My gracious, she will certainly never~~ *"Ah, she'll never do it."*   **replace**
>
> ~~do it."~~ Those words made her grab the rope
>
> and push off. *(swinging high)*
>
> Gina felt herself ∧ over the water, and   **add**
>
> then she let go. She ~~fell~~ *plunged* into the cool water.   **replace**
>
> (She had jumped in just the right spot!)   **reorder**
>
> Almost immediately, she felt her toes touch
>
> the soft bottom of the canal. She heard the
>
> hooting and clapping as she swam to
>
> shore.

1. In the first and third sentences, why does the writer change *I* to *she*?
2. In the first paragraph, why does the writer replace Mark's dialogue? [Hint: Review pages 235–236.]
3. In the first sentence of the second paragraph, why does the writer add the words *swinging high*?
4. In the second sentence of the second paragraph, why does the writer change the word *fell* to *plunged*?
5. Why does the writer change the order of the third sentence in the second paragraph?

EXERCISE 5 ▶ **Evaluating a Story**

Here's part of a story about a teenager who spends three days collecting marine life near the shore. How would you edit this story? Get together with two or three of your classmates and evaluate the paragraph. What can be done to improve it? Use the evaluating and revising chart on page 234 to help you decide.

> He spent three days tide-pooling, wading in the pools left by the tide and looking at the marine life. In school, he was considered strange, but here he was accepted by the other beach bums who wandered the beach. He caught sea anemones and other things. He didn't talk to many people. He saw abalone and mussels and a few sand dollars. He spent all his time outside with nature. My trip was working out just as I had planned.

| WRITING ASSIGNMENT | PART 6: **Evaluating and Revising Your Story** |

Try out your story with a real audience. Exchange stories with another classmate and use the evaluation/revision guidelines on page 234 to evaluate each other's stories. Take notes on your partner's evaluation of your story. Then, evaluate your own story with a cold, objective eye. Using your classmate's suggestions and your own evaluation, make changes to improve your story.

 REFERENCE NOTE: For reminders about peer evaluation, see pages 49–50.

Proofreading and Publishing

Proofreading. Going over your clothes with a lint brush gets them ready for that special occasion. Proofreading does the same thing for your story. Look for mistakes in mechanics, grammar, and usage.

MECHANICS HINT

Punctuating Dialogue

These suggestions will help you punctuate the dialogue in your stories.

1. If the dialogue tag comes first, put a comma after it, before the quotation marks.

EXAMPLE   The sportscaster said, "The game has just been tied!"

2. Sometimes the dialogue tag comes last. If the quote ends in an exclamation point or a question mark, don't use a comma before the tag.

EXAMPLES   "I won the race!" exclaimed Joaquin as he crossed the finish line.

"How many syllables are in a haiku?" asked Mona's teacher.

3. Sometimes the tag comes in the middle of the quote. When this happens, put a comma before quotation marks in front of the tag. Then, put a comma after the tag.

EXAMPLE   "Josh," said Maria, "I still love you, even if you do have 'Go Cougars' shaved into your hair."

☞ REFERENCE NOTE: For more information on punctuating dialogue, see pages 792–798.

Publishing Your Story.   People of all ages enjoy reading and hearing stories. Think about the best way to share your story with others. Here are three ideas:

- Make your story into a puppet show, and stage it for a class at a nearby elementary or day-care school.
- Compile a booklet of your class's stories and make copies for everyone in the class.
- Distribute a booklet of your class's stories to area retirement homes or hospitals. Volunteer to read your stories aloud to those who can't see or read.

WRITING ASSIGNMENT   PART 7:
Proofreading and Publishing Your Story

Challenge yourself to eliminate all the errors from your story. (Remember to check the dialogue carefully for punctuation.) Then publish or share your story with others.

EXERCISE 6   **Speaking and Listening: Reading Your Story Aloud**

People have always told stories—around the fire in a cave, in the great halls of medieval castles, in living rooms and kitchens. Now's your chance to join in this long tradition. Get together with a small group and read your story aloud. Take turns until everyone has had a chance.

  Reflecting on Your Writing

If you decide to include your story in your **portfolio,** answer the following questions and attach the answers to your story.

- Which part of your story do you like best? least?
- Did you include dialogue in your story? How did this affect your story?
- What was the most difficult part of writing a story?

A STUDENT MODEL

Imagine summer days. Abigail Smigel, a student at Watkins Mill High School in Gaithersburg, Maryland, describes catching bees, leaving echoes in mailboxes, and climbing tall trees. Notice Abigail's attention to detail and effective dialogue as you read this passage from her story.

<u>from</u> Spearhead Days
by Abigail Smigel

With a loud "Humph," I slumped down into the pile of garden sacks in the back of the garage. The stench of old gardening tools, fertilizer, and trash seeped into my head as I shifted my position to a more comfortable one. I grabbed an old lime sack to cover myself before it was too late: He was coming and I knew it. The unmistakable sound of his feet grew closer. Suddenly a pail of rotten tulip bulbs fell onto the table near me and then to the floor with a crash. A cloud of dust forced me to let out a small sputter as I burrowed deeper into the heap of unexplored belongings. I knew I would be found in a minute . . . if only I could reach that old sled to cover . . . "GOTCHA!"

I screamed, and in the confusion, that sled landed directly on my left baby toe. I hollered some more. "How did you find me?" I cried out.

"My magic spearhead showed me," he said. Laughing hysterically, he held the prize as it shone in the light of the garage. Jason rolled on the floor laughing as I emerged with a layer of crud covering my face, body, and clothing. Tears were streaming down my face, creating a muddy mess, as he began to laugh even harder. Between gasps he hollered, "Come . . . into the . . . garage! I . . . got her!" Looming in the afternoon light of the doorway was another figure, seized with laughter.

First appeared in *Merlyn's Pen: The National Magazine of Student Writing.*

WRITING WORKSHOP

 **A News Story**

Writing news stories is different from writing the story you've written in this chapter. For one thing, news stories usually rely on facts rather than an imagined event. The news writer's purpose isn't to be creative. News stories also follow a very tight structure. The first paragraph is called the *lead*. There the writer tries to answer the *5W-How?* questions about the story—Who? What? When? Where? Why? and How? In other words, the lead summarizes the important facts of the story. Then the rest of the news story fills in the details.

As you read the following news story, notice how the writer quickly gives the facts in the lead and then moves on.

Flood Is Called Right Tonic for Grand Canyon

WASHINGTON (AP)—An effort to help restore the Grand Canyon to a more natural state by inundating it with water released from an upstream dam "worked brilliantly," Interior Secretary Bruce Babbitt said on Thursday.

"The flood is over; the waters have receded," Mr. Babbitt said. "What we have found is really quite extraordinary." He spoke at a briefing two weeks after water was released at the base of the Glen Canyon Dam, sending a torrent from Lake Powell into the canyon.

The dam, on the Colorado River, has meant that years have gone by without annual spring floods. That has depleted the sandy beaches in the canyon and damaged the spawning grounds for fish, researchers say. The goal of the deliberate flood was to stir up sediment and help restore natural conditions.

Mr. Babbitt said that the canyon appeared to have up to a third more beaches and that the flooding had created many channels that could serve as habitats for endangered fish like the humpback chub.

"It was exactly what we needed to do," said David Wegner, program manager for the Bureau of Reclamation. "We have more beaches now than we had three weeks ago. The challenge for us now is to see how long they will last."

In addition to creating beaches, stirring up the sediment provides nutrients for plants and helps improve conditions for fish, he said.

The discharge peaked at 45,000 cubic feet of water per second. It continued for seven days, lowering the level of Lake Powell by three and a half feet, Mr. Babbitt said.

Mr. Babbitt said that 80 percent of the new beach sediment had been deposited in the first 40 hours of flooding and that all the new deposits had been in place within 100 hours.

The New York Times

1. Which *5W-How?* questions does the news writer answer in the lead paragraph?
2. What facts do the other paragraphs give you about the deliberate flood?
3. Why didn't the writer try to put some of these facts in the lead?
4. What order does the writer use to present information? What words signal this type of order?

Writing a News Story

Prewriting. What events are making news in your school, community, or state? Did the mayor just approve funding for a new teen center? Look around to see what local, national, and even international events interest you and deserve a news story. Once you've chosen a story to cover, find out all the facts through research and, if possible, by interviewing. Use the *5W-How?* questions to start. Keep asking questions until you feel you have the whole story.

Writing, Evaluating, and Revising. Begin by writing your lead, the most important part of a news story. Summarize the story, but grab the reader's attention. Writing a lead sounds easier than it is, so keep trying. Even the most experienced reporters write lead after lead until they get it just right. Fill in the rest of the story with the important facts, beginning with the most important. A news story is usually short, so decide what's really important to understanding the story. Keep your sentences short and simple. Use direct quotations from key people. And stick to just the facts. Your own opinions and feelings don't belong in a news story.

Evaluate your draft by asking yourself if the story is clear and the facts are accurate. Ask someone unfamiliar with the story to read your account and tell you if it's clear. Then, revise your story to make it clearer and more informative and as short and direct as possible.

Proofreading and Publishing. A news story belongs in the media—the newspaper, TV, or radio. Your school newspaper is a good place to start, but you can also try your local TV and radio stations. They might be interested in student news that they don't know about. News stories are always checked by copyeditors, but you'll want to make yours as error-free as possible. Check your spelling, grammar, and punctuation very carefully.

You may want to add your news story to your **portfolio.** If you do not publish your story immediately, update your news and try submitting it later. Was it difficult keeping your opinions out of the story? Explain.

MAKING CONNECTIONS

A HUMOROUS SKIT

A *humorous skit* is a short play that involves one or two characters and a single conflict, or problem. The humor comes from exaggeration and from improbable situations—events that wouldn't likely happen in real life. Much of the humor is also physical—exaggerated or strange movements, for example.

You've seen skits in many TV shows that use these ideas of humor. In one episode of *Cheers,* for example, the characters have a food fight instead of a friendly Thanksgiving dinner at Carla's house. In a classic *I Love Lucy* skit, Lucy and her neighbor Ethel struggle with a huge mound of bread dough. In another episode, Lucy performs a Western song, complete with cowboy hat, chaps, and fake mustache.

Get together with two or three classmates and write a short, humorous skit. Remember to rely on exaggeration of speech and movement and improbable situations. As you write your draft, label each character's lines. Also include stage directions—such as *Mario slowly slides down to the floor*—to guide the characters' actions. You might want to base your skit on one of these situations.

1. Some students experience an improbable event that keeps them from finishing an important group project.
2. A clerk in a department store has trouble understanding exactly what a customer wants.
3. An alien from outer space dresses like a human and attends school.
4. Two preschoolers lead their baby sitters into an adventure.

A BIOGRAPHICAL SKETCH

Do you ever read *People Weekly* magazine? If so, you're like many others who are interested in reading about the lives of famous people. Stories that tell the history of a person's life are called *biographies.* Shorter versions are known as *biographical sketches,* which use many of the same techniques found in story writing. The difference is that a story can be fiction; a biographical sketch must be nonfiction. The writer can't make up details just because they seem more interesting than the actual details.

Try your hand at writing a biographical sketch. Below are some details about the performer Ray Charles. After doing some more research, write a one- to three-paragraph sketch on Charles. Or if you prefer, choose another famous person—perhaps an entertainer, an athlete, or a government or military leader. Research and write a biographical sketch on your subject.

His career milestones

► Began losing sight to glaucoma at age 6.
► First musical job with country band Florida Play-boys, at age 16.
► First major pop hit, *What'd I Say*, 1959.
► First country hit, 1962 album *Modern Sounds in Country and Western Music*, and its single *I Can't Stop Loving You*.
► 10th Grammy, 1983, for *Born to Love Me*.
► Inducted into Rock and Roll Hall of Fame and awarded Kennedy Center Honors medal, 1986.

Copyright 1990, USA TODAY

7 WRITING TO INFORM: EXPOSITION

TOTALLY EXCELLEN PIZZA

STEP 1 Collect and s
your favorite veggies—
mushrooms, onions,
olives, peppers,
artichokes—even
broccoli!
Collect and grate
your favorite
low-fat
pizza cheese.
Remember—it's not a
totally excellent pizza
if it's not heaped with veggie.

STEP 2 The fun begins!
Prepare a whole wheat crust. Combine eqc
parts of whole wheat flour and unbleached
flour with prepared yeast, water as needed, and
olive oil. Knead and let dough rise. Shape it
with your fingertips
to fit the pizza pan.

STEP 3 Now for the good stuff!
Start with the tomato sauce (lightly
seasoned with garlic and basil) and
then add the veggies and _cheese._
Bake at 475° until the cheese is
bubbly and golden.
The best step: Eat and enjoy!

Working and Playing

Did you know hikers found a 4,000-year-old body in the Austrian Alps? How do you get to Kansas City from here? How does a faucet work? How do you make a pizza? Everybody wants information, even needs it. Without it we wouldn't be able to survive. And since we spend so much of our lives **working and playing,** much of the information we share has to do with processes—how to do something or how something works.

Writing and You.   You'll find examples of writers sharing information about processes in many places. In a magazine a scientist explains how Egyptians made mummies. The writer of an instruction manual tells you how to play a new video game. When was the last time you needed information about how something works or how to do something?

As You Read.   In the following passage from *Alice's Adventures in Wonderland,* two unusual creatures share some information with Alice—how to perform a dance. After reading their instructions, could you dance the Lobster-Quadrille?

from

THE LOBSTER-QUADRILLE

by Lewis Carroll

T HE MOCK TURTLE sighed deeply, and drew the back of one flapper across his eyes. He looked at Alice and tried to speak, but for a minute or two sobs choked his voice. "Same as if he had a bone in his throat," said the Gryphon, and it set to work shaking him and punching him in the back. At last the Mock Turtle recovered his voice, and, with tears running down his cheeks, he went on again:

"You may not have lived much under the sea"— ("I haven't," said Alice)—"and perhaps you were never introduced to a Lobster"— (Alice began to say "I once tasted"— but checked herself hastily, and said, "No, never") —"so you can have no idea what a delightful thing a Lobster-Quadrille is!"

"No, indeed," said Alice. "What sort of a dance is it?"

"*Y*ou may not have lived

much under the sea . . .

so you can have no idea

what a delightful thing

a Lobster-Quadrille is!"

"Why," said the Gryphon, "you first form into a line along the seashore—"

"Two lines!" cried the Mock Turtle. "Seals, turtles, salmon, and so on: then, when they cleared all the jelly-fish out of the way—"

"*That* generally takes some time," interrupted the Gryphon.

"You advance twice—"

"Each with a lobster as a partner!" cried the Gryphon.

"Of course," the Mock Turtle said: "advance twice, set to partners—"

"Change lobsters, and retire in same order," continued the Gryphon.

"Then, you know," the Mock Turtle went on, "you throw the—"

"The lobsters!" shouted the Gryphon, with a bound into the air.

"As far out to sea as you can—"

"Swim after them!" screamed the Gryphon.

"Turn a somersault in the sea!" cried the Mock Turtle, capering wildly about.

"Change lobsters again!" yelled the Gryphon at the top of its voice.

"Back to land again, and—that's all the first figure," said the Mock Turtle, suddenly dropping his voice, and the two creatures, who had been jumping about like mad things all this time, sat down again very sadly and quietly, and looked at Alice.

"It must be a very pretty dance," said Alice timidly.

"Would you like to see a little of it?" said the Mock Turtle.

"Very much indeed," said Alice.

"Come, let's try the first figure!" said the Mock Turtle to the Gryphon. "We can do it without lobsters, you know. Which shall sing?"

"Oh, *you* sing," said the Gryphon. "I've forgotten the words."

So they began solemnly dancing round and round Alice, every now and then treading on her toes when they passed too close, and waving their forepaws to mark the time. . . .

from *Alice's Adventures in Wonderland*

READER'S RESPONSE

1. Could you do the Lobster-Quadrille following the Mock Turtle and Gryphon's directions? Try it and see.
2. Imagine that aliens from outer space are teaching earthlings to perform a strange dance. In your journal, explain how the dance would be performed.

WRITER'S CRAFT

3. Lewis Carroll's purpose was to create a literary work, not to inform. But fictional characters can share information, just like real people. Can you think of any other fictional characters that have shared information?
4. To help readers, steps in a process are usually listed in the order they're performed. In what order are the steps for the quadrille given?

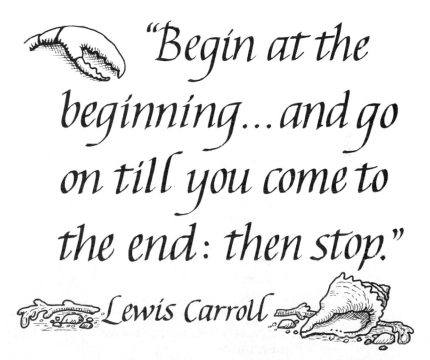

"Begin at the beginning...and go on till you come to the end: then stop."

Lewis Carroll

Ways to Inform

In this chapter you're going to concentrate on one way of writing to inform—explaining a process. But what other ways are there to share information? Where does explaining a process fit in? Here are examples of how you can share information.

- in a science report, telling how a caterpillar turns into a butterfly
- in a paper for English class, explaining how to fix a flat tire on a bicycle
- in a letter to a friend, describing the way your house looks so he or she can visualize it
- in an essay for history class, describing the Vietnam Veterans Memorial
- in an article for the school newspaper, explaining the differences between in-line skates and regular skates
- in a letter to your eight-year-old cousin, explaining what *responsibility* means
- in a book report, explaining how the characters and plot are developed
- in a report to your supervisor, explaining the strengths and weaknesses of a new type of software program

LOOKING AHEAD

In the main assignment in this chapter, you'll use narration to explain a process you are familiar with. You will write about how to do something. As you work, remember that a "how-to" process paper

- presents the steps of the process in the order they're done
- includes all necessary steps
- defines any terms the audience may not understand

Writing a Process Paper

Prewriting

Choosing a "How-to" Process to Explain

Everyone knows how to do a variety of things. You may be able to bake the world's best carrot bread or make bracelets from buttons and embroidery thread or do a "180" on a skateboard. All these topics would be suitable for a "how-to" process paper. The purpose of a "how-to" process paper is for readers to learn how to do the process themselves. To choose a topic, think about these things:

- What do you know how to do well?
- Why would someone else want to learn to do it?
- Can you thoroughly explain the topic in a short paper?

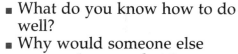

An Inventory of Your Interests. To choose a topic for your "how-to" process paper, consider not only what you know but also what you like. Maybe you know how to clean a kitchen until it sparkles, but if you don't enjoy doing it, then cleaning a kitchen probably isn't a good topic for you.

The Value of the Skill.   Think about whether the skill or process is a valuable one. In other words, what will your readers gain from learning how to do it? Don't consider only "serious" topics, however. Some activities are valuable because they are fun to do. Also think about whether it's a process your audience is interested in—something they may not know how to do but want to learn about.

The Scope of the Topic.   Consider, also, whether the topic is suitable for a short paper. Some skills—like frying an egg—can be explained in a paragraph, but some processes—like building a house—require a book-length explanation. In this chapter, you're not interested in writing a book.

When choosing a "how-to" process to explain, remember to

- brainstorm (pages 25–26), making a list of all the things you enjoy doing
- consider the value of learning how to do the process you're explaining
- decide whether the topic is narrow enough (or broad enough) to write an explanation in the time you have

---

EXERCISE 1 ▶   **Choosing Topics**

What's a good topic for your "how-to" process paper? Decide which of the following topics are suitable for you to explain. Be certain that the topics you select meet the three criteria, or standards, you've just read about.

1. how to perform modern dances
2. how to dry a plate
3. how to raise a child
4. how to organize your closet
5. how to make a better score on a computer game

Exploring Possible Topics

Now give some thought to your own topic. With a small group of your classmates, discuss possible topics for "how-to" process papers. What topics seem especially interesting? What topics are suitable for a paper?

WRITING ASSIGNMENT

PART 1:
Choosing a Topic to Write About

Think about your group's ideas before deciding on a topic of your own. Select a topic your group suggested or another topic that you especially like and that you know a lot about. Then, write a sentence or two explaining why the process you've chosen is valuable.

COMPUTER NOTE: If your school computers are arranged in a network, you may be able to use them to do collaborative prewriting or drafting.

 *Prewriting*

Thinking About Purpose, Audience, and Tone

Why are you writing this paper? Who will read it? How do you want your paper to sound? Now's the time to think about the purpose, audience, and tone of your "how-to" process paper.

Purpose. The primary purpose of your "how-to" process paper is to *inform* your audience about something they don't already know how to do. If your grandfather is the world's expert on growing kumquats, there's no point in telling him how to do it. Likewise, there would be no point in teaching a group of ninth-graders how to button a shirt—they've known how to do that for years.

Audience. Your purpose is to share information about a process, but your readers have to want that information. You may have to get them interested by explaining the value of the process to them. You want to let them know, for example, that they'll earn better grades, or make their homes safer, or have more fun on Saturday afternoons.

Tone. A "how-to" process paper is usually friendly and casual in tone. You want to make your audience feel at ease. You also want to use specific, clear language. If your approach is friendly and your directions are clear, your audience will be more likely to understand the process you're explaining.

EXERCISE 3 ▶ **Analyzing the Audience for a "How-to" Process Paper**

Who might be interested in your topic? Who may want to know the process you plan to discuss? Match suitable audiences with the following topics. Ask yourself *why* a topic is suitable or unsuitable for each audience. (There may be more than one suitable audience for a topic.)

EXAMPLE **1.**

	Topic:	how to bathe a dog
	Audiences:	fifth-graders who own dogs
		professional dog groomers
		circus trainers

1. *Suitable audience:* *fifth-graders who own dogs*

1. Topic: how to buy a used car
   Audiences: families on a limited budget
   seventh-graders
   high school students

2. Topic: how to prepare for college entrance
   exams
   Audiences: high school juniors
   college professors
   high school teachers

3. Topic: how to discipline young children
   Audiences: new parents with young children
   day-care workers
   first-graders

4. Topic: how to change a tire
   Audiences: garage mechanics
   first-time car owners
   people who use the subway for
   transportation

Prewriting

Gathering Your Information

An effective "how-to" process paper explains clearly how to perform a process. To do that, you'll need to consider *everything* your readers might need to know. What materials are needed? What terms may need to be defined? What steps have to be performed?

Often, going to a book or a videotape that explains your "how-to" process is a way to begin gathering details. You can get suggestions on the steps to follow, and you can also find out how someone else has explained the process. Cookbooks, hobby books, and "how-to" manuals are storehouses of information and details you can use to get started. Your local video store probably carries instructional videotapes that are also good sources of background information.

Materials. What will your readers need to have on hand before they begin the task? Will they need scissors, construction paper, tape, and thumbtacks, or will they need only a comfortable chair? Will they need a special salad mold, or will any one-quart bowl do? Will they need to make a special trip to the hardware store, or will they have everything at home?

Definitions. You'll need to explain (define) terms your audience isn't familiar with. How much you'll need to explain depends on your readers. An experienced cook will know what "sauté on low heat" means, but an inexperienced cook may not. Someone familiar with computers will know what "booting up" means, but a novice will be left in the dark.

Steps. Many "how-to" process papers involve a series of steps or directions. The writer tells the reader exactly what to do and when to do it. For example, if you were to tell readers how to get somewhere on a public bus, you would first have to tell them the number of the bus and when and where to catch it. Here's one writer's list of steps for washing a car.

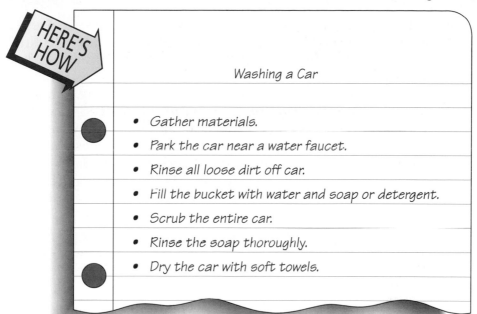

To gather details for your "how-to" process paper

- make a list of all materials your readers will need
- list and define words or terms your audience may not understand
- list all the necessary steps, arranging them in their correct order

---

CRITICAL THINKING

Arranging Details

When you explain a process, think carefully about how to present the information. Consider, for example, the case of Mr. Martínez, who is putting together a bookshelf following the manufacturer's instructions. He has the shelves almost together—only to discover that he needs a pair of pliers, something the manufacturer failed to tell him. If he lets go of the bookshelves at this point to find some pliers, the shelves will fall down. Imagine his frustration.

Help your readers avoid such situations by thinking about how to arrange the information they need to know. Consider *what* they need to know and *when* they need to know it. And remember that "how-to" process papers nearly always use chronological order: what comes first, what comes second, and so on. Make sure your readers will understand *why* they need to do Step *A* before Step *B*.

 CRITICAL THINKING EXERCISE:
Arranging Details

Can you do a better job of arranging information than Mr. Martínez's manufacturer? Here are some notes one writer made on training monkeys to work with people who have disabilities. Working with one or two classmates, read the notes carefully, and then decide how the writer might arrange the information so that it's easier to follow.

> Training monkeys for use with people who have disabilities
>
> > monkey gets reward for fetching object
> > monkey fetches object and brings to trainer
> > monkey cared for by foster family until age three
> > monkey's training begins at age three
> > trainer rings bell when monkey performs well
> > monkey usually learns tasks in thirty minutes
> > trainer uses laser to show monkey what to fetch

 **EXERCISE 4** ▶ **Speaking and Listening: Explaining and Following a Process**

Taking turns with your classmates, give one classmate a simple process to perform. The process might be to draw a simple object like a square or circle on the board. Or it might be to walk across the room and bring back some object. Explain the process one step at a time, but don't give away the end result.

Shoe reprinted by permission: Tribune Media Services.

PART 2:
Gathering Information for Your "How-to" Process Paper

Help your readers out by giving them all the information they'll need. Begin by listing *all* the necessary materials. Next, list each step in the process in the correct order, and decide what terms need defining. You may want to make a chart like the one below to list all this information.

Topic:

Materials:

Steps in the Process:

Terms to Define:

Writing Your First Draft

The Basic Elements of "How-to" Process Papers

"How-to" process papers may vary a bit in how they are put together. They often open with a lively *introduction* (a paragraph or two) designed to interest the reader in the topic. Often the introduction explains the advantages of learning how to perform the process. Usually, the writer establishes a friendly tone right away and maintains that tone throughout the essay.

The *body* of the essay is devoted to explaining the steps in the process and to giving any explanation and background the reader needs. Usually, the writer begins by listing the essential materials. Then the writer presents the steps exactly in the order they're to be performed. Often the writer gives helpful hints about each step.

A *conclusion* often discusses more of the advantages—and maybe the disadvantages—of learning the process. A conclusion might also include further hints or advice.

The writer of this "how-to" essay has made his topic interesting to his readers. He maintains a friendly, lively tone, and he tries to make his directions clear and complete. As you read, think about whether you could follow his directions. Could you make your own video?

A MAGAZINE ARTICLE

How to Shoot Your Own Video
by David Hajdu

INTRODUCTION
Attention grabber

You really want to see a movie, but there's nothing on TV except rerun cop shows and dopey sitcoms; the twenty-screen multiplex theater is playing nothing but *Friday the 13th,* parts one through twenty; and all the videos at the video store are rented out except for the operas.

BODY
Advantages
of learning
process

Don't despair. There is a creative new way to satisfy your movie craving: *Make your own.* All it takes is a video camcorder, a few friends/movie stars, and a basic understanding of the principles of good moviemaking. Any movie you make will be both fun and challenging to shoot as well as a thrill to watch, even if it turns out less than perfect. Who knows? Your homemade video production might even be *good.*

List of
materials

The only piece of equipment you'll need is a camcorder, which can record both sights and sounds on videocassette. (Of course, you'll need a TV and a VCR to play your video *on,* but you won't need them to shoot the video itself.) . . .

Explanation/
Background

The first thing young Spielberg did—as every video moviemaker should do—was to *plan* the production thoroughly in advance. He prearranged every shot by sketching out a storyboard, best described as a movie in comic-strip form. While creating a story-board may be too involved for most home moviemakers, it is essential at least to out-line the principal scenes that will make up your movie.

Step

Director Steven Spielberg on the site of *Close Encounters of the Third Kind* (1977).

Helpful hint

Don't wing it and just start shooting, or your movie will almost certainly be a shapeless series of incongruous, confusing sequences. Rather, apply the two-thousand-year-old rudiments of classic dramatic structure, and *tell a story*. Give your movie a beginning, a middle, and an end (preferably in that order). . . .

Step

Explanation

Before you even unpack the camcorder from its case, jot down the particulars of each scene you'd like to shoot. Once you start shooting, this outline—your scaled-down screenplay—will serve as a guide, or "step sheet." You won't be able to edit your film after it's shot, so you must essentially edit in advance by shooting only what you want to appear in the final movie. . . .

Helpful hint

Your movie should run no longer than fifteen to twenty minutes, because the attention span of your eventual audience isn't likely to be much longer than that. Production time is typically five to ten times longer than viewing time, so your movie will probably take an hour and a half to three hours to shoot.

Step

When you're planning what to shoot, remember that movies are predominantly a visual medium (although sound is also an important ingredient). It sounds obvious, but think in *visual terms.* Let's say you want to show a certain emotion in one of your characters. How would you convey such an internal event in visual terms? First, try to picture how real-life people behave when they have that feeling.

Helpful hint

If, for instance, you want to convey that your heroine has a crush on your hero, you might show her darting away and quickly fixing her hair when she hears that he's approaching. If you want to convey that she's tense, you might have her twist her hair or pick at imaginary pieces of lint on her shirt.

The camera captures action—nothing more—so your job as a filmmaker is to shoot the action that will visually tell the story.

Step

The next hurdle is figuring out the best way to use your camcorder to show that action. When should you shoot a close-up, use a pan, opt for a zoom, or try something fancier? The answer under most circumstances is to follow one simple, critical rule: Cover the action. That's all. Use nice, straightforward shots; fill the viewfinder with the person, object, or activity that is key to that shot.

Step

Before you ever attempt to zoom, pan, or fade, it's important to understand exactly what you'd be *communicating* by doing so. These videotaping techniques aren't just arbitrary tricks; they're distinctive ways to accent a shot and affect the viewer's perceptions. This glossary of the seven basic video shots will help you decide how best to shoot each sequence of your movie.

Explanation

Definition/ Explanation	**Long shot:** Taken at a good twenty or thirty feet from your subject. A long shot lets you capture the largest amount of territory in your viewfinder. This often serves as an opening, or "establishing," shot at the beginning of a movie or scene, which helps to root the audience in a time and place.
Definition/ Explanation	**Medium shot:** Essentially full-body coverage. Ideal for most home-movie purposes, the medium shot is the "vanilla" shot—the most straightforward and popular frame-up.
Definition/ Explanation	**Close-up:** For head shots and closer. Strictly for dramatic emphasis, a close-up increases the viewer's expectations because it intensifies attention on a particular detail. It also puts strong demands on the acting ability—and looks—of your subject.
Definition/ Explanation	**Pan:** A horizontal, hand-pivoted camera movement used as a transitional device. By changing focal points within a shot, a pan is a setup that demands you also give the viewer a payoff—a new focal point worth changing to.

**Definition/
Explanation**

Zoom: A gradual closing in or easing back from one perspective by changing the lens setting. The zoom is essentially a combination of pan and close-up—a powerful effect best reserved strictly for melodramatic or shock purposes. Much misused by beginners, the zoom can give audiences "see sickness."

**Definition/
Explanation**

Cut: An ordinary change of shots made by turning the camera on and off. A cut indicates a change in focal point within an established scene, usually without a break in continuity or a change in time or place.

**Definition/
Explanation**

Fade: Gradual emergence into or fading out of an image, to or from complete black. A fade should only be used to mark a distinct departure from the established time and place. Never fade in and out within one scene; your viewers are likely to think your characters all went out to have dinner or something and then came back.

Seventeen

EXERCISE 5 ▶ **Analyzing the Organization of a "How-to" Process Paper**

Are you ready to shoot your own video? After you've read the essay, meet with two or three classmates to discuss the following questions.

1. How does David Hajdu begin his essay? Why do you think he chose this method?
2. What are the basic steps in making a video, according to David Hajdu?
3. Why do you think he gives such detailed explanations with each step? How careful is the author to describe the steps in the order they're done?
4. Would you have trouble following Hajdu's directions? Explain.
5. Some people might think that Hajdu's conclusion is a bit abrupt. What do you think?

A Basic Framework for a "How-to" Process Paper

The model you've just read is by a professional writer, one whose business it is to make a living with words. For student writers, such a model can be intimidating. The less experienced writer tends to think "I could never be that good!" Actually, you might be surprised at how good you can be. The following writer's model is an example of the kind of essay you can write.

A WRITER'S MODEL

INTRODUCTION
Attention grabber

It's Saturday afternoon. The car is filthy, and you've got big plans for the night. Will a dirty car be bad for your image? You could drive down to the local car wash, but that costs money, and you've budgeted the last penny of your money for tonight. Maybe it's time to do things the way they did in the good old days—wash the car by hand. Washing a car by hand really isn't hard, and it saves money. It's also easier on your car's paint job.

Advantages of learning process

List of materials

To wash a car by hand, all you need is a water hose, a five- to ten-gallon bucket, some mild dish-washing soap or laundry detergent, and three old, soft towels. One of these towels should be small like a dish towel and two should be regular-sized bath towels. If you have a chamois, a soft leather cloth used by professional car washers, you can use it instead of the two large towels, but you don't have to.

Definition of term

Step

First, park the car in a place with good drainage near a water faucet. Then, attach the water hose and use it to rinse all the loose dirt off the car.

Step

Next, fill the bucket with water and add the soap or detergent. Use about the same amount of soap as you would use to wash a sink full of dishes or a small load of clothes. Now you're

Explanation

Step

Explanation

Step

Helpful hint

Step

Explanation

CONCLUSION
**Restatement of
advantages**

ready to scrub. Dip the small towel in the bucket and begin to wash the car. Some people think it's best to start with the top of the car. But it really doesn't matter much where you begin just as long as you use a system and scrub the entire car, including windows, bumpers, and mirrors.

After the car has been completely washed and all foreign materials have been removed, start the process of rinsing with the hose. Use as much water pressure as possible and be sure to remove all the soap film. Soap film can damage the paint and dull the finish of your car.

When you've finished rinsing, the car is ready for drying. Using a chamois or very soft towels is important. You wouldn't want to scratch the car's paint after all your hard work. Rub gently.

Once the car has dried, it should be clean and shiny, and you should feel proud.

WRITING NOTE In the essay on how to wash a car, the writer uses transitions like *first, then, next,* and *after* to guide the reader through the process. Transitions help make the order of the steps clear to the reader. (For more information on transitions, see pages 83–86, 124.)

You may find it helpful to model your essay after the one on how to wash a car. It follows the framework given below:

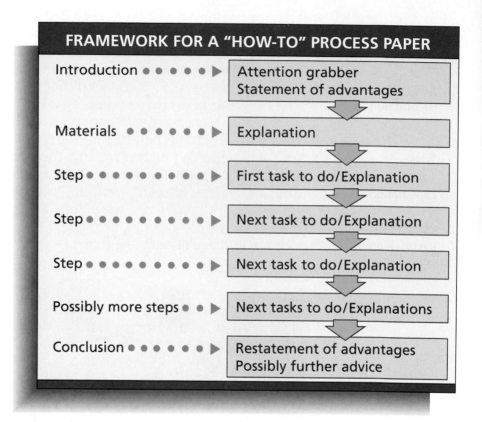

FRAMEWORK FOR A "HOW-TO" PROCESS PAPER

Introduction • • • • • • ▶ | Attention grabber
Statement of advantages

Materials • • • • • • • ▶ | Explanation

Step • • • • • • • • • ▶ | First task to do/Explanation

Step • • • • • • • • • ▶ | Next task to do/Explanation

Step • • • • • • • • • ▶ | Next task to do/Explanation

Possibly more steps • • ▶ | Next tasks to do/Explanations

Conclusion • • • • • • ▶ | Restatement of advantages
Possibly further advice

PART 3:
Writing a Draft of Your "How-to" Process Paper

By this time, you're an "expert" on your process. As you draft your paper, keep in mind the basic framework above. You can follow this order: (1) write an introductory paragraph, (2) tell what materials are needed, (3) present the steps in order, explaining them as necessary, and (4) conclude with a restatement of the advantages or with further advice.

 REFERENCE NOTE: For help in writing interesting introductions and conclusions, see pages 120–123 and 126–129.

Evaluating and Revising

You can use the following chart to evaluate your paper and to revise it. Begin by asking yourself each question in the left-hand column. If your paper has that weakness, use the revision technique in the right-hand column.

EVALUATING AND REVISING PROCESS ESSAYS

EVALUATION GUIDE	REVISION TECHNIQUE
1 Does the introduction interest the reader and explain the advantages of learning the process?	**Add** an interesting anecdote or details. **Add** (or **replace**) a sentence that explains the advantages of learning the process.
2 Does the essay explain what materials the reader will need **before** telling how to perform the task?	**Add** a list of all the materials needed before explaining the process.
3 Are the steps in the process listed in the order they are to be performed? Are all the steps included?	**Reorder** the steps so that they are in the order they are to be performed. **Add** necessary steps.
4 Are all the terms that the audience may not understand clearly defined?	**Add** definitions of any unfamiliar terms.
5 Does the conclusion restate the advantages or include further hints?	**Add** sentences that discuss the advantages of learning the process or that give more helpful hints.

GRAMMAR HINT

Using Varied Sentences

The subject of an **imperative** sentence is always the pronoun *you*, but the pronoun is not in the sentence. The sentence usually begins with the verb. When you write "how-to" process papers, you often use a series of imperative sentences and can sound as though you're barking out orders. So it's best to vary your sentences to avoid sounding abrupt.

EXAMPLES   *Imperative Sentences.* Tear the paper into tiny pieces. Make the pieces about one-quarter-inch square. Add the pieces to the paste mixture. Stir the mixture with a wooden spoon until the paper is soaked.

Varied Sentences. You will need to tear the paper into tiny pieces. Make the pieces about one-quarter-inch square. The next step is to add the pieces to the paste mixture. After you add them, stir the mixture with a wooden spoon until the paper is soaked.

☞ **REFERENCE NOTE:** For more information on sentence variety, see pages 436–437.

"The language must be careful and must appear effortless. It must not sweat."

Toni Morrison

EXERCISE 6 ▶ **Analyzing a Writer's Revisions**

Here is a revised first draft of a paragraph from the writer's model on page 270. Study the writer's changes and then answer the questions that follow the paragraph.

One of these towels should be small like a dish towel and two should be regular size bath towels. To wash a car by hand, all ~~one~~ *you* needs is a water hose, a five- to ten-gallon bucket, some mild dishwashing soap or laundry detergent, and three old soft towels. If you have a chamois *a soft leather cloth,* used by professional car washers, you can use it instead of the two large towels, *but you don't have to.*

reorder

replace

cut

add

add

1. Why did the writer move the first sentence to later in the paragraph?
2. In the second sentence, why did the writer replace the word *one* with *you*? [Hint: Review page 258.]
3. In the last sentence, why did the writer add the words *a soft leather cloth*? How does this information help the reader?
4. Why did the writer add the words *but you don't have to* to the last sentence?

WRITING ASSIGNMENT

PART 4:
Evaluating and Revising Your "How-to" Paper

Now it's time to work on improving your own process paper. Exchange papers with another student. Then use the questions from the chart on page 273 to evaluate each other's essays. Read and think about your partner's evaluation. Then, evaluate your own paper and revise it to correct any weaknesses.

Proofreading and Publishing

Proofreading is important in a "how-to" process paper when a little mistake like *add to cups of oil* instead of *add two cups of oil* can make a big difference. Proofread, also, for errors in spelling, capitalization, punctuation, and usage.

When you wrote your essay, you had some readers in mind. Here are two ways to reach other readers.

- Volunteer for a "how-to" day at a local kindergarten or day-care center. Teach appropriate activities from your "how-to" papers to the children.
- Stage a "Here's How-to" day in class. You and your classmates can present your essays as speeches.

PART 5:
Proofreading and Publishing Your Paper

Proofread your paper very carefully, and correct any errors you find. Proofreading with a partner will help you catch mistakes you might otherwise miss. When you have a clean, final copy of the paper, try one of the publishing suggestions above, or collaborate with a few classmates to come up with other creative ways to share your work.

 Reflecting on Your Writing

If you decide that you would like to add your "how-to" paper to your **portfolio,** include with the paper your written responses to the following questions.

- How did you decide on a topic? Would you pick the same topic next time?
- Did you find it difficult to include all the necessary steps? Explain.
- How can writing directions help you with other kinds of writing assignments? How will this activity improve your oral skills?

A STUDENT MODEL

Chris McDowell, a student at Oxon Hill High School in Oxon Hill, Maryland, has some good ideas about how you can turn "trash into cash." And according to Chris, "the easiest thing to do in this paper was writing the final draft."

How to Turn Trash into Cash
by Chris McDowell

If your closets are anything like mine, overcrowded and messy, then you are in sore need of a garage sale. Garage sales provide you with money and some much needed space. Items such as old toys, baseball or football cards, old furniture, and used clothes are easy to fix up, appraise, and finally sell.

First of all, you need to go through your house, attic, or garage and find items that you have no use for. Generally, any item that you have not used in a year's time should be sold. Collect everything you want to sell, and check for things like faded paint or missing parts.

Next, you need to repair the items. The items may need to be dusted, but a few may require a fresh coat of paint. When painting, make sure to select appealing colors and styles. You'll need to order parts to repair items that you don't have all the pieces for.

By now you should be ready to set prices for your items. You should base the price on several factors. Many people will pay more for an item if its warranty is not expired. Jewelry can be appraised, and price guides list the value of stamps, comic books, and football or baseball cards.

The last step (and my personal favorite) is that you sell the item. You might haggle over the price with some people. Try not to be too firm about the price, as it's bad for business.

WRITING WORKSHOP

The Cause-and-Effect Essay

Informative writing may answer many different kinds of questions. The "how-to" process paper that you've written in this chapter answers the question *How do you do that?* Another form of informative writing answers the question *Why does that happen?* or *What are the effects?* The essay that answers these last two questions is usually called a *cause-and-effect essay.* Writers of cause-and-effect essays use narration to explain why certain actions or situations (causes) produce certain results (effects).

Some cause-and-effect relationships are easy to describe. For example: You're sunburned (an effect). Why? You stayed in the sun too long (cause). But most cause-and-effect relationships—the kind worth writing informative essays about—are more complex. One effect may be the result of many causes.

Here's an essay about one of the most popular animals in the world—the panda. But the panda is in danger of disappearing forever. Why? As you read the essay, look for the causes of this sad effect.

from The Secret World of Pandas
by Byron Preiss and Gao Xueyu

Pandas are rarely seen together in the wild except for a few weeks during the spring mating season, and even then their encounters may not last long. A female can conceive only two or three days a year and can't deliver a healthy cub until she is six or seven years old. Her litter usually consists of two newborns, but she is likely to focus on a single cub—not necessarily the healthier—and let the other die. Because she takes 18 months to rear her offspring, she will reproduce only once every two years. By the time she reaches age 14, she will become infertile. In the best of circumstances, a female panda will raise four, perhaps five, cubs. But faced with the stresses of limited feeding areas, attacks by poachers and other catastrophes, only two cubs are

likely to survive to adulthood—zero population growth, at best. Attempts to save the species through breeding programs in zoos have been disheartening. Only six pandas born in zoos outside China have survived. Of 90 born in Chinese zoos, only 37 lived six months.

In China, pandas and people compete for the same territory. Though humans sometimes will assist an ailing panda, . . . they also invade panda territory to clear land for crops, to log or build new roads. When highways and clearings slice up panda preserves, the isolated animals may end up mating with first cousins and diluting their gene pool. Scientists estimate that panda communities of fewer than 100 animals face serious inbreeding problems; of all the panda communities in China, only three have populations of 100 or more. A sweeping plan proposed by the Chinese Ministry of Forestry last year would nearly double the land preserved for pandas, establish corridors to connect disjointed populations and transfer small groups to larger forests. "The panda is a very simple animal to maintain in the wild," says American zoologist George B. Schaller. "But if we can't protect the wilderness, we can't protect the panda."

Life

1. How is the female panda herself a possible cause for the disappearance of her species (the effect)?
2. What are two ways that humans cause part of the problem for pandas?

Writing a Cause-and-Effect Essay

Prewriting. Think about an effect that concerns you, and ask yourself if you could explain its causes. Is the dropout rate low or high in your school? Can you explain why? Write a sentence that gives an effect and several main causes for the effect. List facts and reasons to explain each cause.

Writing, Evaluating, and Revising. A common way to organize a cause-and-effect essay is to state an effect (America's youth are physically unfit, for example) and then to explain the causes (too much TV, too little exercise, and so on). If the causes are not equally important, then the least important cause is usually stated first and the most important last. To evaluate and revise, make sure you have included the information and background readers will need.

Proofreading and Publishing. Check your spelling, capitalization, and punctuation carefully before sharing your essay. You may want to add your cause-and-effect essay to your **portfolio.** Return to the essay, and reflect on your writing. What did you learn about your topic? Are your ideas presented clearly? How can you improve the essay?

For Better or For Worse copyright 1991 Lynn Johnston Productions, Inc. Reprinted with permission of Universal Press Syndicate. All rights reserved.

MAKING CONNECTIONS

Science

Much of the study of science is the study of process explanations. In the following passage from a textbook, language and illustrations together explain a scientific or natural process. Here's the way the textbook explains how cold and warm fronts form.

> Where a cold air mass moves in on a warm air mass, a *cold front* occurs. The cold air mass wedges itself under the warm air mass and raises it. The rising warm air expands and cools. Water vapor condenses and precipitation occurs.
>
> When a warm air mass moves over cold air, a *warm front* occurs. As the warm front continues to move, the warm air rises and cools. Water vapor condenses and precipitation occurs.
>
> A cold front and a warm front move in different ways. A cold front moves toward a warm area, while a warm front moves toward a cold area.

A cold front

A warm front

What scientific processes can you explain? How a tadpole becomes a frog? Photosynthesis? How the human eye works? Choose some scientific process you understand well, or use the following information (about how clouds form). Then, create an illustrated explanation of the process similar to the textbook's explanation of cold and warm fronts. To do this, draw a picture of each of the following steps in the process of cloud formation.

- air currents rise, air cools
- temperature reaches dew point
- water vapor condenses, clings to dust particles
- droplets formed on dust particles group together, become clouds
- large droplets fall through rising air, become rain

(Just for fun, you may want to see how one writer/ illustrator treats a range of scientific processes. Go to your library and check out David Macaulay's *The Way Things Work.*)

SPEAKING AND LISTENING

The "How-to" Video

If you're a regular TV viewer, you know that television presents a variety of "how-to" spots. You've probably heard the local weatherperson explain what to do in case of a tornado or hurricane. Daytime talk shows often have instructions in cooking or home decorating. Sometimes whole shows are devoted to how to catch fish or how to make a home more energy efficient.

Your local video store probably has a shelf or two devoted to "how-to" videos—everything from how to exercise safely to how to tour London.

You and some of your classmates might enjoy making your own "how-to" video. Your first step is to select a topic. Next you might want to watch one or two video "how-to" shows to see how they are put together.

Once you get a clear idea of how these videos work, you'll be ready to put together your script and your storyboard. For further hints on how to make a video, study the essay, "How to Shoot Your Own Video," on pages 264–269 of this chapter. You may also want to include in your video someone who knows American Sign Language. This person can present your instructions to viewers who are deaf or hard of hearing.

INVEST IN
VICTORY LIBER[T]

THEY KEPT THE
SEA LANES
OPEN

L.A. SHAFER

THE W.P. POWERS CO. LITHO, N.Y.

HE
LOAN

Taking a Stand

People are always trying to convince you to do or think something. Sometimes they give you logical reasons. But sometimes they simply try to appeal to your emotions.

Writing and You. Everybody does it. Your best friend argues that his choice of a movie is better than yours. Advertisers try to convince you to drink their juice, wear their jeans, or read their magazine. As this World War I poster shows, governments aim to convince you to support their efforts. When was the last time you tried to convince someone to do or think something?

As You Read. The poster on these pages tries to persuade you with dramatic images. But persuasion also occurs in literature, where writers use words to persuade. As you read the following excerpt from *The Piano Lesson,* notice how Boy Willie tries to talk Berniece into selling a piano.

L.A. Shafer, *They Kept the Sea Lanes Open* (1919). Collection of Walton Rawls.

from
The Piano Lesson
by August Wilson

BERNIECE: Boy Willie . . . you gonna play around with me one too many times. And then God's gonna bless you and West is gonna dress you. Now set that piano back over there. I done told you a hundred times I ain't selling that piano.

BOY WILLIE: I'm trying to get me some land, woman. I need that piano to get me some money so I can buy Sutter's land.

BERNIECE: Money can't buy what that piano cost. You can't sell your soul for money. It won't go with the buyer. It'll shrivel and shrink to know that you ain't taken on to it. But it won't go with the buyer.

BOY WILLIE: I ain't talking about all that, woman. I ain't talking about selling my soul. I'm talking about trading that piece of wood for some land. Get something under your feet. Land the only thing God ain't making no more of. You can always get you another piano. I'm talking about some land. What you get something out the ground from. That's what I'm talking about. You can't do nothing with that piano but sit up there and look at it.

BERNIECE: That's just what I'm gonna do. Wining Boy, you want me to fry you some pork chops?

"You can always get you another piano. I'm talking about some land. What you get something out the ground from."

BOY WILLIE: Now, I'm gonna tell you the way I see it. The only thing that make that piano worth something is them carvings Papa Willie Boy put on there. That's what make it worth something. That was my great-grandaddy. Papa Boy Charles brought that piano into the house. Now, I'm supposed to build on what they left me. You can't do nothing with that piano sitting up here in the house. That's just like if I let them watermelons sit out there and rot. I'd be a fool. Alright now, if you say to me, Boy Willie, I'm using that piano. I give out lessons on it and that help me make my rent or whatever. Then that be something else. I'd have to go on and say, well, Berniece using that piano. She building on it. Let her go on and use it. I got to find another way to get Sutter's land. But Doaker say you ain't touched that piano the whole time it's been up here. So why you wanna stand in my way? See, you just looking at the sentimental value. See, that's good. That's alright. I take my hat off whenever somebody say my daddy's name. But I ain't gonna be no fool about no sentimental value. You can sit up here and look at the piano for the next hundred years and it's just gonna be a piano. You can't make more than that. Now I want to get Sutter's land with that piano. I get Sutter's land and I can go down and cash in the crop and get my seed. As long as I got the land and the seed then I'm alright. I can always get me a little something else. Cause that land give back to you. I can make me another crop and cash that in. I still got the land and the seed. But that piano don't put out nothing else. You ain't got nothing working for you. Now, the kind of man my daddy was he would have understood that. I'm sorry you can't see it that way. But that's why I'm gonna take that piano out of here and sell it.

READER'S RESPONSE

1. Does Boy Willie convince you that the family ought to sell the piano?
2. Berniece feels a personal attachment to the piano and wants to keep it. Have you ever had to sell or give away something that you cared about, even though you knew there was no practical reason to keep it? Take a few minutes to write about how you felt. If you haven't had this experience, write about how you imagine it would make you feel.

WRITER'S CRAFT

3. What practical reasons does Boy Willie give Berniece for selling the piano?
4. Does he appeal to her emotions as well as her practical side? How?
5. Berniece also tries to persuade. Does she appeal to Boy Willie's head or to his heart? How?

Ways to Persuade

Writers trying to persuade are like Boy Willie in *The Piano Lesson*—they want to get someone to accept their opinions or move someone to action. There is more than one way that you can develop a persuasive message. Here are some examples of different ways to persuade.

- in an essay for history class, writing a biography to persuade readers that a person should be admired for his or her leadership
- in a letter to the editor, trying to convince sports fans that poor refereeing caused your team's loss
- in a letter to a pen pal, describing your town to persuade him or her that it's a great place
- in a bulletin board notice, describing your used skateboard to persuade someone to buy it
- in a student handbook, comparing two courses in your school to convince students that one is more interesting than the other
- in an article for the school newspaper, evaluating a movie to convince readers that it's not worth seeing
- in a letter to your principal, stating an opinion about recycling and trying to persuade him or her to start recycling school paper

LOOKING AHEAD

In this chapter, you'll use evaluation to develop a persuasive essay and a letter of opinion. Keep in mind that an effective persuasive essay or letter of opinion

- states the writer's opinion, or point of view, about the topic
- provides convincing support for the writer's opinion
- often appeals to the reader's emotions

Writing a Persuasive Essay

Prewriting

Choosing a Topic

All of us have opinions on a variety of topics—the minimum age for a driver's license, the three-point shot in basketball, or the best person for president of the United States. Most of these topics would be suitable for a persuasive essay. To choose a topic, think about four things:

1. Does the topic matter to you?
2. Is it a topic you have an opinion about?
3. Can people have different opinions about the topic?
4. Is there a group of people—an audience—you'd like to convince of your opinion?

A Topic That Matters to You.   The topic you choose for a persuasive essay should be one that concerns you or affects your life. It might be a topic of national interest, such as spending more money on the space program. Or it might be a topic of local interest, such as the curfew for teenagers in your community.

Be sure to choose a topic worth arguing about. There's no point, for example, in arguing that roses are prettier than daisies. That's a matter of personal taste. But it might be important to argue for or against planting flowers to beautify the school.

An Opinion, Not a Fact.   With a topic in mind, you need to be sure you have a definite opinion about the topic. Remember that an *opinion* is a belief or attitude— what you think—about a topic. Opinions vary from person to person and are different from facts. A statement of *fact* can be proven true or false. It is a fact, for example, that the South American rain forests are endangered. It is an opinion that the United States should act to save the rain forests.

Different Opinions.   A suitable topic for a persuasive essay is one on which people can have opposing or conflicting opinions. And each person thinks his or her opinion is "right." For example, one group of people believes that the three-point rule has improved college basketball and should be retained; another group believes it has ruined the game and should be eliminated.

An Audience to Convince.   When you write your persuasive essay, you'll need to have an audience in mind. To decide on an audience, consider what group of people might disagree with your opinion. After all, there's no point in trying to convince people who already agree with you. (You'll also find this to be true when you have to be persuasive on the job.)

A Statement of Opinion

You can pull topic, opinion, and audience together in your mind by writing a sentence that clearly states the topic and your opinion on it. Here are some examples.

> The three-point rule has ruined college basketball and should be abolished.
> We must act now to save the South American rain forests.
> The weeknight curfew for teenagers should be extended to 11:00 P.M.

Writing this statement will help you focus your thinking about the topic and will guide you in planning your essay.

When choosing a topic for a persuasive essay

- use some of the techniques you've already learned—brainstorm, talk to other people, listen to radio and television, or look through newspapers and magazines to find a topic that concerns you (See pages 22–35.)
- be sure you can identify opposing opinions on the topic
- target a particular audience
- write a sentence that clearly states the topic and your opinion on it

---

E X E R C I S E 1 ▶ **Distinguishing Fact from Opinion**

With a small group, identify whether each statement below is a *fact* or an *opinion*. [Remember: A fact is a statement whose truth can be checked, and an opinion is a belief or attitude.] Some of these items are tricky—to get the right answers you'll have to think carefully.

1. Bobby Orr was the greatest defenseman in National Hockey League history.
2. The first Olympic games in modern times were held in Athens, Greece, in April 1896.
3. Six descendants of the American writer Edgar Allan Poe played varsity football at Princeton University.
4. The American crawl, most often used in freestyle, is the fastest of all swimming strokes.
5. Chris Evert was the most popular women's tennis player on the international circuit in the 1980s.

EXERCISE 2 ▶ Exploring Possible Topics

Working with a small group, collect a stockpile of topics that you think would be interesting for persuasive essays. Include in your collection some school or educational topics, some topics of local interest, and some topics of national or worldwide interest. Be sure the topics focus on a belief or opinion.

Education Bill Cut

COMMUNIST REGIME COLLAPSES

Budget-cutters should heed opinion poll

Conservation must preserve local heritage

WRITING ASSIGNMENT

PART 1:
Choosing a Topic to Write About

Select a topic to write about, either one your group identified in Exercise 2 or another topic you really care about. For example, is the school board planning to adopt a school-wide uniform? Are budget cuts forcing your community to cancel programs for teenagers? After choosing a topic, write a sentence that states the topic and your opinion about it.

Prewriting

Thinking About Purpose, Audience, and Tone

The purpose of your persuasive essay is not just to share information. You want to convince someone else to (1) do as you suggest or (2) think as you suggest. For that reason, you have to be very much aware of the beliefs and interests of the people you're writing for—your audience. What do they think is important? What will it take to convince them? What are their concerns? Why might they disagree with you? For example, if you and your friends want to have a ninth-grade formal dance, you might have to convince a number of people that it's a good idea. Generally, those people could be divided into groups. You could analyze their interests and concerns in this way.

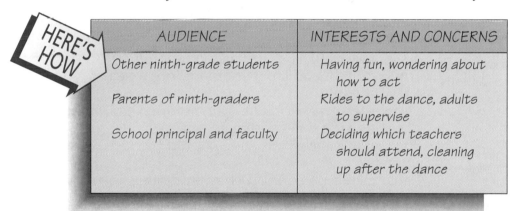

	AUDIENCE	INTERESTS AND CONCERNS
HERE'S HOW	Other ninth-grade students	Having fun, wondering about how to act
	Parents of ninth-graders	Rides to the dance, adults to supervise
	School principal and faculty	Deciding which teachers should attend, cleaning up after the dance

Usually a persuasive essay is serious and logical, with a formal tone. It's true that a humorous tone can be effective in some types of persuasive writing. But you have to be careful not to go too far with it. If your essay sounds casual or silly, or too emotional, your audience will probably not take your opinion seriously and will not be persuaded. That would defeat your purpose. Remember that your audience has to believe you in order to be convinced.

EXERCISE 3 ▶ **Speaking and Listening: Analyzing an Audience's Point of View**

When you think about the audience for your persuasive essay, ask yourself two questions: *What group in my audience will most strongly disagree with my opinion? What reason(s) would they have for disagreeing?* Practice this technique in a small group. Let one person in your group choose one of the opinions given below and name an audience that would disagree with it. Then, have the other group members act as a "disagreeable" audience by giving a reason for disagreeing with the opinion. Take turns until each group member plays both parts.

> *Example opinion:* The Parents' Association should sponsor a ninth-grade formal dance.
> *What group will strongly disagree?* The Parents' Association.
> *What reasons will they have for disagreeing?*
> **1.** Ninth-grade students are not mature enough for a formal dance.
> **2.** Formal dances are too expensive—new clothes, tickets, and flowers.

1. A bus fare of $1.00 is unfair to students.
2. The local school district should adopt a year-round class schedule.
3. Midwestern power plants must reduce emissions of sulfur dioxide that cause acid rain.
4. The driving age in our state should be raised to age eighteen.
5. Cable television companies should offer free service to low-income families.

DRIVER **MISSOURI** LICENSE

09876543210

No. YZ012 - 3456 - 7890 - 1234

• SAWYER, THOMAS
• 100 STEAMBOAT ST
• HANNIBAL   MO 63401

Class 1	Expiration Date 07 - 06 - 03	
Birth Date 07 - 04 - 80	Social Security Number 100 - 00 - 0001	
Sex M	Height 5'11"	Weight 160	Eyes BRN

Thomas Sawyer

 *Prewriting*

Supporting Your Opinion

Remember that your purpose in writing a persuasive essay is to convince others to think and, perhaps, to behave in a certain way. As you know, you can't convince people to accept your opinion just by telling them you're right. To convince your readers, you can use *logical appeals* and *emotional appeals* to support your opinion.

Logical Appeals

Logical appeals are aimed at your readers' minds, at their thinking side. They are made up of

- **logical reasons** why your audience should believe you (keep in mind that not all reasons are equally persuasive for all audiences)
- **evidence** that proves or explains your reasons

Reasons. *Reasons* tell *why* an opinion should be accepted. For example:

Opinion	We need a stoplight at the corner next to the high school.
Reasons	It is a heavily trafficked intersection at the opening and closing of each school day.
	It is a dangerous intersection.

But reasons alone aren't always enough to persuade your audience. Your readers usually want proof that the reasons are sound, or well-founded.

Evidence. With *evidence,* you provide proof that your opinion and your reasons are sound. Evidence consists of

- **facts and statistics**—information that can be checked by testing, observing firsthand, or reading reference materials.

  Each school day, 150 vehicles and 350 pedestrians go through the intersection between the hours of 7:00 and 8:00 A.M. and 2:00 and 3:00 P.M. [evidence for first reason]
  Three students have been hit by cars in the last two years. [evidence for second reason]

- **expert opinion**—statements by people who are recognized as authorities on the subject

   Chief of Police Emile Galceran explained, "A stoplight is needed at that intersection to force cars to slow down."

Sources of Reasons and Evidence.   Where can you find reasons and evidence? For some topics, you will be able to rely almost totally on what you already know— your own observations and common knowledge. For other topics, you'll have to go beyond yourself to what other people know and to written sources.

To find reasons and evidence to support your opinion

- review your writer's journal, brainstorm, or ask yourself questions to discover what you already know (See pages 22–29.)
- talk to people who know something about the topic
- read books, magazine articles, or newspapers for data on the issue
- research facts and statistics on your topic

Collect all the reasons and evidence you can think of or find. Later on you'll find that some ideas are stronger than others.

Emotional Appeals

Has anyone ever told you, "You're tugging on my heart-strings"? That's what *emotional appeals* are all about— aiming at your readers' feelings.

Emotional appeals are often just examples—ones chosen to awaken specific feelings in your audience. For example, to convince readers to contribute to an animal shelter, you might discuss the plight of a particular abandoned cat. You'd want to appeal to your readers' sense of sympathy and to their love of animals. To persuade students to participate in a campus clean-up day, you might describe the litter located around the school. Here you'd aim to touch their sense of pride and their school spirit.

Your own experiences—what you've done and observed—are a rich source of these kinds of emotional appeals. Think about how you want your audience to feel about your topic. Then include an example that will appeal to that emotion. But remember: Emotional appeals alone aren't always convincing enough. And sometimes—especially in the classroom—you may be expected to rely *only* on reasons and evidence.

WRITING NOTE Persuasive writing that uses emotional appeals can be very convincing when the emotional appeal parallels, or goes along with, the logical appeal. For example, you can sell a car not only because of its efficiency and speed (logical), but also because of its beauty (emotional). Sometimes the two appeals are just two different views of the same thing. For example, if you get a part-time job, you'll be able to make some money (logical) and buy the car you want to buy (emotional).

CRITICAL THINKING

Evaluating Your Reasoning

The whole point of a persuasive essay is to provide convincing support for your opinion. That mainly means using strong, clear reasons and believable, factual evidence. Don't fall into the trap of using statements that look like reasons but aren't reasons at all. It's true that some people who aren't on guard might be persuaded by the four types of statements listed below. But any audience that is reading critically won't be persuaded by these "impostors."

Statements Masquerading as Reasons

1. **Circular Reasoning.** You may think you are giving a reason to support your opinion, but all you may be doing is restating your opinion in different words.

Statement of Opinion	Pablo has the best qualifications to be class president.
Circular Reasoning	Pablo's qualifications are superior to his opponent's.

Saying Pablo has superior qualifications is the same as saying he has the best qualifications.

2. **False Cause and Effect.** You may assume that one event caused another event, just because one came before the other. That isn't necessarily true.

First Event	The city created a 10:00 P.M. curfew for teenagers.
Second Event	Three teenagers were in a wreck at 9:30 P.M. on their way home from a party.
False Cause and Effect	The wreck occurred because there was a curfew and the teenagers had to be home by 10:00 P.M.

Other events and actions probably caused the wreck, not the curfew. The curfew and the time of the wreck just happened to be close.

3. **Attacking the Person.** You may be tempted to attack the character or judgment of people who don't agree with your opinion. (In politics this is called "negative campaigning.") Not facing the issue can weaken the case you're trying to present to your audience.

Attacking the Person	People who grow tobacco or make and sell cigarettes are more concerned with their own pocketbooks than with the lives of other human beings.
Confronting the Issue	Thirty years of research has shown that smoking cigarettes can cause cancer.

Talking about the people who grow tobacco or sell cigarettes doesn't deal with the real issue: the health hazards of smoking.

4. **Hasty Generalization.** You may assume that just because something is true in a few instances, it's true in all cases. That's not necessarily so.

> *First Instance* The taxi driver who drove me from the airport was rude to me.
>
> *Second Instance* The waiter in the café was rude to me.
>
> *Hasty Generalization* Everyone in this town is rude.

Although a few people were rude, it does not necessarily follow that all the people in the town don't mind their manners.

CRITICAL THINKING EXERCISE:
Evaluating Reasons

Are you on alert for statements pretending to be reasons? After you read the following opinion and its supporting statements, indicate whether each statement is (1) circular reasoning, (2) false cause and effect, (3) attacking the person, or (4) hasty generalization. Then, in place of each weak statement, write a "true" reason. You may want to talk to someone who knows something about the topic—a parent, a theater owner, a movie critic for your local newspaper, or a frequent moviegoer.

> *Opinion:* The practice of showing advertisements before feature films should be continued in our local movie theaters.
>
> *Supporting Statements:*
> 1. Anyone who thinks that theaters should eliminate commercials has not thought very carefully about the subject.
> 2. One of our local movie theaters eliminated advertisements two months ago, and fewer people came to see the feature films.

3. It is a good idea to show commercials in movie theaters.

4. One theater showed advertisements before the feature film and made enough money to increase its number of screens. Every theater here can do the same.

WRITING ASSIGNMENT

PART 2:
Finding Support for Your Opinion

What reasons and evidence do you have to support your opinion statement from Writing Assignment, Part 1 (page 294)? List them. If your list seems too brief or unconvincing for your audience, collect more support by talking with other people ("experts") and reading about the topic. One way you can think about your ideas is to complete a chart like the one below. Unless your teacher has asked you to write a paper that is strictly logical, you might also include an emotional appeal.

OPINION	
AUDIENCE	
REASONS	EVIDENCE
1.	1.
2.	2.
3.	3.

Writing Your First Draft

Now that you have your ideas, you need to think about how to bring them together in an effective persuasive essay—one that will convince your audience.

The Basic Elements of Persuasive Essays

Keep in mind that a persuasive essay

- states an opinion about a topic people disagree on
- aims to convince an audience to think or to behave as the writer suggests
- uses reasons and evidence to convince the audience
- often appeals to the audience's emotions
- makes the writer appear credible, or believable

Borgman reprinted with special permission of King Features Syndicate, Inc.

The writer of the following essay makes creative use of the basic persuasive essay elements. Notice how his headline, a joking reference to the founder of a chain of ballroom dance schools, sets the stage for the conversational, witty tone of the whole essay.

A MAGAZINE EDITORIAL

Calling Arthur Murray

Opinion

Ballroom dancing has as much right to be in the Olympics as, say, rhythmic gymnastics

by E. M. Swift

Background

Left, right, left, right . . . forward, backward . . . hop, hop, hop.

Pardon me, but I'm in training for the 2000 Olympics. In case you missed the big news that has set the Olympic world atwitter, on April 3 the International Olympic Committee granted provisional recognition to ballroom dancing and surfing. The decision was a small but essential step in the two activities' long waltz toward their eventual goal of medal status. . . .

Opposing opinion

There are naysayers, of course, those who do not see ballroom dancing—officially known in the U.S. as dance sport since changing its name in 1989—as Olympian fare. One is John Krimsky, interim executive director of the U.S. Olympic Committee. After the IOC announcement, Krimsky said, "I would hope some sanity will come back into the selection of Olympic sports."

Emotional appeal

Right. As if the traditional Olympic sports, like modern pentathlon, are examples of sanity. About 15 people worldwide . . . participate in that arcane event, which is about as modern as a windup watch. The modern pentathlon, which combines fencing, horseback riding, pistol shooting, running, and swimming, achieves an almost impossible trifecta: It's expensive, it's time-consuming, and it has no fan base. Yet Mr. Krimsky chooses to question the sanity of dance sport. . . .

American reaction to dance sport continues the country's long tradition of sporting isolationism. Abroad, the International Dance Sport Federation is robust and growing, with 62 member countries on six continents. The U.S. has about 2,000 competitive dancers; Germany has 100,000. Dance sport competitions fill 10,000-seat arenas in Asia and Europe. It's shown on prime time television, attracting deep-pocketed sponsors. "And

don't tell me it isn't athletic," says Peter Pover, past president of the U.S. Dance Sport Council. . . . "In competitions couples have to do five 90-second dances in a row, with only 20 seconds between dances. Plus, the girls have to do it going backwards! All a runner has to do is jog around the track. . . ."

Plus it's cheap, drug-free, and politically correct, encouraging equal participation by both sexes. Facilities can be found everywhere, and the television ratings promise to be as strong as they are for figure skating. So

it's time for the curmudgeons at the USOC to tone down the disparaging rhetoric and turn up the sounds of samba.

Sports Illustrated

EXERCISE 4 ▶   **Analyzing the Organization of a Persuasive Essay**

Read the essay on Olympic ballroom dancing (pages 304–305). Then, meet with two or three classmates to discuss the following questions.

1. Does this essay convince you that ballroom dancing should be an Olympic sport? Why or why not?
2. What kind of opposing view does the essay express? Is the opposing opinion valid? Why?
3. Swift begins the essay with an opinion and background information. Do you think this approach helps the writer build a convincing essay? Do you think the essay should use more emotional appeals?
4. What kind of evidence does Swift use? Why do you think Swift includes that kind of evidence?
5. Swift includes an expert opinion in this essay. Does including this opinion make Swift's essay more or less convincing? Why?
6. Does Swift seem believable? Explain.

WRITING NOTE   Persuasive essays may vary a great deal in the way they are put together. The statement of opinion may be the first sentence in the essay, or it may not appear until much later. The opinion may be stated in one sentence, in two sentences, or even as a question. One writer may use only one reason, but another may use several reasons, each supported by solid evidence. The most important reason or evidence may come first—or it may come last. An emotional appeal may tug on the reader's feelings, or the writer may be strictly logical. One writer may include a clear call to action, saying what he or she wants readers to do. But another may omit it entirely or only hint at it. Every writer tries to do what's most convincing for his or her topic.

A Simple Framework for a Persuasive Essay

The professional essay you've studied shows how a persuasive essay can be put together. But that essay was written by a professional writer—someone who makes his living by writing. When you're learning to write a persuasive essay, it's often helpful to have some kind of framework or basic structure to follow. The following essay illustrates a useful framework for your own writing.

A WRITER'S MODEL

INTRODUCTION   Warm spring weather has arrived. You get in your car, roll down the windows, pop a tape in the stereo, turn up the volume, and head out for the lake. A great feeling and harmless fun, right? Some state senators don't think so. To them, extremely loud car stereos are a public nuisance and even dangerous. They've proposed a law that bans car speakers above a certain size and sets legal volume levels. Playing a loud car stereo shouldn't be a crime, and this legislation must be defeated.

Attention grabber

Emotional appeal

Background

Statement of opinion

EXPLANATION   A main reason for defeating the proposed law is that existing state laws already cover the problems the senators mention. According to Richard Tharpe, Hamilton County sheriff, "Right now we can arrest people for disturbing the peace, and state rules even set noise-pollution levels." In addition, if a stereo does cause a traffic accident—which Tharpe notes is uncommon and hard to prove—the driver can be charged. Your good judgment will tell you that we do not need to duplicate laws.

Reason

Evidence/ Expert opinion and fact

Reason

Emotional appeal

EXPLANATION   A second reason is that singling out car stereos is a form of discrimination, because many other "public noises" are just as loud. Parades and rallies use high-volume sound trucks. Radio stations broad-

Reason

Evidence/ Facts

cast live from stores and parking lots. Loudspeakers, bands, and cheering crowds at football games can be heard for blocks. Sound from any of these events could infringe on the public's right to peace. But a law to eliminate these noises would be considered unfair and illogical. No one wants to go to a quiet football game. It would spoil the fun. Why should driving to the lake be different?

Emotional appeal

CONCLUSION
We all want our streets to be calm and safe, but the senators' approach is misguided. A law restricting the volume of car stereos is unnecessary and unfair, and each of us should write or call our legislators to say so.

Restatement of opinion and call to action

V O L U M E

WRITING NOTE In the essay about loud car stereos, the writer presents two reasons along with some explanations and evidence. There is no magic number of reasons or pieces of evidence you need to support your opinion. But most people think you need at least two or three reasons plus some evidence. You have to decide what will work best for your audience.

You may find it helpful to model your own persuasive essay after the one on loud car stereos. It follows the framework given below:

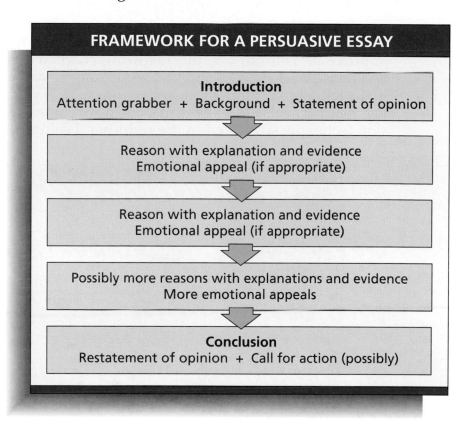

FRAMEWORK FOR A PERSUASIVE ESSAY

Introduction
Attention grabber + Background + Statement of opinion

Reason with explanation and evidence
Emotional appeal (if appropriate)

Reason with explanation and evidence
Emotional appeal (if appropriate)

Possibly more reasons with explanations and evidence
More emotional appeals

Conclusion
Restatement of opinion + Call for action (possibly)

WRITING
ASSIGNMENT

PART 3:
Writing a Draft of Your Persuasive Essay

Are you ready to write? Keeping the basic framework in mind as a model, write a rough draft of your persuasive essay. Use the topic, opinion statement, and support you developed in Writing Assignment, Part 1 (page 294) and Part 2 (page 302). As you write, keep your readers in mind. What support will they find most convincing? Consider what tone will be most effective in persuading them, too.

Evaluating and Revising

You have a draft of your essay, but you're not really finished yet. Now you have to take time to see how to improve it. You can use the following chart to evaluate and revise your essay. Begin by asking yourself a question in the left-hand column in the following chart. If you identify that particular weakness in your essay, use the revision technique suggested in the right-hand column.

What convinces is conviction. Believe in the argument you're advancing. If you don't, you're as good as dead.

Lyndon Baines Johnson
36th President of the United States

EVALUATING AND REVISING PERSUASIVE ESSAYS

EVALUATION GUIDE	REVISION TECHNIQUE
1 Do the first one or two sentences grab the audience's attention?	**Add** an interesting statistic or example or **replace** existing sentences with one.
2 Does a clear statement of the writer's opinion appear early in the essay?	**Add** a sentence (or **replace** an existing sentence) that clearly states the topic and your opinion on it.
3 Is background information needed to help explain the issue?	**Add** facts or examples that will help your readers understand the topic.
4 Are there enough reasons and evidence provided to convince the audience of the writer's opinion?	Find additional reasons, facts, or expert opinions and **add** them to the essay.
5 Are all of the reasons strong?	**Cut** any statements that aren't reasons at all (circular reasons, false cause-effect, attacking the person, hasty generalization). **Add** reasons your readers can understand and accept.
6 If appropriate, is there an emotional appeal designed to make the audience feel a certain way?	**Add** a sentence (or **replace** an existing one) that clearly appeals to the reader's emotions.
7 Is the essay's conclusion effective?	Rewrite the conclusion and **add** a sentence that restates your opinion in different words. **Add** a call to action.
8 Is the tone of the essay appropriate?	**Cut** any frivolous remarks and **replace** them with statements that reveal your concern about the topic.

EXERCISE 5 ▶ **Analyzing a Writer's Revisions**

Study the writer's revision of the second paragraph in the composition on pages 307–308. Then, answer the questions that follow the paragraph.

A main reason for defeating the proposed law is that existing state laws already cover the problems the senators mention. ~~The real problem is that they just don't like rock and roll.~~ **cut** According to Richard Tharpe, ~~who knows the law,~~ ^Hamilton County sheriff^ "Right now we can **replace** arrest people for disturbing the peace, and state rules even set noise-pollution levels." ^In addition,^ ~~If~~ a stereo does cause a traffic accident— **add** which Tharpe notes is ^uncommon and^ hard to prove—the **add** driver can be charged. ~~It just isn't wise to pass this law.~~ ^Your good judgment will tell you that we do not need to duplicate laws.^ **replace**

1. Why did the writer remove the second sentence? [Hint: Review pages 299–301.]
2. What is the effect of the replacement in the third sentence? Why is the change important?
3. Why did the writer add *In addition* to the beginning of the fourth sentence? How does this improve the paragraph?
4. Why did the writer add *uncommon and* to the fourth sentence?
5. Why did the writer replace the last sentence? Do you think the new sentence is a good addition to the paragraph? Why?

USAGE HINT

Using Active Voice

Persuasive writing should be strong, not weak. Your persuasive essay will sound strong if you use verbs in the active voice. When the subject in a sentence does the acting, the verb is in the active voice. When the subject is acted upon, the verb is in the passive voice. The passive voice always includes a form of the verb *be*.

EXAMPLES   Active Voice. With an extended school day, students **could take** additional academic courses.

Passive Voice. With an extended school day, additional academic courses **could be taken** by students.

 REFERENCE NOTE: For more information on the active and passive voice, see pages 633–635.

 PART 4:

Evaluating and Revising Your Persuasive Essay

Exchange essays with another student and use the questions from the chart on page 311 to evaluate each other's essays. Read your partner's evaluation. Then, evaluate your essay yourself and revise it to correct any problems you've found.

 COMPUTER NOTE: Use your word-processing program's Cut and Paste commands to find the best placement for a sentence or paragraph within a document. You can always move back the sentence or paragraph if you change your mind.

Proofreading and Publishing

Proofreading. As usual in proofreading, look for problems with wording, spelling, capitalization, punctuation, and usage. If you really want to convince your audience to agree with you, you need to avoid distracting them with errors. Remember to recopy your essay before you share it with an audience.

Publishing. You had an audience in mind when you wrote your essay—the school board, community officials, other teenagers, parents. Unless your audience reads your essay, however, there is no way you can convince them to accept your opinion. Here are three ways you can reach your audience.

- Send your essay to your school newspaper and invite readers to respond in writing.
- Stage an "opinion forum." Present your essays as speeches, with discussion afterward.
- Compile a booklet of your class's persuasive essays. Distribute it to other English classes and place it in your school library.

PART 5:
Proofreading and Publishing Your Essay

Proofread your essay carefully and correct the errors. Proofreading for spelling is easier when you read your paper backwards, reading from right to left one word at a time. Then, publish or share your essay with others.

 Reflecting on Your Writing

To add this essay to your **portfolio,** date the paper and write a brief reflection answering these questions.

- Did your opinion change as you wrote the paper? How?
- Did you shape your support by keeping the audience in mind? How?
- What skills did you improve while writing this paper?

A STUDENT MODEL

In her essay "Discipline by Suspension," Sara Schille argues that there are better ways to deal with disruptive students. Sara, a student at Van Buren Junior High School in Tampa, Florida, explains why she chose school suspension for her topic: "An essay could possibly give me a chance to express my feelings against it." As you read the following paragraph from Sara's essay, ask yourself if she persuades you that another approach might be more effective.

from Discipline by Suspension
by Sara Schille

The inability of suspension to produce effective results calls for a newer and better discipline to replace it. Some type of community service could be a solution. Only a small number of hours would show a student the working world. Being involved in the scene could, in addition, provide some education. There are also other benefits to this solution. A student who likes the type of work being assigned may realize that he or she could be paid for the work. From this a student may then seek a job in the field of interest. Instead of suspension, community hours would be a more realistic solution.

WRITING WORKSHOP

A Letter to the Editor

Like persuasive essays, persuasive letters try to get the reader to act or believe as the writer wants. You might, for example, write a letter to your state senator urging his or her support for a particular bill. Or, you might write an open letter asking students to support the school soccer team. You might even write a letter to a friend urging him or her to attend the same summer camp you're going to. You might also write a letter to the editor, another type of persuasive letter.

Usually such letters are written not just to the editor of the newspaper or magazine, but also to a specific group of readers—other taxpayers, political officials, people who litter. Most of the time, something has upset the writer—taxes are increasing to pay for the schools, or speeders are making a street dangerous. As you read this letter to the editor of the *Austin American-Statesman*, think about the topic that concerns the writer and his opinion about it.

To the Editor:

Parking meter poles are springing up in the downtown area like toadstools after rain, and presumably meters will soon follow. Installing meters is a mistake. Eliminating free hourly parking may provide modest revenues for the city, but it strongly discourages people from spending time or money downtown. The dollar or two extra to go to a restaurant for lunch or to the library or to shop is a burden for some and an annoyance to all. At present there is a good balance between paid and free parking. Let's leave it that way!

Peter Flagg Maxson
Architectural Historian
Texas

1. What issue concerns the writer? What is his opinion about it?
2. What support—reasons and evidence and emotional appeals—does the writer use to convince the reader? Does he convince you?
3. What audience do you think the writer is trying to reach? Do you think this letter will convince them?
4. What do you think might have caused Mr. Maxson to write this letter?

Writing a Letter to the Editor

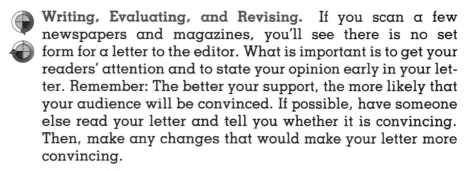

Prewriting. What bothers or concerns you? Are you worried that the school board will require students to wear uniforms? Are you upset because litter and refuse are left in public places in your town? When you've thought of a topic you really care about, write a sentence stating your opinion about it. Think about how you can support your opinion. If necessary, gather some additional support by reading or talking to knowledgeable people.

Writing, Evaluating, and Revising. If you scan a few newspapers and magazines, you'll see there is no set form for a letter to the editor. What is important is to get your readers' attention and to state your opinion early in your letter. Remember: The better your support, the more likely that your audience will be convinced. If possible, have someone else read your letter and tell you whether it is convincing. Then, make any changes that would make your letter more convincing.

Proofreading and Publishing. A letter to the editor is meant to be read by many people, so decide where you want to mail it—your school newspaper, your local newspaper, or a special-interest magazine. Your letter may be printed in a newspaper or magazine where many people can read it, so proofread very carefully. Most editorial pages contain notices telling writers how to address their letters.

A letter to the editor may be an effective piece of persuasive writing you can add to your **portfolio**, along with a written response to the following question: What have you learned about your ability to use sound reasoning?

MAKING CONNECTIONS

SPEAKING AND LISTENING

Advertising and Persuasion

Ads are one form of persuasion you can't escape. In fact, one estimate is that by the time you're sixty years old, you will have seen or heard fifty million ads. Most ads try to convince you to buy something, but some ads also promote an idea or a cause.

Select five ads to analyze—from television or radio or both. Then use the following questions to examine the persuasive techniques of the ads. Give an oral presentation of your findings to your class.

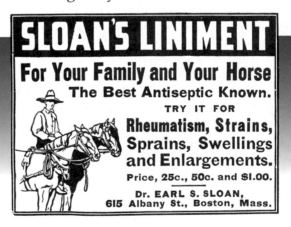

- Who is the audience for each ad?
- What is each ad's aim—to sell a product or to urge you to support a cause? What product or cause?
- Do any of the ads use reasons and evidence to persuade you? Which ones?
- Do any of the ads use circular reasoning, false cause and effect, attacking the person, or hasty generalization? Which ones?

- Which ads appeal more to the emotions than to logic and judgment?
- Which ad do you think is the most persuasive? Why?
- What can you say in one or two sentences to summarize what you've discovered about the ads?

Now that you've analyzed several ads, you should have a good sense of how they're put together. Try your hand at writing an advertisement for a new product—perhaps a new brand of blue jeans or athletic shoes or even a new kind of frozen dinner. If you decide to write a television or magazine ad, it's also a good idea to consider what kinds of pictures you'd use. A good way to begin is to think about the people most likely to buy the product. Ask yourself what would appeal to that audience. Share your ad with your classmates—would they use some of their hard-earned money to buy your product? Why?

> The codfish lays ten thousand eggs,
> The homely hen lays one.
> The codfish never cackles
> To tell you what she's done.
> And so we scorn the codfish,
> While the humble hen we prize,
> Which only goes to show you
> That it pays to advertise.
>
> *Anonymous*

PERSUASION ACROSS THE CURRICULUM

Social Studies

One of the most effective uses of persuasion occurs in speeches our senators and representatives give before the United States Congress. Presented according to the formal rules of the House or the Senate, their speeches usually address topics of serious national interest. Sometimes, however, they reflect a not-so-serious national interest, as in the following speech by Illinois Representative Richard Durbin. His speech is "tongue-in-cheek," or playful in tone, even though it is presented formally.

Study this speech (you may even enjoy reading it aloud to get its full flavor). Then, think of a topic that you care about, even though you know it is not one of serious national consequence—for example, people whose haircuts spell words, lights for baseball on Wrigley Field, children having to eat broccoli (or fish), people over twenty-five being allowed to wear shorts. You're a member of the United States Congress. Present a tongue-in-cheek persuasive speech on your topic to your class.

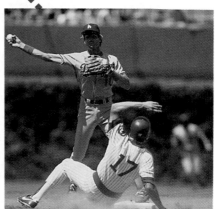

A Great American Symbol
by Richard Durbin

Mr. Speaker, I rise to condemn the desecration of a great American symbol. No, I am not referring to flag burning; I am referring to the baseball bat.

Several experts tell us that the wooden baseball bat is doomed to extinction, that major league baseball players will soon be standing at home plate with aluminum bats in their hands.

Baseball fans have been forced to endure countless indignities by those who just cannot leave well enough alone: designated hitters, plastic grass, uniforms that look like pajamas, chicken clowns dancing on the baselines, and, of course, the most heinous sacrilege, lights in Wrigley Field.

Are we willing to hear the crack of a bat replaced by the dinky ping? Are we ready to see the Louisville Slugger replaced by the aluminum ping dinger? Is nothing sacred?

Please do not tell me that wooden bats are too expensive, when players who cannot hit their weight are being paid more money than the President of the United States.

Please do not try to sell me on the notion that these metal clubs will make better hitters.

What will be next? Teflon baseballs? Radar-enhanced gloves? I ask you.

I do not want to hear about saving trees. Any tree in America would gladly give its life for the glory of a day at home plate.

I do not know if it will take a constitutional amendment to keep our baseball traditions alive, but if we forsake the great Americana of broken-bat singles and pine tar, we will have certainly lost our way as a nation.

From a speech made on the floor of the U.S. House of Representatives on July 26, 1989, by Richard Durbin, a Democrat from Illinois.

Reading and Responding

It's hard to **read** or view anything without **responding.** Whether it's wonderful or terrible, the urge is there to say what you think about it.

Writing and You. For every book and movie, there seems to be a critic. Sometimes, critics just give a personal response—giving five stars, three stars, no stars. But sometimes they go further, analyzing the book or movie in detail to see what works and what doesn't. How did you respond to the last book you read or movie you saw?

As You Read. In the following review of the film *Apollo 13*, the writer looks closely at the movie—its plot, characters, camera work, and so on. As you read, consider the critic's response. Based on his review, would you want to see this movie?

Jacob Lawrence, *The Library* (1960). National Museum of American Art, Washington, D.C. (1969.47.24)/Art Resource, N.Y.

DARK SIDE OF THE MOON

by Owen Gleiberman

Tom Hanks is a steadfast astronaut caught in America's most calamitous lunar mission in "Apollo 13," Ron Howard's you-are-there docudrama.

There's a moment in Ron Howard's *Apollo 13* (Universal, PG) that is so powerfully ironic it's hard to know whether to laugh or cringe. It's April 11, 1970, and NASA has just launched Apollo 13, the spaceflight that's to culminate in America's third walk on the moon. The three astronauts on board—Jim Lovell (Tom Hanks), Fred Haise (Bill Paxton), and Jack Swigert (Kevin Bacon)—are putting on a live-from-the-capsule demonstration for the folks back home. As they float around their cramped quarters, making cornball jokes and playing with a futuristic device (check it out, folks—a handheld video camera!), it's clear that, in their aw-shucks way, they're reveling in the role of the all-American hero. Lovell, the one who has been chosen to walk on the moon, understands that the mission is showbiz, a kind of sequel to Neil Armstrong's triumph less than a year before. There's just one problem: America is no longer watching. The major television networks, picking up on the nation's collective lack of interest, have all gone with their regularly scheduled programming, stranding Lovell and his comrades—without their even knowing it—in the broadcast void. The year before, a trip to the moon was a religious experience; now it's a rerun.

Of course, America soon begins to tune in, if not for the reasons anticipated. Shortly into the flight, there's an explosion, and the capsule starts leaking oxygen. The plans for the moon walk are instantly abandoned. The only question now is whether Lovell

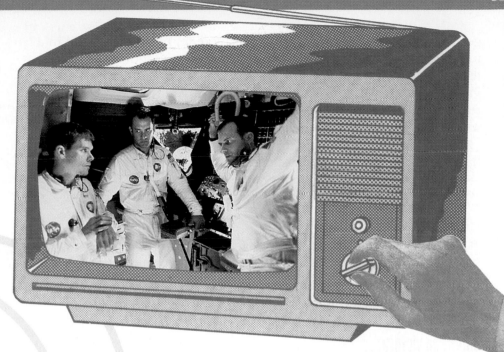

and his crew can get back to earth alive. This disaster in the making, unfolding in a high-tech tin can hundreds of thousands of miles from earth, ought to be ominously thrilling. Yet the weight of that earlier scene—of a nation's indifference to space travel—hangs over the movie.

Apollo 13 is an uncanny experience. It chronicles one of the most dramatic of all spaceflights, an American catastrophe that became an American victory, and it does this in a way that's so authentic, so brilliant in its technical details, that it succeeds in putting us *on* that ship. Visually, the film's re-creation of space travel is flat-out stunning. And the intercutting of actual news reports, principally from Walter Cronkite, adds to the eerie sense that we're seeing history in all its verisimilitude. For all the grandeur of its scale, though, the film is still a bit of a stunt. *Apollo 13* engrosses us in the nuts and bolts of what its astronaut heroes are doing, but it never quite tells us who they are. Despite some tense and beautiful moments, the film left me feeling like the American public of 1970, detached from an experience I should have been finding supremely gripping.

One might have expected a director like Howard to play this story at full inspirational throttle. But no, he has made a true docudrama, maintaining fealty to the tiniest facts. Most of the action hinges on the technical maneuvers of the astronauts: the way they get the capsule to dock with the lunar module, or pilot the ship in a fuel-saving trajectory around the dark side of the moon (one of the few times Howard indulges in wistfulness), or build makeshift devices to suck out the carbon dioxide that's invading the cabin. The revelation of the movie is how low-tech much of their activity seems, as if they were '50s mechanics in a 21st-century vehicle. Yet Howard's decision to let the inherent drama of the mission dictate his entire scenario has a downside. In a sense, he hasn't done enough shaping himself. He has made a movie of objective events—an epic of tinkering.

> "*Apollo 13* . . . chronicles one of the most dramatic of all spaceflights, an American catastrophe that became an American victory. . . . "

Hanks, Paxton, and Bacon try to get inside the skins of these space-age pilot jocks. But the roles, as written, simply don't give them enough to work with. We know that Hanks's Lovell is a chummy family man who's desperate to walk on the moon . . . and that Paxton's Haise falls ill on board. Where, though, are the tensile group dynamics among these three? Philip Kaufman's wonderful adaptation of *The Right Stuff* showed us that astronauts, beneath their square-jawed facades, could be complex men driven by pride, anger, even deceit. Howard buys back into the myth of the astronaut as honorable

dullard. Even Hanks, with his jovial charisma, seems too much like *Hanks* to convince us he's playing a historical figure. There is more fear, passion, and lightning in Ed Harris's performance as Gene Kranz, the Mission Control commander who's trying to get the spacecraft back through sheer will, than there is in any of the astronauts. Harris takes chances; he surprises you in every scene. But Hanks's solid-guy performance is encased in nobility. You look at him now, and you know *exactly* what you're gonna get.

Entertainment Weekly

READER'S RESPONSE

1. If you have seen this film, tell whether you agree or disagree with the reviewer. Explain why.
2. Did you find the review interesting? What did you like or dislike about it? What do you think of the writer's sense of humor?

WRITER'S CRAFT

3. What strengths of the film does the writer point out? What weaknesses does the writer point out?
4. Does the writer give enough details from the film to support the opinions in the review? Give some examples.

> "A good critic is the sorcerer who makes some hidden spring gush forth unexpectedly under our feet."
>
> François Mauriac

Purposes for Writing About Literature

If you're writing for your school newspaper, you may already be writing reviews of popular books, films, and even television shows. In class assignments, you'll often be asked to write a review, called a *literary analysis,* in which you analyze works you study, such as poems, plays, novels, and short stories. There are many different purposes for writing about literature and nonprint media. Here are some examples.

- in a journal entry, expressing why a book has special meaning for you
- in a letter to a friend, explaining why you've rented the same video fifteen times
- in a college entrance essay, expressing how the books you've read have shaped your life
- in a letter to the editor, encouraging members of the community to boycott a certain TV show
- in a letter to the school board, asking them to purchase certain books for the school library
- in a paper for your English class, analyzing the theme of a novel
- in a workplace memo, informing your coworkers about a book you think they might like to read
- in a notice for the library bulletin board, giving brief summaries of new books
- in a script for a skit, spoofing an eyewitness report from a television newscast
- in a poem, describing how you were affected by a short story you read when you were younger

In this chapter you will learn how to write a literary analysis of a story or stories. In an analysis you examine the elements, or parts, of the story to gain a deeper understanding of it. In turn, this knowledge will enhance your own personal feelings toward the work, regardless of whether the story makes you laugh or cry or even bores you to the last page.

LOOKING
AHEAD

In the main assignment in this chapter you'll write a literary analysis. Its basic purpose will be to inform. As you work through this chapter, keep in mind that an effective literary analysis

- examines the work's separate elements—plot, character, setting, and so on
- provides support in the form of quotations and other details from the work
- has the characteristics of a well-developed composition

"Literature is news that stays news."
Ezra Pound

Writing a Literary Analysis

Reading and Responding to Stories

How does a movie critic review a movie? By watching the movie. The critic may first have strong feelings about the film. It may be the best film ever made, or the critic may want to walk out before the ending. But that's not the critic's job. The critic is there to write a critical analysis—to explain to an audience what makes the movie tick. It's the same when you read a story. Your first reaction is a personal response. Then you may move on to a critical analysis.

Responding to Stories

Did you ever think that writers need you? Well, they do. Any story is just words on a page until some real live person starts reading it—and thinking about it, feeling it, watching the events unfold.

And that's precisely where you start—with your own personal response. Does a character make you furious or give you the creeps? Do you find a scene laugh-out-loud funny, goose-bump scary, or just plain dull? Do you like the story, hate it, or just feel lukewarm?

As you read the following story, start with your personal response. Tune in to your own thoughts, feelings, and memories.

A SHORT STORY

A Man Who Had No Eyes
by MacKinlay Kantor

A beggar was coming down the avenue just as Mr. Parsons emerged from his hotel.

He was a blind beggar, carrying the traditional battered cane, and thumping his way before him with the cautious, half-furtive effort of the sightless. He was a shaggy, thick-necked

fellow; his coat was greasy about the lapels and pockets, and his hand splayed over the cane's crook with a futile sort of clinging. He wore a black pouch slung over his shoulder. Apparently he had something to sell.

The air was rich with spring; sun was warm and yellowed on the asphalt. Mr. Parsons, standing there in front of his hotel and noting the *clack-clack* approach of the sightless man, felt a sudden and foolish sort of pity for all blind creatures.

And, thought Mr. Parsons, he was very glad to be alive. A few years ago he had been little more than a skilled laborer; now he was successful, respected, admired. . . . Insurance. . . . And he had done it alone, unaided, struggling beneath handicaps. . . . And he was still young. The blue air of spring, fresh from its memories of windy pools and lush shrubbery, could thrill him with eagerness.

He took a step forward just as the tap-tapping blind man passed him by. Quickly the shabby fellow turned.

"Listen, guv'nor. Just a minute of your time."

Mr. Parsons said, "It's late. I have an appointment. Do you want me to give you something?"

"I ain't no beggar, guv'nor. You bet I ain't. I got a handy little article here"—he fumbled until he could press a small object into Mr. Parsons's hand—"that I sell. One buck. Best cigarette lighter made."

Mr. Parsons stood there, somewhat annoyed and embarrassed. He was a handsome figure with his immaculate gray suit and gray hat and malacca stick. Of course the man with the cigarette lighters could not see him. . . . "But I don't smoke," he said.

"Listen. I bet you know plenty people who smoke. Nice little present," wheedled the man. "And, mister, you wouldn't mind helping a poor guy out?" He clung to Mr. Parsons's sleeve.

Mr. Parsons sighed and felt in his vest pocket. He brought out two half dollars and pressed them into the man's hand.

"Certainly, I'll help you out. As you say, I can give it to some-one. Maybe the elevator boy would—" He hesitated, not wish-ing to be boorish and inquisitive, even with a blind peddler. "Have you lost your sight entirely?"

The shabby man pocketed the two half dollars. "Fourteen years, guv'nor." Then he added with an insane sort of pride: "Westbury, sir. I was one of 'em."

"Westbury," repeated Mr. Parsons. "Ah, yes. The chemical explosion. . . . The papers haven't mentioned it for years. But at the time it was supposed to be one of the greatest disasters in—"

"They've all forgot about it." The fellow shifted his feet wearily. "I tell you, guv'nor, a man who was in it don't forget about it. Last thing I ever saw was C shop going up in one grand smudge, and gas pouring in all the busted windows."

Mr. Parsons coughed. But the blind peddler was caught up with the train of his one dramatic reminiscence. And, also, he was thinking that there might be more half dollars in Mr. Par-son's pocket.

"Just think about it, guv'nor. There was a hundred and eight people killed, about two hundred injured, and over fifty of them lost their eyes. Blind as bats—" He groped forward until his dirty hand rested against Mr. Parsons's coat. "I tell you, sir, there wasn't nothing worse than that in the war. If I had lost my eyes in the war, okay. I would have been well took care of. But I was just a workman, working for what was in it. And I got it. You're right I got it, while the capitalists were making their dough! They was insured, don't worry about that. They—"

"Insured," repeated his listener. "Yes. That's what I sell—"

"You want to know how I lost my eyes?" cried the man. "Well, here it is!" His words fell with the bitter and studied drama of a story often told, and told for money. "I was there in C shop, last of all the folks rushing out. Out in the air there was a chance, even with buildings exploding right and left. A lot of guys made it safe out the door and got away. And just when I was about there, crawling along between those big vats, a guy behind me grabs my leg. He says, 'Let me past, you—!' Maybe he was nuts. I dunno. I try to forgive him in my heart, guv'nor. But he was bigger than me. He hauls me back and climbs right over me! Tramples me into the dirt. And he gets out, and I lie there with all that poison gas pouring down on all sides of me, and flame and stuff. . . ." He swallowed—a studied sob—and stood dumbly expectant. He could imagine the next words: *Tough luck, my man. Now, I want to—* "That's the story, guv'nor."

The spring wind shrilled past them, damp and quivering.

"Not quite," said Mr. Parsons.

The blind peddler shivered crazily. "Not quite? What do you mean, you–?"

"The story is true," Mr. Parsons said, "except that it was the other way around."

"Other way around?" He croaked unamiably. "Say, guv'nor—"

"I was in C shop," said Mr. Parsons. "It was the other way around. You were the fellow who hauled back on me and climbed over me. You were bigger than I was, Markwardt."

The blind man stood for a long time, swallowing hoarsely. He gulped: "Parsons. I thought you—" And then he screamed fiendishly: "Yes. Maybe so. Maybe so. But I'm blind! I'm blind, and you've been standing here letting me spout to you, and laughing at me every minute! I'm blind!"

People in the street turned to stare at him.

"You got away, but I'm blind! Do you hear? I'm—"

"Well," said Mr. Parsons, "don't make such a row about it, Markwardt. . . . So am I."

EXERCISE 1 ▶ Responding to a Story

Were you ready for those last three words? What's your personal response to "A Man Who Had No Eyes"? Take a few minutes to write in your journal. Here are some questions to get you started. Did you like the way the story ended? Or did you feel tricked? How do you feel about Parsons and Markwardt?

Understanding the Basic Elements of Stories

With many stories, you just stop with personal response. And that's good. However, there are times when you need to go beyond those personal feelings. Perhaps the story fascinates you for some reason, and you find yourself thinking about it more carefully. More often, however, you'll be reading more closely (more critically) because you've been given a class assignment. You have to prepare for a class discussion, or you have to write a literary analysis.

To go beyond your personal response, you have to know more about what makes a story a story. You need a basic understanding of the elements of a story—those features writers use to create stories. When you write a literary analysis, you'll base it on one or more of these elements.

Here are the elements you can use to analyze a story. These elements let you look inside a story so you can talk about it clearly and specifically.

Plot.   *Plot* is most simply what happens in a story—the unfolding events. And what sets a plot in motion are the conflicts, or problems, that the main character or characters face. In an *external conflict,* a character struggles against another person (or people), nature, society, or chance. In an *internal conflict,* a character's struggle is within himself or herself.

The *climax* of a story—usually the most exciting or tense scene—is the moment when the main conflict is settled, one way or another. In a story with a *surprise,* or *twist, ending,* the climax may end the story.

Setting.   A story's *setting* is its time and place. It includes such details as the weather, the landscape, buildings, and streets. Setting can be important in at least three ways. It may provide background for understanding characters and events, create the conflict (think of a wide river that a swimmer must cross), or create the *mood,* a story's emotional effect (think of an ancient, spooky house).

Characters. *Characters* are the individuals in a story, whether people, animals, angels, or robots. Besides simply telling readers what a character is like, writers have other methods of making characters real and vivid. They can reveal personality through a character's *appearance, speech, thoughts,* and *actions,* and also through *effects on other characters* (how others respond to and talk about the character).

In analyzing characters, also keep in mind these two good questions: (1) What is the character's *motivation* for an action? (2) Does the character change in the story, and how?

Point of view. In everyday conversation, point of view means the way you look at things, and in literature its meaning is similar: *Point of view* is the vantage point, or position, from which a writer tells a story. It's important because it determines what—and how much—readers are told.

In *first-person point of view,* the narrator is a character in the story. This narrator speaks as *I* (the first-person pronoun) and can tell readers only what he or she *personally* sees, hears, thinks, and imagines. A first-person narrator may not know, or tell, everything.

In the *third-person point of view,* the narrator uses third-person pronouns—*he, she, them,* and so on. This narrator may vary in how much he or she can enter into the thoughts of the characters, telling as much or as little as the writer wants. Some third-person narrators restrict themselves to the mind of just one character.

As you read the story, remember that the author isn't telling it—one of these narrators is. And that's important. Is the narrator telling the whole truth? Is he or she trying to hide something from you?

Theme. *Theme* is an important idea about life or human nature that is shown in a story. You might think of theme as what the story "says" to you, its message or point. A theme is more than one word—like *friendship.* It's an idea—like *Sometimes you have to hurt friends to help them.* Sometimes the writer doesn't state the theme directly.

CRITICAL THINKING

Analyzing a Short Story

When you write about literature, you're usually analyzing it: looking closely at a story's different parts and how they fit together. That's why active reading is so valuable. When you read actively, you're already starting to pay attention to some story parts, or elements—the characters, for example.

Actually, you analyze many familiar things this way—even a favorite team's football plays: what worked and what went wrong. On the job, you might analyze a procedure to see how to streamline it. By analyzing, you come to a better understanding.

CRITICAL THINKING EXERCISE:
Analyzing a Short Story

Working with some other students, use these questions to analyze "A Man Who Had No Eyes," page 330. If you have trouble with a question, remember that you can review the discussion of story elements (pages 334–335), and you can go back to the story. Listen to and discuss everyone's ideas—you may not all agree.

1. **Plot:** What important conflicts—external and internal—do the two characters face? What is the story's climax, the outcome of the central conflict?
2. **Setting:** Where and when does the story take place? Does the setting help explain characters and events, cause a conflict, set a mood? Does the setting change at any point? (Hint: Think about the weather.)
3. **Character:** What are the two characters like? (Think about appearance, speech, thoughts, actions, and the reactions of other characters.)
4. **Point of view:** Is the point of view first person or third person? If it's third person, is the narrator restricted just to the thoughts of one character? Or does the narrator go into the minds of both characters? How does this point of view affect what you know or feel about the characters and their actions?
5. **Theme:** What point about life or people does the story seem to make?

WRITING
ASSIGNMENT

PART 1:
Choosing a Story to Read

Find a story that seems interesting to you. It may be one you've read before or one your teacher recommends. Read it once just for enjoyment. When you've finished your reading, jot down your personal responses in your journal. What do you find interesting about the story? Do you think it's a good story?

Structuring Your Literary Analysis

There are two ways to structure a literary analysis. You can examine individual elements within a story, or you can compare and contrast elements.

Examining Individual Elements.   You can examine one or more individual elements within a story. Here are three examples of literary analyses with this structure.

1. "The Birds," by Daphne du Maurier, is a story about a family living on a farm that is attacked by birds. You might analyze the *plot* in this story. At what point is it obvious that there will be a conflict between the people and the birds? When does the conflict build? When does the outcome become definite?

2. "The Scarlet Ibis," by James Hurst, is a story about a young boy who has a brother named Doodle, who cannot walk. The boy is so ashamed of Doodle that he's determined to teach Doodle to walk. In a terrible thunderstorm, the brother runs away from Doodle. You might analyze the *theme* in this story. Doodle's brother is cruel to him and is ashamed of him and yet loves him at the same time. Is that true of human nature and love?

3. "The Cask of Amontillado" is a horror story by Edgar Allan Poe. As in most Poe stories, the *setting* adds to the feeling of horror. In a literary analysis, you might examine the sights, sounds, and smells that are part of the frightening setting. What effect do they have on the characters? on the plot?

In this type of literary analysis, your teacher might also ask you to examine more than one element within a story. In "The Scarlet Ibis," for example, the first-person narrator is Doodle's own brother. You can increase your understanding of the story by looking at how his role as narrator adds to the theme.

Comparing and Contrasting Elements. Another way to structure a literary analysis is to compare and contrast two elements within a single story or two elements in two different stories. You must be sure, however, that the two elements share some important feature. Here are examples of literary analyses you can structure this way.

1. "A Man Who Had No Eyes" and Guy de Maupassant's famous story "The Necklace" both have surprise, or twist, endings. ("The Necklace" is about a poor woman who loses what she believes is a valuable necklace.) You can compare and contrast the endings of the two stories. Do the authors use the surprise endings to make similar statements about human nature?

2. "A Man Called Horse" is about a young man from New England who is captured by members of the Crow nation. At first, he is treated like a horse and used as a slave. Later, he becomes a member of the Crows. You can compare and contrast Horse before and after his acceptance by the Crows. How does he change? What does he learn about himself?

3. In Pearl Buck's story "The Old Demon," an old woman who lives in a farming village is faced with two conflicts—one from the threat of a flood and the other from a Japanese enemy. You can compare and contrast how the woman deals with these two conflicts. What do they say about her character and about human nature?

WRITING
ASSIGNMENT

PART 2:
Thinking About Structure

Look at the story you chose for Writing Assignment, Part 1 (page 337). Does any element stand out that you might examine in a literary analysis? Are there two similar elements that you might compare and contrast? Do you know of another similar story that might be compared and contrasted with your first one? Don't make a definite decision now. Just let some ideas play around in your mind. Jot your ideas down on a sheet of paper.

Prewriting

Developing Your Literary Analysis

Deciding how to develop and focus your analysis involves several steps:

1. reading one or two stories closely
2. choosing one or two elements for analysis
3. identifying a main idea
4. thinking about your purpose, audience, and tone

Reading Stories Closely

You can't analyze a story until you've studied it carefully. Here are the strategies for close reading:

1. Read the story a second time, more slowly and thoughtfully than before.
2. As you read, make predictions about what will happen next.
3. Look up unfamiliar words and expressions.
4. Try to figure out the writer's purpose. Is there some point the writer is trying to make?
5. Ask yourself questions about each of the elements—plot, characters, setting, point of view, and theme. (See page 337 for questions you can ask.)

It's a good idea to take notes as you do your close reading. Here are one writer's notes for a close reading of "A Man Who Had No Eyes."

CLOSE READING NOTES

What do I think will happen next?	*When Mr. Parsons learns that it was Markwardt who almost killed him, I thought he would be angry at Markwardt. Why isn't he?*
What are some words I don't know or questions I have?	*Why does the narrator call Markwardt "half-furtive"? Why does Markwardt use the word <u>guv'nor</u>? Is this a British story? Why is this story called "A Man Who Had No Eyes"? Aren't there two blind men in this story?*
What does the writer's purpose seem to be?	*Markwardt almost killed Parsons to get out, but it's Parsons who makes a success out of his life. Is the author saying something about how we have to make our own way in life, even when someone else hurts us?*
What do I notice about characters, setting, and point of view?	*This story's definitely got a surprise ending. And the characters are alike in one way, but they're both very different—they were both blinded in the same explosion, and one made his way in life afterwards and one didn't. I guess the "eyes" in the title means the way you look at life as well as your eyesight. The narrator tells us a little bit about Parsons's thoughts, but not much. That's why the ending's such a surprise.*

EXERCISE 2 ▶ **Speaking and Listening: Reading Actively**

Read "A Man Who Had No Eyes" again—out loud—with three or four classmates. Have one person read a few paragraphs. Next, have the next person tell some active-reading thoughts. Then, have the next person give an additional thought. Keep on until you've finished the story.

PART 3:
Reading Your Story Critically

Now that you've allowed yourself time for a personal response to the story you've chosen, look at it more closely and critically. Read the story again, this time using the strategies for close reading. Take notes as you read. You can use the Here's How notes on page 341 as a guide for your own.

Choosing Story Elements for Analysis

After your close reading, the next step is to decide which element or elements to analyze. For many school assignments, your teacher will identify the element. But if you decide, how do you make the decision? First, start with what interests you. As you were reading the story, did you think the cliff-hanger plot was great or the characters were just like people you know? Then, think about what elements seem to be important in the story. Perhaps the point of view doesn't seem to be very important, but the characters are complex and striking.

Identifying Your Main Idea

You've almost focused your literary analysis. Now you're ready to decide on your main idea. For example, you've decided you're going to write about the element of theme in "The Scarlet Ibis." Your main idea might be "The theme of this story is that we are sometimes ashamed of and cause pain to people we love." Or you might compare and contrast the two characters in "A Man Who Had No Eyes." Your main idea might be "Even though both men are sightless, only one man has no eyes."

PART 4:
Focusing Your Literary Analysis

It's hard to make a final decision, but decide now about the elements you'll examine or the elements you'll compare and contrast in your literary analysis. Then, write a sentence or two that states your main idea.

Thinking About Audience, Purpose, and Tone

When you write a literary analysis, your purpose is to analyze the story by examining its elements. With this purpose in mind, you won't go off the track in two common ways: (1) writing just a summary of the plot, or (2) writing only your personal reaction. Your goal is to give readers a richer understanding of the story by examining parts of it closely.

When you write an analysis, assume that your audience has read the story. (Remember, your audience is probably your teacher and your classmates.) To understand your ideas, these readers need story details as examples, but not a whole retelling of the story.

The tone in essays about literature is fairly formal—which doesn't mean it can't be lively. If you're excited about a story, you can certainly show your excitement. Just be sure your tone shows careful thought about the literature. That way your readers will take you seriously while they also enjoy what you have to say.

EXERCISE 3 ▶	Thinking About Purpose, Audience, and Tone

You're writing a literary analysis of the plot in "A Man Who Had No Eyes" for your teacher and classmates. With your purpose, audience, and tone in mind, which of these items would you *not* include in your analysis?

1. "A Man Who Had No Eyes" is about these two guys who both lose their eyesight in a bad accident. What actually happens is that Markwardt almost killed Parsons in the accident.
2. The surprise ending of "A Man Who Had No Eyes" depends on the point of view. The narrator must keep from the reader until the end the fact that Parsons, too, was blinded in the explosion.
3. Boy! I really liked this story. English would be a lot better if we could read more stories like this one.
4. There's no indication until the end that Parsons cannot see. When Markwardt tries to sell Parsons a lighter, the narrator says only, "Of course the man with the cigarette lighters could not see him."

 *Prewriting*

Collecting and Organizing Details

Collecting Details. When you're writing about literature, your support comes *from the literature itself*. If you say that a setting causes a depressing mood, then you must find details that show this to readers. You have to *prove* to your readers that your ideas are sound. Reread the story to support your ideas. You can use plot events, dialogue, and details of all kinds—like a description of setting. To present the evidence, you can quote, paraphrase, or summarize. Just be sure you use something specific from the story for each idea. Here are some notes for "A Man Who Had No Eyes."

 **HERE'S HOW**

"A Man Who Had No Eyes"	
Idea	*Support*
Parsons seems snobby and selfish.	nice clothes, rich from insurance, "annoyed and embarrassed" by beggar
Markwardt seems pitiful.	greasy clothes, "shabby," blind and helpless (can't work) after accident
Narrator holds back facts and makes us think a certain way.	Starts story with "Mr. Parsons" and "a blind beggar." We think <u>Parsons</u> is watching a beggar.

 WRITING NOTE There's no rule about how many details you need to support a point. You may use only one, you may use more—whatever makes your idea *clear* and *convincing*. At this stage, though, you're wise to gather as much support as you can. You can choose the best examples later. Also, be sure that any quotations are exact (word for word), so you don't have to recheck them later.

Organizing Details. How you organize details depends on the structure of your literary analysis. If you are discussing plot, for example, you may use a *chronological* organization. But if you're analyzing character, you might use *order of importance*, beginning with the character's most (or least) important trait. These patterns can also help you order ideas if you plan to compare and contrast elements. You might want to set up a chart like the following one.

HERE'S HOW

Comparing and Contrasting the Characters		
	Parsons	*Markwardt*
Appearance	"still young"; "handsome figure"; clean suit and stick	carrying cane; shaggy; greasy coat; "half-furtive"; shabby
Speech	"correct" English —"Well, . . . don't make such a row about it . . . "	slang; wheedling talk; "incorrect" English—"I ain't no beggar, guv'nor"; "poor guy"
Attitude	pity for the blind; "glad to be alive"; "still young"; buys lighter even though he doesn't smoke	feels sorry for himself: " . . . mister, you wouldn't mind helping a poor guy out?"; "They've all forgot about it."

WRITING ASSIGNMENT

PART 5:
Collecting and Organizing Details

Now reread the story. Write down quotations, story details, and plot events to use as examples in your paper. (You may want to use note cards.) Then, organize your ideas in the order you'll discuss them, by making an outline or by setting up a chart like the one above. Use quotations from the story as well as ideas in your own words.

Writing Your First Draft

You should now have a nicely detailed plan for your essay. The next step is putting that plan into the sentences, paragraphs, and form of an essay.

You'll need an *introduction* that (1) tells readers the title and author of your story or stories and (2) includes your main idea. A literary analysis doesn't have to have a flashy introduction, but you still want to interest readers.

The *body* of your essay comes from your outline or chart. In the body, you present and develop your ideas about the story or stories.

The *conclusion* brings your essay to a close. Two good ways to end an analysis are by (1) restating your main idea—bringing the focus back to it, and (2) summarizing your points—gathering in one paragraph the ideas you developed in the essay's body.

Here's a model analysis that compares and contrasts the two characters in "A Man Who Had No Eyes." The analysis might also have analyzed the plot with its surprise ending, or it might have analyzed the point of view. This writer, however, found distinct differences between two men who were so similar in one important way.

A WRITER'S MODEL

**INTRODUCTION—
Author and
title of story**

Story details

MacKinlay Kantor's "A Man Who Had No Eyes" begins "on a warm spring day." On that day, two sightless men—Parsons and Markwardt—meet in front of a hotel. At the beginning of the story, the reader does not know that Parsons cannot see. That lack of knowledge makes the differences between the two men seem even more distinct. It isn't until the end of the story that the reader learns that Parsons, too, is blind.

Main idea

By then, the reader knows that even though both men are sightless, only one cannot see.

First point of comparison— appearance

Quotations from story

The two men are obviously different in appearance. Although Parsons carries a "malacca stick," he gives no evidence of being blind. He is a "handsome figure with his immaculate gray suit." Markwardt, on the other hand, carries the "traditional battered cane" and is dressed in a "greasy" coat.

Second point of comparison— speech

Quotations from story

The speech of the two men also points up their differences. Parsons speaks with dignity, like an educated man: "It's late. I have an appointment. Do you want me to give you something?" Markwardt, however, speaks in a wheedling tone, using slang and words that show his self-pity: "And, mister, you wouldn't mind helping a poor guy out?" His self-pity is carried to an extreme when he speaks about the explosion when he was "just a workman, working for what was in it."

Third point of comparison— attitudes

Quotations from story

Story details

Story details

Parsons and Markwardt both have different attitudes toward life. Parsons, though blind, has made a success of his life by selling insurance. "A few years ago," the narrator says, "he had been little more than a skilled laborer; now he was successful, respected, admired. . . ." But Markwardt is little more than a beggar who wants others to feel sorry for him. It's almost as though he believes the story that he tells Parsons about the man who, during the explosion, "hauls me back and climbs right over me!"

CONCLUSION

Restatement of main idea

At the beginning of the story, when the two men first meet, the air is "rich with spring." Later, when Markwardt is telling his lie, the wind becomes "damp and quivering." It's obvious that the memory of the explosion and Markwardt's role in it are painful for Parsons to remember. In spite of that, however, Parsons has gone on to make a success of his life. In contrast, Markwardt—as his appearance, speech, and attitude show—has allowed his self-pity to dominate him. In this story, both men are sightless. But Markwardt is "A Man Who Had No Eyes."

A Simple Framework for a Literary Analysis

It's helpful to follow a simple framework when you're writing a literary analysis. You could use the first framework that follows if you were writing about a single element in a story. You could use either of the other two frameworks if you were comparing and contrasting elements in one or two stories.

SINGLE ELEMENT FRAMEWORK

Introduction (statement of main idea)

Main Point 1

Main Point 2

Main Point 3 (and so on)

Conclusion (restatement or summary of main idea)

COMPARISON AND CONTRAST FRAMEWORKS

POINT BY POINT	BLOCK
Introduction (statement of main idea about *A* and *B*)	Introduction (statement of main idea about *A* and *B*)

Main Point 1
  Discussion of *A*
  Discussion of *B*
	Discussion of *A*
	  Main Point 1
	  Main Point 2
	  Main Point 3

Main Point 2
  Discussion of *A*
  Discussion of *B*
	Discussion of *B*
	  Main Point 1
	  Main Point 2
	  Main Point 3

Main Point 3
  Discussion of *A*
  Discussion of *B*
	Conclusion (restatement or summary of main idea)

Conclusion (restatement or summary of main idea)	

WRITING NOTE The writer's model on pages 346–347 uses the *point-by-point* method of development. As you can see, the writer compares each point—appearance, speech, and attitude—for both Parsons and Markwardt. Using the *block method* of comparison and contrast, the writer would have described the appearance, speech, and attitude of Parsons and then the appearance, speech, and attitude of Markwardt.

WRITING ASSIGNMENT

PART 6:
Writing Your First Draft

You've worked hard to read closely and to collect and organize support for your ideas. Now put your writing plan into action. Following your outline or chart, write a rough draft of your literary analysis.

Reminder

As you draft your literary analysis, make sure it has

- an introduction that includes author(s), title(s), and main idea
- a body that presents your main points and gives specific support from the stories
- transitions to move readers from one point to the next
- a conclusion that restates your main idea or summarizes your main points

---

"The difficulty of literature is not to write, but to write what you mean."

Robert Louis Stevenson

Evaluating and Revising

No writer gets everything perfect the first time. When you're drafting, you have many things on your mind (you may even come up with new ideas), so the next step is a step back. Read your essay to see exactly what you said—evaluate and revise it.

Sometimes it helps to evaluate what someone else has written, too. This isn't something that happens only in school, by the way. Writers often analyze each other's work. In the following selection, African American writer Ralph Ellison describes how he spent his time during the recession of 1937, learning the craft of writing.

> I went to Dayton, Ohio, where my brother and I hunted and sold game to earn a living. At night I practiced writing and studied Joyce, Dostoevski, Stein, and Hemingway. Especially Hemingway; I read him to learn his sentence structure and how to organize a story. I guess many young writers were doing this, but I also used his description of hunting when I went into the fields the next day. I had been hunting since I was eleven, but no one had broken down the process of wing-shooting for me, and it was from reading Hemingway that I learned to lead a bird. When he describes something in print, believe him; believe him even when he describes the process of art in terms of baseball or boxing; he's been there.
>
> Ralph Ellison, *Writers at Work*

You can use the following chart to find weaknesses and ways to correct them. Ask yourself each question in the left-hand column of the chart. If you find a problem, use the revision technique in the right-hand column.

EVALUATING AND REVISING LITERARY ANALYSES

EVALUATION GUIDE	REVISION TECHNIQUE
1 Does the literary analysis reveal a close reading of the story?	**Replace** any incorrect details from the story.
2 Is the analysis suitable for its purpose, audience, and tone?	**Cut** plot details not related to your purpose. **Cut** informal expressions.
3 Does the introduction give the authors and titles of the stories? Does it include a main idea?	**Add** the authors and titles of the stories. **Add** a sentence (or **replace** an existing one) that states the main idea.
4 Does the body include enough support from the story for the writer's ideas?	**Add** quotations, story details, and plot events.
5 Is the essay's organization clear and consistent?	**Reorder** ideas so that the organization makes sense to the reader and is appropriate to the elements that are examined.
6 Does the conclusion bring the essay to a definite close?	**Add** a sentence or sentences (or **replace** existing ones) that restate your main idea or summarize existing points.

> **EXERCISE 4** ▶ **Analyzing a Writer's Revisions**

Here's the first draft of the third paragraph about "A Man Who Had No Eyes" (page 347). With several classmates, use the chart on page 351 to figure out why the writer made these changes. Then, answer the questions that follow.

∧ ~~The old guy~~ Parsons speaks with	**cut**
dignity, ~~you know,~~ like an educated man:	**cut**
⟨⟨It's late. I have an appointment. Do you	**add**
want me to give you something? ″⟩The	**add**
speech of the two men also points up their	**reorder**
differences. Markwardt, however, speaks in	
a wheedling tone, using slang and words	
"And, mister, you wouldn't mind helping a poor guy out?"	
that show his self-pity. His self-pity is	**add**
carried to an extreme when he speaks	
about the explosion when he was just a	**add**
workman, working for what was in it.″⟩	**add**

1. Why did the writer delete the words *The old guy* and *you know* from the first sentence?
2. Why did the writer add quotation marks to the second sentence?
3. Why did the writer move the third sentence? How does this change the organization of the paragraph?
4. Why did the writer add the words *And, mister, you wouldn't mind helping a poor guy out?* to the next-to-the-last sentence?
5. Why did the writer add quotation marks to the last sentence?

WRITING ASSIGNMENT

PART 7:
Evaluating and Revising Your Literary Analysis

Exchange papers with another student, and use the questions from the evaluation/revision chart on page 351 to evaluate each other's papers. Then, revise your paper.

Proofreading and Publishing

Proofreading. Now is the time to make sure your final revision is clean—free from distracting errors. A good plan for this essay is to proofread once as you usually do and then double-check quotation marks and the spelling of the names of characters, cities, and so on.

COMPUTER NOTE: Most spell-checkers flag proper nouns, but many let you skip over often-used proper nouns (such as the names of story characters) that are spelled correctly.

MECHANICS HINT

Using Quotation Marks

Put quotation marks before and after any words taken directly from a story. Sometimes you'll quote a passage that already contains quotation marks—a character's dialogue, for example. In a case like this, you have a quotation within a quotation, so you enclose the dialogue in single quotation marks.

EXAMPLES   *Quotation.* Parsons is **"**annoyed and embarrassed**"** by the beggar.

Quotation Within a Quotation. The last line brings the even bigger shock of Parsons's blindness: **"** 'Well,' said Mr. Parsons, 'don't make such a row about it, Markwardt. . . . So am I.' **"**

Remember that commas and periods always go inside quotation marks, whether double or single.

 REFERENCE NOTE: For more information on quotation marks, see pages 792–799.

Publishing.   You may think that students' essays about literature have a special and limited audience: the teacher. But, in fact, writing about literature has a very big potential audience: anyone who reads stories, novels, poems, and plays.

Part of the pleasure of *reading* literature is *talking about* it, and that's just what you've done—in written form—in your analysis. With your teacher's help, plan some special days for sharing papers. Here are two ideas for sharing your analysis.

- With your teacher's help, group together papers that analyze the same elements—papers that focus on setting, for example, or on characters or on plot. Read each group of essays aloud. Then compare and contrast them. What did you notice about how setting works in different stories? about different ways to analyze a character?
- Stage your own story review program. You might use the format of TV shows that give reviews of current movies. If possible, videotape your program to share with other classes.

PART 8:
Proofreading and Publishing Your Literary Analysis

After all the work on your analysis, don't neglect the finishing touches. Proofread your final draft carefully, correct any errors, and then share it with others.

 Reflecting on Your Writing

You may want to add your literary analysis to your **portfolio.** If so, date it and write a brief reflection by answering these questions.

- How did you choose which literary element to focus on?
- Did writing a literary analysis help you gain insights into writing or understanding literature? If so, how?

A STUDENT MODEL

Yolanda Doss offers you this advice about writing
a literary analysis: "Read and understand the
story thoroughly before you try to write about it.
And please take your time!" Yolanda, who attends
Fenger High School in Chicago, Illinois, writes about
two well-known story characters.

Studies in Contrast
by Yolanda Doss

"The Gift of the Magi" by O. Henry and "The
Necklace" by Guy de Maupassant are studies in
contrast between the egocentric, materialistic
Madame Loisel and the kind-hearted Della.

Madame Loisel was a pretty, middle-class
woman, obsessed with trying to be something she
wasn't. She was so obsessed that it made her a
greedy, ungrateful, and self-centered person,
caring for no one but herself. The result of her
materialism was ironic and tragic.

Della was an extremely sweet, caring, and
thankful young woman. Her personality was as
beautiful as her appearance. Della loved to give and appreciated anything she received in return. She sacrificed her most
prized possession for the sake of the man she loved, and he
did the same for her. Della was not obsessed with materialistic things and was very much satisfied with what she had.

Although both Della and Madame Loisel faced a need for
money, Madame Loisel wanted it for the things it could buy
her, while Della thought of money only as a means to show
her love to her husband.

WRITING WORKSHOP

A Definition

If you use comparison and contrast in a literary analysis, you're using one of the strategies in a kind of writing called *classification*. (This is what you see in the writer's model on pages 346–347.) **Classifying** is grouping together things that have common characteristics. In literature, for example, "story" is a classification whose members share the characteristics (or elements) of plot, characters, setting, and so on. "Poem" is a classification whose members share the characteristics (or elements) of rhythm, figurative language, and imagery.

Now, however, you'll try your hand at a different kind of classification: defining. You'll determine the characteristics that make up a certain kind of story. After all, there are all sorts of stories (some that you like better than others): The large classification of "story" includes such smaller classifications as "horror story," "adventure story," and "detective story."

As you read the following definition of detective stories, decide what characteristics define a detective story.

Ever since I read the Encyclopedia Brown stories in fifth grade (about a boy who solved every puzzle in his hometown), I've been hooked on detective stories. When I begin one, I can't wait to get to the end, but when I finish, I'm sorry it's over. What is it about detective stories that makes them so special?

First: murder. Actually, any crime will do, but murder is most common and most exciting. The story's plot must be a suspenseful, well-crafted one in which a crime is committed, a detective follows clues, and logic solves the case. It's very important, too, that readers learn all the clues that the detective does, so that they at least have a chance to be as smart as the detective.

The brilliant detective who misses nothing is, of course, the central character. The detective always sees much more than other characters—even when they're looking at the same things—and maybe that's why many detectives are so arrogant and impatient. Sherlock Holmes, who constantly makes fun of Scotland Yard inspectors, is the best example. But even if the detectives aren't as conceited as Holmes (Agatha Christie's Miss Marple is <u>very</u> polite), or even if they're police officers themselves (like P. D. James's Adam Dalgliesh), they make other people who try to solve the crime look pretty dim.

Besides off-the-track police, the story's other characters must include several likely suspects. Part of the fun of detective fiction is finding out that almost everyone has a good motive for committing the crime, even the "nice" characters that readers don't really want to suspect.

The settings can be anywhere, but at some point in the story, the setting almost always contributes to suspense or a feeling of danger. Big houses with lots of rooms (and especially a secret or locked room), towers and basements, dark streets, even trains—all these settings can be good ones because they're either ominous or create many possibilities for a sneaky, smart criminal.

Finally, when a detective story ends, everything is crystal clear and the crime is punished. All the

uncertainty and fear ends at the climax, when the criminal is revealed and caught. Detective fiction always carries a message that makes readers feel better: even though bad things do happen, bad people are never as smart as detectives.

1. According to the writer, what characteristics define detective stories?
2. What variations—differences—in detective stories does the writer mention?
3. Does the writer's definition seem accurate when you think of detective stories you've read? Why or why not?

Writing a Definition

Prewriting. What's your favorite kind of story? Do you like science fiction, horror, adventures, westerns, YA (young adult) fiction, or some other type? Choose one form, and list some particular stories. (You can use both novels—*long* stories—and short stories.) Then, decide what special characteristics the stories have in common. To help your thinking, focus on the story elements you studied in this chapter.

Writing, Evaluating, and Revising. A good way to organize a definition is to begin with the most important characteristic. As you write, use examples and refer to actual stories to make the characteristics clear and interesting. Also, point out variations when you need to—your definition doesn't have to be an ironclad rule. When you finish, have someone read your definition to look for missing characteristics, suggest other examples, and identify characteristics that are too narrow. Then revise.

Proofreading and Publishing. Proofread carefully to catch mistakes, and then let others read your definition. You might join with other students who have defined the same or a similar type of story to read and discuss your papers in a small group.

If you add your definition to your **portfolio,** date the definition and attach responses to these questions: How did you organize your definition? What did you learn about defining kinds of literature?

MAKING CONNECTIONS

WRITING ACROSS THE CURRICULUM

Creative Writing

You probably remember a short story that didn't end the way you wanted it to. The ending was a letdown, too sad, or too silly, and you said, "What *should* have happened is. . . ." Well, "A Man Who Had No Eyes" gives you a perfect chance to show your writing talents. What happens to Parsons and Markwardt? Does Markwardt change after his meeting with Parsons, or does he remain the same? Do you have a better idea for the ending than the author? Put what you've learned about stories into action, and write a new ending. Collaborate with someone else if you like.

INFORMING THROUGH EVALUATION

Writing a Review

A review not only tells you what a movie, play, or book is about, it also helps you decide whether to go see it or read it. That's because a good review does two things: It analyzes the elements of the book or movie, and it gives a judgment about it. Would you want to see the movie *Stand and Deliver* after reading the review below? Does reviewer Roger Ebert think the movie is good or not?

Stand and Deliver
by Roger Ebert

There were moments in *Stand and Deliver* that moved me very deeply, and other moments so artificial and contrived that I wanted to edit them out, right then and there. The result is a film that makes a brave, bold statement about an unexpected subject—but that lacks the full emotional power it really should have.

Olmos (left) with the real Escalante

Stand and Deliver tells the story of a high school mathematics teacher who takes a class of losers and potential drop-outs and transforms them, in the course of one school year, into kids who have learned so much that eighteen of them are able to pass a tough college credit calculus exam at the end of the year—an exam so hard that only two percent of students nationwide can pass it, although everyone in this class does.

The story is based on fact, on the life of Jaime Escalante, an actual East Los Angeles man who left a higher-paying job in business to return to education and prove something. What he proved is that motivation and hard work can rewrite the destinies of kids that society might be willing to write off.

Escalante, played in the film by Edward James Olmos, faces a disheartening challenge on the first day of school. His class is undisciplined, unmotivated, and rebellious. He doesn't confront them; he outflanks them. Adopting a weird sideways shuffle and a strange habit of talking to himself, he strikes them at first as simply bizarre; they stop making noise because they want to hear what foolish thing he'll say next.

Then he starts teaching, using examples out of the everyday lives of his students, making them think things out for themselves, announcing that the "punishment" for not working hard in class is to be banished from the class—a class most of the kids would rather be out of, anyway. The kids themselves are amazed that this strategy works, and more amazed still to find that they're expected to do thirty hours of homework a week, and come in on Saturday morning for extra classes.

All of this material is fine and strong. Not so fascinating, however, are the vignettes of student life outside the school. Some of these scenes are important to the story—as when we discover why it is so hard for some of the kids to find time for their homework—but others, including a high school romance, are simply marking time.

from *ROGER EBERT'S MOVIE HOME COMPANION 1990 EDITION*

Now try your hand at writing a review about a movie you've really liked. You might mention enough about the plot and the characters (as reviewer Ebert does) to get your readers really interested.

Exploring Your World

Research is a way of **exploring the world,** of discovering what has been and what is. When you write a research report, you're sharing with others the worlds you've explored.

Writing and You. Reports of research are everywhere—in books, magazines, newspapers. Biographers share what they've learned about famous people. Scientists report on space, our brains, or the history of the earth. Reporters write about events at home and around the world. What have you learned recently that you would like to share?

As You Read. As you read Richard Wolkomir's research report, notice two things. How does he get your interest in the beginning? How does he let you know where he discovered the information he is sharing?

The stone giants on Easter Island, located in the South Pacific 2,400 miles west of Chile

The COLD FACTS

About Human Survival

by Richard Wolkomir

When rescuers pulled the two-year-old from a frigid creek near Salt Lake City, Utah, she had been underwater more than an hour. She was not breathing, and at 66 degrees F, her body temperature was some 30 degrees below normal.

Using resuscitation devices and a machine that gradually warmed her blood, doctors brought the little girl's temperature up to 77 degrees. Her heart, stimulated by the equipment, resumed pumping. Her pupils slowly began reacting to light. Eight weeks later, when she finally left the hospital, her only complication was a slight tremor. A year later, in 1988, pediatricians at the Primary Children's Medical Center in Salt Lake City reported the tremor was fading.

It seemed a medical impossibility. Indeed, had it not been for the numbing cold of the creek, chances are the toddler would not have survived. Physicians believe the 41-degree water chilled her, shutting down her metabolism and minimizing damage.

As scientists learn more about the ability of some animals to withstand cold, other researchers are making fascinating discoveries about the human body's own defense strategies when the mercury plummets. What they learn in the lab could mean the difference between life and death to a person left too long out in the cold.

> "... researchers are making fascinating discoveries about the human body's own defense strategies when the mercury plummets."

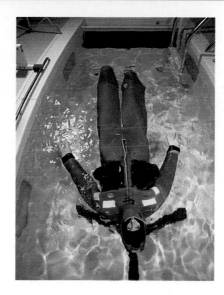

At the University of Minnesota Medical School in Duluth, physiologists wire sensors to volunteers—some frantically pedaling exercise bicycles in a chilled indoor pool, others splashing in icy Lake Superior or shivering in a refrigerated chamber—in an effort to study reactions to hypothermia, or extreme chilling. As they have found, our primary strategy for combating cold is a process called blood shunting.

"We have nerves designed to detect cold," says physiologist Lorentz Wittmers, director of the university's Hypothermia Laboratory. If our body cools below its normal 98.6 degrees, our cold detectors switch on. The brain commands the blood vessels to contract (a condition known as vasoconstriction), and less blood flows to the body's surface, keeping heat loss to a minimum. Meanwhile, warm blood shunts to the body's vital core.

"If the need arises," says physiologist Robert Pozos, the laboratory's former director, "blood flow to the finger, for example, can be reduced by 99 percent." But too little blood for too long can lead to frost-nipped skin, or frostbite, with tissues freezing perhaps to the bone. So the chilled body periodically dilates its blood vessels, sending a surge of warmth and oxygen to the freezing extremities.

Another defense is shivering, involuntary muscle contractions that generate heat. "Once it was thought shivering was controlled by the hypothalamus in the brain," notes David Israel, a researcher at the lab. "But now we're finding that the spinal cord has an effect, too."

Surprisingly, physical fitness often *reduces* resistance to cold. Says Wittmers, "Athletes don't handle cold so well because they've trained their bodies to be more efficient heat dissipators." Grant Gwinup, a researcher at the University of California at Irvine, has found that while most athletes burn away fat—the body's natural insulation—swimmers gain back whatever they lose. Because water absorbs 32 times more heat from the body than does air, he says, swimmers compensate for the loss with increased appetite.

Cold water also triggers what's known as the "mammalian dive reflex," an involuntary reaction that probably helped save the Utah toddler. Many people, especially children, respond to cold water on the face with a lower heart rate, higher blood pressure and reduced blood flow to all organs except the heart and brain. The response may be some sort of evolutionary vestige. "When a seal, beaver or other aquatic animal submerges, it stops breathing and its heart rate drops," says Wittmers. "Seals go from 100 beats per minute to just 6, reducing the heart's workload."

In children, the ratio of surface area to mass is large, so they chill quickly. Their metabolism drops, and therefore their cells demand much less oxygen. The effect on the body is similar to that of a car slowing to an idle: It uses less fuel.

National Wildlife Magazine

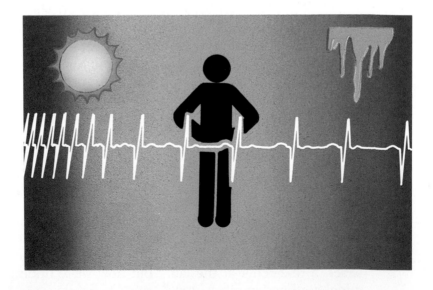

READER'S RESPONSE

1. Is the information in this article interesting to you? Do you learn anything about the body's responses to cold that you didn't know before?
2. Would you like to learn more about what happens to our bodies when they are subjected to extreme cold? What would you like to know?

WRITER'S CRAFT

3. How did Wolkomir attempt to get our attention in the beginning of the article? Was his attempt successful?
4. Wolkomir presents several facts in this article. What facts does he present about frostbite? about shivering? about athletes?
5. Wolkomir did not conduct original research (his own laboratory tests and experiments) on the body's reactions to cold. Where did he get his information? How do you know?

"It is better to ask some of the questions than to know all of the answers."

James Thurber

Ways to Develop Research

Report writing appears in ordinary magazines and newspapers, in scientific journals, in marketing reports for businesses, and even in speeches and ads. Some reports of research, like the article on pages 364–366, are informal. The readers of such articles don't expect detailed references to show where the writer got the information. Other reports—the ones you write in school and those in scientific journals—are more formal. Readers *do* expect to see exactly where the information came from.

But all reports have one thing in common. They present factual information to readers. Here are examples of how reports on research can be developed.

- in a report for biology class, writing a biographical report on a scientist's life
- in a report for earth science class, describing rock formations in the Grand Canyon
- in an essay for history class, describing an archaeological site in Arizona on the Navajo Indian Reservation
- in a report to the yearbook committee, relating the results of a search for a printing company
- in a paper for math class, reporting on a car's gas mileage
- in an article for the school newspaper, reporting on a series of tests to determine which brand of athletic shoes is most durable

LOOKING AHEAD

In the main part of this chapter, you'll learn how to write a formal research report. You'll use narration or classification to report the results of your research. Keep in mind that a formal research paper

- presents factual information about the topic
- presents information from several sources
- tells readers the source of the information

Writing a Research Paper

Prewriting

Finding a Topic for Your Report

Ideas for research subjects are all around you. You can find them by being curious about what you read, what you see, and what you hear.

Identifying a General Subject for Your Research

You may find ideas for research from books, from your own interests, or even from a casual conversation with your next-door neighbor. Here's a list of sources and some examples of subjects they might suggest to you.

SOURCES FOR SUBJECTS		
SOURCES	EXAMPLES	SUBJECTS
Hobbies and interests	an interest in computer games; a collection of baseball cards	computer color graphics; baseball records
Family and neighbors	a parent who is a nurse; a neighbor from Lithuania	nursing careers; life in Lithuania
Neighborhood and community	local jazz festival; an interesting building	jazz musicians; Victorian architecture
Books, magazines, and newspapers	"The First Shark: To Bite or Not to Bite" (*Science News*, Feb. 1996)	sharks; fossils; paleontology; ichthyology
Movies and television	*Toy Story;* "A History of U.S. 'Spy Machines'" (*NOVA*, PBS)	special effects in a movie; spies and spying

Limiting Your Subject to a Specific Topic

So much has been written about broad subjects such as "movies" or "sharks" that you could never read all of the material. The solution is to limit your subject to a specific topic, one you can explore in the specified time.

Most large subjects are made up of many smaller topics. For example, within the broad subject "sharks," you could identify these specific topics: feeding patterns of sharks, sharks in captivity, sharks in literature, and the economic importance of sharks. Here are some ways you can identify specific topics within a subject.

- Look up your subject in your library's card catalog or online catalog (a computerized version of the card catalog) or in the *Readers' Guide to Periodical Literature* or other electronic indexes. Notice the topics that are listed there.
- Find some books on your subject. Look through their tables of contents and indexes.
- Read an article about your subject in a print or CD-ROM encyclopedia. Many encyclopedias list related topics at the end of articles.
- Search the World Wide Web for pages or sites that contain keywords related to your subject.

Selecting a Suitable Topic

Don't think your work is finished just because you've thought of a limited topic. It may not be suitable for a research report. Not all topics will work equally well as topics for a research report. To select the best possible topic from all your ideas, choose one that

- *will inform your audience*—Your audience will want to learn something new or unusual.
- *is interesting*—Think of all the times you've switched TV channels because you were bored. It isn't quite as easy to switch topics once you're in the middle of a research project.
- *you can find information about*—The most interesting topic in the world can't be developed if there isn't enough information. When a topic is very recent or very technical—for instance, a medical breakthrough just announced—you may not be able to find much information about it.
- *will allow you to use outside sources*—A good research topic is developed from a variety of sources. "My experiences in Hurricane Zelda" has only one source: you.

EXERCISE **1** ▶ **Exploring Possible Subjects**

Get together with a small group and make a list of subjects for a research report. To get started, use the Sources for Subjects chart on page 369. For more ideas, look at the book titles on the nonfiction shelves in your library, or survey titles of documentary tapes in video stores.

EXERCISE **2** ▶ **Limiting Subjects to Specific Topics**

To practice finding specific topics, choose two of the subjects listed below. Then use the suggestions on page 370 to develop at least three specific topics from the subject.

1. the environment
2. the human brain
3. television
4. sports

PART 1

Identifying a Topic for Research

Choose a subject for your research report, either one your group identified in Exercise 1 or another subject that really interests you. Next, identify at least three specific topics from your subject. Then, using the guidelines on page 371, select one of these topics for your report.

Thinking About Purpose, Audience, and Tone

Purpose. The basic purpose of your research report is to inform your readers—to share the facts and details you've learned through your research. It's also an opportunity to share any insights or conclusions that you've reached. For example, imagine that you've discovered the following information through your research:

> Humpback whales communicate through "whale songs."
> New research suggests that whales are peaceful, friendly creatures.
> Whales have the largest brains on earth.

From these facts, you might conclude that "whales should be respected rather than feared." Your purpose would be to share the conclusion as well as the facts.

Audience. If your audience doesn't come away from your report with a better understanding of your topic, you haven't accomplished your purpose. As you research and write your report, ask yourself these questions about your audience.

1. Who will read my report?
2. What do my readers already know about my topic?
3. What information can I give my audience that will be surprising or new to them?
4. How can I be sure to give my audience complete information, not leaving out any important area my readers want to hear about?

Tone. A research report usually has a serious, fairly formal tone. If you've given serious thought to your topic, you also want your audience to think about it seriously.

WRITING NOTE At any point in your research, feel free to "step aside" and evaluate your progress. For example, you may find that your topic simply isn't working and that you need to change it. Or you may begin with two or three research questions and then find that you need to go in an entirely different direction. Changing or adding to your ideas is a natural and important part of the process.

EXERCISE 3 ▶ **Speaking and Listening: Analyzing Purpose and Audience**

Suppose that you're writing a report on the topic "Hispanic American contributions to the American Revolution." With a small group of classmates, discuss these questions about your purpose and audience. Your audience is a group of typical ninth-grade students.

1. Which of these pieces of information do you know? Which do you think your readers might know?
   a. During the 1500s, Spain established colonies in what is now the United States.
   b. Spaniards and Hispanic Americans played an important role during the American Revolution.
   c. Jorge Farragut—the father of the Civil War hero Admiral David Glasgow Farragut—was a Hispanic American who joined the Continental Army and became a major in the cavalry.
2. Junípero Serra, the founder of the Spanish missions in California, requested that each Spaniard contribute two pesos to the colonists' efforts against Britain. Would you need to define *pesos* for your audience?
3. In your opinion, the thirteen original colonies would not have been able to defeat the British without the aid of Hispanic Americans. Should you include this opinion in your report? Why or why not?

Junípero Serra

The Granger Collection, New York.

4. For the Bicentennial of the Declaration of Independence, in 1976, King Juan Carlos I of Spain presented a statue of General Bernardo de Gálvez to the United States. During the Revolutionary War, Gálvez captured five British forts and broke the rule of the British along the Mississippi River. Why might you want to mention this statue in your report?

Calvin & Hobbes copyright 1989 Watterson. Distributed by Universal Press Syndicate. Reprinted with permission. All rights reserved.

Developing Research Questions

Even if you have a specific topic in mind, doing research can sometimes seem like stumbling around in the dark. To give yourself a sense of direction as you begin your research, start with a list of questions.

The easiest way to develop research questions is to rely on your natural curiosity. What do *you* want to know about your topic? For example, for a report on "the role of African American soldiers in the Civil War," you might ask the following questions.

GENERAL QUESTIONS	QUESTIONS FOR A SPECIFIC TOPIC
1. What is the topic? (How can you define it?)	1. What exactly was the role of the African American soldier in the Civil War?
2. What groups, or classes, make up the topic?	2. What were the names of the individual African American regiments?
3. What are the topic's parts, and how do they work together?	3. What ranks did black soldiers hold, and how did they perform as a group?
4. How has the topic changed over time?	4. How did the role of African American soldiers change during the course of the war?
5. How is the topic similar to or different from related topics?	5. How did the role of black soldiers differ from that of white soldiers?
6. What are the topic's advantages or disadvantages?	6. What were the advantages to African Americans who chose a military career?

Reminder

To find a topic and begin your research

- preview resource materials to find a general subject
- limit the subject to a suitable topic
- stop to think about your purpose and your audience
- develop a list of research questions about your topic

PART 2:
Beginning Your Research

Use your curiosity and what you already know about the topic to begin your research. Start by thinking about your purpose and audience. Then, make a list of research questions, similar to the examples given above.

Prewriting

Finding and Evaluating Sources of Information

Now you're ready to look for up-to-date, reliable sources of information in your library and your community. You'll also have to decide which sources to use.

Locating Sources of Information

At one time (not so very long ago) you would have confined your research to print sources in the library. But that's not the case today. Your search for information can take you beyond books and magazines.

LIBRARY RESOURCES	
RESOURCE	**SOURCE OR INFORMATION**
Card catalog or online catalog	books listed by title, author, and subject; in some libraries this catalog also lists audiovisual materials— videotapes, records, CDs, audiotapes, filmstrips, and films
Readers' Guide to Periodical Literature	articles in magazines and journals
Microfilm or microfiche or online databases	indexes to major newspapers such as *The New York Times*, back issues of newspapers
Vertical file	pamphlets, news clippings
General and specialized reference books and CD-ROMs	encyclopedias (electronic or print), biographical references, atlases, almanacs
Videotapes and audiotapes	movies, documentaries, instructional tapes, audiotapes of books
Librarian	help in using reference materials and finding sources, including audiovisual materials

COMMUNITY RESOURCES	
RESOURCE	SOURCE OR INFORMATION
World Wide Web and online services	articles, interviews, bibliographies, pictures, videos, sound recordings
Local government agencies	facts and statistics on various subjects, information on local government policies, experts on local government
Local offices of state and federal government officials	voting records, recent or pending legislation, experts on state and federal government
Local newspaper offices	accounts of events of local interest, historical information on city or area
Museums and historical societies	historical events, scientific achievements, art and artists, special exhibits, and experts on these subjects
Schools and colleges	print and nonprint sources in libraries, experts on various subjects
Video stores	documentary and instructional videotapes and audiotapes

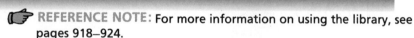 **REFERENCE NOTE:** For more information on using the library, see pages 918–924.

WRITING NOTE An important part of doing research is keeping track of your sources. Be sure to keep complete and accurate information about every source you use. This will help you let your readers know where you found your ideas and will also help you to avoid plagiarism. *Plagiarism* is using someone else's words or ideas as though they were your own. No matter how you use your sources (direct quotation, paraphrase, or summary), be sure to give credit to the person whose ideas you use. If you download material from a computer to your personal disk, do not simply cut and paste information onto your report. Remember to use quotation marks and to cite the source.

Evaluating Sources of Information

Not all information is equally helpful. To evaluate sources, ask yourself these questions.

1. *Does the information seem outdated?* Even historic topics, such as "the drafting of the Declaration of Independence," continue to be researched. Be sure that at least some of your sources are as up-to-date as possible.
2. *Does the information seem factual—reliable and accurate?* If the information in a source is inconsistent with your knowledge or with information from other sources, it may be inaccurate.
3. *Does the source seem objective and logical?* Some sources may be based on poor logic or slanted to one particular point of view. For example, an article by the president of the Organization of Believers in Unidentified Flying Objects would probably not give you objective information about UFOs.

☞ **REFERENCE NOTE:** For more information on sources such as the Internet and online CD-ROMs, see page 922.

Preparing Source Cards

If you've ever read something and then forgotten where you read it, you know why source cards are important. One method for keeping track of your sources is to write each one on a different 3″ × 5″ card (sometimes called a bibliography card). Another method is to create a separate computer file for each source.

No matter which method you choose, if you use the following guidelines to record the information, you'll have a head start on the final list of sources for your paper.

GUIDELINES FOR RECORDING SOURCE INFORMATION

1. **Book with One Author.** Write author's name, last name first; book title; place of publication; publishing company's name; and year of publication.
2. **Book with More Than One Author.** First author: write last name first. Other authors: first name first.
3. **Magazine Article.** Write author's name, last name first; article title; magazine name; day (if given), month, and year of publication; and beginning and ending page numbers. If no author, start with article title.
4. **Newspaper Article.** Write author's name, last name first; article title; newspaper name; day, month, and year of publication; section number (if there is one) and page number. If the newspaper has different editions (morning, afternoon), write the edition and *ed.* before the page number. If no author, start with article title. (Example: . . . New York Times 1 Aug. 1997, early ed., sec. A2.)
5. **Encyclopedia Article.** Write author's name, last name first; article title; encyclopedia name; and year of publication, followed by the abbreviation *ed.* If no author, start with article title.
6. **Radio or Television Program.** Write episode or segment title (if any); program name; series title (if any); network name; local station call letters and city (if any); and day, month, and year of broadcast.
7. **Film or Video.** Write title; director or producer; medium (for video recordings); distributor; and year of release.
8. **Personal or Telephone Interview.** Write interviewee's name; interview type (personal or telephone); and day, month, and year of interview.
9. **Electronic Materials.** Write author's name (if any); title (include publisher, date, and page numbers if material was first in a print source); date of posting (online); CD-ROM title or database title (if any, for online sources); type of source (*CD-ROM* or *Online*); location of source (*Internet,* online service, or city, if given, for CD-ROMs); distributor (CD-ROMs); date of publication (CD-ROMs) or access date; and Internet address (if any).

The following sample source cards show how the writer of the model research paper in this chapter recorded her sources. Pay particular attention to the way she used punctuation: This will be important when she prepares her final list of sources. Also notice that she numbered each source card. Later, when she is taking notes, she'll be able to identify the source by number.

HERE'S HOW

MacPherson, James M. <u>Marching Toward Freedom:</u>   1
    <u>Blacks in the Civil War 1861–1865</u>.
    New York: Facts on File, 1991.

Fincher, Jack. "The Hard Fight Was Getting into   2
    the Fight at All." <u>Smithsonian</u>
    Oct. 1990: 46–61.

"Black Soldiers." <u>Software Toolworks Multimedia</u   3
    <u>Encyclopedia</u>. CD-ROM. Novato: Grolier
    Electronic Publishing, 1992.

<u>The Civil War</u>. Dir. Ken Burns. Videocassette.   4
    PBS Video, 1990.

Grant, Linda. Telephone Interview. 26 April 1996.   5

MECHANICS HINT

Punctuating Titles

Underline the titles of books, magazines, newspapers, movies, television series, CDs, record albums, and audiotapes. Also underline titles of CD-ROMs, World Wide Web sites, and videotapes. (In print, this underlining appears as *italics*.)

> The television series <u>Dr. Quinn, Medicine Woman</u> features an actor who portrays a prairie doctor.

Put quotation marks around the titles of stories, articles, poems, individual TV episodes, and songs. But don't put quotation marks around the title of your own report.

> In his article "Honoring the Buffalo Soldiers," Roger J. Spiller discusses the dedication of a new memorial.

👉 **REFERENCE NOTE:** For more information on the punctuation of titles, see pages 789–790, 799.

When you prepare your source cards, be sure to

- record all the information accurately
- use punctuation and capitalization correctly
- follow the special guidelines for recording references

EXERCISE 4 ▶ **Using Library and Community Resources**

Working with a partner or small group, choose one of the following research questions. Identify four possible sources of answers to this question. Try to think of two library sources and two community sources. The sources you identify should be up-to-date, reliable, and specific, including titles, names, and so on.

1. What would be a healthful, low-calorie menu for lunch at various local fast-food restaurants? What fast-food dishes are lowest in fat, sugar, sodium, and cholesterol? [Hint: Ask at fast-food restaurants for nutrition guides. Talk with home economics, health, or science teachers.]
2. What are some opportunities for teenage volunteers in your city or rural area? What contributions are teenage volunteers making in your community? [Hint: Check with religious and volunteer groups. Check your telephone directory for a volunteer hot-line number.]

PART 3:
Locating Sources of Information

Working alone or with a research partner, answer the following questions on sources of information about your topic. Don't stop until you've identified at least five or six sources of reliable, up-to-date information.

1. How many books on your topic are listed in your library's catalog? What are two titles?
2. Does your library have any pamphlets on your topic? (Check the vertical file.)
3. Does a keyword search of the World Wide Web return Internet addresses for sites containing information on your subject? What are the names of the sites?
4. Does your community have any other sources of information on your topic? If so, what are they?

PART 4:
Preparing Source Cards

Use the guidelines on page 379 to prepare a card for each of your sources of information.

Prewriting

Planning, Recording, and Organizing Information

With your sources in hand, you have three major tasks at this point. You need to develop a plan, collect information, and organize it.

Preparing an Early Plan

You'll save time in the long run if you take a little time right now to plan. For example, after some preliminary reading about the role of African American soldiers in the Civil War, one writer developed this early plan.

> *Forgotten Heroes*
>
> *History of African American soldiers*
>   *Early in war*
>   *1862*
>   *1863*
>
> *Discrimination*
>
> *Heroism*
>
> *Effects on society*
>   *Attitude of Northerners*
>   *Pride and self-respect*
>   *Drive for civil rights*

With this kind of plan in hand, the writer was able to focus the rest of her research. Knowing what to look for helped her research to go smoothly.

Taking Notes

You may have a great memory for details. Still, you're not going to be able to remember everything you read about your topic. But if you take good notes, you'll have a record of the important information when it's time to sit down and draft your report.

HINTS FOR TAKING NOTES

1. Use 4″ × 6″ note cards, $8\frac{1}{2}$″ × 11″ paper folded in half, or computer files.
2. Use a separate note card or computer file for each item of information and for each source.
3. Put a heading of two or three key terms in the upper left-hand corner for each note.
4. Write the source number in the upper right-hand corner and the page numbers at the bottom.
5. Keep computer printouts in a folder. Highlight keywords and make notes in the margin.

When you take notes, you can *quote directly, summarize,* or *paraphrase.* Here are three different ways to record notes on the same passage.

Direct Quotation.   If the author has an especially good way of saying something, you may want to quote him or her. Be sure to copy the author's exact words, using the same capitalization and punctuation marks. To avoid plagiarism, put quotation marks at the beginning and end of any quoted passage.

Direct Quotation

African American Soldiers	1

"Even as black troops were fighting for their freedom and their country, they also had to struggle for fair treatment and equal rights within the army itself, for black soldiers were often victims of discrimination. African American regiments were sometimes issued inferior guns and ammunition and black soldiers were assigned more than their share of heavy labor and fatigue duty."

p. 91

Summary. A *summary note* includes only the main ideas and the most important supporting ideas. Shorter than the original material, it allows you to save space. Write the note in your own words and sentence structure. Most of your notes will be summary notes.

Summary Note

African American Soldiers	1
African American soldiers were often discriminated against in the army. They were often given poorer-quality equipment and had to do heavier labor than whites.	
	p. 91

Paraphrase. A *paraphrase note* includes most of the author's ideas, not just the main ones. Like the summary note, it's written in your own words. You paraphrase to simplify the material you've read. Begin by identifying the writer whose words you're paraphrasing.

Paraphrase Note

African American Soldiers	1
Author James McPherson claims that African American soldiers had to fight for equality in the army just as they fought for freedom and the Union, for they were often discriminated against. These regiments were sometimes given poor-quality guns and ammunition. Soldiers were also given an unfair share of heavy, physical work.	
	p. 91

REFERENCE NOTE: For more help with taking notes, see
page 912.

 WRITING NOTE During the planning stage of your research, you should be able to identify the thesis, or main idea, of your report. At first your thesis will probably be informal, perhaps not even stated in a sentence. Eventually, as you develop your paper, the thesis will become a sentence or two in your paper—your thesis statement. For example, here's how one writer began to identify the thesis for a research report on African American soldiers in the Civil War: *African American soldiers experienced discrimination, but they fought with great courage, and they profoundly affected the country.*

 REFERENCE NOTE: For more information on writing thesis statements, see pages 111–112.

WRITING ASSIGNMENT

PART 5:
Planning and Note Taking

Begin your research with some preliminary reading. Then create an early plan and use it as a guide when you continue your reading. Remember to take accurate notes and to keep a careful record of your sources.

Preparing an Outline

Your early plan guided your research, but you may need a more thorough plan, or outline, to help you organize the information you've collected. Although you may well reorganize some of your information as you're writing or revising your first draft, an outline can be helpful as you are putting your ideas on paper.

You might begin by sorting your note cards or computer note files into groups according to the headings in your early plan. If you have some information that won't fit under those headings, you may have to create new headings for your final outline.

Here's an outline based on the early plan on page 383. Notice that it is a *formal* outline, with Roman numerals and capital letters. A formal outline is usually typed and included with the research paper. It serves as a kind of table of contents for the reader.

Forgotten Heroes

I.   History of African American soldier
   A.   Rejection at beginning of war
   B.   Authorization of first units—1862
   C.   Emancipation Proclamation—1863
II. Discrimination against African American soldiers
III. Courage of African American soldiers
   A.   54th Massachusetts
      1.   Battle at Fort Wagner
      2.   Medal of Honor winner
   B.   Other regiments
IV. Effects of African American soldiers
   A.   Changing attitude of Northerners
   B.   Pride and self-respect
   C.   Drive for civil rights
V.   Debt to African American soldiers— Washington, D.C., monument

After you've finished your outline, put your note cards in the same order as your headings. When you begin to write, you will be able to follow your outline and to refer to your cards for facts and information.

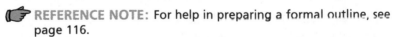 **REFERENCE NOTE:** For help in preparing a formal outline, see page 116.

PART 6:
Preparing a Final Outline

Revise your early plan and prepare a final outline. What changes have you made? Why have you made them?

Writing Your First Draft

Half your work is done. You've thought of a topic, located sources, and collected and organized information. The next step is to pull all this information together in a first draft that includes proper credit for your sources.

Combining the Basic Elements of a Report

When you write your first draft, you can't just copy down a series of notes from your note cards. You have to pull the information together in a way that will interest your readers and help them understand the topic. To do that, you begin with the basic form of a composition. A good research report, like any good essay or article, has these basic elements:

- an *introduction* that grabs the reader's attention and presents a clear statement of the thesis
- a series of *body* paragraphs that develop and support the thesis
- a *conclusion* that ties your main points together

You can use your final outline as a guide to developing your draft. Each heading of your outline may become a separate paragraph, or even two paragraphs, in your paper.

 REFERENCE NOTE: For more information about thesis statements and composition form, see pages 111–112, 120–129.

 CRITICAL THINKING

Synthesizing Ideas and Information

When you synthesize, you bring pieces of information together from different sources and draw your own conclusions. It's important that your report be more than a string of someone else's ideas.

To synthesize information, look for a common idea, or element, among the various facts and information you have collected. Then, express this idea in your own words and use an example or two to support your point. For instance, you might read three different opinions of the performance of African American soldiers. Since each source gives high marks to African American soldiers, you might write something like this:

Northern generals agreed that African Americans were excellent soldiers. After the Battle of Honey Spring, for example, General Blunt said that they "make better soldiers in every respect than any troops I have ever had under my command" (Carle 90).

Statement of common idea

Example to prove point

 CRITICAL THINKING EXERCISE:
Synthesizing Ideas and Information

Synthesizing ideas is not easy, but here's your chance to practice your skill. Read through the following information about whale songs. What main idea is common to all this information? Write a sentence stating the main idea you find.

- whale songs—complex, have distinct, repeated themes
- songs can change from one year to next
- Biologist Katharine Payne of Cornell University says, "Whales, it seems, are fashion-oriented. We found that when a song is in fashion among a particular population of whales, all the whales are going to sing it."
- song changes gradually during the season— completely changed by end
- new breeding season, whales "start with the same song they were singing at the end of the previous season" (Bernd Würsig)
- end of second breeding season—new song

"A Louie, Louie . . . wowoooo . . . We gotta go now . . ."

Giving Credit to Your Sources

In a research report you borrow the ideas of other people, but you have to acknowledge that you borrowed them. You need to give credit, or document, your sources in the body of your report and in a list at the end of your report.

Giving Credit in the Body of Your Report.   When you're writing the body of your report, you must make a couple of decisions about crediting sources: what to credit and how to credit.

1. *How do you know what to give credit for?* Here's the test: if the same information can be found in several sources, it is considered common knowledge. You don't have to give credit. For example, it's common knowledge that Martin Luther King, Jr., gave his "I Have a Dream" speech in Washington, D.C., in 1963. You wouldn't have to document that fact.

2. *How do you show the credit?* Do you use footnotes at the bottom of each page? Do you use parenthetical notes (called parenthetical citations)? What kind of punctuation do you use? There isn't any one way to give credit, but in this chapter, you'll see examples of the format recommended by the Modern Language Association of America (MLA). You'll need to follow your teacher's recommendation.

GUIDELINES FOR GIVING CREDIT WITHIN THE REPORT

Place the information in parentheses at the end of the sentence in which you've used someone else's words or ideas.

1. **Source with One Author.** Last name of the author followed by the page number(s) (if any): (McPherson 93)

2. **Source with No Author Given.** Title, or a shortened form of it, followed by the page number(s) (if any): ("Fort Pillow")

3. **Source with Two or More Authors.** All authors' last names, followed by the page number(s) (if any): (Ward, Burns, and Burns 253)

4. **More Than One Source by the Same Author.** Author's last name, followed by title or shortened version of it, followed by page number(s) (if any): (Cohen, Mysterious Places 3)

WRITING NOTE   In this chapter you're learning to use parenthetical notes, or citations, to document your research. But it's possible that your teacher will ask you to use footnotes, another style of documentation. All you really need to do is follow the exact style recommended by your teacher, but here's an example of one style of footnote for a book by one author. The number *1* at the beginning of the footnote refers to a number in the report where there is information to document. Notice that the footnote gives the author's first and last names (in that order), the book's title, publication information, and a page reference.

¹ James M. McPherson, Marching Toward Freedom: Blacks in the Civil War 1861–1865 (New York: Facts on File, 1991) 21.

Preparing the List of Sources.   The documentation you give in the body of your report is not meant to be complete. Anyone who might want to read more about your topic will turn to the list of sources at the end of your report. This list, usually called *Works Cited,* includes all the sources you've used in your report. Another name for this listing is *Bibliography.* You can use the heading *Bibliography* if your sources are print ones only. If you use any nonprint sources—such as films or electronic materials— *Works Cited* is a more appropriate heading.

GUIDELINES FOR PREPARING THE LIST OF WORKS CITED

1. Follow the format you used for your source cards. (See pages 379–380).
2. List your sources in alphabetical order by the authors' last names (or, if no author is listed, by the title). Put your list of Works Cited on a separate sheet of paper in your final report.
3. Begin each listing at the left margin. If the listing is longer than one line, indent the remaining lines five spaces. (See the list of Works Cited on page 396.)

Now, read the following report on African American soldiers. Notice how the report combines basic composition form with parenthetical documentation and a list of Works Cited.

A WRITER'S MODEL

Forgotten Heroes

INTRODUCTION

Specific details about one African American soldier

"I felt freedom in my bones" (Fincher 52). Those are the words of escaped slave Elijah Marrs as he stripped away his old rags and donned his new army blues. Marrs was only one of nearly 180,000 African American soldiers who served in the Union Army during the Civil War

Thesis Statement

(Fincher 52). African American soldiers faced a struggle. Although they experienced discrimination, they served with great courage, and their effect on the United States was profound.

**BODY
History of African American soldier—first event in struggle**

From the very beginning of the Civil War, African American soldiers attempted to enlist in the Union Army. At first, they were rejected. At the time, most Northern whites were prejudiced against African Americans and believed they were not bold enough to fight (McPherson 52).

Source with one author—author's name

Initially, Abraham Lincoln was also opposed to the idea. He believed that African American soldiers would anger the border states, causing them to turn against the Union (McPherson 52).

Second event in struggle—details arranged in chronological order

In 1862, however, as the North lost several major battles and morale began to drop, public opinion began to change. In the fall of 1862, Lincoln authorized the formation of the first African American regiments: the First South Carolina Volunteers (McPherson 53) and the First Kansas Colored Volunteers (Carle 79).

Source with one author—author's name

Third event in struggle

On January 1, 1863, Lincoln issued the Emancipation Proclamation; slaves who escaped to the North were legally considered free citizens. After the proclamation, blacks could be widely recruited for the Union Army (McPherson 20). Of course, if the North did not win the war, the proclamation would be worthless. Historian Barbara Fields notes that African American soldiers knew that "the Emancipation Proclamation did nothing to get them their freedom. It said they had a right to put their bodies on the line if they had the nerve to believe in it" (The Civil War).

Direct quotation —expert opinion

Source with no author given— title

Discrimination against soldiers

Even though African Americans joined the army, they still experienced discrimination. Men in these regiments received ten dollars a month and no clothing allowance. White soldiers received thirteen dollars a month plus a clothing allowance. In addition, African American soldiers could not serve as officers. In practice, the African American regiments often received

Source with three authors— authors' names

inferior arms and ammunition. White doctors refused to serve with the regiments, and black soldiers died of disease at a much higher rate than white soldiers (Ward, Burns, and Burns 253).

It was risky for African American soldiers to enlist in the Union Army. Angry at the idea of African American troops, the Confederate forces would not allow them to surrender. Instead, they were shot or enslaved (Ward, Burns, and Burns 335).

Source with no author given— title

Courage of soldiers

At the fierce Battle of Fort Pillow, hundreds of black soldiers were massacred after they surrendered ("Fort Pillow").

Discrimination and risk did not dampen the enthusiasm of the African American soldiers. In battle after battle, the soldiers showed great courage. For example, at Fort Wagner, South Carolina, the most famous of the African American regiments, the 54th Massachusetts, led the attack on the Confederate stronghold. Half of the six hundred volunteers were killed, wounded, or captured, including the commander, twenty-five-year-old Colonel Robert Gould Shaw (Fincher 46).

Source with one author—author's name

One soldier, Sergeant William Carney, became the first African American soldier to win the Congressional Medal of Honor (Fincher 56).

The courage shown by the 54th Massachusetts at Fort Wagner is one of the great moments in American military history. A reporter of the time made this comment:

Direct quotation —set off from text

> It is not too much to say that if this Massachusetts 54th had faltered when its trial came, 200,000 troops for whom it was a pioneer would never have been put into the field, but it did not falter. It made Fort Wagner such a name for the colored race as Bunker Hill has been for ninety years to the white Yankees (The Civil War).

Source with no author given— title

Effects of soldiers

In battle after battle, African American soldiers showed their heroism. Their courage changed the way that Northerners viewed them.

Direct quotation

Assistant Secretary of War Charles Dana said that "the bravery of blacks in the battle at Milliken's Bend completely revolutionized the sentiments of the Army" (Fincher 54). General Butler said, "I swore to myself a solemn oath . . . 'to defend the rights of those men who have given their blood for me and my country that day and for their race forever'" (Fincher 60–61).

Source with one author—author's name

Bruce Catton, author of <u>The Centennial History of the Civil War</u>, describes the change:

Direct quotation —set off from text

Source named in sentence— volume and page number

> Under the revolution involved in the act of changing slaves into free men, even into soldiers, there lay a profounder revolution involving the way individual men looked at their fellow human beings (3: 120).

The service of African Americans in the Civil War had two other profound effects. For one thing, the experience "contributed to the development of their racial pride and self-respect" (McPherson 96). For another, "the blacks' struggle to get fair treatment from the military began to quicken their drive for equal rights in civilian life" (McPherson 96).

Direct quotation

CONCLUSION

The country has been slow to acknowledge its debt to the African American soldier. In September 1996, a major memorial to honor African American soldiers who served in the Civil War was dedicated in Washington, D.C. As part of the memorial, the names of 178,000 African American soldiers and 7,000 white officers who served with them are inscribed on stainless steel plaques (Grant).

Interviewee's name

The monument of steel and stone is mute. The words of Commander Carleton Philpot, describing the men of the 9th and 10th Cavalry regiments, are a fitting tribute for African American soldiers of the Civil War: "This is a group of heroes—true heroes that you don't have to create. Not football players, not singers, just guys who did a tough job and nobody gave a hoot" (Spiller 86).

Direct quotation

Source with one author—author's name

Works Cited

Carle, Glenn L. "The First Kansas Colored." <u>American Heritage</u>. Feb./March 1992: 79–91.

Catton, Bruce. <u>The Centennial History of the Civil War</u>. 3 vols. Garden City, New York: Doubleday, 1965.

<u>The Civil War</u>. Dir. Ken Burns. Videocassette. PBS Video, 1990.

Fincher, Jack. "The Hard Fight Was Getting into the Fight at All." <u>Smithsonian</u> Oct. 1990: 46–61.

"Fort Pillow." <u>ENCARTA</u>™ Multimedia Encyclopedia. CD-ROM. Redmond: Microsoft, 1994.

Grant, Linda. Telephone Interview. 26 April 1996.

McPherson, James M. <u>Marching Toward Freedom: Blacks in the Civil War 1861–1865</u>. New York: Facts on File, 1991.

Spiller, Roger J. "Honoring the Buffalo Soldiers." <u>American Heritage</u>. Feb./March 1992: 84–86.

Ward, Geoffrey C., Ken Burns, and Ric Burns. <u>The Civil War: An Illustrated History</u>. New York: Knopf, 1990.

PART 7:
Writing a First Draft

Using your final outline and note cards as a guide, write the first draft of your report. Unless your teacher gives you different instructions, follow the MLA format in this chapter to give credit to your sources. Then, prepare your works cited list. Be sure to list only the sources you actually used in the report.

 COMPUTER NOTE: When you're working on your list of works cited, word-processing programs make it easy to create and change indents, tabs, and special formatting.

Peanuts reprinted by permission of United Feature Syndicate, Inc.

Evaluating and Revising

You've probably invested a great deal of time and effort in your report. Spending a little more time now can help you improve the final product. Ask yourself the questions in the left-hand column of the chart on page 398 to evaluate your report. If you uncover weaknesses, use the revision techniques in the right-hand column to correct them.

WRITING NOTE Now is a good time to look at how you've incorporated direct quotations into your paper.

At first you may find it awkward to work direct quotations into your report. But it will become more natural with practice. You'll find, for example, that you can use a phrase or a clause from quoted material to complete a sentence: *The service of the African American soldiers "contributed to the development of their racial pride and self-respect" (McPherson 96).* To incorporate a longer quotation, you can identify the writer of the quoted material, followed by the quotation itself: *Historian Barbara Fields says, "The Emancipation Proclamation did nothing to get them freedom. It said they had a right to put their bodies on the line if they had the nerve to believe in it" (The Civil War).*

"I can't write five words but that I change seven."

Dorothy Parker

EVALUATING AND REVISING RESEARCH REPORTS

EVALUATION GUIDE	REVISION TECHNIQUE
1 Does the introduction grab the reader's attention and present a clear thesis statement?	Start with an interesting fact or quotation. **Add** a sentence that presents your conclusions about your research.
2 Are ideas and information pulled together (synthesized) and stated in the writer's own words?	Be sure that the topic sentence of each paragraph in your report is in your own words and expresses your own ideas. **Add** or **replace** topic sentences as necessary.
3 Are ideas supported with enough information? Will readers find the information complete?	**Add** information such as facts and statistics, expert opinions, examples, and explanations. **Add** surprising details.
4 Are enough print and non-print sources of information used? Are they recent, reliable, and objective?	Use your library's online or card catalog and the *Readers' Guide* to find more sources. Interview someone. **Add** information from these sources to your report.
5 Does all the information relate directly to the topic?	**Cut** information not directly related to your topic.
6 Is proper credit given for each source of information used?	**Add** documentation for any information that isn't everyday knowledge.
7 Is the format for giving credit to sources within a report and at the end of a report carefully followed?	**Replace** incorrect items in your documentation so that it follows the MLA format or another format recommended by your teacher.

E X E R C I S E 5 ▶   **Analyzing a Writer's Revisions**

Study the following revised paragraph from the sample report on pages 392–396. Then answer the questions.

> *Even though*
> ₍ₐ₎African Americans joined the army,   add
>
> ~~and~~ they still experienced discrimination.   cut
>   *ten dollars a month*
> Men in these regiments received ₍ₐ₎~~a little~~   replace
>
> ~~money~~ and no clothing allowance. White   cut
>   *thirteen dollars a month*
> soldiers received ₍ₐ₎~~more money~~ plus a   replace
>
> clothing allowance. ~~(Even thirteen dollars~~   cut
>
> ~~wasn't much money, was it?)~~ In addition,   cut
> *African American soldiers*
> ~~they~~ could not serve as officers. In practice,   replace
>
> the African American regiments often
>   *and ammunition*
> received inferior arms₍ₐ₎ White doctors   add
>
> refused to serve with the regiments, and
>   *of disease*
> black soldiers died ₍ₐ₎at a much higher rate   add
>   *(Ward, Burns, and Burns 253)*
> than white soldiers₍ₐ₎   add

1. Why did the writer add *Even though* to the topic sentence?
2. Why did the writer replace the words *a little money* and *more money* with *ten dollars a month* and *thirteen dollars a month*?
3. Why did the writer cut the fourth sentence?
4. Why did the writer replace *they* with *African American soldiers*?
5. Why did the writer add *(Ward, Burns, and Burns 253)*?

| **WRITING** ASSIGNMENT | PART 8: **Evaluating and Revising Your Research Report** |

Exchange papers with a classmate, and use the guidelines on page 398 to evaluate each other's reports. Use your classmate's evaluation to improve your report.

Proofreading and Publishing

Don't keep what you've learned a secret. Proofread to clean up all those careless errors, and then share your knowledge with others. Try one of these suggestions.

- Prepare a copy of your report to present to an elementary school library for reference.
- Volunteer to make an oral report about your research to your science or history class.

PART 9:
Proofreading and Publishing Your Research Report

Proofread your report carefully, and correct any errors. Publish or share your report with others.

 Reflecting on Your Writing

Will you add your report to your **portfolio?** If so, date it and write a brief reflection answering these questions.

- What did you learn about research while working on this report?
- What would you do differently if you were just beginning?

A STUDENT MODEL

Emily Courtney, a student at Bret Harte Junior High School in Oakland, California, believes that research is easy when you write about a subject that you are "genuinely interested in." Although Emily presents theories about the Anasazi in the passages on the following page, the mystery surrounding these people still remains.

<u>from</u> The Mysteries of the Anasazi
by Emily Courtney

The Anasazi are the source of a great mystery to the archaeological world. The list of theories dealing with their arts, religion, everyday life, and, most of all, their disappearance, is endless. There are so many conflicting ideas about how the past took place that it is hard to get a clear picture of the most likely scenario. In this report, I'll try to give you the most accurate account of Anasazi history and general culture I can, using several sources and my own personal knowledge and experience.

Researchers believe the Anasazi descended from a nomadic people who moved frequently throughout the Southwest for about 10,000 years, traveling where food led them. Archaeologists generally consider 2,300 years before the present to be when that nomadic tribe settled down to form the Anasazi culture (Jaffe 81). . . .

Communication with Mesoamerican cultures helped the Anasazi develop culturally. By 750, the Anasazi began building complex masonry structures. Chaco Canyon is praised as the most awesome archaeological site in the United States. Until as late as 1882, Chaco could have been considered the largest apartment complex in the world (Jaffe 81). The building called Pueblo Bonito has a D-shaped layout of more than 650 rooms (Lekson, Windes, Stein, and Judge 100). . . . Around 1115, the Anasazi began to leave Chaco and other small and large villages in the surrounding area. Within fifteen years, Chaco was abandoned, leaving behind no apparent reason for its desertion (Jaffe 83). Archaeologists speculate the cause to have been anything from invasion, drought, or overuse of resources, to ritual exodus (Ortiz). There is no shortage of explanations, yet none can be proven or fully explained. . . .

In my opinion, the most believable ending to the Pueblo era took place when a severe drought lasting twenty-three years came in 1276 ("Ancient Mansions of Chaco Canyon" 77). Many people believe that it is because of the drought that the Anasazi moved south and east. They settled along the Rio Grande, where some of their descendants (the Hopi and Pueblo people) still reside today (Ceram 86).

WRITING WORKSHOP

The I-Search Report

The I-Search paper is a personal research report. It begins with a topic that has personal meaning for you. The I-Search paper tells the story of your search for information. It includes these parts:

- information you want to learn about your topic
- your early thoughts about the topic
- the sources you explored for information
- information you found about the topic
- your reaction to the information you found

An I-Search paper is much more personal and less formal than the typical research report. The writer addresses the reader directly, using the pronoun *I*. However, the I-Search paper and the research paper share many characteristics. The I-Search paper involves many forms of research including interviews, surveys, polls, and experiments. Information from outside sources is documented the same way as information in a formal research report. Unless your teacher tells you otherwise, use the MLA format that you learned in this chapter.

In the following excerpt from an I-Search report, the writer explores the topic of left-handedness. Which parts of the report are included here?

Lefty

There's a box that belongs to my parents in the back of the storage closet that I'm allowed to rummage through. . . . Recently, I found a crumpled, lined paper with simple sentences written out in a child's handwriting. My mother's name is on the paper, but the handwriting could never have been hers. My mother has neat, firm handwriting. The handwriting on this paper is very messy. Not surprisingly, the grade on the paper is D.

"Oh, yes," my mother said, looking at the paper, "that's the year they tried to make me right-handed." . . .

How many people, I wondered, have gone through experiences like my mother? Is there discrimination in our society against left-handed people? What causes left-handedness, anyway? Are left-handed people unusually creative or intelligent? . . .

Using the trusty Readers' Guide to Periodical Literature, I quickly found an article in Smithsonian magazine with an intriguing title: "The Sinister Difference: Why Lefties Have It So Hard." I was shocked to learn that discrimination against left-handed people is very real. Also, according to the article, left-handers are more prone to accidents (Shute 131).

1. Why is the writer interested in left-handedness?
2. What does the writer want to learn about the topic?
3. What are the writer's early thoughts about the topic?
4. In the last sentence, what do the name and number in parentheses mean?

Writing an I-Search Paper

Prewriting. What topic do you care about? Ask yourself what you want to learn about your topic, and jot down a list of questions. As you do your research, you'll uncover ideas you didn't think about at this early stage. Finally, ask yourself what you think about the topic at this point.

Writing, Evaluating, and Revising. As you write your report, keep in mind the parts of an I-Search paper. You're also writing the story of your research. This includes your thoughts about the topic as well as your reaction to the information that you find. Write your report in an informal tone, using first person and addressing the reader directly.

Proofreading and Publishing. Since other people will be reading your report, take the time to proofread it carefully. Correct any errors in spelling, capitalization, and mechanics. Consider sharing your findings with an appropriate class, perhaps history or science.

If you decide to add your I-Search report to your **portfolio,** date it and write a brief reflection based on these questions. How did you choose your topic? What discoveries did you make about your topic? What surprises did you find?

MAKING CONNECTIONS

INFORMING THROUGH EVALUATION

Writing a Book Report

The writer of a book report evaluates a book so that readers will know whether they might enjoy reading it. The writer gives enough information about the book to support the evaluation. The most common features of a book report include

- the title of the book and the author
- an introduction to interest the reader
- a brief description of the setting and main character(s)
- a brief summary of the plot that hints at the main conflict without ruining the suspense
- an evaluation of the book—why the audience should or should not read the book

In this excerpt from a book report, how does the writer evaluate the book without destroying the suspense?

Hisako's Mysteries
by Yoshiko Uchida

On Hisako's birthday, an intriguing envelope arrives. In it is a blank sheet of paper and a 1000-yen note. Who sent this money? No one knows. And why won't anyone talk to Hisako about the letter she found in the upstairs closet? Hisako has many questions about it because the letter is about her father, who died when Hisako was two.

One day, Hisako's best friend Fusa invites Hisako to accompany her family on a trip to Tokyo. Just before Hisako leaves, Hana, the housekeeper, gives the girl a picture of a grinning young man. "Study it carefully," Hana says, "and let me know if you ever see such a man in Tokyo, perhaps at your uncle's home" (50). Although Hisako wants to know the man's identity, the housekeeper refuses to say much about him.

Write a book report of your own, perhaps about a book your teacher asked you to read or one that a friend recommended. These hints will help you write your report.

- Read the book once for pleasure, and then go back over it.
- Note where you learn something important about characters, conflict, plot, and setting.
- Take notes about details that will help you explain the book and your opinion about it.
- Decide whether to recommend the book.
- Keep in mind the common features of a book report.
- Include quotations from the book if they help support your recommendation.

SPEAKING AND LISTENING
Research and Nonprint Media

Producers of television news programs often do extensive research to prepare their shows. Watch one of the daily news programs for two days. As you watch, take notes.

- Identify one story about a person. What facts do you learn about the person?
- Identify one story about another country. What do you learn about the country or the people who live there? How many people were interviewed?
- Identify one story about a current problem in the United States. What background information about the problem does the news give us? Do any experts give their opinions?

Review your notes, and then get together with two or three classmates. Discuss what you've learned about research and the news.

11 WRITING COMPLETE SENTENCES

LOOKING
AHEAD

This chapter will give you some practice in evaluating your sentences for completeness. You will learn how to

- identify and correct sentence fragments
- identify and correct run-on sentences

Sentence Fragments

A *sentence* is a word group that has a subject and a verb and expresses a complete thought. A *sentence fragment* is a word group that does not have all the basic parts of a complete sentence. Unlike a sentence, a fragment does not express a complete thought. It is missing some important information.

Sentence fragments usually occur when you are writing in a hurry or are a little careless. You may leave out a word, or you may chop off a part of a sentence by putting in a period too soon.

To find out whether you have a complete sentence or a sentence fragment, you can use a simple three-part test:

1. Does the group of words have a subject?
2. Does it have a verb?
3. Does it express a complete thought?

If you answer *no* to any of these questions, your word group is a fragment. It is missing at least one basic part.

FRAGMENT   Was the best sharpshooter in the United States. [The subject is missing. *Who* was the best sharpshooter in the United States?]

SENTENCE   Annie Oakley was the best sharpshooter in the United States.

FRAGMENT   Annie Oakley with "Buffalo" Bill Cody's Wild West show. [The verb is missing. *What* did she do with the Wild West show?]

SENTENCE   Annie Oakley performed with "Buffalo" Bill Cody's Wild West show.

FRAGMENT   As it fell through the air ninety feet away. [This group of words has a subject and a verb, but it doesn't express a complete thought. *What happened* as something fell through the air?]

SENTENCE   Annie could shoot a playing card as it fell through the air ninety feet away.

STYLE NOTE By itself, a fragment doesn't express a complete thought. But fragments can make sense if they are clearly related to the sentences that come before or after them. These sentences give the fragments meaning because they help us fill in the missing parts.

The following passage is from an essay that describes the death and the cutting down of a great white oak on the writer's family homestead. The author's grandfather has carefully cut at the dead tree and is about to aim the final blows. See how the author uses fragments to describe the fall of the great tree.

> Then came the great moment. A few last, quick strokes. A slow, deliberate swaying. The crack of parting fibers. Then a long "swoo-sh!" that rose in pitch as the towering trunk arced downward at increasing speed.
>
> Edwin Way Teale, "The Death of a Tree"

Experienced writers like Teale sometimes use sentence fragments for effect. As a beginning writer, however, you need to become accomplished at writing complete sentences before you begin to experiment with fragments.

E X E R C I S E 1 ▶ **Identifying Sentence Fragments**

Some of the following items are sentence fragments. To find out which items are fragments and which are complete sentences, apply the three-part test (page 407). If the item is a complete sentence, write *C*. If the subject is missing, write *S*. If the verb is missing, write *V*. If the item has a subject and verb but doesn't express a complete thought, write *I*.

EXAMPLE   **1.** Who wrote "A Christmas Memory."
          1. *I*

1. Truman Capote was an American author.
2. Was born in New Orleans in 1924.
3. Grew up in Alabama.
4. Because he hated attending boarding schools.
5. *Breakfast at Tiffany's* probably his most famous novel.
6. When he moved to New York City.
7. "A Christmas Memory" was made into a television movie.
8. His characters lively and eccentric.
9. Is one of his most moving stories.
10. Spent six years researching his nonfiction book *In Cold Blood*.

Phrase Fragments

A *phrase* is a group of words that does not have a subject and a verb. There are three kinds of phrases that can easily be mistaken for complete sentences: *verbal phrases, appositive phrases,* and *prepositional phrases.*

Verbal Phrases

Verbals are forms of verbs that are used as other parts of speech. They sometimes fool us into thinking that a group of words has a verb when it really doesn't. One type of verbal usually ends in *-ing, -d,* or *-ed* and doesn't have a helping verb (such as *is, were,* or *have*) in front of it. Another type of verbal has the word *to* in front of the verb (*to go, to play*).

A *verbal phrase* is a phrase that contains a verbal. By itself, a verbal phrase is a fragment because it doesn't express a complete thought.

FRAGMENT	Seeing the movie *Glory.*
SENTENCE	I enjoyed seeing the movie *Glory.*
FRAGMENT	To become good soldiers.
SENTENCE	Black volunteers in the Civil War trained hard to become good soldiers.
FRAGMENT	Gaining glory for itself and for all black soldiers.
SENTENCE	Gaining glory for itself and for all black soldiers, the 54th Massachusetts Regiment led the attack on Fort Wagner.

Appositive Phrases

An *appositive* is a word that identifies or explains the noun or pronoun it follows. An *appositive phrase,* a phrase made up of an appositive and its modifiers, is a fragment. It does not contain the basic parts of a sentence.

FRAGMENT	A twenty-five-year-old soldier.
SENTENCE	The 54th Massachusetts Regiment was commanded by Colonel Shaw, a twenty-five-year-old soldier.

Prepositional Phrases

A *prepositional phrase* is a group of words beginning with a preposition and ending with a noun or pronoun. A prepositional phrase can't stand alone as a sentence because it doesn't express a complete thought.

FRAGMENT	With great courage on the battlefield.
SENTENCE	The 54th Massachusetts Regiment acted with great courage on the battlefield.

WRITING NOTE Usually a phrase needs to stay as close as possible to the word it modifies in the sentence. However, some phrases, such as the infinitive phrase "to become good soldiers," make sense at the beginning or the end of the sentence. (To learn more about placing phrases in sentences, see pages 686–690.)

| EXERCISE 2▶ | **Revising Phrase Fragments** |

Use your imagination to create sentences from the following phrases. You can either (1) attach the fragment to a complete sentence, or (2) develop the phrase into a complete sentence by adding a subject, a verb, or both.

EXAMPLE **1.** landing on the planet
      1. *Landing on the planet, the astronauts immediately began to explore.*
          or
      The astronauts were landing on the planet.

1. in a huge spaceship
2. setting foot on the planet
3. to explore the craters
4. walking around in a spacesuit
5. finding no sign of life
6. the astronaut's spaceship
7. checking the spaceship for damage
8. the planet's moon
9. to return to Earth
10. on a successful mission

Subordinate Clause Fragments

A *clause* is a group of words that has a subject and a verb. One kind of clause, an ***independent clause,*** expresses a complete thought and can stand on its own as a sentence. For example, the group of words *I ate my lunch* is an independent clause. However, another kind of clause, a ***subordinate clause,*** does not express a complete thought. This clause is a fragment and can't stand alone as a sentence.

FRAGMENT When Paris stole the beautiful Helen of Troy. [*What happened* when Paris stole Helen?]

SENTENCE When Paris stole the beautiful Helen of Troy, he started the Trojan War.

FRAGMENT Who was a great hero of the Greeks. [Note that this would be a complete sentence if it ended with a question mark.]

SENTENCE Odysseus, who was a great hero of the Greeks, took part in the Trojan War.

FRAGMENT   Because of the trick with the wooden horse. [*What was the result of the trick?*]

SENTENCE   Because of the trick with the wooden horse, the Greeks finally won the Trojan War.

WRITING NOTE   A subordinate clause telling *why, where, when,* or *how* is called an **adverb clause.** You can place an adverb clause either before or after the independent clause in a sentence.

EXAMPLE   **After he started home from the Trojan War,** Odysseus had many more adventures.

or

Odysseus had many more adventures **after he started home from the Trojan War.**

If you put the subordinate clause first, use a comma to separate it from the independent clause. The comma makes the sentence easier for the reader to understand.

EXERCISE 3▶   **Revising Subordinate Clause Fragments**

The following paragraph contains some subordinate clause fragments. First, find these clause fragments. Next, revise the paragraph, joining the subordinate clauses with independent clauses. (There may be more than one way to join them.) Change the punctuation and capitalization as necessary.

People have been using cosmetics for thousands of years. In Africa, the ancient Egyptians used perfumes, hair dyes, and makeup. That they made from plants and minerals. While they often used cosmetics to be more attractive. They also used them to protect their skin from the hot sun. Today, cosmetics are made from over five thousand different ingredients, including waxes, oils, and dyes. The cosmetics business is a huge industry. Advertisers sell cosmetics. By appealing to our sensitive nature. They often hint. That their products will make us beautiful, happy, and successful.

Although modern-day cosmetics ads look different from the ads of eighty years ago. They still appeal to our emotions.

"Mother, here she is"

OF all moments the most trying—when the son brings *her* to his mother, of all critics the most exacting. Mother-love causes her to look with penetrating glance, almost *trying* to find flaws. No quality of beauty so serves to win an older woman as a skin smooth, fresh and healthy *in a natural way*, as easily provided by

POMPEIAN CREAM

EXERCISE 4▶ **Using Subordinate Clauses in Sentences**

Use each of the following subordinate clause fragments as part of a complete sentence. Add whatever words are necessary to make the meaning of the sentence complete. Add capitalization and punctuation as necessary.

1. as we watched the spaceship land
2. who approached the house in long leaps
3. which startled the dog
4. if we go outside the house
5. when they handed me a glowing sphere

WRITING NOTE   A series of items is another kind of fragment that's easily mistaken for a sentence. Notice that, in the following example, the series of items in dark type isn't a complete sentence.

FRAGMENT   I ate several things for lunch. **A sandwich, an apple, four pieces of celery, and some popcorn.**

To correct the fragment, you can

- make it into a complete sentence

or

- link it to the previous sentence with a colon

SENTENCE   I ate several things for lunch. **I ate** a sandwich, an apple, four pieces of celery, and some popcorn.

or

I ate several things for lunch**:** a sandwich, an apple, four pieces of celery, and some popcorn.

| EXERCISE 5 ▶ | **Identifying and Revising Fragments** |

Some of the following groups of words are sentence fragments. Identify each fragment and make it part of a complete sentence, adding commas where necessary. When you find a complete sentence that doesn't need revision, write C.

EXAMPLE   **1.** Originally raised to hunt badgers. Dachshunds are now popular as pets.
            1. *Originally raised to hunt badgers, dachshunds are now popular as pets.*

1. Humans have kept dogs as pets and helpers. For perhaps ten thousand years.
2. Herding sheep and cattle and guarding property. Many dogs more than earn their keep.
3. Descended from wolves. Some dogs are still somewhat wolflike.
4. There are over one hundred breeds of dogs now.
5. If you have a Saint Bernard. You have one of the largest dogs.
6. Because Yorkshire terriers are very tiny. Many people keep them as pets.
7. Since they are all born blind and unable to take care of themselves. Puppies need their mothers.
8. Most dogs are fully grown by the time they are one year old.
9. Dogs live an average of twelve years. Although some live to be nearly twenty.
10. If you like dogs. Consider having one for a pet.

Run-on Sentences

A **run-on sentence** is two or more complete sentences run together as one. Because they don't show where one idea ends and another one begins, run-on sentences can confuse your reader. There are two kinds of run-ons. In the first kind, called a **fused sentence,** the sentences have no punctuation at all between them.

RUN-ON Schools in the Middle Ages were different from ours students usually did not have books.

CORRECT Schools in the Middle Ages were different from ours**.** Students usually did not have books.

In the other kind of run-on, the writer has linked together sentences with only a comma to separate them from one another. This kind of run-on is called a **comma splice.**

RUN-ON Schools today have books for every student, many schools also have televisions and computers.

CORRECT Schools today have books for every student**.** Many schools also have televisions and computers.

Shoe reprinted by permission: Tribune Media Services.

One way to spot run-on sentences is to read your writing aloud. A natural, distinct pause in your voice usually means that you need to separate sentences in some way. You can also check for run-ons by identifying subjects and verbs. That will help you find where one complete thought ends and another one begins.

Revising Run-on Sentences

There are several ways you can revise run-on sentences. As shown in the examples on page 415, you can always make two separate sentences. But if the two thoughts are equal to one another in importance, you may want to make a *compound sentence.*

RUN-ON Canada has ten provinces each province has its own government. [fused]
Canada has ten provinces, each province has its own government. [comma splice]

1. You can make a compound sentence by using a comma and a coordinating conjunction (such as *and, but,* or *or*).

CORRECTED Canada has ten provinces, **and** each province has its own government.

2. You can make a compound sentence by using a semicolon.

CORRECTED Canada has ten provinces; each province has its own government.

3. You can make a compound sentence by using a semicolon and a word such as *therefore, instead, meanwhile, still, also, nevertheless,* or *however.* These words are called *conjunctive adverbs.* Follow a conjunctive adverb with a comma.

CORRECTED Canada has ten provinces; **also,** each province has its own government.

WRITING NOTE   Before you join two sentences in a compound sentence, make sure that the ideas in the sentences are closely related to one another. If you link unrelated ideas, you may confuse your reader.

UNRELATED Canada is almost four million square miles in size, and I hope to visit my relatives there someday.
RELATED Canada is almost four million square miles in size, but most of its people live on a small strip of land along the southern border.

REFERENCE NOTE: For more information on compound sentences and how to form them, see pages 428–429 and 577–578.

EXERCISE 6 ▶ **Revising Run-on Sentences**

The following items are confusing because they're run-on sentences. See if you can clear up the confusion by revising the run-ons to form clear, complete sentences. To revise, use the method given in parentheses after each sentence. (The examples on page 416 will help you.)

EXAMPLE 1. Hollywood is still a center of American movie making fine films are made in other places, too. (comma and coordinating conjunction)

1. *Hollywood is still a center of American movie making, but fine films are made in other places, too.*

1. Movies entertain millions of people every day they are popular all over the world. (two sentences)
2. Many films take years to make they require the skills of hundreds of workers. (comma and coordinating conjunction)
3. The director of a movie has an important job the cast and crew all answer to the director's instructions. (semicolon)

4. The director makes many decisions, the producers take care of the business end of moviemaking. (semicolon and conjunctive adverb)

5. The first movie theaters opened in the early 1900s they were called *nickelodeons.* (two sentences)

6. Thomas Edison was a pioneer in early moviemaking he invented the first commercial motion-picture machine. (semicolon)

7. The machine was called a *kinetoscope,* it was a cabinet that showed moving images through a peephole. (two sentences)

8. Early movies were silent, sometimes offscreen actors would fill in the dialogue for the audience. (comma and coordinating conjunction)

9. The first sound films were shown in the late 1920s they marked a milestone in moviemaking history. (semicolon)

10. Movies are great entertainment they are also an art form. (semicolon and conjunctive adverb)

REVIEW ▶ **Revising Fragments and Run-on Sentences**

The following paragraph contains several sentence fragments and run-on sentences. First, identify each word group as a fragment or run-on. Then, revise the fragments and run-ons, changing the punctuation and capitalization as necessary to make each sentence clear and complete.

During the Civil War. Women nurses showed remarkable heroism. They took care of sick and wounded soldiers, they risked their lives carrying supplies. To military hospitals. Sally L. Tompkins one such woman. She ran a military hospital in the South she was one of two women captains in the Confederate Army. Clara Barton was another heroic Civil War nurse, she worked tirelessly. Caring for sick and wounded soldiers in the North. In 1864, Barton superintendent of nurses for the Union Army. She later founded the American Red Cross Society. Served as president of the Red Cross. Until 1904.

MAKING CONNECTIONS

Sentences in Poetry

Poets use language in different and creative ways. They often use unconventional sentence structure as part of their poetic technique. But sometimes they also use plain, ordinary complete sentences just as prose writers do. The difference is not in the structure of the sentences but in the shape of the sentences—the way they are arranged on the page. This poetic shaping adds to the meaning of the sentences, and sometimes it even reflects their meaning.

Read the following poem by Leslie Marmon Silko. What are the sentences in the poem? How does Silko use line breaks and stanza breaks to help express the thoughts of these sentences? How does the overall shape of the poem reflect its meaning?

The Time We Climbed Snake Mountain
by Leslie Marmon Silko

seeing good places
                for my hands
I grab the warm parts of the cliff
                and feel the mountain as I climb.

somewhere around here
        yellow spotted snake is sleeping
                        on his rock
                                in the sun.

so please
        I tell them,
                watch out,
don't step on yellow spotted snake,
                he lives here.
                        The mountain is his.

Write three or four sentences describing an object that's part of your everyday life, such as a baseball glove, a tree outside your window, or even a favorite pair of sneakers. After you write your sentences, experiment with different ways of setting them up on the page. Try breaking each sentence into several lines and arranging the lines into different shapes as Silko did in her poem. If you like, you can even try imitating the shape of Silko's poem.

Read each arrangement of your sentences aloud. Does the placement of the words make a difference in how you read the sentences? How does it affect the meaning of the sentences?

12 WRITING EFFECTIVE SENTENCES

LOOKING AHEAD

You probably like to try on different clothing combinations for style. When you write, you can try on different sentence combinations for style, too. In this chapter, you will learn how to

- use sentence-combining techniques
- make your sentences clear and precise
- vary the structure of your sentences

Combining Sentences

Short sentences are often effective, but a long, unbroken series of them can sound choppy. For example, notice how dull and tiresome the following paragraph sounds.

I've seen a lot of earthling-meets-alien movies. I saw <u>The Last Starfighter</u>. I saw all the <u>Star Trek</u> movies. I have noticed something about these movies. I've noticed that there are good humans in these movies. There are bad humans. There are good aliens. There are bad aliens. The humans and aliens are actually not so different from each other.

Notice how much more interesting the paragraph sounds when the short, choppy sentences are combined into longer, smoother sentences.

I've seen a lot of earthling-meets-alien movies, including <u>The Last Starfighter</u> and all the <u>Star Trek</u> movies. I have noticed that there are good and bad humans in these movies as well as good and bad aliens. The humans and aliens are actually not so different from each other.

Inserting Words

You can combine short sentences by inserting a key word from one sentence into another. You usually need to eliminate some words in sentences that are combined. You may also need to change the form of the key word.

USING THE SAME FORM	
ORIGINAL	Edgar Allan Poe led a short life. His life was tragic.
COMBINED	Edgar Allan Poe led a short, **tragic** life.
CHANGING THE FORM	
ORIGINAL	Edgar Allan Poe wrote strange stories. He wrote horror stories.
REVISED	Edgar Allan Poe wrote strange, **horrifying** stories.

WRITING NOTE When you change the form of a word, you often add an ending that makes the word an adjective or an adverb. Usually this ending is *–ed, –ing,* or *–ly.*

EXERCISE 1 ▶	**Combining Sentences by Inserting Words**

In the following sets of sentences, some words have been italicized. Combine each set of sentences by inserting the italicized word (or words) into the first sentence. The directions in parentheses will tell you how to change the word form if it is necessary to do so.

EXAMPLE   **1.** Edgar Allan Poe was a writer who wrote stories and poems. Edgar Allan Poe was an *American* writer.
   1. *Edgar Allan Poe was an American writer who wrote stories and poems.*

1. Poe's mother died three years after he was born. His mother was an *actress*.
2. Poe was taken in by Mrs. John Allan and her husband. He was taken in *later*. Their taking him in was *fortunate*. (Add *–ly* to *fortunate*.)
3. Poe created stories. He created *detective* stories.
4. Poe inspired the author of the Sherlock Holmes stories. The author had *talent*. (Add *–ed* to *talent*.)
5. Poe had theories about the writing of fiction. His theories were *original*.

EXERCISE 2 ▶	**Combining Sentences by Inserting Words**

In Exercise 1, the words you needed to insert were italicized. Now try using your own judgment to combine sentences. There may be more than one way to combine each set; do what sounds best to you. Add commas and change the forms of words whenever you need to.

EXAMPLE   **1.** Luis Valdez is a famous playwright. He is a Mexican American.
   1. *Luis Valdez is a famous Mexican American playwright.*

1. Valdez was born in Delano. Delano is in California.
2. He grew up in a family of farm workers. They were migrant workers.
3. As a child, Valdez began to work in the fields. He was six years old.

4. He champions the cause of underpaid migrant farm workers. He also champions the cause of migrant farm workers who suffer from overwork.
5. He organized the Farm Workers' Theater, a troupe of actors and musicians. The troupe travels.

Inserting Groups of Words

You also can combine closely related sentences by taking a phrase from one sentence and inserting it into another sentence.

Prepositional Phrases

A *prepositional phrase,* a preposition with its object, can usually be inserted in another sentence with no changes. All you have to do is leave out some of the words in one of the sentences.

ORIGINAL   Twelve million immigrants came to the shores of the United States. They came through Ellis Island.

REVISED   Twelve million immigrants came to the shores of the United States **through Ellis Island.**

Participial Phrases

A *participial phrase* contains a verb form that usually ends in *–ing* or *–ed.* It acts as an adjective, modifying a noun or a pronoun. Sometimes, you can change the verb from one sentence into a participle by adding *–ing* or *–ed.*

Then you can combine the two sentences. Place the participial phrase close to the noun or pronoun it will modify to avoid confusing your reader.

ORIGINAL   Many immigrants faced long months of waiting at Ellis Island. They were weakened by their journeys.

REVISED   Many immigrants, **weakened by their journeys,** faced long months of waiting at Ellis Island.

Appositive Phrases

An *appositive phrase* follows a noun or pronoun and helps to explain it. Sometimes you can combine sentences by changing one of the sentences to an appositive phrase.

ORIGINAL   My grandfather was an immigrant. My grandfather brought with him photographs that are now souvenirs.

REVISED   My grandfather, **an immigrant,** brought with him photographs that are now souvenirs.

 COMPUTER NOTE: Don't be afraid to use your word-processing program's Cut and Paste commands to insert different phrases.

EXERCISE 3 ▶   **Combining Sentences by Inserting Phrases**

Revise each of the following sets of sentences to create one sentence. There may be more than one way to combine the sentences. In the first five sets, the words you need to insert are italicized. After that, change the forms of words as indicated in parentheses, and add commas wherever you need to.

EXAMPLE   **1.** Auguste Piccard was a Swiss physicist who studied the upper atmosphere. He studied it by going up in balloons.
   1. *Auguste Piccard was a Swiss physicist who studied the upper atmosphere by going up in balloons.*

1. Auguste Piccard was an inventor, scientist, and explorer. He was *from Switzerland.*
2. Piccard once spent sixteen hours in a balloon. He was *floating across Germany and France.*
3. Piccard attended the Swiss Institute of Technology. The institute is *in Zurich, Switzerland.*

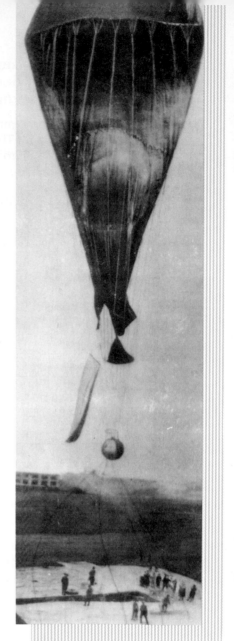

4. Piccard was a young man when he became a professor. He became a professor *at the Swiss Institute.*

5. Piccard created an important invention. He invented *an airtight gondola.*

6. The gondola took Piccard ten miles into the air. The gondola was attached to a balloon.

7. Piccard then made numerous balloon trips. He studied electricity. (Change *studied* to *studying.*)

8. Piccard turned his interest to the ocean depths. He designed a deep-sea diving ship. (Change *designed* to *designing.*)

9. Piccard and his son Jacques went two miles below the surface of the Adriatic Sea. They went in 1953.

10. Another deep-sea diving ship went almost ten miles below the surface of the ocean. It set the world's depth record in 1960. (Change *set* to *setting.*)

Using Compound Subjects and Verbs

Another way to combine sentences is to make compound subjects and verbs. Just look for sentences that have the same subject or the same verb. Then make the subject or verb compound by adding a coordinating conjunction such as *and, but, or, nor,* or *yet.*

ORIGINAL   The Angles were fierce people. The Jutes were fierce people. [different subjects with same verb]

REVISED   **The Angles and the Jutes** were fierce people. [compound subject with same verb]

ORIGINAL   The Angles and Saxons invaded Britain. The Angles and Saxons conquered Britain. [different verbs with same subject]

REVISED   The Angles and Saxons **invaded and conquered** Britain. [compound verb with same subject]

ORIGINAL   The Angles conquered Britain. The Saxons also conquered Britain. They both ran off the native Celts. [different subjects and different verbs]

REVISED   **The Angles and the Saxons conquered** Britain and **ran off** the native Celts. [compound subject and compound verb]

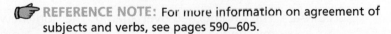

USAGE HINT

Checking for Subject-Verb Agreement

When you combine sentences by making compound subjects and compound verbs, make sure that your new subjects and verbs agree in number.

ORIGINAL   The dialect of the Angles is an ancestor of Modern English. The dialect of the Saxons is also an ancestor of Modern English.

REVISED   The **dialects** of the Angles and the Saxons **are** ancestors of Modern English. [Plural subject *dialects* takes the verb *are*.]

☞ REFERENCE NOTE: For more information on agreement of subjects and verbs, see pages 590–605.

EXERCISE 4 ▸ **Creating Compound Subjects and Compound Verbs**

Here are five series of short sentences. Combine each series into one sentence that has a compound subject, a compound verb, or a compound subject and a compound verb.

1. Bananas are a tropical fruit. Coconuts are also a tropical fruit.
2. Brazil produces bananas. India produces bananas. Both countries export bananas.
3. Some bananas are cooked like vegetables. They are eaten like vegetables.
4. By A.D. 600, the Egyptians were eating coconuts. Indians and Koreans were also eating coconuts.
5. Coconuts are not a major crop in the United States. Bananas are not a major crop in the United States, either.

Creating a Compound Sentence

You can combine two sentences by creating a compound sentence. A *compound sentence* is really two or more simple sentences linked by

- a comma and a coordinating conjunction
  or
- a semicolon
  or
- a semicolon and a conjunctive adverb

Before linking two thoughts in a compound sentence, make sure that the thoughts are related to one another and equal in importance. That's what a compound sentence tells the reader.

☞ REFERENCE NOTE: For more information about how to create compound sentences, see pages 416 and 577–578.

ORIGINAL The cat knocked over a lamp. The dog chewed up my shoe.

REVISED The cat knocked over a lamp, **and** the dog chewed up my shoe. [comma and coordinating conjunction]
The cat knocked over a lamp; the dog chewed up my shoe. [semicolon]
The cat knocked over a lamp; **meanwhile,** the dog chewed up my shoe. [semicolon and conjunctive adverb]

You can use the coordinating conjunctions *and, but, nor, for, yet,* and *so* to form compound sentences. However, because *so* is often over-worked in writing, you should think twice about using it.

When you join two sentences with a coordinating conjunction, remember to use a comma before the conjunction.

EXERCISE 5 ▶ **Combining Simple Sentences into Compound Sentences**

The sentences in the following pairs are closely related. Using the methods you've learned, combine each pair into a compound sentence. Remember to add commas where they are needed in your combined sentences.

1. The Hopi Indians live on a reservation. They have many separate villages.
2. Many Hopi Indians grow crops. Some make jewelry, baskets, pottery, and wooden dolls.
3. The dolls are called kachina dolls. They have a special meaning for the Hopi.
4. Kachina dolls represent spirits. They play an important part in Hopi religious ceremonies.
5. The Hopi are peaceful people. Their religion is important to them.

Creating a Complex Sentence

A *complex sentence* includes one *independent clause*—a clause that can stand alone as a sentence. It also has one or more *subordinate clauses*—clauses that cannot stand alone as sentences.

Adjective Clauses

You can make a sentence into an *adjective clause* by inserting *who, which,* or *that* in place of the subject. Then you can use the adjective clause to give information about a noun or a pronoun in another sentence.

ORIGINAL   Many people are afraid of bats. They are usually harmless creatures.

REVISED   Many people are afraid of bats, **which are usually harmless creatures.**

Adverb Clauses

You can turn one sentence into an *adverb clause* and combine it with another sentence. The adverb clause may modify a verb, an adjective, or another adverb in the sentence (the independent clause) that it is attached to.

Adverb clauses begin with subordinating conjunctions like *after, although, because, if, when,* and *where.* You have to choose these conjunctions carefully. They show the relationship between the ideas in the adverb clause and the independent clause. For example, *when* shows how the ideas are related in time, and *where* shows how the ideas are related in space. When you use an adverb clause at the beginning of a sentence, you need to separate it from the independent clause with a comma.

ORIGINAL   Bats are considered dangerous. They rarely attack humans.

REVISED   **Although bats are considered dangerous,** they rarely attack humans.

Noun Clauses

You can make a sentence into a *noun clause* and insert it into another sentence just like an ordinary noun. You create a noun clause by inserting a word like *that, how, what,* or *who* at the beginning. When you place the noun clause in the other sentence, you may have to change or remove some words.

ORIGINAL   Dracula is such a frightening character. This doesn't help the bats' reputation.

REVISED   **That Dracula is such a frightening character** doesn't help the bats' reputation. [The word *that* introduces the noun clause, which becomes the subject of the verb *does help.*]

EXERCISE 6 ▶	**Combining Sentences into Complex Sentences**

Following are five sets of short, choppy sentences that need improving. Use subordinate clauses to combine each set of sentences into a single complex sentence. You may see different ways to combine some of the sets; just choose the way that sounds best to you. You may need to change or delete some words to make smooth combinations.

1. The shark is a member of a fish family. The family includes the largest and fiercest fish.
2. Sharks have long bodies, wedge-shaped heads, and pointed back fins. The back fins sometimes stick out of the water.
3. Sharks live mostly in warm seas. Some sharks have been found in bodies of cold water.
4. The whale shark is harmless to people. It feeds on plankton.
5. However, many sharks are ruthless killers. They feed on flesh.

REVIEW A ▶	**Revising a Paragraph by Combining Sentences**

Using all of the sentence-combining techniques you have learned, revise and rewrite the following short paragraph. Use your judgment about what sentences to combine and how to combine them. Work for clear, varied sentences that read smoothly, but don't change the meaning of the original paragraph.

Stonehenge is in southwestern England. It is a series of stones. They are huge stones. They weigh as much as fifty tons. Stonehenge was built about five thousand years ago. The stones were moved to their present site. They were moved by as many as one thousand people. There are many theories about the purpose of the stones. One popular theory is that the stones served as an observatory. The observatory was astrological. At one point in the summer, the sun rises directly. It rises over one of the stones.

Improving Sentence Style

In the first part of this chapter, you learned some techniques for making smooth sentence combinations. Now you'll learn how to style your sentences by making them clear, balanced, and varied.

Using Parallel Structure

When you combine several related ideas in one sentence, it's important to make sure that your combinations are balanced. You create balance in a sentence by using the same form or part of speech to express each idea. For example, you balance a noun with a noun, a phrase with a phrase, and a clause with a clause. This balance is called parallelism, or *parallel structure.*

NOT PARALLEL   I'm not much of an athlete, but I like softball, soccer, and to play hockey. [two nouns and a phrase]

PARALLEL   I'm not much of an athlete, but I like **softball, soccer,** and **hockey.** [three nouns]

NOT PARALLEL	Dominic doesn't have enough time to play soccer, join the debating team, and band. [two phrases and a noun]
PARALLEL	Dominic doesn't have enough time **to play soccer, join the debating team,** and **participate in band.** [three phrases]
NOT PARALLEL	I knew that soccer was popular in Europe and its popularity in Latin America, too. [clause and phrase]
PARALLEL	I knew **that soccer was popular in Europe** and **that it was popular in Latin America, too.** [two clauses]

EXERCISE 7 ▶ **Revising Sentences to Create Parallel Structure**

Bring balance to the following sentences by putting the ideas in parallel form. You may need to add or delete some words. If a sentence is already correct, write C.

1. Paris, the capital of France, is famous for its history, culture, and to eat in excellent restaurants.
2. The Seine River runs through the city and supplies water to all Parisians.
3. Visiting the Notre Dame Cathedral, walking through the Louvre Museum, and the Eiffel Tower are all favorite pastimes of tourists.
4. It is interesting that Paris has always attracted artists and refugees have always been welcome.
5. Many famous Americans, including Ernest Hemingway, lived and writing in Paris during the 1920s.

Revising Stringy Sentences

Linking together related ideas is a good way to bring variety to your writing. But if you overdo it, you may end up with a *stringy sentence.*

A *stringy sentence* just goes on and on. It usually has too many independent clauses strung together with coordinating conjunctions like *and* or *but.* Since all the ideas are treated equally, the reader has trouble seeing how they are related.

There are two ways you can fix stringy sentences. You can

- break the sentence into two or more sentences
- turn some of the independent clauses into subordinate clauses or phrases

STRINGY   The fire alarm bell rang, and everyone started to file out of school, but then our principal came down the hall, and he said the bell was a mistake, and we went back to our classes.

BETTER   The fire alarm bell rang, and everyone started to file out of school. Then our principal came down the hall to say the bell was a mistake. We went back to our classes.

BETTER   When the fire alarm bell rang, everyone started to file out of school. Then our principal came down the hall. He said the bell was a mistake, and we went back to our classes.

EXERCISE 8 ▶ Revising Stringy Sentences

Decide which of the following sentences are stringy and need improving. Then revise the stringy sentences. You can do this by (1) breaking each sentence into two or more sentences or (2) turning some of the independent clauses into subordinate clauses or phrases. If you find a sentence that is effective and doesn't need to be improved, write C.

EXAMPLE   **1.** Alexandre Gustave Eiffel was a French engineer, and he designed the Eiffel Tower, and he also designed the frame for the Statue of Liberty, but his greatest accomplishment may have been proving that metal was an important building material.

1. *Alexandre Gustave Eiffel was a French engineer who designed the Eiffel Tower and also the frame for the Statue of Liberty. His greatest accomplishment may have been proving that metal was an important building material.*

1. Alexandre Gustave Eiffel was a famous Frenchman, and he was born in 1832, and he died in 1923.
2. Eiffel was an engineer, and he designed the Eiffel Tower, and it was built for the World's Fair of 1889.

3. Eiffel's chief interest was bridges, and the Eiffel Tower displays his bridge-designing skills, but so does another historical monument, and it's a monument that you're familiar with.

4. In 1885, Eiffel used his engineering knowledge to design part of a great American symbol, the Statue of Liberty in New York Harbor.

5. Toward the end of his life, Eiffel studied the effects of air on airplanes, and then in 1912, he built a wind tunnel and an aerodynamics laboratory, and later he conducted experiments from the Eiffel Tower, which is now a favorite tourist attraction.

Revising Wordy Sentences

If someone says, "It would please me greatly if you would diminish the volume of your verbalizing during the time I am perusing this reading material," you might wonder what language is being spoken. How much easier and clearer to say, "Please be quieter while I'm reading."

Here are three tips for creating sentences that aren't too wordy.

- Don't use more words than you need to.
- Don't use fancy words where simple ones will do.
- Don't repeat yourself unless it's absolutely necessary.

WORDY	Ken is a talented drummer who plays the drums with great skill.
IMPROVED	Ken is a talented drummer.

WORDY	In the event that we are unable to go to the movie, we can play basketball at home.
IMPROVED	If we can't go to the movie, we can play basketball at home.

> **EXERCISE 9** ▶ **Revising Wordy Sentences**

The writer of the following letter wants to make a complaint, but the wordiness of the letter gets in the way. Revise the letter, making it clearer and more effective. You may add details if you wish.

Dear Mr. and Mrs. Wilson,

At this point in time, it is my unhappy duty to inform you of the fact that I will no longer be available to baby-sit with Charles. On the evening of July 13, I was hired by you to perform the duties of baby sitter for your three-year-old son. These duties were performed by me to the best of my ability. However, I do not feel that any baby sitter should be in a position of having to deal with the threat of harm to the baby sitter's person. I feel that Charles's hurling of objects at my person and his action of locking me in the closet were possible threats to my safety. The situation being what it is, I feel that I cannot safely perform my duties, and I will no longer place myself in danger by sitting with your son.

Sincerely,

Miguel Garza

Varying Sentence Beginnings

The basic structure of an English sentence is a subject followed by a verb. But following this pattern all the time makes your writing dull. Notice how boring the following paragraph sounds:

The theater was packed. Jan and I managed to find our seats. The play began thirty minutes late. We were bored. We read the program four times. Jan wanted to find out the reason for the delay. She asked an usher. The usher was amused. The usher said that the star's costume had been damaged by her dog. We laughed because the play was Cats.

Now notice how much more interesting the same paragraph sounds with varied sentence beginnings. To create the varied beginnings, the writer has combined sentences. Some sentences became subordinate clauses, and others became phrases.

> Although the theater was packed, Jan and I managed to find our seats. The play began thirty minutes late. Bored, we read the program four times. To find out the reason for the delay, Jan asked an usher. Amused, the usher said that the star's costume had been damaged by her dog. We laughed because the play was <u>Cats</u>.

You can use the following methods to vary sentence beginnings.

VARYING SENTENCE BEGINNINGS

SINGLE-WORD MODIFIERS

Excitedly, Marcia opened her presents. [adverb]
Hungry, the family stopped at the restaurant. [adjective]

PHRASES

With tears of joy, Carla received her prize.
[prepositional phrase]
Smiling happily, Tanya told us the good news.
[participial phrase]
To make good grades, you must study. [infinitive phrase]

SUBORDINATE CLAUSES

Because the coach was angry, the team ran ten laps.
[adverb clause]
When Tom found the kitten on his doorstep, he decided to keep it. [adverb clause]

EXERCISE 10 ▶ **Varying Sentence Beginnings**

The following sentences are all good, but they would make a boring paragraph. Here's your chance to practice varying sentence beginnings. The notes in parentheses tell you whether to start your revised sentence with a single-word modifier, a phrase, or a clause. In some cases, you may also want to add or delete a word to make the sentence sound better.

1. Animals are in danger of extinction in many different parts of the world. (phrase)
2. The aye-aye is a small animal related to the monkey. (phrase)
3. The aye-aye is endangered because the rain forest on its home island is being destroyed. (subordinate clause)
4. You must travel to the Pyrenees, Portugal, or the former Soviet Union to see the desman, a water-dwelling mammal. (phrase)
5. People are threatening the desmans' survival by damming mountain streams. (phrase)
6. The giant otter of South America is protected, but poachers continue to threaten its survival. (subordinate clause)
7. Mountain lions are hunted and thus generally stay away from humans. (single-word modifier)
8. The great peacock moth of Europe is in trouble because its home is being damaged by acid rain. (subordinate clause)
9. Wolves are expert hunters, and they prey on large animals. (phrase)
10. Gray wolves, sadly, are an endangered species. (single-word modifier)

EXERCISE 11 ▶ **Revising Sentences to Create Variety**

Use what you have learned about varying sentence beginnings to revise the following paragraph. Reword some sentences so that they begin with single-word modifiers, phrases, or clauses. Some sentences may be reworded in several ways; choose the way that sounds best to you. (Consult the chart on page 437 for help.)

> Ocean animals unfortunately are often on endangered lists. Penguins are at risk in oceans of the Southern Hemisphere. Many penguin species have problems today because of oil pollution and commercial fishing. Turtles are endangered because they are slaughtered for food and for their shells. Lobsters become threatened when people overfish. Mediterranean monk seals also are threatened by increased land development and tourism.

REVIEW B ▶ Revising a Paragraph

The following paragraphs have many of the problems you have reviewed in this section. Show your writing style by rewriting and revising the paragraphs so that (1) each sentence has parallel structure, (2) stringy and wordy sentences are corrected, and (3) sentences have varied beginnings. You may add or delete details as necessary.

> One time in the recent past, we went on a picnic in Big Bend National Park in Texas. It had rained heavily all night north of the park. A friend of ours, Mrs. Brown, went with us. She had lived in that part of Texas for a large number of years and knowing all about what to expect if it rained. She said there could be a flash flood in the park. The park could be dangerous even if it didn't rain there because the water could run across the dry desert sand.
>
> Mrs. Brown made us turn our cars around to face in the other direction because she wanted us to be able to leave the low area fast if a flood came. The sun was shining with great brightness, and everyone thought Mrs. Brown was crazy, and we started to eat our picnic.
>
> A very high wall of water four feet high came toward us suddenly. We jumped into the cars and to get away just in time. Our picnic floated away, but we were glad to be alive, and we thanked Mrs. Brown.

MAKING CONNECTIONS

Sentence Craft

Professional writers craft their sentences with care. They know that sentence structure matters. It is important for the sound and for the sense of what they write.

In the following paragraph, notice the varied sentences the writer uses to describe a childhood experience. How does her style help express her feelings about her home town?

from "Marigolds"
by Eugenia W. Collier

When I think of the home town of my youth, all that I seem to remember is dust—the brown, crumbly dust of late summer—arid, sterile dust that gets into the eyes and makes them water, gets into the throat and between the toes of bare brown feet. I don't know why I should remember only the dust. Surely there must have been lush green lawns and paved streets under leafy shade trees somewhere in town; but memory is an abstract painting—it does not present things as they are, but rather as they *feel*. And so when I think of that time and that place, I remember only the dry September of the dirt roads and grassless yards of the shanty-town where I lived. And one other thing I remember, another incongruency of memory—a brilliant splash of sunny yellow against the dust—Miss Lottie's marigolds.

Write a paragraph about a neighborhood that you remember fondly. Describe the neighborhood, and then tell why it has special meaning for you. Work to create clear, lively sentences that fit together smoothly.

13 ENGLISH: ORIGINS AND USES

LOOKING AHEAD

In this chapter, you will get a glimpse of the amazing variety and flexibility of the English language. You will learn

- where English came from
- how English continues to grow and change
- what the varieties and uses of English are
- how to choose the best words for a specific purpose, audience, and situation

From Yesterday to Tomorrow

The English language has been around for longer than we have records of. It was first written about 1,300 years ago and was spoken long before that. Over the centuries, English has grown and changed to become the rich, expressive language we use today. And it's still growing and changing, along with its many users (over 750 million!) throughout the world.

To get a picture of how English changes, you might compare your everyday expressions with those that the adults you know used when they were young. For example, people didn't use the word *veejay* twenty years ago; the word wasn't invented until the 1980s, when music videos became popular. And computer terms like *byte* and *software* have been around for only a few decades.

The difference between your English and that of the previous generation is only a small part of the continuing change that has taken place in the language since its beginnings. The history of this development is like any history. It is a story of people, places, and times.

The Beginnings of English

Many of the world's languages come from an early language called ***Proto-Indo-European.*** We have no records of this parent language, but it was probably spoken by people in Eastern Europe six or seven thousand years ago. Tribes of these people slowly migrated across Europe and to India. As the tribes wandered in different directions, each tribe developed its own ***dialect,*** or distinct version of the language. The dialects eventually developed into separate languages. This map shows how the Indo-European root word *māter* ("mother") developed in some of these languages. The arrows indicate directions of migration.

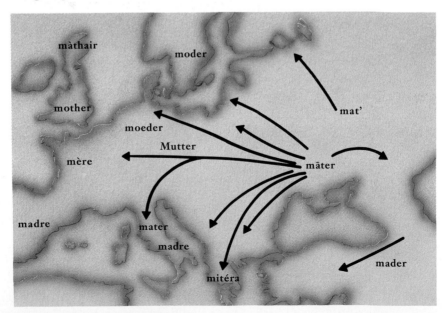

Old English

Around A.D. 450, tribes known as the Angles and the Saxons invaded Britain. They took over the areas of the island that had been settled earlier by a people called the Celts. The separate dialects these tribes spoke eventually blended into one language—*Old English,* sometimes called Anglo-Saxon.

You'd have a difficult time talking with the Anglo-Saxons—not just because they were different from us but also because English has changed so much in 1,500 years. Yet even after centuries of change, the language still bears traces of its Anglo-Saxon roots. For example, the words *eat, drink,* and *sleep* come from the Old English words *etan, drincan,* and *slæp.* And the Anglo-Saxons used an *–s* to form the plurals of many nouns, just as we do. We also have Old English to thank for irregular verb forms such as *swim, swam, swum.*

EXERCISE 1 ▶ Decoding Old English

Many of our everyday words existed in Old English in somewhat different forms. For example, *egg, milk,* and *cheese* come from the Old English *æg, meolc,* and *cese.* Look closely at the following Old English words, and see if you can figure out what they are in present-day English.

1. heofon, sunne, mona, steorra
2. haer, eage, eare, toth
3. thicce, thynne, eald, geong
4. sealt, mete, hunig
5. dæg, niht, wicu, monaþ, gear

Middle English

In 1066, the Normans from France seized control of England, and for the next 150 years a few thousand French-speaking people ruled the country. French was declared the official language—the language of government, business, and law. Because of this, many English words that are connected with wealth and power come from the French.

OLD FRENCH	governeor	atourne	faceon
MODERN ENGLISH	governor	attorney	fashion

While French was the language of the educated and was used for almost all written communication, English didn't die. The common people of England still spoke English in their everyday lives. However, their language was changing into a form we call *Middle English.* The grammar of English was becoming simpler as many of the complicated word endings disappeared.

The following lines are matching excerpts from the Lord's Prayer (Matthew 6:9–13) in Old English and Middle English. As you can see, Middle English looks much more like the English you know.

OLD ENGLISH	Fæder ure þu þe eart on heofonum, si þin nama gehalgod.
MIDDLE ENGLISH	Fader oure þat art in hevene, i-halwed bee þi name.

English was eventually reestablished as the national language of England. Three hundred years after the French invasion, educated people were again using English—that is, Middle English—for writing as well as for speaking.

The Birth of Modern English

Two very different things happened to English as it moved into the period of *Modern English.* It became standardized, and it expanded into an international language.

London Sets the Standard

Before William Caxton set up the first printing press in England around 1476, speakers and writers of English used many different versions of the language. Often, people from one part of the country had trouble understanding the English spoken and written in other sections. In those days, there was no such thing as correct spelling.

Caxton and other early printers changed all this. They standardized spelling, and since London was the center of English trade and culture, they printed all books in London English. London English soon became the standard throughout England.

Once standards were set, people wanted to learn the "proper" way to speak and write their language. Grammar and usage handbooks sprang up, along with the first English dictionaries.

English Travels Abroad

From the sixteenth century through the nineteenth century, English merchants, explorers, and settlers played a twofold role in the growth of English. They brought English to other parts of the globe, helping to make it an important world language. They also learned many new words from other languages, enriching English with imports such as the following ones.

AFRICAN	DUTCH	JAPANESE	SPANISH	TURKISH
okra	cruise	soy	siesta	yogurt

> **E X E R C I S E 2** ▶ **Identifying the Origins of Borrowed Words**

Each of the following words in Modern English was borrowed from another language. Look up each word in a dictionary that gives word origins, and tell what language it was borrowed from.

1. compute
2. hammock
3. plaza
4. ghoul
5. noodle

6. ketchup
7. hickory
8. canoe
9. drill
10. carnival

American English

Immigration to the American colonies opened a new chapter in the history of English. Separated from London by an ocean, the English colonists began to develop their own version of the language—*American English*. At the same time, regional dialects sprang up in different parts of the new nation. These dialects were the beginnings of the Southern, Northern, and Midwestern accents that you can hear in the United States today.

Like the United States itself, American English represents a wonderful variety of cultures and peoples. Native Americans, Africans who came as slaves, and immigrants from most countries around the world have enriched the language with words from their native tongues. For example, Native Americans gave us *coyote* and *squash; jazz* and *gumbo* come from Africa; and Italian immigrants added *spaghetti* and *ravioli* to the American menu.

Shoe reprinted by permission: Tribune Media Services.

EXERCISE 3 ▶	**Identifying Word Origins**

Each of the following foods was added to the American menu by a different group of people. Using a dictionary that gives word origins, find out what language gave us the word for the food.

1. burrito   **3.** waffle   **5.** succotash
2. zucchini   **4.** chop suey

English: The Twentieth Century and Beyond

Fifteen hundred years ago, English was the language of a few migrating tribes. What will it be in the world of the twenty-first century? We can't know for certain, but we do have signs that point to possibilities.

Vocabulary Growth

Dictionary makers can't keep up with the growth of English vocabulary. The last count was over 600,000 words—and the count grows every day as people around the world contribute to the language.

World Use

English has become the most widely used language in the history of the world. It is an official language in eighty-seven nations and territories. It is the world language of

- diplomacy
- science, technology, and aviation
- international trade

EXERCISE 4 ▶	**Identifying Word Origins**

Each of the following words is a twentieth-century newcomer to English. Look up each word in a dictionary or an encyclopedia, and then write a sentence or two describing its origin.

1. sitcom   **3.** brunch   **5.** boycott
2. radar   **4.** nylon

The Varieties of English

Our lives would be easier in some ways if there were strict rules for every writing and speaking situation. We would always know what kinds of words to use in a particular situation. But at the same time, our language would be boring because it would have no variety.

It's important to know that English is much more than a set of rules. It is a rich and flexible language that offers you many choices. To speak and write effectively—at home, at school, and on the job—you need to know what the varieties of English are and how to choose among them.

Dialects of American English

Like all languages, English has many distinct versions, called *dialects*. Everyone uses a dialect, and no dialect is better or worse than another. Each has unique features of grammar, vocabulary, and pronunciation.

You are already familiar with one version of English— the *standard American English* used in schools, in newspapers, and on radio and television. In addition to standard American English, there are two kinds of dialects used in the United States: *regional dialects* and *ethnic dialects*.

Regional Dialects

You've probably noticed that people in one area of the country tend to talk differently from people in another area. That's because each area has its own **regional dialect.** There are four major regional dialects in the United States: *New England, Northern, Midland,* and *Southern.*

Pronunciations of words often vary from one dialect region to another. For example, some Northerners tend to drop the *r* sound from words, so that *barn* sounds like "bahn." People in some parts of the Midland and Southern areas tend to add an *r* sound, so that *wash* sounds like "warsh."

Regional dialects also vary in grammar and vocabulary. For example, you may say "sick *to* my stomach" if you come from New York but "sick *at* my stomach" if you come from Georgia. And you may drink *soda, tonic,* or *pop,* depending on what part of the country you come from.

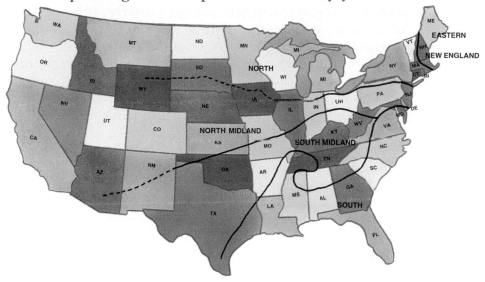

Ethnic Dialects

An *ethnic dialect* is a dialect used by people who share the same cultural heritage. Because Americans come from many different cultures, American English includes many different ethnic dialects. The most widely used ethnic dialects are the Black English of many African Americans and the Hispanic English of many people from Cuba, Mexico, Central America, and Puerto Rico.

Many everyday words began as ethnic dialect words but then became part of the general English vocabulary. For example, *tote* and *chigger* came into English through Black dialect, and *avocado* and *taco* were added to English by Hispanic Americans.

Standard American English

Every variety of English has its own set of rules and guidelines. No variety is the best or the most correct. However, one kind of English is more widely used and accepted than others in the United States. This variety is called *standard American English.*

Standard American English is the one variety that

belongs to all of us. Because it's commonly understood, it allows people from many different regions and cultures to communicate with one another clearly. It is the variety of English you read and hear most often in books and magazines, on radio and television. It is the kind of English that people are expected to use in most school and business situations.

The **Handbook of Grammar, Usage, and Mechanics** in this textbook gives you some of the rules and guidelines for using standard American English. To identify the differences between standard American English and other varieties of English, the **Handbook** uses the labels *standard* and *nonstandard*. *Nonstandard* doesn't mean wrong language. It means language that is inappropriate in situations where standard English is expected.

☞ **REFERENCE NOTE:** For more about standard English, see page 697.

E X E R C I S E 5 ▶   Identifying Features of Dialects

A good way to appreciate a dialect is to hear it. In the following passage, an eleven-year-old girl and her grandfather are speaking Southern dialect. Emilu insists that she remembers everything that has ever happened to her. Her grandfather thinks that remembering things is not such a simple matter. Read the passage aloud, pronouncing the words as the author has spelled them. Is the characters' language different from yours? How would you express the same thoughts in your own dialect?

> She swung her feet. "I know ever dadblasted thing ever happen to me."
>
> "You think so, little daughter. But there is things gittin away from you in the night when you fergit to hold on."
>
> She shook her head. "Not me. I got it all somewhere. In my head, I reckon."
>
> "Course you ain't live long. There just ain't that much."
>
> "There's a plenty, I guarantee. There is plenty done happen."
>
> Helen Norris, "The Singing Well"

Standard English—Formal to Informal

Just as you can change your clothes to suit different occasions, you can "dress up" or "dress down" your language to suit your audience and your purpose. Depending on the circumstances, your language can be formal, informal, or somewhere in between. This chart shows some of the appropriate uses of very formal and very informal English.

USES OF FORMAL AND INFORMAL ENGLISH		
	FORMAL	INFORMAL
SPEAKING	formal, dignified occasions, such as banquets and dedication ceremonies	everyday conversation at home, school, work, and recreation
WRITING	serious papers and reports	personal letters, journal entries, and many newspaper and magazine articles

You can say the same thing in many different ways. For example, *chow down* and *dine* both mean "eat," but one is much more formal than the other. The main differences between formal and informal English are in sentence structure, word choice, and tone.

FEATURES OF FORMAL AND INFORMAL ENGLISH		
	FORMAL	INFORMAL
SENTENCE STRUCTURE	long and difficult	short and easy
WORD CHOICE	precise; often technical or scientific	simple and ordinary; often includes contractions, colloquialisms, and slang
TONE	serious and dignified	conversational

EXERCISE 6▶   **Writing an Informal Invitation**

Your school is holding a student recognition night, and you've been selected to receive an award for your participation in a school or community activity. The school provides you with five invitations like the one printed here. But the invitation sounds too stiff and formal to send to the person (such as an aunt, uncle, counselor, coach, or minister) who first got you interested in the activity. Write the *informal* invitation that you would send to that person.

The Administration and Faculty of Central High School

cordially invite you to attend the

Second Annual Student Recognition Ceremony

in the Town Hall Auditorium

on Friday evening the twelfth of April

at eight o'clock

Uses of Informal English

In informal speaking and writing, people constantly make up new words and give new uses and meanings to old ones. This makes informal English flexible. Dictionaries help you to see this flexibility by giving labels to different informal uses of words. The two most commonly listed usage labels are *colloquialism* and *slang*.

☞ REFERENCE NOTE: See pages 926–927 for a sample dictionary entry showing usage labels.

Colloquialisms

Colloquialisms are the informal words and phrases of conversational language. They bring flavor and color to everyday speech and a friendly, conversational tone to writing. Many colloquialisms are figures of speech that aren't meant to be taken literally.

EXAMPLES   I may have made a mistake, but you don't have to **fly off the handle** about it.

The bride's parents are usually expected to **foot the bill** for the wedding.

The judge, who had been convicted of accepting bribes, swore that he had been **framed.**

LOOKING AT Language

Where Do Colloquialisms Come From?

Many colloquialisms have interesting histories. For example, the phrase *barking up the wrong tree* originally referred to dogs trained to hunt raccoons and opossums. When a dog chased and cornered the wrong kind of animal, the hunter would find it "barking up the wrong tree." Eventually, the phrase came to refer to anybody who had the wrong idea about something.

In a book such as *Why Do We Say It?* (Castle, 1985), look up the original meanings of two colloquialisms, such as *jerkwater town* and *pass the buck.*

Slang

Slang is made up of newly coined words or of old words used in unconventional ways. It is usually clever and colorful. It is often a special language for specific groups of people, such as students and military personnel. Some people use slang to be up-to-date.

The following words, when used with the given meanings, are all marked *slang* in *Webster's New World Dictionary.* Can you think of other slang words used today to mean the same things?

bummer —a depressing experience
cool —pleasing, excellent
cop out —to quit, abandon
hassle —to annoy, harass
weirdo —a bizarre or strange person

Jump Start reprinted by permission of United Feature Syndicate, Inc.

Sometimes a slang word becomes a lasting and widely used part of the language. But more often than not, it lives a short and limited life. Slang is generally used only in the most informal speaking situations.

STYLE NOTE Colloquialisms and slang often fit well in short stories. They can help make your characters believable. For example, in the following excerpt, colloquialisms and slang help make the narrator seem like a real teenager.

> At the last minute Annie couldn't go. She was invaded by one of those twenty-four-hour flu bugs that sent her to bed with a fever, moaning about the fact that she'd also have to break her date with Handsome Harry Arnold that night. We call him Handsome Harry because he's actually handsome, but he's also a nice guy, cool, and he doesn't treat me like Annie's kid brother, which I am, but like a regular person.
> Robert Cormier, "The Moustache"

However, do not use colloquialisms or slang in test answers, essays, reports, or other types of formal writing.

EXERCISE 7 ▶ **Replacing Slang and Colloquialisms with More Formal English**

Can you explain the slang or colloquial expression in each of the following sentences? Use a dictionary to find the meanings of any that you can't explain. Then rewrite each sentence to say the same thing in more formal English.

1. "Bought another pack of *coffin nails,* huh? Haven't you heard about the Surgeon General's report?"

2. Maria may seem *stuck-up,* but she's really just shy.
3. If I can't get my parents to *cough up* the money, I won't be able to have my bike repaired.
4. She plays a *wicked* game of tennis.
5. He tried to *butter up* his sister with compliments, but she still wouldn't lend him her car.

Worlds of Meaning

Words have many layers of meaning. Their messages can change depending on the time, the place, and the situation in which they are used. It is important to understand some of the possible meanings and associations of the words you choose. You want to be sure that your words are going to say what you want them to.

Idioms

Have you ever been struck by how funny some of our everyday expressions would seem if they were taken word-for-word? For example, what if you literally *lost your temper* or *ran across* some friends from school? Expressions like these are called *idioms.*

Idioms are phrases in a language that mean something different from the literal meanings of the words. Idioms often can't be explained grammatically, and they make no sense if translated word-for-word into another language.

EXAMPLES   I tried to call you, but you were **on the phone.**
Carla really **gets into** waterskiing.
We **talked out** the problem.

Jargon

The word *jargon* often means "wordy, confusing, unintelligible language." But it can also refer to words and phrases that have special meanings for particular groups of people, such as people who share the same profession, occupation, hobby, or field of study. In this second sense, jargon can be a practical and effective way to communicate because it reduces a group of many words to just one or two words. A good example is the word *pan,* which has a special meaning in television and movie production. It is a brief and simple way of saying "move a camera across a wide angle."

A single word can be used as jargon by two or more groups, with each group giving it a different meaning.

EXAMPLE **Lead:**
Card players—the act of playing first
Electricians—a wire that carries current
Journalists—the opening paragraph of a news story
Musicians—the main melody in a musical composition

Jargon is effective only if the reader or listener is familiar with its special meaning. It is inappropriate for a general audience.

EXERCISE 8 ▶ **Defining Words with Specialized Uses**

What is the general, ordinary meaning of each of the following italicized words? What special meaning does the word have for the field or sport indicated? Look up each word in a dictionary to find the special meaning.

1. *noise*—electronics
2. *track*—television
3. *mole*—espionage
4. *steal*—baseball
5. *platform*—politics

Denotation and Connotation

The *denotations* of a word are its direct, plainly expressed meanings—the meanings a dictionary lists. In addition to their denotations, many words have ***connotations*** — meanings suggested by or associated with the word.

Because connotations often stir people's feelings, they can have powerful effects on the listener or reader. For example, the words *proud* and *arrogant* have similar denotative meanings, but they suggest different ideas. *Proud* can suggest self-respect and a sense of accomplishment. *Arrogant*, on the other hand, has negative connotations of snobbishness or a kind of superior attitude.

Your writing will be more effective if you are aware of the connotations words have. You can choose words for their connotations, but be careful to avoid words that might send the wrong message to your audience.

| EXERCISE 9 | **Analyzing the Connotations of Words** |

The words in each of the following pairs have similar meanings. Which word would you prefer if someone were describing you? Why?

1. thin, scrawny
2. thrifty, stingy
3. curious, nosy
4. humble, meek
5. tidy, fussy
6. choosy, picky
7. determined, stubborn
8. commanding, bossy
9. intelligent, brainy
10. critical, faultfinding

Loaded Words

Words that are intended to provoke strong feeling, either positive or negative, are called ***loaded words.*** A writer or speaker who wants to prejudice you for or against something may use loaded words because of their appeal to your emotions. For example, advertisers, politicians, and writers of newspaper editorials often use loaded words to convince or influence their readers.

EXAMPLES   After suffering **defeat** in last week's presidential primary, Senator Blank addressed a **mere handful of people** last night at the Civic Center.

After suffering a **setback** in last week's presidential primary, Senator Blank addressed a **small but spirited audience** last night at the Civic Center.

> **E X E R C I S E 10▶**   **Analyzing Loaded Words**

Senator Blank is running against Governor Blab for president. The following account of Senator Blank's speech at a political rally was written by Governor Blab's press agent. What words are loaded against Senator Blank? As Senator Blank's campaign manager, write your account of the same scene. The first sentence has been done for you on page 457.

> After suffering defeat in last week's presidential primary, Senator Blank addressed a mere handful of people last night at the Civic Center. Looking drained and feverish, the senator threatened to continue his futile bid for the nomination. His voice rose hysterically as he ended his speech with these foolhardy words: "I intend to beat Governor Blab next week right here in his home state."

Euphemisms

Words that mean basically the same thing can have very different effects on an audience. Sometimes a word or phrase may be considered offensive because it is too direct. A writer or speaker may replace it with a *euphemism.* Euphemisms are agreeable-sounding terms that are substituted for more direct, less pleasant-sounding ones.

EUPHEMISM	MORE DIRECT TERM
sanitation engineer	garbage collector
dentures	false teeth
house of correction	prison
passed away	died
underprivileged	poor

Some euphemisms are used as a courtesy to avoid offending people or hurting their feelings. For example, if a friend asks you what you think of his unattractive new shirt, you might call the shirt "colorful" instead of "loud." However, other euphemisms are used to mislead people—to hide unpleasant truths or misrepresent the facts. For example, an accident in a workplace might be called a *safety-related occurrence*. And an official might report that troops are *engaging the enemy on all sides* when the troops are actually being ambushed.

E X E R C I S E 11 ▶ **Translating Euphemisms into Straightforward Language**

List five of the euphemisms that you hear and read in your everyday life. Then translate each euphemism into straightforward language, telling what it really means.

EXAMPLE   1. *Euphemism: previously owned car*
            Translation: used car

STYLE NOTE   Always be aware of the effect your words are likely to have on your reader. Loaded words and euphemisms will have a place in some of your writing. However, you should choose them carefully and use them sparingly.

Tired Words

A *tired word* is a word that has lost its freshness and force. It has been used so often and so carelessly that it has become worn-out and almost meaningless. The words *nice, fine, pretty, wonderful, terrific,* and *great* are good examples of tired words.

Tired words are usually acceptable in everyday conversation. But in most cases, they are not exact enough to be effective in writing. For example, how much do you learn about a movie if the reviewer in your local newspaper writes that it is a "great" movie? How much do you tell the reader of your book report if you say that the book is "wonderful" or "terrific"? In both cases, the answer is "not much."

Clichés

A tired expression is often called a *cliché* (klē-shā´). Many of the most common clichés are overused comparisons: *busy as a bee, clear as crystal, quick as a flash, white as a sheet, straight as an arrow, thin as a rail.* Other clichés include the expressions *few and far between, accidents will happen, gala occasion, last but not least.*

You might say I'm a HEAD in the clouds, SHOULDER to the wheel, NOSE to the grindstone, TONGUE in the cheek, HEART on the sleeve, FEET on the ground kind of guy!

Bob Quigman: World's Greatest Contortionist.

STYLE NOTE   Tired words and clichés are weak and boring. Watch for them as you evaluate and revise your writing. Keep a thesaurus or a dictionary of synonyms handy for finding livelier, more precise words.

E X E R C I S E 12▶   **Identifying Tired Words and Clichés**

Spend a week watching and listening for tired words and expressions—including any that you use yourself. Each day, jot down at least one that you've heard or read. Compare your list with those of your classmates. By combining lists, you will have a collection of expressions to avoid when you write.

MAKING CONNECTIONS

Write an Advertisement

Ad writers can't afford to waste words. They have to choose each word carefully for its likely effect on listeners and readers. For this reason, they often use loaded words—words that have strong emotional appeal.

Working with a classmate, write and act out a script for a short television commercial. Advertise any product you like—for example, a new breakfast cereal, a line of "designer" clothing, or an imaginary brand of laundry detergent. Your commercial can be funny or serious, as long as it's convincing.

Getting Started

To help you get started, sketch a few pictures of the product you want to advertise. Then, create a list of positive, appealing words and phrases that might help you sell the product. Write down as many words as you can think of; you can narrow down your list later.

Developing Your Ad

Next, decide what kind of scene you will write and act out—for example, a conversation at a family's breakfast table or a trip to a department store. Work with your partner to write short lines of dialogue for your scene, using the most effective words from your list. Decide which part each of you will play and what simple props you can make or bring from home.

Testing Your Ad

You won't know if your ad works until you test it on an audience. Act out your script for your classmates. Then, ask them for feedback. Would they buy the product you've advertised? Why or why not?

PART TWO

HANDBOOK

GRAMMAR

14 The Parts of Speech
15 The Parts of a Sentence
16 The Phrase
17 The Clause

USAGE

18 Agreement
19 Using Verbs Correctly
20 Using Pronouns Correctly
21 Using Modifiers Correctly
22 A Glossary of Usage

MECHANICS

23 Capital Letters
24 End Marks and Commas
25 Semicolons and Colons
26 Italics and Quotation Marks
27 Apostrophes
28 Hyphens, Dashes, Parentheses
29 Spelling
30 Correcting Common Errors

14 THE PARTS OF SPEECH

The Work That Words Do

Diagnostic Test

Identifying Parts of Speech

Identify the part of speech of each italicized word in the following paragraph.

EXAMPLE   Everyone [1] *has* favorite summer [2] *places.*
　　　　　　1. *verb*
　　　　　　2. *noun*

　　　For [1] *me,* no [2] *spot* is [3] *better* than the beach. On [4] *hot,* sunny days, when the sand [5] *burns* my feet, I am always [6] *careful* [7] *about* putting on [8] *sunscreen.* I like to run [9] *through* the foaming surf and later relax under a beach umbrella. Most of the time, I [10] *enjoy* being with friends, [11] *but* sometimes I prefer to be by [12] *myself.* With only [13] *strangers* around me, I [14] *feel* free to think my [15] *own* thoughts. I wander [16] *slowly* along the water-line, poking through all the interesting things [17] *that* the sea has washed up. Once I accidentally stepped on a [18] *jellyfish* and couldn't help but yell [19] *"Ouch!"* when it stung my foot. Since then, I've learned to be [20] *more* careful about where I step.

	The Eight Parts of Speech		
noun	adjective	adverb	conjunction
pronoun	verb	preposition	interjection

The Noun

14a. A *noun* is a word used to name a person, place, thing, or idea.

PERSONS	Sharon, Captain Brown, hairstylist, swimmers
PLACES	Iowa, district, Mars, Antarctica, library
THINGS	okra, Great Pyramid, toothpicks, U.S.S. *Enterprise*, merry-go-round
IDEAS	peace, truth, justice, excellence, honesty

Born Loser reprinted by permission of Newspaper Enterprise Association, Inc.

Common and Proper Nouns

A *proper noun* names a particular person, place, thing, or idea and is always capitalized. A *common noun* names any one of a group of persons, places, things, or ideas and is not generally capitalized.

COMMON NOUNS	PROPER NOUNS
scientist	Marie Curie, Charles Drew
woman	Coretta Scott King, Rita Moreno, Maria Tallchief
city	Cairo, St. Louis, Paris
building	World Trade Center, Buckingham Palace
continent	North America, South America, Africa
mountain	Mount Everest, Kilimanjaro, Pike's Peak
day	Monday, Thursday, Labor Day

Concrete and Abstract Nouns

A *concrete noun* names an object that can be perceived by the senses. An *abstract noun* names an idea, a feeling, a quality, or a characteristic.

CONCRETE NOUNS	cloud, tulip, thunder, silk, yogurt
ABSTRACT NOUNS	freedom, joy, beauty, kindness

▶ EXERCISE 1 **Identifying and Classifying Nouns**

The following paragraph contains twenty-five nouns. Write all the nouns that you find in each sentence. Then circle the proper nouns. A name counts as one noun even if it has more than one part.

EXAMPLE [1] English grows every day with the addition of new words.
1. *English, day, addition, words*

[1] Many useful and amusing new words came into our language during World War II. [2] Now these words are familiar to most Americans. [3] One of these odd words is *gremlin*. [4] During the war, fliers were often troubled by mysterious mechanical malfunctions. [5] Not knowing what caused these problems, they joked that gremlins—small, mischievous creatures—were in the aircraft. [6] These gremlins could be helpful as well as harmful. [7] Many fliers claimed they had miraculously escaped danger only because the gremlins had come to their rescue. [8] Artists drew the imps as little men with beards and top hats who played all over the planes.

▶ EXERCISE 2   **Classifying Nouns**

Identify each of the following nouns as a *common noun* or a *proper noun*. If the noun is proper, name a corresponding common noun.

EXAMPLE   1. Zora Neale Hurston
           1. *proper noun—writer*

1. man	**8.** movie	**15.** Alice Walker
2. month	**9.** Virginia	**16.** airport
3. Vietnam	**10.** ocean	**17.** cousin
4. singer	**11.** Mount Hood	**18.** automobile
5. Athena	**12.** Australia	**19.** blues
6. city	**13.** Detroit	**20.** Christopher
7. gumbo	**14.** street	Columbus

Compound Nouns

A *compound noun* consists of two or more words used together as a single noun. The parts of a compound noun may be written as one word, as two or more words, or as a hyphenated word.

ONE WORD	firefighter, Iceland, newspaper
TWO OR MORE WORDS	prime minister, Red River Dam, fire drill
HYPHENATED WORD	sister-in-law, Stratford-on-Avon, push-up

NOTE: If you are not sure how to write a compound noun, look in a dictionary. Some dictionaries may give two correct forms for a word. For example, you may find the word *vice-president* written both with and without the hyphen. As a rule, use the form the dictionary lists first.

▶ EXERCISE 3   **Identifying Compound Nouns**

Each of the following sentences contains at least one compound noun. Identify the compound noun(s) in each sentence.

EXAMPLE   1. My cousin John is a political scientist.
           1. *political scientist*

1. I use a word processor or a typewriter in class.
2. We went swimming in the Gulf of Mexico.
3. My brother-in-law lives in Council Bluffs, Iowa.
4. My Old English sheepdog is still a puppy.
5. Benjamin Banneker's almanac gave exact times for sunrises and sunsets.
6. We used to play hide-and-seek in the old barn.
7. Sitting Bull was the war chief who masterminded the Sioux victory at the Battle of the Little Bighorn.
8. Meet me at the bowling alley near the post office.
9. The fountain pen is not as popular as the ballpoint.
10. Luis Valdez is a playwright, actor, and director.

▶ EXERCISE 4 **Identifying Nouns**

Identify all the nouns in each numbered sentence in the following paragraph.

EXAMPLE [1] To enter the wildlife park, we walked through the mouth of a huge fake alligator.
    1. *park, mouth, alligator*

[1] Businesses sometimes use gigantic objects to advertise their products. [2] A stand that sells fruit might look like an enormous orange, complete with doors and windows. [3] Huge dogs, dinosaurs, and figures of Paul Bunyan are formed with cement or fiberglass to help sell chain saws, trucks, or souvenirs. [4] This old hotel in New Jersey was built to look like an elephant!

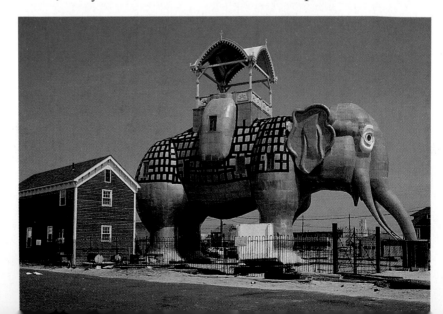

▶ EXERCISE 5   **Identifying Nouns**

Everything you see in these photographs—the people, the objects, the place itself—is named by at least one noun. Time yourself to find out how many nouns you can list in five minutes. What three items would you be tempted to buy? Why?

The Pronoun

14b.   A *pronoun* is a word used in place of one or more nouns or pronouns.

EXAMPLES   Where is Lian? **She** said **she** would be here on time. [The pronoun *she* takes the place of the proper noun *Lian* twice in the second sentence.]

Our teacher and Mr. Barnes said **they** would go to the meeting. [The pronoun *they* takes the place of two nouns: *teacher* and *Mr. Barnes.*]

Many in the crowd had brought cameras with **them.** [The pronoun *them* takes the place of the pronoun *Many.*]

Antecedents

A pronoun usually refers to a noun that comes before it. This noun, called an *antecedent,* gives the pronoun its meaning. In the following examples, the arrows point from the pronouns to their antecedents.

EXAMPLES   Tomás closed his **book** and put **it** down.

The coach showed the **players** how **they** should throw the ball.

Why did **Janet** take **her** dog to the veterinarian?

Have the **birds** flown south yet? **They** should start migrating soon.

Lee hit a **home run. It** was his first of the season.

Notice that a pronoun may appear in the same sentence as its antecedent or in a following sentence.

▶ EXERCISE 6   **Identifying Pronouns and Antecedents**

Find all the pronouns in each sentence in the following paragraph. [Note: Not all sentences contain a pronoun.] Give the antecedent for each pronoun.

EXAMPLE   [1] In about A.D. 1150, a historian wrote down a strange tale English villagers had told him.
     1. *him—historian*

[1] Since many people told the same story, the historian believed it. [2] Supposedly, a young boy and girl with bright green skin had been found wandering in the fields. [3] They spoke a foreign language and wore clothing made of an unknown material. [4] At first, the two children would eat only green beans, but after they learned to eat bread, their skin gradually lost its greenness. [5] After learning English, the girl said she and her brother had come from a land called Saint Martin. [6] This story sounds like science fiction, doesn't it? [7] Perhaps the villagers invented it to amuse their friends and fool historians.

Personal Pronouns

	SINGULAR	**PLURAL**
FIRST PERSON	I, my, mine, me	we, our, ours, us
SECOND PERSON	you, your, yours	you, your, yours
THIRD PERSON	he, his, him she, her, hers it, its	they, their, theirs, them

NOTE: Many possessive forms, such as *my, your,* and *her,* may also be classified as adjectives. See pages 473 and 811–814.

Other Commonly Used Pronouns

REFLEXIVE AND INTENSIVE PRONOUNS
(used to refer to or to emphasize a noun or another pronoun)

myself	ourselves
yourself	yourselves
himself, herself, itself	themselves

RELATIVE PRONOUNS
(used to introduce adjective and noun clauses)

who	whom	whose	which	that

INTERROGATIVE PRONOUNS
(used to begin questions)

Who . . . ?	Whose . . . ?	What . . . ?
Whom . . . ?	Which . . . ?	

DEMONSTRATIVE PRONOUNS
(used to point out a specific person, place, thing, or idea)

this	that	these	those

INDEFINITE PRONOUNS
(used to refer to people, places, things, or ideas in general; frequently used without antecedents)

all	each	more	one
another	either	most	other
any	everybody	much	several
anybody	everyone	neither	some
anyone	everything	nobody	somebody
anything	few	none	someone
both	many	no one	

▶ EXERCISE 7 **Identifying Pronouns**

Identify all the pronouns in each sentence in the following paragraph.

EXAMPLE   [1] My friend Hideko invited me to a Japanese tea ceremony at her house.

    1. *My, me, her*

[1] The tea ceremony at Hideko's house was more like some I have seen in the movies than the one shown here. [2] Hideko said that in Japan people have special rooms for their tea ceremonies, but we used her family's living room. [3] Hideko told me that the purpose of the tea ceremony, a custom which dates back hundreds of years, is to create a peaceful mood. [4] In the ceremony, everyone sits quietly and watches the tea being made. [5] Hideko's mother was our tea master, the person who conducts the ceremony and prepares the tea. [6] Before entering the room for the ceremony, we took our shoes off. [7] During the ceremony, each of us kneeled on straw mats. [8] Hideko's mother served us sweet cakes called *kashi* (KAH-shee). [9] Then she prepared the tea and served it in bowls that had been in their family for generations. [10] Afterward, Hideko gave me a poster to remember the ceremony by.

The Adjective

14c. An *adjective* is a word used to modify a noun or a pronoun.

To *modify* a word means to describe the word or to make its meaning more definite. An adjective modifies a noun or a pronoun by telling *what kind, which one,* or *how many.*

WHAT KIND?	WHICH ONE?	HOW MANY?
gray sky	**that** girl	**five** fingers
old shoes	**next** day	**many** rivers
clever dog	**either** way	**fewer** hours
low price	**last** chance	**some** problems

GRAMMAR

Pronoun or Adjective?

Some words may be used as either pronouns or adjectives. When used as pronouns, these words take the place of nouns. When used as adjectives, they modify nouns.

PRONOUN	ADJECTIVE
I like **that**.	I like **that** shirt.
Either will do.	**Either** car will do.
Sheila bought **some**.	Sheila bought **some** books.

The words *my, your, his, her, its, our,* and *their* are called pronouns throughout this book. They are the ***possessive*** forms of personal pronouns, showing ownership or relationship. Some teachers, however, prefer to call these words adjectives because they tell *which one* about nouns: *my* sister, *your* book, *our* team, *their* tents.

Nouns Used as Adjectives

COMMON NOUNS	COMMON NOUNS USED AS ADJECTIVES
cheese	**cheese** sandwich
snow	**snow** sculpture
winter	**winter** sale

PROPER NOUNS	PROPER NOUNS USED AS ADJECTIVES
Sioux	**Sioux** tradition
Texas	**Texas** coast
Picasso	**Picasso** painting

▶ EXERCISE 8   **Identifying Nouns Used as Adjectives**

Identify whether each italicized word in the following paragraph is used as a *noun* or an *adjective*.

EXAMPLE   Do you want to see my new [1] *baseball* card?
                1. *baseball*—adjective

I love anything that has to do with [1] *baseball.* I save the money I make mowing the [2] *golf* course, and then I go to the [3] *card* [4] *store*. The [5] *store* owner sold me a terrific [6] *Don Mattingly* [7] *card* today. It came in its own [8] *plastic* case. I'll display my new card with my other favorites in a special [9] *glass* [10] *case* on the wall in my room.

When a noun is used as an adjective, your teacher may prefer that you call it an adjective. Proper nouns used as adjectives are called *proper adjectives.*

☞ REFERENCE NOTE: Sometimes a proper adjective and a noun are used together so frequently that they become a compound noun: *Brazil nut, French bread, India ink.* See page 467 for more on compound nouns.

Articles

The most frequently used adjectives are *a, an,* and *the.* These words are usually called *articles.*

A and *an* are *indefinite articles.* They indicate that the noun refers to one of a general group. *A* is used before words beginning with a consonant sound. *An* is used before words beginning with a vowel sound. Notice that *an* is used before a word beginning with the consonant *h* when the *h* is not pronounced.

EXAMPLES   **A** girl won.
An elephant escaped.
This is **an** honor.

The is a *definite article.* It indicates that a noun refers to someone or something in particular.

EXAMPLES   **The** girl won.
The elephant escaped.
The honor goes to her.

Adjectives in Sentences

An adjective usually comes before the noun or pronoun it modifies.

EXAMPLES   Ms. Farrell tells **all** students that **good** workers will be given **special** privileges.

A **sweating, exhausted** runner crossed the line.

In some cases, adjectives follow the word they modify.

EXAMPLE   A dog, **old** and **overweight,** snored in the sun.

Other words may separate an adjective from the noun or pronoun it modifies.

EXAMPLES   Beverly was **worried.** She felt **nervous** about the play.

Cheered by the crowd, the band played an encore.

▶ EXERCISE 9   ## Revising Sentences by Using Appropriate Adjectives

Add adjectives to make two entirely different sentences from each of the following five sentences.

EXAMPLE   1. The waiter showed the woman to a table in the corner.

1. *The kindly waiter showed the shy woman to a pleasant table in the sunny corner.*
   The haughty waiter showed the elegant woman to a private table in the shadowy corner.

1. The blossoms on the trees filled the air with a scent.
2. As the clouds gathered in the sky, the captain spoke to the crew.
3. At the end of the hall were stairs that led to a room.
4. Jerome's car had an engine and wheels.
5. The singers and comedians gave a performance for the audience.

▶ EXERCISE 10   ## Using Adjectives in a Descriptive Paragraph

Inside this castle are hundreds of rooms—a throne room, banquet halls, dungeons, and so on. Write a paragraph that describes a room in the castle as it might have looked when a king or a queen lived there. In your paragraph, use adjectives that clearly describe the room. Underline the adjectives you use and be prepared to identify the noun that each adjective modifies.

GRAMMAR

WRITING APPLICATION

Using Adjectives to Make Your Writing Exact

When you describe something, you use adjectives to help your reader "see" clearly what you are describing. The more specific your adjectives are, the clearer your word-picture will be. More than one adjective can modify a noun or pronoun to make your description even more precise.

NOT EXACT   The dog chased the man.
EXACT   The tiny, hairless dog chased the large, hairy man.

Think of other adjectives you could use to make the inexact sentence more specific.

▶ WRITING ACTIVITY

Your science class visited the wildlife habitat, but one of your friends was sick and could not go. Write a paragraph telling your friend about the field trip. Use specific adjectives to help your friend picture what he or she missed.

Prewriting   Make a list of the animals and the scenes that will interest your friend. Beside each item on your list, write one or two specific adjectives.

Writing   You may want to look at pictures of wildlife in magazines or books to help you think of exact descriptions as you write your first draft.

Evaluating and Revising   Have a friend or a classmate read your paragraph to see if you have created clear word-pictures. Revise your paragraph by adding specific adjectives if any descriptions are unclear or too general.

Proofreading   Check your paragraph for errors in spelling and punctuation. Be sure that you have capitalized any proper nouns used as adjectives. (See pages 474 and 721 for more about proper adjectives.)

▶ REVIEW A   **Identifying Nouns, Pronouns, and Adjectives**

Identify each of the italicized words in the following paragraph as a *noun*, a *pronoun*, or an *adjective*.

EXAMPLE   [1] Most high school *students* read at least *one* play by William Shakespeare.

1. *students—noun; one—adjective*

[1] *This* article tells about Shakespeare's *life*. [2] *Shakespeare*, perhaps the most *famous* playwright of all time, was born in Stratford-on-Avon in 1564. [3] He was baptized in the *small* church at Stratford shortly after *his* birth. [4] In 1616, *he* was buried in the *same* church. [5] If *you* visit his grave, you can find an *inscription* placing a curse on *anyone* who moves his bones. [6] Out of *respect* for his wish or because of fear of his curse, *nobody* has disturbed the grave. [7] As a result, his body has never been moved to Westminster Abbey, where many *other* famous *English* writers are buried. [8] Visitors to *Stratford* can also see the house in *which* Shakespeare was born. [9] At *one* time tourists could visit the large house that Shakespeare bought for *himself* and his family. [10] *This* was where they lived when he retired from the London *theater*.

The Verb

14d.   A *verb* is a word used to express an action or a state of being.

Action Verbs

An *action verb* expresses physical or mental activity.

| PHYSICAL | come | go | inquire | proceed |
| MENTAL | believe | know | remember | understand |

▶ EXERCISE 11   **Writing Action Verbs**

Write twenty action verbs, not including those listed above. Include and underline at least five verbs that express actions that cannot be seen.

Transitive and Intransitive Verbs

A *transitive verb* is an action verb that expresses an action directed toward a person or thing named in the sentence.

EXAMPLES   Neil **rang** the bell. [The action of the verb *rang* is directed toward *bell.*]

Juanita **mailed** the package. [The action of *mailed* is directed toward *package.*]

The action expressed by a transitive verb passes from the doer—the subject—to the receiver of the action. Words that receive the action of a transitive verb are called *objects.*

☞ REFERENCE NOTE: For more information about objects and their uses in sentences, see pages 522–524.

An *intransitive verb* expresses action (or tells something about the subject) without passing the action from a doer to a receiver.

EXAMPLES   Last Saturday we **stayed** inside.
The children **laughed.**

A verb may be transitive in one sentence and intransitive in another.

EXAMPLES   Marcie **studied** her notes. [transitive]
Marcie **studied** very late. [intransitive]

The poet **wrote** a sonnet. [transitive]
The poet **wrote** carefully. [intransitive]

☞ REFERENCE NOTE: Like intransitive verbs, linking verbs (*be, seem, appear,* etc.) never take direct objects. See page 480 for more information about linking verbs.

▶ EXERCISE 12   **Using Transitive and Intransitive Verbs**

Choose a verb from the following list for each blank in the paragraph on the next page. Then identify each verb as *transitive* or *intransitive.*

drifted	landed	admired	experienced
floated	rode	met	watched
climbed	arrived	left	did
awaited	suggest	tried	drove

EXAMPLE   Can you [1] _____ an activity for this weekend?
1. *suggest—transitive*

Aunt Pam and I [1] _____ something really different last summer. We [2] _____ on inner tubes down a river in the wilderness. A guide [3] _____ our group with a truckful of giant tubes and picnic lunches, and [4] _____ us upstream about twenty miles. Then everyone [5] _____ into a tube in the water. The guide [6] _____ in the truck to a picnic spot downstream, halfway back to the base. All morning, we [7] _____ lazily along in the sunshine and [8] _____ the wildlife along the shore. When we [9] _____ at the picnic spot, a delicious lunch [10] _____ us.

PICTURE THIS

You are the sports commentator for a local radio station and are recapping Friday night's high school football game. Write a short commentary on the game. Then, describe the dramatic tackle shown in the picture. As a commentator, you are known for your creative use of verbs not usually associated with sports, such as "Logan *microwaved* the ball to his receiver." Be sure to tell what teams were playing, when and where, and who won. Use a variety of interesting action verbs to make your news report lively. After completing your news story, trade with a partner and underline all the action verbs.

Subject: a high school football game
Audience: local sports fans
Purpose: to inform

Linking Verbs

A *linking verb* is a verb that connects the subject to a word that identifies or describes it. The most commonly used linking verbs are forms of the verb *be*.

LV or HV

be	shall be	should be
being	will be	would be
am	has been	can be
is	have been	could be
are	had been	should have been
was	shall have been	would have been
were	will have been	could have been

Here are some other frequently used linking verbs.

appear	feel	look	seem	sound	taste
become	grow	remain	smell	stay	turn

The noun, pronoun, or adjective that follows a linking verb completes the meaning of the verb and refers to the noun or pronoun that comes before the verb.

EXAMPLES   The answer **is** three. [answer = three]
The answer **is** correct. [correct answer]
The casserole **tasted** strange. [strange casserole]

Many linking verbs can be used as action (nonlinking) verbs as well.

EXAMPLES   The wet dog **smelled** horrible. [linking verb—horrible dog]
The dog **smelled** the baked bread. [action verb]

The motor **sounded** good. [linking verb—good motor]
The engineer **sounded** the horn. [action verb]

Even *be* is not always a linking verb. It is sometimes followed only by an adverb.

EXAMPLE   I was **there.**

REFERENCE NOTE: See pages 485–489 for a discussion of adverbs.

To be a linking verb, the verb must be followed by either a noun or a pronoun that names the subject or by an adjective that describes it.

▶ EXERCISE 13   **Identifying Linking Verbs and the Words They Link**

Identify the linking verb in each of the following sentences. Then give the words that are linked by the verb.

EXAMPLE   1. Dixie can be a very obedient dog.
1. *can be—Dixie, dog*

1. He felt foolish when his car ran out of gas.
2. Suddenly, it turned very dark, and the wind began to blow fiercely.
3. We had waited so long for dinner that anything would have tasted wonderful.
4. The plot of that fantasy novel seems awfully childish to me now.
5. Kevin and I stayed best friends throughout middle school.
6. I am happy that you won the chess match.
7. If the coach had let me play, this game would have been my first one with the Tigers.
8. My father thinks that you should become a lawyer.
9. After practicing hard, Stef's band sounded great in the concert.
10. For a confusing moment, Dr. Kostas thought the planet's rings appeared smaller.

▶ EXERCISE 14   **Writing Appropriate Linking Verbs**

Choose a linking verb for each blank. Use a different verb for each sentence.

EXAMPLE   1. The baby _____ sleepy after he was fed.
1. *The baby grew sleepy after he was fed.*

1. That building _____ the new public library.
2. The car _____ funny.
3. The moose _____ huge.
4. I _____ very nervous about the driving test.
5. Her garden _____ dried and brown in the drought.
6. Let's hope the evening _____ cool.
7. We can eat the raspberries when they _____ red.
8. Burt _____ grouchy early in the morning.
9. The soup _____ too salty.
10. The puppy _____ healthy and playful.

▶ EXERCISE 15   **Writing Sentences with Action Verbs and Linking Verbs**

Choose five nouns from the following list. For each noun, write two sentences. Make the noun the subject of each sentence. Use an action verb in one sentence and a linking verb in the other. Identify which sentence contains the action verb and which contains the linking verb.

EXAMPLE   1. fireworks
1. *The fireworks filled the night sky with bursts of color.* [action verb]
The fireworks grew more colorful toward the end of the program. [linking verb]

1. pilot
2. locomotive
3. taco
4. skater
5. football
6. coins
7. foghorn
8. Mrs. Wu
9. Lincoln
10. movie

Verb Phrases

A *verb phrase* consists of a main verb preceded by at least one *helping verb* (also called an *auxiliary verb*). Besides all forms of the verb *be,* helping verbs include

✓has	shall	may	could	✓do
✓have	will	should	might	✓did
✓had	can	would	must	✓does

[handwritten: Some may be AV]

Notice how helping verbs work together with main verbs to make a complete verb phrase.

EXAMPLES   **is** leaving   **may** become   **might have** remained
had seemed   **should** move   **must have** thought
shall be going   **could** jump   **does** sing

Sometimes the parts of a verb phrase are interrupted by other parts of speech.

EXAMPLES   She **had** always **been thinking** of her future.
We **could** never **have moved** the car alone.
Did you **hear** the Rev. Jesse Jackson's speech?
Has my sister **played** her new CD for you?

NOTE: The word *not* is always an adverb. It is never part of a helping verb, even when it is joined to a verb as the contraction *–n't.*

EXAMPLES She **should** not **have borrowed** that necklace.
She **shouldn't have borrowed** that necklace.

☞ **REFERENCE NOTE:** For more on contractions, see pages 818–819.

▣▶ EXERCISE 16 **Identifying Helping Verbs**

Identify all the helping verbs in each of the following sentences.

EXAMPLE **1.** How well did your brother recover from his back injury?
1. *did*

1. Fortunately, he didn't need surgery.
2. His physical therapist has designed an exercise program for him.
3. Before exercising, he must spend at least five minutes warming up.
4. Does he walk indoors on a treadmill or outdoors on a track?
5. He will be using a back-extension machine.
6. In his exercise program at home, he will be using a gymnastic ball.
7. The doctor is always reminding my brother about proper techniques for lifting.
8. When lifting heavy objects, my brother must wear a back brace.
9. Should he try acupuncture or massage therapy?
10. Without physical therapy, he might not have healed as quickly and as completely.

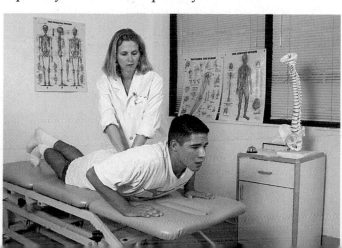

▶ EXERCISE 17 **Identifying Verbs and Verb Phrases**

Identify all the verbs and verb phrases in the following sentences. Include all helping verbs, even if the parts of a verb phrase are separated by other words.

EXAMPLE   1. We will probably go to the movie if we can finish our assignment.
1. *will go, can finish*

1. Mr. Jensen always sweeps the floor first.
2. Then he washes the chalkboards.
3. He works slowly but steadily.
4. The weather forecaster had not predicted rain.
5. All morning the barometer was dropping rapidly.
6. The storm was slowly moving in.
7. Your dog will become fat if you feed it too much.
8. Dogs will usually eat everything you give them.
9. Cats will stop when they have had enough.
10. After our team has had more practice, we will win.

▶ EXERCISE 18 **Revising Dialogue Using Verbs**

Using a variety of verbs can make dialogue more interesting. Rewrite the dialogue below. In five of the eight items, replace *said* with one of the verbs from this list.

wailed	bellowed	gloated	gasped
whispered	teased	soothed	confessed
shouted	replied	whined	accused
snapped	cried	muttered	called

EXAMPLE   1. "Mom, I'm home!" said Tony, sprinting in the door.
1. *"Mom, I'm home!" bellowed Tony, sprinting in the door.*

1. "Guess what? I won the spelling bee," he said.
2. "Honey, that's wonderful," said his mother.
3. "Who cares?" said his sister Amy.
4. "You're just jealous," said Tony.
5. "I am not!" Amy said, running out of the kitchen.
6. "Don't let her bother you," said his mother. "Enjoy your success."
7. "Oh, I am," said Tony, "but I wish I could share it with Amy."

8. "She'll come around," his mother said. "Meanwhile, sit down and tell me all about it."

The Adverb

14e. An *adverb* is a word used to modify a verb, an adjective, or another adverb.

Just as an adjective makes the meaning of a noun or a pronoun more definite, an adverb makes the meaning of a verb, an adjective, or an adverb more definite.

Adverbs Modifying Verbs

In the following examples, each boldfaced adverb makes the meaning of a verb more definite by telling *where, when, how,* or *to what extent* (*how long* or *how much*).

WHERE?	WHEN?
We lived **there.**	May we go **tomorrow?**
Please step **up.**	Water the plant **weekly.**
I have the ticket **here.**	We'll see you **later.**

HOW?	TO WHAT EXTENT?
She **quickly** agreed.	I am **completely** happy.
The rain fell **softly.**	He **hardly** moved.
Drive **carefully.**	Did she hesitate **slightly?**

Adverbs may come before or after the verbs they modify. Sometimes adverbs interrupt the parts of a verb phrase. Adverbs may also introduce questions.

EXAMPLE **Where** in the world did you **ever** find that pink-and-purple necktie? [The adverb *where* introduces the question and modifies the verb phrase *did find*. The adverb *ever* interrupts the verb phrase and also modifies it.]

GRAMMAR

▷ EXERCISE 19   **Completing Sentences by Supplying Appropriate Adverbs**

Complete each of the following sentences by supplying an appropriate adverb. The word in parentheses tells you what information the adverb should give about the action.

EXAMPLE   1. He moved his hand (*how*).
           1. *gracefully*

1. The soldiers must travel (*how*).
2. You will probably sleep well (*when*).
3. They whispered (*how*) to Mr. Baldwin.
4. Tonya took a deep breath and dived (*where*).
5. Did you study (*to what extent*)?
6. Handle the baby kittens (*how*).
7. My uncle Hans is (*when*) in a bad mood.
8. Your taxi should be (*where*) soon.
9. I could (*to what extent*) taste the tangy pizza.
10. (*When*), you should paste the pictures on the poster.

Adverbs Modifying Adjectives

EXAMPLES   Beth did an **exceptionally** fine job. [The adverb *exceptionally* modifies the adjective *fine*, telling *how fine*.]

Slightly cooler temperatures are forecast for this Sunday. [The adverb *slightly* modifies the adjective *cooler*, telling *how cool*.]

The most frequently used adverbs are *too, so,* and *very*. In fact, these words are often overworked. To make your speaking and writing clearer and more definite, try to find more precise adverbs to take the place of these inexact, overused words.

Adverbs That Frequently Modify Adjectives		
completely	especially	quite
dangerously	extremely	rather
definitely	largely	surprisingly
dreadfully	mainly	terribly
entirely	mostly	unusually

▶ EXERCISE 20 **Identifying Adverbs That Modify Adjectives**

Identify the ten adverbs that modify adjectives in the following paragraph. For each adverb, give the adjective it modifies.

EXAMPLE   [1] The compass I had bought was incredibly cheap.
          1. *incredibly—cheap*

[1] If you are ever really lost in the woods at night, knowing how to find the North Star may be extremely important. [2] Here is one method that is often useful. [3] First, find the constellation Ursa Major, which many people call the Big Dipper. [4] This constellation is especially easy to find. [5] It consists of seven rather bright stars in the northern sky that are arranged in the shape of a large dipper. [6] Do not confuse it with the Little Dipper, which is somewhat smaller. [7] After you have found the Big Dipper, you must be very careful to sight along the two stars that form the front of the dipper bowl. [8] They are two points on an almost straight line that leads to Polaris, the North Star. [9] This method for getting your bearings is completely reliable—except when the clouds are so dense that you cannot see the stars.

▶ EXERCISE 21 **Revising with Adverb Modifiers**

Revise the following phrases and sentences by adding one adverb modifier for each of the italicized adjectives. Use a different adverb in each item.

EXAMPLE   1. a *confusing* sentence
          1. *an especially confusing sentence*

1. a *sharp* turn
2. *playful* kittens
3. an *easy* question
4. a *swept* floor
5. Her little brother has a *bright* smile.
6. Terri felt *satisfied* that she had done her best.
7. The old mansion was *silent*.
8. Robert became *sick* and had to leave early.
9. Had Clara been *safe*?
10. Most of the questions on the test were *difficult*.

Adverbs Modifying Other Adverbs

EXAMPLES   Calvin was **almost** never there. [The adverb *almost* modifies the adverb *never*, telling *to what extent.*]

We'll meet **shortly** afterward. [The adverb *shortly* modifies the adverb *afterward*, telling *to what extent.*]

She slept **too** late. [The adverb *too* modifies the adverb *late*, telling *to what extent.*]

EXERCISE 22   **Identifying Adverbs That Modify Other Adverbs**

Identify all the adverbs that modify other adverbs in the following sentences. After each, give the adverb it modifies.

EXAMPLE   1. Brian is so terribly shy that he blushes when people speak to him.
       1. *so, terribly*

1. The cat leapt to the windowsill quite agilely.
2. The books were stacked rather haphazardly.
3. Corrie knew she'd have to get up incredibly early to watch the eclipse.
4. The tornado almost completely destroyed the barn.
5. The famous diamond was more heavily guarded than any other exhibit at the museum.
6. My brother is nearly always finished with his paper route before I am finished with mine.
7. She registered too late to be eligible for the first sweepstakes drawing.
8. In the final four minutes of the game, Isiah Thomas shot extremely accurately.
9. Usually it seems that each month goes more rapidly than the month before.
10. They walked onto the stage most calmly, as if they felt completely relaxed.

Forms of Adverbs

Although many adverbs end in *–ly*, the *–ly* ending does not automatically mean that a word is an adverb. Many adjectives also end in *–ly*: the *daily* newspaper, an *early* train, an *only* child, a *friendly* person. Some words such as *now, then, far, already, somewhat, not,* and *right* are often used as adverbs, yet they do not end in *–ly*. To identify a word as an adverb, ask yourself:

- Does this word modify a verb, an adjective, or an adverb?
- Does it tell *when, where, how,* or *to what extent*?

▶ EXERCISE 23   Identifying Adverbs and the Words They Modify

Identify the adverb or adverbs in each numbered sentence in the following paragraph. Then give the word or expression that the adverb modifies. [Note: Not all sentences contain an adverb.]

EXAMPLE   [1] Have you ever thought about writing a movie script?
       1. *ever—have thought*

[1] Successful movie scripts, or screenplays, are written according to a very rigid formula. [2] The main character and the story idea must grab an audience's interest quickly. [3] Almost exactly twenty-five minutes into the movie comes a "plot point." [4] This is a surprising event that swings the story around in another direction. [5] Most of the action and conflict occurs in the next hour of the movie. [6] Then comes another plot point, about eighty-five minutes into the movie. [7] Finally we learn what happens to the characters. [8] The last time I went to a movie I really liked, I checked my watch. [9] It was quite interesting to find that the movie's timing matched this formula.

▶ EXERCISE 24   Revising Sentences by Using Appropriate Adverbs

Revise each of the following sentences by adding at least one appropriate adverb. Try not to use the adverbs *too, so,* and *very*.

1. Angelo promised me that he would try to meet the train.
2. My coat was torn during the long hike, and Barbara lent me her poncho.

3. Engineering degrees are popular with students because job opportunities are good.
4. The Wallaces are settled into a new house, which they built by themselves.
5. When the baseball season begins, I will be attending games every day.
6. Ronald dribbled to his left and threw the ball into a crowd of defenders.
7. Visits to national monuments and parks remind us that our country has an exciting history.
8. We returned the book to Marcella, but she had planned her report without it.
9. Georgia O'Keeffe displayed her paintings and received the admiration of a large audience.
10. The recipe calls for two eggs, but I did not have time to buy any at the store.

 REVIEW B   **Identifying Nouns, Pronouns, Adjectives, Verbs, and Adverbs**

Identify the italicized words in each numbered sentence in the following paragraph as *nouns, pronouns, adjectives, verbs,* or *adverbs.*

EXAMPLE   [1] *You* may know that Brazil is the *largest* country in South America.
     1. *You—pronoun; largest—adjective*

[1] My *best* friend's mother just *came* back from visiting her family in Brazil. [2] *She* showed us these pictures she took in Brasília, the *capital*, and told us about it. [3] It was

amazing to learn that this area had been jungle until construction began in the 1950s. [4] At first, few people lived in Brasília because it was *so isolated*. [5] However, over the *years* hundreds of thousands of people *have* moved *there*. [6] Several other Brazilian cities *also* lie within one hundred *miles* of Brasília. [7] Several good highways *connect* Brasília with other major cities. [8] Residents enjoy the wide streets and open spaces *that* are *shown* in these pictures. [9] *One* of Brasília's *most* striking features is its bold architecture. [10] Aren't the government *buildings* at the Plaza of the Three Powers *fantastic*?

The Preposition

14f. A *preposition* is a word used to show the relationship of a noun or a pronoun to some other word in the sentence.

By changing the prepositions in the following examples, you can change the relationship of *Saint Bernard* to *bed* and *everything* to *beach*.

The Saint Bernard slept **near** my bed.	Everything **about** the beach was wonderful.
The Saint Bernard slept **under** my bed.	Everything **except** the beach was wonderful.
The Saint Bernard slept **on** my bed.	Everything **from** the beach was wonderful.

Commonly Used Prepositions			
aboard	around	besides	during
about	as	between	except
above	at	beyond	for
across	before	but (meaning	from
after	behind	*except*)	in
against	below	by	inside
along	beneath	concerning	into
among	beside	down	like

(continued)

GRAMMAR

Commonly Used Prepositions *(continued)*

near	past	toward	with
of	since	under	within
off	through	underneath	without
on	throughout	until	
out	till	up	
over	to	upon	

NOTE: Many words in the preceding list can also be adverbs. To be sure that a word is a preposition, ask whether the word relates a noun or a pronoun following it to a word that comes before it. Compare the following sentences:

> Welcome **aboard.** [adverb]
> Welcome **aboard** our boat. [preposition]

Prepositions that consist of more than one word are called *compound prepositions.*

Compound Prepositions

according to	in addition to	next to
as of	in front of	on account of
aside from	in place of	out of
because of	in spite of	owing to
by means of	instead of	prior to

☞ **REFERENCE NOTE:** The preposition and the noun or pronoun that follows it combine to form a *prepositional phrase.* For a discussion of prepositional phrases, see pages 533–538.

▶ EXERCISE 25 **Revising Sentences by Using Appropriate Prepositions**

Revise the numbered sentences in the following paragraph by using appropriate prepositions or compound prepositions to fill the blanks.

EXAMPLE   [1] Tasty, fresh lobster is a treat _____ many diners.
            1. *Tasty, fresh lobster is a treat for many diners.*

[1] Lobsters are large shellfish that live __in__ the sea. [2] The people who fish __for__ these creatures are hardy and

independent. [3] Using small, specially built boats and a number _of_ cratelike traps made _from_ wood, they go to work. [4] Lobster fishing _in_ the United States has been practiced only _during_ the last century; before that time people thought lobster was not good to eat. [5] For centuries, farmers used the plentiful lobsters as fertilizer _or_ their gardens. [6] To catch lobsters, the fishers first lower traps _with_ chunks _of_ bait _into_ the sea. [7] Then the fishers mark the location ____ colorful floats that identify the owners. [8] If the fishers are lucky, the lobster enters the trap ____ the part called the *kitchen*, tries to escape ____ another opening called the *shark's mouth*, and then is trapped ____ the section called the *parlor*. [9] Fishers call a lobster ____ only one claw a *cull*; one ____ any claws is called a *pistol* or a *buffalo*. [10] By law, undersized lobsters must be returned _to_ the sea.

The Conjunction

14g. A *conjunction* is a word used to join words or groups of words.

Coordinating conjunctions always connect items of the same kind. Sometimes they join single words, or they may join groups of words.

Coordinating Conjunctions			
and	but	or	nor
for	yet	so	

EXAMPLES   streets **and** sidewalks [two nouns]
on land **or** at sea [two prepositional phrases]
Judy wrote down the number, **but** she lost it. [two complete ideas]

   Correlative conjunctions also connect items of the same kind. However, unlike coordinating conjunctions, correlatives are always used in pairs.

GRAMMAR

Correlative Conjunctions	
both . . . and	not only . . . but also
either . . . or	neither . . . nor
whether . . . or	

EXAMPLES **Both** Jim Thorpe **and** Roberto Clemente were outstanding athletes. [two proper nouns]

We want to go **not only** to Ontario **but also** to Quebec. [two prepositional phrases]

Either we will buy it now, **or** we will wait for the next sale. [two complete ideas]

☞ REFERENCE NOTE: A third kind of conjunction—the *subordinating conjunction*—is discussed on pages 571–572.

▶ EXERCISE 26 **Identifying and Classifying Conjunctions**

Write all the conjunctions in each sentence in the following paragraph. Be prepared to tell whether they are *correlative* or *coordinating conjunctions.*

EXAMPLE [1] For my family and me, moving is both an exciting and a dangerous experience.
1. *and, both . . . and*

[1] When we bought our new house, my mother wanted to hire movers, but my father said we could do the moving more efficiently. [2] He said that doing the job ourselves would be not only much faster but also far less expensive than having movers do it. [3] Neither my mom nor I was enthusiastic, but at last Dad convinced us. [4] Luckily, Uncle Waldo and my cousin Fred volunteered to help, for they thought it was a great idea. [5] Both Uncle Waldo and Fred lift weights, and they love to show off their muscles. [6] On the day of the move, Dad rented a truck, but it wasn't large enough, and we had to make several trips. [7] At the new house, we could get the sofa through neither the back door nor the front door, and Uncle Waldo strained his back trying to loosen the sofa from the door frame. [8] On the second load, either Fred or my father lost his grip, and the refrigerator fell on Dad's

foot. [9] His enthusiasm was somewhat dimmed, yet he said his foot didn't hurt much and told us we were doing a wonderful job. [10] Whether we saved money or not after paying both Uncle Waldo's and Dad's doctor bills and having the doorway widened is something we still don't discuss in our family.

▶ EXERCISE 27 **Using Conjunctions**

Look at this camp schedule. If you were at this camp, how would you spend your day? Write five sentences about what you would and would not do. In each sentence, use a coordinating conjunction or a pair of correlative conjunctions. Write at least two sentences that contain different pairs of correlative conjunctions.

EXAMPLE 1. *If I go to the movie, I can neither sing campfire songs nor listen to storytelling.*

Camp Schedule	
personal time	early swim
BREAKFAST	
nature hike	computer seminar
art class	aerobics
	volleyball
LUNCH	
your choice: water-ski trip or scuba trip	swimming
	sailing class
	crafts
DINNER	
video games	
movie	campfire songs
	storytelling

The Interjection

14h. An *interjection* is a word used to express emotion. It has no grammatical relation to the rest of the sentence.

Since an interjection is unrelated to other words in the sentence, it is set off from the rest of the sentence by an exclamation point or by a comma or commas.

EXAMPLES **Hey!** Be careful of that wire!
There's a skunk somewhere, **ugh!**
I like that outfit, but, **wow,** it's really expensive.
Well, I guess that's that.

▶ EXERCISE 28   **Using Interjections**

In the following dialogue, Jason is telling his friend Michelle about a concert he attended. Use appropriate interjections to fill in the numbered blanks. Be sure you punctuate each interjection correctly.

EXAMPLE   [1] " ____ You mean you actually got to go?" Michelle gasped.

1. *"Wow! You mean you actually got to go?" Michelle gasped.*

[1] " ____ how was the concert?" asked Michelle. "Tell me all about it."

Jason shook his head. "The opening act was terrible. [2] ____ It seemed like they played forever!"

"But how was the rest of the show? [3] ____ Give me some details, Jason!"

"The drummer was fantastic. [4] ____ He acted like a wild man. He was all over the drums! But the best part was Stevie's twenty-minute guitar solo. [5] ____ he really let loose. The crowd went crazy!"

Determining Parts of Speech

14i.   A word's use determines its part of speech.

The same word may be used as different parts of speech. For instance, to figure out what part of speech *down* is in each of the following sentences, read the entire sentence. What you are doing is studying the word's *context*—the way the word is used in the sentence. From the context, you can identify the part of speech that *down* is in each of the following sentences.

EXAMPLES   The fine feathers of young birds are called **down**.
           [noun]
           She wore a **down** vest. [adjective]
           Do you think the tackle will **down** the runner before reaching the end zone? [verb]
           Her poster fell **down**. [adverb]
           My cousin lives **down** the street. [preposition]

▶ EXERCISE 29 **Identifying Words as Different Parts of Speech**

Read each of the following sentences. Then, identify the part of speech of the italicized word. Be ready to justify your answer by telling how the word is used in the sentence.

1. Did the pond *ice* over?
2. An *ice* storm struck.
3. *Ice* covered the walk.
4. The light flashed *on*.
5. We rode *on* the subway.
6. They went to the *park*.
7. We can *park* the car here.
8. They waited by the *park* entrance.
9. We are all here *but* Jo.
10. I slipped, *but* I didn't fall.

▶ EXERCISE 30 **Determining Parts of Speech**

A soldier in the American Revolution brings his general this spy message he found in a hollow tree. Unfortunately, termites have eaten holes in the paper. For each hole, supply one word that makes sense, and give its part of speech. [Note: Each missing word is a different part of speech.]

EXAMPLE   Please _____ this message to General Baxter immediately.

Please <u>deliver</u> this message to General Baxter immediately.—(verb)

! The Redcoats are chasing me. I expect them to _____ me soon. They are camped _____ the river and they are well rested. They will attack your _____ at dawn's _____ light tomorrow. General, _____ must prepare your troops to leave.

Yours in haste, John Cadrain

Review: Posttest 1

Identifying Parts of Speech

Write the part of speech of each italicized word in the following paragraph. Be ready to explain the use of the word in the sentence.

EXAMPLE   Pioneers [1] *learned* how to recognize [2] *danger.*
   1. *verb*
   2. *noun*

The [1] *first* pioneers on the Great Plains [2] *encountered* many kinds [3] *of* dangerous animals. Grizzly bears and [4] *huge* herds of bison were menaces to [5] *early* settlers. One of the [6] *most* ferocious beasts of the plains [7] *was* a [8] *grizzly* protecting her cubs. However, [9] *neither* the bison nor the grizzly was the most feared animal [10] *on* the frontier. Not even the deadly [11] *rattlesnake*—nor [12] *any* of the other prairie creatures—was dreaded so much as the skunk. You may think, [13] *"Oh,* that is [14] *ridiculous."* [15] *Yet* it is true. Skunks were not feared because they [16] *smelled* bad but, instead, because they [17] *so* often carried [18] *rabies.* Since there was no vaccine for rabies in [19] *those* days, the bite of a rabid skunk spelled certain [20] *doom* for the unlucky victim.

Review: Posttest 2

Writing Sentences Using the Same Words as Different Parts of Speech

Write twenty sentences, using each of the words on the next page as two different parts of speech. Underline the word and give its part of speech in parentheses after each sentence.

EXAMPLE   1. up
      1. *We looked up. (adverb)*
         We ran up the stairs. (preposition)

1. light	5. cook	9. below
2. run	6. ride	10. picture
3. over	7. in	
4. line	8. love	

SUMMARY OF PARTS OF SPEECH

Rule	Part of Speech	Use	Examples
14a	noun	names	**Lydia** reads **novels.**
14b	pronoun	takes the place of a noun	**You** and **they** saw **it.**
14c	adjective	modifies a noun or a pronoun	I got a **new** bike. We were **hungry.**
14d	verb	shows action or a state of being	We **swam** and **surfed.** She **was** a candidate.
14e	adverb	modifies a verb, an adjective, or another adverb	They are **here.** We were **quite** surprised. You worked **very quickly.**
14f	preposition	relates a noun or a pronoun to another word	Some **of** the kittens **in** the pet store window had bows **on** their necks.
14g	conjunction	joins words or group of words	Whitney **or** Jan will sing. We plan to hike **and** to camp.
14h	interjection	expresses emotion	**Hey! Hooray! Well,** here we are.

15 THE PARTS OF A SENTENCE

Subject, Predicate, Complement

Diagnostic Test

A. Identifying the Parts of Sentences

Identify the italicized words in the following passage. Use these abbreviations.

s.	subject	*p.a.*	predicate adjective
v.	verb	*d.o.*	direct object
p.n.	predicate nominative	*i.o.*	indirect object

EXAMPLE   Raising money is hard **[1]** *work.*
            1. *p.n.*

A carwash can be a good **[1]** *fund-raiser.* Knowing this, the freshman class **[2]** *planned* a carwash for last Saturday. On Saturday morning, the **[3]** *sky* did not look **[4]** *good.* In fact, the weather forecast predicted **[5]** *thunderstorms.* Did **[6]** *any* of this discourage **[7]** *us?* No, we had our carwash anyway. Our first customer, at 9 A.M., was a **[8]** *woman* in a pickup truck. Glancing at the sky, she paid **[9]** *us* a compliment. "You're really **[10]** *brave,*" she said. The rain

[11] *began* as she was speaking, and our disappointment must have been **[12]** *obvious.* "Don't worry," she added, "there is **[13]** *nothing* like a rainwater rinse." We charged **[14]** *her* only one **[15]** *dollar* because she had cheered us up so much.

B. Identifying and Punctuating the Kinds of Sentences

Write the last word of each of the following sentences, and then give the correct mark of punctuation. Classify each sentence as *imperative, declarative, interrogative,* or *exclamatory.*

EXAMPLE   1. My uncle from Turkey is visiting us
            1. *us.* —*declarative*

16. What delicious foods the Turks eat
17. A *doner kebab* is grilled lamb served in pita bread
18. Would you like to taste this yogurt with garlic
19. Look at his fascinating pictures of Istanbul
20. How beautiful Istanbul's crowded skyline is

The Sentence

In casual conversation, people often leave out parts of sentences. In writing, however, it is better to use complete sentences most of the time. They help to make meaning clear to the reader.

15a.   A *sentence* is a group of words that contains a subject and a verb and expresses a complete thought.

If a group of words does not express a complete thought, it is a *fragment,* or piece of a sentence. It is not a sentence.

FRAGMENT   the room with the high ceiling
SENTENCE   We looked into the room.

FRAGMENT	waiting by the door
SENTENCE	The clerk was waiting by the door.

FRAGMENT	after you have finished the test
SENTENCE	Who has finished the test?

Notice that a sentence always begins with a capital letter and ends with a mark of punctuation—a period, a question mark, or an exclamation point.

▶ EXERCISE 1   ### Identifying Sentences and Revising Fragments

Decide whether each of the following groups of words is a sentence or a fragment. If the word group is a sentence, correct its capitalization and punctuation. If the word group is a fragment, revise it to make a complete sentence. Be sure to add correct capitalization and punctuation.

EXAMPLES   1. here are your glasses
           1. *Here are your glasses.*

           2. before going out
           2. *Before going out, I always turn off the lights.*

1. on Monday or later this week
2. patiently waiting for the mail carrier
3. will you be there tomorrow
4. four people in a small car
5. just yesterday I discovered
6. two strikes and no one on base
7. it runs smoothly
8. leaning far over the railing
9. give me a hand
10. while waiting in line at the theater

Subject and Predicate

15b.   A sentence consists of two parts: the subject and the predicate. The *subject* names the person, place, thing, or idea spoken about in the rest of the sentence. The *predicate* says something about the subject.

In the following examples, the subjects are separated from the predicates by blue vertical lines. Notice that the subject and the predicate may be only one word each, or they may be more than one word.

> Coyotes | were howling in the distance.
> The telephone in the lobby | rang.
> The woman in the red blouse | is my aunt.

In these three examples, the words to the left of the vertical line make up the *complete subject.* The words to the right of the vertical line make up the *complete predicate.*

Often, however, the subject is in the middle or at the end of a sentence.

> In the dim light, **the eager scientist** examined the cave walls.
> Does **Brian's car** have a tape deck?
> On the table stood **a silver vase.**

▶ EXERCISE 2   **Identifying the Complete Subject**

Identify the complete subject of each sentence in the following paragraph.

EXAMPLE   [1] The art of quilting has been popular in America for a long time.
> 1. *The art of quilting*

[1] Ever since colonial times, Americans have made quilts. [2] Traditional designs, with names like Honeycomb, Tumbling Blocks, and Trip Around the World, have been handed down from generation to generation. [3] The designs on this page are quilt blocks from a modern

quilt. [4] They certainly don't look like the ones Great-Grandmother used to make! [5] However, quilting techniques have stayed basically the same for well over a hundred years. [6] Small scraps of bright cloth are still painstakingly stitched together to create each block. [7] As in many antique quilts, each block in this quilt was designed and sewn by a different person. [8] Some of the designs are simple. [9] In others, colorful details bring circus scenes to life. [10] To set off the brilliant colors, a dark background was chosen for the quilt.

▶ EXERCISE 3 **Writing Complete Predicates**

Write complete sentences by supplying complete predicates for the following subjects. Be sure to use correct capitalization and punctuation.

EXAMPLE   1. that famous painting
          1. *That famous painting sold for three million dollars.*

1. justice
2. some commercials
3. the store on the corner
4. the woman next door
5. one way to study

The Simple Subject

| 15c. | The *simple subject* is the main word or group of words within the complete subject. |

The *complete subject* consists of the simple subject and any words, phrases, or clauses that modify the simple subject.

EXAMPLES   Their scientific discoveries made them famous.

Complete subject   Their scientific discoveries
Simple subject   discoveries

The talented Georgia O'Keeffe is known for her paintings of huge flowers.

Complete subject   The talented Georgia O'Keeffe
Simple subject   Georgia O'Keeffe

GRAMMAR

☞ **REFERENCE NOTE:** Compound nouns such as *Georgia O'Keeffe* are considered one noun. For more about compound nouns, see page 467.

NOTE: In this book, the term *subject* refers to the simple subject unless otherwise indicated.

▶ EXERCISE 4   **Writing Complete Sentences**

Make each of the following fragments a sentence by adding a complete subject. Underline each simple subject.

EXAMPLE   1. Did _____ watch the Super Bowl?
            1. *Did your little <u>brother</u> watch the Super Bowl?*

1. _____ was baying at the moon.
2. _____ can make the pizza.
3. _____ is needed for this recipe.
4. Was _____ the person who won the match?
5. _____ rose and soared out over the sea.
6. _____ stood on the stage singing.
7. _____ were late for their classes.
8. Over in the next town is _____ .
9. Buzzing around the room was _____ .
10. In the middle of the yard grew _____ .

The Simple Predicate

15d. The *simple predicate*, or *verb*, is the main word or group of words within the complete predicate.

EXAMPLE   The ambulance raced out of the hospital drive and down the crowded street.

    Complete predicate   raced out of the hospital drive and down the crowded street
    Simple predicate   raced

The simple predicate may be a single verb or a verb phrase. Verb phrases always have more than one word.

EXAMPLES   will sing   has been broken   have been trying

When you are asked to pick out the simple predicate in a sentence, be sure to include all parts of the verb phrase. Keep in mind the various helping verbs, such as

am	were	have	might	can
are	do	has	must	should
is	does	had	shall	would
was	did	may	will	could

EXAMPLE   Diego couldn't have taken my book.

Complete predicate   couldn't have taken my book
Verb   could have taken

NOTE: Throughout this book, the word *verb* refers to the simple predicate unless otherwise indicated.

Shoe reprinted by permission: Tribune Media Services.

EXERCISE 5 Identifying the Complete Predicate and Verb

For each sentence in the following paragraph, write the complete predicate. Then underline the verb in each complete predicate.

EXAMPLE   [1] Surfing and snow skiing are different in many ways.
1. *are different in many ways*

[1] The warm-weather sport of surfing is powered by the force of incoming waves. [2] The wintertime activity of snow skiing relies instead on gravity. [3] Surfers can pursue their sport with only a surfboard, a flotation vest, a swimsuit, and a safety line. [4] A skier's equipment includes ski boots, skis with bindings, safety cables, ski poles, warm clothing, and perhaps goggles. [5] Surfers paddle out to their starting place under their own power. [6] Skiers must usually buy tickets for a ski-lift ride to the top of the mountain. [7] Oddly enough, some important similarities exist between surfing and skiing. [8] Both

depend on the cooperation of nature for pleasant weather and good waves or good snow. [9] Both sports require coordination and balance more than strength. [10] In fact, each of these sports would probably make an excellent cross-training activity during the other's off-season.

EXERCISE 6   **Writing Complete Sentences**

Make each of the following fragments a complete sentence by adding a subject or a predicate. Proofread for correct capitalization and punctuation.

1. the trouble with my class schedule
2. the legs of the table
3. appeared deserted
4. my billionaire aunt from Detroit
5. thousands of screaming fans

REVIEW A   **Distinguishing Between Fragments and Sentences; Identifying Subjects and Predicates**

Identify each word group as either a sentence (*S*) or a fragment (*F*). Then, for each sentence, copy the simple subject, underlining it once, and the simple predicate, underlining it twice.

EXAMPLE   1. The talented musicians played well together.
         1. *S—musicians—played*

1. Jazz music filled the room.
2. Supporting the other instruments, the piano carried the melody.

3. The saxophonist, with lazy, lingering notes.
4. Beside him, the bass player added depth to the band.
5. A female vocalist with a deep, rich voice.
6. Charmed the audience with her delivery.
7. However, the star of the show was the drummer.
8. Most of the evening, she stayed in the background.
9. Until the last half-hour.
10. Then she dazzled everyone with her brilliant, high-speed technique.

 EXERCISE 7 | **Identifying Complete Subjects and Complete Predicates**

Write each of the following sentences, underlining the complete subject once and the complete predicate twice. Be sure to include all parts of compound subjects and compound predicates.

EXAMPLE   1. Gary Soto is my favorite author.
           1. *Gary Soto* *is my favorite author*.

1. His poetry and short stories are often about his life.
2. He will read from his works and sign books tonight.
3. Carlos, Charles, and I will find front-row seats.
4. My cousin just bought the book *Too Many Tamales*.
5. Gary Soto's latest collection of poetry is wonderful!
6. His realistic way of presenting life appeals to me.
7. This particular poem brings back many memories.
8. Something similar happened to me in first grade.
9. Sandra Cisneros and Rudolfo Anaya are also successful Mexican American authors.
10. Their stories reflect a rich cultural heritage.

Finding the Subject

The best way to find the subject of a sentence is to find the verb first. Then ask "Who?" or "What?" in front of it.

EXAMPLES   Here you can swim year-round. [The verb is *can swim*. Who can swim? *You* can swim. *You* is the subject.]
            The price of those tapes seemed too high to us. [The verb is *seemed*. What seemed? *Price* seemed. *Price* is the subject.]

▶ EXERCISE 8 **Identifying Subjects and Verbs**

Identify the verb and its subject in each of the following sentences. Be sure to include all parts of a verb phrase.

EXAMPLE **1.** Long before the equal rights movement of the 1960s, women in the United States were excelling in their professions.
1. *were excelling—verb; women—subject*

1. Anne Bissell successfully ran her husband's carpet sweeper business after his death in 1889.
2. For a time, she served as corporation president.
3. Because of her management, the company sold millions of carpet sweepers.
4. A courageous and clever journalist of the late 1800s, Nellie Bly reported on social injustice.
5. On assignments, she would often wear disguises.
6. Another journalist, Ida Wells-Barnett, became editor and part owner of the *Memphis Free Speech* in 1892.
7. By the early 1930s, she had been crusading for forty years against racial injustice and for suffrage.
8. At the end of her fourth term as general of the Salvation Army, Evangeline Booth retired in 1939.
9. The financial stability of the Salvation Army has been credited to her.
10. She also improved many Salvation Army services.

15e. The subject of a verb is never part of a prepositional phrase.

EXAMPLE Most **of the women** voted.

When you ask "Who voted?" you may be tempted to answer, "*Women* voted." But look closely. The sentence does not say the *women voted*. It says *most* of the women voted. *Women* is the object in the prepositional phrase *of the women*.

Prepositional phrases can be especially misleading when the subject follows the verb.

EXAMPLE **Around the corner from here is a store.** [Neither *corner* nor *here* can be the subject because each word is part of a prepositional phrase. *Store* is the subject of the verb *is*.]

A *prepositional phrase* begins with a preposition and ends with a noun or a pronoun, which is called the object of the preposition.

EXAMPLES

to the bank	by the door	in the picture
of a book	on the floor	after class
at intermission	for them	except him

☞ **REFERENCE NOTE:** For more about prepositional phrases, see pages 533–541.

▶ EXERCISE 9 **Identifying Subjects and Verbs**

Identify the verb and the subject in each of the following sentences.

EXAMPLE   [1] Most of the students in our class have enjoyed discussing our town's folklore.
1. *have enjoyed—verb; Most—subject*

[1] Many regions of the United States have local legends. [2] One pine-forested area in New Jersey is supposedly haunted by the Jersey Devil. [3] This fearsome monster reportedly chases campers and wayward travelers through the woods. [4] In contrast, Oregon is haunted by legends of the less aggressive Bigfoot. [5] This humanlike creature secludes itself in heavily forested areas. [6] Its shaggy coat of hair looks like a bear's fur. [7] According to legend, Bigfoot is gentle and shy by nature, avoiding contact with strangers. [8] Elsewhere, stories around the Lake Champlain area tell about a monster resembling a sea serpent in the depths of the lake. [9] Many sightings of this beast have been reported to authorities. [10] Over the years, a number of people have tried unsuccessfully to photograph the monster.

Sentences That Ask Questions

Questions often begin with a verb, a helping verb, or a word such as *what, when, where, how,* or *why.* The subject usually follows the verb or helping verb.

EXAMPLES   How is the **movie** different?
Does **she** have a ride home?

In questions that begin with a helping verb, like the last example on the previous page, the subject always comes between the helper and the main verb. You can also find the subject by turning the question into a statement and then finding the verb and asking "Who?" or "What?" in front of it.

EXAMPLES   **Was the train late? becomes The train was late.** [What was late? The *train* was.]
Has she answered the letter? becomes She has answered the letter. [Who has answered? *She* has.]

Sentences Beginning with *There*

Never mistake the word *there* for the subject of a sentence. *There* is often used to get a sentence started when the subject comes after the verb. In this use, *there* is called an *expletive.*

                              V   S
EXAMPLES   **There is a drawbridge over the river.**

                              V   S
           There are insects in our garden.

To find the subject in such a sentence, ask "Who?" or "What?" before the verb followed by *there*.

EXAMPLE   **There was a clerk at the counter.** [Who was there? A *clerk* was.]

NOTE: Like *there*, the adverb *here* is often used to get a sentence started.

EXAMPLE   **Here is your pencil.**

To find the subject, ask "Who?" or "What?" before the verb followed by *here*.

EXAMPLE   **Here is your pencil.** [What is here? *Pencil* is.]

▶ EXERCISE 10   **Identifying Subjects and Verbs**

Identify the subjects and the verbs in the following sentences.

EXAMPLE   1. Will you help me study for my history test?
          1. *you—subject; will help—verb*

1. There are many questions on American history in my book.
2. Naturally, there are answers, too.
3. Under whose flag did Columbus sail?
4. Where is Plymouth Rock?
5. How much do you know about the Lost Colony?
6. What does *squatter's rights* mean?
7. In what area did most of the early Dutch colonists settle?
8. Was there disagreement among settlers in Massachusetts?
9. What kinds of schools did the colonists' children attend?
10. How did people travel in colonial America?

PICTURE THIS

The little-known Caribbean island of Coquille wants to advertise to attract tourists. The minister of tourism has asked you to write a paragraph for a new travel brochure. You are excited because the Caribbean islands conjure up images of white beaches, palm trees, tropical sunsets, buried treasures, and calypso bands. In your paragraph, refer to these images and the scenes pictured here. Vary the position of the subjects in your sentences to make your writing more interesting. Include at least one question and one statement beginning with *there*.

Subject: a Caribbean island
Audience: people planning their vacations
Purpose: to persuade

The Understood Subject

In a request or a command, the subject of a sentence is usually not stated. In such sentences, *you* is the **understood subject.**

REQUEST   Please answer the phone.
COMMAND   Listen carefully to his question.

In the first sentence, who is to answer the phone? *You* are—that is, the person spoken to. In the second sentence, who is to listen? Again, *you* are.

Sometimes a request or a command will include a name.

EXAMPLES   Ellen, please answer the phone.
Listen carefully to his question, class.

Ellen and *class* are not subjects in these sentences. These words are called **nouns of direct address.** They identify the person spoken to or addressed. *You* is still the understood subject of each sentence.

EXAMPLE   Ellen, (you) please answer the phone.

▶ EXERCISE 11   **Writing Requests or Commands**

Using five of the seven situations listed on the next page, write sentences that are requests or commands. In three of your sentences, use a noun of direct address.

EXAMPLE   *Setting*   *Person Speaking*   *Person Addressed*
          1. medieval castle   queen   wizard
          1. *Wizard, make this straw into gold.*

Setting	Person Speaking	Person Addressed
1. restaurant	diner	server
2. kitchen	parent	teenager
3. desert oasis	Aladdin	genie
4. courtroom	judge	defense attorney
5. child's room	child	baby sitter
6. spaceship	alien invader	crew member
7. forest	Big Bad Wolf	Little Red Riding Hood

Compound Subjects

15f. A *compound subject* consists of two or more subjects that are joined by a conjunction and have the same verb.

The conjunctions most commonly used to connect the words of a compound subject are *and* and *or*.

EXAMPLE **Antony** and **Mae** baked the bread. [Who baked the bread? Antony baked it. Mae baked it. *Antony* and *Mae* form the compound subject.]

When more than two words are included in the compound subject, the conjunction is generally used only between the last two words. Also, the words are separated by commas.

EXAMPLE **Antony, Mae, and** Pamela baked the bread. [Compound subject: *Antony, Mae, Pamela*]

Correlative conjunctions may be used with compound subjects.

EXAMPLE **Either** Antony **or** Mae baked the bread. [Compound subject: *Antony, Mae*]

▶ EXERCISE 12 **Identifying Compound Subjects and Their Verbs**

Identify the compound subjects and their verbs in the following sentences.

EXAMPLE 1. Roast turkey and cranberry sauce are often served at Thanksgiving.
1. *turkey, sauce—compound subject; are served—verb*

1. Moles and bats supposedly have very poor eyesight.
2. April, May, and June are the best months for studying wildflowers in Texas.
3. Kettles of soup and trays of sandwiches were prepared.
4. Both you and I should go downtown.
5. Either *Macbeth* or *Othello* features witches in its plot.
6. In that drawer must be her scissors and ruler.
7. Gerbils and goldfish are popular pets.
8. There are many good jokes and riddles in that book.
9. Where are you and your family going on your vacation this year?
10. There are a dozen eggs and a pound of margarine in the refrigerator.

Compound Verbs

15g. A *compound verb* consists of two or more verbs that are joined by a conjunction and have the same subject.

EXAMPLES Jim Thorpe **entered** and **won** several events in the 1912 Olympics.
They **looked** but **saw** nothing.
The committee **met, voted** on the issue, and **adjourned.**
My sister **will buy** or **lease** a car.

Notice in the last sentence that the helping verb *will* is not repeated before *lease.* In compound verbs, the helping verb may or may not be repeated before the second verb if the helper is the same for both verbs.

▶ EXERCISE 13 **Identifying Subjects and Compound Verbs**

Identify the compound verbs and the subjects in the following sentences. Be sure to include helping verbs.

EXAMPLE   1. Should I buy this pair of jeans now or wait for a sale?
           1. *should buy, wait—compound verb; I—subject*

1. Visit, shop, and relax.
2. Toshiro sings, acts, and dances in the show.
3. At the fair, Dan ran faster than the other boys and won the prize of twenty-five dollars.
4. Will you walk home or wait for the four o'clock bus?
5. This kitchen appliance will slice, dice, or chop.
6. Velma will not only bring the salad but also bake bread for the party.
7. Pick your socks up and put them either in the hamper or downstairs by the washer.
8. The marching band practiced hard and won the state competition.
9. Geraldo rewound the cassette and then pressed the playback button.
10. The newborn calf rose to its feet with a wobble and stood for the first time.

Both the subject and the verb may be compound.

EXAMPLES   The **students** and **teachers wrote** the play and **produced** it.
          Either **Jan** or **Beverly will write** the story and **send** it to the paper.

▶ REVIEW B   **Finding Subjects and Verbs**

Write each of the ten sentences in the paragraph on the next page. Then, complete the following steps to find the subject and the verb in each sentence. [Note: Not all steps apply to every sentence.]

1. Cross out all prepositional phrases so that you can isolate the verb and the subject.
2. Cross out *Here* or *There* at the beginning of a sentence to eliminate these words as possible subjects.
3. Underline all verbs twice, including all helpers and all parts of a compound verb.
4. Underline all subjects once, including all parts of a compound subject.

EXAMPLE [1] Quicksand can be dangerous to a hiker.
       1. *Quicksand* <u>*can be*</u> *dangerous* ~~to a hiker~~.

[1] In quicksand, you need to remain calm. [2] Violent movement, such as kicking your legs, will only worsen the situation. [3] There are several steps to follow to escape from quicksand. [4] First, discard your backpack or any other burden. [5] Next, gently fall onto your back and spread your arms. [6] In this position, you will be able to float. [7] Only then should you slowly bring your feet to the surface. [8] Perhaps a companion or someone else nearby can reach you with a pole or a rope. [9] Are you alone? [10] Then you should look for the shortest distance to solid ground and paddle slowly toward it.

Complements

15h. A *complement* is a word or group of words that completes the meaning of a predicate.

It is possible for a group of words to have a subject and a verb and not express a complete thought. Notice how the following sentences need the boldfaced words to complete their meaning.

EXAMPLES This stew tastes **strange.**
          She always was a **leader.**
          I told **them.**
          Mr. Garcia gave **me directions.**

The words *strange, leader, them, me,* and *directions* are complements. Each one of these words completes the meaning of the predicate. The complement may be a noun, a pronoun, or an adjective.

             S   V   C
EXAMPLES Marcella might become a **chemist.**

              S   V   C
          The cat watched **us.**

              S   V   C
          The clerks at that store are **helpful.**

NOTE: The complement of a sentence is never part of a prepositional phrase.

EXAMPLES　She watched the cheering **crowd**. [*Crowd* is the complement.]
She watched from the cheering **crowd**. [*Crowd* is part of the prepositional phrase *from the cheering crowd.*]

▶ EXERCISE 14　**Identifying Subjects, Verbs, and Complements**

Identify the subject, verb, and complement in each sentence in the following paragraph.

EXAMPLE　[1] Many modern slang expressions sound okay to my great-grandfather.
1. *expressions—subject; sound—verb; okay—complement*

[1] Like every generation, my great-grandfather's generation had its own slang. [2] He still uses it all the time, particularly in telling stories. [3] Great-grandpa played the trombone in a jazz band during the 1920s and '30s. [4] He and other musicians developed many slang expressions. [5] Their language was called *jive talk*. [6] A lot of Great-grandfather's expressions are sayings of entertainer Cab Calloway. [7] Great-grandpa uses phrases such as Calloway's *beat to my socks* (tired) and *out of this world* (perfect). [8] His speech is full of words like *hepcat* and *hip* (wise) and *groovy* (wonderful). [9] Such language became popular all over the United States. [10] And my great-grandfather, at least, still speaks it.

▶ EXERCISE 15　**Writing Sentence Complements**

Write five complete sentences by adding a complement to each of the following groups of words.

1. Jesse usually seems
2. Tomorrow the class will hear
3. That broiled fish looks
4. Last week our class visited
5. Do you have

The Subject Complement

15i. A *subject complement* is a noun, pronoun, or adjective that follows a linking verb. It describes or identifies the simple subject.

EXAMPLES Mark Twain's real name was **Samuel Clemens.**
     The surface felt **sticky.**

In the first sentence, the complement *Samuel Clemens* follows the linking verb *was* and identifies the subject *name.* In the second sentence, the complement *sticky* follows the linking verb *felt* and describes the subject *surface.*

☞ REFERENCE NOTE: Linking verbs are discussed on page 480.

(1) A *predicate nominative* is a noun or pronoun in the predicate that explains or identifies the subject of the sentence.

EXAMPLES A whale is a **mammal.**
     The only people in line were **they.**
     Angela has become a very talented **soloist.**

(2) A *predicate adjective* is an adjective in the predicate that modifies the subject of the sentence.

EXAMPLES The soup is **hot.** [hot soup]
     That soil seems awfully **dry.** [dry soil]

Subject complements may be compound.

EXAMPLES The prizewinners are **Jennifer** and **Marcus.** [compound predicate nominatives]
     The corn tastes **sweet** and **buttery.** [compound predicate adjectives]

To find the subject complement in an interrogative sentence, rearrange the sentence to make a statement.

EXAMPLES Is Darnell the treasurer?
     Darnell is the **treasurer.** [predicate nominative]

To find the subject complement in an imperative sentence, insert the understood subject *you.*

EXAMPLE Be a winner!
    (You) Be a **winner!** [predicate nominative]

EXERCISE 16 **Identifying Subject Complements**

Each of the following sentences has at least one subject complement. For each sentence, give the complement or complements and tell whether each is a *predicate nominative* or a *predicate adjective*.

EXAMPLE 1. Gloria is my favorite character on the show.
　　　　 1. *character—predicate nominative*

1. Does the lemonade taste too sour?
2. The constant chirping of the birds became more and more shrill as the cat approached.
3. The window washers on the fifteenth floor appeared tiny.
4. Why does he always look so serious?
5. Our candidate for the city council was the winner in the primaries.
6. You should feel proud of yourself for keeping your word.
7. Will the hall monitors for Wednesday be Charlene and LaReina?
8. Soft and cool was the grass under the catalpa tree.
9. Be a friend to animals.
10. The crowd grew quiet when Governor Markham began the speech.

EXERCISE 17 **Writing Subject Complements**

Make sentences of the following groups of words by adding nouns, pronouns, or adjectives as subject complements. Use five compound complements. Tell whether each subject complement is a *predicate nominative* or a *predicate adjective*.

EXAMPLE 1. The sky turned
　　　　 1. *The sky turned cloudy and dark. —predicate adjectives*

1. The artist frequently was
2. Those are
3. Sara Brown became
4. It could be
5. The house looked
6. Are you
7. The weather remained
8. The test seemed
9. Manuel had always felt
10. That recording sounds

WRITING APPLICATION

Using Linking Verbs to Express Sensory Details

Sensory details tell how something looks, sounds, feels, smells, or tastes. They appeal to the reader's senses and help the reader share the writer's experience more fully. Sensory details often follow linking verbs because these verbs "link" a subject with another word that describes it.

TOUCH LINK   The treehouse walls **feel** smooth, almost velvety.

SIGHT LINK   The weathered plywood **is** a dignified shade of gray.

These details do more than describe a place. They capture the writer's feelings about it. How does the writer feel about the treehouse? How do you know?

▶ WRITING ACTIVITY

Think about a place you enjoyed being in. Then write a paragraph describing this place. Include sensory details based on your memory and your imagination. Use a variety of linking verbs to express those sensory details.

Prewriting   Make a list of the five senses, noting several details about your place that appeal to each sense.

Writing   As you write your first draft, think about making your sensory details interesting and vivid.

Evaluating and Revising   Does your paragraph capture the feeling of your special place? Delete or add details to make your descriptions clearer. Check to see that you have used linking verbs that apply to all of the senses.

Proofreading   As you find and correct errors in spelling, punctuation, and grammar, pay special attention to the agreement of subjects and verbs. (See pages 590–608 for more about subject-verb agreement.)

Objects

Objects are complements that do not refer to the subject.

EXAMPLE   Lee Trevino sank the **putt.**

In this sentence, the object *putt* does not explain or describe the subject *Lee Trevino.* Notice that *sank* is an action verb rather than a linking verb.

☞ **REFERENCE NOTE:** Action verbs are discussed on pages 477–478.

15j. A *direct object* is a noun or pronoun that receives the action of the verb or shows the result of the action. It answers the question "Whom?" or "What?" after an action verb.

EXAMPLES   Dot asked **Ira** about the game.
Her poem won an **award.**

In the first sentence, *Ira* receives the action expressed by the verb *asked* and tells *whom* Dot asked. Therefore, *Ira* is the direct object. In the second sentence, *award* names the result of the action expressed by the verb *won* and tells *what* her poem won. *Award* is the direct object.

You can find the object of an action verb by asking the question "Whom?" or "What?" after the verb.

```
              S     V    DO
EXAMPLES   Lucy visited me. [Lucy visited whom? Lucy visited me.]

              S     V     DO
           Germs cause illness. [Germs cause what? Germs cause
           illness.]

              S       V        DO
           They were taking snapshots. [They were taking what?
           They were taking snapshots.]
```

Direct objects are never found in prepositional phrases.

EXAMPLE   Josh was riding his bicycle. [*Bicycle* is the direct object.]
Josh was riding on his bicycle. [*Bicycle* is part of the prepositional phrase *on his bicycle.*]

▶ EXERCISE 18   **Identifying Direct Objects**

Identify the direct object in each of the following sentences.

EXAMPLE   1. I enjoy this magazine very much.
         1. *magazine*

1. This article gives interesting facts about libraries.
2. The city of Alexandria, in Egypt, had the most famous library of ancient times.
3. This library contained the largest collection of plays and works of philosophy in the ancient world.
4. The Roman emperor Augustus founded two public libraries.
5. Fire destroyed all of these libraries.
6. Readers could not borrow books from either the library in Alexandria or the Roman libraries.
7. During the Middle Ages, the monastery libraries introduced the idea of a circulating library.
8. By the sixth century, Benedictine monks were borrowing books from their libraries for daily reading.
9. Nowadays in the United States, we have thousands of circulating libraries.
10. Readers borrow millions of books from them every year.

15k.   An *indirect object* is a noun or pronoun that precedes the direct object and usually tells *to whom* or *for whom* (or *to what* or *for what*) the action of the verb is done.

INDIRECT OBJECTS   Sheila told the **children** a story.
                  Frank gave the **Red Cross** a donation.

In the sentences above, *story* and *donation* are direct objects answering the question "What?" after action verbs. Sheila told a story *to whom*? *Children*, the answer, is an indirect object. Frank gave a donation *to whom*? *Red Cross* is the indirect object.

    You can find the indirect object of an action verb by asking "To whom?" or "For whom?" something is done.

                  S   V   IO   DO
EXAMPLES   My little sister sang **me** a song. [My little sister sang a song to whom? To *me*.]

                  S   V   IO   DO
           Natalie knitted her **friend** a sweater. [Natalie knitted a sweater for whom? For her *friend*.]

If the word *to* or *for* is used, the noun or pronoun following it is part of a prepositional phrase and cannot be an indirect object.

| PREPOSITIONAL PHRASES | My teacher showed the bird's nest **to the class.** |
| | I left some dessert **for you.** |

| INDIRECT OBJECTS | The teacher showed **the class** the bird's nest. |
| | I left **you** some dessert. |

☞ **REFERENCE NOTE:** For more information about prepositional phrases and objects of prepositional phrases, see pages 533–541.

NOTE: Both direct and indirect objects may be compound.

EXAMPLES   Lydia sold **cookies** and **lemonade.** [compound direct object]
Lydia sold **Freddy** and **me** lemonade. [compound indirect object]

▶ EXERCISE 19   **Identifying Direct Objects and Indirect Objects**

Identify the direct and indirect objects in the following sentences. You will not find an indirect object in every sentence. Make sure that you give both words for compound direct and indirect objects.

EXAMPLE   1. Sometimes I read my little brother stories from Greek mythology.
1. *indirect object—brother; direct object—stories*

1. In one myth, a famous artist and inventor named Daedalus built the king of Crete a mysterious building known as the Labyrinth.
2. The complicated passageways of this building give us the word *labyrinth,* meaning "a confusing maze of possibilities."
3. After the completion of the Labyrinth, the king imprisoned Daedalus and his son, whose name was Icarus.
4. To escape, Daedalus made Icarus and himself wings out of feathers and beeswax.
5. He gave Icarus careful instructions not to fly too near the sun.
6. But Icarus soon forgot his father's advice.

7. He flew too high, and when the sun melted the wax in the wings, he plunged to his death in the ocean.
8. Though saddened by the death of his son, Daedalus flew on and reached Sicily in safety.
9. Mythology tells us many other stories of Daedalus's fabulous inventions.
10. Even today, the name Daedalus suggests genius and inventiveness.

▶ REVIEW C   **Identifying Complements**

Identify the complements in the following sentences. Then tell whether each complement is a *predicate nominative*, a *predicate adjective*, a *direct object*, or an *indirect object*. Some sentences may have no complements; others may have more than one.

EXAMPLE   [1] **My brother Bill gave Mom a birthday surprise.**
　　　　　　　1. *Mom—indirect object; surprise—direct object*

[1] My brother made Mom a birthday cake. [2] However, the project soon became a fiasco. [3] First, Bill cracked three eggs into a bowl. [4] But bits of the shells went in, too. [5] Then he added the flour and other dry ingredients. [6] The electric mixer whirled the batter right onto the ceiling. [7] The batter was so sticky that it stayed there and didn't fall off. [8] Bill did not clean the ceiling immediately, and the sticky substance hardened overnight. [9] Mom was not angry, but she did give Bill a suggestion for a gift. [10] "A clean kitchen would be a great birthday present," she said.

▶ EXERCISE 20   **Identifying Complements**

The picture on the next page, *House by the Railroad*, was painted by the American artist Edward Hopper in 1925. Very few old houses like this one are still standing. Who might have lived there? What were their names and occupations, their thoughts and feelings? Write ten sentences about the house and its inhabitants. Use at least one complement in each sentence. Underline each complement and be prepared to tell whether it is a *predicate adjective*, a *predicate nominative*, a *direct object*, or an *indirect object*.

EXAMPLE 1. *This old house looks <u>empty</u> and <u>lonely</u>. —predicate adjective; predicate adjective*

Edward Hopper, *House by the Railroad*, (1925), Oil on canvas, 24 × 29″, The Museum of Modern Art, New York. Given anonymously.

▶ REVIEW D   **Identifying the Parts of a Sentence**

Identify the italicized words in the following passage. Use these abbreviations.

s.	subject	*p.a.*	predicate adjective
v.	verb	*d.o.*	direct object
p.n.	predicate nominative	*i.o.*	indirect object

EXAMPLE   When you draw faces, do they look [1] *realistic?*
          1. *p.a.*

Before this winter, I couldn't draw a human [1] *face* well. However, our [2] *neighbor*, Mr. Teng, is a portrait [3] *painter*, and he has been giving [4] *me* some instructive [5] *tips*. He says that the most important [6] *feature* is the correct [7] *placement* of the eyes. Apparently, most [8] *people* draw the [9] *eyes* too high. In fact, [10] *they* should be placed halfway down the head. Many people also [11] *make* the ears too small. The [12] *top* of each ear [13] *should align* with the eyebrow, and the [14] *bottom* should align with the tip of the nose. Getting the width of the face right is also [15] *important*. Mr. Teng says, "Use one eye's [16] *width* as a unit of measure and make the head five eye-widths wide." There are many other [17] *guidelines*, but these tips from Mr. Teng are the most [18] *basic.* By following them, I can now draw a human [19] *face* that [20] *looks* realistic.

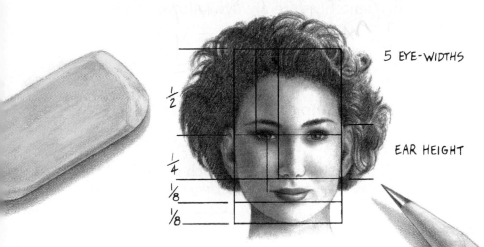

5 EYE-WIDTHS

EAR HEIGHT

½

¼

⅛

⅛

Classifying Sentences by Purpose

15l.   Sentences may be classified as *declarative, imperative, interrogative,* or *exclamatory.*

(1) A ***declarative sentence*** makes a statement. All declarative sentences are followed by periods.

EXAMPLE   Dr. Rosalyn Yalow won a Nobel Prize in medicine in 1977.

(2) An ***imperative sentence*** gives a command or makes a request. Imperative sentences are usually followed by periods. Very strong commands, however, may take an exclamation point.

EXAMPLES   Please open your books to page 3.
Be careful of the undertow.
Stop!

Notice in these examples that a command or a request has the understood subject *you.*

(3) An ***interrogative sentence*** asks a question. Interrogative sentences are followed by question marks.

EXAMPLES   Can she finish in time**?**
            How did she find Yoshi and Sarah**?**

(4) An *exclamatory sentence* expresses strong feeling. Exclamatory sentences are always followed by exclamation points.

EXAMPLES   Oh, no**!** The battery is dead**!**
            I can't believe this is happening**!**

▶ EXERCISE 21   ### Identifying the Four Kinds of Sentences

For each of the following sentences, choose the correct end mark of punctuation. Classify each sentence as *imperative, declarative, interrogative,* or *exclamatory.*

EXAMPLE   1. There are many delicious foods from India
           1. *period—declarative*

1. Do you like spicy food
2. Some Indian food is hot, and some isn't
3. *Sambar* is a soup made with lentils and vegetables
4. Save me some of those curried shrimp
5. What is that wonderful bread called
6. *Palek alu* is a spicy dish of potatoes
7. Watch out for the hot chilies
8. Isn't this yogurt drink called *lassi* good
9. Be sure to add the curry and other spices to the onions
10. Wow, wait until you taste this rice-and-banana pudding

▶ EXERCISE 22   **Writing Four Kinds of Sentences**

The picture on the next page shows a still shot from a completed movie scene. Now the director wants to add close-ups of the crowd's reactions. Write ten complete sentences that might be spoken by people in the crowd. Use at least two sentences of each kind: *imperative, declarative, interrogative,* and *exclamatory.* Be prepared to identify the kind of sentence each one is.

EXAMPLE   1. *YOUNG MOTHER: "Stay behind that rope, Billy!"—imperative*

Review: Posttest 1

A. Identifying the Parts of a Sentence

In the following paragraphs, identify each of the numbered italicized words, using these abbreviations:

s.	subject	*p.a.*	predicate adjective
v.	verb	*d.o.*	direct object
p.n.	predicate nominative	*i.o.*	indirect object

EXAMPLE   Are you a mystery **[1]** *fan*?
          1. *fan—p.n.*

Sir Arthur Conan Doyle certainly gave **[1]** *readers* a wonderful **[2]** *gift* when he **[3]** *created* the character of Sherlock Holmes. **[4]** *Holmes* is a **[5]** *master* of the science of deduction. He **[6]** *observes* seemingly insignificant **[7]** *clues*, applies logical reasoning, and reaches simple yet astounding conclusions.

The Hound of the Baskervilles is an excellent **[8]** *example* of how Holmes solves a baffling **[9]** *mystery*. The **[10]** *residents* of a rural area are afraid of a supernatural dog that **[11]** *kills* people at night. Helpless against this beast, they seek the **[12]** *services* of Sherlock Holmes. Using logic, he solves the mystery and relieves the people's **[13]** *fear*. This story is **[14]** *one* of Conan Doyle's best because it is both **[15]** *eerie* and mystifying.

B. Identifying and Punctuating the Kinds of Sentences

Copy the last word of each of the following sentences and then give the correct end mark of punctuation. Classify each sentence as *imperative, declarative, interrogative,* or *exclamatory.*

EXAMPLE 1. Sherlock Holmes has many dedicated fans
            1. *fans*. —*declarative*

16. How clever Sherlock Holmes is
17. Sir Arthur Conan Doyle wrote four novels and fifty-six short stories about Holmes
18. Have you read any of these stories
19. I particularly like the stories in which Holmes confronts the evil Professor Moriarty
20. Read just one of these stories and see why millions of mystery fans love Sherlock Holmes

Review: Posttest 2

Writing Sentences

Write your own sentences according to the following guidelines. Underline the specified part or parts.

EXAMPLE 1. a sentence beginning with *There* and containing a compound subject
            1. *There were* <u>*games*</u> *and* <u>*contests*</u> *for the children.*

1. a declarative sentence with a compound verb
2. an interrogative sentence with a compound subject
3. an imperative sentence with a noun of direct address
4. a sentence with a direct object
5. a sentence with an indirect object
6. a sentence with a predicate nominative
7. a sentence beginning with an adverb
8. a sentence with an adjective modifying a complement
9. a sentence with a compound complement
10. a sentence ending with a verb

16 THE PHRASE

Prepositional, Verbal, and Appositive Phrases

Diagnostic Test

A. Identifying and Classifying Prepositional Phrases

Identify the ten prepositional phrases in the following sentences. Then give the word(s) modified by each phrase and the type of phrase (*adj.* for adjective phrase, *adv.* for adverb phrase).

EXAMPLE **[1]** Our whole family reads the newspaper in the morning.
1. *in the morning—reads—adv.*

[1] A daily newspaper has something for almost everyone. [2] In addition to news, the paper offers recipes, entertainment, classified ads, and much more. [3] My family never argues over the sections of the paper. [4] Dad always begins with the sports pages; Mom prefers the general news. [5] My favorite part, the comics, appears in many newspapers. [6] My sister and I enjoy characters like

Garfield and Snoopy. **[7]** I also find the editorial and opinion pages interesting, especially when a debate between two sides develops. **[8]** Sometimes I can see the logic behind an argument, while other times I wonder why grown people argue about some trivial issue.

B. Identifying Verbals and Appositives

Identify each italicized word in the following sentences as a *participle*, a *gerund*, an *infinitive*, or an *appositive*.

EXAMPLE **[1]** The young woman, an excellent *athlete*, wanted *to earn* a gold medal for her *swimming*.
1. *athlete—appositive*
   to earn—infinitive
   swimming—gerund

[9] *Enjoyed* by people throughout history, amateur athletic competition involves more than **[10]** *winning* an event. When talented amateurs compete **[11]** *to test* their skills, they learn a great deal about their sports. In addition, the love of a sport, the best **[12]** *reason* for **[13]** *entering* into competition, usually grows as an athlete's performance improves. Furthermore, **[14]** *sharing* hard work with teammates leads a person **[15]** *to appreciate* cooperative effort. Competitions **[16]** *organized* on many levels give amateur athletes frequent opportunities **[17]** *to put* their abilities to the test. Many young people dream of participating in state, national, and international competitions, **[18]** *events* that draw the best athletes.

16a. A *phrase* is a group of related words that is used as a single part of speech and does not contain both a predicate and its subject.

EXAMPLES **has been sitting** [verb phrase; no subject]
about you and me [prepositional phrase; no subject or verb]

A group of words that has *both* a subject *and* a verb is not a phrase.

EXAMPLES   **We found** your pen. [*We* is the subject of *found.*]
if **she will go** [*She* is the subject of *will go.*]

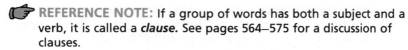 **REFERENCE NOTE:** If a group of words has both a subject and a verb, it is called a *clause.* See pages 564–575 for a discussion of clauses.

EXERCISE 1   **Identifying Phrases**

Identify each of the following groups of words as a *phrase* or *not a phrase*.

EXAMPLES   1. with a hammer   2. because we agree
1. *phrase*   2. *not a phrase*

1. was hoping
2. if she really knows
3. with Abdul and me
4. will be writing
5. inside the house
6. since Donna wrote
7. after they leave
8. has been cleaned
9. on Ricardo's desk
10. as the plane lands

Prepositional Phrases

16b.   A *prepositional phrase* is a group of words beginning with a preposition and ending with a noun or a pronoun.

EXAMPLES   **to** the pool   **at** the Jacksons' house   **instead of** them

Some prepositions are made up of more than one word, like *instead of* in the last example. Notice that an article or other modifier often appears in the prepositional phrase. The first example contains *the,* the second *the Jacksons'.*

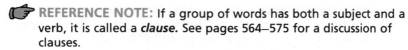 **REFERENCE NOTE:** For a list of commonly used prepositions, see pages 491–492.

16c.   The noun or pronoun that ends a prepositional phrase is the *object* of the preposition that begins the phrase.

EXAMPLES   Every weekend, Pedro works **in his parents' store.**
[*Store* is the object of the preposition *in.*]

Are you going **with them?** [*Them* is the object of the preposition *with.*]

Objects of prepositions may be compound.

EXAMPLES **Kyoko called to Nancy and me.** [Both *Nancy* and *me* are objects of the preposition *to.*]
The marbles were scattered under the table and chairs. [The preposition *under* has a compound object, *table* and *chairs.*]

Do not be misled by a modifier coming after the noun or pronoun in a prepositional phrase. The noun or pronoun is still the object.

EXAMPLE **Mom and Mrs. Braun worked at the polls** today. [The object of the preposition *at* is *polls.* The adverb *today* tells *when* and modifies the verb *worked.*]

EXERCISE 2 **Identifying Prepositions and Their Objects**

Identify each preposition and its object in the following paragraph.

EXAMPLE [1] **I've been studying Spanish in school for three years.**
1. *in—school; for—years*

[1] Last Tuesday, my Spanish class went on a field trip to Juarez, Mexico, across the Río Grande from El Paso, Texas, where we live. [2] Señora Ayala, our teacher, wanted us to practice speaking and reading Spanish outside the classroom. [3] Everyone was supposed to speak only Spanish during the trip. [4] We first went to the *Muséo de Arte e Historia* and saw colorful displays of art and crafts as well as many archaeological exhibits. [5] J. D., Leo, Yolanda, and I looked around the museum and read the information about each exhibit. [6] Besides the museum, we visited the Pueblito Mexicano, a beautiful shopping area owned by the Mexican government. [7] Later, we decided to go to a restaurant near the *mercado*, the big marketplace. [8] As Señora Ayala walked among our tables, she listened to us order our tacos, enchiladas, and frijoles in Spanish. [9] We walked around the mercado for a few minutes and then went into the Nuestra Señora de Guadalupe mission,

which was built in 1659. [10] As we got ready to leave, we chatted in Spanish about all of the interesting things we had seen.

The Adjective Phrase

Prepositional phrases used as adjectives are called *adjective phrases.*

EXAMPLES The members **of the club** want sweatshirts **with the club emblem.**

The prepositional phrase *of the club* is used as an adjective to modify the noun *members. With the club emblem* is used as an adjective to modify the noun *sweatshirts.*

Unlike a one-word adjective, which usually precedes the word it modifies, an adjective phrase always follows the noun or pronoun it modifies.

EXAMPLE Annie closed the cellar door.
Annie closed the door **to the cellar.**

More than one adjective phrase may modify the same word.

EXAMPLE The bottle **of vitamins on the shelf** is mine. [The prepositional phrases *of vitamins* and *on the shelf* both modify the noun *bottle.*]

An adjective phrase may also modify the object of another prepositional phrase.

EXAMPLE The horse **in the trailer with the rusted latch** broke loose. [The phrase *in the trailer* modifies the noun *horse. Trailer* is the object of the preposition *in.* The phrase *with the rusted latch* modifies *trailer.*]

Often you can convert the objects of adjective phrases into nouns used as adjectives. Doing this makes your writing less wordy.

ADJECTIVE PHRASES	NOUNS USED AS ADJECTIVES
The light **in the kitchen** is on.	The **kitchen** light is on.
The airports **in Chicago and New York** are crowded.	The **Chicago** and **New York** airports are crowded.

However, not all adjective phrases can be changed into one-word modifiers that make sense. Sometimes, changing an adjective phrase makes a sentence confusing.

CLEAR Please hand me the book **on the table.**
CONFUSING Please hand me the **table** book.

▶ EXERCISE 3 **Identifying Adjective Phrases and the Words They Modify**

Identify the ten adjective phrases in the following paragraph and give the word that each modifies. [Note: Some sentences contain more than one phrase.]

EXAMPLE [1] The year before last, our family visited South Dakota and saw a famous monument to great American leaders.
1. *before last—year; to great American leaders—monument*

[1] My mom took this picture of our guide Ben Black Elk with my brother, sister, and me when we were visiting this scenic spot in front of Mount Rushmore National Memorial. [2] As you can see, the mountainside behind us is a lasting tribute to George Washington, Thomas Jefferson, Theodore Roosevelt, and Abraham Lincoln. [3] Tourists on the viewing terrace gaze up nearly five hundred feet to see these works of art along the opposite granite wall. [4] Almost sixty feet in height, these four massive faces are an inspiration to all who visit Mount Rushmore.

The Adverb Phrase

An *adverb phrase* is a prepositional phrase used as an adverb to tell *when, where, how, why,* or *to what extent.*

EXAMPLES   **By Wednesday** Christopher will be finished. [The adverb phrase *By Wednesday* tells *when* Christopher will be finished.]

They sailed **across the lake** yesterday. [The adverb phrase *across the lake* tells *where* they sailed.]

She answered **with a smile.** [The adverb phrase *with a smile* tells *how* she answered.]

The calculations erred **by more than two inches.** [*By more than two inches* is an adverb phrase telling *to what extent* the calculations erred.]

In the previous examples, the adverb phrases all modify verbs. An adverb phrase may also modify an adjective or an adverb.

EXAMPLES   Mom is good **at tennis** but better **at volleyball.** [The adverb phrase *at tennis* modifies the adjective *good.* The adverb phrase *at volleyball* modifies the adjective *better.*]

Is the water warm enough **for swimming**? [The adverb phrase *for swimming* modifies the adverb *enough.*]

Adjective phrases always follow the words they modify, but an adverb phrase may appear at various places in a sentence.

EXAMPLES   **Before noon** the race started.
The race started **before noon.**

Be sure to place phrases carefully so that they express the meaning you intend.

EXAMPLES   **In the park,** we waved to the children. [Both we and the children were in the park. The phrase *in the park* acts as an adverb and modifies the verb *waved.*]

We waved to the children **in the park.** [We were outside the park, and the children were in it. The phrase *in the park* acts as an adjective and modifies *children.*]

Like adjective phrases, more than one adverb phrase may modify the same word.

GRAMMAR

GRAMMAR

EXAMPLE **During summers,** my older sister works **at the museum.**
[The adverb phrases *during summers* and *at the museum* both modify the verb *works*. The first phrase tells *when* my sister works; the second phrase tells *where* she works.]

▶ EXERCISE 4 **Identifying Adverb Phrases**

Identify the ten adverb phrases in the following sentences and give the word or words each phrase modifies. [Note: Some sentences contain more than one phrase.]

EXAMPLE [1] **The concept of time has inspired many artists over the years.**
1. *over the years—has inspired*

[1] This weathered sculpture, *Fountain of Time,* stands in Chicago's Washington Park. [2] This work shows humanity as it struggles through time. [3] Father Time appears as a dark, mysterious outsider who stands apart from the other figures and gazes at their efforts. [4] Another artist's concept of time is displayed in New York City's Rockefeller Center. [5] Three figures representing Past, Present, and Future are painted on the ceiling. [6] Wherever you stand in the room, Past's eyes are turned away from you, while Future's eyes look upward. [7] The eyes of Present, however, always look straight at you.

 EXERCISE 5

Combining Sentences Using Adjective and Adverb Phrases

You are a reporter for your school newspaper. The Young Business Leaders Club has given you an announcement for its upcoming banquet. Write an article about this event, using the information from the announcement below. Use five adjective phrases and five adverb phrases to help you include the necessary information in your article.

Young Business Leaders Club

What?   Annual Banquet
Where?   Executive Inn Restaurant
           North Highway 53
When?   Friday, May 11, 6:30 to 9:00 p.m.

Tickets are $10.00 per person, available from Alonzo Jackson.

Program

6:30   **Welcome Address**—Anna Wong, president
6:45   **Introductory Remarks**—J. Zarr, club sponsor
7:00   **Dinner**
8:00   **Speakers' Forum: "Planning Now for Your Future"**—
       Rebecca López, nutritionist, Memorial Hospital
       John Perri, owner, Computer Solutions
       Susanne Drennan, financial planner, United Savings Bank
8:45   **Presentation of Young Business Leader Award**

 REVIEW A

Identifying and Classifying Prepositional Phrases

List all the prepositional phrases in each of the following sentences. After each phrase, identify how the phrase is used. Write *adj.* if the phrase is used as an adjective; write *adv.* if the phrase is used as an adverb. Be prepared to identify the word each phrase modifies.

EXAMPLE   1. Theories about the universe have changed over the years.
          1. *about the universe—adj.; over the years—adv.*

1. About seventy years ago, Edwin Hubble discovered the existence of galaxies outside the Milky Way.
2. Now we know that there are perhaps a million galaxies inside the bowl of the Big Dipper alone.
3. Astronomers believe that our galaxy is only one among billions throughout the universe.
4. Galileo, Copernicus, and other early scientists who were curious about outer space would be amazed at the extent of space exploration today.

WRITING APPLICATION

Using Prepositional Phrases to Add Detail to Your Writing

Prepositional phrases add information to a sentence. Adjective phrases tell details about *what kind, which one,* and *how many.* Adverb phrases give details about *when, where, why, how, how much,* and *how far.*

WITHOUT PHRASES We have been planning a treasure hunt.
WITH PHRASES For three weeks we have been planning a treasure hunt for the younger children in our neighborhood.

▶ WRITING ACTIVITY

You are planning a treasure hunt for a group of neighborhood children. The treasure hunt will include six stops for clues. For each clue, write a sentence containing at least one prepositional phrase. Use a combination of adjective and adverb phrases.

Prewriting First, think about your neighborhood and pick a good place to hide a treasure. Then think of six places to hide clues.

Writing Write a sentence giving a clue about each location. The final sentence should lead the children directly to the hidden treasure.

Evaluating and Revising Ask someone who is familiar with the area of the treasure hunt to look over your clues. Revise any clues that are not clear. Be sure that each clue contains at least one prepositional phrase and that you have used both adjective and adverb phrases in your clues.

Proofreading Check to be sure that your prepositional phrases are properly placed. Remember that an adjective phrase always follows the noun or pronoun it modifies. An adverb phrase may occur at various places in a sentence.

Verbals and Verbal Phrases

Verbals are formed from verbs. Like verbs, they may be modified by adverbs and may have complements. However, verbals are used as other parts of speech.

There are three kinds of verbals: *participles, gerunds,* and *infinitives.*

The Participle

| **16d.** | A *participle* is a verb form that can be used as an adjective. |

EXAMPLES **Waxed** floors can be dangerously slippery. [The participle *waxed,* formed from the verb *wax,* modifies the noun *floors.*]
We saw the raccoon **escaping** through the back door. [The participle *escaping,* formed from the verb *escape,* modifies the noun *raccoon.*]

There are two kinds of participles: *present participles* and *past participles.*

(1) Present participles end in *–ing.*

EXAMPLES We ran inside to get out of the **pouring** rain. [*Pouring* is a present participle modifying the noun *rain.*]

Watching the clock, the coach became worried. [The present participle *watching* modifies the noun *coach—watching coach.*]

Although participles are forms of verbs, they do not stand alone as verbs. However, a participle may be used with a helping verb to form a verb phrase.

EXAMPLES   The rain **was pouring.**
The coach **had been watching** the clock.

When a participle is used in a verb phrase, it is part of the verb, not an adjective.

(2) Past participles usually end in *−d* or *−ed.* Other past participles are irregularly formed.

EXAMPLES   A **peeled** and **sliced** cucumber can be added to a garden salad. [The past participles *peeled* and *sliced* modify the noun *cucumber.*]
The speaker, **known** for her strong support of recycling, was loudly applauded. [The irregular past participle *known* modifies the noun *speaker—known speaker.*]

Like a present participle, a past participle can also be part of a verb phrase. When a past participle is used in a verb phrase, it is part of the verb, not an adjective.

EXAMPLES   I **have peeled** and **sliced** the cucumber.
The speaker **was known** for her strong support of recycling.

 **REFERENCE NOTE:** For more information on participle forms, see pages 618–622 and 630–631. For a discussion of irregular verbs, see pages 620–622.

EXERCISE 6   **Identifying Participles and the Words They Modify**

Identify the participles used as adjectives in each of the following sentences. After each participle, give the noun or pronoun it modifies. [Note: Some sentences contain more than one participle used as an adjective.]

EXAMPLE   1. We searched the island for buried treasure.
1. *buried—treasure*

1. The prancing horses were loudly applauded by the delighted audience.
2. The colorful flags, waving in the breeze, brightened the gloomy day.
3. Swaggering and boasting, he made us extremely angry.
4. The game scheduled for tonight has been postponed because of rain.
5. Leaving the field, the happy player rushed to her parents sitting in the bleachers.
6. Branches tapping on the roof made an eerie sound.
7. We thought the banging shutter upstairs was someone walking in the attic.
8. Painfully sunburned, I vowed never to be so careless again.
9. Terrified by our big dog, the burglar turned and fled across the yard.
10. The platoon of soldiers, marching in step, crossed the field to the stirring music of the military band.

▶ EXERCISE 7 **Choosing Appropriate Participles**

For each blank in the following sentences, choose a participle that fits the meaning of the sentence.

EXAMPLE   1. The ＿＿ tide washed over the beach.
　　　　　　 1. *rising*

1. Mr. Ortiz explained the effects of pollution and drought on plants ＿＿ in a rain forest.
2. ＿＿ from the point of view of a firefighter, the story is full of accurate detail.
3. The tiger, ＿＿ by the hunters, swam across the river to safety.
4. ＿＿ at the traffic light, the driver put on his sunglasses.
5. The tourists ＿＿ in the hotel were given a free meal.
6. ＿＿ as an excellent place to camp, the park lived up to its reputation.
7. ＿＿ by a bee, Candace hurried to the infirmary.
8. The poem describes a spider ＿＿ on a thread.
9. We stumbled off the race course, ＿＿.
10. ＿＿, I quickly phoned the hospital.

▶ EXERCISE 8 **Writing Sentences with Participles**

Write five sentences, using a different one of the follow-ing participles in each. Be careful to use the participle as an adjective and not as part of a verb phrase.

EXAMPLE 1. locked
         1. *We couldn't open the locked door.*

1. running   3. challenged   5. written
2. cooked   4. missing

The Participial Phrase

16e. A *participial phrase* is a phrase containing a participle and any complements or modifiers it may have.

EXAMPLES **Seeing the cat,** the dog barked loudly.
The cat hissed at the dog **barking in the yard next door.**
We yelled at the dog **noisily barking at the cat** and finally had to bring him in.

In each of the following sentences, an arrow points from the participial phrase to the noun or pronoun that the phrase modifies.

EXAMPLES **Switching its tail,** the panther paced back and forth. [participle with object *tail*]

She heard me **sighing loudly.** [participle with the adverb *loudly*]

Living within his budget, he never needs to borrow money. [participle with prepositional phrase modifier *within his budget*]

Quickly grabbing the keys, I dashed for the door. [participle with preceding adverb *quickly* and object *keys*]

A participial phrase should be placed very close to the word it modifies. Otherwise the phrase may appear to modify another word, and the sentence may not make sense.

MISPLACED	He saw a moose riding his motorcycle through the woods. [The placement of the modifier calls up a silly picture. *He*, not *the moose*, is riding the motorcycle.]
IMPROVED	Riding his motorcycle through the woods, he saw a moose.

👉 **REFERENCE NOTE:** The punctuation of participial phrases is discussed on pages 750–755. The participle as a dangling modifier is discussed on pages 686–687. Combining sentences using participles is discussed on pages 424–425 and 437.

▶ EXERCISE 9   **Identifying Participial Phrases**

Identify the participial phrases in the following paragraph and give the word each phrase modifies.

EXAMPLE [1] The sight of skyscrapers towering against the sky moves almost anyone.
1. *towering against the sky—skyscrapers*

[1] How are skyscrapers created, and what keeps them standing tall? [2] As the drawing shows, columns of steel or concrete reinforced with steel are sunk into bedrock beneath the building. [3] If a layer of rock isn't present, these columns are sunk into a thick concrete pad spread across the bottom of a deep basement. [4] From this foundation rises a steel skeleton, supporting the walls and floors. [5] The cutaway drawing below shows how this skeleton, covered with a "skin" of glass and metal, becomes a safe working and living space for people.

REVIEW B

Identifying Participles and Participial Phrases

Identify the participles and participial phrases in the following paragraph and give the words they modify. Some sentences contain more than one participle or participial phrase.

EXAMPLE [1] **Cats, known for their pride and independence, are supposed to be hard to train.**

1. *known for their pride and independence—cats*

[1] One day I was giving Chops, my very spoiled cat, treats. [2] Standing on her hind legs, she reached up with her paw. [3] Grabbing for my fingers, Chops tried to bring the tasty morsel closer. [4] Pulling my hand back a little, I tugged gently on her curved paw, and she stepped forward. [5] Praising my clever cat, I immediately gave her two more treats. [6] The next time I held a treat up high, Chops, puzzled but eager, repeated the grab-and-step movement. [7] Soon Chops was taking steps toward treats held out of her reach. [8] I now have an educated cat who can walk on two legs. [9] Grabbing the treats and gobbling them down, she has learned that certain moves always get her a snack. [10] Sometimes after Chops has had her treat, she just sits and looks at me, no doubt thinking that humans are truly a strange bunch!

The Gerund

16f. A *gerund* is a verb form ending in *-ing* that is used as a noun.

Like nouns, gerunds are used as subjects, predicate nominatives, direct objects, or objects of prepositions.

EXAMPLES **Singing** is fun. [subject]

Their favorite exercise is **running**. [predicate nominative]

Shelly likes **swimming**. [direct object]

Get specially designed shoes for **jogging**. [object of a preposition]

Like nouns, gerunds may be modified by adjectives and adjective phrases.

EXAMPLES   We listened to **the beautiful** singing **of the famous soprano.** [The article *the,* the adjective *beautiful,* and the adjective phrase *of the famous soprano* modify the gerund *singing. Singing* is used as the object of the preposition *to.*]

The loud ringing **of my alarm** wakes me every morning. [The article *the,* the adjective *loud,* and the adjective phrase *of my alarm* modify the gerund *ringing,* which is the subject of the sentence.]

Like verbs, gerunds may also be modified by adverbs and adverb phrases.

EXAMPLES   Floating **lazily in the pool** is my favorite summer pastime. [The gerund *floating* is used as the subject of the sentence. It is modified by the adverb *lazily* (telling *how*) and also by the adverb phrase *in the pool* (telling *where*).]

Brandywine enjoys galloping **briskly on a cold morning.** [The gerund *galloping* is the direct object of the verb *enjoys.* The adverb *briskly* (telling *how*) and the adverb phrase *on a cold morning* (telling *when*) both modify *galloping.*]

Gerunds, like present participles, end in *-ing.* To be a gerund, a verbal must be used as a noun. In the following sentence, three words end in *-ing,* but only one of them is a gerund.

EXAMPLE   **Following** the coach's advice, she was **planning** to go on with her **training.** [*Following* is a present participle modifying *she. Planning* is part of the verb phrase *was planning.* Only *training,* used as the object of the preposition *with,* is a gerund.]

▶ EXERCISE 10   **Identifying and Classifying Gerunds**

Identify each gerund in the following sentences. Then write how each is used: *subject, predicate nominative, direct object,* or *object of a preposition.*

EXAMPLE   1. Instead of driving, let's walk.
          1. *driving—object of a preposition*

1. Her laughing attracted my attention.
2. By studying, you can improve your grades.
3. Why did the birds stop chirping?
4. Writing in my journal has helped me understand myself better.
5. Frowning, Dad said that we had to finish our homework before we could go skating.
6. Yvette's favorite exercise is hiking.
7. Before leaving the beach, we sat and watched the fading light.
8. Yesterday, Mrs. Jacobs was discussing flying.
9. One of Alvin's bad habits is boasting.
10. Without knocking, the crying child threw open the door.

The Gerund Phrase

16g. A *gerund phrase* contains a gerund and any modifiers or complements it may have.

EXAMPLES **The gentle pattering of the rain** was a welcome sound. [The gerund phrase is the subject of the sentence. The gerund *pattering* is modified by the article *the,* the adjective *gentle,* and the prepositional phrase *of the rain.* Notice that the modifiers preceding the gerund are included in the gerund phrase.]

I feared **skiing down the mountain alone.** [The gerund phrase is used as the object of the verb *feared.* The gerund *skiing* is modified by the prepositional phrase *down the mountain* and by the adverb *alone.*]

His job is **giving the customers their menus.** [The gerund phrase is used as a predicate nominative. The gerund *giving* has a direct object, *menus,* and an indirect object, *customers.*]

Evelyn Ashford won a gold medal for **running the 100-meter dash.** [The gerund phrase is the object of the preposition *for.* The gerund *running* has a direct object, *dash.*]

NOTE: Whenever a noun or a pronoun comes before a gerund, the possessive form should be used.

EXAMPLES **Pedro's** constant practicing improved **his** playing.
My playing the radio loudly is a bad habit.

> EXERCISE 11 **Identifying and Classifying Gerund Phrases**

Find the gerund phrases in the following paragraph. Then identify how each phrase is used: as a *subject*, a *predicate nominative*, an *object of a preposition*, or a *direct object*.

EXAMPLE [1] The best hunting trophies are the ones you get by photographing wild animals.
1. *photographing wild animals—object of a preposition*

[1] Exciting and challenging, wildlife photography is surprisingly similar to hunting with a gun. [2] In both activities, knowing the animals' habits and habitats is vital to success. [3] Other important skills are being quiet and keeping your aim steady. [4] In photography, you must also consider lighting the prey and choosing the correct film. [5] Your patience and skill are rewarded when you "capture" a wild creature without killing it.

> REVIEW C **Identifying and Classifying Gerunds and Gerund Phrases**

Identify each gerund or gerund phrase in the following sentences. Then tell how each is used: as a *subject*, a *predicate nominative*, a *direct object*, or an *object of a preposition*.

EXAMPLE [1] Drawing a good caricature is hard to do.
1. *Drawing a good caricature—subject*

[1] A caricature is a picture, usually of a person, that draws attention to key features by emphasizing them. [2] Usually, caricature artists enjoy poking fun at famous people. [3] When you look at this sketch of Teddy Roosevelt, you can't help

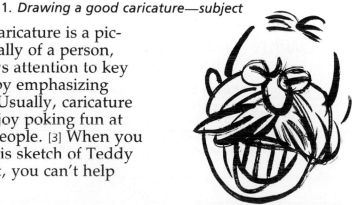

smiling. [4] The artist began by simplifying the shape of his subject's head. [5] Then he started outlining the temples and round cheeks with bold strokes. [6] As you have probably guessed, observing is important to good caricature. [7] By enlarging Roosevelt's wide grin and bristly mustache, the artist emphasizes these features and suggests Roosevelt's energetic, outgoing personality. [8] The artist also used his subject's narrowed eyes and oval glasses for comic effect by drawing them smaller and placing them closer together than they really are. [9] Exaggerating has resulted in an amusing but unmistakable likeness.

The Infinitive

16h. An *infinitive* is a verb form, usually preceded by *to,* that can be used as a noun, an adjective, or an adverb.

Infinitives are used as nouns.

EXAMPLES **To love** is **to care.** [*To love* is the subject of the sentence; *to care* is the predicate nominative.]

Cheryl wanted **to work** on the play in any way but **to act.** [*To work* is the object of the verb *wanted. To act* is the object of the preposition *but.*]

Infinitives are used as adjectives.

EXAMPLES The place **to visit** is Williamsburg. [*To visit* modifies the noun *place.*]

That was the record **to beat.** [*To beat* modifies the noun *record.*]

Infinitives also are used as adverbs.

EXAMPLES Sabina Miller jumped **to shoot.** [*To shoot* modifies the verb *jumped.*]

Ready **to go,** we loaded the car. [*To go* modifies the adjective *ready.*]

NOTE: *To* plus a noun or a pronoun (*to school, to him, to the beach*) is a prepositional phrase, not an infinitive.

GRAMMAR

 EXERCISE 12 **Identifying and Classifying Infinitives**

Identify the infinitives in the following sentences. Then tell how each infinitive is used: as a *noun,* an *adjective,* or an *adverb.*

EXAMPLE   1. I would like to help you.
          1. *to help—noun*

1. Tamisha's ambition is to fly.
2. According to the map, the road to take is the one on the left.
3. Chen has learned to tap-dance.
4. I am happy to oblige.
5. An easy way to win at tennis does not exist.
6. The grass began to grow after we watered it.
7. The hockey team went to Coach Norton's house to study last night.
8. We met at the lake to swim.
9. That is not the correct amount of paper to order for this project.
10. To persist can be a sign of stubbornness.

The Infinitive Phrase

16i. An *infinitive phrase* consists of an infinitive together with its modifiers and complements.

Infinitive phrases, like infinitives alone, can be used as nouns, adjectives, or adverbs.

EXAMPLES   **To proofread your writing carefully** is important. [The infinitive phrase is used as a noun, as the subject of the sentence. The infinitive has a direct object, *writing,* and is modified by the adverb *carefully.*]

She is the player **to watch in the next game.** [The infinitive phrase is used as an adjective modifying the predicate nominative *player.* The infinitive is modified by the adverbial phrase *in the next game.*]

We are eager **to finish this project.** [The infinitive phrase is used as an adverb modifying the predicate adjective *eager.* The infinitive has a direct object, *project.*]

NOTE: An infinitive may have a subject.

EXAMPLE I wanted **him to help me with my algebra.** [*Him* is the subject of the infinitive *to help.* The infinitive, together with its subject, complements, and modifiers, is sometimes called an *infinitive clause.*]

The Infinitive with *to* Omitted

Sometimes the *to* of the infinitive is omitted in a sentence.

EXAMPLES I've done all my chores except [to] **feed** the cat.
I'll help you [to] **pack.**
Marla let the dogs [to] **run** loose in the field.

▶ EXERCISE 13 **Identifying and Classifying Infinitives and Infinitive Phrases**

Identify the infinitives and infinitive phrases in the following sentences. After each one, give its use: *noun, adjective,* or *adverb.* A sentence may contain more than one infinitive or infinitive phrase.

EXAMPLE 1. Scott is the person to elect.
1. *to elect—adjective*

1. To dance gracefully requires coordination.
2. She wanted to join the chorus.
3. Sandy needs to study.
4. I'm going to the pond to fish.
5. A good way to lose weight is to eat moderately.
6. After our long vacation, we needed to get back in training.
7. The best way to get there is to take the bus.
8. Don't dare open that present before your birthday.
9. Juanita and Matt shopped to find the perfect gift.
10. He lives to swim and water-ski.

▶ EXERCISE 14 **Identifying and Classifying Infinitive Phrases**

Identify the infinitive phrases in the following paragraph. Then tell how each phrase is used: as a *noun,* an *adjective,* or an *adverb.*

EXAMPLE [1] **To create a miracle fabric was the aim of chemist Joe Shivers.**
1. *To create a miracle fabric—noun*

[1] He succeeded with spandex, and athletes of all shapes and sizes have come to appreciate the qualities of his "power cloth." [2] This strong material has the ability to stretch and to snap back into shape. [3] Its sleek fit lessens friction to give the wearer faster movement through air or water. [4] Its slick surface makes an athlete such as a wrestler hard to hold on to. [5] To say that spandex has athletes covered is not stretching the truth.

REVIEW D | Identifying and Classifying Infinitives and Infinitive Phrases

Identify the infinitives and infinitive phrases in the following paragraph. After each one, give its use: *noun, adjective,* or *adverb.* Remember that the *to* of an infinitive is sometimes omitted.

EXAMPLES [1] **Laurel and Hardy were a comic team to remember.**
1. *to remember—adjective*

[1] Together, slender Stan Laurel and roly-poly Oliver Hardy have made millions of moviegoers laugh. [2] In their day, to be funny in the movies required the use of body language. [3] Both of them proved to be geniuses in their ability to keep audiences laughing. [4] For his famous head scratch, Stan grew his hair long so that he could scratch and pull it to make a comic mess. [5] Stan also developed a hilarious cry to show his character's

childish nature. [6] He would shut his eyes tightly, pinch up his face, and begin to wail. [7] Ollie, too, had an uncanny ability to create his own distinctive mannerisms. [8] For example, he put on a long-suffering look to express frustration. [9] He would also waggle his tie at a person he and Stan had managed to offend and then start giggling nervously. [10] Ollie's intent was to make the person less angry, but his gesture usually had the opposite effect.

▶ REVIEW E ### Identifying and Classifying Verbals and Verbal Phrases

Identify the verbal or verbal phrase in each of the following sentences as a *gerund, gerund phrase, infinitive, infinitive phrase, participle,* or *participial phrase.*

EXAMPLE 1. Building the railroad across the United States in the late 1800s required thousands of workers.
    1. *Building the railroad across the United States in the late 1800s—gerund phrase*

1. The government commissioned two companies to build railway tracks between Omaha, Nebraska, and Sacramento, California.
2. Building eastward from Sacramento, the Central Pacific Railroad relied on Chinese workers.
3. One fourth of the Chinese immigrants in the United States in 1868 helped with laying the track.
4. The terrain was difficult to cover, but the laborers rose to the challenge.
5. Known for their dependability and endurance, the Chinese were strong workers who learned quickly.
6. Complaining was a problem with some workers, but seldom with Chinese laborers.
7. It was often necessary to blow up parts of mountains, and the Chinese workers became experts at this task.
8. Chinese and Irish workers set a record on April 28, 1869, by spiking ten miles and fifty-six feet of track in twelve hours.
9. The railroad company divided the Chinese immigrants into working groups, or gangs, each with twelve to twenty men.

10. Keeping many of their traditional ways, the Chinese workers had food shipped to them from San Francisco's Chinatown.

EXERCISE 15   **Writing Sentences with Verbals and Verbal Phrases**

Making home videos has become a favorite pastime of many Americans. Everyone, it seems, wants to become an amateur movie producer. Friends and family members become actors in these planned or unplanned movies.

Verbals and verbal phrases are also "actors." Verbs that play the role of nouns, adjectives, and adverbs can liven up a piece of writing.

You are entering an amateur moviemaking contest. What film would you like to produce? Describe the movie you would make. Use ten verbals and verbal phrases as "actors" in your description. Underline each verbal or verbal phrase you use. Be able to identify each as a *gerund*, a *participle*, or an *infinitive*.

EXAMPLE   *My singing dog will play the role of Dawgsy, the nightclub performer.—participle*

PICTURE THIS

Ah, romance is in the air! You are watching this scene from your window. Who are these people? What are they doing? You are amazed and begin to imagine explanations for their unusual behavior. You decide to compose a poem about the scene. In your poem, you might describe what is happening,

Tête à tête am Wolkenkratzer 968 étage. Moriz Jung, Austrian, 1885–1915, color lithograph, Vienna, the Wiener Werkstatte.

or you might tell about the feelings of one or both of these characters. Use verbals to enliven your writing. Include at least one participle, one gerund, and one infinitive. You and your classmates might enjoy reading your poems aloud or displaying them on the bulletin board.

Subject: an unusual scene
Audience: classmates
Purpose: to entertain

Appositives and Appositive Phrases

16j. An *appositive* is a noun or a pronoun placed beside another noun or pronoun to identify or explain it.

EXAMPLES   The sculptor **Noguchi** has designed sculpture gardens.
[The noun *Noguchi* identifies the noun *sculptor.*]
Eric, a talented **musician,** plans to study in Europe.
[The noun *musician* explains the noun *Eric.*]

Like any noun or pronoun, an appositive may have adjective and adjective phrase modifiers. If it does, it is called an *appositive phrase.*

16k. An *appositive phrase* is made up of the appositive and its modifiers.

EXAMPLES   My neighbor, **Dr. Jackson,** got her degree in entomology, **the scientific study of insects.**

Lucy Sánchez, **my longtime friend from my old neighborhood,** has a new Scottish terrier.

NOTE: An appositive phrase usually follows the noun or pronoun it refers to. Sometimes, however, the appositive precedes the noun or pronoun explained.

EXAMPLE   **The terror of our block,** little Alisha was on the warpath.

Appositives and appositive phrases are usually set off by commas unless the appositive is a single word closely related to the preceding noun or pronoun. Commas are always used with appositives that refer to proper nouns.

EXAMPLES My brother **Richard** goes to college. [The writer has more than one brother. The appositive is necessary to tell which brother is referred to. Because this information is *essential* to the meaning of the sentence, it is *not* set off by commas.]

My brother, **Richard,** goes to college. [The writer has only one brother. The appositive is not necessary to identify the brother. Because the information is *nonessential,* it is set off by commas.]

Linda, **the editor,** assigned the story.

☞ REFERENCE NOTE: For a discussion of essential and nonessential phrases, see pages 750–751.

▶ EXERCISE 16 **Identifying Appositives and Appositive Phrases**

Identify the appositives and appositive phrases in the following sentences. Then give the word that each appositive or appositive phrase identifies or explains.

EXAMPLE 1. I write haiku, a verse form invented in Japan.
1. *a verse form invented in Japan—haiku*

1. Our community has a new organization, a writers' club called Writers, Inc.
2. Marquita Wiley, a college instructor, started the group at the request of former students.
3. A published author, Ms. Wiley conducts the meetings as workshops.
4. The writers meet to read their works in progress, fiction or poetry, and to discuss suggestions for improvement.
5. The members, people from all walks of life, have varied interests.
6. A mechanic by trade, J. D. Ellis writes funny poems about his hobby, bird-watching.
7. My friend Lusita just had a short story about her people, the Zuni, published in a national magazine.

8. Next week, we'll meet at our regular time, 3:30 P.M.
9. Our speaker is Pat Mora, a Mexican American poet whose work emphasizes harmony between cultures.
10. Have you read the poem "Mending Wall"?

▷ REVIEW F   **Identifying Verbal Phrases and Appositive Phrases**

Find the ten verbal phrases and appositive phrases in the following paragraph. Identify each phrase as a *participial phrase,* a *gerund phrase,* an *infinitive phrase,* or an *appositive phrase.*

EXAMPLE   [1] Florence Griffith Joyner and Jackie Joyner-Kersee, two superstars of track, showed the world how to win big at the 1988 Olympic games.
1. *two superstars of track—appositive phrase to win big at the 1988 Olympic games—infinitive phrase*

[1] Florence, called Flo-Jo by her fans, smashed the women's records in the 100-meter and the 200-meter dash at the games in South Korea. [2] Realizing that she was winning the 100-meter race, Flo-Jo began raising her arms in triumph. [3] This gesture and her brilliant smile, shown on the previous page, seem to illustrate perfectly her supreme confidence and talent. [4] Jackie Joyner-Kersee, Flo-Jo's sister-in-law, gained fame by winning gold medals in the women's long jump and heptathlon. [5] The heptathlon, combining seven different track-and-field events, is a tough two-day competition in which athletes earn points for each event. [6] Earning a total of 7,291 points, Jackie broke the old world record. [7] After she won a third gold medal in the heptathlon at the 1992 Olympics, Jackie began to train for the 1996 games, which she said would be her last.

Review: Posttest 1

A. Identifying and Classifying Prepositional Phrases

Identify each prepositional phrase in the following sentences. Some sentences have more than one prepositional phrase. After each phrase, write the word(s) it modifies and the type of phrase it is (*adj.* for adjective phrase, *adv.* for adverb phrase).

EXAMPLE   **[1]** The museums of different cities are fascinating to tourists.
  1. *of different cities—museums—adj.*
  to tourists—fascinating—adv.

[1] Among its many attractions, New York City offers tourists a number of museums. [2] Perhaps the best-known one is the American Museum of Natural History. [3] This huge museum has exhibits concerning human history and culture and also shows animals, even dinosaurs, in natural-looking displays, called dioramas. [4] Exhibits about earth and space interest young and old alike. [5] In

addition to these exhibits, the museum houses the Hayden Planetarium, which features shows about the heavens. **[6]** The entire complex is popular because it offers something for everyone. **[7]** The city's other museums, which are also fascinating, attract visitors who are interested in specific topics. **[8]** People who enjoy art can visit museums like the Metropolitan Museum of Art, the Museum of Modern Art, and the Guggenheim Museum. **[9]** New York is also home to the Museum of Broadcasting, which is filled with old films and radio broadcasts. **[10]** One of the city's newest museums, Ellis Island Immigration Museum, opened during 1990, displaying many artifacts that had been owned by immigrants who entered this country through Ellis Island.

B. Identifying Verbals and Appositives

In the following paragraph, identify each italicized word or word group as a *participle*, a *gerund*, an *infinitive*, or an *appositive*.

EXAMPLE   **[1]** For some reason, *cleaning* a room, that *dreaded project*, always seems *to create* new projects.
      1. *cleaning—gerund; dreaded—participle; project—appositive; to create—infinitive*

[11] John began with every intention of *cleaning* his entire room, the official disaster *area* of his home. **[12]** He first tackled the pile of CDs *lying* near his *unused* sound system. **[13]** *Sorting* through them, he found them mostly *outdated.* **[14]** John reasoned that his *broken* stereo system, a *gift* from his parents, was the culprit. **[15]** By *repairing* the stereo, he could give himself a reason *to update* his music collection. **[16]** *Trained* in electronics, John soon saw the problem and set *to work* on it. **[17]** Some hours later, John had a *working* stereo system but an *uncleaned* room. **[18]** He had a rude *awakening* when his sister announced, "Mom's coming *to see* how your room looks!" **[19]** A tough *taskmaster*, Mom wanted him *to have* it spotless. **[20]** She applauded his success in *fixing* his stereo but insisted that he clean the room before *doing* anything else.

Review: Posttest 2

Writing Sentences with Phrases

Write ten sentences, following the directions given below. Underline the specified phrase in each sentence.

EXAMPLE 1. Use an *adjective phrase* modifying the subject of a sentence.
     1. *The store <u>on the corner</u> sells video games.*

1. Use an *adjective phrase* modifying the object of a preposition.
2. Use an *adverb phrase* modifying an adjective.
3. Use an *adverb phrase* modifying a verb.
4. Use a *participial phrase* modifying a subject.
5. Use a *participial phrase* modifying a direct object.
6. Use a *gerund phrase* as a subject.
7. Use a *gerund phrase* as a predicate nominative.
8. Use an *infinitive phrase* as a noun.
9. Use an *infinitive phrase* as an adverb.
10. Use an *appositive phrase* that explains or identifies the subject of a sentence.

GRAMMAR

17 THE CLAUSE

Independent and Subordinate Clauses

Diagnostic Test

A. Identifying and Classifying Clauses

Identify the italicized clauses in the following sentences as *independent* or *subordinate*. If a clause is subordinate, label it as an *adjective,* an *adverb,* or a *noun*.

EXAMPLES **1.** *Emily Dickinson,* who was a great American poet, *was born in 1830.*
1. *independent*

2. I have noticed *that her poems do not have titles.*
2. *subordinate—noun*

1. Emily Dickinson appeared to have a fairly normal life *until she became a recluse in her family's home.*
2. *There she wrote poems* that critics now call "great American poetry."
3. Unfortunately, *only a few of Dickinson's poems were published* while she was alive.

4. *After she died in 1886,* her other poems were published.
5. My teacher, Mrs. Brooks, thinks *that everyone should read at least some of Dickinson's poetry.*
6. Emily Dickinson is a poet *whose work I read often.*
7. *The poems* I have just finished reading *are "A Narrow Fellow in the Grass" and "Apparently with No Surprise."*
8. Dickinson's imagery in "Apparently with No Surprise" is *what impresses me most.*
9. *I read her poems aloud* so that I can listen to their rhythms.
10. *Whatever I read by Emily Dickinson* inspires me.

B. Identifying and Classifying Subordinate Clauses

Identify each subordinate clause in the following sentences according to its use: as an adjective (*adj.*), an adverb (*adv.*), or a noun (*n.*). If the clause is used as an adjective or an adverb, write the word or phrase it modifies. If the clause is used as a noun, write *subj.* for subject, *d.o.* for direct object, *i.o.* for indirect object, *p.n.* for predicate nominative, or *o.p.* for object of a preposition.

EXAMPLES   **[1]** Since my family has always wanted to see Alaska, we decided to drive there last summer.
   1. *Since my family has always wanted to see Alaska—adv.—decided*

   [2] After three long days on the road, I doubted that we would ever reach our destination.
   2. *that we would ever reach our destination—n., d.o.*

   [11] To get to Alaska, we drove along the Alaska Highway, which goes through the Yukon Territory in Canada. **[12]** Since this highway is 1,397 miles long, most tourists choose to fly to Alaska. **[13]** However, by driving, we were able to take pictures of whatever caught our attention along the way. **[14]** At a rest stop, I thought that I heard some small animals rustling in the brush, and I grabbed my camera. **[15]** What I saw disappearing into the bushes certainly surprised me; it was an enormous moose and her calf.

GRAMMAR

C. Classifying Sentences According to Structure

Classify each of the following sentences according to its structure: *simple, compound, complex,* or *compound-complex.* Be sure that you can identify all subordinate and independent clauses.

EXAMPLE   [1] Before my history class visited the Senate chamber, we read about the United States Senate.
1. *complex*

[16] Since the passage of the Seventeenth Amendment in 1913, senators have been chosen by popular elections in their states. [17] Unlike presidents, senators are elected to six-year terms, and they can be reelected any number of times. [18] To be eligible for the Senate, a person must have been a United States citizen for at least nine years and be at least thirty years old; a candidate must also live in the state that he or she would like to represent. [19] One important job that senators have is to introduce bills in the Senate. [20] Senators are also responsible for approving or rejecting certain presidential appointments, such as those of federal judges and ambassadors.

17a.   A *clause* is a group of words that contains a verb and its subject and is used as part of a sentence.

Although every clause contains a subject and a verb, not all clauses express a complete thought. Clauses that do are called *independent clauses.* Clauses that do not make sense by themselves are called *subordinate clauses.*

Kinds of Clauses

17b.   An *independent* (or *main*) *clause* expresses a complete thought and can stand by itself as a sentence.

EXAMPLES   **Ms. Santana works in a law office in downtown Concord,** and **she has a successful practice.**

Each independent clause has its own subject and verb and expresses a complete thought. In the example just given, the clauses are joined by a comma and the coordinating conjunction *and*. They could also be written with a semicolon between them:

> Ms. Santana works in a law office in downtown Concord; she has a successful practice.

or with a semicolon and a conjunctive adverb:

> Ms. Santana works in a law office in downtown Concord; **indeed,** she has a successful practice.

or as separate sentences:

> Ms. Santana works in a law office in downtown Concord. She has a successful practice.

☞ **REFERENCE NOTE:** For more information on using semicolons and conjunctive adverbs to join independent clauses, see pages 772–773.

17c. A *subordinate* (or *dependent*) *clause* does not express a complete thought and cannot stand alone.

Words such as *whom, because, what, if,* and *until* signal that the clauses following them are subordinate. *Subordinate* means "lesser in rank or importance." To make a complete sentence, a subordinate clause must be joined to an independent clause.

SUBORDINATE CLAUSES	whom you know because I told him the truth what the show is about
SENTENCES	Will the player **whom you know** give us his autograph? **Because I told him the truth,** Dad wasn't too angry about the broken window. Amy wants to know **what the show is about.**

Notice in these examples that subordinate clauses may appear at the beginning, in the middle, or at the end of a sentence. The placement of a subordinate clause depends upon what kind of clause it is: an adjective clause, an adverb clause, or a noun clause.

▶ EXERCISE 1   **Identifying Independent and Subordinate Clauses**

In each sentence in the following paragraph, identify the clause in italics as *independent* or *subordinate*.

EXAMPLE   [1] *When you think of baseball,* you may think of lightning-fast pitches, bat-splitting home runs, or secret hand signals from coaches and catchers.

1. *subordinate*

[1] *Baseball is a game* that depends heavily on good eyesight. [2] For this reason, until recently, playing the great American game has been something *that people with visual impairments could not hope to do.* [3] At least, this was true *until an engineer named Charley Fairbanks invented beep baseball.* [4] *In this version of baseball, the ball beeps* and the bases buzz so that visually impaired players like the one pictured here can tell when to swing and where to run. [5] Each team has a sighted pitcher and a sighted catcher, *who never get a turn at bat,* and six visually impaired fielders who wear blindfolds so that all players are equally impaired. [6] The pitcher shouts "Ready!" *before the ball is pitched* and "Pitch!" when the ball is released. [7] When the bat strikes the ball, the umpire activates the buzzer in one of the two bases, *which the batter must then run to.* [8] When a team is on defense, the pitcher and catcher cannot field the batted ball themselves; *they can only shout directions to help the fielders.* [9] *Beep baseball is fun to play,* and its challenges create a bond between sighted and visually impaired players. [10] Sighted persons *who put on blindfolds and join in* come away from a game with a new respect for the abilities of their teammates.

Uses of Subordinate Clauses

Like phrases, subordinate clauses can be used as adjectives, adverbs, or nouns.

The Adjective Clause

17d. An *adjective clause* is a subordinate clause used as an adjective to modify a noun or a pronoun.

An adjective clause follows the word it modifies. If a clause is necessary, or *essential,* to the meaning of the sentence, it is not set off with commas. If a clause only gives additional information and is *nonessential* to the meaning of a sentence, it is set off by commas.

EXAMPLES   This is the new music video **that I like best.** [The clause *that I like best* is necessary to tell which video is being referred to. Because this information is *essential* to the meaning of the sentence, it is *not* set off by commas.]

Griffins, **which are mythological beasts,** are seen on many coats of arms. [The clause *which are mythological beasts* is not necessary to identify *griffins.* Because this information is *nonessential* to the meaning of the sentence, it is set off by commas.]

☞ REFERENCE NOTE: For help in deciding whether a clause is essential or nonessential, see pages 750–751, rule 24i.

Relative Pronouns

Adjective clauses are often introduced by *relative pronouns.*

RELATIVE PRONOUNS	who whom whose which that

These words are called *relative pronouns* because they *relate* an adjective clause to the word that the clause modifies. Besides introducing an adjective clause and relating it to another word in the sentence, the relative pronoun has a function in the adjective clause.

GRAMMAR

EXAMPLES   Luís, **who enjoys running,** has decided to enter the marathon. [The relative pronoun *who* relates the adjective clause to *Luís. Who* is used as the subject of the adjective clause.]

Janice, **whom I have known for years,** is my lab partner this semester. [The relative pronoun *whom* relates the adjective clause to *Janice. Whom* is used as the direct object of the verb *have known* in the adjective clause.]

The students questioned the data **on which the theory was based.** [The relative pronoun *which* is the object of the preposition *on* and relates the adjective clause to *data.*]

We met the singer **whose record was released this week.** [The relative pronoun *whose* relates the adjective clause to *singer. Whose* is used as a possessive pronoun in the adjective clause.]

☞ **REFERENCE NOTE:** For more information on using *who* and *whom* correctly, see pages 663–664.

In many cases, the relative pronoun in the clause may be omitted. The pronoun is understood and still has a function in the clause.

EXAMPLE   Here is the salad **you ordered.** [The relative pronoun *that* is understood. The pronoun relates the adjective clause to *salad* and is used as the direct object in the adjective clause.]

Occasionally an adjective clause is introduced by the relative adverbs *where* or *when.*

EXAMPLES   They showed us the stadium **where the game would be held.**
Summer is the season **when I feel happiest.**

▶ EXERCISE 2   **Identifying Adjective Clauses**

Each sentence in the following paragraph contains an adjective clause. Write the adjective clause and underline the relative pronoun or relative adverb that introduces it. If the relative pronoun has been omitted, write the relative pronoun in parentheses and then underline it.

GRAMMAR

EXAMPLE [1] Do you know anyone who is familiar with briffits, swalloops, and waftaroms?

    1. *who is familiar with briffits, swalloops, and waftaroms*

[1] Cartoonists use a variety of unusual names for the symbols that commonly appear in funnies. [2] For example, a *briffit* is the little puff of dust hanging in the spot where a swiftly departing character had just been standing. [3] For times when cartoonists want to make something appear hot or smelly, they use wavy, rising lines called *waftaroms*. [4] *Agitrons* are the wiggly lines around an object that is supposed to be shaking. [5] The limbs of a character who is moving are usually preceded or trailed by curved lines called *blurgits* or *swalloops*. [6] *Plewds,* which look like flying droplets of sweat, are drawn around the head of a worried character. [7] In fact, there are very few motions or emotions for which cartoonists have not invented a clever, expressive symbol. [8] Almost everyone who likes to doodle and draw has used some of these symbols, probably without knowing the words for them. [9] Look at the example cartoon, where you will find the names of other common symbols from the world of cartooning. [10] Now you know a "language" almost nobody outside the cartooning profession knows!

▶ EXERCISE 3   **Revising Sentences by Supplying Adjective Clauses**

Revise the following sentences by substituting an adjective clause for each italicized adjective. Add details to make your sentences interesting. Underline the adjective clause in your sentence.

EXAMPLES   1. The *angry* citizens gathered in front of City Hall.
           1. *The citizens, <u>who were furious over the recent tax increase</u>, gathered in front of City Hall.*

           2. The *old* history books lay on the shelf.
           2. *The history books, <u>which were yellow and tattered from many years of use</u>, lay on the shelf.*

1. As we entered the building, a *colorful* painting caught our attention.
2. The *patient* photographer sat on a small ledge all day.
3. The two attorneys argued all week over the *important* contract.
4. The team of mountain climbers decided to try to reach the top of the *high* peak.
5. At the assembly, Ms. Leon made a *surprising* announcement.
6. Saburo and his friends cautiously entered the *dark* cave.
7. Edna Jackson easily won her *first* political campaign.
8. The trainer spoke harshly to the *disobedient* dog.
9. Dodging to his left and then to his right, Manuel scored the *winning* goal.
10. The veterinarian told Pamela that she was taking good care of her *lame* horse.

The Adverb Clause

17e.   An *adverb clause* is a subordinate clause that modifies a verb, an adjective, or an adverb.

An adverb clause tells *how, when, where, why, how much, to what extent,* or *under what condition* the action of the main verb takes place.

EXAMPLES **After I proofread my paper,** I typed it. [The adverb clause *After I proofread my paper* tells *when* I typed it.]

Because manicotti takes so long to prepare, Joy makes it only on special occasions. [*Because manicotti takes so long to prepare* tells *why* Joy makes it only on special occasions.]

You and your brother may come with us **if you want to.** [*If you want to* tells *under what condition* you and your brother may come with us.]

☞ REFERENCE NOTE: Introductory adverb clauses are usually set off by commas. See page 756.

Like adverbs, adverb clauses may also modify adjectives or adverbs.

EXAMPLES His pitching arm is stronger today **than it ever was.** [The adverb clause modifies the adjective *stronger,* telling *to what extent* his arm is stronger.]

My cousin Adele reads faster **than I do.** [The adverb clause modifies the adverb *faster,* telling *how much* faster my cousin Adele reads.]

☞ REFERENCE NOTE: When using adverb clauses to make comparisons, be sure your comparisons are complete. See pages 682–684.

Subordinating Conjunctions

Adverb clauses are introduced by *subordinating conjunctions.*

Common Subordinating Conjunctions		
after	even though	unless
although	if	until
as	in order that	when
as if	once	whenever
as long as	since	where
as soon as	so that	wherever
because	than	whether
before	though	while

Some subordinating conjunctions, such as *after, before, since,* and *until,* may also be used as prepositions.

EXAMPLES   Be sure to hand in your report **before the end** of class today. [prepositional phrase]
Be sure to hand in your report **before class ends today.** [adverb clause]

EXERCISE 4   ### Identifying and Classifying Adverb Clauses

Identify each adverb clause in the following paragraph. Then write what the clause tells: *when, where, how, why, to what extent,* or *under what condition.* A sentence may have more than one adverb clause.

EXAMPLE   [1] When you see this humble man at his spinning wheel, can you believe that he is considered one of this century's greatest leaders?
1. *When you see this humble man at his spinning wheel—when*

[1] If you look through newspapers from the first half of this century, you will see many pictures of Mohandas K. Gandhi. [2] This man led India to independence from Britain, and he took his spinning wheel wherever he went. [3] He did so because he viewed spinning as a symbol of the peaceful, native Indian lifestyle. [4] He also hoped to encourage the Indian people to make their own clothes so that they would not have to depend on British industry. [5] Although he used only nonviolent methods,

Gandhi fought hard for India's independence. [6] Sometimes he led marches or fasted until the government met his requests. [7] As India's Congress and people increasingly supported Gandhi's nonviolent program, the British government was forced to listen. [8] Gandhi was certainly prepared to represent India as a diplomat because he had studied law in London before he became involved in India's freedom movement. [9] After independence was assured, Gandhi turned his attention to helping India's many poor people. [10] Because he was loved throughout India and the world, Gandhi was called *Mahatma*, meaning "Great Soul."

EXERCISE 5   **Building Sentences That Have Adverb Clauses**

Write five sentences, using clauses from the list below. For each sentence, choose two clauses and a subordinating conjunction from the list on page 571. Do not use the same subordinating clause twice. Underline the adverb clauses in the sentences you create. Begin at least three sentences with a subordinating conjunction. Be sure your capitalization and punctuation are correct.

EXAMPLE   1. *Katrina is a nice cat,* <u>*unless we happen to be out of cat food.*</u>

Clauses

Mom usually plays the piano	I will go myself
someone must go to the market	she can be annoying
I am hungry	I always do
she jumps onto the keyboard	you let her
she likes the rhythms	the dry food is kept
you might think	she meows loudly
we happen to be out of cat food	it gets our attention
she plays sonatas	she is a better musician
we eat dinner	it is raining
you feed her	dinner is over
Katrina is a nice cat	she is in a good mood
	my sister begins to dance
	she knows

PICTURE THIS

This movie crew is filming on location in your town or city. You find out that the director wants to shoot some scenes at a local school, and you decide to convince him to choose your school. Write a paragraph telling the director why your school is interesting and would be a good site for filming. You could consider your school's students, faculty, courses, buildings, and setting. Use adverb clauses to modify a verb, an adjective, and an adverb. Exchange paragraphs with a classmate. Then underline each adverb clause and draw an arrow from it to the word it modifies.

Subject: what's interesting about my school
Audience: a movie director
Purpose: to persuade

The Noun Clause

17f.   A *noun clause* is a subordinate clause used as a noun.

A noun clause may be used as a subject, a complement (predicate nominative, direct object, indirect object), or the object of a preposition.

SUBJECT	**What Mary Anne did** was brave and earned her praise from everyone.
PREDICATE NOMINATIVE	The winner will be **whoever runs fastest.**
DIRECT OBJECT	She finally discovered **what the answer was.**
INDIRECT OBJECT	The clerk should tell **whoever calls** the sale prices.
OBJECT OF PREPOSITION	He checks the ID cards of **whoever visits.**

Noun clauses are usually introduced by *that, what, whatever, who, whoever, whom, whomever,* and *how.*

EXAMPLES   They did not know **who it could be.** [The introductory word *who* is the predicate nominative in the noun clause—*it could be who.*]

Show us **what you bought.** [The introductory word *what* is the direct object in the noun clause—*you bought what.*]

She wished **that she were older.** [The introductory word *that* simply introduces the noun clause and has no function within the noun clause.]

Noun clauses sometimes do not have a stated introductory word.

EXAMPLE   His mother said **he could go.** [The introductory word *that* is understood.]

▶ EXERCISE 6   **Identifying and Classifying Noun Clauses**

Most of the following sentences contain noun clauses. A few do not. If a sentence contains a noun clause, identify the clause. Then tell how the clause is used: as a *subject,* a *predicate nominative,* a *direct object,* an *indirect object,* or an *object of a preposition.* If a sentence does not contain a noun clause, write *no noun clause.*

EXAMPLE   [1] We moved to Massachusetts and did not know what we would find there.

   1. *what we would find there—direct object*

[1] What surprised me first were the yellowish green fire engines. [2] I had thought that fire engines were always red. [3] Our neighbors said that this color kept the fire engines from being confused with other large, red trucks. [4] My sister Michelle made another discovery at the bowling alley. [5] The grapefruit-sized bowling balls with no holes weren't what she was used to! [6] Whoever can knock down the pins with one of those bowling balls must be an expert. [7] We learned that this sport is called candlepin bowling. [8] Later on, I was pleasantly surprised by the delicious baked beans. [9] Someone should give whoever invented Boston baked beans an award. [10] Now, after we have lived in New England for a year, both Michelle and I are happy in our new home.

▶ REVIEW A   **Identifying Subordinate Clauses**

For each sentence in the following paragraph, identify the subordinate clause or clauses. Then tell whether each clause is an *adjective clause,* an *adverb clause,* or a *noun clause.* [Hint: One sentence has no subordinate clause.]

EXAMPLE   [1] In paintings created before 1880, horses are usually shown in poses that now look quaint and unnatural.
      1. *that now look quaint and unnatural—adjective clause*

[1] If you stop to think about it, you can see why painters had a problem. [2] Stop-action photography had not yet been invented, and when painters looked at rapidly moving horses, they could not see exactly where the legs and hooves were at any one instant. [3] Whenever painters wanted to portray a galloping horse, they made up a position that they thought suggested speed. [4] The horses in this painting have both front legs extended far to the

front and both hind legs stretched far out behind.
[5] Today, we know instantly that this is an impossible
position for a horse. [6] Stop-action photography was first
used in the 1870s by a Californian named Eadweard Muy-
bridge, who took this series of photographs of a galloping
horse. [7] Along a racetrack, he set up many cameras
whose shutters were controlled by threads stretched
across the track. [8] As the horse ran by, it broke the
threads and tripped the cameras' shutters one after the
other. [9] Painters of the time thought this new technology
was truly amazing! [10] They were the first artists in history to know exactly what a horse really looked like at
each point in its stride.

Sentences Classified According to Structure

Sentences may be classified according to *purpose* as declarative, imperative, interrogative, or exclamatory (see pages
527–528). Sentences may also be classified according to
structure. The term **structure** refers to the number and
types of clauses in a sentence.

17g. According to their structure, sentences are
classified as *simple, compound, complex,* and
compound-complex.

(1) A *simple sentence* has one independent clause and
no subordinate clauses. It may have a compound subject, a compound verb, and any number of phrases.

FXAMPLE   After eating dinner and washing the dishes, Rita and
          Carlos decided to see a movie.

(2) A *compound sentence* has two or more independent clauses but no subordinate clauses.

GRAMMAR

In effect, a compound sentence consists of two or more simple sentences joined by a comma and a coordinating conjunction, by a semicolon, or by a semicolon and a conjunctive adverb.

EXAMPLES Rita wanted to see an adventure film, but Carlos preferred a comedy.

On the way to the theater, they agreed to toss a coin; Rita won the toss.

Carlos tried to persuade Rita to see the comedy; however, he was unsuccessful.

(3) A *complex sentence* has one independent clause and *at least* one subordinate clause.

EXAMPLES Carlos argued that the coin toss was unfair.

When they got to the theater where the movie was playing, Carlos apologized to Rita.

(4) A *compound-complex sentence* contains two or more independent clauses and *at least* one subordinate clause.

EXAMPLES Rita knew that being stubborn wouldn't solve anything, and she accepted Carlos's apology.

Before the feature started, Carlos offered to buy popcorn; Rita said that she would save his seat.

▶ EXERCISE 7 **Classifying Sentences According to Structure**

Classify each sentence in the following paragraph as *simple, compound, complex,* or *compound-complex*. Be sure that you can identify all subordinate and independent clauses.

EXAMPLE [1] The Five Nations of the Iroquois are Native American tribes in New York State.
1. *simple*

[1] The Five Nations of the Iroquois—Mohawk, Oneida, Onondaga, Cayuga, and Seneca—have an ancient history of storytelling. [2] In the early days, profes-

sional storytellers went from house to house, and they were paid for their storytelling with small gifts. [3] Most of what is known today about Iroquois folk tales comes from the Senecas, whose stories were written down by historians. [4] Some of the most popular stories are about Naked Bear, who was hairless except for one strip of fur up his back. [5] He was so huge that his back could be seen above the trees. [6] He was a man-eater, and he could not be killed in any ordinary way. [7] The tales about Naked Bear are even more frightening than the ones about Stone Coat, who had a skin like stone. [8] Fortunately, Stone Coat was not very smart, and many of the folk tales tell of ways that the Iroquois outsmarted him. [9] There are also tales about the Whirlwinds, who usually appeared as bodiless heads with fiery eyes; in some stories, the Whirlwinds ate sticks and rocks when they couldn't catch people. [10] Other Iroquois stories tell about the adventures of Elk, Partridge, Skunk, and Rattlesnake.

▶ EXERCISE 8   ## Classifying Sentences According to Structure

Classify each sentence in the following paragraph as *simple, compound, complex,* or *compound-complex.*

EXAMPLE   [1] In all the world, there is only one art museum for children's art, and it is located in Norway.
           1. *compound*

Three-year-old Michiru Shioji of Japan expressed an unmistakable image in *My Father is Angry*.

A Picassoid piece, a bike made from scrap wire, is the creation of a 10-year-old boy from Rwanda.

[1] This museum is the International Museum of Children's Art, which occupies a big, old house in Oslo. [2] The

walls are covered from top to bottom with brilliantly colored creations by young artists up to age seventeen. [3] Many of the 100,000 works, which come from 150 countries, deal with objects from nature, but a few, like the bicycle, focus on manufactured objects. [4] Of course, a few of the paintings depict troubles or problems, but most of the works express happiness, energy, and the beauty of nature. [5] Rafael Goldin, the museum's director, says a child's first meeting with exhibited art is very important. [6] Children visit the museum, and they "see that a museum can mean joy and color. [7] If their first visit is to a boring, dusty museum, children will always associate museums with *dusty* and *boring*." [8] Rafael Goldin has even hung some of the paintings at toddlers' eye level to encourage the youngest visitors to begin their own personal relationship with art. [9] Young visitors are very excited when they learn that all the artwork was created by children, and they are often inspired to start painting. [10] Wouldn't it be great if there were a museum like this one in the United States?

WRITING APPLICATION

Using a Variety of Sentence Structures in Writing

Writing that uses the same type of sentence structure over and over can sound childish as well as boring. Good writers vary the type of sentence structure that they use—simple, compound, complex, or compound-complex—to reflect the complexity of their ideas. Writers also adjust the complexity of their language and sentence structure so that it is appropriate to their audience.

BIRD FACTS A   Crows are noisy and large. They land in the trees, and they scare off the other birds.

BIRD FACTS B   Crows, which are abundant all over the world, are noisy and large birds, but they are also intelligent

GRAMMAR

and useful. Some people get annoyed with crows because they land in the trees and scare off the other birds.

What sentence structures are used in the Bird Facts above? Which set of Bird Facts would be more suitable for a first-grade student? Why?

▶ WRITING ACTIVITY

You are at summer camp and are writing home about your experiences. Write a short letter telling your six-year-old sister about a few experiences that you think would interest her. Write another letter to an adult friend or relative about experiences that you believe he or she would find interesting. Use sentence structures and language that are appropriate to each audience.

Prewriting If you have been to a summer camp, make a list of experiences that you could write about. If you haven't been to a camp, use activities that you have read about or seen on television or in movies, or make up activities that you would imagine a camp to have.

Writing As you write your first draft, make sure to include details that would interest your different audiences. Show the relationships between your details by using a variety of subordinate adjective, adverb, and noun clauses.

Evaluating and Revising Read your letters to a classmate, without telling which letter is to your sister and which is to your adult friend or relative. If the classmate can't tell which letter is to which person, you should revise your information and sentence structures. Check to be sure that you have used simpler sentence structures in the letter to your sister, and a variety of structures in the other letter. Also make sure that adjective and adverb clauses clearly modify the words you want them to modify.

Proofreading Check to be sure that all your sentences are complete sentences. Pay special attention to the use of commas to separate clauses. (See pages 746–762 for rules about comma usage.)

▶ REVIEW B   **Identifying and Classifying Subordinate Clauses**

Identify the subordinate clause or clauses in each of the following sentences. Tell whether each clause is used as an *adjective*, an *adverb*, or a *noun*. If a clause is used as an adjective or an adverb, write the word(s) the clause modifies. If a clause is used as a noun, write *subj.* for subject, *d.o.* for direct object, *p.n.* for predicate nominative, or *o.p.* for object of a preposition.

EXAMPLE   1. When our science teacher described insect-eating plants, we listened with amazement.
1. *When our science teacher described insect-eating plants—adverb—listened*

1. Plants that eat insects usually live in swampy areas.
2. Because the soil in these regions lacks nutrients, these plants do not get enough nitrogen through their roots.
3. The nitrogen that these plants need comes from the protein in insects.
4. How these plants catch their food is interesting.
5. A pitcher plant's sweet scent attracts whatever insect is nearby.
6. The insect thinks that it will find food inside the plant.
7. What happens instead is that the insect drowns in the plant's digestive juices.
8. The Venus' flytrap has what look like small bear traps at the ends of its stalks.
9. When a trap is open, an insect can wander in and trigger the trap to shut.
10. The insect is then digested by the plant in a process that takes several days.

▶ REVIEW C   **Classifying Subordinate Clauses**

Classify each of the following italicized clauses as *adjective*, *adverb*, or *noun*. Be prepared to explain your answers.

EXAMPLES   [1] *Until our class visited the county courthouse,* we had imagined [2] *that most court cases were like the ones on TV.*
1. *adverb*
2. *noun*

[1] *As we left the courtroom,* we thought about the men [2] *who had been on trial.* [3] *Although they had not committed a serious crime,* they had broken the law. The law says [4] *that removing sand from a beach is illegal.* A police officer caught the men [5] *when they could not move their truck,* [6] *which had become stuck in the sand.* [7] *After the judge had read the law to them,* the men claimed [8] *that they had never heard of it.* The judge, [9] *who did not believe them,* fined each man twenty-five dollars. The men promised [10] *that they would not take any more beach sand.*

▶ REVIEW D **Rewriting a Paragraph to Include a Variety of Sentence Structures**

You and a partner are working together on an essay. While researching the topic, your partner has jotted down the following information. Your job is to rewrite the paragraph to improve its style. You will need to vary the sentence structure, and you may want to add or delete details to improve the organization. Write at least one sentence with each kind of structure: *simple, compound, complex,* and *compound-complex.* Be prepared to identify the structure of each sentence you write.

Barbara Sneyd lived more than one hundred years ago. Her home was in the English countryside. She came from a wealthy family. Her family loved to ride and hunt.

Barbara had a governess. The governess kept Barbara very busy studying. Barbara did have time to pursue her greatest passion. Her greatest passion was riding. Her mother encouraged her to keep a diary. The diary would be about her life. She started the diary. She was fourteen. It took the form of a sketchbook. In it she recorded her family's life. She painted many small pictures of her family's activities. They went fishing, visiting, and picnicking. Barbara was also a keen observer of nature. She drew and painted her family's horses and pets and the flowers from the garden. She painted many small landscapes. The landscapes showed the countryside around her home. Above all, her diary is full of paintings of horses. She loved horses. You may want to see what her paintings look like. Some pictures from her diary are shown on the previous page.

Review: Posttest 1

A. Identifying and Classifying Subordinate Clauses

Write the subordinate clause in each of the following sentences. Identify the clause as *adj.* (adjective), *adv.* (adverb), or *n.* (noun). If the clause is used as an adjective or adverb, write the word or phrase it modifies. If the clause is used as a noun, write *subj.* for subject, *d.o.* for direct object, *p.n.* for predicate nominative, or *o.p.* for object of a preposition.

EXAMPLES   **1.** After our last class, Elena, Frieda, and I agreed that we would go bicycling in the park.
           1. *that we would go bicycling in the park—n.—d.o.*

           2. As we set out for the park, we had no idea of the difficulties ahead.
           2. *As we set out for the park—adv.—had*

  1. Since none of us own bicycles, we decided to rent them there.
  2. The man who rented us the bikes was helpful.

3. The three of us had bicycled six miles when Frieda's bike got a flat tire.
4. What we found was a nail in the tire.
5. We decided to take the bike to whatever bike shop was the nearest.
6. The woman at the bike shop told us that she could fix the tire quickly.
7. After we had paid for the repair, we rode back to the park and bicycled for an hour.
8. Our only worry was that the man at the rental shop might not pay us back.
9. When we returned our bikes, we showed the man the bike with the repaired tire.
10. He refunded us the money we had spent to fix the tire.

B. Classifying Sentences According to Structure

Classify each of the following sentences as *simple, compound, complex,* or *compound-complex.* Be sure that you can identify all subordinate and independent clauses.

EXAMPLE   **1.** Amanda now plays the violin because of a winter concert that she heard when she was in the third grade.
   1. *complex*

11. Amanda loved the sound of the orchestra at her school's winter concert, and she decided then to study the violin.
12. Because Amanda was still quite small, her first violin was not full-sized.
13. When she started the sixth grade, however, Amanda was playing a full-sized violin.
14. Amanda did not always enjoy the many hours of practice, but they were necessary because the instrument is so complicated.
15. Just playing the proper notes, without being too sharp or too flat, can be difficult on a violin.
16. On a keyboard instrument, you press a key and hear the note for that key.
17. On a violin, however, the placement of a finger on the string can affect the pitch of the note.

18. If the pitch of each note is not exactly correct, the result can be a barely recognizable tune.
19. Once a student has mastered pitch to some extent, he or she still has a great deal to think about; for posture, hand position, and bowing technique all require great concentration.
20. When students can actually create music with this stubborn instrument, they have reason to be proud.

Review: Posttest 2

Writing a Variety of Sentence Structures

Write your own sentences according to the following guidelines.

EXAMPLE   1. a compound sentence with two independent clauses joined by a semicolon and a conjunctive adverb
        1. *We wanted to go to the mall; instead, we went to the flea market.*

1. a simple sentence with a compound verb
2. a complex sentence with an adjective clause
3. a compound-complex sentence
4. a compound sentence with two independent clauses joined by the conjunction *but*
5. a complex sentence with a noun clause used as a subject
6. a simple sentence with a compound subject
7. a complex sentence with an adverb clause placed at the end of the sentence
8. a complex sentence with a noun clause used as a direct object
9. a compound sentence with two independent clauses joined by the conjunction *or*
10. a complex sentence with a noun clause used as the object of a preposition

18 AGREEMENT

Subject and Verb, Pronoun and Antecedent

Diagnostic Test

A. Correcting Errors in Subject-Verb and Pronoun-Antecedent Agreement

Most of the following sentences contain an agreement error. For each sentence, identify the incorrect verb or pronoun, and supply the correct form. If the sentence is correct, write C.

EXAMPLE   1. Peter and Mark likes to play baseball.
　　　　　　1. *likes—like*

1. Computer science, in addition to foreign languages, are offered at our junior high school.
2. Since either Janet or Brian always bring a camera, we are sure to have pictures of the school carnival.
3. The faculty at our school want to give the student body more privileges.

   4. *Romeo and Juliet* are required reading in our class.
   5. Neither Heather nor Rosa usually forgets to bring their running shoes.
   6. Promises is all I have ever gotten from your company, and I want my money back.
   7. There is some slices of bread left, but some of them are hard and stale.
   8. Two gallons of milk was all the bucket would hold.
   9. Either Alexis or the other girls are going to bring decorations for the party.
   10. Each of the children completed their own project, which was an animal figure made out of clay.

B. Identifying and Correcting Errors in Subject-Verb and Pronoun-Antecedent Agreement

Each sentence in the following paragraph contains an error in agreement. Identify each incorrect verb or pronoun, and supply the correct form.

EXAMPLE   [1] Tapes and CDs of popular music is getting very expensive.
     1. *is—are*

[11] The economics of this situation hit young people right in the wallet! [12] Every one of my friends like music. [13] However, nobody ever have enough money to buy all the best new songs. [14] Teenagers have to use his or her intelligence to save money in the music store. [15] Several of my friends buys a single instead of an album if they want only one song from the album. [16] Danny, one of my best friends, take another approach. [17] The Caterpillars are his favorite group, and Danny tapes every new Caterpillars' song straight from the radio. [18] He don't have to pay for anything but the blank tape. [19] Copying tapes is perfectly legal if all of the music that you tape are just for your own use. [20] Two of my friends, Carla and Stephanie, save as much as four or five dollars per tape by buying her tapes on sale.

Number

Number is the form of a word that indicates whether the word is singular or plural.

18a. When a word refers to one person or thing, it is *singular* in number. When a word refers to more than one, it is *plural* in number.

SINGULAR	PLURAL
student	students
child	children
it	they
berry	berries

 EXERCISE 1 **Classifying Nouns and Pronouns by Number**

Identify each italicized word as either *singular* or *plural*.

EXAMPLE As a child, the girl in the [1] *photograph* was sure she was not very good at anything.
1. *singular*

She was overshadowed by the other [1] *children* in her family, especially by her older sister Madge, who wrote [2] *stories* and plays. Lonely and full of self-doubt, the girl surrounded herself with imaginary [3] *companions*. But

USAGE

[4] *everything* changed when she caught influenza and became restless during her recovery. Her mother brought her a [5] *notebook* and suggested that, like Madge, she might write a story. After practicing on short stories, she decided to tackle a detective [6] *novel*. [7] *"They* are very difficult to do," said Madge. "I don't think you could write one." But Madge was wrong, because the young author was Agatha Christie, who became the most successful mystery [8] *writer* in history. Her mystery novels and story collections have sold many millions of copies in [9] *English* and in at least sixty other [10] *languages*.

Agreement of Subject and Verb

18b. A verb should always agree with its subject in number.

(1) Singular subjects take singular verbs.

EXAMPLES **He washes** the dishes. [The singular verb *washes* agrees with the singular subject *he.*]
A girl in my neighborhood **plays** in the school band. [The singular subject *girl* takes the singular verb *plays.*]

(2) Plural subjects take plural verbs.

EXAMPLES **They wash** the dishes.
Several **girls** in my neighborhood **play** in the school band.

In the examples above, the main verbs agree in number with their subjects. Like single-word verbs, verb phrases also agree with their subjects. However, in a verb phrase, only the first helping (auxiliary) verb changes its form to agree with a singular or plural subject.

EXAMPLES **A girl** in my neighborhood **was playing** in the school band.
Several **girls** in my neighborhood **were playing** in the school band.
He has been washing the dishes.
They have been washing the dishes.

☞ REFERENCE NOTE: Generally, nouns ending in *–s* are plural (*friends, girls*), but verbs ending in *–s* are singular (*sees, hears*). For guidelines on forming plurals, see pages 844–847.

▶ EXERCISE 2   **Identifying Verbs That Agree in Number with Their Subjects**

For each sentence in the following paragraph, choose the verb in parentheses that agrees with the subject.

EXAMPLE   [1] It might surprise you to know that people in Japan often (*eat, eats*) noodles.
     1. *eat*

[1] These pictures (*show, shows*) how noodles are prepared. [2] First, the noodle maker (*roll, rolls*) the dough out as thin as possible. [3] Then, the cook (*slice, slices*) the folded layers. [4] Next, the strands of noodles (*is, are*) separated and dusted with flour to prevent sticking. [5] After the noodles have dried a little, they (*go, goes*) into boiling water or broth to cook. [6] The Japanese (*enjoy, enjoys*) noodles made from either wheat flour, called *udon*, or buckwheat flour, called *soba*. [7] Cooked noodles, mixed with sauce, broth, vegetables, or fish, (*makes, make*) a popular lunch. [8] Noodle shops all over Japan (*serves, serve*) a variety of noodle dishes. [9] These shops (*resemble, resembles*) our fast-food restaurants. [10] For lunch or a snack, customers go to a noodle shop and (*order, orders*) noodles with their favorite toppings.

USAGE

18c. The number of the subject is not changed by a phrase following the subject.

Remember that a verb agrees in number with its subject. *The subject is never part of a prepositional phrase.*

EXAMPLES   The **sign** near the glass doors **explains** the theme of the exhibit.
Several **paintings** by Emilio Sánchez **were hanging** in the gallery.

Compound prepositions such as *together with, in addition to, as well as,* and *along with* following the subject do not affect the number of the subject.

EXAMPLES   **Anne,** together with her cousins, **is** backpacking in Nevada this summer.
Robert, along with Kimberly and Elvin, **has** been nominated for class president.

▶ ORAL PRACTICE 1   **Using Verbs That Agree in Number with Their Subjects**

Read the following sentences aloud, stressing the italicized words.

1. The *rules* in this textbook *are* guidelines for using standard English.
2. *Mastery* of these rules *leads* to improvement in speaking and writing.
3. The correct *use* of verbs *is* especially important.
4. Correct *spelling,* in addition to correct usage of verbs, *is* an essential writing skill.
5. *People* in the business world *look* carefully at letters of application.
6. *Letters* with nonstandard English *do* not *make* a good impression.

▶ EXERCISE 3   **Identifying Subjects and Verbs That Agree in Number**

Identify the subject of each verb in parentheses in the following paragraph. Then, choose the form of the verb that agrees with the subject.

EXAMPLE   Units of measure sometimes [1] (*causes, cause*)
           confusion.
           1. *Units—cause*

Confusion among shoppers [1] (*is, are*) understandable
because the traditional system for indicating quantities
[2] (*makes, make*) shopping a guessing game. For example,
the quantity printed on yogurt containers [3] (*is, are*) the
number of ounces in a container. A shopper on the look-
out for bargains [4] (*does, do*) not know whether liquid or
solid measure is indicated. In addition, different brands of
juice [5] (*shows, show*) the same quantity in different ways.
A can labeled "twenty-four ounces" [6] (*contains, contain*)
the same quantity as a can labeled "one pint eight
ounces." Shoppers' confusion over such labeling, along
with rising prices, [7] (*is, are*) a matter of concern to consumer groups. These groups believe that the metric
system, in use in European countries, [8] (*clears, clear*) up
most of the confusion. The units in the metric system
[9] (*has, have*) fixed relationships to one another. As a result,
consumer groups in this country [10] (*continues, continue*)
to advocate our adopting this system of measurement.

▶ EXERCISE 4   **Choosing Verbs with the Correct
                  Number**

Each sentence in the following paragraph contains an italicized pair of verbs in parentheses. From each pair,
choose the form of the verb that agrees with its subject.

EXAMPLE   [1] Of all numbers, the number 12 (*is, are*) one of the
           most fascinating.
           1. *is*

[1] The even division of 12 by 1, 2, 3, 4, and 6 (*is, are*)
possible. [2] Curiously, the sum of these five numbers (*is,
are*) a square, 16; and their product is 144, which is the
square of 12 itself. [3] When the Greek philosopher Plato
devised his ideal state, the system of weights and measures (*was, were*) based on the number 12 because it could
be evenly divided in so many ways. [4] To this day, many
quantities in our lives (*involve, involves*) the number 12.
[5] The number of months in a year, inches in a foot,
and items in a dozen (*is, are*) 12. [6] In our courts of law, 12

members of a jury (*decide, decides*) a defendant's guilt or innocence. [7] Each player in a game of checkers (*begin, begins*) with 12 pieces. [8] In bowling, 12 consecutive strikes (*give, gives*) you a perfect game. [9] The number of black pentagons on a soccer ball (*equal, equals*) the number of buttons on a push-button telephone—12. [10] Samuel Clemens even used this interesting number as his pen name—the riverboat slang for 2 fathoms, or 12 feet, (*are, is*) *Mark Twain*!

18d. The following pronouns are singular: *each, either, neither, one, everyone, everybody, no one, nobody, anyone, anybody, someone, somebody.*

EXAMPLES **Each** of the athletes **runs** effortlessly. [Each one runs.]
Neither of the women **is** ready to start. [Neither one is ready.]
Someone was waving a large flag.
Does everyone in your family **enjoy** playing tennis?

18e. The following pronouns are plural: *several, few, both, many.*

EXAMPLES **Several** of the runners **are exercising.**
Few of the athletes **have qualified.**
Were both of the games **postponed?**
Many on the team **practice** daily.

18f. The pronouns *some, all, most, any,* and *none* may be either singular or plural.

These pronouns are singular when they refer to a singular word and plural when they refer to a plural word.

EXAMPLES **Some** of the show **is** funny. [*Some* refers to the singular noun *show.*]
Some of the entertainers **are** funny. [*Some* refers to the plural noun *entertainers.*]

All of the cast **looks** young.
All of the performers **look** young.

Most of his routine **sounds** familiar.
Most of his jokes **sound** familiar.

Was any of the criticism positive?
Were any of the reviews positive?

None of the music **is** catchy.
None of the tunes **are** catchy.

The words *any* and *none* may be singular even when they refer to a plural word if the speaker is thinking of each item individually. *Any* and *none* are plural only if the speaker is thinking of several items as a group.

EXAMPLES   **Any** of these books **is** worth reading. [*Any one book* is worth reading.]
None of the books **was** overdue. [*Not one book* was overdue.]

Any of these books **are** worth reading. [*All the books* are worth reading.]
None of the books **were** overdue. [*No books* were overdue.]

USAGE

▶ EXERCISE 5   **Identifying Subjects and Verbs That Agree in Number**

Identify the subject of each verb in parentheses. Then choose the form of the verb that agrees with that subject.

EXAMPLE   1. Several of the kittens (*has, have*) been adopted.
1. *Several—have*

1. Each of the comedians (*tries, try*) to outdo the other.
2. Somebody on the bus (*was, were*) whistling.
3. (*Is, Are*) all of the apples spoiled?
4. Neither of these books (*has, have*) an index.
5. (*Do, Does*) everybody in the class have a pencil?
6. Few of these jobs (*sounds, sound*) challenging.
7. Several of those plants (*grows, grow*) better indoors.
8. She said that no one in the office (*leaves, leave*) early.
9. Both of her parents (*has, have*) offered us a ride.
10. (*Do, Does*) most of those CDs belong to her?

▶ REVIEW A   **Proofreading a Paragraph for Subject-Verb Agreement**

Identify the ten agreement errors in the following paragraph. Then supply the correct form of each incorrect verb.

USAGE

EXAMPLE   [1] On weekends, I often goes with my mother to antique shops.
      1. *goes—go*

[1] Until recently, this hunt for old things were very boring. [2] Then one day, I noticed that a dusty shoe box full of antique postcards were sitting near me on a counter. [3] Soon, I was flipping through the cards, and before you knows it, I had decided to start a postcard collection! [4] The cards in my collection is very precious to me. [5] On one card, the flames of a campfire glows in front of several Plains Indian tepees under a colorful sunset. [6] Several other cards has pictures of tribal leaders and warriors. [7] There is so many cards on American Indians, I has decided to specialize in cards about the Navajo. [8] On my favorite card, a Navajo mother wrapped in beautiful blankets are posing with her baby on her back. [9] Collecting postcards are not an expensive hobby either. [10] Many of my cards was priced at a dollar or less.

WRITING APPLICATION

Using Correct Subject-Verb Agreement

When the subject and the verb of a sentence do not agree, a reader may not clearly understand what the writer means.

CONFUSING   Your prizes is in the mail.
    CLEAR   Your prize is in the mail.

After reading the first sentence, you wouldn't know whether you were getting one prize or more than one. The second sentence makes it clear—one prize is on the way.

▶ WRITING ACTIVITY

During Career Day, the school counselor asks you to write a paragraph beginning with this statement: "People I know work at a variety of jobs." Using subjects and verbs that agree, describe the jobs of three people you know.

Prewriting   Start by listing at least three people you know who have different kinds of jobs. Think of action verbs that describe what these people do. For example, instead of saying "Mrs. Ruíz is a chemistry teacher," say "Mrs. Ruíz teaches chemistry."

Writing   As you write your first draft, be sure to include some details that clearly show how the jobs differ from one another.

Evaluating and Revising   Check your rough draft to be sure that the examples you have chosen show a variety of jobs. If not, you may want to replace some examples or add new ones. Identify the subjects and verbs in each sentence, and be sure that they agree.

Proofreading and Publishing   Read your paragraph aloud to help you recognize any errors in usage, spelling, and punctuation. Be sure that you have capitalized all proper names. Your class might photocopy and display their paragraphs during a Career Day. With the permission of the people you wrote about, you could also prepare a job information directory.

The Compound Subject

A *compound subject* is a subject that contains two or more nouns or pronouns that are the subject of the same verb.

18g. Subjects joined by *and* usually take a plural verb.

The following compound subjects joined by *and* name more than one person or thing and take plural verbs.

EXAMPLES   **Leslie Marmon Silko** and **Mari Evans are** poets. [Two persons are poets.]
Rhyme, rhythm, and **imagery help** poets express their feelings. [Three things help.]

Compound subjects that name only one person or thing take a singular verb.

EXAMPLES   My **pen pal and best friend is** my cousin. [One person is your friend and pen pal.]
Pumpkin seeds and raisins makes a tasty snack. [The one combination makes a snack.]

18h. Singular subjects joined by *or* or *nor* take a singular verb.

EXAMPLES   After dinner, either **Anne** or **Tony loads** the dishwasher. [*Either* Anne *or* Tony loads the dishwasher, not both.]
Neither the **coach** nor the **principal is** happy with the team's performance. [Neither *one* is happy.]

18i. When a singular subject and a plural subject are joined by *or* or *nor,* the verb agrees with the subject nearer the verb.

ACCEPTABLE   Neither the losers nor the **winner was** happy with the outcome of the match.
ACCEPTABLE   Neither the winner nor the **losers were** happy with the outcome of the match.

Try to avoid such awkward constructions by rephrasing the sentence.

BETTER   The **losers were** not happy with the outcome of the match, and neither **was** the **winner.**
or
The **winner was** not happy with the outcome of the match, and neither **were** the **losers.**

▶ EXERCISE 6   **Choosing Verbs That Agree in Number
with Their Subjects**

Choose the correct form of the verb in parentheses in each of the following sentences.

EXAMPLE   1. In August, eager players and their fans (*looks, look*) forward to the start of football season.
1. *look*

1. The coach and the player (*was, were*) surprised by the referee's call.
2. (*Is, Are*) Drew or Virgil going out for the pass?
3. Neither the quarterback nor the wide receiver (*hear, hears*) the whistle.
4. The marching band or the pep squad (*has, have*) already performed.
5. (*Do, Does*) Josh and Brian enjoy football as much as Rachel does?

▶ ORAL
PRACTICE 2   **Using Verbs That Agree in Number
with Their Subjects**

Read the following sentences aloud, stressing the italicized words.

1. The *books* on that shelf *need* dusting.
2. A *carton* of duck eggs *is* in the refrigerator.
3. *Tina and Betty are* first cousins once removed.
4. *Playing* games *or listening* to old records *is* an enjoyable way to spend a rainy Saturday.
5. *Several* of these insects *eat* through wood.
6. Every *one* of you *has* met my friend Phil.
7. *Neither* Eileen *nor* Greg *enjoys* listening to that kind of music.
8. *Both* Mr. *and* Mrs. Chen *agree* to be chaperons for our spring dance.

▶ REVIEW B   **Revising Sentences for Subject-Verb
Agreement**

Revise each of the following sentences according to the directions given in parentheses. Change the verb in the sentence to agree with the subject as necessary.

EXAMPLE   1. The teachers have finished grading the tests.
(Change *The teachers* to *Each of the teachers.*)
1. *Each of the teachers has finished grading the tests.*

1. My aunt is planning a trip to Nairobi National Park in Kenya. (Change *aunt* to *aunts.*)
2. Have Yoko and Juan already seen that movie? (Change *and* to *or.*)
3. Nobody on the team plans to attend the award ceremonies. (Change *Nobody* to *Many.*)
4. My grandmother, as well as my mother and aunts, raises tropical fish to earn extra money. (Change *grandmother* to *grandparents.*)
5. Most of the food for the party is in the refrigerator. (Change *food* to *salads.*)
6. Neither the librarian nor the aides have found the missing book. (Change *Neither the librarian nor the aides* to *Neither the aides nor the librarian.*)
7. Black bean soup and a tossed salad make an inexpensive meal. (Change *Black bean soup and a tossed salad* to *Macaroni and cheese.*)
8. Some of my friends take the bus to school. (Change *Some* to *One.*)
9. The puppy playing with my sisters is two months old. (Change *puppy* to *puppies* and *sisters* to *sister.*)
10. Few of the reporters' questions were answered in detail. (Change *Few* to *Neither.*)

▶ EXERCISE 7   **Using Verbs That Agree in Number with Compound Subjects**

Was Christopher Columbus really the first person to discover the Americas? To answer this question, you look for information in the school media center. The notes and map on the next page represent some of your findings. Using your map and notes, write five sentences about these explorations. In each sentence, use a compound subject joined by *and, or,* or *nor.* Include at least one example of two singular subjects joined by *either/or* or *neither/nor* and one singular and one plural subject joined by *either/or* or *neither/nor.*

EXAMPLE   **1.** *Neither Eric the Red nor his son was the first person to come to the Americas.*

Asians

Asians may have come to the Americas 10,000 to 25,000 years ago. Thought to have traveled from Siberia to Alaska
Came by boat or over a land bridge that has since disappeared
Went all over North America, Central America, and South America
Descendants are Native Americans

Vikings

Vikings, or Norsemen, came from ancient Scandinavia
Probably first Europeans to land in the Americas
Norwegian explorer Eric the Red had a settlement in Greenland in the 900s
His son Leif and crew in A.D. 1000 came to northeast coast of North America

Columbus

Italian explorer Christopher Columbus made voyages under Spanish flag
Crew mainly Spanish
Ships the Niña, the Pinta, and the Santa María
On October 12, 1492, Columbus reached an island in Bahamas, near the coast of North America

Other Problems in Agreement

18j. *Don't* and *doesn't* must agree with their subjects.

Contractions are two words combined into one, with one or more letters omitted. *Don't* is the contraction for *do not*. *Doesn't* is the contraction for *does not*.

With the subjects *I* and *you* and with plural subjects, use *don't (do not)*.

EXAMPLES   I **don't** know.   They **don't** give up.
You **don't** say.   These **don't** shrink.
We **don't** want to.   Apathetic people **don't** care.

With other subjects, use the singular *doesn't (does not)*.

EXAMPLES   He **doesn't** know.   One **doesn't** give up.
She **doesn't** say.   This **doesn't** shrink.
It **doesn't** want to. Donna **doesn't** care.

▶ EXERCISE 8   **Using *Doesn't* and *Don't* Correctly**

Write the correct form (*doesn't* or *don't*) for each of the following sentences.

EXAMPLE   1. ____ that bouquet of roses look great?
1. *Doesn't*

1. This apple ____ taste sweet.
2. ____ he want to see the game?
3. These ____ impress me.
4. One of the players ____ plan to go.
5. ____ Jason and Tanya like the new band uniforms?

18k. Collective nouns may be either singular or plural.

Collective nouns are singular in form, but they name a *group* of persons or things.

Collective Nouns				
army	class	family	group	public
assembly	club	fleet	herd	swarm
audience	committee	flock	jury	team

Use a plural verb with a collective noun when you are referring to the individual parts or members of the group acting separately. Use a singular verb when you refer to the group acting together as a unit.

EXAMPLES   The class **have completed** their projects. [*Class* is thought of as individuals.]
          The class **has elected** its officers. [*Class* is thought of as a unit.]

☞ REFERENCE NOTE: Be sure that any pronoun referring to a collective noun has the same number as the noun. See pages 608–611 for more on pronoun-antecedent agreement.

▶ EXERCISE 9   **Writing Sentences with Collective Nouns**

Select five collective nouns and write five pairs of sentences showing clearly how the nouns you choose may be either singular or plural.

EXAMPLE   1. *The jury is ready.*
             The jury are still arguing among themselves.

18l. A verb agrees with its subject, not with its predicate nominative.

                              S   PN
STANDARD   The marching **bands are** the main attraction.

                          S   PN
STANDARD   The main **attraction is** the marching bands.

☞ REFERENCE NOTE: For a discussion of standard and nonstandard English, see pages 449–450.

18m. When the subject follows the verb, find the subject and make sure that the verb agrees with it.

The most common cases in which the subject follows the verb are in sentences beginning with *here* and *there* and in questions.

EXAMPLES   Here **is a list** of addresses.
          Here **are** two **lists** of addresses.

USAGE

USAGE

There **is** my **notebook.**
There **are** my **notebooks.**

Where **is** Heather? Where **is** Chris?
Where **are** Heather and Chris?

Contractions such as *here's, where's, how's,* and *what's* include the verb *is.* Do not use one of these contractions unless a singular subject follows it.

NONSTANDARD	There's some facts on that topic in a chart at the back of the book.
STANDARD	There **are** some **facts** on that topic in a chart at the back of the book.
STANDARD	At the back of the book, there**'s** a **chart** with some facts on that topic.

☞ REFERENCE NOTE: For more on contractions, see pages 818–820.

18n. Words stating an amount are usually singular.

A word or a phrase stating a weight, a measurement, or an amount of money or time is usually considered one item and takes a singular verb.

EXAMPLES **Thirty dollars is** too much for a concert ticket.
Two hours is a long time to wait.
Three fourths of the show **is** over.

Sometimes, however, the amount is thought of as individual pieces or parts. If so, a plural verb is used.

EXAMPLES **Five** of the dollars **were borrowed.**
Two of the hours **were spent** in line.
Three fourths of the songs **are** new.

18o. The title of a work of art, literature, or music, even when plural in form, takes a singular verb.

EXAMPLES *Blue Lines* **is** an early painting by Georgia O'Keeffe. [one work of art]
The Souls of Black Folk **is** often **cited** as a classic of African American literature. [one book]
"Greensleeves" is an old English folk song. [one piece of music]

18p.   *Every* or *many a* before a subject calls for a singular verb.

EXAMPLES   **Every** homeowner and storekeeper **has joined** the cleanup drive.
Many a litterbug **was surprised** by the stiff fines.

18q.   A few nouns, although plural in form, take singular verbs.

EXAMPLES   **Politics is** a controversial topic.
The **news** of the nominee for the Supreme Court **was** a surprise to many observers.
Rickets is a serious health problem in some countries.

NOTE: Some nouns that end in *-s* take a plural verb even though they refer to a single item.

EXAMPLES   The **scissors need** to be sharpened.
Were these **pants** on sale?
The **pliers are** next to the wrench.

USAGE

▶ EXERCISE 10   **Identifying Subjects and Verbs That Agree in Number**

Identify the subject of each verb in parentheses. Then, choose the form of the verb that agrees with the subject.

EXAMPLE   1. Many a book (*has, have*) been written about the beauties of our country.
1. *book—has*

1. The class (*has, have*) chosen titles for their original plays.
2. First prize (*was, were*) two tickets to Hawaii.
3. Three quarters of the movie (*was, were*) over when we arrived.
4. Rattlesnakes (*was, were*) the topic of last week's meeting of the hiking club.
5. (*Has, Have*) every student in the class memorized a poem?
6. *War and Peace* (*is, are*) a world-famous novel.
7. Two thirds of the missing books (*was, were*) returned.

8. Mathematics (*is, are*) an important part of many everyday activities.
9. Where (*is, are*) the paragraphs you wrote?
10. Four weeks (*is, are*) enough time to rehearse the play.

> **ORAL PRACTICE 3** **Using Subject-Verb Agreement**

Read each of the following sentences aloud, stressing the italicized words.

1. His main *concern is* his two horses.
2. *Many a* writer and scholar *has* puzzled over that problem.
3. *Is economics* taught at your high school?
4. *Are* there any green *apples* in that basket?
5. *Romeo and Juliet has* been made into a ballet, a Broadway musical, and at least two movies.
6. *Two weeks is* more than enough time to write a report.
7. My *family is* planning to hold its reunion in October.
8. My *family are* planning their schedules now.

> **REVIEW C** **Identifying Verbs That Have the Correct Number**

Choose the correct form of the verb in parentheses in each of the following sentences.

1. Mumps (*is, are*) a common childhood disease.
2. Taxes (*is, are*) always a main issue during an election year.
3. Not one of the ushers (*knows, know*) where the lounge is.
4. The team (*is, are*) on a winning streak.
5. Carol, as well as Inés, (*writes, write*) a column for the *East High Record*.
6. "Beauty and the Beast" (*is, are*) a folk tale that exists in many different cultures.
7. Ten pounds (*is, are*) far too much weight for a young child to carry in a backpack.
8. It is difficult to concentrate when there (*is, are*) radios and stereos blasting away.

USAGE

9. (*Has, Have*) either of you read *To Kill a Mockingbird*?
10. In most situation comedies, there (*is, are*) a very wise character, a very foolish character, and a very lovable character.

▶ EXERCISE 11   **Using Titles That Agree with Verbs in Number**

Terence and Janeese are at the video rental store deciding what movies they will rent for the weekend. In the following sentences, wherever TITLE appears, supply the name of one of the movies shown below or of a movie of your own choice. Then choose the correct form of the verb to complete each sentence.

EXAMPLE   1. Look, Terence. TITLE (*is, are*) supposed to be very funny.
1. *Horse Feathers—is*

1. Terence: According to LaShonda, TITLE and TITLE (*is, are*) very exciting.
2. Janeese: Well, TITLE or TITLE (*sounds, sound*) more interesting to me.
3. Terence: Sir, (*is, are*) TITLE in stock?
4. Clerk: I'm afraid not, but TITLE (*entertain, entertains*) almost everyone, and you might enjoy it.
5. Terence: Janeese, TITLE (*is, are*) a fairly recent movie, but TITLE (*are, is*) an old-timer.
6. Janeese: Well, I like animated films, and TITLE (*fit, fits*) that category.

7. Clerk: If you ask me, TITLE (*beat, beats*) every other film we have, but someone just rented my last copy.

8. Janeese: Both TITLE and TITLE (*are, is*) good, but I've seen each of them twice.

9. Terence: (*Isn't, Aren't*) TITLE any good? I'm surprised.

10. Janeese: All right, here's my vote. TITLE (*is, are*) tonight's movie, and either TITLE or TITLE (*is, are*) the movie for Saturday night's party.

Agreement of Pronoun and Antecedent

A pronoun usually refers to a noun or another pronoun that comes before it. The word that a pronoun refers to is called its ***antecedent.***

☞ REFERENCE NOTE: For a further discussion of antecedents, see pages 469–470.

18r. A pronoun should agree with its antecedent in number and gender.

A few singular personal pronouns have forms that indicate the gender of the antecedent. Masculine pronouns refer to males; feminine pronouns refer to females. Neuter pronouns refer to things and often to animals.

MASCULINE	FEMININE	NEUTER
he	she	it
him	her	it
his	hers	its

EXAMPLES   **Colette** performs **her** solo today.
James makes **his** lunch every day.
The **show** has the Old West as **its** theme.

When the antecedent of a personal pronoun is another kind of pronoun, look in a phrase following the antecedent to determine gender.

EXAMPLES   **One** of the **women** in the acting class designs **her** own costumes.
Each of the **boys** rode **his** bicycle to school.

When the antecedent may be either masculine or feminine, use both the masculine and the feminine forms connected by *or*.

EXAMPLES   **Every one** of the students shouted **his or her** approval.
A **person** should always choose **his or her** friends carefully.

In many cases you can avoid the awkward *his or her* construction by rephrasing the sentence and using the plural form of the pronoun.

EXAMPLES   **All** of the students shouted **their** approval.
People should always choose **their** friends carefully.

USAGE

(1) Use a singular pronoun to refer to *each, either, neither, one, everyone, everybody, no one, nobody, anyone, anybody, someone,* or *somebody.*

EXAMPLES   **Someone** left **his or her** hat on the field.
One of the parakeets escaped from **its** cage.

NOTE: Sometimes the meaning of *everyone* and *everybody* is clearly plural. In such cases, the plural pronoun should be used.

CONFUSING   Everyone laughed when he or she saw the clowns.
CLEAR   **Everyone** laughed when **they** saw the clowns.

(2) Two or more singular antecedents joined by *or* or *nor* should be referred to by a singular pronoun.

EXAMPLES   Neither **Richard nor Bob** distinguished **himself** in the finals.
Paula or Janet will present **her** views on the subject.

Sentences of this type can sound awkward if the antecedents are of different genders. If a sentence sounds awkward, revise it to avoid the problem.

AWKWARD   Ben or Maya will read his or her report.
REVISED   Ben will read his report, or Maya will read hers.

NOTE: In conversation, plural personal pronouns are often used to refer to singular antecedents that can be either masculine or feminine. This form is becoming increasingly popular in writing as well and may someday become acceptable as standard written English.

EXAMPLES **Everybody** has packed **their** lunch in insulated coolers.

Each member of the Senior Citizens Club received **their** tickets in advance.

(3) Two or more antecedents joined by *and* should be referred to by a plural pronoun.

EXAMPLES **Mona and Janet** left early because **they** had to be home before ten o'clock.

Mom and Dad celebrated **their** twentieth wedding anniversary yesterday.

▶ EXERCISE 12 **Identifying Antecedents and Writing Pronouns**

Each of the following sentences contains a blank where a pronoun should be. Complete each sentence by inserting a pronoun that agrees with its antecedent. Identify the antecedent.

EXAMPLE 1. Carmen and Tina said that ____ thought my idea was sensible.
1. *they—Carmen and Tina*

1. A person should always try ____ best.
2. The uniform company finally sent Jerome and Ken the shirts that ____ had ordered.
3. Claire or Ida will go to the nursing home early so that ____ can help the residents into the lounge.
4. Several of the volunteers contributed ____ own money.
5. Are you sure that each of the contestants answered ____ questions correctly?
6. Both of the girls packed ____ suitcases carefully for the trip.
7. Everyone on the baseball team wore a name tag on ____ jacket.

8. Neither of the women withdrew ____ job application.
9. Anyone can belong if ____ is interested.
10. Neither the coaches nor the players blamed ____ for the loss.

PICTURE THIS

You are a member of this nineteenth-century family. Tired of packing and moving, you are ready for a rest before you begin unpacking. You decide to use this time to write a brief letter to a friend back home about your journey to this place and your reactions to your new home. Use the details in the painting and make up any other details that you need. In your letter, use the following pronouns: *his, her, its, their, each, everybody, he, she,* and *all.* Be sure that the pronouns you use agree with their antecedents in number and gender.

Subject: a family's move
Audience: a friend
Purpose: to inform or to entertain

USAGE

Henry Mosler, *Just Moved* (1870). Oil on canvas. The Metropolitan Museum of Art, Arthur Hoppock Hearn Fund, 1962 (62.80). © 1981 By The Metropolitan Museum of Art.

USAGE

▶ EXERCISE 13 **Proofreading Sentences for Pronoun-Antecedent Agreement**

Many of the following sentences contain errors in agreement between pronouns and their antecedents. If a sentence is correct, write C. If there is an error in agreement, identify the error and give the correct form of the pronoun so that it will agree with its antecedent.

EXAMPLE 1. All of us need to choose a topic for his or her reports.
1. *his or her—our*

1. George has chosen Walt Disney as the subject of his report.
2. Several other people in our class have also submitted his or her topics.
3. Dominic, one of the Perrone twins, has chosen Alfred Hitchcock as their subject.
4. Neither George nor Dominic will have difficulty finding material for their report.
5. Each of these moviemakers' films has left their mark on the entertainment world.
6. Both Ming Chin and Sue offered their help with proofreading to George and Dominic.
7. Each boy refused politely, saying that they would proofread the report on their own.
8. Does everyone, including George and Dominic, know that they must assemble facts, not opinions?
9. Neither George nor Dominic should forget to include anecdotes about their subject.
10. Nobody likes to discover that they just read a list of dull facts about an interesting subject.

▶ EXERCISE 14 **Creating Sentences That Demonstrate Pronoun-Antecedent Agreement**

Create ten sentences that describe the students pictured on the next page. Begin each sentence with the word or words given. Include at least one pronoun to make each sentence demonstrate rule 18r. Be prepared to identify the pronouns and their antecedents in your sentences. [Note: Be sure subjects and verbs agree.]

EXAMPLE   1. One
          1. *One of the boys is wearing his cowboy boots.*

1. Each
2. Nobody
3. All
4. Both girls
5. Somebody

6. One boy and one girl
7. Neither Viviana nor LaShonda
8. Ved and Jason
9. One person
10. Several

Review: Posttest

A. Proofreading Sentences for Subject-Verb and Pronoun-Antecedent Agreement

Each of the following sentences contains an error in agreement. Identify each incorrect verb or pronoun, and supply the correct form.

EXAMPLE   1. Rochelle Richardson, one of our city's former
             mayors, live next door to me.
          1. *live—lives*

USAGE

1. When the truck overturned, a herd of cattle were set free on the expressway.
2. The teacher reminded everyone to sharpen their pencils before the test began.
3. Not one of our tomato plants are producing any fruit, but the green beans seem to be thriving.
4. Everybody have been talking about the class picnic ever since you thought of the idea.
5. I thought that either Carla or Tiffany hadn't gotten their grade on the test yet.
6. Many of their experiments have failed, but neither Dr. Jenkins nor his assistants ever gives up hope.
7. My entry in both flower shows were three specimens of a new strain of orchid.
8. There is a brush, a comb, and a mirror on the dresser top.
9. Many a sailor have perished when his or her ship ran aground on that reef.
10. Measles have been almost completely conquered in the United States by a vaccine.

B. Proofreading a Paragraph for Subject-Verb and Pronoun-Antecedent Agreement

Most of the sentences in the following paragraph contain at least one agreement error. For each error, identify the incorrect verb or pronoun and supply the correct form. If the sentence is correct, write *C*.

EXAMPLE   [1] Filming an animal in its natural surroundings present many problems.
1. *present—presents*

[11] One problem is that the photographer, in most cases, have to get quite close to the animal. [12] Ten yards often make the difference between a good scene and no scene at all. [13] A zoom lens or a telephoto lens are generally used, but even then, getting good photographs can be very difficult. [14] Before filming, the crew usually watch the animal for weeks to learn its habits and find good vantage points for taking pictures. [15] In addition, the photographer and the crew uses every trick of the trade in filming wild animals. [16] For example, *Foxes at Night* were

almost certainly not filmed at night! **[17]** "Nighttime" films are generally made during daylight hours, when there is plenty of natural light. **[18]** Later, all of the daytime footage are darkened using filters. **[19]** Also, many of the animals used in a nature film has been trained or partially tamed. **[20]** For example, if a photographer or a crew member take care of a bird from the moment it hatches, it will instinctively follow him or her everywhere. **[21]** The photographer can then easily take close up pictures of the bird after it matures. **[22]** In many films, scenes of animals giving birth and raising their young is filmed in a studio, not in the wild. **[23]** Photographers accomplish this by building a den where he or she can film the baby animals through a window beside the nest. **[24]** This film, along with footage taken in the natural habitat, are then skillfully edited. **[25]** As a result, few of the viewers ever suspects that he is watching film that has been shot indoors.

USAGE

19 USING VERBS CORRECTLY

Principal Parts, Tense, Voice

Diagnostic Test

A. Using the Past and Past Participle Forms of Irregular Verbs

For each of the following sentences, give the correct form (past or past participle) of the verb in parentheses.

EXAMPLE   1. I have (*write*) a story about the big snowstorm we had last winter.
           1. *written*

1. The wind (*blow*) all night long during the snowstorm.
2. When Latisha and I looked outside in the morning, at least a foot of snow had (*fall*).
3. Instead of a brown, lifeless yard, we (*see*) a glittering fantasy world.
4. Never in our lives had we (*eat*) cereal as fast as we did that morning!

5. We quickly put on our parkas and (*run*) out the door to build a snow fort.
6. To our surprise, Mom (*come*) outside, too, with a mischievous smile on her face.
7. We should have (*know*) she would start a snowball fight!
8. Before we could get our revenge, Mom (*go*) back into the house to warm up.
9. Pretty soon our feet felt as if they had (*freeze*) solid.
10. When we finally went inside, Mom (*bring*) us mugs of hot apple cider as a peace offering.

B. Revising Verb Tense or Voice

Some of the following sentences have a verb in the wrong tense, an awkward use of the passive voice, or both. Revise each incorrect sentence to correct these errors. If a sentence is correct, write *C*.

EXAMPLE   [1] Some money was lost by someone at the beach.
     1. *Someone lost some money at the beach.*

[11] Ever since he was a boy, my grandfather loves to go beachcombing. [12] Last Saturday, two ten-dollar bills and two twenty-dollar bills were found by him among some dark green seaweed. [13] He ran right home and shouts to Grandma that he had found a bunch of money. [14] Of course, by the time Grandpa got back down to the ocean, the seaweed is being inspected by his neighbor Joe. [15] Between the two of them, Grandpa and Joe found over two hundred dollars that day.

C. Identifying Errors in the Use of *Lie* and *Lay*, *Sit* and *Set*, and *Rise* and *Raise*

For each of the following sentences, write *C* if the sentence is correct. If the sentence is incorrect, write the correct verb form.

EXAMPLE   1. We lay the boxes down and took a break.
     1. *laid*

16. Aunt Janet loves to set by the sunny window on winter afternoons.
17. I'll sit in a chair; the cat can lay in the hammock.
18. If you set the bread dough over a pan of warm water, the dough will rise faster.
19. The dogs are either laying under the porch or sitting by the gate.
20. The curtain rose just as we set down to watch the production of *Miss Saigon*.

The Principal Parts of Verbs

The four basic forms of a verb are called the *principal parts* of the verb.

19a. The four principal parts of a verb are the *base form*, the *present participle*, the *past*, and the *past participle*.

The principal parts of the verb *ring*, for example, are *ring* (base form), *ringing* (present participle), *rang* (past), and *rung* (past participle). These principal parts are used to form all of the different verb tenses.

EXAMPLES The bells **ring** every day.
The bells **are ringing** now.
The bells **rang** at noon.
The bells **have rung** for the last time today.

Notice that the tenses made from the present participle and past participle contain helping verbs, such as *am, is, are, has, have*.

NOTE: Some teachers refer to the base form as the infinitive. Follow your teacher's directions in labeling these forms.

Regular Verbs

19b. A *regular verb* is a verb that forms its past and past participle by adding *–d* or *–ed* to the base form.

BASE FORM	PRESENT PARTICIPLE	PAST	PAST PARTICIPLE
use	(is) using	used	(have) used
suppose	(is) supposing	supposed	(have) supposed
risk	(is) risking	risked	(have) risked

Notice that the present participle of most regular verbs ending in *–e* drops the *–e* before adding *–ing*.

One common error in the use of the past and the past participle forms is to leave off the *–d* or *–ed* ending.

NONSTANDARD We use to play soccer.
STANDARD We **used** to play soccer.

NONSTANDARD She was suppose to come early.
STANDARD She was **supposed** to come early.

☞ **REFERENCE NOTE:** For a discussion of standard and nonstandard English, see pages 449–450.

Another common error is to misspell or mispronounce verbs.

NONSTANDARD We were attackted by mosquitoes.
STANDARD We were **attacked** by mosquitoes.

NONSTANDARD Someone has drownded.
STANDARD Someone has **drowned.**

NOTE: A few regular verbs have an alternate past form ending in *–t.* For example, the past form of *burn* is *burned* or *burnt.*

▶ ORAL
PRACTICE 1

Pronouncing the Past and Past Participle Forms of Regular Verbs Correctly

Read each sentence aloud, stressing the italicized verb.

1. Aunt Rosie *used* to do needlepoint.
2. What has *happened* to your bicycle?
3. Several people were *drowned* in the flood.
4. The agents *risked* their lives.
5. Aren't you *supposed* to sing?
6. The game was well *advertised.*
7. The critics *praised* Amy Tan's new book.
8. He *carried* the suitcases to the car.

USAGE

USAGE

Irregular Verbs

19c. An *irregular verb* is a verb that forms its past and past participle in some other way than by adding *–d* or *–ed.*

An irregular verb forms its past and past participle by

- changing vowels *or* consonants
- changing vowels *and* consonants
- making no change at all

BASE FORM	PAST	PAST PARTICIPLE
begin	began	(have) begun
bring	brought	(have) brought
ride	rode	(have) ridden
go	went	(have) gone
put	put	(have) put

Since most English verbs are regular, people sometimes try to make irregular verbs follow the same pattern. However, such words as *throwed, knowed, shrinked,* or *choosed* are considered nonstandard. If you are not sure about the parts of a verb, look in the dictionary, which lists the principal parts of irregular verbs.

© 1984 by Sidney Harris.

"WHEN I SAY 'RUNNED', YOU KNOW I MEAN 'RAN'. LET'S NOT QUIBBLE."

IRREGULAR VERBS FREQUENTLY MISUSED			
BASE FORM	**PRESENT PARTICIPLE**	**PAST**	**PAST PARTICIPLE**
begin	(is) beginning	began	(have) begun
blow	(is) blowing	blew	(have) blown
break	(is) breaking	broke	(have) broken
bring	(is) bringing	brought	(have) brought
burst	(is) bursting	burst	(have) burst
choose	(is) choosing	chose	(have) chosen
come	(is) coming	came	(have) come
dive	(is) diving	dove	(have) dived
do	(is) doing	did	(have) done
drink	(is) drinking	drank	(have) drunk
drive	(is) driving	drove	(have) driven
eat	(is) eating	ate	(have) eaten
fall	(is) falling	fell	(have) fallen
freeze	(is) freezing	froze	(have) frozen
give	(is) giving	gave	(have) given
go	(is) going	went	(have) gone
grow	(is) growing	grew	(have) grown
know	(is) knowing	knew	(have) known
put	(is) putting	put	(have) put
ride	(is) riding	rode	(have) ridden
ring	(is) ringing	rang	(have) rung
run	(is) running	ran	(have) run
see	(is) seeing	saw	(have) seen
shake	(is) shaking	shook	(have) shaken
shrink	(is) shrinking	shrank	(have) shrunk
sink	(is) sinking	sank	(have) sunk
speak	(is) speaking	spoke	(have) spoken
steal	(is) stealing	stole	(have) stolen
sting	(is) stinging	stung	(have) stung
strike	(is) striking	struck	(have) struck
swear	(is) swearing	swore	(have) sworn
swim	(is) swimming	swam	(have) swum
take	(is) taking	took	(have) taken
tear	(is) tearing	tore	(have) torn
throw	(is) throwing	threw	(have) thrown
wear	(is) wearing	wore	(have) worn
write	(is) writing	wrote	(have) written

When the present participle and past participle forms are used as main verbs (simple predicates) in sentences, they always require helping verbs.

PRESENT PARTICIPLE	+	HELPING VERB	=	MAIN VERB
taking walking going	+	⎡ forms ⎤ of ⎣ **be** ⎦	=	am taking was walking have been going

PAST PARTICIPLE	+	HELPING VERB	=	MAIN VERB
taken walked gone	+	⎡ forms ⎤ of ⎣ **have** ⎦	=	have taken has walked had gone

To help you avoid nonstandard usage, include *is* with the present participle and *have* with the past participle. For example, say *do, is doing, did, have done* or *see, is seeing, saw, have seen.*

NONSTANDARD We already seen that program.
   STANDARD We **have** already **seen** that program.

☞ REFERENCE NOTE: Sometimes a past participle is used with a form of *be: was chosen, are known, is seen.* This use of the verb is called the *passive voice.* See pages 633–635.

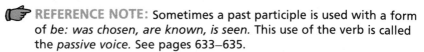

ORAL
PRACTICE 2

Using the Past and Past Participle Forms of Irregular Verbs Correctly

Read each of the following sentences aloud, stressing the italicized verbs.

1. *Have* you *begun* the research for your report?
2. Last week we *saw* The Long Walk Home and Havana.
3. The bell *rang,* and the door *burst* open.
4. I *have known* her since the first grade.
5. He *brought* his rock collection to school.
6. They *risked* their lives to rescue the survivors.
7. Elizabeth *has written* a short article for the school newspaper.
8. She *has given* us her permission.

EXERCISE 1

Writing the Past and Past Participle Forms of Irregular Verbs

Change each of the following verb forms. If the base form is given, change it to the past form. If the past form is given, change it to the past participle. Use *have* before each past participle form.

EXAMPLES   **1.** eat   **2.** took
                 1. *ate*   **2.** *have taken*

1. do	**6.** know	**11.** choose	**16.** shrank
2. began	**7.** spoke	**12.** broke	**17.** ran
3. see	**8.** stole	**13.** drink	**18.** ring
4. rode	**9.** blew	**14.** drove	**19.** fell
5. went	**10.** bring	**15.** froze	**20.** swim

EXERCISE 2

Identifying Correct Forms of Irregular Verbs

For each of the following sentences, choose the correct form of the verb in parentheses.

EXAMPLE   **1.** Mai's parents (*telled, told*) her about their journey in a boat from South Vietnam to Malaysia.
          1. *told*

1. They (*rode, rid*) in a crowded boat like the one you see in this picture.
2. Along with many other people, Mai's parents (*chose, choosed*) to make such a journey rather than stay in South Vietnam after the Vietnam War ended.

USAGE

USAGE

3. These refugees (*came, come*) to be called "boat people."
4. Mai's parents abandoned their home after the South Vietnamese capital, Saigon, had (*fell, fallen*) to North Vietnamese forces.
5. The people on the boat (*brang, brought*) few possessions or supplies.
6. After they (*drank, drunk*) what little water was on board, they went thirsty.
7. Mai's father said the people had (*ate, eaten*) all the food in a few days.
8. When another boat of refugees (*sank, sunk*), its people crowded onto Mai's parents' boat.
9. They spent many days and nights on the ocean before they (*saw, seen*) land again.
10. Then it (*took, taken*) months for Mai's parents to be moved from Malaysian refugee camps to the United States.

▶ EXERCISE 3   **Identifying Correct Forms of Irregular Verbs**

Choose the correct past or past participle of the verb given in parentheses.

EXAMPLE   I just [1] **(*wrote, written*)** my fourth letter to my Russian pen pal!
1. *wrote*

Joining the Russian American pen-pal club Druzhba is one of the most important things I have ever [1] (*did, done*). The founder of the club [2] (*chose, chosen*) the name Druzhba because it means "friendship" in Russian. This club has [3] (*given, gave*) American and Russian students the chance to become friends. I [4] (*began, begun*) to write to my pen pal Vanya last September. His reply to my first letter [5] (*took, taken*) weeks to get to me. (I wish it could have [6] (*flew, flown*) here faster from the other side of the globe.) In his letters, Vanya has [7] (*written, wrote*) about his daily life, his family, and his thoughts and feelings. We have [8] (*become, became*) good friends through our letters, even though we have never [9] (*spoke, spoken*) to each other. Reading each other's essays in the club newsletter has also [10] (*brung, brought*) us closer together.

▶ EXERCISE 4   **Using the Past and Past Participle Forms of Verbs**

You are on a family vacation in Florida, and you have just bought the postcards shown below to send to a friend. Write a message describing your trip so far. Use five past and five past participle forms of the verbs listed below. Underline each verb form. Use the portion of the road map shown beside the postcards to find real numbers for highways you have traveled on and real names for towns, parks, and attractions you have visited. Invent the other details of your trip.

drive	ride	stay	visit	see	reach
do	swim	eat	buy	write	take
fall	run	come	give	begin	go

▶ REVIEW A   **Writing the Past and Past Participle Forms of Verbs**

For each of the following sentences, write the correct past or past participle form of the verb given.

EXAMPLE   1. *run*   Yesterday we ＿＿ around the track three
                             times.
                      1. *ran*

1. *sing*   Luther Vandross ＿＿ last night.
2. *burst*   The car suddenly ＿＿ into flames.
3. *drink*   Yesterday they ＿＿ juice with their
             sandwiches.
4. *use*   He ＿＿ to camp out every summer.
5. *do*   They ＿＿ their best to repair the damage.
6. *give*   Grandma has ＿＿ us some old photos.
7. *risk*   The detective ＿＿ her life.
8. *ring*   My alarm ＿＿ at six o'clock.
9. *speak*   Toni has not ＿＿ to me since our argument.
10. *fall*   A tree has ＿＿ across the highway.

▶ REVIEW B   **Writing the Past and Past Participle Forms of Verbs**

Write the correct past or past participle form of each italicized verb in the following paragraph.

EXAMPLE   All my life I have [1] (*know*) that I must make my own
                    choices.
                    1. *known*

I have never [1] (*choose*) to be on a sports team because I am not a very athletic person. Everyone is amazed at this because my brother and sister have [2] (*drive*) themselves very hard and have [3] (*become*) excellent athletes. For example, my brother, Emilio, [4] (*break*) three swimming records this year alone. He has [5] (*swim*) better than anyone else in our school. He also [6] (*go*) out for tennis and track this year. My sister, Elena, is only a junior, but she has already [7] (*run*) the 100-yard dash faster than any senior girl. I [8] (*use*) to think I wanted to follow in my brother's and sister's footsteps, but now I have [9] (*take*) a different path in life. My English teacher just [10] (*give*) me a chance to lead the debating team, and I am going to grab it!

▶ REVIEW C

Writing the Past and Past Participle Forms of Verbs

For each of the following sentences, write the correct form of the verb given.

EXAMPLE   1. *go*   We ____ to the Ozark Mountains.
           1. *went*

1. *throw*   Kerry should have ____ the ball to Lee.
2. *freeze*   Has the water ____ yet?
3. *write*   Theo has ____ me a long letter.
4. *see*   Have you ____ that actor in person?
5. *shrink*   The curtains have ____ two inches.
6. *throw*   I finally ____ my old running shoes away.
7. *drown*   Nobody has ever ____ in this lake.
8. *give*   Taro ____ me a bowl of miso soup.
9. *blow*   The strong wind this afternoon ____ our treehouse down.
10. *take*   I have already ____ a picture of you, Molly.

USAGE

▶ REVIEW D

Writing the Past and Past Participle Forms of Verbs

Each sentence in the following paragraph has at least one verb in italics. Write the correct form of each verb.

EXAMPLE   [1] Have you ever (*take*) a trip to the country?
           1. *taken*

[1] We have always (*spend*) summer vacations at Uncle Dan's farm in Vermont. [2] We (*do*) the most wonderful things there last year! [3] We (*swim*) in the millpond and (*eat*) watermelon on the back porch. [4] A few times, we (*ride*) our bikes into town to get groceries. [5] We also (*take*) turns riding Horace, the mule. [6] I have (*fall*) off Horace twice, but I never (*break*) any bones. [7] Both times, I (*come*) down in a pile of soft hay. [8] Then I dusted myself off and (*climb*) right back on.

▶ REVIEW E

Proofreading Sentences for Correct Verb Forms

Some of the following sentences contain an incorrect verb form. If the sentence is correct, write *C*. If the form of a verb is wrong, write the correct form.

EXAMPLE   1. Marian Anderson sung her way out of poverty.
          1. *sang*

1. She went on to earn worldwide fame and the Presidential Medal of Freedom.
2. Can you tell from the costumes and scenery in the picture below that she use to perform in operas?
3. In 1955, Marian Anderson become the first African American singer to perform with the Metropolitan Opera in New York City.
4. She performed in concerts and operas all over the world, but she begun her career as a child, singing hymns in church.
5. Anderson, who was from a poor Philadelphia family, was awarded a scholarship to study music in Europe.
6. European audiences soon taked notice of her as a talented performer.
7. Audiences in the United States also loved her and admired her determination and courage.
8. In 1939, Anderson was not permitted to sing at a hall in Washington, D.C., so she give a free concert at the Lincoln Memorial, attended by 75,000 people.
9. In the 1950s, the U.S. government choosed her to go on a goodwill tour of Asia and to be a United Nations delegate.
10. Anderson has wrote of her experiences in her autobiography, *My Lord, What a Morning.*

▶ REVIEW F   **Proofreading a Paragraph for Correct Verb Forms**

The following paragraph contains ten incorrect verb forms. If the sentence is correct, write *C*. If a verb form is wrong, write the correct form.

EXAMPLE   [1] A Confederate search party had went out to get boots for their soldiers and saddles for their horses.
   1. *had gone*

[1] By chance, the searchers run into the Union cavalry. [2] It is not clear who attackted first, but a battle begun near Gettysburg, Pennsylvania, on July 1, 1863. [3] The fighting go on for three days. [4] First one side and then the other got the upper hand. [5] Shells bursted in the air, and cannonballs whistled in all directions. [6] At one point, some Confederate soldiers clumb to the top of Cemetery Ridge, and their flag flown there a brief time. [7] However, the Union army drived them back. [8] By the time the battle had ran its course, more than 20,000 Union soldiers and 25,000 Confederate soldiers had fell.

Tense

The time expressed by a verb is called the **tense** of the verb. Every verb in English has six tenses:

present	present perfect
past	past perfect
future	future perfect

The following list shows the six tense forms of *give*. Presenting all the forms of a verb in this way is called *conjugating* the verb.

CONJUGATION OF THE VERB *GIVE*	
PRESENT TENSE	
SINGULAR	*PLURAL*
I give	we give
you give	you give
he, she, *or* it gives	they give

(continued)

CONJUGATION OF THE VERB *GIVE (continued)*

PAST TENSE

SINGULAR	PLURAL
I gave	we gave
you gave	you gave
he, she, *or* it gave	they gave

FUTURE TENSE

SINGULAR	PLURAL
I will (shall) give	we will (shall) give
you will give	you will give
he, she, *or* it will give	they will give

PRESENT PERFECT TENSE

SINGULAR	PLURAL
I have given	we have given
you have given	you have given
he, she, *or* it has given	they have given

PAST PERFECT TENSE

SINGULAR	PLURAL
I had given	we had given
you had given	you had given
he, she, *or* it had given	they had given

FUTURE PERFECT TENSE

SINGULAR	PLURAL
I will (shall) have given	we will (shall) have given
you will have given	you will have given
he, she, *or* it will have given	they will have given

NOTE: The helping verb *shall* can be used in the second person (*you*) and third person (*he, she, it, they*), as well as in the first person.

Each of the six tenses has an additional form called the *progressive form,* which expresses continuing action. It consists of a form of the verb *be* plus the present participle of a verb. The progressive is not a separate tense but an additional form of each of the six tenses.

Present Progressive	am, are, is giving
Past Progressive	was, were giving
Future Progressive	will (shall) be giving
Present Perfect Progressive	has, have been giving
Past Perfect Progressive	had been giving
Future Perfect Progressive	will (shall) have been giving

Consistency of Tense

19d. Do not change needlessly from one tense to another.

NONSTANDARD Cara fielded the ball and throws the runner out. [*Fielded* is past tense; *throws* is present tense.]

STANDARD Cara **fielded** the ball and **threw** the runner out. [*Fielded* and *threw* are both past tense.]

NONSTANDARD He stands on the mound and stared at the batter. [*Stands* is present tense; *stared* is past tense.]

STANDARD He **stands** on the mound and **stares** at the batter. [*Stands* and *stares* are both present tense.]

The perfect tenses are used to express completed action.

NONSTANDARD I regretted that I chose such a broad topic. [Since the action of choosing was completed before the action of regretting, the verb should be *had chosen,* not *chose.*]

STANDARD I regretted that I **had chosen** such a broad topic.

WRITING APPLICATION

Using Verb Tense to Make Instructions Clear

When you give instructions, you break a process into steps. Usually, you give the steps in the order in which they must be done. The correct verb tense can help make your instructions clear by showing whether an action occurs before, after, or at the same time as another action.

| BEFORE/AFTER | When you **have washed** the apple, **cut** it into pieces. |
| SAME TIME | When you **wash** the apple, **cut** it into pieces. |

Which of the steps above might leave you with a soapy snack?

▶ WRITING ACTIVITY

You have been asked to teach your eight-year-old brother to make his own after-school snack. Write instructions for making a nutritious treat. Use correct verb tense so that your directions are easy to follow.

Prewriting   You will need to choose a snack that a child would be able to make and would enjoy. You may want to list all of the steps first and then go back and number them in order.

Writing   As you write your first draft, think about how to define or clarify words that an eight-year-old might not know. Make sure that your verb tenses show the sequence of the steps.

Evaluating and Revising   Ask a friend or a young child you know to act out your instructions. Revise any steps that confuse your assistant. Add time signal words (such as *first, second, then,* and *next*) and check to be sure your verb tenses are correct.

Proofreading and Publishing   Use your textbook to check the spelling of the verbs in your instructions. Pay special attention to the irregular verbs. (See pages 620–622 for more about irregular verbs.) Your class may decide to make its own snack cookbook to share with elementary school students or your local parent-teacher organization. Photocopy your recipes or input them on a computer. Then group them by ingredients or ease of preparation and publish your cookbook.

▶ EXERCISE 5 **Proofreading a Paragraph to Make the Tenses of the Verbs Consistent**

Proofread the following paragraph, looking for needless changes of verb tense. Decide whether the paragraph should be written in the present or past tense. Then change the verbs to make the tenses consistent.

It all started as soon as I came home from school. I am in my room, and I have planned to study for two hours. It was about five o'clock. To my surprise, Nancy Chang decided to drop by. She dashes into the house, slams the door behind her, and yells for me. What she wanted is a fishing companion. She has been thinking about going fishing all week. Getting my gear together, I become excited and can almost see the fish fighting over which one is to be my first catch. On our way out to the lake, we see clouds beginning to form, and we knew we are in for trouble. It rains all right, for the whole weekend. The fish were safe for another week.

Active and Passive Voice

A verb in the *active voice* expresses an action done *by* its subject. A verb in the *passive voice* expresses an action done *to* its subject.

ACTIVE VOICE **The coach instructed us.** [The subject, *coach*, performs the action.]

PASSIVE VOICE **We were instructed by the coach.** [The subject, *we*, receives the action.]

Compare the following related sentences:

         S   O

ACTIVE **The author provides helpful diagrams.**

         S

PASSIVE **Helpful diagrams are provided by the author.**

In the two sentences above, the object of the active sentence becomes the subject of the passive one. The subject of the active sentence is now expressed in a prepositional phrase. In fact, this phrase can be omitted.

PASSIVE **Helpful diagrams are provided.**

In a passive sentence, the verb phrase always includes a form of *be* and the past participle of the main verb. Other helping verbs may also be included.

ACTIVE   Willa Cather **wrote** *My Ántonia.*

PASSIVE   *My Ántonia* **was written** by Willa Cather.

ACTIVE   Someone **has erased** the tapes.

PASSIVE   The tapes **have been erased.**

☞ **REFERENCE NOTE:** For more information on helping verbs, see pages 482–483.

The following list shows the conjugation of the verb *give* in the passive voice. Compare this conjugation to the one on pages 629–630.

CONJUGATION OF THE VERB *GIVE* IN THE PASSIVE VOICE	
PRESENT TENSE	
SINGULAR	**PLURAL**
I am given	we are given
you are given	you are given
he, she, *or* it is given	they are given
PAST TENSE	
SINGULAR	**PLURAL**
I was given	we were given
you were given	you were given
he, she, *or* it was given	they were given
FUTURE TENSE	
SINGULAR	**PLURAL**
I will (shall) be given	we will (shall) be given
you will be given	you will be given
he, she, *or* it will be given	they will be given

(continued)

CONJUGATION OF THE VERB *GIVE* IN THE PASSIVE VOICE *(continued)*	
PRESENT PERFECT TENSE	
SINGULAR	***PLURAL***
I have been given	we have been given
you have been given	you have been given
he, she, *or* it has been given	they have been given
PAST PERFECT TENSE	
SINGULAR	***PLURAL***
I had been given	we had been given
you had been given	you had been given
he, she, *or* it had been given	they had been given
FUTURE PERFECT TENSE	
SINGULAR	***PLURAL***
I will (shall) have been given	we will (shall) have been given
you will have been given	you will have been given
he, she, *or* it will have been given	they will have been given

USAGE

Using the Passive Voice

The passive voice emphasizes the person or thing receiving the action rather than the one performing the action. It may be used when the speaker does not know or does not wish to say who performed the action.

In general, you should avoid overusing the passive voice because it makes your writing sound weak and awkward. Using the active voice helps make your writing direct and forceful.

PASSIVE   The ball was hit over the outfield fence by Jody.
ACTIVE   Jody hit the ball over the outfield fence.

PASSIVE   The totals for the new budget were carefully checked.
ACTIVE   The club treasurer carefully checked the totals for the new budget.

▶ EXERCISE 6   **Classifying Sentences by Voice**

Identify each of the following sentences as *active* or *passive*.

EXAMPLE   1. In the morning, I am awakened by the alarm clock.
1. *passive*

1. The album was not reviewed by most critics.
2. The student body elects the council president.
3. Angelo's courageous act prevented a tragedy.
4. W. C. Handy composed the famous jazz classic "St. Louis Blues."
5. Your generous contribution to help the homeless is greatly appreciated.
6. The half-time show was performed by the band.
7. This afternoon the baby stood up by himself.
8. Was Saul Bellow awarded the Nobel Prize?
9. I don't understand this math problem.
10. Brian has been appointed captain of the team.

▶ EXERCISE 7   **Using Verbs in the Active Voice and the Passive Voice**

Identify the verb in each of the following sentences as either *active* or *passive*. Then, revise each sentence in the passive voice to make it active voice.

EXAMPLE   1. My 4-H project was just completed.
1. *passive; I just completed my 4-H project.*

1. For my project I grew vegetables in containers.
2. Initially, 4-H clubs were joined only by farm children.
3. Their projects focused on crops and livestock.
4. Later projects, such as automobile safety and career studies, interested young people in the city.
5. Completed projects are often exhibited by members at local or county fairs.
6. 4-H club members also learn about good citizenship.
7. Summer camps are attended by many 4-H members.
8. Community projects are planned by our club yearly.
9. The city appreciated our tree-planting project.
10. Young people worldwide are helped by participation in 4-H.

PICTURE THIS

You are a sportswriter for the *Chicago Tribune.* The home team is playing the final game of the World Series. Hopes have been high, but they are dashed as these players watch a teammate strike out. Write a short news article about this event. Begin with something that will grab your readers' interest, and be sure to include the answers to the *who, what, when, where, why,* and *how* questions. Use active-voice verbs to help your readers "see" the action. After finishing your article, trade papers with a partner, and underline all the active-voice verbs.

Subject: the final game of the World Series

Audience: sports fans in Chicago

Purpose: to inform

Norman Rockwell (1894–1978), *The Dugout,* 1948, Watercolor, 19 × 17⅛", The Brooklyn Museum. 71.124

USAGE

Special Problems with Verbs

Lie and *Lay*

The verb *lie* means "to rest" or "to recline," "to remain in a lying position." *Lie* never takes an object.

The verb *lay* means "to put" or "to place" (something). *Lay* usually takes an object.

PRINCIPAL PARTS OF *LIE* AND *LAY*			
BASE FORM	**PRESENT PARTICIPLE**	**PAST**	**PAST PARTICIPLE**
lie (rest)	(is) lying	lay	(have) lain
lay (put)	(is) laying	laid	(have) laid

These examples show how the verb *lie* is used.

> I sometimes **lie** on the floor.
> The bills **are lying** on the table.
> Yesterday Lambert **lay** on the grass.
> How long **have** the bills **lain** there?

The following examples show how the verb *lay* is used. Notice how these examples differ from the ones above.

> **Lay** those books down.
> I **am laying** the clean towels on this chair.
> Yesterday Lambert **laid** the bricks on the patio.
> **Have** you **laid** your report aside?

NOTE: The verb *lie* may be used to describe the lying position of inanimate objects as well as people and animals. Even though someone or something put the object down, it *lies* (not *lays*) there.

> EXAMPLE   The jacket is still **lying** where Brian dropped it in the corner.

When deciding whether to use *lie* or *lay,* ask yourself two questions.

QUESTION 1:   What do I want to say? Is the meaning "to be in a lying position," or is it "to put something down"?

QUESTION 2:   What time does the verb express, and which principal part is used to show this time?

The following two examples show how you can apply these questions to determine which verb—*lie* or *lay*— should be used.

EXAMPLE: How long have you (*lain, laid*) there?

QUESTION 1:   **Meaning?** The meaning here is "to be in a lying position." Therefore, the verb should be *lie.*

QUESTION 2:   **Principal part?** The time is past, and the sentence requires the past participle with *have.* The past participle of *lie* is *lain.*

ANSWER: How long **have** you **lain** there?

EXAMPLE: Calvin (*lay, laid*) the jacket on the bed.

QUESTION 1:   **Meaning?** The meaning here is "to put." Therefore, the verb should be *lay.*

QUESTION 2:   **Principal part?** The time is past and requires the past form, which is *laid.*

ANSWER: Calvin **laid** the jacket on the bed.

■► ORAL **Using the Forms of *Lie* and *Lay***
   PRACTICE 3 **Correctly**

Read each of the following sentences aloud. Be able to explain why the italicized verb is correct.

1. The pilgrim *laid* his prayer rug on the ground.
2. Yesterday afternoon all the cows *lay* under a shade tree.
3. A wet towel is *lying* on the sand.
4. Kimiko was carefully *laying* the tiles on the floor.
5. The best route *lay* to the west.
6. That box has *lain* in your closet for weeks.
7. His thoughts *lie* miles away.
8. Yesterday I *laid* the pliers on the bench, and they should still be *lying* there.

■► EXERCISE 8 **Choosing the Correct Forms of *Lie* and *Lay***

Choose the correct form of *lie* or *lay* for each of the following sentences.

EXAMPLE   1. Jennifer ＿＿ the flowers on the table and looked for a vase.
           1. *laid*

1. He ＿＿ the report aside and called for order.
2. Alma will ＿＿ down for a siesta.
3. She has ＿＿ on the couch all morning.
4. The baby was ＿＿ quietly in the nurse's arms.
5. Is that today's paper ＿＿ in the mud?
6. I have ＿＿ the shoes near the fire to dry.
7. ＿＿ down.
8. The lace had ＿＿ in the trunk for years.
9. Our cat ＿＿ in the sun whenever it can.
10. After reading for almost three hours, I ＿＿ back and rested my head on the cushions.

Sit and *Set*

The verb *sit* means "to rest in an upright, seated position." *Sit* almost never has an object.

The verb *set* means "to put" or "to place" (something). *Set* usually takes an object. Notice that *set* does not change form in the past or past participle.

PRINCIPAL PARTS OF *SIT* AND *SET*			
BASE FORM	**PRESENT PARTICIPLE**	**PAST**	**PAST PARTICIPLE**
sit (rest)	(is) sitting	sat	(have) sat
set (put)	(is) setting	set	(have) set

EXAMPLES **Sit** down.
Set it down.
The cups **sat** on the tray.
I **set** the cups there.

ORAL
PRACTICE 4   **Using the Forms of *Sit* and *Set* Correctly**

Read each of the following sentences aloud. Be able to explain why the italicized verb is correct.

1. I *set* the chairs on the lawn.
2. The campers *were sitting* around the fire.
3. Rosa *sat* next to Scott.
4. Please *set* the won tons on that plate.
5. Will you please *sit* still?
6. The car *sat* there all week.
7. Have we really *sat* here that long?
8. Dolores *sat* down and *set* the teapot in front of me.

EXERCISE 9   **Writing the Forms of *Sit* and *Set***

For each of the blanks in the following sentences, write the correct form of *sit* or *set*.

EXAMPLE   1. Will you ____ with me, Josh?
            1. *sit*

1. Please ____ here, Mrs. Brown.
2. Have you ____ the seedlings in the sun?
3. We were ____ in the park during the fireworks.
4. Someone has already ____ the kettle on the stove.

5. Grandpa is busily ____ tomato plants in the garden.
6. At the concert, Keith ____ near Isabelle.
7. Mrs. Levine ____ the menorah on the mantel.
8. They were ____ on the rocks, watching the surf.
9. We had ____ still for almost an hour.
10. Have you ever ____ on the beach at sundown?

Rise and Raise

The verb *rise* means "to go in an upward direction." *Rise* never has an object.

The verb *raise* means "to move something in an upward direction." *Raise* usually takes an object.

PRINCIPAL PARTS OF *RISE* AND *RAISE*			
BASE FORM	**PRESENT PARTICIPLE**	**PAST**	**PAST PARTICIPLE**
rise (go up)	(is) rising	rose	(have) risen
raise (move something up)	(is) raising	raised	(have) raised

EXAMPLES   I always **rise** early.
Someone **will raise** that question.
The price index **rose** sharply.
The publisher **raised** the price of the paper.

ORAL
PRACTICE 5

Using the Forms of *Rise* and *Raise* Correctly

Read each of the following sentences aloud. Be able to explain why each italicized verb is correct.

1. The tide *rises* early this weekend.
2. We *raised* our hands to vote.
3. A woman *rose* from her seat and *raised* an objection.
4. The teacher *raised* his eyebrows.
5. Everyone in my house *rises* early except me.
6. Has the sun *risen* yet?
7. Everyone *rose* when the judge entered the room.
8. The builders *had raised* the large beam into place.

▶ EXERCISE 10   **Writing the Forms of *Rise* and *Raise***

For each of the blanks in the following sentences, write the correct form of *rise* or *raise*.

EXAMPLE   1. The river has been _____ rapidly since noon.
          1. *rising*

1. Please _____ and face the audience.
2. After the speech, the reporters _____ several questions.
3. Will the governor _____ the sales tax again?
4. The price of fuel has _____ steadily.
5. Let's get there before the curtain _____.
6. Jerry, one of the stagehands, will _____ the curtain for each act.
7. The bread has _____ beautifully.
8. The moon _____ and slipped behind a cloud.
9. The candidate _____ to address her supporters.
10. The children _____ their flag for Cinco de Mayo.

▶ REVIEW G   **Writing Sentences Using the Forms of *Lie* and *Lay*, *Sit* and *Set*, and *Rise* and *Raise***

Write ten sentences, using each of the following verbs.

EXAMPLE   1. was sitting
          1. *The puppy was sitting beside its mother.*

1. rise
2. raised
3. have sat
4. have set
5. was lying
6. was laying
7. will sit
8. had lain
9. has been rising
10. has been setting

▶ REVIEW H   **Identifying the Correct Forms of *Lie* and *Lay*, *Sit* and *Set*, and *Rise* and *Raise***

For each of the following sentences, choose the correct verb in parentheses.

EXAMPLE   1. The number of European immigrants coming to the United States (*rose, raised*) steadily during the late 1800s and early 1900s.
          1. *rose*

1. This Hungarian mother (*sat, set*) with her children for this picture around 1910.
2. They were among thousands of immigrant families who (*sat, set*) their baggage on American soil for the first time at the immigration station on Ellis Island in New York Harbor.
3. (*Lying, Laying*) down was often impossible on the crowded ships that brought these immigrants to the United States.
4. Most immigrants were thankful to be able to (*lie, lay*) their few belongings on the deck and think of the future.
5. Their hopes for new lives must have (*risen, raised*) as they drew closer to the United States.
6. The history book (*lying, laying*) on the desk states that eleven million immigrants came to the United States between 1870 and 1899.
7. (*Sit, Set*) down and read more about the immigrants who came from Germany, Ireland, Great Britain, Scandinavia, and the Netherlands in the early 1800s.
8. After 1890, the number of immigrants from Austria-Hungary, Italy, Russia, Poland, and Greece (*rose, raised*).

USAGE

The Granger Collection, New York.

9. Many United States citizens were (*rising, raising*) concerns that there would not be enough jobs for everyone in the country.
10. But we know now that immigrant workers helped the country to (*rise, raise*) to new industrial heights.

▶ REVIEW I

Choosing the Correct Form of Easily Confused Verbs

The verbs *lie, lay, sit, set, rise,* and *raise* are used in many common expressions. For each of the following questions, choose the letter of the phrase that gives the correct use of the verb.

EXAMPLE 1. How might you help someone out?
  a. set her on the right course
  b. sit her on the right course
  1. *a*

1. What do people do at a noisy party?
   a. raise a ruckus   **b.** rise a ruckus
2. Instead of slumping, what should you do?
   a. sit up straight   **b.** set up straight
3. How might you react to an injustice?
   a. not take it lying down
   b. not take it laying down
4. What does a court officer say when the judge enters the courtroom?
   a. All raise.   **b.** All rise.
5. What is someone doing who can't make up his or her mind?
   a. sitting on the fence   **b.** setting on the fence
6. How might you describe a fidgety child?
   a. She can't set still.   **b.** She can't sit still.
7. When your meal is ready, what do you do?
   a. set down to dinner   **b.** sit down to dinner
8. If you're being direct about something, what are you doing?
   a. laying it on the line   **b.** lying it on the line
9. If you are not doing your best, what are you doing?
   a. lying down on the job
   b. laying down on the job
10. After days of heavy rain, what may a river do?
    a. raise over its banks   **b.** rise over its banks

REVIEW J   **Writing Sentences Using the Correct Forms of Verbs**

Write ten sentences, using each of the following verbs. Supply appropriate helping verbs if needed.

EXAMPLE   1. chosen
      1. *Have you chosen a topic for your paper?*

1. set   **4.** drank   **7.** chose   **9.** lain
2. laid   **5.** laying   **8.** sat   **10.** lying
3. rose   **6.** risen

REVIEW K   **Identifying Correct Uses of Verbs**

USAGE

Read the following paragraph. Each sentence has at least one pair of words or phrases in parentheses. For each pair, choose the correct item.

EXAMPLE   [1] Look at this great old photograph that Grandma has just (*gave, given*) me.
      1. *given*

[1] Grandma told me that the Pop Corn King (*been, was*) her grandfather and, consequently, was my great-great-grandfather. [2] This warmhearted man (*rose, raised*) Grandma and her sister after their parents had (*drowned, drownded*) in a flood. [3] He is the one (*sitting, setting*) in the driver's seat. [4] The picture was (*took, taken*) in 1914 in the resort town of Petoskey, Michigan. [5] During the summer, my great-great-granddad (*use, used*) to drive

through the streets in late afternoon. [6] He (*rang, rung*) a bell, and children (*run, ran*) out to buy treats just as kids do today. [7] Look—the popcorn (*cost, costed*) only five cents! [8] The last time (*popcorn was bought by me, I bought popcorn*) at the movies, I had to pay $3.25!

Review: Posttest

Proofreading Paragraphs for Correct Verb Forms

Read the following paragraphs. If a sentence contains an incorrect or awkward verb form, write the correct form or revise the sentence. If a sentence is correct, write C. Some sentences may have more than one incorrect verb.

EXAMPLES   [1] I have always wanted a pet.
           1. *C*
           [2] As a child, I use to dream about having a dog or cat.
           2. *used*

[1] Every time I ask my parents, they said, "No, not in an apartment." [2] One day last year, I was setting on the front steps reading the newspaper when I spot an ad for a female ferret. [3] Deciding to investigate, I fold the paper, hop on my bike, and rode to the pet shop that had placed the ad.

[4] When I walked into the store, I seen the ferret right away. [5] She was laying in a cardboard box on top of the counter. [6] I told the owner I wanted to hold her, and he reaches into the box. [7] When he withdrew his hand, the ferret was holding onto his finger with what looked like very sharp teeth.

[8] I cautiously reached out and takes the ferret's hindquarters in my cupped hands. [9] The rest of her long body poured slowly into my hands until she was sitting on her haunches. [10] She looked up at me and suddenly clamps her teeth on my thumb. [11] The ferret done that to show me who was boss. [12] I should have knowed then that my troubles had just began.

[13] I ran all the way home and persuaded my parents to let me keep the ferret on a trial basis. [14] I had already give her a name—Ferris the Ferret—and I lose no time rushing back to the pet shop. [15] When I come home with Ferris, I sit a dish of cat food in front of her. [16] She stuck her snout into the dish and ate greedily. [17] After she had went into each room in the apartment, she choosed the top of the TV as her special place. [18] When my parents objected, I made a cardboard house with two entry holes and set it in a corner of my bedroom. [19] Ferris sniffed around her new home; then she goes in and laid down for a nap.

[20] For the next few days, Ferris spent her time either napping or nipping. [21] She always attackted me when I least expected it. [22] Once, as she lies on my desk while I am studying, she suddenly locked her teeth onto my earlobe. [23] I was so startled that I jump up quickly, and Ferris wound up laying on the floor with a look that makes me feel guilty. [24] The next day the bad news was gave to me by my parents: Ferris had to go back to the pet shop. [25] I no longer want a pet ferret, but I have wrote to the local zookeeper to ask about snakes.

USAGE

20 USING PRONOUNS CORRECTLY

Nominative and Objective Uses

Diagnostic Test

A. Identifying Correct Forms of Pronouns

For each of the following sentences, give the correct form of the pronoun in parentheses.

EXAMPLE   1. (*We, Us*) girls have built a picnic table.
          1. *We*

1. Janell and (*I, me*) painted the room together.
2. Alan, (*who, whom*) I did the typing for, said that he will pay me on Friday.
3. The young Amish couple drove us and (*they, them*) into town in a horse-drawn wagon.
4. Carolyn has been playing the guitar longer than (*she, her*).
5. The last two people to arrive, Tranh and (*I, me*), had trouble finding the skating rink.
6. Hector wrote this song for you and (*I, me*).
7. The winner is (*whoever, whomever*) finishes first.

8. Ellis was worried about his project, but Mrs. Asato gave (*he, him*) an A.
9. Was the winner of the race (*he, him*) or Aaron?
10. The pictures of the Grand Canyon impressed them more than (*we, us*), for we had seen the real thing.

B. Proofreading a Paragraph for Correct Pronoun Forms

Some of the following sentences contain a pronoun that has been used incorrectly. If a pronoun is incorrect, write the correct form. If the sentence is correct, write *C*.

EXAMPLE   [1] Between you and I, I'd like to see a blue rose.
          1. *me*

[11] Are you as interested in plants as me? [12] Nowadays, scientists are hard at work trying to develop a truly blue rose for us plant enthusiasts to enjoy. [13] That surprises Ms. Phillips, my science teacher, and I. [14] She doubts even more than me that breeding a blue rose is possible. [15] Us modern rose-lovers have never seen a blue rose. [16] Yet, an Arab agriculturist in the thirteenth century said that he had done it. [17] For centuries, rose breeders who have tried to produce the legendary blue rose have failed. [18] However, genetic engineering makes this more possible today than ever before. [19] In fact, some genetic engineers who I read about are working on this project now. [20] Finally, other rose-lovers and me can hope that we will someday see a truly blue rose.

USAGE

Case

Case is the form of a noun or pronoun that shows its use in a sentence. In English, there are three cases: *nominative*, *objective*, and *possessive*.

Choosing the correct case form for a noun is no problem, because the form remains the same in the nominative and objective cases.

EXAMPLE   My **dentist** has opened a new practice with another **dentist.**

Only in the possessive case does a noun change its form, usually by adding an apostrophe and an *s*.

EXAMPLE   My **dentist's** business is thriving.

☞ REFERENCE NOTE: For more about forming possessives with apostrophes, see pages 807–815.

Personal pronouns, however, have various case forms. In the following example, the pronouns in bold-faced type all refer to the same person. They have three different forms because of their different uses.

EXAMPLE   **I** [nominative] **forgot to bring my** [possessive] **notebook with me** [objective].

The Case Forms of Personal Pronouns

PERSONAL PRONOUNS		
SINGULAR		
NOMINATIVE CASE	OBJECTIVE CASE	POSSESSIVE CASE
I	me	my, mine
you	you	your, yours
he, she, it	him, her, it	his, her, hers, its
PLURAL		
NOMINATIVE CASE	OBJECTIVE CASE	POSSESSIVE CASE
we	us	our, ours
you	you	your, yours
they	them	their, theirs

Notice that *you* and *it* have the same form in the nominative and the objective case. All other personal pronouns have different nominative and objective forms.

☞ REFERENCE NOTE: For more about possessive case, see pages 811–815. For more about pronouns, see pages 469–473.

The Nominative Case

20a. The subject of a verb is always in the nominative case.

EXAMPLE **She** was glad that **they** were elected.

In the example, *she* is the subject of *was; they* is the subject of *were elected.*

Sometimes you may be unsure about which pronoun to use when both parts of a compound subject are pronouns. To help you choose the correct form, try each pronoun separately with the verb.

EXAMPLE: (*She, Her*) and (*they, them*) answered the ad.
She answered the ad.
Her answered the ad.
They answered the ad.
Them answered the ad.

ANSWER.   **She** and **they** answered the ad.

Sometimes the pronouns *we* and *they* sound awkward when used as parts of a compound subject. In such cases, it is a good idea to revise the sentence.

AWKWARD   We and they hope to sit together at the game.
BETTER   **We** hope to sit with **them** at the game.

ORAL
PRACTICE 1   **Using Pronouns as Subjects**

Read the following sentences aloud, stressing the italicized pronouns.

1. *She* made the shrimp tempura that *we* liked so much.
2. My brother and *I* are planning to paint the inside of the garage tomorrow.
3. It was apparent that *he* and *I* had won the debate.
4. *We* heard that Tim and *she* were disappointed.
5. *He* and *she* said that *we* were responsible for counting the ballots.
6. Where are my parents and *they*?
7. Will you and *he* help us with the book sale?
8. *She* and her sister have made posters for the party at the Senior Citizens Center.

▶ EXERCISE 1   **Identifying Pronouns Used as Subjects**

The following paragraph contains ten pairs of pronouns in parentheses. For each pair, choose the correct pronoun to use as a subject.

EXAMPLE   [1] *(They, Them)* may be the most famous husband and wife scientist team ever.
   1. *They*

Although Marie and Pierre Curie were both brilliant physicists, [1] *(she, her)* is better known than her husband is today. In fact, [2] *(I, me)* was surprised to learn that [3] *(them, they)* both received the Nobel Prize in physics in 1903. [4] *(We, Us)* tend to remember only Marie because [5] *(her, she)* was the first woman to win a Nobel Prize. In 1911, [6] *(she, her)* was again honored by the Nobel committee when [7] *(she, her)* was awarded the prize in chemistry. Despite her individual honors, Marie Curie always felt that [8] *(her, she)* and her husband were a team. Working in this small laboratory in Paris, [9] *(they, them)* didn't have room for independent research. As a result, [10] *(them, they)* collaborated on almost every project.

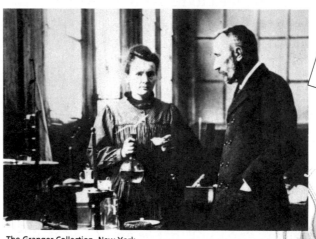

The Granger Collection, New York.

▶ ORAL PRACTICE 2   **Using Compound Subjects**

Read each of the following sentences aloud, stressing the italicized pronouns.

1. *He* and *I* agree that lacrosse is the most exciting game we've ever played.
2. *They* and their friends enjoyed the field trip.
3. Will Sue Ann and *she* enter the art contest?
4. *You* and *we* will compete in the playoffs.
5. *We* and our teacher are glad that *he* and *she* are returning.
6. Could Tyrone and *we* go to the pep rally with you?
7. *She* and her father put the paper model together.
8. How excited *you* and *they* must be!

20b. A predicate nominative is always in the nominative case.

A *predicate nominative* is a noun or pronoun that follows a linking verb and explains or identifies the subject of the sentence.

☞ REFERENCE NOTE: For more about predicate nominatives, see pages 517–520.

A pronoun used as a predicate nominative always follows a form of the verb *be* or a verb phrase ending in *be* or *been*.

EXAMPLES   This is **he**.
            It may be **she**.
            It should have been **they**.

NOTE: Widespread usage has made such expressions as *It's me, That's him,* or *Could it have been her?* acceptable in speaking. You should avoid them in your written work unless you are writing conversational English in a dialogue.

▶ EXERCISE 2   **Writing Pronouns Used as Predicate Nominatives**

Complete the following sentences by adding pronouns used as predicate nominatives. Use a different pronoun in each sentence. Do not use *you* or *it*.

1. Do you know if it was ____?
2. I thought it was ____.
3. The winner of the marathon is ____.
4. That was not ____.
5. Can the valedictorian be ____?

The Objective Case

Objective case pronouns are used as direct objects, indirect objects, and objects of prepositions.

☞ **REFERENCE NOTE:** For more information about the different types of objects, see pages 522–524 and 533–538.

20c. The direct object of a verb is always in the objective case.

A *direct object* is a noun or pronoun that receives the action of the verb or shows the result of the action.

EXAMPLES Clem called **her** on the telephone last night. [*Clem* is the subject of the verb *called*. Clem called *whom?* The answer is *her.*]

He paid **us** generously for our work. [*He* is the subject of the verb *paid*. He paid *whom?* He paid *us.*]

When the object is compound, try each pronoun separately. All parts of the compound must be correct for the sentence to be correct.

NONSTANDARD Clem's call surprised her and I. [*Clem's call surprised her* is correct. *Clem's call surprised I* is incorrect. Therefore, *Clem's call surprised her and I* is incorrect. The second pronoun should be *me.*]

STANDARD Clem's call surprised her and **me.**

▶ ORAL PRACTICE 3 **Using Pronouns as Direct Objects**

Read the following sentences aloud, stressing the italicized pronouns.

1. They saw Liang and *me* at the fair.
2. Julia said that she recognized *him* and *me* at once.
3. Has anyone called *her* or *him* lately?
4. They took *us* to the reggae concert.
5. Thelma often visits Charlene and *her*.
6. A dog chased *her* and *me* out of the yard.
7. The search party found Duane and *him* in the woods.
8. Did you ask *them* or *us*?

USAGE

▶ EXERCISE 3   **Choosing Pronouns Used as
Direct Objects**

Choose appropriate pronouns for the blanks in these sentences. Use a variety of pronouns. Do not use *you* or *it*.

1. I found Nina and ___ in the library.
2. Will you help ___ or ___?
3. Sylvia Chu drove Candy and ___ to the movies.
4. We all watched Aaron and ___.
5. These gloves fit both Carl and ___.

20d.   The indirect object of a verb is always in the objective case.

An *indirect object* is a noun or pronoun that tells *to whom* or *for whom* something is done. Pronouns used as indirect objects are in the objective case: *me, him, her, us, them.*

EXAMPLES   The librarian gave **her** a pass.
Molly lent **me** two books.

▶ ORAL
PRACTICE 4   **Using Pronouns as Indirect Objects**

Read each of the following sentences aloud, stressing the italicized pronouns.

1. Mrs. Petratos offered *them* delicious moussaka.
2. Show Yolanda and *her* your snapshots of Chicago.
3. Sara made Dad and *me* mittens and matching scarves.
4. Send Tom and *me* your new address.
5. My parents told *her* and *me* the news.
6. Mrs. Maranjian gave *him* and *her* applications.
7. Tell Willie and *me* the story that you told Erin.
8. The judges awarded *us* the trophy.

▶ EXERCISE 4   **Writing Pronouns Used as
Indirect Objects**

Write appropriate pronouns for the blanks in the following sentences. Use a variety of pronouns.

1. Hassan asked ___ the most difficult question.
2. Alex baked ___ a loaf of banana bread.

3. The teacher handed ____ and ____ the homework assignments.
4. Linda threw ____ the ball.
5. Mr. Young has never told ____ and ____ the real story.
6. Writing stories gives ____ great pleasure.
7. We brought ____ T-shirts from California.
8. Mr. Cruz sent ____ a pen as a graduation gift.
9. My little sister gave ____ an animal carved out of soap.
10. Lee's cousin knitted ____ a sweater.

▶ REVIEW A **Identifying Correct Forms of Pronouns**

Identify the correct pronoun in parentheses for each of the following sentences. Then give its use in the sentence—as *subject, predicate nominative, direct object,* or *indirect object.*

EXAMPLE 1. Brian and (*I, me*) visited the computer fair.
  1. *I—subject*

1. A guide showed (*we, us*) the latest models.
2. She told Brian and (*I, me*) some interesting facts about computer technology.
3. In a short time, we had surprised (*she, her*) and several bystanders with our ability.
4. The new computer wizards were (*we, us*)!
5. Another guide showed Brian and (*I, me*) all kinds of walking machines.
6. (*He, Him*) and his twin sister danced with two robots.
7. The watching crowd and (*they, them*) seemed to enjoy the dance.
8. One robot reached out and touched (*us, we*) with a plastic hand.
9. Brian and (*I, me*) asked our guides how the robots worked.
10. (*They, Them*) patiently explained the control panels.

▶ REVIEW B **Identifying Correct Forms of Pronouns**

Identify the correct pronoun for each pair given in parentheses in the following paragraph.

USAGE

EXAMPLE   My cousin Felicia showed [1] (*I, me*) some photographs
of buildings designed by I. M. Pei.
1. *me*

Felicia, who is studying architecture, told [1] (*I, me*) a little about Pei. [2] (*He, Him*) is a famous American architect who was born in China. In 1935, [3] (*him, he*) came to the United States to study, and in 1954, [4] (*him, he*) was granted citizenship. Pei's reputation grew quickly, and by the 1960s many people easily recognized the structures designed by [5] (*he, him*). His buildings, such as the East Building of the National Gallery of Art in Washington, D.C., are quite distinctive; consequently, many people greatly admire [6] (*they, them*). [7] (*He, Him*) has designed numerous projects in the United States, Europe, and Canada. Did you know that the architect of this glass pyramid at the Louvre is [8] (*him, he*)? Some people don't like the pyramid because [9] (*they, them*) think it looks out of place alongside the buildings that surround it. But Felicia says that Pei has given [10] (*we, us*) a work of art.

20e. The object of a preposition is always in the objective case.

The *object of a preposition* is a noun or pronoun that follows a preposition. Together, a preposition, its object, and any modifiers of that object make up a prepositional phrase.

EXAMPLES   with **me**   before **her**   next to **them**
              for **us**   behind **him**

Drabble reprinted by permission of United Feature Syndicate, Inc.

USAGE

    Errors often occur when the object of a preposition is compound. You can usually figure out the correct pronouns by trying each one separately in the prepositional phrase.

NONSTANDARD   The company sent a letter to her and I. [*The company sent a letter to her* is correct. *The company sent a letter to I* is incorrect. The correct forms of the pronouns are *her* and *me*.]

STANDARD   The company sent a letter to her and **me**.

NOTE: Many people use incorrect pronoun forms with the preposition *between.* You have probably heard phrases like *between he and I* and *between you and they.* These phrases are incorrect. The pronouns are objects of a preposition and should be in the objective case: *between him and me, between you and them.*

☞ **REFERENCE NOTE:** For a list of prepositions, see pages 491–492.

▶ ORAL   **Using Pronouns as Objects of**
    PRACTICE 5   **Prepositions**

Read each of the following sentences aloud, stressing the italicized words.

1. Talk over your problems *with her* and *them*.
2. I addressed cards *to* my mother and *her*.
3. *Between you* and *me*, I am worried *about them*.
4. She is always very polite *to him* and *me*.
5. The coaches rode in a bus *in front of us*.
6. A stray dog was running *toward* Luke and *her*.
7. First prize was shared *by* Jen and *me*.
8. May I play mah-jongg *with you* and *them*?

> EXERCISE 5 **Proofreading a Paragraph for Correct Pronoun Forms**

Identify the personal pronouns in each sentence in the following paragraph. If a pronoun is incorrect, write the correct form. If a pronoun is correct, write C.

EXAMPLE [1] She thinks all of we should have the experience of working at a store checkout counter.
1. *She—C; we—us*

[1] Mrs. Jenkins, the home economics teacher whom Tricia and me admire, told us about the Universal Product Code (UPC) yesterday. [2] All of we have seen the black-striped UPC symbols on nearly everything that we have bought. [3] Mrs. Jenkins showed the other classes and we how to interpret the eleven-digit number in this UPC. [4] Her explained to we that the first digit identifies the product, the next five digits stand for the manufacturer, the next five digits tell things about the product (such as its color and size), and the last digit is a check number that tells the computer if another digit is not correct. [5] Gregory and her found the lesson especially interesting. [6] The two of they had used the code when they worked as clerks in a store last summer.

> REVIEW C **Identifying Correct Pronoun Forms**

For each of the following sentences, choose the correct pronoun in parentheses. Then give its use in the sentence—as *subject, predicate nominative, direct object, indirect object,* or *object of the preposition.*

EXAMPLE 1. Did Alva or (*she, her*) leave a message?
1. *she—subject*

1. I'm positive it was (*they, them*).

USAGE

2. (*He, Him*) and (*I, me*) are working on a special science project.
3. Excuse me, is that package on the table for Mother or for (*I, me*)?
4. No one told Otis or (*I, me*) about the game.
5. I hope that you and (*she, her*) will be able to get there on time.
6. The teacher gave Rosa and (*I, me*) extra math homework.
7. That's (*he, him*) on the red bicycle.
8. Between you and (*I, me*), I like your plan better than George's plan.
9. When are your parents and (*they, them*) coming home?
10. Everyone in the class except (*she, her*) and (*I, me*) had read the selection from the *Mahabharata*.

REVIEW D   **Identifying Correct Pronoun Forms**

Identify the correct pronoun for each pair given in parentheses in the following paragraph.

EXAMPLE   You may not know [1] (*they, them*) by name, but you may recognize these actors in this scene from the movie *Do the Right Thing*.
1. *them*

For many years, actors Ossie Davis and Ruby Dee have entertained [1] (*we, us*) fans of movies and television with their talented performances. My friend Elvin and [2] (*me, I*) like both of [3] (*they, them*) a lot. Did you know that [4] (*they, them*) have been married since 1948? When Davis worked on Broadway, [5] (*he, him*) wrote and starred in *Purlie Victorious*, and critics raved about [6] (*he, him*). More recently, [7] (*him, he*) has appeared on the TV show *Evening Shade*. You might have seen [8] (*she, her*) in the movie *The Jackie Robinson Story*.

What Elvin and [9] (*me, I*) admire most about Davis and Dee is that [10] (*them, they*) are fine performers who actively support civil rights and other humanitarian causes.

▶ EXERCISE 6 **Using Pronouns Correctly**

You are the leader of an ancient or isolated tribe that knows little about modern science. Going about your daily routine, you notice that the sky does not look normal. In fact, it looks as though the sun may disappear. Your people are crying and wailing, for they fear that the world may end. They look to you, their leader, for answers. Luckily, your grandfather told you about the time the sun disappeared when he was a boy. The sun came back again, he told you, but anyone who had looked straight at the darkened sun went blind. Write ten sentences telling your people the story of the darkened sun. Use these pictures and your imagination to tell the story as a folk legend. In your sentences, use ten of the following pronouns: *I, he, she, we, they, me, him, her, us, them, you, it.* Underline the pronouns you use.

EXAMPLES 1. *Kamila looked upon the face of the darkened sun, and he went blind.*
2. *When the sun returned, our ancestors welcomed it back.*

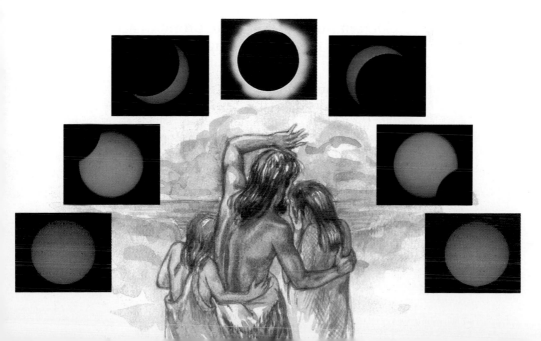

USAGE

Special Pronoun Problems

Who and *Whom*

NOMINATIVE	OBJECTIVE
who	whom
whoever	whomever

NOTE: In spoken English, the use of *whom* is becoming less common. In fact, when you are speaking, you may correctly begin any question with *who* regardless of the grammar of the sentence. In written English, however, you should distinguish between *who* and *whom*. *Who* is used as subject or predicate nominative, and *whom* is used as an object.

20f. The use of *who* or *whom* in a subordinate clause depends on how the pronoun functions in the clause.

When you are choosing between *who* or *whom* in a subordinate clause, follow these steps:

STEP 1: Find the subordinate clause.
STEP 2: Decide how the pronoun is used in the clause—as subject, predicate nominative, object of the verb, or object of a preposition.
STEP 3: Determine the case of the pronoun according to the rules of standard English.
STEP 4: Select the correct form of the pronoun.

EXAMPLE: Do you know (who, whom) she is?
STEP 1: The subordinate clause is *(who, whom) she is.*
STEP 2: In this clause, the subject is *she,* the verb is *is,* and the pronoun is the predicate nominative: *she is (who, whom).*
STEP 3: As predicate nominative, the pronoun is in the nominative case.
STEP 4: The nominative form is *who.*
ANSWER: Do you know **who** she is?

Remember that no words outside the clause affect the case of the pronoun. In the example above, the entire clause is used as a direct object of the verb *do know,* but the pronoun is used as a predicate nominative (nominative case) within the clause.

EXAMPLE: Margaret Mead, *(who, whom)* I read about in several articles, wrote interesting books.

STEP 1: The subordinate clause is *(who, whom) I read about in several articles.*

STEP 2: In this clause, the subject is *I,* and the verb is *read.* The pronoun is the object of the preposition *about: I read about (who, whom).*

STEP 3: The object of a preposition is in the objective case.

STEP 4: The objective form is *whom.*

ANSWER: Margaret Mead, **whom** I read about in several articles, wrote interesting books.

Frequently, *whom* in subordinate clauses is omitted (understood).

EXAMPLES   The woman (whom) I admire most is Dr. Mead.
The woman (whom) I read about is a well-known anthropologist.

ORAL PRACTICE 6   **Using the Pronouns *Who* and *Whom* in Subordinate Clauses**

Read each of the following sentences aloud, stressing the italicized pronouns.

1. Take this book to Eric, *whom* you met yesterday.
2. Mr. Cohen is the man *who* lives next door to us.
3. Can you tell me *who* they are?
4. Toni Morrison is an author *whom* many readers admire.
5. *Whom* Mona finally voted for is a secret.
6. The coach will penalize anyone *who* misses the bus.
7. *Whoever* wins the race will get a prize.
8. The woman to *whom* I was speaking is conducting a survey.

EXERCISE 7   **Classifying Pronouns Used in Subordinate Clauses and Identifying Correct Forms**

For each of the following sentences, choose the correct pronoun in parentheses. Then give its use in the sentence—as a *subject, predicate nominative, direct object, indirect object,* or *object of the preposition.*

EXAMPLE   1. I know (*who, whom*) you are.
           1. *who—predicate nominative*

1. Mrs. James, (*who, whom*) I work for, owns a pet shop in the mall.
2. Is there anyone here (*who, whom*) needs a bus pass?
3. She is the only one (*who, whom*) everybody trusts.
4. Both of the women (*who, whom*) ran for election to the City Council were elected.
5. I helped Mr. Thompson, (*who, whom*) was shingling his porch roof.
6. Eileen couldn't guess (*who, whom*) it was.
7. It was Octavio Paz (*who, whom*) won the Nobel Prize in literature in 1990.
8. Her grandmother, to (*who, whom*) she sent the flowers, won the over-fifty division of the marathon.
9. The author (*who, whom*) you admire is scheduled to visit the local bookstore next Tuesday.
10. Shirley Chisholm, (*who, whom*) we are studying in history class, was the first African American woman elected to Congress.

PICTURE THIS

Long ago, kings and queens kept jesters and clowns around to cheer them up. You are a member of an ancient royal household, and this jester is your friend. One day,

Norman Rockwell, *Jester*, Oil on canvas, from *Saturday Evening Post*, February 11, 1939. Collection of Mrs. G. A. Godwin. Printed by permission of the Norman Rockwell Family Trust. Copyright 1939 the Norman Rockwell Family Trust.

you overhear him and his puppet deep in conversation. What are they saying to each other? Write a short conversation between the two. In your dialogue, include the pronouns *who* and *whom*. Use *who* as a subject or a predicate nominative. Use *whom* as an object of a verb or an object of a preposition. With a hand puppet, you could present the finished dialogue to your class.

Subject: a conversation between a jester and his puppet
Audience: your classmates
Purpose: to entertain

20g. **Pronouns used as appositives are in the same case as the word to which they refer.**

An *appositive* is a noun or pronoun that follows another noun or pronoun to identify or explain it.

EXAMPLES   The winners, **he, she,** and **I,** thanked the committee. [Since *winners* is the subject of the sentence, the pronouns in apposition with it (*he, she, I*) must be in the nominative case.]

Every volunteer except two, **him** and **her,** received an award. [Since *two* is the object of the preposition *except,* the appositives *him* and *her* must be in the objective case.]

The teacher introduced the speakers, Laura and **me.** [Since *speakers* is the direct object of *introduced,* the pronoun *me,* which is in apposition to *speakers,* must be in the objective case.]

To figure out the correct form for a pronoun used with an appositive or as an appositive, read the sentence with only the pronoun.

EXAMPLES   **(*We, Us*) scouts offered to help.** [Omit the appositive, *scouts:* We offered to help.]

Ms. Fernandez asked two students, Stephanie and (*he, him*), to help the librarian. [Omit the direct object, *students:* Ms. Fernandez asked Stephanie and him to help the librarian.]

☞ **REFERENCE NOTE:** For a further discussion of appositives, see pages 556–557.

▶ EXERCISE 8   **Identifying the Correct Pronoun Forms as Appositives**

For each of the following sentences, give the correct form of the pronoun in parentheses.

EXAMPLE   1. The principal named the winners, Julia and (*I, me*).
           1. *me*

1. The coach showed (*we, us*) boys the new uniforms.
2. Our friends, (*she, her*) and Lucas, helped us make the refreshments.
3. All of the class saw the movie except three, Floyd, Ada, and (*I, me*).
4. Mrs. López hired (*we, us*) boys for the summer.
5. (*We, Us*) girls are expert players.
6. Kiole listed her three favorite actors, Emilio Estevez, Tom Cruise, and (*he, him*).
7. Come to the game with (*we, us*) girls.
8. The best singers may be the quartet, Ellen and (*they, them*).
9. I want to go to the concert with two friends, Iola and (*he, him*).
10. The librarian gave the best readers, Craig and (*I, me*), two books.

▶ REVIEW E   **Correcting Pronoun Forms**

For each of the following sentences, choose the correct pronoun in parentheses. Then give its use in the sentence—as *subject, predicate nominative, direct object, indirect object, object of the preposition,* or *appositive.*

EXAMPLE   1. The cyclist gave (*we, us*) a smile as she rode past.
           1. *us—indirect object*

1. Students (*who, whom*) want to help organize the Kamehameha Day celebration should speak to Kai or me.
2. Give these magazines to (*whoever, whomever*) you wish.
3. Don't (*they, them*) know that (*we, us*) students do our best?
4. The candidates, Ralph and (*he, him*), will speak at the rally tomorrow.
5. The community Earth Day planners are (*they, them*).
6. Len and (*I, me*) had planned to watch the laser light show together.
7. Will you pass (*I, me*) the dictionary, please?
8. Whitney Houston, (*who, whom*) I saw in concert, sings many songs that (*I, me*) like.
9. It would be a great help to (*we, us*) beginners if (*they, them*) would give us more time.
10. Visiting Australia is an exciting opportunity for Clay and (*she, her*).

▶ REVIEW F   **Identifying Correct Pronoun Forms**

Choose the correct pronoun from each pair in parentheses in the following paragraph.

EXAMPLE   [1] My sister Angela is one of many women in our society (*who, whom*) use makeup.
          1. *who*

   The use of makeup to enhance female beauty has a longer history than most of [1] (*we, us*) might imagine. In fact, [2] (*we, us*) cosmetic historians must look back to ancient times for the origins of makeup. For example, heavy black eye makeup was worn by the ancient Egyptians, [3] (*who, whom*) originally used it as protection from reflected sunlight. It was [4] (*they, them*) who felt that the eyes were the most important facial feature. Both men and women lined their eyes with a dark liquid called *kohl*, which [5] (*they, them*) applied with a small wooden or ivory stick. As you can see from the statue of Queen Nefertiti, [6] (*she, her*) and her noblewomen used not only *kohl* but other cosmetics as well. To [7] (*they, them*) dark, heavily made up eyes and rosy red lips were the marks of female beauty. European noblewomen in the Middle Ages and the Renaissance wanted to emphasize their pale skin, so [8] (*them, they*) dusted their faces with chalk-white powder. It was Queen Elizabeth I, a monarch like Nefertiti, [9] (*who, whom*) set this style in the English court. Although we might think that [10] (*them, they*) look strange today, both Nefertiti and Queen Elizabeth I were making themselves beautiful according to the fashion of their times.

The Granger Collection, New York.

The Pronoun in an Incomplete Construction

Notice how pronouns change the meaning of sentences with incomplete constructions.

EXAMPLES   Everyone knows that you like Jo better than **I**.
Everyone knows that you like Jo better than **me**.

In the first sentence above, the nominative case pronoun *I* is the subject of an understood verb: *Everyone knows that you like Jo better than I [like Jo].* In the second example sentence, the objective case pronoun *me* is the object of the understood verb: *Everyone knows that you like Jo better than [you like] me.*

The case of the pronoun depends upon how the omitted part of the sentence would be completed.

20h. After *than* and *as* introducing an incomplete construction, use the form of the pronoun that would be correct if the construction were completed.

EXAMPLES I wrote you more often than **he** [wrote you].
I wrote you more often than [I wrote] **him.**

Did you help Ada as much as **I** [helped Ada]?
Did you help Ada as much as [you helped] **me?**

EXERCISE 9 ## Completing Incomplete Constructions and Classifying Pronoun Forms

Beginning with the *than* or *as,* write the understood clause for each sentence, using the correct form of the pronoun. Then, tell whether the pronoun in the completed clause is a *subject* or an *object.* [Note: Some items may have more than one correct answer.]

EXAMPLE   1. Kim was as surprised as (*I, me*).
1. *as I was—subject*

1. Justin plays the guitar better than (*I, me*).
2. The story mystified him as well as (*we, us*).
3. Is your sister older than (*he, him*)?
4. Have they studied as long as (*we, us*)?
5. We have known him longer than (*she, her*).
6. Are you more creative than (*he, him*)?
7. Did you read as much as (*I, me*)?
8. I like René better than (*they, them*).
9. Many people are less fortunate than (*we, us*).
10. Are you as optimistic as (*she, her*)?

Inexact Pronoun Reference

20i. A pronoun should always refer clearly to its antecedent.

Using a pronoun that refers to either of two antecedents produces an *ambiguous reference.*

INEXACT   My uncle called my brother after he won the relay.
[Who won the relay, my uncle or my brother?]
EXACT   After my brother won the relay, my uncle called him.
EXACT   After my uncle won the relay, he called my brother.

Using the pronouns *it, this, that, such,* and *which* to refer to a general idea rather than to a specific antecedent produces a *general reference.*

USAGE

INEXACT   The ski jumper is scheduled to compete today. That explains why he's been practicing.

EXACT   The ski jumper has been practicing because he is scheduled to compete today.

Suggesting a word or idea without actually stating it can produce a *weak reference.*

INEXACT   Paul likes many of the photographs I have taken; he thinks I should choose this as my profession.

EXACT   Paul likes many of the photographs I have taken; he thinks I should choose photography as my profession.

An *indefinite reference* occurs when a pronoun (often *it, they,* or *you*) refers to no particular person or thing.

INEXACT   In the book it explains how cells divide.

EXACT   The book explains how cells divide.

NOTE: Familiar expressions such as *it seems as though . . . , it is raining,* and *it's early* are correct even though they contain inexact pronoun references. In these cases, the antecedents to *it* are commonly understood to be weather, time, and so forth.

▶ EXERCISE 10   **Correcting Inexact Pronoun References**

Revise each of the following sentences, correcting each inexact pronoun reference.

EXAMPLE   1. Have you ever been physically unable to prepare meals for yourself? That can be a serious problem.
           1. *Being physically unable to prepare meals for yourself can be a serious problem.*

1. Older persons, people with disabilities, and people who are ill sometimes cannot prepare meals for themselves, which is when Meals on Wheels can help.
2. Meals on Wheels is an organization in which they arrange to have meals delivered to people's homes.
3. As a nonprofit organization, Meals on Wheels has a limited budget, which is why it relies on volunteers.
4. Many businesses, churches, clubs, and organizations supply volunteers, and they contribute money.
5. People who receive services provided by Meals on Wheels usually help to pay for these services, but it's voluntary and based on a person's ability to pay.
6. In some Meals on Wheels organizations, they offer clients a variety of services.

7. Grocery shopping is a service provided to clients by volunteers who purchase and then deliver them.
8. Some clients depend on volunteers for rides when they have appointments and errands to run.
9. To lift their spirits, some volunteers regularly call clients on the phone; other volunteers help clients by performing minor home safety repairs.
10. Volunteers not only provide needed services but also often form personal bonds with their clients; that is why you may want to volunteer at a local Meals on Wheels.

▶ REVIEW G   **Writing Sentences with Pronouns**

The director of the local animal shelter has asked you to write a short brochure that will be mailed to potential contributors. Write ten sentences for the brochure, using the following words and phrases.

EXAMPLE   1. as much as she
        1. *Our mayor believes in helping animals, and I hope that you will want to help them as much as she.*

1. who
2. whom
3. we members
4. us members
5. you and I

6. you and me
7. as much as she
8. as well as him
9. more than I
10. more than me

Review: Posttest

A. Correcting Pronoun Forms

If a pronoun is used incorrectly, write the correct form of the pronoun. If the sentence is correct, write *C*.

EXAMPLE   1. This arrangement is strictly between Carl and I.
        1. *me*

1. The author spoke to us students of the history class about Slavic culture in Eastern Europe.
2. During the Olympic trials, every diver except she received a low score from the judges.

3. The instructor, who seemed nervous during the show, was proud of Lani's performance.
4. It couldn't have been her.
5. Van is more energetic than me.
6. Rick couldn't spot Maura and I in the crowd at the fair.
7. Tyrone and he are playing backgammon at Regina's house.
8. Laura handed a copy of her new book to Darla.
9. Angie's neighbors, Mrs. Brandt and he, helped plant the tree.
10. How soon will they announce who the finalists are?

B. Proofreading a Paragraph for Correct Pronoun Forms

Some of the sentences in the following paragraph contain pronouns that have been used incorrectly. If the sentence is correct, write *C*. If the form of a pronoun is incorrect, write the correct form.

EXAMPLE   [1] To Velma and I, Dizzy Dean is one of the greatest baseball players of all time.
1. *me*

[11] There never has been another baseball player like him. [12] Fans still talk about he and his teammates. [13] Dean played for the St. Louis Cardinals, to who his fastball was a great help, especially during the 1934 World Series. [14] Dean was such a character that his fans never knew what crazy notion might come to he during games. [15] He always had an air of confidence about himself, too, which added to his popularity. [16] A boss once talked about his bragging to Dean, who glibly replied, "'Tain't braggin' if you kin really do it!" [17] When Dean became a sportscaster, him and his informal speech appealed to fans. [18] He liked watching baseball games and reporting on they. [19] A big honor for him was being elected to baseball's Hall of Fame. [20] The Dizzy Dean Museum in Jackson, Mississippi, is a good place for we fans to find out more about Dean's career.

21 USING MODIFIERS CORRECTLY

Comparison and Placement

Diagnostic Test

A. Correcting Forms of Modifiers

For each of the following sentences, write the error in comparison, followed by the correct form. If the sentence is correct, write C.

EXAMPLE   1. His problem is more worse than yours.
          1. *more worse—worse*

1. Which did you like best, the book or the movie?
2. The sun is brighter than anything in our solar system.
3. The tomatoes from our garden taste sweeter than those from the store.
4. This is the most nicest surprise I've ever had in my entire life!
5. Raymond likes my brother more than you.

6. Did you know that the Nile is longer than any river in the world?
7. The price of apples is lower than grapes.
8. Don't you feel more better now that you've had a rest?
9. Trees growing near the ocean are often much smaller than in more protected areas.
10. Which route do you think is better, upstream, downstream, or overland?

B. Correcting Dangling and Misplaced Modifiers

Each of the following sentences contains either a dangling or a misplaced modifier. Rewrite each sentence so that it is clear and correct.

EXAMPLE   1. Every morning that young girl walks her dog in a jogging outfit.
　　　　　 1. *Every morning that young girl in a jogging outfit walks her dog.*

11. Alone, the hours before dawn seemed to drag on endlessly.
12. To paint miniatures, patience and a steady hand are helpful.
13. Running the last lap of the race, my calf muscle cramped, and the other runners passed me.
14. In different parts of the world, we have read about unusual customs.
15. A tree was destroyed by a bulldozer that was almost two hundred years old.
16. Sharon relaxed in the sun and watched her fishing line happily whistling a tune.
17. The prisoners were caught by the police trying to escape from jail.
18. Together, the project can be completed before the end of this week.
19. Almost hidden under the pile of old books, Janelle saw the letter.
20. The mayor pledged that he would build more parks at the political rally.

Comparison of Modifiers

A *modifier* describes or limits the meaning of another word. There are two kinds of modifiers: *adjectives* and *adverbs.* Adjectives state qualities of nouns or pronouns. Adverbs modify verbs, adjectives, and adverbs.

Adjectives are used to compare one noun with another noun that has the same quality.

EXAMPLE   This beach is **sandier** than that one.

Adverbs are used to make comparisons between verbs.

EXAMPLE   I changed into my bathing suit **quickly,** but Lois changed into hers even **more quickly**.

21a.   The forms of modifiers change when they are used to show comparison.

There are three degrees of comparison: *positive, comparative,* and *superlative.*

POSITIVE	COMPARATIVE	SUPERLATIVE
young	younger	youngest
fearful	more fearful	most fearful
rapidly	more rapidly	most rapidly
bad	worse	worst
good	better	best

Regular Comparison

(1) A one-syllable modifier regularly forms its comparative and superlative degrees by adding *−er* and *−est.*

POSITIVE	COMPARATIVE	SUPERLATIVE
low	lower	lowest
large	larger	largest
deep	deeper	deepest

USAGE

(2) Some two-syllable modifiers form their comparative and superlative degrees by adding *–er* **and** *–est.* **Other two-syllable modifiers form their comparative and superlative degrees with** *more* **and** *most.*

POSITIVE	COMPARATIVE	SUPERLATIVE
gentle	gentler	gentlest
lovely	lovelier	loveliest
careful	more careful	most careful
slowly	more slowly	most slowly

☞ **REFERENCE NOTE:** For guidelines on how to spell comparative and superlative forms correctly, see pages 840–843.

NOTE: Some two-syllable modifiers may take either *–er, –est* or *more, most: common, commoner, commonest* or *common, more common, most common.*

If you are unsure of how a two-syllable modifier is compared, look in an unabridged dictionary.

▶ EXERCISE 1 **Spelling Comparative and Superlative Forms**

Give the forms for the comparative and superlative degrees of the following words.

EXAMPLES 1. bright   2. quickly
          1. *brighter, brightest*   2. *more quickly, most quickly*

1. fast   **3.** happy   **5.** simple   **7.** safe   **9.** anxious
2. soon   **4.** careful **6.** hazy   **8.** wisely   **10.** pretty

(3) Modifiers that have more than two syllables form their comparative and superlative degrees with *more* **and** *most.*

POSITIVE	COMPARATIVE	SUPERLATIVE
energetic	more energetic	most energetic
significantly	more significantly	most significantly

> ORAL
> PRACTICE 1

Using Comparative and Superlative Forms

Give the comparative and superlative degrees of the following words.

1. original
2. appropriately
3. reasonably
4. pessimistic
5. important
6. confident

(4) Modifiers that indicate less of a quality use the word *less* or *least* before the modifier.

POSITIVE	COMPARATIVE	SUPERLATIVE
helpful	less helpful	least helpful
frequently	less frequently	least frequently

> ORAL
> PRACTICE 2

Using Comparisons to Indicate Less or Least of a Quality

Give the comparisons to indicate *less* and *least* of the six words listed in Oral Practice 1.

Irregular Comparison

Some modifiers do not follow the regular methods of forming their comparative and superlative degrees.

POSITIVE	COMPARATIVE	SUPERLATIVE
bad	worse	worst
good/well	better	best
many/much	more	most

NOTE: Do not add the *–er*, *–est* or *more, most* forms to irregularly compared forms: *worse*, not *worser* or *more worse*.

> EXERCISE 2

Using Comparative and Superlative Forms

For the blank in each of the following sentences, write the correct form of the word in italics before that sentence.

EXAMPLE 1. *bad* My notebook looks ____ than Joshua's.
1. *worse*

1. *well* I can skate ____ now than I could last year.
2. *many* She caught the ____ fish of anyone in our group.
3. *bad* That is the ____ movie I have ever seen.
4. *much* We have ____ homework than we had last week.
5. *good* Felicia has the ____ attendance record of anyone.
6. *many* Are there ____ plays than short stories in your literature book?
7. *good* Tyrone is the ____ pitcher on our baseball team this year.
8. *much* Of the three groups of volunteers, our group cleaned up the ____ litter.
9. *good* Both of the poems were well written, but I thought that Sarah's was ____ than his.
10. *bad* My cold is ____ than hers.

▶ REVIEW A **Writing Comparative and Superlative Forms**

Write the comparative and superlative forms of the following modifiers. If you are unsure about the forms of a two-syllable modifier, look up the modifier in an unabridged dictionary.

EXAMPLE 1. meaningful
1. *more meaningful, most meaningful*

1. bad
2. good
3. early
4. many
5. fuzzy
6. loose
7. well
8. noisy
9. patiently
10. graceful

▶ EXERCISE 3 **Proofreading Sentences for Correct Comparative and Superlative Forms**

Identify the comparative and superlative forms of the modifiers in the following sentences. If the form is correct, write C. If the form of a modifier is wrong, write the correct form.

EXAMPLE 1. Gypsies make up one of Europe's interestingest
cultures.
  1. *interestingest—most interesting*

1. Gypsies are more commonly found in Eastern Europe than anywhere else in the world.
2. Although most Gypsies live in Romania, Hungary, and other European countries, the culture of the Gypsies suggests that they migrated there from other lands.
3. The bestest theory about the Gypsies' origin is that they came from India.
4. As the photograph below shows, Gypsies wear some of their colorfulest traditional clothing for their celebrations.
5. They also brighten their lives with the most wildest violin music they can play and dance to.

6. On the move more oftener than most other Europeans, they used to travel in wagons like the one pictured here.
7. Gypsies usually live in groups, with the larger group consisting of several hundred families.
8. The most high law in Gypsy society is the *kris,* a system of rules based on the Gypsies' religious beliefs.
9. Gypsies generally earn their living as migrant agricultural workers and, less frequently, as entertainers.
10. Although change has come slowlier to these wanderers than to most other ethnic groups in Europe, some Gypsies now are settling in communities.

USAGE

Use of Comparative and Superlative Forms

21b. Use the comparative degree when comparing two things. Use the superlative degree when comparing more than two.

COMPARATIVE   Writing mysteries seems **more challenging** than writing nonfiction.

In my opinion, Dorothy L. Sayers is a **better** writer than Agatha Christie.

SUPERLATIVE   This is the **best** Sherlock Holmes story that I have ever read.

Writing a mystery story is the **most challenging** assignment I've had so far.

NOTE: In everyday conversation, people sometimes use the superlative degree in comparing two things: *Put your best foot forward.*

EXERCISE 4   **Identifying Correct Comparative and Superlative Forms**

Each of the following sentences contains a comparative or superlative modifier. If the form is correct for the number of items compared, write *C*. If the wrong form is used, write the correct form.

EXAMPLE   1. Nina's report on Native Americans' star legends was the more interesting report in the class.
    1. *most interesting*

1. Although Nina and I both researched our reports carefully, her report was the most thorough one.
2. The Native Americans' stories about the stars and the sky are even better than the Greek myths, in my opinion.
3. Nina told two dozen stories, but the six myths she told about the cluster of stars known as the Pleiades are the more fascinating.
4. The stranger tale, which is from the Monache Indians of central California, relates how a little girl and six women who wouldn't give up eating onions became the Pleiades.
5. The scariest of the tales is the Skidi Pawnee myth about six brothers and an adopted sister who fight the Rolling Skull.

6. That story was not only the more interesting but also the longer legend that Nina told.
7. Of all the earthly creatures in the stories Nina told, Coyote is perhaps the more important.
8. In fact, people often play a least important role than Coyote plays in some stories.
9. After class, I told Nina that compared with my report, hers was the best.
10. She said that telling the stories was easier than finding them.

▶ EXERCISE 5   **Using Modifiers Correctly**

Your pen pal in Monaco, one of the smallest countries in the world, has written to you that his family may be moving to the United States and needs some information about major cities. You have done some research and have made this chart showing the ten largest cities in the United States. Using the chart and what you know about these and other cities in the United States, write a short letter to your friend. In your letter, use at least five comparative modifiers and five superlative modifiers. Be sure to use the proper forms of modifiers and to make your comparisons clear.

EXAMPLE   *Dear Louis,*

I'm excited that you may move here! Our biggest city, of course, is New York, which has a population of more than seven million.

Largest Cities in the United States	
City	Population
New York, NY	7,332,564
Los Angeles	3,485,398
Chicago	2,783,726
Houston	1,630,553
Philadelphia	1,585,577
San Diego	1,110,549
Detroit	1,027,974
Dallas	1,006,877
Phoenix	983,403
San Antonio	935,933

21c. Include the word *other* or *else* when comparing one thing with others that belong in the same group.

NONSTANDARD   Ruth is more agile than any member of her gymnastics team. [Ruth is a member of her team, and she cannot be more agile than herself. The word *other* should be added.]

STANDARD   Ruth is more agile than any **other** member of her gymnastics team.

NONSTANDARD   Carlos ran faster than everyone. [The word *everyone* includes all people, and Carlos is a person. Since he cannot run faster than himself, the word *else* should be added.]

STANDARD   Carlos ran faster than everyone **else.**

☞ **REFERENCE NOTE:** For a discussion of standard and nonstandard English, see pages 449–450.

ORAL PRACTICE 3   **Using Comparisons Correctly**

Read the following sentences aloud, stressing the italicized words.

1. My grandmother is wiser than anyone *else* I know.
2. My sister has more cassettes than anyone *else* in the family.
3. Your report is more imaginative than any *other* report submitted so far.
4. Brent can pass better than anyone *else* on the team.
5. This ring is more valuable than any *other* piece of jewelry I own.

EXERCISE 6   **Revising Faulty Comparisons**

Revise each of the following sentences by adding *other* or *else*.

EXAMPLE   1. Rodney spells better than anyone in his class.
         1. *Rodney spells better than anyone else in his class.*

1. Today has been colder than any day this year.
2. Kumiko eats more slowly than anybody in this cafeteria.

USAGE

3. Flying is faster than any type of travel.
4. My sunflowers grew taller than any flowers I planted this year.
5. Luís enjoys swimming more than anything.

21d. Avoid double comparisons.

A *double comparison* is incorrect because it contains both *–er* and *more* or *–est* and *most.*

NONSTANDARD	She is **more** funnier than he.
STANDARD	She is **funnier** than he.

NONSTANDARD	This is the **most** cheapest bicycle in the store.
STANDARD	This is the **cheapest** bicycle in the store.

▶ EXERCISE 7   **Revising Modifiers by Eliminating Double Comparisons**

Write each incorrect modifier in the following sentences. Then revise the modifier by crossing out the unnecessary part to eliminate the double comparison.

EXAMPLE   1. Today is more colder than yesterday.
            1. ~~more~~ colder

1. That is the most softest sweater that I have ever had.
2. You seem to be trying more harder in school this year.
3. She is the most fastest runner on the team.
4. Illustrations help make the explanations more clearer to the readers.
5. Georgia is more larger in area than any other state east of the Mississippi.

21e. Be sure your comparisons are clear.

UNCLEAR	The average temperature in Dallas is higher than Spokane. [This sentence incorrectly compares a temperature to a city.]
CLEAR	The average temperature in Dallas is higher than the average temperature in Spokane.

UNCLEAR	Is the skin of the rhinoceros harder than the alligator?
CLEAR	Is the skin of the rhinoceros harder than the skin of the alligator?

USAGE

Both parts of an incomplete comparison should be stated if there is any chance of misunderstanding.

UNCLEAR	I visited her more than Elise.
CLEAR	I visited her more than I visited Elise.
CLEAR	I visited her more than Elise visited her.

WRITING APPLICATION

Using Comparative and Superlative Forms of Modifiers

Each day, people make decisions about what to buy or what to do. They base their decisions on comparisons. For instance, they may look for *more reliable* cars, *less expensive* shoes, the *fastest* rollercoaster, or the *most exciting* movie. Accurate comparisons help people express exactly what they mean.

INACCURATE	My brother is more taller than anyone I know.
ACCURATE	My brother is **taller** than anyone **else** I know.

or

My brother is the **tallest** person I know.

▶ WRITING ACTIVITY

As the restaurant critic for *Good Food* magazine, you always give a year-end summary of the best eateries and their food. Discuss your choices in a paragraph, using five comparative and five superlative forms of adjectives and adverbs.

Prewriting Using either real or imaginary restaurants, make a list of several places and their best dishes. Think of some ways to compare the restaurants (food, atmosphere, service, price). If your local paper has a food columnist, you may want to read some of his or her restaurant reviews to get ideas about what to say.

Writing As you write your first draft, use your list to help you make accurate comparisons.

Evaluating and Revising   Read your paragraph to a class-mate to see if your comparisons are clearly stated. Revise any comparisons that are confusing. Pay special attention to adjectives and adverbs that have irregular comparative forms. Be sure, too, that you have correctly used the word *other* when comparing one restaurant or dish with others in the same group.

 Proofreading and Publishing   As you correct any mistakes in spelling, grammar, and punctuation, pay special attention to the spelling of comparative and superlative forms made by adding –*er* and –*est*. You and your classmates could prepare a newcomer's guide to local restaurants. Decide how you want the guide to look. Then, type it and make photocopies or input it on a computer. Give copies of your guide to new students and their families.

 REVIEW B   **Revising Sentences in a Paragraph by Correcting Modifiers**

Each sentence in the following paragraph has at least one incorrect use of a comparative or superlative modifier. Some sentences contain more than one error. Correct each error or unclear comparison.

EXAMPLE   [1] Eagles are widely regarded as more majestic than any bird in the world.
     1. *Eagles are widely regarded as more majestic than any other bird in the world.*

[1] Many cultures have revered the eagle as one of their most strongest symbols of bravery and power. [2] In the United States, early colonial leaders thought that the image of the bald eagle would be a more better symbol for their new country than the turkey. [3] Benjamin Franklin had argued that the turkey was the most practical choice of the two birds, but he was outvoted. [4] I think most people would agree that the eagle is the best choice. [5] Even though eagles are not more larger than all birds, they are

among the more effective hunters and fliers. [6] As you can see from these pictures, the eagle's sharp beak and long claws are more powerful than the turkey. [7] And I think the eagle is more handsomer, too.

Dangling Modifiers

21f. A modifying word, phrase, or clause that does not clearly and sensibly modify a word or a group of words in a sentence is a *dangling modifier.*

DANGLING	Together, the litter along the highway was picked up, bagged, and hauled away.
CORRECT	Together, we picked up, bagged, and hauled away the litter along the highway.

When a modifying phrase containing a verbal comes at the beginning of a sentence, the phrase is followed by a comma. Immediately after that comma should come the word that the phrase modifies.

DANGLING	Jogging in the park, a rabbit peered out at me from the underbrush.
CORRECT	Jogging in the park, I saw a rabbit peering out from the underbrush.
DANGLING	To understand Countee Cullen's poetry, some knowledge of figurative language is necessary.
CORRECT	To understand Countee Cullen's poetry, **the reader** needs some knowledge of figurative language.

DANGLING   Equipped with even the best gear, the rock cliff was difficult to climb.

CORRECT   Equipped with even the best gear, the **mountaineers** had difficulty climbing the rock cliff.

A sentence may appear to have a dangling modifier when *you* is the understood subject. In such cases, the modifier is not dangling; instead, it is modifying the understood subject.

EXAMPLE   To find the correct spelling, (you) look up the word in a dictionary.

☞ **REFERENCE NOTE:** For more information on verbals and verbal phrases, see pages 541–556. For more information about understood subjects, see page 513.

▶ EXERCISE 8   **Writing Sentences with Introductory Modifiers**

Write complete sentences, using the following list of introductory modifiers.

EXAMPLE   1. Having solved one problem,
            1. *Having solved one problem, Joe Harris found that another awaited him.*

1. Leaping from branch to branch,
2. Suddenly,
3. While eating our lunch,
4. Surrounded by the cheering crowd,
5. To make sure he wouldn't be late,

Correcting Dangling Modifiers

To correct a dangling modifier, rearrange the words in the sentence, and add or change words to make the meaning logical and clear.

DANGLING   To become a physicist, years of study and research are required.

CORRECT   To become a physicist, **you** [*or* a person] must spend years studying and doing research.

or

If you want to become a physicist, **you** must spend years studying and doing research.

USAGE

DANGLING   While lighting the birthday candles, the cake started to crumble.

CORRECT   While **I was** lighting the birthday candles, the cake started to crumble.

or

While lighting the birthday candles, **I noticed** the cake **starting** to crumble.

▶ EXERCISE 9   **Revising Sentences by Eliminating Dangling Modifiers**

Most of the following sentences contain dangling modifiers. If a sentence is correct, write *C* after the corresponding number. If it is incorrect, revise the sentence to eliminate the dangling modifier.

EXAMPLE   1. While mopping the kitchen, my baby brother woke up from his nap.

1. *While I was mopping the kitchen, my baby brother woke up from his nap.*

1. Walking through the main gate, the swimming pool lies to your right.
2. Lost, the small village was a more than welcome sight.
3. To earn spending money, Mother gave me a job addressing envelopes.
4. After studying hard, a long walk can be refreshing.
5. While walking in the woods, the sound of singing birds is an enjoyable experience.
6. To understand the meaning of a sentence, even the little words can be important.
7. To become a great athlete, you need dedication and self-discipline.
8. Standing on the beach, a school of dolphins suddenly appeared.
9. After winning the last game of the season, the celebration lasted nearly all night.
10. Tired and sore, the job was finally finished.

▶ EXERCISE 10   **Revising Sentences by Eliminating Dangling Modifiers**

Each of the following sentences contains a dangling modifier. Revise each sentence to eliminate the problem.

EXAMPLE
1. While climbing the tower, Niagara Falls looked magnificent to us.
1. *While we were climbing the tower, Niagara Falls looked magnificent.*

or

1. *While climbing the tower, we thought Niagara Falls looked magnificent.*

1. Trying to see and do everything around Niagara Falls, the days passed quickly.
2. While riding in a tour boat called the *Maid of the Mist,* the spray from the base of the falls drenched us.
3. Roaring constantly, an awesome amount of power is generated.
4. After walking through Queen Victoria Park, a hearty lunch at the restaurant was refreshing.
5. To see the waterfalls at their most beautiful, a visit at night when they are illuminated was recommended by the tour guide.

Misplaced Modifiers

21g. A word, phrase, or clause that sounds awkward because it modifies the wrong word or group of words is a *misplaced modifier.*

Modifying words, phrases, and clauses should be placed as near as possible to the words they modify.

MISPLACED — My cousin's dog was chasing the geese, yapping and barking.

CORRECT — **Yapping and barking,** my cousin's dog was chasing the geese.

MISPLACED — Born eight weeks ago, we adopted one of the beagle puppies.

CORRECT — We adopted one of the beagle puppies **born eight weeks ago.**

MISPLACED — I read about the bank robbers who were captured in this morning's paper.

CORRECT — I read **in this morning's paper** about the bank robbers who were captured.

▶ EXERCISE 11   **Revising Sentences by Correcting Misplaced Modifiers**

Revise the following sentences so that they make sense. Be sure that you do not misplace another modifier in revising a sentence.

1. Michiko went outside to trim the bonsai trees with Uncle Saburo.
2. I could see the scouts marching over the hill through my binoculars.
3. As a child, my grandfather taught me how to make tortillas.
4. One advertiser handed out roses to customers with dollar bills pinned to them.
5. I borrowed a radio from my sister with a weather band.
6. Did you look for a collection of hats worn by your grandmother in the attic?
7. Our cat was waiting on the front porch for us to come home patiently.
8. She ate two peaches and a plate of strawberries watching TV.
9. In a tank at the aquarium, we watched the seals play.
10. We gave the boxes of cereal to the children with prizes inside.

Misplaced Clause Modifiers

Adjective clauses and adverb clauses should be placed where they are clearly linked to the words they modify.

MISPLACED   I bought a new lock for my bicycle that has simple a combination.

CORRECT   I bought a new lock that has a simple combination for my bicycle.

To correct misplaced clauses, place the modifying clause as close as possible to the word or words that it modifies.

MISPLACED   There is a car in the garage that has only one door and no windshield.

CORRECT   In the garage, there is a car that has only one door and no windshield.

MISPLACED	The money and tickets are still in my wallet that I meant to return to you.
CORRECT	The money and tickets that I meant to return to you are still in my wallet.

☞ **REFERENCE NOTE:** For more information on phrase and clause modifiers, see Chapters 16 and 17.

EXERCISE 12 ## Revising Sentences by Correcting Misplaced Clauses

Revise each of the following sentences, placing the misplaced clause near the word it modifies. Remember to use a comma after introductory verbal phrases.

1. Birds are kept away by scarecrows, which eat seeds.
2. The disabled truck is now blocking the overpass that suddenly went out of control.
3. There was a bird in the tree that had a strange-looking beak.
4. A huge dog chased me as I rode my bicycle that was growling and barking loudly.
5. An old log sat on the kitchen table that was covered with moss.
6. We thanked the clerk at the post office that had helped us with our overseas packages.
7. There are several books on our shelves that were written by Rolando Hinojosa-Smith.
8. A boy was standing at the bus stop that looked remarkably like my cousin.
9. She crossed the river on a ferry, which was more than a mile wide.
10. There is a flower garden behind the shed that is planted with prize-winning dahlias.

REVIEW C ## Revising Sentences by Correcting Dangling and Misplaced Modifiers

Revise each of the following sentences by placing the dangling or misplaced modifier near the word it modifies or by rephrasing the sentence.

1. Awaking from a nap, the island of Puerto Rico came into view through my airplane window.

USAGE

2. Our guide was waiting to take us to our hotel inside the airport terminal.
3. To understand the guide's Spanglish dialect, some knowledge of both Spanish and English proved to be helpful.
4. Driving along the Panoramic Route, the scenery was breathtaking!
5. We stopped for lunch at a stall along the road that was made from palm branches.
6. Hungry, the spicy rice and beans were delicious.
7. We bought souvenir rocks from a young boy decorated with island scenes.
8. Look at that strange fish in the water that is puffing up!
9. Anxious to shower and unpack, our hotel room was the next stop.
10. To fully appreciate all the island had to offer, more time was needed.

▶ REVIEW D   **Using Modifying Phrases and Clauses Correctly**

You are writing a science fiction story. To help you get started, you have jotted down the following list of phrases and clauses:

  roaring and breathing fire as it approached
  shooting up into the night sky
  squashed beneath the huge spaceship
  that had a head on each finger
  whether they had come in peace
  to communicate with the aliens
  which seemed to be everywhere
  in wonder at what they were seeing
  to defend themselves from the strange creatures
  that hissed when anyone moved

Now you can use some of these ideas to start the story. Use five of the phrases and clauses correctly, making sure that you don't have any dangling or misplaced modifiers.

EXAMPLE   to communicate with the aliens
                   To communicate with the aliens, Martin tried playing
                   samba music at half-speed.

Review: Posttest

A. Revising Sentences by Correcting Modifiers

Each of the following sentences contains at least one error in the use of modifiers: mistakes in comparisons, or dangling or misplaced modifiers. Revise each sentence so that it is clear and correct.

EXAMPLE   1. When traveling through Scotland, I discovered that stories about monsters were more popular than any kind of story.
   1. *When traveling through Scotland, I discovered that stories about monsters were more popular than any other kind of story.*

1. Having received a great deal of publicity, I had already read several articles about the so-called Loch Ness monster.
2. One article described how a young veterinary student spotted the monster who was named Arthur Grant.
3. While cycling on a road near the shore of Loch Ness one day, Grant came upon the most strangest creature he had ever seen.
4. Cycling closer, the monster took two great leaps and plunged into the lake.
5. Numerous theories have been discussed about the origin and identity of the monster in the local newspapers.
6. Of all the proposed theories, the better and more fascinating one was that the monster must be a freshwater species of sea serpent.
7. Having found a huge, dead creature on the shore of the lake in 1942, the mystery of the monster was thought to be solved finally.
8. One famous photograph of the monster has recently been revealed to be a hoax, which had seemed to confirm the creature's existence.
9. Doubtful, stories about the Loch Ness monster have always struck some people as unbelievable.
10. However, people continue to report seeing the monster, perhaps more than any mysterious creature.

USAGE

B. Using Modifiers Correctly in a Paragraph

Most of the sentences in the following paragraph have mistakes in the use of modifiers. Revise each incorrect sentence to correct these errors. If a sentence is correct, write C.

[11] Kay has a better understanding of both solar and geothermal energy than anyone I know. [12] Yoko isn't sure she agrees, but I have talked with Kay more than Yoko. [13] Kay thinks that solar energy is the best of the two methods for generating power. [14] She claims that the energy from the sun will soon be more easy to harness than geothermal energy. [15] Arguing that the sun's energy could also be less expensive to use, Kay says that more research into solar energy is needed. [16] Yoko disagrees and thinks that geothermal energy is more cheaper than solar energy. [17] She told me that for centuries people in other countries have been using geothermal energy, such as Iceland and Japan. [18] However, she added that geothermal energy is less well known than any source of power in our country. [19] Although often ignored in the United States, Yoko feels that geothermal energy has already proven itself to be safe and efficient. [20] Unconvinced, both points of view seem to me to offer promising new sources of energy.

22 A GLOSSARY OF USAGE

Common Usage Problems

Diagnostic Test

A. Solving Common Usage Problems

In each of the following sets of expressions, one expression contains an error in usage. First, write the letter of each incorrect expression. Then, write the correct expression after it.

EXAMPLE 1. **a.** between the two of us **b.** not going anywheres
   c. the woman whom I saw
   1. *b. not going anywhere*

1. **a.** among the three puppies **b.** where he lives at
   c. less water in the pond
2. **a.** will effect her health **b.** a short way to go
   c. raised the rent
3. **a.** traveled a long ways **b.** two others besides her
   c. could have called
4. **a.** that type of wrench **b.** accepted the trophy
   c. learned him how to swim

5. **a.** busted a jar **b.** runs well **c.** haven't any
6. **a.** a look at them stars **b.** improved somewhat
   c. lions, tigers, bears, etc.
7. **a.** as fast as we can **b.** without I say so
   c. have but one hour
8. **a.** all students except her **b.** a person that I trust
   c. read in the newspaper where
9. **a.** in an hour **b.** should of asked
   c. fell off the wall
10. **a.** these kind of shoes **b.** ought to wait his turn
    c. discovered the North Pole

B. Proofreading a Paragraph for Standard Usage

The following paragraph contains ten errors in English usage. Copy the error or errors in each numbered sentence, and write the correct usage after it.

EXAMPLE **[1]** I started wondering about left-handedness because of that there left-handed boy which is in my class.

1. *that there—that; which—who* (or *that*)

[11] Please bring me a dictionary so that I can look up what *left-handed* means, like I started to do earlier. **[12]** *Left-handedness* is where a person uses the left hand more then the right hand. **[13]** It don't matter which hand a person mainly uses because a left-hander functions just as good as a right-hander does. **[14]** Being left-handed couldn't hardly be a handicap since the great artists Leonardo da Vinci and Michelangelo were left-handed. **[15]** Of course, less people, only about ten percent of the population, are left-handed. **[16]** Scientists ain't certain, but they think that left-handedness is determined by which side of the brain is more dominant in a individual. **[17]** Some scientists they say that the left side of the brain is more dominant in a right-handed person and that the right side of the brain is more dominant in a left-handed person.

This chapter provides a compact glossary of common problems in English usage. You will notice that some examples are labeled *standard* or *nonstandard*. ***Standard English*** is the most widely accepted variety of English. It is the language used in most books, newspapers, and magazines. ***Nonstandard English*** is language that doesn't follow the rules and guidelines of standard English. For more discussion of standard and nonstandard English, see pages 449–454.

☞ REFERENCE NOTE: Many points of usage covered in this glossary are also discussed elsewhere in the book. Use the index at the back of the book to find these discussions.

USAGE

a, an These *indefinite articles* refer to one of a general group.

> EXAMPLES   We saw **a** bluejay and **an** owl.
> **A** hawk flew over us **an** hour ago.

Use *a* before words beginning with a consonant sound; use *an* before words beginning with a vowel sound. In the examples above, *a* is used before *hawk* because the *h* in *hawk* is pronounced. *An* is used before *hour* because the *h* in *hour* is not pronounced.

accept, except *Accept* is a verb that means "to receive." *Except* may be either a verb or a preposition. As a verb, it means "to leave out" or "to omit." As a preposition, *except* means "excluding."

> EXAMPLES   We **accept** your apology.
> Club members will be **excepted** from the fee.
> Everyone **except** me has seen the exhibit.

affect, effect *Affect* is a verb meaning "to influence." *Effect* used as a verb means "to accomplish." Used as a noun, *effect* means "the result of some action."

> EXAMPLES   The bright colors **affect** how the patients feel.
> The doctors hope the treatment will **effect** a cure for the disease.
> The bright colors have a beneficial **effect** on the patients.

ain't Avoid this word in speaking or writing; it is nonstandard English.

all the farther, all the faster Used in some parts of the country to mean "as far as" or "as fast as."

> DIALECT   This is all the faster I can go.
> STANDARD   This is **as fast as** I can go.

a lot Do not write the expression *a lot* as one word. It should always be written as two words.

> EXAMPLE   I have **a lot** of homework tonight.

among See **between, among.**

and etc. *Etc.* is an abbreviation of the Latin phrase *et cetera,* meaning "and other things." Thus, *and etc.* means "and and other things." Do not use *and* with *etc.*

> EXAMPLE   My younger sister collects string, bottle caps, stickers, **etc.** [not *and etc.*]

anywheres, everywheres, nowheres, somewheres Use these words without the final *s*.

> EXAMPLE   That bird is described **somewhere** [not *somewheres*] in this book.

as See **like, as.**

as if See **like, as if.**

at Do not use *at* after *where.*

> NONSTANDARD   This is where I live at.
> STANDARD   This is **where** I live.

beside, besides *Beside* is a preposition that means "by the side of" someone or something. *Besides* as a preposition means "in addition to." As an adverb, *besides* means "moreover."

> EXAMPLES   Sit **beside** me on the couch.
>
> **Besides** songs and dances, the show featured several comedy sketches.
>
> I don't want to go. **Besides,** it's starting to snow.

between, among Use *between* when you are referring to two things at a time, even though they may be part of a group consisting of more than two.

EXAMPLES   Take the seat **between** Alicia and Noreen in the third row.
There was some confusion The manager could not decide which of the four players to select because there was not much difference **between** them. [Although there are more than two players, each one is being compared with the others separately.]

Use *among* when you are thinking of a group rather than of separate individuals.

EXAMPLES   We were able to collect only ten dollars **among** the four of us.
There was some confusion **among** the jurors about one part of the defendant's testimony. [The jurors are thought of as a group.]

bring, take *Bring* means "to come carrying something." *Take* means "to go carrying something." Think of *bring* as related to *come, take* as related to *go.*

EXAMPLES   **Bring** that box over here.
Now **take** it down to the basement.

bust, busted Avoid using these words as verbs. Use a form of either *burst* or *break.*

EXAMPLES   The balloon **burst** [not *busted*] loudly.
The firefighters **broke** [not *busted*] a window.

EXERCISE 1   **Solving Common Usage Problems**

For each sentence, choose the correct word or words in parentheses, according to standard usage.

EXAMPLE   1. Everyone seemed greatly (*affected, effected*) by her speech on animal rights.
1. *affected*

1. There was complete agreement (*between, among*) the members of the council.
2. Is that (*all the farther, as far as*) you were able to hike?
3. The (*affects, effects*) of lasers on surgical procedures have been remarkable.
4. My schedule this year includes English, social studies, science, (*etc., and etc.*).
5. The boiler (*busted, burst*) and flooded the cellar.

6. Liza promised to (*bring, take*) me the new cassette.
7. I don't know where it (*is, is at*).
8. Please (*bring, take*) this note to the manager's office.
9. (*Beside, Besides*) my aunts and uncles, all my cousins are coming to our family reunion.
10. Ms. Yu (*accepted, excepted*) my excuse for being late.

EXERCISE 2   **Proofreading a Paragraph for Standard Usage**

The following paragraph contains ten errors in standard English usage. Identify the error or errors you find in each sentence. Then, write the correct usage.

EXAMPLE   [1] It isn't pretty, but this fossilized skull has caused alot of talk in the scientific world.
           1. *alot—a lot*

[1] The San Juan, Argentina, area is one of the best places anywheres to find dinosaur fossils. [2] In 1988, Paul Sereno's discovery there broke a previous record between fossil hunters for the oldest dinosaur remains. [3] On a expedition with students from the University of Chicago, where he was a biologist at, Sereno found the oldest dinosaur fossils ever unearthed up to that time. [4] Sereno's herrerasaurus fossil was in good shape; in fact, this skull doesn't even look busted. [5] Beside being extremely old, the 230-million-year-old skeleton was amazingly complete accept for the hind limbs. [6] That sort of find certainly ain't ordinary. [7] Sereno and his herrerasaurus have effected the work of biologists and dinosaur-lovers everywheres.

could of Do not write *of* with the helping verb *could.* Write *could have.* Also avoid *had of, ought to of, should of, would of, might of,* and *must of.*

EXAMPLE   Diane could **have** [not *of*] telephoned us.

discover, invent *Discover* means "to be the first to find, see, or learn about something that already exists." *Invent* means "to be the first to do or make something."

EXAMPLES   Marguerite Perey **discovered** the element francium.
The zipper was **invented** in 1893.

don't, doesn't *Don't* is the contraction of *do not. Doesn't* is the contraction of *does not.* Use *doesn't,* not *don't,* with *he, she, it, this,* and singular nouns.

EXAMPLES   It **doesn't** [not *don't*] matter.
The bus **doesn't** [not *don't*] stop at this corner.

effect See **affect, effect.**

everywheres See **anywheres,** etc.

fewer, less *Fewer* is used with plural words. *Less* is used with singular words. *Fewer* tells "how many"; *less* tells "how much."

EXAMPLES   There are **fewer** gypsy moths this year.
They have done **less** damage to the trees.

good, well *Good* is always an adjective. Never use *good* to modify a verb; use *well,* which is an adverb.

NONSTANDARD   Pancho Gonzales played good.
STANDARD   Pancho Gonzales played **well.**

Although it is usually an adverb, *well* is used as an adjective to mean "healthy."

EXAMPLE   She does not feel **well.**

NOTE: *Feel good* and *feel well* mean different things. *Feel good* means "to feel happy or pleased." *Feel well* simply means "to feel healthy."

EXAMPLES   The news made her feel **good.**
I didn't feel **well,** so I went home.

Good is often used as an adverb in conversational English, but it should not be used that way in writing.

USAGE

▶ EXERCISE 3 **Solving Common Usage Problems**

For each sentence, choose the correct word in parentheses, according to standard usage.

EXAMPLE 1. Today's Americans are using (*fewer, less*) salt than
they did years ago.
1. *less*

1. You should (*of, have*) written sooner.
2. Who (*discovered, invented*) what makes fireflies glow?
3. (*Don't, Doesn't*) Otis know that we're planning to leave in five minutes?
4. I usually do (*good, well*) on that kind of test.
5. Our doctor advised my uncle to eat (*fewer, less*) eggs.
6. He (*don't, doesn't*) look angry to me.
7. If I had known, I might (*of, have*) helped you with your project.
8. We had (*fewer, less*) snowstorms this year than last.
9. Our teacher (*doesn't, don't*) require us to type our reports.
10. Whoever (*discovered, invented*) the escalator must have been ingenious.

▶ REVIEW A **Solving Common Usage Problems**

Most of the following sentences contain errors in standard usage. If a sentence is correct, write *C*. If a sentence contains an error in standard usage, write the correct form.

EXAMPLE 1. Don't anyone know when this game will start?
1. *Doesn't*

1. Perhaps I should of called before visiting you.
2. Who discovered the cellular phone system?
3. The beautiful spring weather is effecting my powers of concentration.
4. We can't decide between this movie and that one.
5. That box contains less cookies than this one.
6. We felt good because practice went so well.
7. What affect did the quiz have on your grade?
8. Why won't you except my help?
9. We stood beside the lake and watched the swans.
10. Did you bring flowers to your aunt when you went to visit her in her new home?

▶ REVIEW B   **Solving Common Usage Problems**

Choose the word or expression in parentheses that is correct according to standard usage.

EXAMPLE   Alvin Ailey significantly [1] (*affected, effected*)
            modern dance in America.
            1. *affected*

Alvin Ailey [1] (*could of, could have*) just dreamed of being a famous choreographer; instead, he formed [2] (*a, an*) interracial dance company that is known all over the world. Ailey started his dance company with [3] (*less, fewer*) than ten dancers in New York City in 1958. Today, the Alvin Ailey American Dance Theater has a very [4] (*good, well*) reputation [5] (*between, among*) modern dance lovers [6] (*everywhere, everywheres*). Ailey also ran a dance school and [7] (*discovered, invented*) many fine young dancers there. [8] (*Beside, Besides*) teaching, he choreographed operas, television specials, and numerous ballets. This scene is from Ailey's ballet *Survivors* (1987), an energetic celebration of the anti-apartheid movement in South Africa. Ailey and his company have [9] (*accepted, excepted*) much praise, countless compliments, numerous rave reviews, [10] (*and etc., etc.*), for their creativity.

USAGE

USAGE

had of See **could of.**

had ought, hadn't ought Unlike other verbs, *ought* is not used with *had*.

NONSTANDARD   Lee had ought to plan better; he hadn't ought to leave his packing until the last minute.

STANDARD   Lee **ought** to plan better; he **ought not** to leave his packing until the last minute.

or

Lee **should** plan better; he **shouldn't** leave his packing until the last minute.

hardly, scarcely See **The Double Negative** (pages 711–712).

he, she, they Do not use an unnecessary pronoun after the subject of a clause or a sentence. This error is called the *double subject.*

NONSTANDARD   My mother she grows all her own herbs.
STANDARD   My mother grows all her own herbs.

invent, discover See **discover, invent.**

kind, sort, type The words *this, that, these,* and *those* should always agree in number with the words *kind, sort, type.*

EXAMPLE   I like **this kind** of jeans better than any of **those** other **kinds.**

learn, teach *Learn* means "to acquire knowledge." *Teach* means "to instruct" or "to show how."

EXAMPLE   Some of our coaches **teach** classes in gymnastics, where young gymnasts can **learn** many techniques.

leave, let *Leave* means "to go away" or "to depart from." *Let* means "to allow" or "to permit."

NONSTANDARD   Leave her speak if she insists.
STANDARD   **Let** her speak if she insists.
STANDARD   Let's **leave** on time for a change.

less See **fewer, less.**

like, as In informal English, the preposition *like* is often used as a conjunction meaning "as." In formal English, use *like* to introduce a prepositional phrase, and use *as* to introduce a subordinate clause.

EXAMPLES   She looks **like** her sister. [The preposition *like* introduces the phrase *like her sister.*]
We should do **as** our coach recommends. [*Our coach recommends* is a clause and needs the subordinating conjunction *as* to introduce it.]

☞ REFERENCE NOTE: For more on phrases, see Chapter 16. For more about clauses, see Chapter 17.

like, as if In formal written English, *like* should not be used for the compound conjunction *as if* or *as though*.

EXAMPLE   Scamp looks **as though** [not *like*] he has been in the swamp again.

might of, must of See **could of**.

no, none, nothing See **The Double Negative** (pages 711–712).

nowheres See **anywheres,** etc.

of Do not use *of* with prepositions such as *inside, off,* or *outside.*

EXAMPLES   He fell **off** [not *off of*] the ladder **outside** [not *outside of*] the garage.
What's **inside** [not *inside of*] that box?

ought to of See **could of**.

USAGE

▶ EXERCISE 4   **Solving Common Usage Problems**

For each sentence, choose the correct word or words in parentheses, according to standard usage.

EXAMPLE   1. I (*had ought, ought*) to write my report on the Chinese inventions of paper and printing.
1. *ought*

1. The report must be on ancient Chinese history, (*like, as*) my teacher directed.
2. For (*this, these*) kind of report, I should start with the information that the Chinese had invented paper as we know it early in the second century A.D.
3. If I (*had of, had*) seen them make paper by soaking, drying, and flattening mulberry bark, I would have been amazed.
4. (*The Chinese they, The Chinese*) didn't have the technology to mass produce paper for another four hundred years.

USAGE

5. By A.D. 200, the Chinese were using paper for writing and painting (*like, as if*) they always had done so.
6. I (*hadn't ought, ought not*) to forget that the Chinese also used paper for making umbrellas, fans, and lanterns.
7. In addition to (*this, these*) sorts of uses, the Chinese were using paper money by the seventh century.
8. You could have knocked me (*off of, off*) my chair when I learned that the Chinese were printing by A.D. 600—some eight hundred years before the invention of modern printing in Germany.
9. (*Leave, Let*) me tell you how they used wooden blocks with characters carved on them for printing.
10. By the tenth century, the Chinese had (*learned, taught*) themselves how to print entire books with wooden blocks and had invented movable type.

▶ REVIEW C   **Writing Sentences with Standard Usage**

As you can see, poor Charlie Brown needs some words of comfort or wisdom. But he's not getting them from Lucy. Take Lucy's place in the doctor's booth and try to cheer up Charlie Brown. Write five sentences that offer positive, reassuring advice to help him cope with life's frustrations. In your sentences, use five words from the list on the following page.

Peanuts reprinted by permission of United Feature Syndicate, Inc.

EXAMPLE 1. fewer
1. *More smiles mean fewer frowns.*

as if	let	ought
learn	like (prep.)	sort
leave	nothing	teach

PICTURE THIS

You are the editor of the lifestyle section of the local newspaper. One of your photographers has taken this amusing picture of her pets, Mitten the cat, Tosen the dog, and Kim the mouse. Write four different captions for this photograph—one from the point of view of each of the animals, and one as an outside observer. In your captions, demonstrate the correct usage of five of these words: *effect, among, anywhere, doesn't, good, ought, let, like, fewer.* Use each word only once. Underline the words you use.

Subject: humorous animal picture
Audience: newspaper readers
Purpose: to entertain

USAGE

A Pet's Best Friend?

rise, raise See page 641.

sit, set See pages 639–640.

some, somewhat In writing, do not use *some* for *somewhat* as an adverb.

NONSTANDARD My grammar has improved some.
STANDARD My grammar has improved **somewhat**.

sort See **kind,** etc.

take See **bring, take.**

teach See **learn, teach.**

than, then Do not confuse these words. *Than* is a conjunction; *then* is an adverb.

EXAMPLES This box is heavier **than** that one.
We went swimming; **then** we ate lunch.

them *Them* should not be used as an adjective. Use *those.*

EXAMPLE I like **those** [not *them*] jeans, don't you?

this here, that there The words *here* and *there* are unnecessary after *this* and *that.*

EXAMPLE I'm buying **this** [not *this here*] cassette instead of **that** [not *that there*] one.

this kind, sort, type See **kind,** etc.

type See **kind,** etc.

way, ways Use *way,* not *ways,* in referring to a distance.

EXAMPLE We hiked a long **way** [not *ways*].

well See **good, well.**

when, where Do not use *when* or *where* incorrectly in writing a definition.

NONSTANDARD A "bomb" in football is when a backfield player throws a long pass.
STANDARD A "bomb" in football is a long pass thrown by a backfield player.

where Do not use *where* for *that.*

EXAMPLE I read in this magazine **that** [not *where*] Carol Clay is a champion parachutist.

which, that, who The relative pronoun *who* refers to people only; *which* refers to things only; *that* refers to either people or things.

EXAMPLES Here is the man **who** will install the new carpet. [person]
We decided to replace our old carpet, **which** we have had for nearly ten years. [thing]
The dealer is a person **that** stands behind a product. [person]
It is the kind of carpet **that** will wear well. [thing]

who, whom See pages 662–663.

without, unless Do not use the preposition *without* in place of the conjunction *unless*.

EXAMPLE I will not be able to sing **unless** [not *without*] my cold gets better.

would of See **could of.**

USAGE

▶ EXERCISE 5 **Solving Common Usage Problems**

For each sentence, choose the correct word or words in parentheses, according to standard usage.

EXAMPLE 1. (*That, That there*) motorbike belongs to my cousin.
1. *That*

1. Don't use more paper (*than, then*) you need.
2. (*Them, Those*) dogs have impressive pedigrees.
3. Manuel prefers (*this, these*) kind of skateboard.
4. It is only a short (*way, ways*) to the video store.
5. Tricia relaxed (*some, somewhat*) after she began to speak.
6. On the news, I heard (*where, that*) the game was called off because of rain.
7. Please (*sit, set*) the books on the desk.
8. Is she the player (*who, which*) is favored to win at Wimbledon this year?
9. He would not have released the report (*without, unless*) he had first verified his sources.
10. The rattlesnake on the trail spooked the horse, causing it to (*rise, raise*) up and throw the rider.

EXERCISE 6   **Revising a Paragraph by Correcting Usage Errors**

Identify all of the usage problems that you find in each sentence in the following paragraph. Then write the correct usage.

EXAMPLE   [1] This legendary statue, the Sphinx at Giza in Egypt, would of weathered away completely if it had not been rescued by modern technology.
            1. *would of—would have*

[1] The Sphinx, who has the head of a human and the body of a lion, was suffering some from old age, exposure, and bad restoration attempts, so Egyptian museum officials began a major renewal project in 1990. [2] Scientists knew that the world eventually would lose that there famous statue without restoration was begun immediately. [3] Workers dismantled many stones, sat new ones in their place, and than added natural mortar to let them stones breathe. [4] Workers also stabilized the water table under the mammoth Sphinx, which raises sixty-six feet above the desert sands. [5] These kind of restorations will help to preserve the Sphinx against the harmful effects of wind, rain, and sand for many years to come.

REVIEW D   **Revising Sentences by Correcting Errors in Usage**

Revise each of the following sentences, correcting the error or errors in usage.

USAGE

EXAMPLE   1. I saw on the news where the mayor don't plan to run for reelection.
1. *I saw on the news that the mayor doesn't plan to run for reelection.*

1. Optimism is when a person always looks on the bright side.
2. Luanne she is a better contestant than Tommy is.
3. Take this here rake and them seedlings to Mrs. Murphy like I asked.
4. I would of begun my report sooner then I did if I had known it would need this much research.
5. I heard where people will not be allowed back in the concert hall after intermission without they show their tickets.
6. The tire came off of the truck and rolled a long ways down the turnpike.
7. Heather Ruiz has promised to learn us karate.
8. The people which witnessed the crime hadn't ought to have left before the police arrived.
9. My parents they refuse to leave me stay out past ten o'clock.
10. Them sailors welcomed us aboard the *Intrepid*.

The Double Negative

In a *double negative,* two negative words are used when one is sufficient. Avoid double negatives in both writing and speaking.

"Dropping out of school never done me no harm."

hardly, scarcely The words *hardly* and *scarcely* convey a negative meaning. They should never be used with another negative word.

EXAMPLES   I **can** [not *can't*] **hardly** turn the key in the lock.
              We **have** [not *haven't*] **scarcely** enough time.

no, nothing, none Do not use these words with another negative word.

NONSTANDARD	That answer doesn't make no sense.
STANDARD	That answer **doesn't make any** sense.
STANDARD	That answer **makes no** sense.

NONSTANDARD	The field trip won't cost us nothing.
STANDARD	The field trip **won't cost us anything**.
STANDARD	The field trip **will cost us nothing**.

NONSTANDARD	We wanted grapes, but there weren't none.
STANDARD	We wanted grapes, but there **weren't any**.
STANDARD	We wanted grapes, but there **were none**.

> **EXERCISE 7**   **Revising Sentences by Correcting Errors in Double Negatives**

Revise each of the following sentences, correcting the usage errors.

EXAMPLE   1. It doesn't make no difference to me.
          1. *It makes no difference to me.*
                 or
        It doesn't make any difference to me.

1. Rachel didn't say nothing to him.
2. There isn't hardly anything left to eat.
3. I haven't borrowed no books from the library this week.
4. Laura couldn't hardly make herself heard.
5. What you're saying doesn't make no sense to me.
6. By the time we wrote for tickets, there weren't none available.
7. Hasn't no one in the class read *And Now Miguel?*
8. There wasn't scarcely enough water in the pond to keep the fish alive.
9. Didn't you never say nothing about the noise?
10. I haven't never told no one about our discovery.

EXERCISE 8   **Using Negatives Correctly**

While on duty as a roving reporter for a local radio station, you receive an urgent call to cover a major story downtown. When you arrive, you discover this remarkable scene and immediately begin a live broadcast. Write the script for a portion of your broadcast. In your script, use five of the following negatives correctly.

can *or* are hardly	nothing *or* anything
can *or* have scarcely	none
no	

EXAMPLE   *I can hardly believe my eyes!*

WRITING APPLICATION

Using Formal Standard English in a Business Letter

Each time you write or speak, you present your ideas, opinions, or feelings to an audience. Without thinking about it, you adjust your presentation to suit the particular group you are with. For instance, in talking with friends, you likely would call people by their nicknames and use slang. You would be speaking informally and might even use some nonstandard English. On the other hand, if you were making a speech in front of the whole school, you probably would use more formal language. You would use standard English to communicate with a wider range of people.

Adjusting your speech to suit the group you're addressing shows respect for your audience, and it encourages your listeners to take you seriously.

| INFORMAL/NONSTANDARD | This here is only my opinion, but Eddie Lee he don't represent the views of the freshman class. It don't make sense to elect a class president who promises less dances! Instead, we had ought to vote for Janelle Johnson. She is the only candidate which supports more school dances. |
| FORMAL/STANDARD | In my opinion, Eddie Lee doesn't represent the views of the freshman class. It doesn't make sense to elect a class president who promises fewer dances! Instead, we ought to vote for Janelle Johnson. She is the only candidate who supports more school dances. |

WRITING ACTIVITY

The school board in your district has proposed a new rule that would require students to wear school uniforms. The board members made the proposal after reading about several studies showing the benefits of school uniforms. One study found that schools that require uniforms experience less vandalism and gang violence. Another study concluded that, over all, students who wore uniforms made better grades. Now, the board has invited concerned citizens—students, parents, and teachers—to submit their opinions. Write a letter to the school board, telling why your district should or should not require students to wear uniforms.

Prewriting If you already have an opinion about school uniforms, jot down some reasons to support your view. If you are undecided, you may want to make two lists—one pro and one con. Give as many reasons as you can to support each position. Then, choose the side that you find more persuasive. Number your reasons in the order in which you want to write about them. See pages 115–129 and 306–309 for how to organize supporting details in persuasive writing.

Writing As you write your first draft, use your prewriting notes to keep you focused on your topic. Choose only the best reasons from your list and expand on these. Think about your audience, and try to use language and arguments that will be convincing to the members of the school board.

 Evaluating and Revising Imagine that you are a member of the school board. Read over your letter and ask yourself the following questions.

- Is the writer's opinion clear?
- Are his or her reasons sound?
- Is the organization logical?
- Is the tone of the letter sincere and courteous?
- Does the letter follow the rules of business correspondence?

If your answer to any of these questions is "no," go back and revise the letter. Add, cut, or rearrange supporting details to make your argument more effective. As you revise, follow the rules for standard English usage to communicate with as wide a range of board members as possible. Also, see that the tone and word choice of your letter conform to the standards of polite business correspondence. Since content and form work together to create an impression, be sure to use proper business letter format as you write your revised draft. (See pages 937–942.)

 Proofreading and Publishing Read over your letter again, checking for errors in grammar, punctuation, and spelling. Use the glossary listing in this chapter to correct common usage errors. Use the index of your textbook to find more information on other points of grammar, usage, and mechanics.

You and your classmates may wish to have a debate or panel discussion on the school uniform issue. Divide the class into two groups—pro and con. The groups can then prepare their arguments using the best reasons from each person's letter. Remember to select reasons and a style of presentation that will appeal to your audience—the students in your class.

USAGE

USAGE

Review: Posttest

Revising a Passage by Correcting Errors in Standard Usage

Each of the sentences in the following passage contains at least one error in standard usage. Revise the passage, correcting all of these errors.

EXAMPLE   [1] Everyone accept him joined this here club.
         1. *Everyone except him joined this club.*

[1] Our school has a hiking club that learns us how to appreciate nature. [2] Our club usually goes to parks that we might not of discovered by ourselves. [3] We go hiking anywheres that can be reached by bus in less than three hours. [4] Before we go, we decide what to bring with us. [5] The less things that we have to carry, the better off we are. [6] Beside water, a hat, and a jacket, little else is needed. [7] Those which pack too much soon wish they hadn't of. [8] After all, a 10-mile hike effects you differently when you are weighted down then when you are not.

[9] Our adviser, Mr. Graham, he knows where all the best hiking areas are at. [10] He always tells us that we won't see nothing interesting without we're willing to exert ourselves. [11] But we can't hardly keep up with him once he starts walking.

[12] We go on these sort of walks because we enjoy them. [13] Although we sometimes think our lungs will bust, everyone wants to keep up with the others. [14] The real reward is when we see an unusual sight, like a fawn, a family of otters, a panoramic view, and etc. [15] Than we're sure that all of our hiking ain't been a waste of time. [16] We also except nature like it is and do not try to change it none. [17] When we find bottles or cans in the woods, we get upset with people who can't go anywheres without leaving some mark.

[18] Everyone in the club feels the same way, so we're going to start an clean-up campaign. [19] People ought to enjoy being inside of a park without busting or changing nothing there. [20] We'd rather have more hikers and less people destroying nature.

23 CAPITAL LETTERS

The Rules for Capitalization

Diagnostic Test

A. Correcting Sentences by Capitalizing Words

Identify the word or words that should be capitalized in each of the following sentences. If a sentence is correct, write *C*.

EXAMPLE   **1.** Aunt claire donated her hoover vacuum cleaner to the salvation army.
　　　　　1. *Claire, Hoover, Salvation Army*

1. The judges of the essay contest are miss helen fry and mr. c. m. gonzalez.
2. Before fishing on sylvan lake in custer state park, we bought bait at a stand on highway 385.
3. The travel section of the *New York times* featured an excellent article on jewel cave national monument.
4. The Industrial Revolution drastically changed American life in the 1800s.

5. During world war II, Gloria's grandmother was a volunteer for the red cross.
6. The bomber the troops called *lady luck* sat in the park on Fifty-third Street, two blocks west of the methodist church.
7. Last August, grandpa Henry and aunt Frances took an amtrak express train from New York to chicago.
8. Students at Adams high school may take spanish, geometry, and chemistry I as sophomores.
9. In english class we compared the tone of Grant Wood's painting *American gothic* and Willa Cather's novel *One of ours.*
10. After hurricane allen struck, the governor declared the region a disaster area.

B. Proofreading a Paragraph for Correct Capitalization

Capitalize the word or words that should begin with a capital letter in each sentence in the following paragraph. If a sentence contains no errors, write *C*.

EXAMPLE [1] Yellowstone National Park, which extends into northwestern wyoming, has to be seen to be believed.
1. *Wyoming*

[11] Early reports about this area arrived back east some two hundred years ago from explorers and trappers such as william Clark and Jim Bridger. [12] Their accounts of boiling mud cauldrons and water spewing hundreds of feet in the air seemed unbelievable. [13] Many people laughed at the native people's stories about angry gods who turned trees to stone and caused tremors and thundering noises. [14] Yet settlers avoided the Yellowstone area and its native inhabitants, the shoshone, until after the American civil war. [15] Then, adventurers and local leaders explored the area and persuaded dr. Ferdinand Hayden, director of the U.S. Geological Survey, to see the wonders himself. [16] In 1871, Dr. Hayden surveyed the region with an artist and a photographer, who recorded the amazing sights they saw. [17] In march of 1872, congress voted to set aside 2.2 million acres as Yellowstone

national park. **[18]** Since then, visitors have taken millions of snapshots of such features as the famous geyser old faithful. **[19]** When mom, dad, and i visited the park last summer, we were amazed at the geysers, mudpots, and other sights. **[20]** Next summer, I'm going to take a course in geology offered by the yellowstone institute.

A capital letter at the beginning of a word is an important signal to the reader. A capital letter not only indicates the beginning of a sentence, but also may mark a significant difference in meaning, such as the difference between *may* and *May*.

23a. Capitalize the first word in every sentence.

EXAMPLES   The world of computers has its own language. **A** complete list of instructions for the computer is a *program.* **C**omputer equipment is called *hardware,* and the programs are called *software.*

Traditionally, the first word of a line of poetry is capitalized.

EXAMPLES   **A** bird came down the walk:
He did not know I saw;
He bit an angleworm in halves
And ate the fellow, raw.
Emily Dickinson, *A Bird Came Down the Walk*

NOTE: Some writers do not follow these practices. When you are quoting, use capital letters exactly as they are used in the source of the quotation.

☞ REFERENCE NOTE: For more about using capital letters in quotations, see page 793.

▶ EXERCISE 1   **Capitalizing Sentences in a Paragraph**

Capitalize the ten words that should begin with a capital letter in the following paragraph. Also add the appropriate mark of punctuation to the end of each sentence.

work has begun on developing a new kind of laser radar this instrument would be especially

MECHANICS

useful for blind people how does the radar work a laser device, which is small enough to fit onto an eyeglass frame, emits invisible infrared light beams when the light strikes an object, it bounces back to a receiver placed in the blind person's ear the receiver, in turn, sounds a small tone with this sort of device, the blind person can "hear" any object nearby the device is very promising in fact, it may one day replace the cane or the guide dog as an aid for the blind there are few better examples of how beneficial laser research can be

23b. Capitalize the pronoun *I* and the interjection *O*.

Although it is rarely used, *O* is always capitalized. Generally, it is reserved for invocations and is followed by the name of the person or thing being addressed. You will more often use the interjection *oh*, which is not capitalized unless it is the first word in a sentence.

EXAMPLES "Exult **O** shores! and ring **O** bells!" is a line from Walt Whitman's poem "**O** Captain! My Captain!"
The play was a hit, but **oh**, how nervous **I** was!

EXERCISE 2 **Correcting Capitalization Errors in Sentences**

Most of the following sentences contain errors in capitalization. If a sentence is correct, write *C*. If there are errors in the use of capitals, identify the word or words that should be changed.

EXAMPLE 1. in "Jazz Fantasia," the speaker tells the musicians, "Go to it, o jazzmen."
1. *In, O*

1. yesterday i learned two psalms that begin, "Bless the Lord, o my soul."
2. I haven't really decided about my future, but Oh, how I'd like to be an astronaut!
3. In the poem "The Fool's Prayer," the jester pleads, "O Lord, be merciful to me, a fool!"
4. The car had to stop suddenly, and Oh, was i glad my seat belt was fastened!

5. My favorite lines from *Romeo and Juliet* are
"see how she leans her cheek upon her hand!
o, that i were a glove upon that hand,
that i might touch that cheek!"

23c. Capitalize proper nouns and proper adjectives.

A *common noun* names one of a group of people, places, or things. A *proper noun* names a particular person, place, or thing. *Proper adjectives* are formed from proper nouns.

☞ REFERENCE NOTE: For more about common and proper nouns, see pages 465–466. For a discussion of proper adjectives, see page 474.

Common nouns are not capitalized unless they begin a sentence or a direct quotation or are included in a title (see pages 731–732). Proper nouns are always capitalized.

COMMON NOUNS	PROPER NOUNS	PROPER ADJECTIVES
a poet	Homer	Homeric simile
a country	Turkey	Turkish border
a queen	Queen Elizabeth	Elizabethan drama
a planet	Mars	Martian landscape

Some proper names consist of more than one word. In these names, short prepositions (generally, fewer than five letters) and articles are not capitalized.

EXAMPLES   Tomb **of** the Unknown Soldier
Society **for** the Prevention **of** Cruelty to Animals
Ivan **the** Terrible

NOTE: Proper nouns and adjectives sometimes lose their capitals through frequent usage.

EXAMPLES   **watt**   **titanic**   **sandwich**

To find out whether a noun should be capitalized, check in a dictionary. The dictionary will tell you if a word should always be capitalized or if it should be capitalized only in certain uses.

MECHANICS

EXERCISE 3 **Using Proper Adjectives and Proper Nouns**

You are probably familiar with theme parks such as the one shown here. Now it's your turn to develop your own theme park. You get to choose a location for the park, its theme, its name, and its rides and attractions. For a theme, you might consider continents or countries, products or brand names, movies, or sports and entertainment personalities. Using a com-

bination of common and proper adjectives and nouns, list the location, theme, and name of the park, three rides, and three attractions.

EXAMPLES   Location: *Hangman's Hollow, Pennsylvania*
Theme: *monsters*
Park name: *Movie Monsterville*
Rides: *Dracula's Dungeon, Werewolf Whirl, Mummy-Go-Round*
Attractions: *European Haunted Castle, Frankenstein's Laboratory, Monster Museum*

(1) Capitalize the names of people.

EXAMPLES   GIVEN NAMES   **A**lana   **M**ark
SURNAMES   **D**iaz   **C**ollins

(2) Capitalize geographical names.

TYPE OF NAME	EXAMPLES	
Towns and Cities	Portland Detroit	San Francisco Rio de Janeiro
Counties and Townships	Kane County Hayes Township	East Baton Rouge Parish
States	Florida Missouri	Alaska North Carolina
Countries	Canada New Zealand	United States of America
Continents	Africa	North America

MECHANICS

TYPE OF NAME	EXAMPLES	
Islands	Long Island the West Indies	the Isle of Palms Florida Keys
Mountains	Rocky Mountains Mount McKinley	the Alps the Mount of Olives
Bodies of Water	Pacific Ocean Adriatic Sea	Red River Lake of the Woods
Parks	Yellowstone National Park Cleburne State Park	
Regions	the North the Southeast	the Middle West New England
Roads, Streets, and Highways	Route 66 Interstate 787	Pennsylvania Turnpike West First Street

NOTE: Words such as *north, west,* and *southeast* are not capitalized when they indicate direction.

EXAMPLES   north of town   traveling southeast

However, these words are capitalized when they name a particular place.

EXAMPLES   states in the Northwest   driving in the Southeast

In a hyphenated number, the second word begins with a small letter.

EXAMPLE   Thirty-first Street

Words like *city, island, river, street,* and *park* are capitalized when they are part of a name. If words like these are not part of a proper name, they are common nouns and are not capitalized.

PROPER NOUNS	COMMON NOUNS
life in New York City	life in a big city
Liberty Island	a small island
crossing the Spokane River	crossing the river
on State Street	on a narrow street

MECHANICS

▶ EXERCISE 4   **Recognizing the Correct Use of Capital Letters**

Give the letter of the correctly capitalized sentence in each of the following pairs.

EXAMPLE   **1. a.** Drive Northeast until you get to New Haven.
            b. Drive northeast until you get to New Haven.
            1. *b*

1. **a.** We went canoeing on the Ohio river.
    b. We went canoeing on the Ohio River.
2. **a.** I read the article on south America.
    b. I read the article on South America.
3. **a.** Farewell Bend State Park is in Oregon.
    b. Farewell Bend State park is in Oregon.
4. **a.** Her address is 1614 Robin Street.
    b. Her address is 1614 Robin street.
5. **a.** I will be at Forty-Second Street and Park Avenue.
    b. I will be at Forty-second Street and Park Avenue.
6. **a.** The North sea is East of Great britain.
    b. The North Sea is east of Great Britain.
7. **a.** Atlanta is a fast-growing City in the south.
    b. Atlanta is a fast-growing city in the South.
8. **a.** Pensacola is on the gulf of Mexico.
    b. Pensacola is on the Gulf of Mexico.
9. **a.** The Hawaiian Islands are southwest of California.
    b. The Hawaiian islands are Southwest of California.
10. **a.** Laredo is on the Mexican Border in Webb county.
    b. Laredo is on the Mexican border in Webb County.

PICTURE THIS

You are a crew member on the first spacecraft sent to explore Thor, a new planet just discovered on the edge of our solar system. The spacecraft's computers have mapped part of Thor. Now the captain wants you to write her a brief memo in which you suggest names for ten of the geographical features on the map shown on the next page. Be sure to give your reason for choosing each name and to use capital letters correctly. Underline each proper noun in your memo.

Subject: names for geographical features on planet Thor
Audience: the captain of your spacecraft
Purpose: to persuade

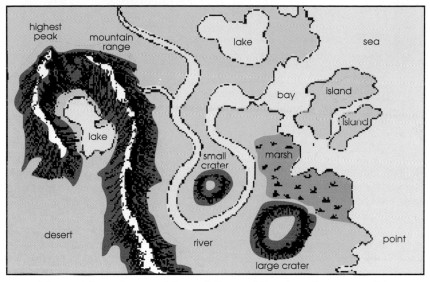

Planet Thor: Survey Map of Coastal Region, Segment 45

(3) Capitalize names of organizations, teams, businesses, institutions, and government bodies.

TYPE OF NAME	EXAMPLES
Organizations	United Nations National Basketball Association Boy Scouts of America B'nai B'rith
Teams	Tampa Bay Buccaneers Golden State Warriors River City Allstars
Businesses	Quaker Oats Company Southern Bell B. F. Goodrich
Government Bodies	Congress Federal Bureau of Investigation House of Representatives State Department

MECHANICS

TYPE OF NAME	EXAMPLES
Institutions	United States Naval Academy Stanford University Bethune-Cookman College North High School Bellevue Hospital

NOTE: The word *party* in the name of a political party may be capitalized or not; either way is correct.

EXAMPLES   Republican **party** *or* **P**arty
Federalist **party** *or* **P**arty

Do not capitalize words like *hotel, theater, college, high school, post office,* and *courthouse* unless they are part of a proper name.

EXAMPLES

Jackson **H**igh **S**chool   a **h**igh **s**chool principal
Copley Square **H**otel   a **h**otel in Boston
Fox **T**heater   a **t**heater in Dallas
Kearney **P**ost **O**ffice   a **p**ost **o**ffice nearby
Victoria County **C**ourthouse   a **c**ourthouse hallway

(4) Capitalize the names of historical events and periods, special events, and calendar items.

TYPE OF NAME	EXAMPLES	
Historical Events and Periods	French Revolution Boston Tea Party	World War II Middle Ages
Special Events	Interscholastic Debate Tournament Gulf Coast Track-and-Field Championship Parents' Day	
Calendar Items	Saturday December New Year's Day	Labor Day Martin Luther King, Jr., Day

NOTE: Do not capitalize the name of a season (summer, winter, spring, autumn, fall) unless it is
personified: "Here is **S**pring in her green dress!"
or
used in the name of a special event: **W**inter Carnival, **S**pring Jubilee.

▶ EXERCISE 5   **Writing Sentences Using Capital Letters**

Correctly use each of the following words in a sentence of your own.

1. river	**3.** motel	**5.** street	**7.** march	**9.** west
2. River	**4.** Motel	**6.** Street	**8.** March	**10.** West

(5) Capitalize the names of nationalities, races, and peoples.

EXAMPLES   **Canadian, Greek, Caucasian, Asian, Hispanic, Zulu, Cherokee, Viking**

NOTE: The words *black* and *white* may or may not be capitalized when they refer to races.

(6) Capitalize the brand names of business products.

EXAMPLES   **Formica, Chevrolet, Teflon**

NOTE: Do not capitalize a common noun that follows a brand name: *Chevrolet van, Teflon pan.*

(7) Capitalize the names of ships, monuments, awards, planets, and other particular places, things, or events.

TYPE OF NAME	EXAMPLES	
Ships and Trains	*Mayflower* *Discovery*	*Yankee Clipper* *Silver Meteor*
Aircraft, Spacecraft, and Missiles	*Pioneer 10* *Columbia*	*The Spirit of St. Louis* *Skylab*
Monuments and Memorials	**Washington Monument** **Lincoln Memorial**	
Buildings	**Chrysler Building** **Rockefeller Center Tower**	
Awards	**Purple Heart** **Academy Award** **Key Club Achievement Award**	
Planets and Other Heavenly Bodies	**Mercury** **Jupiter**	the **Dog Star** **Little Dipper**

NOTE: The word *earth* is not capitalized unless it is used along with the names of other heavenly bodies. The words *sun* and *moon* are not capitalized.

MECHANICS

▶ EXERCISE 6　**Correcting the Capitalization of Words and Phrases**

Correct the following words and phrases, using capital letters as needed.

1. between mars and jupiter
2. a shopping center on north twenty-third street
3. lafayette park in tallahassee, florida
4. some wheaties cereal
5. jefferson racquet club
6. harvard university
7. nike tennis shoes
8. on memorial day
9. an african american
10. the sinking of the *lusitania*

▶ EXERCISE 7　**Identifying Errors in Capitalization**

Each of the following sentences contains errors in capitalization. Correct these errors by changing capital letters to lowercase letters or lowercase letters to capitals.

EXAMPLE　**1.** The earliest African American Folk tales have their roots in africa.
　　　　　1. *folk, Africa*

1. Africans who first came to the americas enjoyed folk tales that blended their own african songs with stories they heard here.
2. Before the civil war, African Americans created new tales that reflected their experiences as Slaves and their desire for Freedom.
3. Many of these tales are about Animals, especially the small but clever character named brer rabbit.
4. Zora neale hurston collected a number of these animal stories and published them in *Mules And Men.*
5. Brer rabbit, who was especially popular in the south in the 1800s, constantly plays tricks on brer fox and brer wolf.
6. In some later tales, the main Character isn't a rabbit but a slave, john, who outsmarts the slave owner.
7. Author virginia hamilton, winner of the newbery medal and the national book award, tells other tales in *The People Could Fly: American Black Folktales.*

8. The title of both that Book and the Painting on its cover refers to another popular kind of black folk tale that developed during the years of slavery.
9. Can you tell that the People on the book's cover are flying above the Earth?
10. "The People Could Fly" is one of many fantasy tales about enslaved people who have Magic Powers to fly away from their troubles.

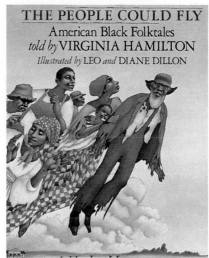

THE PEOPLE COULD FLY
American Black Folktales
told by VIRGINIA HAMILTON
Illustrated by LEO *and* DIANE DILLON

23d. Do *not* capitalize names of school subjects, except for languages or course names followed by a number.

EXAMPLES This year I am taking **algebra, English, civics, Typing I,** and a **foreign language.** Next year I plan to take **American government, English, geometry, Biology I,** and **Spanish.**

NOTE: Do *not* capitalize the name of a class (*freshman, sophomore, junior, senior*) unless it is used as part of a proper noun.

EXAMPLE All **freshmen** should meet after school to discuss the **Freshman-Sophomore Banquet.**

▶ REVIEW A **Correcting Capitalization Errors in Sentences**

Correct the following sentences by changing lowercase letters to capital letters as needed.

1. in tuesday's class, mrs. garcía explained that the diameter of earth is only 405 miles more than that of venus.
2. this year's freshmen will be required to take more courses in english, science, and math than did prior freshmen at briarwood county high school.

3. in chicago we visited soldier field and the museum of science and industry, which is known all over the world.
4. Aboard the space shuttle *columbia* in january 1986, franklin Chang-Díaz became the first astronaut to send a message in spanish back to earth.
5. are german, latin, and science the most helpful courses for someone planning to go into medicine?
6. after i went to the mall and the hardware store, i stopped at quik mart on twenty-second street.
7. we vacationed in the west, stopping to see pikes peak and to go camping and fishing in colorado.
8. in kentucky, one of the border states between the north and the south, you can visit mammoth cave, churchill downs, and the lincoln birthplace national historic site.
9. after labor day last fall, the columbus youth fellowship sponsored a softball tournament at maxwell field.
10. augustus saint-gaudens, a great sculptor who came to the united states from ireland as a child, showed abraham lincoln as a tall, serious man standing with his head bowed.

▶ EXERCISE 8 **Writing a Course Description**

This survey form shows students' suggestions for courses they would like to take. Create a similar form, and list three classes you think would be interesting or would help you to prepare for a career that interests you. Then, for one of the classes, write a brief course description for a student handbook. In your description, give the course title, tell what prerequisites would be necessary, and describe what should be taught in the class.

SUGGESTED NEW COURSE	DEPARTMENT(S) THAT COULD OFFER COURSE	PREREQUISITES
Engine Design I	Science and/or Technology	physics, automotive repair
Screenplay Writing I	English and Computer Science	creative writing, Keyboarding I

23e. Capitalize titles.

(1) Capitalize the title of a person when it comes before a name.

EXAMPLES **President Kennedy** **Mr.** Nakamura
Dr. Dooley **Ms.** Acosta
Professor Simmons **Principal Phillips**

Do not capitalize a title that is used alone or following a person's name, especially if the title is preceded by *a* or *the*.

EXAMPLES We saw the reverend at the park.
Daniel Inouye was first elected **s**enator from Hawaii in 1962.
Cleopatra ruled as the **q**ueen of Egypt from 51–30 B.C.

NOTE: You will notice that for special emphasis or clarity, writers sometimes capitalize a title used alone or following a person's name.

EXAMPLES Many young people admire the **R**everend.
How did the **S**enator vote on this issue?
At the ceremony, the **Q**ueen crowned the winner of the Miss England competition.

When a title is used alone in direct address, it is *usually* capitalized.

EXAMPLES Well, **D**octor, what is your diagnosis?
I think, **S**enator, the issue is critical.
May I speak now, **S**ir [or *sir*]?
Good morning, **M**a'am [or *ma'am*].

(2) Capitalize words showing family relationship when used with a person's name but *not* when preceded by a possessive.

EXAMPLES **Aunt** Clara, **C**ousin Joshua, **G**randfather,
my aunt Clara, your father, Harold's grandmother

(3) Capitalize the first and last words and all important words in titles and subtitles of books, periodicals, poems, stories, historical documents, movies, television programs, works of art, and musical compositions.

Unimportant words in a title are

articles:	*a, an, the*
short prepositions (fewer than five letters):	*of, to, for, from, in, over*
coordinating conjunctions:	*and, but, so, nor, or, yet, for*

TYPE OF TITLE	EXAMPLES
Books	*The Sea Around Us Ordinary People* *I Know Why the Caged Bird Sings*
Periodicals	the *Hispanic Review The Atlantic Monthly*
Poem	"The Charge of the Light Brigade"
Story	"The Pit and the Pendulum" "Raymond's Run"
Historical Documents	Treaty of Paris Declaration of Independence Emancipation Proclamation
Movies	*Dances with Wolves It's a Wonderful Life*
Television Programs	*Meet the Press Nova* *60 Minutes Space: Above and Beyond*
Works of Art	*American Gothic The Thinker*
Musical Compositions	"Tennessee Waltz" "The Flight of the Bumblebee" *The Surprise Symphony*

NOTE: The words *a, an,* and *the* written before a title are capitalized only when they are the first word of a title.

EXAMPLES   *A Tale of Two Cities*
The Autobiography of Malcolm X

Before the names of magazines and newspapers, *a, an,* and *the* are usually not capitalized.

EXAMPLES   the *Saturday Review*
the *Los Angeles Times*

(4) Capitalize names of religions and their followers, holy celebrations, holy writings, and specific deities.

MECHANICS

TYPE OF NAME	EXAMPLES		
Religions and Followers	Judaism Buddhism Catholicism	Mormonism Muslim Taoist	Baptist Quaker
Holy Days	Lent Ramadan	Passover Easter	
Holy Writings	Bible Dead Sea Scrolls	Upanishads Deuteronomy	Koran
Specific Deities	Allah God	Brahma the Holy Ghost	

NOTE: The word *god* is not capitalized when it refers to the gods of ancient mythology.

EXAMPLE   The Greek poet paid tribute to the **god** Zeus.

In some writings, you may notice that pronouns referring to deities are capitalized. In other cases, writers capitalize such pronouns only to prevent confusion.

EXAMPLE   The **Lord** called upon Moses to lead **His** people out of Egypt.

▶ REVIEW B   ## Correcting Capitalization Errors in Phrases and Sentences

If the capitalization in a phrase or sentence below is correct, write *C*. If the capitalization is incorrect, write the correct form.

1. mayor Patterson
2. "Home on The Range"
3. the *Reader's Digest*
4. elected governor
5. the president of the United States
6. was a Roman God

7. my mom and grandma higgins
8. my Cousin's parents
9. N. Scott Momaday won the Pulitzer Prize.
10. *the Mystery of Edwin Drood*

▶ EXERCISE 9   ## Creating a Personal Hall of Fame

What makes a person, a group, an artwork, or anything else great? Think about people and things that you consider to be great. Then make a personal "Hall of Fame,"

MECHANICS

listing your choice of the greatest member in each category listed below. In addition to the categories given, add two categories of your own to the list of things and the list of people. Capitalize titles and other proper nouns appropriately.

THINGS	PEOPLE
movie	sports legend
TV show	business leader
magazine	military leader
song	political leader
novel	writer
poem	inventor
painting	explorer
building	musical group or singer

MECHANICS

WRITING APPLICATION

Using Capital Letters Correctly

What happens if an author ignores the rules of capitalization? Answer: You and other readers must work much harder to understand the author's meaning.

Can you find the five mistakes in the use of capital letters in this movie review?

> The film *Edward scissorhands* is an original twist on the frankenstein theme and is sure to be a Classic. set in suburban america, the film is an enjoyable look at how people learn to accept those who are different.

Which capitalization errors did you find most distracting?

▶ **WRITING ACTIVITY**
Your school's language club plans to publish a booklet about foreign cities that most interest students. Write a paragraph telling about one city and its major attractions.

Prewriting Choose a foreign city that interests you, and jot down the reasons you find it interesting. You may want to gather some information about it from encyclopedias, travel books or brochures, and magazine or newspaper articles. Make a list of the city's major attractions.

Writing As you write your first draft, be sure to include information about the city's location and historical or cultural importance.

Evaluating and Revising Ask a friend who is unfamiliar with the city to read your paragraph. Does the information you have presented make your friend want to visit this city? Add or delete details to make your writing more interesting and informative.

Proofreading Put your paragraph aside for a while and then give it a fresh reading to spot errors. Be sure that you have correctly capitalized geographical names and the names of businesses, institutions, places, and events. Pay particular attention to the spelling of foreign words.

MECHANICS

Review: Posttest

A. Correcting Sentences That Contain Errors in Capitalization

Correct the errors in capitalization in the following sentences. If a sentence contains no errors, write *C*.

EXAMPLE   **1.** My Aunt and I visited the White house in Washington, D.C.
            1. *aunt, House*

1. Val's new schwinn bike had a flat tire.
2. My father is taking a course in public speaking.
3. The atmosphere on venus is about ninety times denser than the atmosphere on earth.
4. We watch Macy's Thanksgiving day parade on television.

5. The opossum can be found as far south as Argentina and as far north as Canada.
6. Our Club raised money for the American heart association.
7. The maya of the Yucatan peninsula worshiped nature Gods such as chac, a god of rain, and Itzamná, a sky god.
8. My uncle Scott works at martha's hardware store.
9. In drama 2, we staged a production of Denise Chavez's *The flying tortilla Man*.
10. The U.S. senate and house of representatives may pass a bill to become a law, but the president can veto it.
11. Mr. Williams is a Reporter for the United Press international.
12. We went to Sea World over easter vacation.
13. Both rabbi Frankel and reverend Stone organized aid for the victims of the fire.
14. The summer Games of the 1996 olympics were held in atlanta, Georgia.
15. Michelangelo's *The creation of the World* and *The Last Judgment* are paintings that depict bible stories.

B. Correcting Capitalization Errors in a Paragraph

Correct the following sentences by adding or deleting capital letters as needed. If a sentence has no errors, write *C*.

EXAMPLE   [1] A gentle elephant named jumbo was once the largest, most popular captive animal in the World.
       1. *Jumbo, world*

[16] When p. t. barnum bought Jumbo in 1882, the elephant had already become a star with the London royal circus. [17] All of england protested the sale when the unhappy elephant refused to board the ship for New York city. [18] however, even queen Victoria and the prince of Wales could not prevent Jumbo's going, since the sale had been completed. [19] Jumbo's Trainer, Matthew Scott, kept the elephant content on the journey across the atlantic ocean. [20] In april, the new addition to "the Greatest Show on earth" arrived in New York, and the 13,500-pound Star marched up broadway to the cheers of

a huge crowd. [21] Soon Jumbo-mania swept across the United States. [22] The elephant was so popular that his name became a common word in the english language— *jumbo,* meaning "extra large." [23] He died tragically on September 15, 1885, in the canadian town of St. Thomas, Ontario. [24] The big-hearted giant, seeing a train bearing down on a baby elephant, pushed the youngster to safety but could not save himself. [25] To keep Jumbo's memory alive, Barnum donated the skeleton of his beloved elephant to the American Museum of natural history.

SUMMARY STYLE SHEET

Names of Persons

Malvina Hoffman	a sculptor
Mr. Jeff Rosenwald	a friend of the family
Dr. Marjorie Hempel	our family doctor

Geographical Names

Mexico City	a city in Mexico
Shetland County	a county in North Carolina
the Canary Islands	some islands in the Atlantic
Great Smoky Mountains	climbing mountains
Pacific Ocean	across the ocean
Sixth Street	a narrow street
Abilene State Park	a state park
in the East, North, Midwest	traveling east, north, west

Organizations, Business Firms, Institutions, Government Bodies

Oakdale Garden Club	a club for gardeners
Your Move Van Lines	a moving company
Vernon High School	a small high school
Supreme Court	a traffic court
Department of Commerce	a department of government

Historical Events and Periods, Special Events, Calendar Items

the Civil War	a bitter war
Atomic Age	an age of progress
National Open Golf Tournament	a golf tournament
Thanksgiving Day	a national holiday
in April or January	in spring or winter

(continued)

MECHANICS

MECHANICS

SUMMARY STYLE SHEET *(continued)*

Nationalities, Races, Religions

Japanese	a nationality
Caucasian	a race
Roman Catholic	a religion
Hanukkah	a holy day
God	a god of mythology

Brand Names

Ford Thunderbird	an automobile
Magnavox	a tape player

Other Particular Places, Things, Events, Awards

Great Republic	a clipper ship
City of New Orleans	a train
Apollo	a spacecraft
Nobel Prize	a prize
North Star	a bright star
Earth, Neptune, Pluto	on the earth
Jefferson Memorial	a memorial to Jefferson
Washington Monument	a monument in Washington
Senior Class Picnic	a senior in high school
Congressional Medal of Honor	a medal for bravery

Specific Courses, Languages

Chemistry I	my chemistry class
French	a foreign language
United States History II	the history book

Titles

Mayor Bradley	a mayor
Good morning, Mayor.	
the President of the United States	the president of the class
the Senator from Iowa	a senator's decision
the Queen of England	a queen's duties
Uncle John	my uncle
A Wrinkle in Time	a novel
the *Boston Herald*	a daily newspaper
Holy Bible	a religious book

24 PUNCTUATION

End Marks and Commas

Diagnostic Test

A. Correcting Sentences by Adding End Marks and Commas

Insert end marks and commas where necessary in the following sentences.

EXAMPLE **1.** After our hike in the woods can we go swimming in the lake

                  1. *After our hike in the woods, can we go swimming in the lake?*

1. Christy says that studying tae kwon do a Korean martial art has improved her concentration and given her self-confidence
2. Well that's the last time that I'll ever ride in a car with Matthew
3. Is the card addressed to Robert Daniels Jr or to Robert Daniels
4. The batter hoping to advance the runners laid down a perfect bunt

5. Use light colors by the way to make a small room seem larger
6. We used to live in Lansing but now we live at 457 Cleveland Rd Huntsville Alabama
7. Did you ask Joe to bring the forks plates and cups to the picnic or shall I bring them
8. What an interesting enjoyable book
9. After we had complained to Mrs Finch about the assignment we had to write letters of apology
10. Reva look out for that pothole in the road

B. Proofreading a Paragraph for End Marks and Commas

Insert the ten end marks and commas that are needed in the following paragraph.

EXAMPLE   [1] By the way have you ever wondered who invented the instant camera

1. *By the way, have you ever wondered who invented the instant camera?*

[11] When Edwin Land's daughter asked him why a camera couldn't immediately produce pictures he started thinking [12] Land, who had taught himself physics quickly worked out the basic principles and design for the instant camera. [13] What a tremendous achievement that was [14] He became head of Polaroid Corp and that company produced the first Polaroid Land camera in 1948. [15] Did you know that Land later made important contributions to the study of color vision and lasers [16] Land died on March 1 1991 [17] Among his honors were the Presidential Medal of Freedom and of course, the National Medal of Science.

___

In speaking, the tone and pitch of your voice, the pauses in your speech, and the gestures and expressions you use all help make your meaning clear. In writing, marks of punctuation, such as end marks and commas, tell readers where these verbal and nonverbal cues occur.

End Marks

End marks—periods, question marks, exclamation points— are used to indicate the purpose of a sentence.

☞ REFERENCE NOTE: For a discussion of how sentences are classified according to purpose, see Chapter 15, pages 527–528.

24a. A statement (or declarative sentence) is followed by a period.

EXAMPLES Nancy López won the tournament.
What Balboa saw below was the Pacific Ocean.
Flora wondered who had already gone.

Notice in the third example that a declarative sentence containing an indirect question is followed by a period.

24b. A question (or interrogative sentence) is followed by a question mark.

EXAMPLES Can a cat see color?
Was the plane late?
Who wrote this note? Did you?

A direct question may have the same word order as a declarative sentence. Since it *is* a question, however, it is followed by a question mark.

EXAMPLES A cat can see color?
The plane was late?

Be sure to distinguish between a declarative sentence that contains an indirect question and an interrogative sentence, which asks a direct question.

INDIRECT QUESTION   He asked me **what worries her.** [declarative]
DIRECT QUESTION   **What worries her?** [interrogative]

24c. An exclamation is followed by an exclamation point.

EXAMPLES Hurrah! What a great play!
Ouch!
Look out!

MECHANICS

Some declarative and interrogative sentences show such strong feeling that they are more like exclamations than statements or questions. If so, an exclamation point should be used instead of a period or a question mark.

EXAMPLES   Here comes the bus!
Can't you speak up!

24d. An imperative sentence is followed by either a period or an exclamation point.

When an imperative sentence makes a request, it is generally followed by a period. Imperative sentences, particularly commands, may also show strong feeling. In such cases, an exclamation point should be used.

EXAMPLES   Please be quiet.
Be quiet!

Sometimes, a command or request is stated in the form of a question. Because of the purpose, however, the sentence is really an imperative sentence and is followed by a period or an exclamation point.

EXAMPLES   May I say a few words now.
Will you stop that!

24e. An abbreviation is usually followed by a period.

TYPES OF ABBREVIATIONS	EXAMPLES
Personal Names	A. E. Housman B. B. King
Titles Used with Names	Mr. Ms. Mrs. Jr. Dr.
States	Calif. Mass. Tex. Nebr.
Time of Day	A.M. P.M.
Years	B.C. A.D.
Addresses	Ave. St. Blvd. Pkwy.
Organizations and Companies	Assn. Co. Inc. Corp.

NOTE: Two-letter state abbreviations without periods are used only when the ZIP Code number is included.

EXAMPLE   Cincinnati, OH 45233

Abbreviations for government agencies and international organizations and some other frequently used abbreviations are written without periods. Abbreviations for most units of measure are usually written without periods, especially in science books. However, a period is always used with the abbreviation for *inch (in.)* to avoid confusion with the word *in*.

EXAMPLES   TV, IQ, FM, UFO, ROTC, USAF, UN
            lb, oz, qt, ft, mi, rpm, km, ml, kg

Shoe reprinted by permission: Tribune Media Services.

If a statement ends with an abbreviation, do not use an additional period as an end mark. However, do use a question mark or an exclamation point if one is needed.

EXAMPLES   Mrs. Tavares visited her relatives in Newark, N.J.
            How long did she stay in Newark, N.J.?

If you are unsure about whether to use periods with abbreviations, look in a dictionary.

MECHANICS

▷ EXERCISE 1   **Correcting Sentences by Adding
                End Marks**

Write the following sentences, adding periods, question marks, or exclamation points as needed.

EXAMPLE   **1.** Does Josh come from Raleigh, NC
           1. *Does Josh come from Raleigh, N.C.?*

1. What a car
2. Whose car is that
3. We asked who owned that car
4. Roman troops invaded Britain in 54 BC
5. By AD 800, Baghdad was already an important city
6. Dr Edward Jenner gave the first vaccination against smallpox in 1796

7. Why do children enjoy using computers
8. Please explain why so many children enjoy using computers
9. When did the Rev. Jesse Jackson run for president
10. Terrific Another coin for my collection

EXERCISE 2 **Using End Marks**

Add periods, question marks, or exclamation points where they are needed in the following sentences. After each sentence, identify the kind of sentence it is.

EXAMPLE [1] Are you familiar with lacrosse, a field game
1. *Are you familiar with lacrosse, a field game?—interrogative*

[1] Just look at these players [2] This picture shows members of Caddo and Choctaw teams competing in a serious game of lacrosse [3] What a rough sport lacrosse must be [4] Did you know that North American Indians actually developed this game [5] Before Columbus came to the Americas in AD 1492, the Iroquois were playing lacrosse around the area of upper New York State and Canada [6] Do you realize that this makes lacrosse the oldest organized sport in America [7] Lacrosse is played by two opposing teams [8] Players use a stick to catch, carry, and throw a ball, which is about 8 in around [9] The head of the stick looks like a bishop's cross, and that's where the name of the game comes from (French, *la crosse*) [10] Lacrosse is especially popular in Canada, the British Isles, and Australia, and it is played in the U S, too

PICTURE THIS

During your vacation to a dude ranch in Texas, you come upon this scene. To record these events for your friends back home, you jot down notes in your vacation journal. Write some of the comments that you overhear while watching these cowboys break the horse and train it to wear a saddle and carry a rider. Write two statements, two questions, two exclamations, and two requests or commands. Use proper end marks (periods, question marks, and exclamation points) for the different types of sentences.

Subject: breaking a horse
Audience: friends
Purpose: to express observations, feelings

Frederic Remington, *His First Lesson*, 1903, Oil on Canvas, Amon Carter Museum, Fort Worth. 1961.231.

MECHANICS

Commas

If you fail to use necessary commas, you may confuse your reader.

CONFUSING   The friends I have invited are Ruth Ann Jerry Lee Derrick Martha and Julie. [How many friends?]

CLEAR   The friends I have invited are Ruth Ann, Jerry Lee, Derrick, Martha, and Julie. [five friends]

24f. Use commas to separate items in a series.

Notice in the following examples that the number of commas in a series is one less than the number of items in the series.

EXAMPLES   All my cousins, aunts, and uncles came to our family reunion. [words]
The children played in the yard, at the playground, and by the pond. [phrases]
Those who had flown to the reunion, who had driven many miles, or who had even taken time off from their jobs were glad that they had made the effort to be there. [clauses]

When the last two items in a series are joined by *and,* you may omit the comma before the *and* if the comma is not necessary to make the meaning clear.

CLEAR WITH
COMMA OMITTED   The salad contained lettuce, tomatoes, cucumbers, carrots and radishes.

NOT CLEAR WITH
COMMA OMITTED   Our school newspaper has editors for news, sports, humor, features and art. [How many editors are there, four or five? Does one person serve as feature and art editor, or is an editor needed for each job?]

CLEAR WITH
COMMA INCLUDED   Our school newspaper has editors for news, sports, humor, features, and art. [five editors]

Some writers prefer always to use the comma before the *and* in a series. Follow your teacher's instructions on this point.

NOTE: Some words—such as *bread and butter, rod and reel, table and chairs*—are used in pairs and may be considered one item in a series.

EXAMPLE   My favorite breakfast is milk, **biscuits and gravy,** and fruit.

(1) If all items in a series are joined by *and* or *or,* do not use commas to separate them.

EXAMPLES   I need tacks and nails and a hammer.
Sam or Carlos or Yolanda will be able to baby-sit tomorrow night.

(2) Independent clauses in a series are usually separated by semicolons. Short independent clauses, however, may be separated by commas.

EXAMPLES   As the day wore on, the sky grew dark; tree branches swayed in the wind; the bitter cold deepened; and the first snowflakes fell.
The sky darkened, branches swayed, the cold deepened, and snow fell.

24g.   Use commas to separate two or more adjectives preceding a noun.

EXAMPLE   Are you going to that hot, crowded, noisy mall?

When the last adjective in a series is thought of as part of the noun, the comma before the adjective is omitted.

EXAMPLES   I study in our small dining room.
I'll drink cool, refreshing orange juice.

Compound nouns like *orange juice, dining room,* and *post office* are considered single units—as though the two words were one word.

When two or more adjectives precede a noun, you can use two tests to determine whether the last adjective and the noun form a unit.

TEST 1:   Insert the word *and* between the adjectives. If *and* fits sensibly between the adjectives, use a comma. In the first example sentence, *and* cannot be logically inserted: *small and dining room.* In the second sentence, *and* sounds logical between the first two adjectives (*cool and refreshing*) but not between the second and third (*refreshing and orange*).

TEST 2:   Change the order of the adjectives. If the order of the adjectives can be reversed sensibly, use a comma. *Refreshing, cool orange juice* makes sense, but *orange cool, refreshing juice* and *dining small room* do not.

REFERENCE NOTE: For more information on compound nouns, see pages 467–468.

MECHANICS

▶ EXERCISE 3 **Correcting Sentences by Adding Commas**

Write each series in the following sentences, adding commas where needed.

EXAMPLE **1.** Rita plays soccer volleyball and softball.
1. *soccer, volleyball, and softball*
or
soccer, volleyball and softball

1. Dr. Charles Drew worked as a surgeon developed new ways of storing blood and was the first director of the Red Cross blood bank program.
2. I am going to take English science social studies algebra and Spanish.
3. The loud insistent smoke alarm woke us just before dawn this morning.
4. Please pass those delicious blueberry pancakes the margarine and the syrup.
5. My twin sister can run faster jump higher and do more push-ups than I can.
6. Where is the nearest store that sells newspapers magazines and paperbacks?
7. Horns tooted tires screeched a whistle blew and sirens wailed.
8. Steel is made from iron other metals and small amounts of carbon.
9. The clown wore a long blue raincoat big red plastic gloves and floppy yellow tennis shoes.
10. Robert Browning says that youth is good that middle age is better and that old age is best.

▶ EXERCISE 4 **Using Commas Correctly in Series**

Your school's new counselor wants to get to know the students better. He has developed the personality questionnaire shown on the next page, and today he's given a copy to all the students in your class. Answer each question by writing a sentence that includes a series of words, phrases, or short independent clauses. Use commas where needed in each series.

EXAMPLE **1.** What do you consider your most outstanding traits?
1. *I am considerate, thoughtful, and loyal.*

PERSONALITY QUESTIONNAIRE

1. What do you consider your most outstanding traits?
2. What qualities do you admire most in a person?
3. Who are the people who have influenced you most?
4. What are your favorite hobbies?
5. What famous people would you like to meet?
6. What countries would you most like to visit?
7. For what reasons do you attend school?
8. What are your favorite subjects in school?
9. What things about the world would you most like to change?
10. What goals do you hope to achieve during the next ten years?

24h. Use commas before *and, but, or, nor, for, so,* and *yet* when they join independent clauses.

Do not be misled by compound verbs, which often make a sentence look as if it contains two independent clauses.

COMPOUND SENTENCE **Mara cleared the table, and Roland did the dishes.** [two independent clauses]

SIMPLE SENTENCE Mara **cleared** the table and **did** the dishes. [one subject with a compound verb]

☞ **REFERENCE NOTE:** For more about compound sentences, see pages 577–578. For a discussion of compound subjects and compound verbs, see pages 514–517.

In the following correctly punctuated compound sentences, notice that independent clauses appear on both sides of the coordinating conjunctions.

Hector pressed the button**, and** the engine started up.
She would never argue**, nor** would she complain to anyone.

NOTE: A comma is always used before *for, so,* and *yet* joining two independent clauses. The comma may be omitted, however, before *and, but, or,* or *nor* when the independent clauses are very short and when there is no possibility of misunderstanding.

EXAMPLE I read that book and I liked it.

MECHANICS

▶ EXERCISE 5   **Correcting Sentences by Adding Commas Between Independent Clauses**

Where a comma should be used, write the word preceding the comma, the comma, and the conjunction following it. If a sentence is correct, write C.

EXAMPLE   **1.** Accident-related injuries are common but many of these injuries could be prevented.
1. *common, but*

1. It is important to know first aid for an accident can happen at any time.
2. More than 83,000 people in the United States die in accidents each year and many millions are injured.
3. Many household products can cause illness or even death yet these products are often stored where small children can reach them.
4. Biking accidents are common wherever cars and bicycles use the same road so bicycle lanes are provided in many communities.
5. Car accidents are the leading cause of childhood fatalities but seat belts have saved many lives.
6. Everyone should know what to do in case of fire and different escape routes should be tested beforehand.
7. To escape a fire, stay close to the floor, and be very cautious about opening doors.
8. Hold your breath and keep low and protected behind a door when opening it for a blast of super-heated air from an adjoining room or hallway can be fatal.
9. An injured person should not be allowed to get up nor should liquid be given to an unconscious victim.
10. Always have someone with you when you swim or you may find yourself without help when you need it.

24i. Use commas to set off nonessential clauses and nonessential participial phrases.

A *nonessential* (or *nonrestrictive*) clause or participial phrase adds information that is not necessary to the main idea in the sentence.

NONESSENTIAL CLAUSES	Eileen Murray**,** **who is at the top of her class,** wants to go to medical school. Texas**,** **which has the most farms in this country,** produces one fourth of our oil.
NONESSENTIAL PHRASES	Tim Ricardo**,** **hoping to make the swim team,** practiced every day. *The Lord of the Rings* **,** **written by J.R.R. Tolkien,** has been translated into many languages.

Each boldfaced clause or phrase above can be omitted because it is not essential to identify the word or phrase it modifies. Omitting such a clause or phrase will not change the meaning of the sentence.

EXAMPLES   Eileen Murray wants to go to medical school.
Tim Ricardo practiced every day.

When a clause or phrase is necessary to the meaning of a sentence—that is, when it tells *which ones* —the clause or phrase is *essential* (or *restrictive*), and commas are *not* used.

Notice how the meaning of the sentence below changes when the essential clause is omitted.

All students **whose names are on that list** must report to Mrs. Washington this afternoon.
All students must report to Mrs. Washington this afternoon.

NOTE: An adjective clause beginning with *that* is usually essential.

EXAMPLE   Was Hank Aaron the first major league baseball player **that** broke Babe Ruth's home run record?

"SURE I GOT ALL THE PUNCTUATION: COMMA, COMMA, PERIOD, PERIOD, QUESTION MARK, COMMA, SEMI-COLON, COMMA, EXCLAMATION POINT, PERIOD..."

©1998 by Sidney Harris.

MECHANICS

EXERCISE 6

Correcting Sentences with Clauses by Adding or Removing Commas

Most of the following sentences contain nonessential or essential clauses. Correctly punctuate each of these clauses. If a sentence is correct, write *C*.

EXAMPLE   **1.** My mother who is a Celtics fan has season tickets to their home games.

         1. *My mother, who is a Celtics fan, has season tickets to their home games.*

1. "Doonesbury" which is my favorite comic strip makes me think as well as laugh.
2. Our math teacher who also teaches gym will leave at the end of the year.
3. The amusement rides that are the most exciting may be the most dangerous.
4. Many of the first settlements in California were founded by Father Junípero Serra who liked to take long walks between them.
5. People, who carry credit cards, should keep a record of their account numbers at home.
6. Amy Kwan who is class president plans to go to Yale.
7. A town like Cottonwood which has a population of five thousand seems ideal to me.
8. All dogs that pass the obedience test get a reward.
9. Have you tried this pemmican which my mother made from an old Cree recipe?
10. "The Gift of the Magi" is a beautiful story, in which the two main characters who are deeply in love make sacrifices in order to buy gifts for each other.

EXERCISE 7

Correcting Sentences with Participial Phrases by Adding or Removing Commas

Correctly punctuate the participial phrases in the following sentences. If a sentence is correctly punctuated, write *C*.

1. People, visiting the reservation, will be barred from burial sites, which are considered holy by Native Americans.
2. Players breaking training will be dismissed from the team.

3. Students, planning to go on the field trip, should bring their lunches.
4. The ants swarming onto the tablecloth made straight for the picnic basket.
5. An owl hooting far away sounded as lonely as I felt.
6. Elizabeth Blackwell completing her medical studies in 1849 became the first female doctor in the United States.
7. Pressure and heat acting on the remains of plants and animals turn them into gas or oil or coal.
8. Every child, registering for school for the first time, must present evidence of certain vaccinations.
9. The astronauts living in space for several days studied the effects of weightlessness.
10. The castle built as a fortress in the sixteenth century is now famous as a tourist attraction.

▶ REVIEW A

Correcting Sentences with Clauses and Participial Phrases by Adding Commas

Some of the following sentences contain clauses and phrases that need to be set off by commas. If a sentence is incorrect, add the necessary comma or commas. If a sentence is correctly punctuated, write C.

EXAMPLE   **1.** Hanukkah which is also called the Feast of Lights is a major Jewish celebration.
   1. *Hanukkah, which is also called the Feast of Lights, is a major Jewish celebration.*

1. The picture on the next page shows a part of the Hanukkah celebration that is very beautiful.
2. The girl following an ancient custom is lighting the menorah.
3. The menorah which is an eight-branched candlestick symbolizes the original festival.
4. Hanukkah which means "dedication" celebrates the rededication of the Temple of Jerusalem in 165 B.C.
5. This event followed the Jewish people's victory over the Syrians who were led by a pagan king.
6. During the first Hanukkah, according to traditional lore, the Jews had a one-day supply of lamp oil that lasted for eight days.

MECHANICS

7. Modern Jews celebrating the memory of this miraculous event light one candle on the menorah each day of the eight-day festival.
8. Hanukkah starts on the twenty-fifth day of the Hebrew month of Kislev which is usually in December on the Gregorian calendar.
9. The festival celebrated all over the world is a time of feasting, gift-giving, and happiness.
10. During Hanukkah, children play a game with a dreidel which is a four-sided toy spun like a top.

 REVIEW B   **Correcting Sentences by Adding Commas**

Add commas where they are needed in the following sentences. If a sentence does not require any commas, write *C*.

EXAMPLE   **1.** The emu is a large flightless bird from Australia.
　　　　　1. *The emu is a large, flightless bird from Australia.*

1. The students sold crafts used books and baked goods at the bazaar.
2. John Wayne whose real name was Marion Morrison won an Academy Award for *True Grit.*
3. Add flour mix the ingredients and stir the batter.
4. People who come to the game early will be allowed to take pictures of the players.
5. *A Raisin in the Sun* written by Lorraine Hansberry will be performed by the Grantville Community Players and will run for three weeks.

MECHANICS

6. The float in the homecoming parade was covered with delicate pink rose petals and small white sunflower seeds.
7. Members of the committee met for three hours but they still have not chosen a theme for the dance.
8. Helium which is used by balloonists deep-sea divers and welders is an inert gas.
9. An eclipse that occurs when the earth blocks the sun's light from the moon is called a lunar eclipse.
10. In one month our little town was hit by a tornado and a flood and a fire yet we managed to survive.

24j. Use commas after certain introductory elements.

(1) Use a comma after words such as *well, yes, no,* and *why* when they begin a sentence.

EXAMPLES   **Yes,** she's going to the cafeteria.
           Ah, there's nothing like cold water on a hot day!

☞ REFERENCE NOTE: These introductory words are called interjections; see pages 495–496.

(2) Use a comma after an introductory participial phrase.

EXAMPLES   **Switching on a flashlight,** the ranger led the way down the path.
           Disappointed by the high prices, we made up a new gift list.

(3) Use a comma after a series of introductory prepositional phrases.

EXAMPLES   **Inside the fence at the far end of her property,** she built a potting shed.
           By the end of the train ride, the children were exhausted.

A short introductory prepositional phrase does not require a comma unless the comma is necessary to make the meaning clear.

EXAMPLES   **At our house** we share all the work.
           At our house, plants grow best in the sunny, bright kitchen. [The comma is necessary to avoid reading *house plants.*]

MECHANICS

(4) Use a comma after an introductory adverb clause.

EXAMPLES **After Andrés Segovia had played his last guitar concert,** the audience applauded for more than fifteen minutes.
When you see smoke, you know there is a fire.

▶ EXERCISE 8 **Correcting Sentences with Introductory Elements by Adding Commas**

Add commas where they are needed after introductory elements in the following sentences. If a sentence is correct, write C.

EXAMPLES **1.** When Marco Polo visited China in the thirteenth century he found an advanced civilization.
1. *When Marco Polo visited China in the thirteenth century,*

1. Although there was a great deal of poverty in China the ruling classes lived in splendor.
2. Valuing cleanliness Chinese rulers took baths every day.
3. Instead of using coins the Chinese used paper money.
4. After marrying a Chinese woman lived in her mother-in-law's home.
5. After one Chinese emperor had died he was buried with more than eight thousand statues of servants and horses.
6. Respected by all their descendants elderly people were highly honored.

Ma Yüan (c. 1160–1225), *Facing the Moon, Southern Sung Dynasty,* The Granger Collection, New York.

MECHANICS

7. Built around 200 B.C. the main part of the Great Wall is about four thousand miles long.
8. Until modern freeways were built the Great Wall was the world's longest construction.
9. In Chinese art people are very small and are usually shown in harmony with nature.
10. As you can see in the painting on the previous page Chinese landscapes look different from those done by Western artists.

24k. Use commas to set off elements that interrupt the sentence.

Two commas are used around an interrupting element—one before and one after.

EXAMPLES That boy, in fact, worked very hard.
Linda, my friend who moved to Ecuador, sent me a long letter.

Sometimes an "interrupter" comes at the beginning or at the end of a sentence. In these cases, only one comma is needed.

EXAMPLES Nevertheless, you must go with me.
I need the money, Josh.

(1) Appositives and appositive phrases are usually set off by commas.

EXAMPLES My dog, **a collie,** is very gentle.
My favorite actress, **Rita Moreno,** stars in the movie I rented.
Everyone, **even his parents,** thinks he is making a mistake.

Sometimes an appositive is so closely related to the word preceding it that it should not be set off by commas. Such an appositive usually has no modifiers; that is, there is no appositive phrase.

EXAMPLES My best friend **Tamisha** lost her wallet.
He recited the second stanza of "Childhood" by the poet **Margaret Walker.**
We **freshmen** made the decorations for the dance.

MECHANICS

EXERCISE 9

Correcting Sentences with Appositives and Appositive Phrases by Adding Commas

Correctly punctuate the appositives in the following sentences. If a sentence is correct as written, write *C*.

EXAMPLE   **1.** My cousin consulted Dr. Moniz an allergy specialist about the harmful effects of pollution.
   1. *My cousin consulted Dr. Moniz, an allergy specialist, about the harmful effects of pollution.*

1. "Ecology" an obscure word thirty years ago has become a popular term today.
2. The word's origin is *oikos* the Greek word meaning "house."
3. Ecology is the study of an enormous "house" the world of all living things.
4. Ecologists study the bond of a living organism to its environment the place in which it lives.
5. Humans one kind of living organism affect their environment in both beneficial and harmful ways.
6. My cousin Claudia is worried about the future of the environment.
7. She and many of her friends attended Earth Day a festival devoted to ecology.
8. An amateur photographer my cousin prepared a slide show on soil erosion in Grant Park.
9. One of many displays at the Earth Day Festival my cousin's presentation attracted wide attention and won a prize.
10. The mayor a member of the audience promised to appoint a committee to study the problem.

(2) Words used in direct address are set off by commas.

EXAMPLES   **Linda,** you know the rules.
   I did that exercise last night, **Ms. Ryan.**
   Your room, **Bernice,** needs cleaning.

EXERCISE 10

Correcting Sentences with Words in Direct Address by Adding Commas

Correct the following sentences by adding commas where they are needed.

1. Dad why can't I go to the movies tonight?
2. As soon as you're ready Virginia we'll leave.
3. Yes Mom I washed the dishes.
4. What we need Mayor Wilson are more playgrounds.
5. Will you answer the last question Jim?

(3) Parenthetical expressions are set off by commas.

Parenthetical expressions are side remarks that add information or relate ideas. In writing, you should ordinarily use commas to set off parenthetical matter.

☞ REFERENCE NOTE: Sometimes parentheses and dashes are used to set off parenthetical matter. For information on using these punctuation marks, see pages 829–834.

Commonly Used Parenthetical Expressions		
after all	generally speaking	nevertheless
at any rate	however	of course
consequently	I believe	on the contrary
for example	in the first place	on the other hand
for instance	moreover	therefore

EXAMPLES **On the contrary,** I am glad that you told me about the error.
She is, **in fact,** a dentist.
You should try out for quarterback, **in my opinion.**

Some expressions may be used both parenthetically and not parenthetically.

EXAMPLES Sandra will, **I think,** enjoy the program. [parenthetical]
I think Sandra will enjoy the program. [not parenthetical]

However, did you finish your report on time? [parenthetical]
However did you finish your report on time? [not parenthetical—similar to "How did you finish?"]

To tell the truth, he tries. [parenthetical]
He tries **to tell the truth.** [not parenthetical]

MECHANICS

NOTE: A contrasting expression introduced by *not* is parenthetical and must be set off by commas.

EXAMPLE   It is the spirit of the giver, **not the cost of the gift,** that counts.

EXERCISE 11

Correcting Sentences with Parenthetical Expressions by Adding Commas

Correctly punctuate the parenthetical expressions in the following sentences.

EXAMPLE   1. In my opinion my little sister Iona has great taste in music.

1. *In my opinion, my little sister Iona has great taste in music.*

© Suzanne Steers; Courtesy Music for Little People.

1. For instance her favorite collection of songs is called *Gift of the Tortoise*.
2. Performed I believe by Ladysmith Black Mambazo, the songs are a blend of English and Zulu words and phrases.
3. The South African performers in fact sing *a cappella* (without musical instruments accompanying them).
4. Not surprisingly their powerful style of music is known worldwide.
5. Fudugazi by the way is the storytelling tortoise who explains the meaning of the songs.
6. By listening to the song "Finger Dance," Iona has learned believe it or not to count to five in Zulu.
7. She has not yet learned to sing any of the songs in Zulu however.

MECHANICS

8. Of course our whole family enjoys listening to these South African songs.
9. The music and sound effects moreover seem to transport us to another land and culture.
10. Everyone should I think follow Fudugazi's advice: "There is magic in these songs; close your eyes and listen, and you will feel the magic too!"

241. Use commas in certain conventional situations.

(1) Use a comma to separate items in dates and addresses.

EXAMPLES   My family moved to Oakland, California, on Wednesday, December 5, 1996.
On December 5, 1996, our address became 25 Peralta Road, Oakland, CA 94611.

Notice that no comma divides the month and day (December 5) or the house number and the street name (25 Peralta Road) because each is considered one item. Also, the ZIP Code is not separated from the abbreviation of the state by a comma: Oakland, CA 94611.

(2) Use a comma after the salutation of a friendly letter and after the closing of any letter.

EXAMPLES   Dear Ms. Chen,   Sincerely yours,
My dear Anna,   Yours very truly,

(3) Use a comma after a name followed by an abbreviation such as *Jr., Sr.,* and *M.D.*

EXAMPLES   Allen Davis, Sr.   Ens. Tanya Jay, U.S.N.
Carol Ferrara, M.D.   Dr. Martin Luther King, Jr.

▶ EXERCISE 12   **Correcting Sentences by Adding Commas**

Add commas where they are needed in the following sentences. If a sentence is correct as it stands, write *C*.

EXAMPLE   1. On July 14 1789 the French people stormed and destroyed the Bastille.
1. *On July 14, 1789, the French people stormed and destroyed the Bastille.*

1. Please send this letter to Ms. Marybeth Correio 1255 S.E. 56th Street Bellevue WA 98006.
2. On April 6 1909 Matthew Henson, assistant to Commander Robert E. Peary, reached the North Pole.
3. I glanced quickly at the end of the letter, which read, "Very sincerely yours Alice Ems Ph.D."
4. The Constitution of the United States was signed on September 17 1787 eleven years after the adoption of the Declaration of Independence on July 4 1776.
5. Did you go on a field trip to the desert in March or April of 1991?

24m. Do not use unnecessary commas.

Too much punctuation is just as confusing as not enough punctuation. This is especially true of commas.

CONFUSING My friend, Jessica, said she would feed my cat and my dog while I'm away, but now, she tells me, she is too busy.

CLEAR My friend Jessica said she would feed my cat and my dog while I'm away, but now she tells me she is too busy.

Have a *reason* for every comma or other mark of punctuation that you use. When there is no rule requiring punctuation and when the meaning of the sentence is clear without it, do not insert any punctuation mark.

EXERCISE 13 **Using Commas Correctly**

A star was born, right in your town, and that star is a friend of yours. Your famous friend has written to you that he or she will soon be coming home for a visit. Now it's your turn to write a friendly letter in response. Write a short letter to your friend, telling about your activities and sharing your thoughts and feelings about your friend's career. You also could plan a reunion or a party during your friend's homecoming. Use commas correctly, especially in the salutation and closing of your friendly letter. Proofread your letter to make sure you have not used any unnecessary commas.

MECHANICS

INCORRECT   When you come home, I'd like to go to our favorite
swimming hole, on the lake, and, maybe, Jeremy,
and Francine, will come with us.

REVISED   *When you come home, I'd like to go to our favorite*
swimming hole on the lake, and maybe Jeremy and
Francine will come with us.

▶ REVIEW C   **Correcting Sentences by Adding Commas**

For each of the following sentences, write all the words
that should be followed by a comma. Place a comma after
each of these words.

EXAMPLE   **1.** Yes Phyllis I know that you want to transfer to
Bayside the high school that has the best volleyball
team in the city.
1. *Yes, Phyllis, Bayside,*

1. Scuttling across the dirt road the large hairy spider a
tarantula terrified Steve Ellen and me.
2. Whitney not Don won first prize.
3. Although German shepherds are most often trained
as guide dogs other breeds that have also been used
include Labrador retrievers golden retrievers and
Doberman pinschers.
4. According to her birth certificate she was born July 7
1976 in Juneau Alaska.
5. Angela and Jennifer are you both planning to write
poems?
6. All poetry entries should be submitted no later than
Friday to Poetry Contest 716 North Cliff Drive Salt
Lake City UT 84103.
7. The best time to plant flower seeds of course is just
before a rainy season not in the middle of a hot dry
summer.
8. Our neighbor Ms. Allen manages two apartment
buildings downtown.
9. As a matter of fact most horses can run four miles
without having to stop.
10. The Comanches like other nomadic Native
Americans once traveled throughout Kansas New
Mexico Texas and Oklahoma.

MECHANICS

▶ REVIEW D **Adding End Marks and Commas**

Add end marks and commas where they are needed in each sentence in the following paragraph.

EXAMPLE [1] As you can see from this map Cabeza de Vaca explored areas in North America and South America

1. *As you can see from this map, Cabeza de Vaca explored areas in North America and South America.*

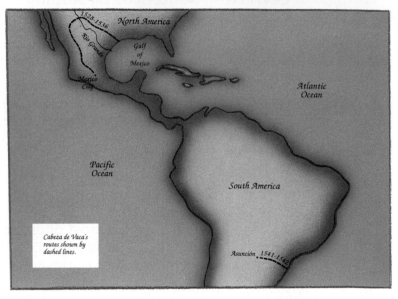

[1] Did you know that Álvar Núñez Cabeza de Vaca a Spanish explorer participated in two trips to this region [2] To tell the truth neither trip ended successfully [3] In the summer of 1527 he was treasurer of an expedition that was sent to conquer and colonize Florida [4] However the invasion didn't work out as planned and he was one of only four survivors [5] These men intended to sail to Mexico but their ship wrecked off the coast of Texas [6] What an unlucky expedition [7] Cabeza de Vaca was captured by Indians but he later escaped and wandered through Texas and Mexico for eight years [8] He tells about his Florida expedition in his book titled *Naufragios* which is the Spanish word for "shipwrecks." [9] In 1541 this adventurer led an expedition to South America and he became governor of Paraguay [10] When the colonists revolted Cabeza de Vaca returned to Spain under arrest but he was later pardoned.

MECHANICS

WRITING APPLICATION

Using Commas to Give Clear Directions

You may think that using commas is confusing, but *not* using commas can be even more confusing.

CONFUSING Quite unexpectedly Mr. Lind my father's friend and co-worker gave us a large antique bird cage four parakeets two parrots and fifty pounds of bird feed.

CLEAR Quite unexpectedly, Mr. Lind, my father's friend and co-worker, gave us a large, antique bird cage, four parakeets, two parrots, and fifty pounds of bird feed.

As you can see, commas in this sentence aren't just for the birds. They are needed to make the meaning clear. What four rules for commas are illustrated in the clear sentence?

▶ WRITING ACTIVITY

A friend asks you for directions from your school to a particular destination. In your instructions, use commas to separate items in a series, to join independent clauses, to set off an introductory adverb clause, to set off a noun of direct address, and to separate items in an address.

Prewriting Choose a destination (real or imagined), and then outline in your mind or on paper the way to get there.

Writing As you write your first draft, think about making the directions clear and easy to follow.

Evaluating and Revising Read through your directions to be sure they are arranged in a logical order. Check to see that your sentences correctly illustrate the five comma usage rules stated in the instructions for this writing activity.

Proofreading Be sure that you have capitalized geographical names and names of persons and businesses, but not words such as *north* and *south* used as compass directions. (See pages 717–738 for more about capitalization.)

MECHANICS

Review: Posttest

Correcting Sentences by Adding End Marks and Commas

Write the following paragraphs, adding end marks and commas where necessary.

EXAMPLE   [1] Computers therefore are not my cup of tea
          1. *Computers, therefore, are not my cup of tea.*

[1] Although TV commercials tell you otherwise computers are not for everyone [2] One day in the showroom of a computer store I stared at a personal computer for more than half an hour but I was still unable to locate the on-off switch [3] The demonstrator Ms Pearl Rangely PhD tried her hardest to be helpful [4] A computer consultant she quickly explained the functions of various switches buttons and boxes [5] She pressed keys she flashed words on the screen and she pushed around a device called a "mouse" [6] I was confused and puzzled and frustrated yet I was also fascinated

[7] Dr Rangely who had often encountered confused consumers before told me that I had "terminal" phobia [8] With a frown I asked her what that meant [9] She replied grinning broadly that it was the fear that bits and bytes can actually bite [10] What a comedian [11] Totally disenchanted I left the store

[12] I headed straight for the library to check out everything that I could find about computers: books magazines catalogs and pamphlets [13] For example I read *The Soul of a New Machine* a fascinating book written by Tracy Kidder [14] When I had finished the book I knew about input output high-level languages and debugging [15] Armed with this knowledge I returned to the store on Friday March 13 [16] Well the same demonstrator was there smiling like a Cheshire cat [17] I rattled off several questions which I think must have surprised her [18] In one afternoon Dr Rangely taught me something about every computer in the store [19] I left however without asking one simple embarrassing question [20] To tell the truth I still don't know where the on-off switch is

SUMMARY OF USES OF THE COMMA

24f Use commas to separate items in a series.

    (1) If all items in a series are joined by *and* or *or*, do not use commas to separate them.

    (2) Independent clauses in a series are usually separated by semicolons. Short independent clauses, however, may be separated by commas.

24g Use commas to separate two or more adjectives preceding a noun.

24h Use commas before *and*, *but*, *or*, *nor*, *for*, *so*, and *yet* when they join independent clauses.

24i Use commas to set off nonessential clauses and nonessential participial phrases.

24j Use commas after certain introductory elements.

    (1) Use a comma after words such as *well*, *yes*, *no*, and *why* when they begin a sentence.

    (2) Use a comma after an introductory participial phrase.

    (3) Use a comma after a series of introductory prepositional phrases.

    (4) Use a comma after an introductory adverb clause.

24k Use commas to set off sentence interrupters.

    (1) Appositives and appositive phrases are usually set off by commas.

    (2) Words used in direct address are set off by commas.

    (3) Parenthetical expressions are set off by commas.

24l Use commas in certain conventional situations.

    (1) Use a comma to separate items in dates and addresses.

    (2) Use a comma after the salutation of a friendly letter and after the closing of any letter.

    (3) Use a comma after a name followed by an abbreviation such as *Jr.*, *Sr.*, and M. D.

24m Do not use unnecessary commas.

MECHANICS

25 PUNCTUATION

Semicolons and Colons

Diagnostic Test

A. Correcting Sentences by Using Semicolons and Colons

Most of the following sentences use a comma or have no punctuation mark at all where there should be a semicolon or a colon. Write each word or number preceding an error, and add the correct punctuation mark. If the sentence is correct, write C.

EXAMPLE **1.** Leon finished his model of the *Apollo 7*, now he is working on a model of the *Eagle*.
1. *Apollo 7;*

1. Cora Mae hurt her ankle when she slid into second base, nevertheless, she finished the game.
2. The most abundant minerals in the human body are calcium, phosphorus, and iron.
3. Nearsightedness is called myopia, farsightedness is called hyperopia.

4. For the opinion survey, Billie will call the Grays, the Mitchells, and the Millers, and Jesse will call the Chuns, the Van Horns, and the Schmidts.
5. Before I began my science project, I reviewed these chapters in my textbook "Sponges," "Mollusks," and "Arthropods The Most Abundant Animals."
6. Dr. Martha Loomis cited Proverbs 29 11 and 29 22 as warnings against letting anger take control of you.
7. In class today, we discussed the contributions of Gutenberg, the inventor of the printing press, Galileo, the inventor of the first complete astronomical telescope, and Newton, the discoverer of the laws of gravity.
8. Ms. Larussa leaves for work at 7 30 every morning and returns promptly at 5 35 every evening.
9. Ahmad was surprised to see Juana, Michelle, and me; we had all kept his birthday party a secret.
10. My dad put the following quotation by Dr. Martin Luther King, Jr., on the wall over his desk "Injustice anywhere is a threat to justice everywhere."

B. Proofreading for Correct Use of Semicolons and Colons

The following advertisement contains ten errors in the use of semicolons or colons. If a semicolon or a colon is needed in a sentence, write the word or number preceding the error and add the needed mark.

EXAMPLE [1] **Your pet probably loves to watch TV therefore, it should have the best in quality entertainment!**
1. *TV;*

[11] Buy your faithful friend the new *Rappin' and Rockin' Pets* video it will make your cat or dog sit up and take notice. [12] With this video, your pet will get the exciting, up-to-date entertainment it has been craving, and, as a concerned owner, you will feel good about what your pet is watching. [13] Science has proven that cats and dogs like the movement and music on television, moreover, they like human contact while watching TV. [14] But are you thinking about your pet's happiness when you turn on the set at 7 00 or 8 00 in the evening? [15] Do you think

your pet really likes to watch the following programs situation comedies, which are about families it doesn't know, movies, which are too long, and news programs, which are too serious? **[16]** You already know the answer order your pet a *Rappin' and Rockin' Pets* video today! **[17]** To place your order, call the following toll-free number 1-000-PET ROCK.

Semicolons

A semicolon looks like what it is: part period and part comma. It says to the reader, "Stop here a little longer than you stop for a comma but not as long as you stop for a period."

25a. Use a semicolon between independent clauses in a sentence if they are not joined by *and, but, or, nor, for, so,* or *yet.*

Notice in the following pairs of examples that the semicolon takes the place of the comma and the conjunction joining the independent clauses.

EXAMPLES   First I had a sandwich and a glass of milk**, and** then I called you for the homework assignment.
First I had a sandwich and a glass of milk**;** then I called you for the homework assignment.

Patty likes to act**, but** her sister gets stage fright.
Patty likes to act**;** her sister gets stage fright.

Similarly, a semicolon can take the place of a period to join two sentences that are closely related.

EXAMPLE   Manuel looked out at the downpour**.** Then he put on his raincoat and boots. [two simple sentences]
Manuel looked out at the downpour**;** then he put on his raincoat and boots. [one compound sentence]

As you can see in the following sentences, a complete thought appears on both sides of each semicolon, and the two independent clauses are not joined by *and, but, or, nor, for, so,* or *yet.*

EXAMPLES   Excellence does not remain alone; it is sure to attract neighbors.

Confucius, *The Sayings of Confucius*

And so, my fellow Americans, ask not what your country can do for you; ask what you can do for your country.

John F. Kennedy, 1961 Inaugural Address

The night was dark, gloomy; the wind moaned over the treetops, and the coyotes howled all around.

Jovita González, *Among My People*

EXERCISE 1
Correcting Sentences by Adding Semicolons Between Independent Clauses

Identify where a semicolon should be placed in each of the following sentences. In some cases, you may prefer to use a period and to capitalize the word after it.

EXAMPLE   **1.** Great earthquakes usually begin gently only one or two slight shocks move the earth.

1. *Great earthquakes usually begin gently; only one or two slight shocks move the earth.*

1. Pressure builds along faults, or cracks, in the earth's crust the weight of this pressure causes earthquakes.
2. As you can see below, the San Andreas fault extends nearly the entire length of California earthquakes often occur along this fault.
3. During an earthquake, huge chunks of the earth's crust begin to move the San Francisco earthquake of 1906, pictured here, was one of the most destructive earthquakes recorded in history.

MECHANICS

4. Energy released during an earthquake is tremendous it can equal the explosive force of 180 metric tons of TNT.
5. Scientists study the force of earthquakes they measure this force on a scale of numbers called the Richter scale.
6. An earthquake measuring less than 5 on the Richter scale is not serious more than 1,000 earthquakes measuring 2 or less occur daily.
7. In 1906, one of the most powerful earthquakes in history occurred in the Pacific Ocean near Ecuador it measured 8.9 on the Richter scale.
8. Tidal waves are a dangerous result of earthquakes geologists use the Japanese word *tsunami* for these destructive waves.
9. Predicting when earthquakes will occur is not yet possible predicting where they will occur is somewhat more certain.
10. Earthquakes seem to strike in a regular time sequence in California, for example, a major earthquake usually occurs every fifty to one hundred years.

25b. Use a semicolon between independent clauses joined by conjunctive adverbs or transitional expressions.

EXAMPLES   Emma felt shy; **however,** she soon made some new friends.
My parents are strict; **for example,** I can watch TV only on weekends.

Notice in the preceding sentences that the conjunctive adverb and the transitional expression are preceded by semicolons and followed by commas.

Commonly Used Conjunctive Adverbs			
also	besides	moreover	accordingly
next	however	nevertheless	consequently
still	indeed	otherwise	furthermore
then	instead	therefore	meanwhile

Commonly Used Transitional Expressions

as a result	for instance	in fact	on the other hand
for example	in addition	that is	in other words

NOTE: When conjunctive adverbs and transitional expressions appear *within* one of the clauses and not *between* clauses, they are usually punctuated as interrupters (set off by commas). The two clauses are still separated by a semicolon.

EXAMPLE   Our student council voted to have a Crazy Clothes Day; the principal, **however,** vetoed the idea.

25c. A semicolon (rather than a comma) may be needed to separate independent clauses joined by a coordinating conjunction when there are commas within the clauses.

CONFUSING   Alana, Eric, and Kim voted for her, and Scott and Vanessa voted for Jason.

CLEAR   Alana, Eric, and Kim voted for her; and Scott and Vanessa voted for Jason.

CONFUSING   Scanning the horizon for the source of the whirring sound, Pedro saw a huge, green cloud traveling in his direction, and, suddenly recognizing what it was, he knew that the crops would soon be eaten by a horde of grasshoppers.

CLEAR   Scanning the horizon for the source of the whirring sound, Pedro saw a huge, green cloud traveling in his direction; and, suddenly recognizing what it was, he knew that the crops would soon be eaten by a horde of grasshoppers.

EXERCISE 2

Correcting Sentences by Adding Semicolons Between Independent Clauses

Identify where a semicolon should be placed in each of the following sentences. In some cases, you may prefer to use a period.

1. My mother and I usually go to Massachusetts in late summer, however, last year we went in July.
2. My grandparents live near Cape Cod, that is why we visit there so often.

MECHANICS

3. I miss my friends and sometimes find the yearly trip to Cape Cod boring, besides, my cousins in Massachusetts are all older than I am.
4. To my great surprise, we had a good time last year, we even did some sightseeing in Boston, Plymouth, and Marblehead.
5. One hot day my mother, grandparents, and I went to the beach, and my grandfather immediately went down to the water for a swim.
6. My grandfather loves the water and is a strong swimmer, nevertheless, we worried when we saw that he was swimming out farther and farther because the currents are strong and tricky.
7. Grandpa, to our great relief, finally turned around and swam back to shore, he was astonished that we had been worried about him.
8. While he was in the water, Mom had gathered driftwood, dug a shallow pit in the sand, and built a fire in it, and Grandma had put lobster, corn, and potatoes on the coals.
9. By the time we had finished eating, it was quite late, consequently, everyone else on the beach had gone home.
10. We didn't leave for home right away, instead, we spent the evening watching the darkening ocean, listening to the whispering waves, and watching the stars come out.

25d. Use a semicolon between items in a series if the items contain commas.

EXAMPLES   I have postcards from Paris, France; Rome, Italy; Lisbon, Portugal; and London, England.
The Photography Club will meet on Wednesday, September 12; Wednesday, September 19; Tuesday, September 25; and Tuesday, October 2.

▶ EXERCISE 3   **Correcting Sentences by Adding Semicolons Between Items in a Series**

Correct the following sentences by adding the needed semicolons. If a sentence needs no semicolons, write *C*.

1. In the fifteenth century, the kings of France, England, and Spain grew stronger as they unified their lands.
2. Africa's then-powerful kingdoms included Mali, on the Niger River, Benin, in what is now Nigeria, and Mwanamutapa, in southern Africa.
3. The Incas in Peru planted crops, such as corn, domesticated animals, such as the llama, and developed crafts, such as weaving.
4. The Mohawks, Senecas, Oneidas, Onondagas, and Cayugas banded together in about the late 1500s to advance peace, civil authority, and righteousness.
5. Mrs. Gillis said that we could choose to write about Dekanawidah, the Huron founder of the Iroquois League, Mansa Musa, the Muslim emperor of Mali, Tamerlane, the Mongol conqueror of the Ottoman Turks, or Alexander the Great, the Macedonian conqueror of Greece and the Persian Empire.

 FXERCISE 4   **Using Semicolons in a Summary**

After seeing the movie *Glory*, you decide to find out more about Civil War reenactors, people who reenact battles of the war. You have gathered the pictures shown here from several newspaper and magazine articles and have made the notes that are shown on the next page. In a paragraph, summarize the material you have gathered. In your paragraph, use a semicolon correctly in four compound sentences and between items in a series that contains commas.

MECHANICS

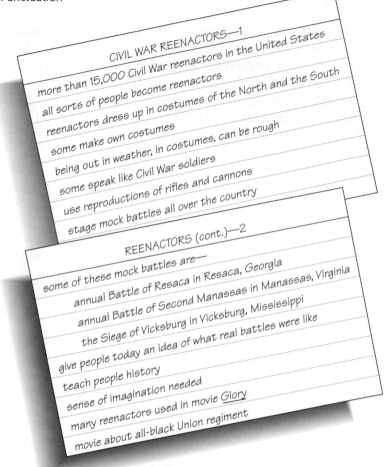

CIVIL WAR REENACTORS—1

more than 15,000 Civil War reenactors in the United States

all sorts of people become reenactors

reenactors dress up in costumes of the North and the South

some make own costumes

being out in weather, in costumes, can be rough

some speak like Civil War soldiers

use reproductions of rifles and cannons

stage mock battles all over the country

REENACTORS (cont.)—2

some of these mock battles are—

annual Battle of Resaca in Resaca, Georgia

annual Battle of Second Manassas in Manassas, Virginia

the Siege of Vicksburg in Vicksburg, Mississippi

give people today an idea of what real battles were like

teach people history

sense of imagination needed

many reenactors used in movie <u>Glory</u>

movie about all-black Union regiment

REVIEW A Correcting Sentences by Adding Semicolons

Most of the following sentences contain at least one error in the use of semicolons. Write the word preceding and following each error, and add the semicolon. If a sentence is correct, write *C*.

EXAMPLE **1.** The largest animal in the world today is the blue whale the largest blue whale ever caught measured slightly more than 113.5 feet and weighed about 170 tons.

    1. *whale; the*

1. Each of the more than seventy-five species of whales is different however, all whales migrate with the seasons.

2. Whales, which are warm-blooded marine mammals, are divided into two main families, these families are the toothed whales (the larger family) and the toothless whales.

3. The biggest toothed whale, the sperm whale, hunts giant squid along the bottom of the ocean, like all other toothed whales, it uses its teeth for catching, not chewing, food.

4. The sperm whale is a record holder in the animal kingdom; it has the largest brain and the thickest skin.

5. Other species of whales include the gray whale, which is probably the best-known toothless whale, the Baird's beaked whale, which is also called the giant bottlenose whale, the bowhead whale, which is also known as the Arctic whale, and the killer whale, which eats almost anything.

6. Whales take very full, deep breaths consequently, they can dive almost a mile below the surface of the ocean and remain underwater for more than an hour at a time.

7. Some whale species exhibit remarkable social behavior; for example, members of a group may stay with a wounded animal or even support it in the water.

8. During the past 250 years, whalers have nearly wiped out many species of whales, the whaling industry continues to threaten those species that have managed to survive.

9. Several countries have banned the killing of certain whale species; but the blue whale, which is close to extinction, remains an endangered species.

10. Whale-watching cruises originated with the public's growing concern over the survival of whales today whale-watching attracts as many as 350,000 people a year.

MECHANICS

▶ REVIEW B   **Correcting Sentences in a Paragraph by Adding Semicolons**

Some sentences in the following paragraph need at least one semicolon. For each incorrectly punctuated sentence, give the word preceding each needed semicolon, the semicolon, and the word following. If a sentence needs no semicolon, write *C*.

EXAMPLE [1] Indian pottery fascinates me, whenever I can, I
watch potters like this woman at the Tigua
(pronounced TEE-wah) Indian Reservation and
Pueblo in El Paso, Texas.
1. *me; whenever*

[1] I could have watched this artist paint designs on the vases for hours, however, I knew that the rest of my family was eager to see more of the reservation. [2] There is much to see there, and they were determined to see it all! [3] The Tiguas have a large adobe visitors center, where they display their arts and crafts and have dance demonstrations, and my younger brothers, Jaime and Lucas, ran all around it. [4] Of course, we had to sample the Tigua specialties at the restaurant, otherwise, we would have missed a unique experience. [5] I've eaten Native American dishes in Phoenix, Arizona, Muskogee, Oklahoma, and Taos, New Mexico, but the food at the Tigua Reservation was my favorite. [6] I especially enjoyed the *gorditas*, which are a kind of taco, the bread, which was fresh out of the oven, and the chili. [7] After lunch, a guide told us that the community was established in 1682 by Tiguas who

were displaced from northern New Mexico; he said the reservation is the oldest inhabited community in Texas boundaries today. [8] The Tiguas are especially proud of their mission they certainly should be. [9] It is a beautiful, restored building, now known as the Ysleta Mission and we enjoyed seeing it. [10] It is the oldest mission in Texas moreover, it is one of the oldest in all of North America.

Colons

Generally, the colon is used to call the reader's attention to what comes next.

25e. Use a colon to mean "note what follows."

(1) Use a colon before a list of items, especially after expressions like *the following* and *as follows.*

EXAMPLES   You will need to bring **the following equipment:** a sleeping bag, a warm sweater, and extra socks.
Additional supplies are **as follows:** a toothbrush, toothpaste, a change of clothes, and a pillow.

Sometimes, the items that follow the colon are used as appositives. If a word is followed by a list of appositives, the colon is used to make the sentence clear.

EXAMPLES   At the crossroads we saw three signs: To Norway, To Paris, and To Lisbon.
You need to shop for several items: brown shoelaces, a quart of milk, and five or six carrots.

☞ REFERENCE NOTE: For more information on appositives and appositive phrases, see pages 556–557.

NOTE: Do not use a colon before a list that follows a verb or a preposition.

INCORRECT   Additional supplies are: a toothbrush and toothpaste, a change of clothes, a towel, a pillow, and an air mattress.
CORRECT   Additional supplies are a toothbrush and toothpaste, a change of clothes, a towel, a pillow, and an air mattress.

MECHANICS

INCORRECT	You need to shop for: brown shoelaces, a quart of milk, and five or six carrots.
CORRECT	You need to shop for brown shoelaces, a quart of milk, and five or six carrots.

(2) Use a colon before a long, formal statement or a long quotation.

EXAMPLE   Horace Mann had this to say: "Do not think of knocking out another person's brains because he differs in opinion from you. It would be as rational to knock yourself on the head because you differ from yourself ten years ago."

25f.   Use a colon in certain conventional situations.

(1) Use a colon between the hour and the minute.

EXAMPLES   9:30 P.M.   8:00 A.M.

(2) Use a colon between chapter and verse in biblical references and between all titles and subtitles.

EXAMPLES   Deuteronomy 25:1–16
"Beware: Do Not Read This Poem"

(3) Use a colon after the salutation of a business letter.

EXAMPLES   Dear Ms. González: Dear Dr. Fenton:
Dear Sir or Madam: To Whom It May Concern:

▶ EXERCISE 5   **Correcting Sentences by Adding Colons**

Correct the following sentences by adding needed colons. If a sentence does not need a colon, write C.

EXAMPLE   **1.** When I came into class at 9 15 A.M., everyone was writing a theme based on this West African proverb "To know nothing is bad; to learn nothing is worse."
1. *When I came into class at 9:15 A.M., everyone was writing a theme based on this West African proverb:* "To know nothing is bad; to learn nothing is worse."

1. Last summer I read "Choices A Tribute to Dr. Martin Luther King, Jr.," by Alice Walker.
2. The wooden desk was littered with papers, pencils, paperback books, food wrappers, and dirty socks.

3. At the festival we bought tacos and refried beans.
4. The qualities she likes most in a person are as follows reliability, a good sense of humor, and a willingness to work.
5. Learn to spell the following new words *aneurysm, fluoroscope, peregrination,* and *serendipity.*
6. An enduring statement of loyalty, found in Ruth 1 16, begins as follows "Entreat me not to leave thee or to return from following after thee, for whither thou goest, I will go."
7. Mrs. Hughes named the three students who had completed extra projects Marshall, Helena, and Regina.
8. From 8 00 A.M. until 6 00 P.M., Mr. Brooks sells brushes, brooms, and cleaning products.
9. Alone in the house at night, I heard some scary sounds the creaking of a board, the scratching of tree branches against a window, and the hissing of steam in the radiator.
10. Tomorrow's test will include the marks of punctuation that we have studied so far commas, semicolons, and colons.

▶ EXERCISE 6   **Using Colons in a Listing Game**

Do you think the picture on the next page is a photograph or a painting? It's difficult to tell, but this is actually a painting in the style called *trompe l'oeil* (trōnp lë´y´). That's French for "deceive the eye." Use this painting to play a listing game with a friend or a classmate. To play, make up categories based on items in the painting. Then list as many items as you can in each category. The winner is the player with the most entries. Here are five categories that you might use to get started.

Uses for a magnifying glass
Presidents with beards
Presidents I've never heard of before
Kinds of money in the painting
People who look like the woman in the photograph

Under each category heading, write a sentence using a colon correctly before your list.

MECHANICS

EXAMPLE

FAVORITE PRESIDENTS

My favorite presidents shown on the border of the painting are as follows: Lincoln, Jefferson, and Washington.

John Haberle, *The Changes of Time*, Oil on Canvas, Manoogian Collection.

WRITING APPLICATION

Using Colons in a Business Letter

Attention-getting signals are everywhere, from the cries of babies to the blasts of train whistles. In writing, the colon is an attention getter. It generally signals readers to "stay tuned" because important information, such as a list or a quotation, follows.

NO SIGNAL   For the party, please bring a bag of chips, some dip, and your favorite music.

SIGNAL   For the party, please bring the following things: a bag of chips, some dip, and your favorite music.

▶ WRITING ACTIVITY

You have volunteered to order the items that the band members of your school will sell to raise money for road trips. Write a short letter to order these items.

Prewriting First, decide what kinds of items to sell (ballpoint pens, dried fruit, candles, book covers, and so on) and how many to order. Also, decide on each item's price, and make up a name and address for a company.

Writing   As you write your first draft, try to keep the body of your letter short and to the point.

Evaluating and Revising   Be sure that you have followed the correct form for a business letter. (See pages 937–942.) Check that you have used a colon after the salutation and before the list of items that you are ordering.

Proofreading   Slowly read your letter aloud, focusing on spelling and punctuation. Have you capitalized all proper names, company names, addresses, and brand names?

▶ REVIEW C   **Correcting Sentences by Adding Semicolons and Colons**

Correct the following sentences by adding semicolons and colons where they are needed.

1. A small, windowless log cabin stood against the rail fence directly behind it ran a muddy stream.
2. Because the club has run out of funds, the following supplies must be brought from home pencils, erasers, paper, and envelopes.
3. I enjoy the following hobbies fly-fishing, reading, and riding my bike.
4. Other jobs take too much time for example, if I worked in a store, I would probably have to work most nights.
5. American cowhands used the ten-gallon hat as protection from the sun and as a dipper for water the leather chaps they wore served as protection from thorny bushes.
6. A rabbi, a minister, and a priest discussed their interpretations of Isaiah 2 2 and 5 26.
7. In his speech Dr. Fujikawa quoted from several poets Rudyard Kipling, David McCord, and Nikki Giovanni.
8. Sojourner Truth, a former slave, could neither read nor write however, this accomplished woman spoke eloquently against slavery and for women's rights.

MECHANICS

9. From 1853 to 1865, the United States had three presidents Franklin Pierce, a Democrat from New Hampshire James Buchanan, a Democrat from Pennsylvania and Abraham Lincoln, a Republican from Illinois.

10. From 12 30 to 1 00 P.M., I was so nervous that I could not sit still I paced up and down, swinging my arms and taking deep breaths, while I rehearsed each play in my mind.

Review: Posttest

A. Correcting Sentences by Adding Semicolons and Colons

For each of the following sentences, write the word or number preceding each punctuation error, and then write the needed semicolon or colon. If the sentence is correct, write C.

EXAMPLE   1. Someday, robots may do many simple household chores, wash windows, answer the telephone, make repairs, and serve dinner.
       1. *chores:*

1. I didn't go to the game last night, instead, I took care of my baby brother.
2. The band members will perform at the civic center on Tuesday, January 15, at the Kiwanis Club on Saturday, January 19, and at the Oak Nursing Home on Friday, January 25.
3. For the lesson on figures of speech, we had to find examples of simile, metaphor, personification, and hyperbole.
4. Dr. Enríquez has traveled to rain forests in many parts of the world, Borneo, Brazil, Costa Rica, and Sri Lanka.
5. The first Spaniards who settled in America built forts, mission churches, and pueblos, evidence of their influence on American architecture can be found in the Southwest.

6. The Tower of Babel, as described in Genesis 11 1–9, closely resembled a ziggurat, or terraced pyramid.
7. Erica never misses a football game on TV, last Saturday, for example, she watched football from noon to 7 00 P.M.
8. The Fast-Track Flashbacks, who were on a one-month tour, performed their most popular songs for the fans, and everywhere they went, they were greeted with cheers and applause.
9. My brother doesn't like violence on television, in the movies, or in books; and he plays only nonviolent games like golf and badminton.
10. The events for the annual Ironman Triathalon, which is held in Hawaii and is open to men and to women, are as follows, swimming 2.4 miles in the ocean, bicycling 112 miles, and running 26.2 miles.

B. Proofreading a Letter for Correct Use of Semicolons and Colons

Find the ten places where a semicolon or a colon needs to be inserted in the following letter. Write each word or number that should be followed by a semicolon or a colon; then add the needed punctuation mark.

EXAMPLE **[1]** Last summer we stayed home during summer vacation, this summer we took a trip in the car.
1. *vacation;*

> 290 Eureka Street
> Dallas, TX 76013
> August 15, 1993

Director
California Department of Parks and Recreation
Box 2390
Sacramento, CA 95811

[11] Dear Sir or Madam,

    [12] While on vacation this summer, my family and I visited the following states New Mexico, Arizona, Oregon, and California. **[13]** We wanted you to know that we especially enjoyed our stay in California, we learned a lot and had a great time.

[14] What we liked best was visiting the Spanish missions in the Los Angeles area they gave us a real sense of history. [15] My favorite places were Mission San Fernando Rey de España, located in Mission Hills, Mission San Gabriel Arcangel, located in San Gabriel, and El Pueblo de Los Angeles. [16] The Old Plaza Church, Nuestra Señora la Reina de Los Angeles, which dates from 1822, was especially wonderful, but unfortunately we couldn't stay long because it was nearly 12 30 P.M. and we had reservations for lunch.

[17] Our stay in California was really great, we hope to return again soon when we have more time. [18] I want to visit some of the missions around San Francisco therefore, I'd like you to send me some information on that area.

Very truly yours,

Angie Barnes

Angie Barnes

26 PUNCTUATION

Italics and Quotation Marks

Diagnostic Test

A. Correcting Sentences by Adding Underlining (Italics) and Quotation Marks

Write each letter, word, or title that should be either underlined (italicized) or put in quotation marks. Then, supply underlining or quotation marks, whichever is needed.

EXAMPLE **1.** According to The Book of Word Histories, there is a close link between the words lettuce and galaxy.
1. The Book of Word Histories, lettuce, galaxy

1. The concert ended with a stirring rendition of The Stars and Stripes Forever.
2. There's Still Gold in Them Thar Hills, an article in Discovery, describes attempts to mine low-grade gold deposits on Quartz Mountain in California.
3. The overture to Mozart's opera The Magic Flute is often played as a concert piece.
4. The fifth unit in African American Literature is titled The Harlem Renaissance.

5. I Am Joaquín is an epic poem that celebrates Mexican American culture.
6. As a baby sitter I have read the children's book The Pokey Little Puppy at least a dozen times.
7. Horace Greeley founded the Tribune, an influential New York newspaper; in it he published his antislavery essay The Prayer of Twenty Millions.
8. Although the poem When You Are Old has three stanzas, it contains only one sentence.
9. The word recommend has two m's but only one c.
10. Robert Fulton's steamboat, Clermont, was the first one that could be operated without losing money.

B. Punctuating Dialogue by Adding Quotation Marks

Insert quotation marks where they are needed in the following dialogue.

EXAMPLE [1] Listen carefully! said Mrs. García. Every student who plans to go on the field trip must have a note from home.

1. *"Listen carefully!" said Mrs. García. "Every student who plans to go on the field trip must have a note from home."*

[11] Before our field trip begins, continued Mrs. García, be sure that you have a notebook and a collection kit.

[12] Will we need binoculars? asked Melvin.

[13] Leave your binoculars at home, answered Mrs. García. Your ears will be more helpful than your eyes on this trip.

[14] What will we be able to hear so far out in the country? asked Arnold.

[15] What a question! exclaimed Felicia. This time of year, you can hear all sorts of sounds.

[16] I hope that we hear and see some birds, said Koko. Didn't someone once say, The birds warble sweet in the springtime?

[17] When, asked James, do we eat lunch? My mom packed my favorite kinds of sandwiches.

[18] Don't worry, said Mrs. García. Most birds are quiet at midday. We can have our lunch then.

MECHANICS

[19] Ruth Ann said, Mrs. García, would you believe that I don't know one birdcall from another?

[20] That's all right, Ruth Ann, laughed Mrs. García. Some birds call out their own names. For example, the bobolink repeats its name: Bob-o-link! Bob-o-link!

Italics

When writing or typing, indicate italics by underlining. If your composition were to be printed, the typesetter would set the underlined words in italics. For example, if you typed the sentence

> Helen Keller wrote The Story of My Life.

it would be printed like this:

> Helen Keller wrote *The Story of My Life*.

NOTE: If you use a personal computer, you can probably set words in italics yourself. Most word-processing software and many printers are capable of producing italic type.

26a. Use underlining (italics) for titles of books, plays, films, periodicals, works of art, television programs, ships, aircraft, and so on.

TYPE OF TITLE	EXAMPLES
Books	*The Diary of Anne Frank* *Invisible Man*
Plays	*The Piano Lesson, Romeo and Juliet*
Films	*Casablanca, Harvey*
Periodicals	*Seventeen, The New York Times*
Works of Art	*The Thinker, Birth of Venus*
Television Series	*60 Minutes, In Living Color*
Ships	*Titanic, Queen Elizabeth II*
Aircraft and Spacecraft	*Spirit of St. Louis, Apollo 1*

Underline (italicize) the title of a poem long enough to be published in a separate volume. Such poems are usually divided into titled or numbered sections, such as cantos, parts, or books. Also, italicize the titles of long musical compositions. Such compositions include operas, symphonies, ballets, oratorios, and concertos.

EXAMPLES   In my report on Coleridge, I plan to quote from Part VII of *The Rime of the Ancient Mariner.*

At her recital, she will play a selection from Tchaikovsky's *Swan Lake.*

Mr. Kellen sang a popular song that came from *Porgy and Bess.*

The words *a, an,* and *the* written before a title are italicized only when they are part of the title. Before the names of newspapers and magazines, however, they are not italicized, even if they are capitalized on the front page of the newspaper or on the cover of the magazine.

EXAMPLES   I am reading John Knowles's *A Separate Peace.*

In the museum we saw Edmonia Lewis's statue *The Death of Cleopatra.*

My parents subscribe to *The Wall Street Journal* and the *San Francisco Examiner.*

☞ REFERENCE NOTE: Magazine articles, chapter headings, and titles of short poems, short stories, short musical compositions, and individual episodes of TV shows should be placed in quotation marks, not italicized. See page 799 for this rule.

26b. Use underlining (italics) for words, letters, and figures referred to as such and for foreign words.

EXAMPLES   The word *Mississippi* has four *s*'s and four *i*'s.

The *3* on that license plate looks like an *8.*

The *corrido,* a fast-paced ballad, evolved from a musical form brought to the New World by early Spanish explorers and settlers.

▶ EXERCISE 1   **Correcting Sentences by Adding Underlining (Italics)**

Underline all the words and word groups that should be italicized in the following sentences.

EXAMPLE   **1.** We gave Mom a subscription to Working Woman magazine.

1. *We gave Mom a subscription to* Working Woman *magazine.*

1. Jason named his ship Argo because Argos had built it.
2. The Marine Corps motto is Semper Fidelis, which means "always faithful."
3. Have you read the novel Dragonsong by Anne McCaffrey?
4. When I spelled occurrence with one r, I was eliminated from the spelling contest.
5. The Gilbert and Sullivan comic opera The Mikado and the Puccini opera Madama Butterfly are both set in Japan.
6. Shari asked if she could borrow my copy of Sports Illustrated.
7. Mrs. Hopkins said that if she had to describe me in one word, the word would be loquacious.
8. My mother, who grew up in Chicago, still subscribes to the Chicago Tribune.
9. My favorite painting is Georgia O'Keeffe's Black Iris; my favorite sculpture is Constantin Brancusi's Bird in Space.
10. My parents own a set of the Encyclopaedia Britannica; and my aunt, who lives within walking distance of us, just bought a set of The World Book Encyclopedia.

PICTURE THIS

You are an art consultant for a publisher. You think that the painting on the next page would make an excellent cover illustration because it would catch people's attention. Now you must look over the publisher's list of new titles and decide where to use the painting. Write a short memo to the art director, pointing out publications that the painting could illustrate. These publications include a novel, a play, a book of poetry, a poster for the movie version of a book, and a specialty magazine. You can make up the titles.

EXAMPLE **1.** *I suggest that we use this painting to illustrate the poster for Raiders of the Lost Rock.*

Subject: the painting *Le Château des Pyrénées*

Audience: an art director
Purpose: to persuade

René Magritte, *Le Château des Pyrénées*, ©1991 C. Herscovici, Brussels/Artists Rights Society (ARS), New York/Art Resource, N.Y.

Quotation Marks

26c. Use quotation marks to enclose a *direct quotation*—a person's exact words.

EXAMPLES   Melanie said, "This car is making a very strange noise."
"Maybe we should pull over," suggested Amy.

Do not use quotation marks for *indirect quotations*.

DIRECT QUOTATION   Stephanie said, "I'm going to wash the car." [the speaker's exact words]
INDIRECT QUOTATION   Stephanie said that she was going to wash the car. [not the speaker's exact words]

Always be sure to place quotation marks at both the beginning and the end of a direct quotation.

INCORRECT   She shouted, "We can win, team!
CORRECT   She shouted, "We can win, team!"

An interrupting expression is not a part of a quotation and therefore should never be inside quotation marks.

INCORRECT	"Let's sit here, Jennifer whispered, not way down there in front."
CORRECT	"Let's sit here," Jennifer whispered, "not way down there in front."

When two or more sentences by the same speaker are quoted together, use only one set of quotation marks.

INCORRECT	Brennan said, "I like to sit close to the screen." "The sound is better there."
CORRECT	Brennan said, "I like to sit close to the screen. The sound is better there."

26d. A direct quotation begins with a capital letter.

EXAMPLES   Explaining the lever, Archimedes said, "Give me a place to stand, and I can move the world."
Miss Pérez answered, "The rest of the chapter, of course." [Although this quotation is not a sentence, it is Miss Pérez's complete remark.]

NOTE: If the direct quotation is obviously a fragment of the original quotation, it may begin with a small letter.

EXAMPLE   Are our ideals, as Scott says, mere "statues of snow" that soon melt? [The quotation is obviously only a part of Scott's remark.]

26e. When a quoted sentence is divided into two parts by an interrupting expression, the second part begins with a small letter.

EXAMPLES   "I wish," she said, "that we went to the same school."
"I know," I answered, "but at least we are friends."

If the second part of a quotation is a new sentence, a period (not a comma) follows the interrupting expression, and the second part begins with a capital letter.

EXAMPLE   "I requested an interview," the reporter said. "She told me she was too busy."

26f. A direct quotation is set off from the rest of the sentence by commas or by a question mark or an exclamation point.

MECHANICS

EXAMPLES   Delores explained, "You know how much I like
              chicken," as she passed her plate for more.
              The plumber shouted, "Turn off that faucet!" when
              the water started gushing out of the pipe.

26g. When used with quotation marks, other marks of punctuation are placed according to the following rules:

(1) Commas and periods are always placed inside closing quotation marks.

EXAMPLES   "I haven't seen the movie," remarked Jeannette,
              "but I understand it's excellent."
              He read aloud "Ode to the End of Summer," a poem
              by Phyllis McGinley.

(2) Semicolons and colons are always placed outside closing quotation marks.

EXAMPLES   Socrates once said, "As for me, all I know is that I
              know nothing"; I wonder why everyone thinks he
              was such a wise man.
              The following actresses were cited for "best
              performance in a leading role": Sally Field, Meryl
              Streep, Cher, and Jodie Foster.

(3) Question marks and exclamation points are placed inside the closing quotation marks if the quotation is a question or an exclamation; otherwise, they are placed outside.

EXAMPLES   "Is it too cold in here?" the manager asked as I
              shivered.
              "Yes!" I answered. "Please turn down the air
              conditioner!"
              Can you explain the saying "Penny wise, pound
              foolish"?
              It's not an insult to be called a "bookworm"!

▶ EXERCISE 2   **Writing Sentences with Direct and Indirect Quotations**

If a sentence contains a direct quotation, change it to an indirect quotation. If a sentence contains an indirect quotation, change it to a direct quotation. Be sure your answers are correctly punctuated.

MECHANICS

EXAMPLES   1. "Where should we go for vacation this year?"
asked my mother.

1. *My mother asked where we should go for vacation this year.*

2. My little brother Jason said that he wanted to see castles like the ones in the brochures.

2. *My little brother Jason said, "I want to see castles like the ones in the brochures."*

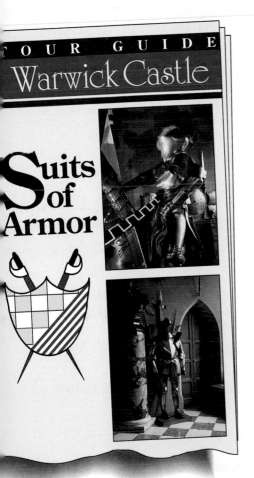

1. When we planned our trip to England, Mom said, "Our stops will include some castles."

2. Our tour book says that Colchester Castle, built in 1080, is a good place to start.

3. Jason asked whether the castles were haunted.

4. "No," said Mom, "but we'll stay close together so that you won't be afraid."

5. In England, Jason told Mom that he wanted to swim in a moat.

6. "Warwick Castle," said our guide, "is one of the most beautiful in England."

7. "One of its towers," he went on to say, "was built in 1066."

8. "Is it still the home of the Earls of Warwick?" I asked.

9. The guide said that the castle contains many works of art.

10. "I like the collection of suits of armor best," said Jason.

MECHANICS

26h. When you write dialogue (a conversation), begin a new paragraph every time the speaker changes.

EXAMPLE   "What's that?" Sally demanded impatiently.
Luisa seemed surprised. "What's what?"
"That thing, what you got in your hand."
"Oh this. . ." and she held it up for Sally to inspect.
"A present."
"A what?"
"A present I picked up."
"Oh." Sally moved her eyes to the house. "Looks
like his place burned down. What d'you find inside?"
"Just this," Luisa said, gazing blankly at the house.
"What d'you want that for?"

Ron Arias, "El Mago"

Notice that a paragraph may be only one line long. Also
notice that a paragraph may consist of only a word or two
treated as a complete sentence even though it is not one.

WRITING APPLICATION

Using Quotation Marks in a Dialogue

Almost any story is much more interesting if it contains dialogue that makes the characters come alive by speaking for
themselves. When you write dialogue, be careful to use
quotation marks correctly, or else your readers won't know
who is saying what.

Where are quotation marks used correctly in the following dialogue?

"I wish, Jerome said to Dolores, "that you'd use quo-
tation marks correctly.
Why? she asked, "and stopped writing."
Because I'm an interesting character, he replied, and
I want your readers to know what I'm saying.
"Oh, very well," Dolores said. "If you're going to be a
difficult character, I will."
"Thanks a lot," Jerome said. "Now start over."
"I wish," Jerome said to Dolores, "that you'd use quo-
tation marks correctly."

▶ **WRITING ACTIVITY**

Write a page of dialogue in which characters tell a story, either fact or fiction, through a conversation.

Prewriting Decide upon a story and a few characters to tell it. You could retell a favorite anecdote, report the exact words of an amusing conversation, or write an imaginary interview with a famous person.

Writing As you write your first draft, think about making the characters sound different from one another.

Evaluating and Revising First, ask a classmate to read your dialogue. Revise any parts that are unclear or uninteresting to your reader. Be sure that you have begun a new paragraph every time the speaker changes. Also, check that you have followed the rules for direct quotations and quotations with interrupting expressions.

Proofreading Read through your dialogue again, this time concentrating on correcting errors in grammar, spelling, and punctuation. [Note: You may have purposefully included some errors to help your dialogue sound like real conversation, as in the dialogue on page 796.]

26i. When a quoted passage consists of more than one paragraph, put quotation marks at the beginning of each paragraph and at the end of the entire passage. Do not put quotation marks after any paragraph but the last.

EXAMPLE   "At nine o'clock this morning," read the news story, "someone entered the Mill Bank by the back entrance, broke through two thick steel doors guarding the bank's vault, and escaped with sixteen bars of gold.

    "No arrests have been made, but state police are confident the case will be solved within a few days."

NOTE: A long passage (not dialogue) quoted from a book or another printed source is usually set off from the rest of the text. The entire passage is usually indented and double-spaced. In some cases, it is also set in small type. When a quoted passage has been set off in one of these ways, no quotation marks are necessary.

26j. Use single quotation marks to enclose a quotation within a quotation.

EXAMPLES   Annoyed, Becky snapped, "Don't tell me, 'That's not the way to do it.'"

My uncle said, "Remember the words of Chief Joseph: 'I have heard talk and talk, but nothing is done. Good words do not last long unless they amount to something.'"

Tiffany shouted, "How dare you say 'Yuck'!"

▶ EXERCISE 3   **Using Quotation Marks in Dialogue**

Calvin, the little boy in the comic strip *Calvin and Hobbes*, definitely has a mind of his own. As you can see from this panel, one thing Calvin has a strong opinion about is baby sitters. Even though Rosalyn, his baby sitter, tells Calvin to go to bed, he probably won't go without a fight. What do you think will happen next? Write a short follow-up conversation between Calvin and Rosalyn. Be sure to follow the rules for the correct use of quotation marks.

EXAMPLE   *"Oh, no, I couldn't possibly go to bed," Calvin replied. "I haven't fed my alligator."*

Calvin & Hobbes copyright 1988 Watterson. Distributed by Universal Press Syndicate. Reprinted with permission. All rights reserved.

▶ REVIEW A   **Correcting Sentences by Adding Quotation Marks for Dialogue**

Correct each of the following passages, adding quotation

marks where necessary. Remember to begin a new paragraph each time the speaker changes.

1

Race-car driver Janet Guthrie, said Chet, reading from his notes, is a trained physicist who has spent many years working at an important job for an aircraft corporation.

2

Who shot that ball? Coach Larsen wanted to know. I did, came the reply from the small, frail-looking player. Good shot, observed the coach, but always remember to follow your shot to the basket. I tried, but I was screened, the player explained.

3

The *Brownsville Beacon*, the editorial began, will never support a candidate who tells the taxpayers, Vote for me, and I will cut taxes.

The reason is simple. Taxes, just like everything else in this inflationary society, must increase. Any candidate who thinks otherwise is either a fool or a liar.

4

In the interview the candidate said, I am a very hospitable person. Yes, her husband agreed, Ralph Waldo Emerson must have been thinking of you when he said, Happy is the house that shelters a friend.

26k. Use quotation marks to enclose titles of articles, short stories, essays, poems, songs, individual episodes of TV shows, chapters, and other parts of books or periodicals.

EXAMPLES   The article "What Teenagers Need to Know About Diets" should be required reading.
The poem "On Ageing" by Maya Angelou is one of my grandmother's favorites.
Edward James Olmos stars in the movie based on the *corrido* "The Ballad of Gregorio Cortez."
Please turn to the chapter titled "Our Solar System."

☞ REFERENCE NOTE: Remember that the titles of long poems and long musical compositions are italicized, not enclosed in quotation marks. See the examples on page 790.

MECHANICS

EXERCISE 4 **Correcting Sentences by Adding Quotation Marks for Titles**

Correct the following sentences by adding quotation marks as needed.

EXAMPLE   **1.** Did O. Henry write The Last Leaf?
            1. *Did O. Henry write "The Last Leaf"?*

1. That address to the United Nations can be found in our literature book, in the chapter titled Essays and Speeches.
2. A popular Old English riddle song is Scarborough Fair.
3. Have you read the story Split Cherry Tree by Jesse Stuart?
4. Which Eve Merriam poem is your favorite, Cheers or How to Eat a Poem?
5. Have you read Fran Lebowitz's essay Tips for Teens?

REVIEW B **Correcting Sentences by Adding Underlining (Italics) and Quotation Marks**

Write the following sentences, adding underlining (italics) and quotation marks where needed.

1. The Bay Area Youth Theater is presenting Lorraine Hansberry's play A Raisin in the Sun.
2. Tyrone announced that he is going to sing Some Enchanted Evening from the musical South Pacific.
3. I have tickets to the opera Carmen, said Karen, and I would like you to be my guest.
4. The Spanish word for goodbye is adiós; the Swahili word is kwa heri.
5. My favorite story by Sir Arthur Conan Doyle is The Adventure of the Dying Detective, which is included in the anthology The Complete Sherlock Holmes.
6. Ms. Loudon said, I like your report on Ernest Hemingway. Remember, however, that Ernest is spelled without an a.
7. In her review of The King and I, the drama critic for the Los Angeles Times commented, This production is an excellent revival of a play that never seems to wear thin.

MECHANICS

8. In my paper, which I titled The Hispanic Soldier in Vietnam, I cited several passages from Luis Valdez's play The Buck Private.
9. Mrs. Howard asked, In Julius Caesar who said, This was the noblest Roman of them all? Which Roman was being described?
10. Have you read Hannah Armstrong, one of the poems in the Spoon River Anthology by Edgar Lee Masters?

 REVIEW C

Writing Titles with Underlining (Italics) and Quotation Marks

You are a member of the scientific exploration team aboard this research ship about to leave for a month-long mission. You forgot to bring along any entertainment for your off-work hours, but before shipping out you can send ashore for supplies. The ship has a VCR and a television, but only limited storage space. Make a list of some items you would like to have with you. Include five books, five movies, three poems, two short stories, five songs, and five television programs. Use underlining (italics) and quotation marks correctly for all the titles. After completing your list, compare it with those of your classmates.

MECHANICS

MECHANICS

▶ REVIEW D **Correcting Paragraphs by Adding Underlining (Italics) and Quotation Marks**

Correct the following paragraphs by adding underlining (italics) and quotation marks where necessary.

EXAMPLE   [1] Are all of these books by or about Benjamin Franklin? asked Bonnie Lou.

1. *"Are all of these books by or about Benjamin Franklin?" asked Bonnie Lou.*

[1] Yes, Bonnie Lou, Mr. Reyes answered. [2] There's even one, Ben and Me by Robert Lawson, that's a biography written from the point of view of Amos, Franklin's pet mouse.

[3] This one, The Many Lives of Benjamin Franklin by Mary Pope Osborne, sounds really interesting, said Jasmine.

[4] It is, Mr. Reyes said. [5] And that's exactly what we're going to talk about today—the many lives of this early American genius. [6] Who can tell me about one of them?

[7] He invented electricity, didn't he? asked Liang.

[8] Well, he didn't exactly invent electricity, corrected Mr. Reyes, but his experiment proved that lightning is a form of electricity.

[9] Franklin also helped draft some of our important historical documents and in addition was a diplomat, a printer, and a publisher. [10] Franklin's writings, such as his Autobiography and Poor Richard's Almanack, have given us many well-known sayings.

Review: Posttest

A. Correcting Sentences by Adding Underlining (Italics) and Quotation Marks

For each of the following numbered items, add underlining (italics) and quotation marks where necessary.

EXAMPLE **1.** Don't forget your umbrella, said Jody. I read in the
Sun Times that it's going to rain today.

          1. *"Don't forget your umbrella," said Jody. "I read in
the <u>Sun Times</u> that it's going to rain today."*

1. My grandmother asked me which one I wanted for
    my birthday, Laura said, a subscription to Time or
    one to Popular Mechanics.
2. Welcome aboard the Elissa, said the skipper. It was
    built in the 1800s, but it has been restored and is still
    a seaworthy ship.
3. Emerson once said, The only way to have a friend is
    to be one; I think he's right.
4. In the book The Complete Essays of Mark Twain,
    you'll find an essay titled Taming the Bicycle.
5. Jennifer said, I never can remember how many c's
    and s's the word necessary has.
6. Beth finally figured out that when Tranh used the
    Vietnamese phrase không biêt, he was telling her
    that he didn't understand.
7. The 18 on her uniform looks like a 13, Earl said.
8. Alexandra replied, I'm surprised you watched Gone
    with the Wind. Two days ago you said, I don't want
    to see the movie until I've read the book.
9. Every week the whole family gathers in front of the
    television to watch In Living Color.
10. The Beatles' song Yesterday has been a favorite of
    several generations.

MECHANICS

B. Correcting Paragraphs of Dialogue by Adding Underlining (Italics) and Quotation Marks

The following dialogue contains ten errors in the use of
underlining (italics) and quotation marks. Correct these
errors by adding the appropriate marks of punctuation.
[Note: Each error in the use of quotation marks involves a
pair of single or double quotation marks.]

EXAMPLE **[1]** I thought the poetry unit in English class would
be dull, Ella said, but it's not. We're studying
Langston Hughes, and he's great!

          1. *"I thought the poetry unit in English class would
be dull," Ella said, "but it's not. We're studying
Langston Hughes, and he's great!"*

[11] Oh, I've heard of him, Chet said. Didn't he write a poem called The Dream Keeper?

[12] Yes, that's one of my favorites, Ella said. An entire book of his poems is called The Dream Keeper, too. And another one of his best-known poems is called Dreams.

[13] I guess he dreamed a lot, Chet replied.

[14] Ella said, He did a lot more than that! Mrs. Berry told us that Langston Hughes traveled a lot. For a time, he was on the crew of a steamer that sailed around Africa and Europe. In fact, one of his autobiographies is called The Big Sea.

27 PUNCTUATION

Apostrophes

Diagnostic Test

A. Correcting Sentences by Using Apostrophes Correctly

In the following sentences, apostrophes are either missing or incorrectly used. Write the correct form of each incorrect word. In some cases, an apostrophe must be added or deleted; in others, the spelling of the word must be changed.

EXAMPLE   **1.** The invention of written mark's to stand for spoken words is one of humanities greatest achievements.
      1. *marks; humanity's*

1. Many ancient peoples felt that writing had a magic power of it's own.
2. Writing was practiced by the elders' of a tribe to preserve the tribes lore as well as its laws.
3. Were not sure when or how writing began, but we do know that it existed several century's before 3000 B.C.

4. Theres plenty of evidence that people communicated through they're drawings long before they had a system of writing.
5. Spain and France's wonderful cave drawings were painted more than thirty thousand year's ago.
6. The ancient Peruvians message system was a complicated arrangement of knots.
7. Someones research has shown that *W*'s and *J*'s werent used in English writing until the Middle Ages.
8. In China, ones mastery of basic reading depends on learning one thousand character's.
9. Hardwick Book Stores window display features early system's of writing.
10. Bess and Robert, who's reports were on the history of writing, asked one of Mr. Hardwicks clerks for permission to examine the stores display.

B. Proofreading a Paragraph for Correct Use of Apostrophes

The following paragraph contains ten errors in the use of apostrophes. For each sentence, write the correct form of each incorrect word. In some cases, an apostrophe must be added or deleted; in others, the spelling of the word must be changed.

EXAMPLE   [1] Sumerian cuneiforms and Egyptian hieroglyphics are early complete system's of writing.
   1. *systems*

[11] Despite many years work, scholars were not able to decipher hieroglyphics until the nineteenth century. [12] In 1799, one of Napoleons soldiers serving in Egypt discovered a stone tablet, which came to be known as the Rosetta Stone. [13] The tablets surface was inscribed in three ancient language's: Greek, Egyptian hieroglyphics, and Coptic, which is an Afroasiastic language derived from ancient Egyptian. [14] The experts translations of the Greek text revealed that the same information had been written in all three languages in 196 B.C. [15] They're next step was to use their knowledge of Greek and Coptic to identify how names' of specific people and places were written in hieroglyphics. [16] It wasnt until 1822, however, that a

Frenchman named Jean-François Champollion deciphered the ancient Egyptians writing. [17] Following another scholars' theory that hieroglyphic symbols represent sounds, Champollion figured out which symbols represent which sounds.

Possessive Case

The *possessive* of a noun or pronoun shows ownership or relationship.

OWNERSHIP   She is a teacher in **Maria's** school.
                     The **Girl Scouts'** cookie sale starts tomorrow.
                     Can I count on **your** vote?
RELATIONSHIP   **Larry's** friend uses a wheelchair.
                     You need a good **night's** sleep.
                     I appreciate **your** waiting so long.

27a. To form the possessive case of a singular noun, add an apostrophe and an *s*.

EXAMPLES   Yuki's problem   a bus's wheel
             the mayor's desk   this evening's paper
             Mrs. Ross's job   a dollar's worth

NOTE: A proper name ending in *s* may add only an apostrophe if the addition of 's would make the name awkward to pronounce.

        EXAMPLES   **Ulysses'** plan
                      Mrs. Sanders' car
                      West Indies' export

► EXERCISE 1   **Using Apostrophes to Form the Possessive Case of Singular Nouns**

Form the possessive case of each of the following words. After each possessive word, give an appropriate noun.

EXAMPLE   **1.** Theresa
              1. *Theresa's pencil*

1. baby	4. cent	7. Ellen	10. Miss Williams
2. uncle	5. class	8. mouse	
3. year	6. Terry	9. Mr. Chan	

MECHANICS

27b. To form the possessive case of a plural noun ending in *s,* add only the apostrophe.

EXAMPLES   birds' feathers   cousins' visit

Although most plural nouns end in *s,* some are irregular. To form the possessive case of a plural noun that does not end in *s,* add an apostrophe and an *s.*

EXAMPLES   children's shoes   deer's food

☞ REFERENCE NOTE: For more examples of irregular plurals, see page 846.

▶ EXERCISE 2   **Forming the Possessive Case of Plural Nouns**

Form the possessive case of each of the following plural nouns.

EXAMPLE   **1.** knives
              1. *knives'*

1. men   **5.** princesses   **9.** mice
2. cats   **6.** dollars   **10.** parents
3. teachers   **7.** elves
4. enemies   **8.** cattle

NOTE: Do not use an apostrophe to form the *plural* of a noun. Remember that the apostrophe shows ownership or relationship.

INCORRECT   Two players' left their gym suits in the locker room.
CORRECT   Two **players** left their gym suits in the locker room. [simple plural]
CORRECT   Two **players'** gym suits were left in the locker room. [The apostrophe shows that the gym suits belong to the two players.]

▶ EXERCISE 3   **Revising Phrases by Forming the Possessive Case of Nouns**

Revise the following phrases by using the possessive case.

EXAMPLE   **1.** parties for seniors
              1. *the seniors' parties*

1. prizes for winners
2. manners for teenagers
3. yokes of oxen
4. duties of nurses
5. names of players
6. suits for women
7. ideas of inventors
8. medals for veterans
9. routines for dancers
10. roles for actresses

▶ EXERCISE 4   **Recognizing Correct Forms of Nouns**

Choose the correct form of each noun given in parentheses in the following paragraph.

EXAMPLE   Several [1] (*photographs, photograph's*) taken by *Voyagers 1* and *2* were combined into the illustration below to show a few of [2] (*Saturns, Saturn's*) many satellites.
   1. *photographs*
   2. *Saturn's*

At least eighteen natural satellites or celestial [1] (*bodies, body's*) revolve around the planet Saturn. Seven of our solar [2] (*systems, system's*) nine planets have satellites, but Saturn and Jupiter have the most. [3] (*Scientists, Scientists'*) figures on the number of [4] (*satellites, satellite's*) vary, and new space [5] (*probes, probe's*) sometimes reveal more satellites. Two [6] (*planets, planets'*), Earth and Pluto, have only one satellite each. Of course, you are familiar with our [7] (*planets, planet's*) satellite, the moon. As you can see from this illustration, [8] (*satellite's, satellites'*) sizes and features vary greatly. Titan, a satellite of Saturn, is the largest of that [9] (*planets, planet's*) satellites. Another of [10] (*Saturns, Saturn's*) satellites, Mimas, has a crater that covers about one third of its diameter.

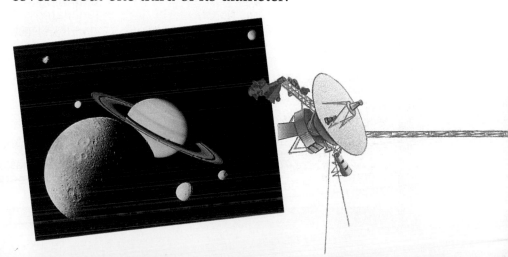

MECHANICS

EXERCISE 5

Using the Possessive Case of Nouns in Writing a Paragraph

The chart below lists the most popular film of each decade since the beginning of the motion picture industry. The entertainment publication *Variety* prepared this listing based on the amount of money that each movie made. How would you complete the chart for the 1990s? Write a paragraph about the movie that you think will be the smash hit of this decade. You may want to compare or contrast your choice with another film in the list. In your paragraph, use the possessive case of at least five of these words:

actors	costumes	friends	setting
audience	decade	movie	special effects
characters	director	music	star
children	film	plot	year

EXAMPLE **1.** friends

1. *My friends' rave reviews of* Dances with Wolves *convinced me to see it.*

MOST POPULAR MOVIES BY DECADES		
TITLE	DECADE	LEADING ACTORS
The Birth of a Nation (1915)	pre-1930s	Lillian Gish, Henry B. Walthall
Gone with the Wind (1939)	1930s	Clark Gable, Vivien Leigh
Cinderella (1949)	1940s	Cinderella, Prince Charming (animated)
The Ten Commandments (1956)	1950s	Charlton Heston, Yul Brynner, Anne Baxter
The Sound of Music (1965)	1960s	Julie Andrews, Christopher Plummer
Star Wars (1977)	1970s	Mark Hamill, Carrie Fisher, Harrison Ford
E.T.—The Extra Terrestrial (1982)	1980s	Henry Thomas, Drew Barrymore
?	1990s	?

27c. Possessive personal pronouns do not require an apostrophe.

> ## Possessive Personal Pronouns
>
> my, mine   our, ours
> your, yours   their, theirs
> his, her, hers, its

My, your, her, its, our, and *their* are used before a noun. *Mine, yours, hers, ours,* and *theirs,* on the other hand, are never used before a noun; they are used as subjects, complements, or objects in sentences. *His* may be used in either way.

EXAMPLES   Lee has **your** sweater. Lee has a sweater of **yours.**
That is **your** watch. That watch is **yours.**
Her idea was wonderful. **Hers** was the best idea.
This is **our** plant. This plant is **ours.**
There is **his** record. There is a record of **his.**

NOTE: The possessive form of *who* is *whose,* not *who's.* Similarly, do not write *it's* for *its,* or *they're* for *their.* For more discussion of these possessive pronouns, see pages 854, 857, and 859.

EXERCISE 6   **Recognizing Correct Forms of Possessive Personal Pronouns**

In each of the following sentences, give the correct form of the pronoun in parentheses.

EXAMPLE   **1.** Ralph Ellison, (*who's, whose*) book *Invisible Man* won a National Book Award, studied music at Tuskegee Institute.
    1. *whose*

1. Did you know, Sumi, that two poems of (*yours, yours'*) have been chosen for the literary magazine?
2. When I first read that book, I was surprised by the quality of (*its, it's*) artwork.
3. (*Hers, Hers'*) is the bicycle with the reflectors on (*its, it's*) fenders.
4. Eudora Welty, (*who's, whose*) short stories involve eccentric characters, is my favorite writer.

MECHANICS

5. "The trophy is (*ours, ours'*)!" shouted the captain as the *Flying S* crossed the finish line.
6. (*Theirs, Theirs'*) is the only house with blue shutters.
7. Penny and Carla worked as gardeners this summer and saved (*their, they're*) money for a ski trip.
8. The students (*who's, whose*) names are called should report backstage.
9. (*Their, They're*) schedule calls for a test on Tuesday.
10. (*Who's, Whose*) signature is this?

27d. Indefinite pronouns in the possessive case require an apostrophe and *s.*

EXAMPLES nobody**'**s wish another**'**s viewpoint
someone**'**s license neither**'**s school

☞ **REFERENCE NOTE:** For a listing of more indefinite pronouns, see page 471.

▶ EXERCISE 7   **Recognizing Correct Forms of Possessive Pronouns**

Choose the correct pronoun in parentheses in each of the following sentences.

1. The reward is (*yours, your's*).
2. (*Ours, Our's*) works better than (*theirs, their's*).
3. (*Who's, Whose*) game is that?
4. (*Theirs, Their's*) is the best frozen yogurt in town.
5. Your car needs to have (*its, it's*) oil changed.
6. It wasn't (*anyone's, anyones'*) fault that we missed the bus yesterday.
7. (*Her's, Hers*) is the best project in the Science Fair.
8. (*Someones, Someone's, Someones'*) choir robe was left on the bus.
9. (*Everybodys, Everybody's, Everybodys'*) trees must be irrigated.
10. That dog of (*their's, theirs*) should be on a leash.

▶ REVIEW A   **Writing the Singular, Plural, and Possessive Forms of Nouns**

On a piece of paper, make four columns headed *Singular, Singular Possessive, Plural,* and *Plural Possessive.* Write each of those forms of the following words. Add a suitable noun to follow each word in the possessive case. If you do not know how to spell a plural form, use a dictionary.

1. friend
2. typist
3. bicycle
4. referee

5. sheep
6. woman
7. penny
8. dress

9. musician
10. lioness

EXAMPLES

SINGULAR	SINGULAR POSSESSIVE	PLURAL	PLURAL POSSESSIVE
dog	dog's owner	dogs	dogs' owners
knife	knife's blade	knives	knives' blades

REVIEW B

Correcting the Forms of Nouns and Pronouns

Identify and correct the ten incorrect possessive forms in the following paragraph.

EXAMPLE [1] These women welcomed us to the Shaker village of Pleasant Hill, Kentucky, during our history class' field trip last spring.
    1. *class's*

[1] As you can see, the style of the womens dresses is quite old. [2] In fact, the villages history goes back to 1806. [3] That was the year that the religious group known as

MECHANICS

the Shakers founded they're own community. [4] We learned that the Shaker's lively way of dancing gave the group it's name. [5] Everyones life in the Shaker village was orderly, simple, and productive. [6] This basic harmony was true even of the childrens' routines. [7] During the days tour of the village, we saw several people, including the man on the previous page, practicing Shaker crafts. [8] One guide of our's told us that the Shakers invented the common clothespin and the flat broom and designed useful furniture and boxes. [9] I enjoyed visiting the gardens and the Centre Family House and imagining how a Shakers' life must have been.

27e. In compound words, names of organizations and businesses, and words showing joint possession, only the last word is possessive in form.

COMPOUND WORDS	everyone **else's** worry
	community **board's** meeting
	vice-**president's** contract
	brother-in-**law's** gift
ORGANIZATIONS	United **Fund's** drive
BUSINESSES	Berkeley Milk **Company's** trucks
JOINT POSSESSION	Peggy and **Lisa's** tent [The tent belongs to both Peggy and Lisa.]
	children and **parents'** concerns

NOTE: The possessive of an acronym is formed by adding an apostrophe and *s*.

EXAMPLES   NASA**'s** latest space probe
CBS**'s** hit television program

When one of the words showing joint possession is a pronoun, both words should be possessive in form.

EXAMPLE   **Peggy's and my tent** [not *Peggy and my tent*]

NOTE: Use a phrase beginning with *of* or *for* to avoid awkward possessive forms.

AWKWARD	the director of the Cazadero Music Festival's son
BETTER	the son of the director of the Cazadero Music Festival
AWKWARD	the Society for the Prevention of Cruelty to Animals' advertisement
BETTER	the advertisement for the Society for the Prevention of Cruelty to Animals

27f. When two or more persons possess something individually, each of their names is possessive in form.

EXAMPLES **Mrs. Martin's** and **Mrs. Blair's** cars [the cars of two different women]
Asha's and **Daniella's** tennis rackets [individual, not joint, possession]

▶ EXERCISE 8 **Revising Phrases by Using the Possessive Case**

Revise the following phrases by using the possessive case.

EXAMPLE **1.** The book owned by Natalie and Stan
1. *Natalie and Stan's book*

1. the ticket of Sylvia and the ticket of Eric
2. an investigation by the FBI
3. the duet of Gwen and Carlos
4. a uniform belonging to the master sergeant
5. the history of the Grand Canyon
6. the job shared by Isabel and me
7. an agent for the Acme Life Insurance Company
8. one tractor belonging to my uncle and one to us
9. the award given by the Sales Department
10. the business of her mother-in-law and the business of her cousin

MECHANICS

WRITING APPLICATION

Using Apostrophes to Make Nouns Possessive

Just as relationships are important in your life, relationships between words are important in your writing. Apostrophes help to make clear the relationship of one noun or pronoun to another.

UNCLEAR The bands new recording is Marcuss favorite.
CLEAR The band's new recording is Marcus's favorite.

MECHANICS

▶ **WRITING ACTIVITY**

Write a paragraph about the musical preferences of your family or your friends. Use at least two singular possessive nouns, two plural possessive nouns, and one indefinite pronoun in the possessive case.

Prewriting   First, make a list of family members or friends, and beside each name write what you know about that person's musical tastes. If you're not sure about someone's preferences, ask him or her.

Writing   As you write your first draft, think about ways of organizing your information (by type of music, age of listener, etc.).

Evaluating and Revising   Ask a family member or friend to read your paragraph. Is it clear whose preferences are discussed? Check your placement of apostrophes.

Proofreading   As you read through your paragraph to correct errors in spelling, grammar, and punctuation, be sure that every pronoun agrees with its antecedent in number and in gender. (See pages 608–610.) Capitalize words such as *aunt* and *uncle* when they are used with a person's name or in the place of a person's name but *not* when they are preceded by a possessive personal pronoun. (See page 731.)

▶ REVIEW C   **Identifying Words That Require Apostrophes**

In the following paragraph, identify the ten words requiring apostrophes, and then insert the apostrophes.

EXAMPLE   [1] Have you ever heard of the U.S. Patent Offices Hall of Fame for inventors?
   1. Offices—Office's

[1] The Hall of Fames members, who are both American and foreign, include many people that you've probably heard of as well as some you haven't. [2] Vladimir

Kosma Zworykin's picture tube helped lead to televisions development. [3] Willis Haviland Carrier changed peoples lives all over the world with his work on air conditioning and refrigerators. [4] Luther Burbanks accomplishment was the development of more than eight hundred new plant varieties. [5] Heart patients pacemakers were invented by Wilson Greatbatch. [6] You'll probably recognize such famous inventors as the Ford Motor Companys founder, Henry Ford. [7] Of course, Thomas Edisons and Alexander Graham Bells achievements assured their enduring fame. [8] Its not surprising that Orville and Wilbur Wrights invention of the airplane landed them in such good company, too.

PICTURE THIS

Don't be startled, but the character in this pop art painting is talking to *you*. Use your imagination to come up with some answers to these puzzling questions. Write the

Roy Lichtenstein, *Image Duplicator.* Oil and magna on canvas, 24 × 20". © Roy Lichtenstein.

MECHANICS

beginning of a short story telling *why* and *what* you asked the person in the painting, and *what* you know about the image duplicator. You can develop your story any way you wish. But be sure to use the possessive case of a plural noun, two indefinite pronouns, the name of an organization, and the name of a business. For the fun of it, you may want to write the whole short story.

Subject: an image duplicator
Audience: classmates
Purpose: to entertain

Contractions

27g. Use an apostrophe to show where letters or numerals have been omitted in a contraction.

A *contraction* is a shortened form of a word, a figure, or a group of words. The apostrophes in contractions indicate where letters or numerals have been left out.

EXAMPLES
who is	who's	I am	I'm
1991	'91	you are	you're
of the clock	o'clock	we had	we'd
let us	let's	she has	she's
she will	she'll	I had	I'd
Bill is	Bill's	we have	we've

Ordinarily, the word *not* is shortened to *n't* and added to a verb without any change in the spelling of the verb.

EXAMPLES
is not	isn't	were not	weren't
are not	aren't	has not	hasn't
does not	doesn't	have not	haven't
do not	don't	had not	hadn't
did not	didn't	would not	wouldn't
was not	wasn't	should not	shouldn't

EXCEPTIONS will not .... won't   cannot .... can't

Do not confuse contractions with possessive pronouns.

CONTRACTIONS	POSSESSIVE PRONOUNS
Who's at bat? [Who is]	**Whose** bat is that?
It's roaring. [It is]	Listen to **its** roar.
You're too busy. [You are]	**Your** friend is busy.
There's a kite. [There is]	That kite is **theirs**.
They're tall trees. [They are]	**Their** trees are tall.

EXERCISE 9 **Correcting Sentences by Using Apostrophes for Contractions**

If any of the following sentences has a contraction without an apostrophe, identify where an apostrophe should be placed. If a sentence is correct as it stands, write *C*.

1. "Youve changed," she said.
2. World War II ended in 45.
3. Whos coming to the party?
4. "The stores about to close," said the clerk.
5. Several stores were closed because of the storm.
6. Well try to make it.
7. Well, try to make it.
8. She gets up at 6 oclock.
9. Im very glad to meet you.
10. Dont you play chess?

EXERCISE 10 **Recognizing the Correct Use of Apostrophes**

For each sentence in the following paragraph, choose the correct word in parentheses.

EXAMPLE [1] (*Your, You're*) likely to see fiesta scenes like this one in Mexican American communities across the United States each year on September 16.
      1. *You're*

[1] (*It's, Its*) a day of celebration that includes parades, speeches, music, and, as you can see, colorful folk dances. Of course, [2] (*theirs, there's*) plenty of food,

including stacks of tortillas and bowls of beans and soup. [3] (*Who's, Whose*) to say how late the merrymaking will last? [4] (*It's, Its*) a joyful holiday of fun, but everyone remembers [5] (*it's, its*) importance, too. Mexican Americans know that [6] (*they're, their*) celebrating the beginning of Mexico's rebellion to gain independence from Spain. [7] On this day in 1810, Father Miguel Hidalgo y Costilla gathered his forces for the rebellion and uttered (*its, it's*) first battle cry. Father Hidalgo, [8] (*who's, whose*) parish was in west central Mexico, led an army across the country. If [9] (*your, you're*) in Mexico City on the eve of September 16, you can hear the president of Mexico ring what is believed to be the bell that Hidalgo rang to summon his people for [10] (*they're, their*) historic march.

Plurals

 To prevent confusion, use an apostrophe and an –*s* to form the plurals of letters, numbers, and symbols, and words that are referred to as words.

EXAMPLES Grandma always tells me to mind my *p*'s and *q*'s.
I got A's on both tests I took last week. [An apostrophe is used because, without one, the plural spells the word *As*.]
His *hi*'s are always cheerful. [An apostrophe is used because without one the plural spells the word *his*.]

Many writers add only an –*s* when forming these four kinds of plurals. However, using both an apostrophe and an –*s* is never wrong and makes your meaning clear.

EXAMPLE   Two different Web site addresses began with ##'s and ended with *.com*'s.
Those *U*'s look like *V*'s.

Notice in the last example above that the plural of *U* would spell *Us* if the apostrophe were omitted. An apostrophe and an –*s* are used to form the plural of *V* to make the style consistent.

▶ EXERCISE 11   **Forming Plurals by Using Apostrophes**

Correctly form the plural of each italicized item.

1. *q* that look like *g*
2. to put *U* at the end
3. all *A* and *B*
4. unclear pronoun references for *his*
5. dotted your *i*

▶ EXERCISE 12   **Using Contractions Correctly**

While showing a small child around an art museum, you stop in front of this painting. You have read that the painting is supposed to suggest the fast movement of a fire truck through the streets of a city. The fire truck is Engine Number Five. To help your young companion enjoy and understand the painting, you ask the child some simple questions and make some simple observations. Write a series of these questions and comments about the painting. Use at least four contractions and at least one example of the plural of a number.

EXAMPLE   *Isn't this painting unusual, Jenny?*

Charles Henry Demuth, *The Figure 5 in Gold.* Oil on composition board, 26 × 29 3/4". The Metropolitan Museum of Art, Alfred Stieglitz Collection, 1949 (49.59.1). © 1986 By The Metropolitan Museum of Art.

MECHANICS

Review: Posttest

Revising Sentences in a Letter by Using Apostrophes Correctly

In the following letter to his pen pal, Josh often left out or incorrectly used apostrophes. Write the correct form of each incorrect word in his letter.

EXAMPLE [1] Im still working on todays assignment.
1. *I'm; today's*

[1] Ive just finished tonights homework. [2] Writing a composition is usually two hours hard work for me, but Im pleased with this one. [3] Ill read it over in the morning to make sure that my handwritings legible. [4] My teacher has trouble with my *d*s, *t*s, and *o*s. [5] He also objects to my overuse of *and*s and *so*s. [6] If theres an error, Ill have to revise my composition a little. [7] Thats one good reason for being careful, isnt it?

[8] My compositions title is "The Reign of Animals." [9] Moms friend suggested that I call it "Whose in Charge Here?" [10] My familys love for animals is well known in the neighborhood and among our friends'. [11] At the moment were owned by two inside cats, three outside cats, our resident dog Pepper, and a visiting dog we call Hugo.

[12] During Peppers walks, Im usually followed by at least one other dog. [13] Some owners care of their dogs never seems to go beyond feeding them. [14] The City Councils decision to fine owners' who let they're dogs run loose makes sense. [15] Theres one huge dog who's always wandering loose in my neighborhood. [16] His names Hugo, and weve taken him in several times after hes narrowly escaped being hit by a car. [17] In fact, Hugos and Peppers feeding dishes sit side by side in our kitchen.

[18] Peter, our senior cat, who was once one of our neighborhoods strays, isnt about to run from anyones dog. [19] At times weve seen him safeguarding other cats of ours' by running in front of them and staring down an approaching dog and it's owner. [20] Our dogs and cats different personalities never cease to fascinate me.

SUMMARY OF USES OF THE APOSTROPHE

Rule	Examples
27a singular possessive nouns	**wife's** career **hostess's** idea **pony's** harness
27b plural possessive nouns	**students'** papers **heroes'** medals **children's** toys
27c possessive personal pronouns	**his** bicycle **our** TV a friend of **theirs**
27d possessive indefinite pronouns	**everyone's** wish **somebody's** jacket **no one's** concern
27e possessive compound nouns, nouns that show joint possession	great-**uncle's** hat Sweeper Broom **Company's** ad Maya and **Theo's** project
27f nouns that show individual possession	**Brad's** and **Nicole's** lunches **Mr. Molina's** and **Ms. Jackson's** jobs
27g contractions	**Who's** there? **It's** ten **o'clock**. during the 1960s and **'70s**
27h plurals of lowercase letters, some uppercase letters, and some words referred to as words	*p*'s and *q*'s I got two **A's**. *ha ha's*

MECHANICS

28 PUNCTUATION

Hyphens, Dashes, Parentheses

Diagnostic Test

A. Using Hyphens, Dashes, and Parentheses Correctly

Add hyphens, dashes, and parentheses where needed in the following sentences. Don't add commas in these sentences.

EXAMPLE **1.** Nancy Wing she is the ex champion will award the golf trophies.

1. *Nancy Wing—she is the ex-champion—will award the golf trophies.*

1. Yori will be twenty one on the twenty first of September this year.
2. "That sounds like" gasped Jeff as he dashed for the window.
3. A former all state quarterback, our coach insists that there is no such thing as a self made star.
4. A dog I think it was a poodle jumped into the lake.

5. The Historical Society the local members, that is will conduct a tour of the harbor.
6. My sister Patricia she is in college now wants to be a marine biologist.
7. The recipe for winter herb bread calls for one and one half cups of whole wheat flour.
8. At the auction someone bid one thousand dollars for a pre Revolutionary desk.
9. The great Incan civilization flourished A.D. 1000 to 1500 until the arrival of Francisco Pizarro in 1531.
10. Next month of course, I'll write you before then we're going on an overnight hike.

B. Adding Hyphens, Dashes, and Parentheses

The following paragraph contains ten errors in the use of hyphens, dashes, and parentheses. Correct each error by inserting the appropriate punctuation. Don't add commas. [Note: A pair of dashes or a pair of parentheses may be needed to correct a single error.]

EXAMPLE   **[1]** Only one woman has served as prime minister of Israel an independent nation since 1948.

     1. *Only one woman has served as prime minister of Israel (an independent nation since 1948).*

[11] You may be surprised to know I certainly was that an exschoolteacher from Milwaukee, Wisconsin, became prime minister of Israel. **[12]** Golda Meir pronounced may-EAR was prime minister from 1969 to 1974. **[13]** She was born in the former Soviet Union the city of Kiev, to be exact in 1898. **[14]** Eight years later her family emigrated to the United States they settled in Milwaukee. **[15]** She grew up and married, and she and her husband emigrated to Palestine, where she became active in pro Jewish affairs. **[16]** She was a signer one of only two women signers, in fact of Israel's Declaration of Independence. **[17]** In her twenty six years with the government, Meir also served as minister of labor, foreign minister, and Israeli ambassador to the Soviet Union. **[18]** She died in 1978 just four years after she retired.

Hyphens

Some compound words are hyphenated (*red-hot*); some are written as one word (*redhead*); some are written as two or more words (*red tape*).

Whenever you need to know whether a word is hyphenated, look it up in a current dictionary.

👉 **REFERENCE NOTE:** For more information on using the dictionary, see pages 925–928.

28a.	Use a hyphen to divide a word at the end of a line.

EXAMPLE   The governor's reelection celebration will be organ-
             ized by her campaign committee.

In the example above, notice that a word is always divided between syllables at the end of a line. If you need to divide a word and are not sure about its syllables, look it up in a dictionary. In addition, keep in mind the following rules for word division.

(1) Do not divide one-syllable words.

INCORRECT   The line of people waiting to buy tickets stret-
              ched halfway down the block.
  CORRECT   The line of people waiting to buy tickets stretched
              halfway down the block.
  CORRECT   The line of people waiting to buy tickets
              stretched halfway down the block.

(2) Divide an already hyphenated word only at a hyphen.

INCORRECT   The conference speaker this morning is my moth-
              er-in-law.
  CORRECT   The conference speaker this morning is my mother-
              in-law.

(3) Do not divide a word so that one letter stands alone.

INCORRECT   The utility company built a dam to generate e-
              lectricity.
  CORRECT   The utility company built a dam to generate elec-
              tricity.

MECHANICS

▶ EXERCISE 1 **Using Hyphens to Divide Words at the Ends of Lines**

Write each of the following words, using a hyphen to indicate where the word may be divided at the end of a line. If necessary, check a dictionary for the proper syllabication. If a word should *not* be divided, write *one-syllable word* after its number.

EXAMPLES **1.** thoroughly **2.** cooked
1. *thor-ough-ly* **2.** *one-syllable word*

1. original **5.** parentheses **9.** through
2. library **6.** tomorrow **10.** son-in-law
3. fourth **7.** breathe
4. unprecedented **8.** corporation

28b. Use a hyphen with compound numbers from *twenty-one* to *ninety-nine* and with fractions used as adjectives.

EXAMPLES twenty-four chairs
one-half cup [but *one half* of the flour]

28c. Use a hyphen with the prefixes *ex-, self-, all-,* and with the suffix *-elect,* and with all prefixes before a proper noun or proper adjective.

EXAMPLES ex-coach mid-July
self-made pro-American
all-star anti-Communist
president-elect pre-Revolutionary

▶ EXERCISE 2 **Hyphenating Words Correctly**

Insert hyphens in the words that should be hyphenated in the following sentences.

1. The exgovernor presented the all American trophy at the competition.
2. Until 1959, the United States flag had forty eight stars.
3. In twenty five days my grandparents will celebrate their forty fifth wedding anniversary; about three fourths of the family will attend the celebration.

4. The exambassador's lecture focused on the post Andean era.
5. He added one half teaspoon of vanilla to the mixture and set the timer for thirty five minutes.

▶ REVIEW A   **Identifying the Correct Use of Hyphens**

You've just received the following letter from your friend Eduardo. His computer is acting up again, and it's putting in hyphens that aren't supposed to be there. You and Eduardo have a running joke about his computer problems, so you plan to tease him about his excess hyphens. Make a list of all the incorrectly used hyphens you find in the letter and another list of the correctly used ones. [Hint: There are ten of each.]

EXAMPLES   <u>Incorrect</u>   <u>Correct</u>
            early-bird   *brother-in-law*

Hey there!

[1] So, how have you-been? [2] I can't believe it's mid-April. [3] I've been running myself ragged with home-work, club-meetings, sports, and ninety-nine other things. [4] You wouldn-t believe how busy I've been!

[5] I've got a part in our spring-play. [6] It's not a big part, but I'm one of an all-star cast. [7] We're doing <u>Our Town</u>. [8] I am managing the props, too.

[9] Enclosed is a recipe that I used last week to make pop-corn topping. [10] I'm president-elect of the foreign language-club, and it was my turn to host the monthly meeting. [11] Thirty-three members came to my house (we have a total of fifty-one members). [12] I served refreshments, and every-one loved this topping.

[13] Mexican Popcorn Topping: Mix together one-fourth cup of chili-powder, one-half teaspoon of salt, and one-teaspoon each of garlic powder, cilantro, and cumin. [14] (Those last two are herbs.) [15] Sprinkle mixture over plain-popcorn.

Take care and write soon.

Eduardo

Dashes

Many words and phrases are used *parenthetically;* that is, they break into the main thought of a sentence.

EXAMPLES   Anne, **however,** does not agree with him.
The decision **(which player should he choose?)** weighed on Coach Johnson's mind.

Most parenthetical elements are set off by commas or by parentheses. Sometimes, however, these elements demand stronger emphasis. In such cases, a dash is used.

28d. Use a dash to indicate an abrupt break in thought or speech or an unfinished statement or question.

EXAMPLES   Judy—Ms. Lane, I mean—will be your new supervisor.
Our dog—he's a long-haired dachshund—is too affectionate to be a good watchdog.
"Why—why can't I come, too?" Janet asked hesitatingly.
"You're being—" Tina began and then stopped.

▶ EXERCISE 3   **Inserting Dashes in Sentences**

Insert dashes where they are appropriate in the following sentences.

1. "I'd like to thank" and then Tom blushed and quickly sat down.
2. We were surprised in fact, amazed to learn that the game had been called off.
3. The valedictorian that is, the student with the highest average will be given a special award.
4. "I I just don't know," she murmured.
5. My brother's engagement it's a secret, by the way will be announced Sunday.

▶ REVIEW B   **Using Hyphens and Dashes Correctly**

Insert hyphens and dashes where they are needed in each of the following sentences. If a sentence is correct, write *C.*

EXAMPLE 1. State flags you can tell by looking at those shown here are as different as the states themselves.

1. *State flags—you can tell by looking at those shown here—are as different as the states themselves.*

OKLAHOMA

Oklahoma

South Carolina

New Jersey

Colorado

Arkansas

New Mexico

Hawaii

Texas

Washington

1. The American Indian shield on the Oklahoma flag reflects that state's prestatehood years as the territorial home of the Cherokee, Osage, and other Native American peoples.

2. "What what kind of tree is in the center of the South Carolina flag?" Emilio asked. "Is it a palmetto?"

3. Two goddesses Liberty and Ceres, the goddess of agriculture are in the center of New Jersey's flag.

4. On the Colorado flag, one third of the background is white and two thirds is blue.

5. Arkansas a major diamond-producing state has a large diamond on its flag.

6. An ancient Pueblo symbol of the all important sun is on New Mexico's flag.

7. The Union Jack of the United Kingdom as you can see is on a corner of the Hawaiian flag.

8. "The Texas flag is red, white, and blue and contains one lone star because" Megan said before she was interrupted.

9. Blue is a dominant color in forty one state flags.

10. Only one state flag it's Washington's has a green background.

Parentheses

28e. Use parentheses to enclose material that is added to a sentence but is not considered of major importance.

EXAMPLES   During the Middle Ages (from about A.D. 500 to A.D. 1500), Muslims and Vikings invaded Europe.
Aunt Constance (Mother's aunt and my great-aunt) will meet us at the airport.

Material enclosed in parentheses may range from a single word to a short sentence. A short sentence in parentheses may stand by itself or be contained within another sentence.

When end marks belong with the parenthetical materials, place them inside the parentheses. When they belong with the sentences as a whole, place them outside the parentheses.

EXAMPLES   Fill in the application carefully. (Use a pen.)
That old house (it was built at the turn of the century) may soon become a landmark.

In general, follow these two guidelines for using parentheses.

1. Any parenthetical material may be omitted without changing the basic meaning and construction of the sentence.
2. Too many parenthetical expressions in a piece of writing can distract from the main idea. Keep your meaning clear by limiting the number of these expressions you use.

▶ EXERCISE 4   **Writing Sentences with Appropriate Use of Parentheses**

Write the following sentences, adding needed parentheses and punctuating the parenthetical elements correctly.

EXAMPLE   **1.** A fly-specked calendar five years out of date hung on the kitchen wall.
1. *A fly-specked calendar (five years out of date) hung on the kitchen wall.*

MECHANICS

1. I reread all the *Oz* books that I own a considerable number.
2. Edna St. Vincent Millay 1892–1950 began writing poetry as a child.
3. In 1850, California entered the Union as a free state. You will read more about free states in Chapter 5.
4. Gwendolyn Brooks *A Street in Bronzeville* was her first book has received high praise from critics.
5. Killer whales they're the ones with the black and white markings often migrate more than one thousand miles annually.

 REVIEW C   **Using Hyphens, Dashes, and Parentheses Correctly**

Insert hyphens, dashes, and parentheses where they are needed in the following sentences.

EXAMPLE   **1.** You can see from this photograph that Comanche chief Quanah Parker 1845–1911 was a man of strong character.
  1. *You can see from this photograph that Comanche chief Quanah Parker (1845–1911) was a man of strong character.*

1. Parker can you tell this from the photograph? was both a great war chief and a great peace chief.
2. He was the son of a Comanche tribal leader and a young woman Cynthia Ann Parker who was captured dur ing a raid on a Texas homestead.
3. In the 1870s, Parker led a band of Comanche war riors in the Texas Panhandle.
4. Parker surrendered with his band the Quahadi in 1875; they were the last Comanches to do so on the southern plains.

5. After surrendering, Parker became a prosperous rancher quite a change of lifestyle and even owned railroad stock.
6. In fact, he embodied the ideal of the self made man.
7. Parker encouraged his children to learn the ways of the settlers.
8. Parker guided the Comanches his title was principal chief during difficult times after the war ended.
9. In later years, he went to Washington, D.C., and this fact may surprise you became a friend of President Theodore Roosevelt.
10. The Texas city Quanah a Comanche word meaning "sweet-smelling" was named after this great chief.

PICTURE THIS

You, too, are "nooning," or daydreaming, under the trees, opposite the person in the picture below. The peacefulness of the setting inspires both of you to let your thoughts roam, and they turn to your dreams and goals. Write a paragraph about these dreams or goals. Your dreams may be remarkable or unremarkable, humorous

MECHANICS

Winslow Homer, *The Nooning* (1872). Oil on canvas, 13$\frac{5}{16}$ × 19$\frac{3}{4}$", Wadsworth Atheneum, Hartford. The Ella Gallup Sumner and Mary Catlin Sumner Collection Fund.

or serious. In your paragraph, use the following: a hyphen with a compound number, a dash to indicate an abrupt break in thought, and parentheses to set off an explanation.

Subject: a personal dream or goal
Audience: yourself
Purpose: to reflect, to describe

Review: Posttest

A. Identifying Appropriate Uses of Hyphens, Dashes, and Parentheses

Add hyphens, dashes, and parentheses where they are needed in the following sentences. (Don't add commas in these sentences.)

EXAMPLE **1.** Henry Viscardi he founded the National Center for Disability Services created opportunities for people who have disabilities.

           1. *Henry Viscardi—he founded the National Center for Disability Services—created opportunities for people who have disabilities.*

1. The soup was three fourths water and one fourth vegetables.
2. Twenty six students most of them from the advanced math class represented our school at the all state chess match.
3. The Battle of Bunker Hill June 17, 1775 damaged the confidence of the British.
4. Grandmother murmured, "Please turn out the" and then fell asleep.
5. My sister she lives in Boston now is studying pre Columbian art.
6. If you have ever dreamed of finding buried treasure and who hasn't? your search could begin on Padre Island.

7. George Grinnell, who was cofounder of the National Audubon Society, was a self taught expert on the American West and helped negotiate treaties with three Native American peoples the Blackfoot, the Cheyenne, and the Pawnee.

8. The ex treasurer of our club he's an extremely self confident person is now running for class president.

9. Rachel Carson was working for the U.S. Fish and Wildlife Service created in 1940 when she first recog nized how pesticides threaten plant and animal life.

10. Her book *Silent Spring* copyright 1962 alerted the public to the dangers of environmental pollution.

B. Using Hyphens, Dashes, and Parentheses

The following paragraph contains ten errors in the use of hyphens, dashes, and parentheses. Correct each error by inserting the appropriate punctuation. Don't add commas. [Note: A pair of dashes or a pair of parentheses may be needed to correct a single error.]

EXAMPLE   **[1]** I listed eight of the countries along the west coast of Africa Morocco, Mauritania, Guinea, Senegal, Gambia, Guinea-Bissau, Sierra Leone, and Liberia.

1. *I listed eight of the countries along the west coast of Africa (Morocco, Mauritania, Guinea, Senegal, Gambia, Guinea-Bissau, Sierra Leone, and Liberia).*

[11] Liberia's history its founding, that is is unique. **[12]** Liberia was settled in pre Civil War days by freed slaves from the United States. **[13]** An antislavery group, the American Colonization Society, it was officially chartered by the U.S. Congress in 1816 began sending freed slaves to Africa in 1822. **[14]** They named their capital Monrovia in honor of President James Monroe in office 1817–1825. **[15]** They also modeled their country's consti tution and government not surprisingly after those in the United States. **[16]** During Liberia's early years, the United States provided aid to the struggling country. **[17]** Twenty five years later, the settlers how proud they must have been! declared Liberia independent. **[18]** However, the U.S. government didn't officially recognize Liberia until 1862 President Lincoln's administration.

29 SPELLING

Improving Your Spelling

Good Spelling Habits

The following techniques can help you spell words correctly.

1. To learn the spelling of a word, pronounce it, study it, and write it. Pronounce words carefully. Mispronunciation can cause misspelling. For instance, if you say *mis • chie • vi • ous* instead of *mis • chie • vous*, you will probably spell the word wrong.

- First, make sure that you know how to pronounce the word correctly, and then practice saying it.
- Second, study the word. Notice especially any parts that might be hard to remember.
- Third, write the word from memory. Check your spelling.
- If you missed the word, repeat the three steps of this process.

2. Use a dictionary. When you find that you have mis-spelled a word, look it up in a dictionary. Don't guess about correct spelling.

3. Spell by syllables. A *syllable* is a word part that can be pronounced by itself.

EXAMPLES   thor • ough [two syllables]
            sep • a • rate [three syllables]

Instead of trying to learn how to pronounce a whole word, break it up into its syllables whenever possible. It's easier to learn a few letters at a time than to learn all of them at once.

☞ REFERENCE NOTE: For information on using the dictionary to determine the pronunciation of a word, see page 926.

▶ ORAL PRACTICE   **Pronouncing Spelling Words Correctly**

Study the correct pronunciations in parentheses after each of the following words. Then, pronounce each word correctly three times.

1. athlete (ath' • lēt)
2. children (chil' • drən)
3. drowned (dround)
4. escape (e • scāp')
5. library (lī' • brer • ē)

6. lightning (līt' • ning)
7. perhaps (pər • haps')
8. probably (prob' • ə • blē)
9. quiet (kwī' • ət)
10. recognize (rek' • əg • nīz')

MECHANICS

▶ EXERCISE 1   **Spelling by Syllables**

Look up the following words in a dictionary, and divide each one into syllables. Pronounce each syllable correctly, and learn to spell the word by syllables.

1. representative
2. fascinate
3. candidate
4. temperature

5. apparent
6. similar
7. benefit
8. definition

9. acquaintance
10. awkward

4. Proofread for careless spelling errors. Reread your writing carefully, and correct any mistakes and unclear letters. For example, make sure that your *i*'s are dotted, your *t*'s are crossed, and your *g*'s don't look like *q*'s.

5. Keep a spelling notebook. Divide each page into four columns:

COLUMN 1   Correctly spell the word you missed. (Never enter a misspelled word.)

COLUMN 2   Write the word again, dividing it into syllables and marking its accents.

COLUMN 3   Write the word once more, circling the spot that gives you trouble.

COLUMN 4   Jot down any comments that might help you remember the correct spelling.

Here is an example of how you might make entries for two words that are often misspelled.

Correct Spelling	Syllables and Accents	Trouble Spot	Comments
probably	prob'•a•bly	prob(ab)ly	Pronounce both b's
usually	u'•su•al•ly	usua(ll)y	usual + ly (Study Rule 29e)

▶ EXERCISE 2   **Spelling Commonly Misspelled Words**

Copy each of the following words, paying special attention to those with the italicized letters. These letters are silent. Then, have a friend dictate the words to you.

1. ans*w*er
2. a*w*kward
3. *w*hole
4. to*w*ard
5. kno*w*
6. *k*now*l*edge
7. *w*ri*t*ten
8. of*t*en
9. condem*n*
10. colum*n*
11. r*h*ythm
12. use*d* to
13. inste*a*d
14. me*a*nt
15. *a*isle
16. toni*gh*t
17. sure*l*y
18. thou*gh*
19. thro*ugh*
20. nine*t*y

▶ EXERCISE 3   **Preparing a Spelling Notebook**

Set up your own spelling notebook, following the guidelines in item 5 above. Enter three or more words you often have trouble spelling, and compare your work with that of a classmate.

MECHANICS

Spelling Rules

Remembering the following rules can help you figure out how to spell many words.

ie and *ei*

29a. Write *ie* when the sound is long *e*, except after *c*.

EXAMPLES   achieve   chief   niece   shield   ceiling
              believe   field   piece   thief   deceit
              brief   grief   relief   yield   receive

EXCEPTIONS   either, leisure, neither, seize, weird

29b. Write *ei* when the sound is not long *e*.

EXAMPLES   counterfeit   height   reign
              foreign   heir   veil
              forfeit   neighbor   weigh

EXCEPTIONS   friend, mischief, kerchief

–cede, –ceed, and *–sede*

29c. Only one English word ends in *–sede: supersede.* Only three words end in *–ceed: exceed, proceed,* and *succeed.* Most other words with this sound end in *–cede.*

EXAMPLES   accede   intercede   recede
              concede   precede   secede

▶ EXERCISE 4   **Proofreading a Paragraph to Correct Spelling Errors**

The following paragraph contains ten spelling errors involving the use of *ie, ei, –ceed, –cede,* and *–sede.* For each sentence, write the misspelled word or words correctly. If a sentence has no spelling error, write *C.*

EXAMPLE   [1] On my birthday I recieved a wonderful gift.
           1. *received*

MECHANICS

[1] My neighbor, who is a good freind of mine, went on a trip out West. [2] He sent me this Dream Catcher, used by the Sioux to sheild themselves against bad dreams. [3] Charms like this once hung in each tepee, and mine hangs from the cieling near my bed. [4] According to legend, bad dreams get caught in the web and only good ones succede in reaching the sleeper. [5] I do not really believe that my Dream Catcher can interceed on my behalf, but I have not had one wierd dream since my birthday! [6] The Plains Indians moved their homes often, so their possessions could be niether bulky nor heavy. [7] Consequently, the Sioux who made the Dream Catcher had to use common, lightweight materials. [8] The twig bent into a ring is willow wood, and tiny glass beads represent nightmares siezed by the web. [9] Gracefully hanging from either side is a beautiful feather or a horsehair tassel. [10] Wonderful peices of workmanship like this ensure that the culture of the Sioux will never resede into the past.

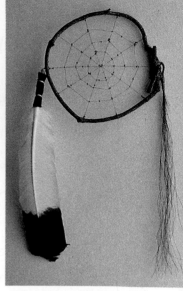

Adding Prefixes

29d. When a prefix is added to a word, the spelling of the original word itself remains the same.

EXAMPLES   im + mortal = **im**mortal   mis + step = **mis**step
                 un + certain = **un**certain   over + rule = **over**rule

Adding Suffixes

29e. When the suffix *–ness* or *–ly* is added to a word, the spelling of the original word remains the same.

EXAMPLES   sure + ly = **surely**   fair + ness = **fairness**
                 real + ly = **really**   late + ness = **lateness**

EXCEPTIONS 1. Words ending in *y* usually change the *y* to *i* before
–*ness* and –*ly:*
empty—emptiness; easy—easily
2. But most one-syllable adjectives ending in *y* follow
Rule 29e:
dry—dryness; sly—slyly
3. *True, due,* and *whole* drop the final *e* before –*ly:*
truly, duly, wholly.

 EXERCISE 5   **Spelling Words with Prefixes and
Suffixes**

Spell each of the following words, including the prefix or
suffix that is given.

1. un + necessary
2. il + legal
3. occasional + ly
4. cleanly + ness
5. mean + ness

29f. Drop the final silent *e* before adding a suffix
that begins with a vowel.

EXAMPLES hope + ing = hoping   strange + est = strangest
noble + er = nobler   admire + ation = admiration
tickle + ish = ticklish   move + able = movable

EXCEPTIONS 1. Keep the final silent *e* in words ending in *ce* or
ge before a suffix that begins with *a* or *o:*
peaceable, knowledgeable
2. To avoid confusion with other words, keep the
final silent *e* in some words:
dyeing and *dying, singeing* and *singing*
3. mile + age = mileage

EXERCISE 6   **Spelling Words with Suffixes**

Add the suffix given for each word, and spell the new
word formed.

1. become + ing
2. guide + ance
3. continue + ous
4. surprise + ed
5. determine + ation

29g. Keep the final silent *e* before adding a suffix
that begins with a consonant.

MECHANICS

EXAMPLES   nine + ty = ni**ne**ty   entire + ly = entire**ly**
                    hope + ful = ho**pe**ful   awe + some = awe**some**
                    care + less = care**less**   pave + ment = pa**ve**ment

EXCEPTIONS   nine + th = ni**n**th   awe + ful = a**w**ful
                      judge + ment = jud**g**ment
                      argue + ment = ar**g**ument

▶ EXERCISE 7   Spelling Words with Suffixes

Spell each of the following words, including the suffix that is given.

1. announce + ment   **4.** care + ful
2. use + age   **5.** write + ing
3. imagine + ary

29h.   When a word ends in *y* preceded by a consonant, change the *y* to *i* before any suffix except one beginning with *i*.

EXAMPLES   fifty + eth = fift**i**eth   mystery + ous = myster**i**ous
                    worry + ed = worr**i**ed   terrify + ing = terrif**y**ing

EXCEPTIONS   1. Some one-syllable words:
                        shy + ness = sh**y**ness   sky + ward = sk**y**ward
                    2. *lady* and *baby* with suffixes:
                        ladylike   ladyship   babyhood

29i.   When a word ends in *y* preceded by a vowel, simply add the suffix.

EXAMPLES   joy + ful = joyful   boy + hood = boyhood
                    array + ed = arrayed   gray + est = grayest

EXCEPTIONS   day + ly = da**i**ly   pay + ed = pa**i**d
                      say + ed = sa**i**d   lay + ed = la**i**d

▶ EXERCISE 8   Spelling Words with Suffixes

Spell each of the following words, including the suffix that is given.

1. extraordinary + ly   **4.** satisfy + ed
2. try + ing   **5.** rely + able
3. deny + al

MECHANICS

Doubling Final Consonants

29j. When a word ends in a consonant, double the final consonant before a suffix that begins with a vowel only if the word

has only one syllable or is accented on the last syllable

and

ends in a *single* consonant preceded by a *single* vowel.

EXAMPLES   drop + ing = dro**pp**ing   occur + ence = occu**rr**ence
plan + ed = pla**nn**ed   propel + er = prope**ll**er
sit + ing = si**tt**ing   refer + ed = refe**rr**ed

Otherwise, simply add the suffix.

EXAMPLES   jump + ed = jumped   tunnel + ing = tunneling
sprint + er = sprinter   appear + ance = appearance

EXERCISE 9   **Spelling Words with Suffixes**

Add the suffix given for each word, and spell the new word formed.

1. swim + er
2. accept + ance
3. number + ing
4. excel + ed
5. riot + ous

REVIEW A   **Spelling Words with Prefixes and Suffixes**

The following paragraph contains ten spelling errors involving the use of prefixes and suffixes. For each sentence, write the misspelled word or words correctly.

EXAMPLE   [1] **Few people know that a teenage boy helped create the awsome Mount Rushmore monument.**
      1. *awesome*

[1] Begining when he was fifteen, Lincoln Borglum helped his famous father, John Gutzon Borglum, as he planed and made this gigantic sculpture. [2] First, John Borglum built a plaster model one-twelfth as large as the completted sculpture would be. [3] On top of this model

MECHANICS

Borglum attached equipment from which he controled a plumb line. [4] The plumb line could be dangled in front of each president's likness to carefuly record each feature. [5] Lincoln Borglum helped in making these measurments. [6] Then, on top of the cliff, he and his father fastenned an identical machine twelve times as large. [7] Lincoln Borglum was one of the workers who operatted this machine. [8] Using it, he copied the movements of the smaller machine and marked where to cut away the rock.

Forming Plurals of Nouns

29k. To form the plurals of most English nouns, simply add *s*.

SINGULAR	boat	house	nickel	radio	teacher
PLURAL	boats	houses	nickels	radios	teachers

29l. To form the plurals of other nouns, follow these rules.

(1) If the noun ends in *s, x, z, ch*, or *sh*, add *es*.

SINGULAR	glass	box	waltz	beach	dish
PLURAL	glasses	boxes	waltzes	beaches	dishes

> **NOTE:** Proper nouns usually follow this rule, too: the *Joneses,* the *Sánchezes.*

MECHANICS

▶ EXERCISE 10 **Spelling the Plurals of Nouns**

Spell the plural of each of the following nouns.

1. guess **2.** ax **3.** tongue **4.** cafeteria **5.** watch

(2) If the noun ends in *y* preceded by a consonant, change the *y* to *i* and add *es*.

SINGULAR	army	baby	sky	story
PLURAL	arm**ies**	bab**ies**	sk**ies**	stor**ies**

EXCEPTION   The plurals of proper nouns: the *Hardys,* the *Carys.*

(3) For some nouns ending in *f* or *fe*, change the *f* to *v* and add *s* or *es*.

EXAMPLES	belief	roof	calf	leaf	wife
	belief**s**	roof**s**	cal**ves**	lea**ves**	wi**ves**

NOTE: Noticing how the plural is pronounced will help you remember whether to change the *f* to *v*.

▶ EXERCISE 11 **Spelling the Plurals of Nouns**

Spell the plural of each of the following nouns.

1. thief   **2.** chef   **3.** theory   **4.** giraffe   **5.** ally

(4) If the noun ends in *o* preceded by a consonant, add *es*.

SINGULAR	echo	hero	tomato
PLURAL	ech**oes**	her**oes**	tomat**oes**

EXCEPTIONS   Nouns for musical terms that end in *o* preceded by a consonant form the plural by adding only *s*.

SINGULAR	alto	piano	solo
PLURAL	alto**s**	piano**s**	solo**s**

A number of nouns that end in *o* preceded by a consonant have two plural forms.

SINGULAR	cargo	grotto	hobo
PLURAL	cargo**s** *or*	grotto**s** *or*	hobo**s** *or*
	cargo**es**	grotto**es**	hobo**es**

The best way to handle plurals of words ending in *o* preceded by a consonant is to check their spelling in a dictionary.

MECHANICS

▶ EXERCISE 12 **Spelling the Plurals of Nouns**

Spell the plural of each of the following nouns.

1. banjo **2.** soprano **3.** lingo **4.** veto **5.** torpedo

(5) The plurals of some nouns are formed in irregular ways.

SINGULAR	child	foot	goose	man	tooth
PLURAL	children	feet	geese	men	teeth

(6) Some nouns have the same form in both the singular and the plural.

SINGULAR AND PLURAL   deer   Japanese   sheep   trout

Compound Nouns

(7) If a compound noun is written as one word, form the plural by adding *s* or *es*.

SINGULAR	spoonful	smashup	icebox
PLURAL	spoonful**s**	smashup**s**	icebox**es**

(8) If a compound noun is hyphenated or written as two words, make the main noun plural. The **main noun** is the noun that is modified.

SINGULAR	sister-in-law	notary public	attorney-at-law
PLURAL	sister**s**-in-law	nota**ries** public	attorney**s**-at-law

▶ EXERCISE 13 **Spelling the Plurals of Nouns**

Spell the plural form of each of the following nouns.

1. ox   **3.** mouse   **5.** deer
2. armful   **4.** man-of-war

Born Loser reprinted by permission of Newspaper Enterprise Association, Inc.

Latin and Greek Loan Words

(9) Some nouns borrowed from Latin and Greek form the plural as in the original language.

SINGULAR alumnus analysis crisis datum
PLURAL alumn**i** analys**es** cris**es** dat**a**

> **NOTE:** A few Latin and Greek loan words have two plural forms.
>
> SINGULAR appendix formula
> PLURAL appendi**ces** *or* appendi**xes** formul**as** *or* formul**ae**

Usually, it is wise to check a dictionary to find the preferred spelling of a plural loan word.

Numerals, Letters, Symbols, and Words Used as Words

(10) To form the plurals of numerals, most capital letters, symbols, and words used as words, add either an *s* or an apostrophe and an *s*.

EXAMPLES Put the **6s** [or **6's**] and the **Rs** [or **R's**] in the second column.
Change the **&s** [or **&'s**] to **ands** [or **and's**].
My parents were teenagers during the **'60s** [or **'60's**].
Many immigrants came to this country during the **1800s** [or **1800's**].

To prevent confusion, always use an apostrophe and an *–s* to form the plurals of lowercase letters, certain capital letters, and some words used as words.

EXAMPLES Your **i's** look like **e's**.
Ramón got all **A's** last semester.
Her muffled **tee hee's** did not interrupt the speaker.

> **NOTE:** Using both an apostrophe and an *s* is never wrong. Therefore, if you have any doubt about whether or not to use the apostrophe, it is better to use it.

▶ EXERCISE 14 **Spelling the Plurals of Nouns and Symbols**

Give the plural forms of each of the following nouns or symbols.

1. + 2. parenthesis 3. *so* 4. 9 5. fulcrum

MECHANICS

▶ REVIEW B   **Spelling the Plurals of Nouns**

In the following silly poem, twenty words are misspelled. Rewrite each misspelled word. [Note: Some lines will no longer rhyme.]

EXAMPLES [1] A group of mans and womens started up a local zoo.
   1. *men; women*
   [2] They bought a lot of animales and put them all on view.
   2. *animals*

[1] They caged the oxes with the deers, the lion with the calfs,

[2] The butterflys and mouses with the burroes and giraffs.

[3] Armys of people soon arrived. In jalopys they were piled,

[4] With wifes and husbands, son-in-laws, and lots of little child.

[5] The boys and girls rode poneys, and they fed the sheeps and deer,

[6] And thought their folks were heros to so nicely bring them here.

[7] The mosquitos had a fine time feasting on the kangarooes;

[8] Most of the other animals minded their *p*s and *q*s.

[9] The moon shone brightly through the leafs as night began to fall.

[10] Why do you think the lion had the nicest day of all?

Spelling Numbers

29m. Always spell out a number that begins a sentence.

EXAMPLE   **One thousand five hundred** band members attended this year's State Marching Band Festival.

29n. Within a sentence, spell out numbers that can be written in one or two words; use numerals for other numbers.

EXAMPLES   I have only **one** week in which to write **four** reports.
We picked **twenty-one** quarts of peaches.
Agnes has sold **116** magazine subscriptions.

EXCEPTION   If you use some numbers with one or two words and some with more than two words, use numerals for all of them.

EXAMPLE   Our school had **563** freshmen, **327** sophomores, **143** juniors, and **90** seniors.

29o. Spell out numbers used to indicate order.

EXAMPLE   My brother graduated **second** [not *2nd*] in his class.

EXCEPTION   Use numerals for dates when you include the name of the month. Always use numerals for years.

EXAMPLES   **School closes on June 6.** [This example could also be written *the sixth of June* but not *June 6th.*]
The Civil War ended in 1865.

▶ EXERCISE 15   **Spelling Numbers**

Write five original sentences, following these directions.

1. Write a sentence beginning with a number.
2. Write a sentence that has two numbers, both of which can be written in one or two words.
3. Write a sentence that has three numbers, two of them with one or two words and one of them with more than two words.

4. Write a sentence using a number to indicate the order in which a person placed in a race.
5. Write a sentence giving the month and date of your birthday.

Words Often Confused

You can prevent many spelling errors by learning the difference between the words grouped together in this section. Some of them are confusing because they are *homonyms* — that is, they're pronounced alike. Others are confusing because they're spelled the same or nearly the same.

advice	[noun] *counsel* He gave me some excellent *advice*.
advise	[verb] *to give advice* She *advised* me to finish high school.
affect	[verb] *to influence* What he said did not *affect* my decision.
effect	[verb] *to accomplish*; [noun] *consequence* OR *result* The mayor has *effected* many changes during her administration. What *effect* will the new factory have on the environment?
all ready	[pronoun plus adjective] *everyone ready* We were *all ready* to go.
already	[adverb] *previously* Sharon has *already* gone.
all right	[This is the only acceptable spelling. Although the spelling *alright* is in some dictionaries, it has not become standard usage.]
all together	*everyone in the same place* When we were *all together*, we voted.
altogether	*entirely* He was *altogether* wrong.

brake	*a stopping device* The *brakes* on our car are good.
break	*to shatter, sever* A high-pitched sound can *break* glass.
capital	[noun] *center of government* OR *money or property used in business;* [adjective] *punishable by death* OR *of major importance* OR *excellent* OR *uppercase* Raleigh is the *capital* of North Carolina. Mrs. Ortiz needs more *capital* to modernize her factory. Killing a police officer is a *capital* crime. I made a *capital* error in my report. This is a *capital* detective story. You need a *capital* letter here.
capitol	[noun] *building, statehouse* In Raleigh, the *capitol* is on Fayetteville Street at Union Square.
choose	[verb, used for present and future tense] *select* You may *choose* your own partner.
chose	[verb, past tense, rhymes with *nose*] The committee *chose* to postpone the meeting.
coarse	*rough* OR *crude* This *coarse* fabric is very durable. He never uses *coarse* language.
course	*path of action or progress* OR *unit of study* OR *track or way* OR *part of a meal;* also used with *of* to mean *naturally* OR *certainly* The airplane strayed off its *course* in the storm. I'm taking an algebra *course.* She's at the golf *course.* The main *course* at the banquet was roasted turkey with dressing. All cats, of *course,* are predators. Of *course,* you're invited.

MECHANICS

▶ EXERCISE 16 **Distinguishing Between Words Often Confused**

Choose the correct word of the pair in parentheses.

1. Betty has (*all ready, already*) handed in her paper.
2. (*All right, Alright*), I'll wrap the package now.
3. The mechanic adjusted the (*brakes, breaks*).
4. Do you know the (*capital, capitol*) of your state?
5. They were (*all together, altogether*) at dinner.
6. The rule goes into (*affect, effect*) today.
7. His (*coarse, course*) manners offended everyone.
8. A fragile piece of china (*brakes, breaks*) easily.
9. Our state (*capital, capitol*) is built of limestone and marble.
10. When will they (*choose, chose*) the winners?

▶ EXERCISE 17 **Proofreading for Words Often Confused**

Correct the ten errors in word usage in the following paragraph.

EXAMPLE   [1] After taking that class, we were already to shoot our own videos.
  1. *all ready*

[1] The best movie-making advise I ever received came from Ms. Herrera, who taught the video coarse I choose as an elective last semester. [2] Once we would-be movie makers were altogether, she said simply, "Rule number one: Take the lens cap off." [3] Everyone laughed, but she said, "It's no joke—in every class at least one person brakes this one basic rule. [4] Of coarse," she added, "forgetting to put film in the camera has much the same affect." [5] If you chose to make your own home videos, I'd advice you to remember Ms. Herrera's words. [6] They will seriously effect the results you'll get.

complement	[noun] *something that completes or makes perfect;* [verb] *to complete or make perfect*
	The office now has a full *complement* of personnel.
	The yellow rug *complemented* the cozy room.

compliment	[noun] *a remark that expresses approval, praise, or admiration;* [verb] *to pay a compliment*
consul	*the representative of a foreign country* The French *consul* was a guest of honor.
council	*a group called together to accomplish a job* The city *council* will debate the issue.
councilor	*a member of a council* At the council meeting, my mother plans to introduce Dr. Watkins, the new *councilor*.
counsel	[noun] *advice;* [verb] *to give advice* I'm deeply grateful for your *counsel*. Did the doctor *counsel* her to get more rest?
counselor	*one who gives advice* I don't think I'm qualified to act as your *counselor*.
des'ert	[noun] *a dry region* The Sahara, in Africa, is the world's largest *desert*.
desert'	[verb] *to leave* She would never *desert* her comrades.
dessert'	[noun] *the final course of a meal* What would you like for *dessert* tonight?

The Far Side copyright 1985 FarWorks, Inc. Distributed by Universal Press Syndicate. Reprinted with permission. All rights reserved.

"Quick, Abdul! Desert! . . . One 's' or two?"

MECHANICS

▶ EXERCISE 18   **Distinguishing Between Words Often Confused**

Choose the correct word of the choices in parentheses.

1. The funds are for a (*desert, dessert*) irrigation project.
2. The Security (*Consul, Council, Counsel*) of the United Nations consists of fifteen members.

3. The new tie will (*complement, compliment*) my suit.
4. Miss Jee is my guidance (*councilor, counselor*).
5. The house looks (*deserted, desserted*).
6. Listen to your parents' (*consul, council, counsel*).
7. I passed on your charming (*complement, compliment*) to Isabel.
8. All the members of the city (*council, counsel*) agreed that the tax proposal was unworkable.
9. Frozen yogurt is my favorite (*desert, dessert*).
10. The American (*consul, counsel*) in Japan announced the trade agreement.

formally	*properly, according to strict rules* Should he be *formally* introduced?
formerly	*previously, in the past* The new consul was *formerly* a professor.
hear	*to receive sounds through the ears* Did you *hear* the president's speech?
here	*at this place* The bus will be *here* soon.
its	[possessive of *it*] The bird stopped *its* singing.
it's	[contraction of *it is*] *It's* an easy problem.
lead	[verb, present tense, pronounced *lēd*] *to go first* I'll *lead* the way.
led	[verb, past tense of *lead*] Last week she *led* us to victory.
lead	[noun, pronounced *led*] *a heavy metal* OR *graphite in a pencil* We made fishing sinkers out of *lead.* Use a sharp *lead* to draw fine lines.
loose	[adjective, rhymes with *noose*] *not tight or not securely fastened* OR *not close together* The string on the package is too *loose.* The car swerved out of the *loose* gravel.
lose	[verb, pronounced *lo͞oz*] *to suffer loss* Don't *lose* your ticket.

MECHANICS

moral	[adjective] *having to do with good or right;* [noun] *a lesson in conduct* It's a *moral* question. These fables all have a *moral*.
morale	[noun] *mental condition, spirit* The employees' *morale* is high.
passed	[verb, past tense of *pass*] He *passed* us in the corridor.
past	[noun] *the history of a person;* [adjective] *former;* [preposition] *farther than* I didn't ask him about his *past*. Her *past* employer recommended her for the job. I went *past* the house.
peace	*absence of conflict* After the long war, *peace* was welcome.
piece	*a part of something* Do you have a *piece* of paper I can borrow?

MECHANICS

▶ EXERCISE 19 **Distinguishing Between Words Often Confused**

Choose the correct word of the pair in parentheses.

1. The coach's praise after the game raised the team's (*morale, moral*).
2. It's already (*passed, past*) nine o'clock.
3. The searchers hoped that the dog would (*lead, led*) them to the lost skier.
4. The hard-driving fullback (*led, lead*) the team to victory.
5. I'm more interested in math than I (*formally, formerly*) was.
6. Several children asked what the (*moral, morale*) of the story was.
7. I need a pencil with a soft (*led, lead*).
8. Everyone at the dance was dressed (*formally, formerly*).
9. Molly (*past, passed*) all her tests.
10. The candidate's (*moral, morale*) standards are well known.

EXERCISE 20 **Proofreading for Words Often Confused**

Correct the ten errors in word usage in the following paragraph.

EXAMPLE [1] My dad's promotion lead to a move for our family.
1. *led*

[1] When we first moved hear, I felt as though I'd been cut lose from everything I formerly cared about. [2] To boost my morale, my parents gave me a peace of advice I didn't really want to here. [3] They said, "If you dwell on the passed, you'll loose out on the present." [4] They both moved a lot when they were young, so I guess they know what its like. [5] Now that a year has past, I realize that every place has it's good points. [6] I've made quite a few new friends, and I'm finally at piece with myself—and with my parents.

plain	[adjective] *clear* OR *not fancy;* [noun] *a flat area of land* She made her point of view *plain.* Steven wears very *plain* clothes. The storm lashed the open *plain.*
plane	[noun] *a flat surface* OR *a level;* also *a tool* OR *an airplane* Each *plane* of the granite block was smooth. The debate was conducted on a high *plane.* Chris smoothed the wood with a *plane.* The *plane* arrived on time.
principal	[noun] *head of a school;* [adjective] *main, most important* Ted had a long talk with the *principal.* Winning is not our *principal* goal.
principle	[noun] *a rule of conduct; a law* OR *a main fact* My friends have high *principles.* I don't know the *principles* of physics.
quiet	[adjective] *silent, still* The library is usually fairly *quiet.*
quite	[adverb] *to a great extent or degree, completely* My little brother is *quite* clever for his age. I'm *quite* pleased with your progress.

shone	[verb, past tense of *shine*] The sun *shone* brightly this morning.
shown	[verb, past participle of *show*] *revealed* Li Hua has just *shown* me her scrapbook.
stationary	*in a fixed position* These chairs are *stationary*.
stationery	*writing paper* Use white *stationery* for business letters.
than	[conjunction, used for comparisons] Jimmy enjoys tennis more *than* golfing.
then	[adverb or conjunction, indicating *at that time* OR *next*] Did you know Bianca *then?* I revised my paper, and *then* I proofread it.
their	[possessive of *they*] The girls gave *their* opinions.
there	[adverb] *at that place* [also an expletive used to begin a sentence (see page 511)] I'll be *there* on time. *There* isn't any milk left.
they're	[contraction of *they are*] *They're* at the station now.

MECHANICS

▷ EXERCISE 21   **Distinguishing Between Words Often Confused**

Choose the correct word of the pair in parentheses.

1. Mrs. Tanaka is our school's (*principal, principle*).
2. One scene of the movie was not (*shone, shown*) on TV.
3. The deer stood (*stationary, stationery*) for a full minute.
4. Gossiping is against his (*principals, principles*).
5. Last night many stars (*shone, shown*) brightly.
6. I wrote the letter on blue (*stationary, stationery*).
7. Rosa learned how to use a (*plain, plane*) in industrial arts class.
8. My (*principal, principle*) problem is learning to spell.
9. We watched a coyote crossing the (*plain, plane*).
10. Tyrone has mastered the basic (*principals, principles*) of chess.

▶ EXERCISE 22 **Proofreading for Words Often Confused**

Correct the ten errors in word usage in the following paragraph.

EXAMPLE [1] Our principle let us out of school early to welcome home our victorious volleyball team.

    1. *principal*

[1] When King High School won the girls' state volleyball championship last year, hundreds of students went to the airport to meet the team's plain. [2] The flight arrived on time, but than it took more then an hour for the aircraft to reach the gate. [3] Finally someone shouted, "Their they are! [4] There coming up the ramp!" [5] Once the entire team was in the waiting area, Coach Janos asked everyone to be quite and introduced each of the girls. [6] They're were loud cheers for each of them, even though quite a few hadn't played in the final game. [7] It was plane that they were quiet excited about there success and looking forward to the official victory rally the next day.

threw	*cast; tossed; pitched* Freddy *threw* three strikes.
through	*in one side and out the opposite side* The fire truck raced *through* the traffic.
to	[preposition; also part of the infinitive form of a verb] They've gone *to* the store. She told us *to wash* the windows.
too	*also* OR *more than enough* I like soccer, and Ted does, *too.* He was *too* tired to think clearly.
two	*the sum of one + one* I noticed *two* packages on the sofa.
waist	[noun] *the middle part of the body* This skirt is too big in the *waist.*
waste	[noun] *unused material;* [verb] *to squander* *Waste* is a major problem in the United States. Don't *waste* your money on that.

MECHANICS

weak	*feeble, lacking force, not strong* The fawn is still too *weak* to walk. We could hardly hear his *weak* voice.
week	*seven days* Carol has been gone a *week*.
weather	*conditions outdoors* The *weather* suddenly changed.
whether	[indicates alternative or doubt] She wondered *whether* to enter the contest.
who's	[contraction of *who is* OR *who has*] I can't imagine *who's* at the door now. *Who's* been marking in my book?
whose	[possessive of *who*] *Whose* bicycle is this?
your	[possessive of *you*] What is *your* idea?
you're	[contraction of *you are*] *You're* my best friend.

▶ EXERCISE 23 **Distinguishing Between Words Often Confused**

Choose the correct word of the pair in parentheses.

1. Next (*weak, week*) the Bears will play the Packers.
2. The ball crashed (*threw, through*) the window.
3. (*Your, You're*) up next, Leshe.
4. Giving a speech makes me (*weak, week*) in the knees.
5. (*Your, You're*) sleeve is torn.
6. Each band member wore a gold sash around the (*waist, waste*).
7. (*Whose, Who's*) bat is this?
8. (*Whose, Who's*) going to be first?
9. No, this isn't a (*waist, waste*) of time.
10. (*Whose, Who's*) seen my black sweater?

▶ EXERCISE 24 **Proofreading for Words Often Confused**

Correct the ten errors in word usage in the following paragraph.

MECHANICS

EXAMPLE   [1] **Have you ever had the whether ruin you're plans?**
            1. *weather, your*

[1] Last Labor Day weekend, my brother Jorge and I got up early Saturday morning and rode our bikes four miles too the beach. [2] The two of us were to busy talking too notice that the sky was growing darker as we rode along. [3] Just as we through our towels on the sand, it started to rain heavily. [4] We waisted the next hour huddled under one of the beach shelters, arguing about weather to stay or to go home. [5] Finally, since the rain showed no signs of letting up, we pedaled miserably back home threw the driving rain. [6] It rained all day Sunday and Monday, to. [7] We ended up spending the whole weekend cooped up in the house while whether forecasters predicted sunny skies for the rest of the weak.

▶ REVIEW C   **Identifying Correctly Spelled Words**

Choose the correct word of the pair in parentheses.

1. a (*brief, breif*) talk
2. (*neither, niether*) one
3. (*course, coarse*) cloth
4. some good (*advice, advise*)
5. fruit for (*desert, dessert*)
6. many (*heros, heroes*)
7. on the (*cieling, ceiling*)
8. two (*copies, copys*)
9. driving (*passed, past*) the theater
10. (*weather, whether*) to stay or not

75 Commonly Misspelled Words

The following list contains seventy-five words that are often misspelled. To find out which words give you difficulty, ask someone to read you the list in groups of twenty-five. Write down each word; then check your spelling. Make a list in your spelling notebook of any word you misspelled. Keep reviewing your list until you have mastered the correct spelling.

ache	belief	coming	eager	guess
across	built	cough	easy	half
again	business	could	every	having
all right	busy	country	February	heard
almost	buy	doctor	forty	hour
always	can't	doesn't	friend	instead
answer	color	don't	grammar	knew

know	ready	speech	together	wear
laid	really	straight	tomorrow	Wednesday
likely	safety	sugar	tonight	where
making	said	surely	tough	which
meant	says	tear	trouble	whole
minute	shoes	though	truly	women
often	since	through	Tuesday	won't
once	speak	tired	until	write

300 Spelling Words

Learn to spell the following words this year if you don't already know how. They're grouped so that you can study them ten at a time.

absence
absolutely
acceptance
accidentally
accommodate
accompany
accomplish
accurate
accustomed
achievement

acquaintance
actually
administration
affectionate
agriculture
amateur
ambassador
analysis
analyze
announcement

anticipate
apology
apparent
appearance
approach
approval
arguing
argument
assurance
attendance

authority
available
basically
beginning
believe
benefit
benefited
boundary
calendar
campaign

capital
category
certificate
characteristic
chief
circuit
circumstance
civilization
column
commissioner

committee
comparison
competent
competition
conceivable
conception
confidential
conscience
conscious
consistency

constitution
continuous
control
cooperate
corporation
correspondence
criticism
criticize
cylinder
debtor

decision
definite
definition
deny
description
despise
diameter
disappearance
disappointment
discipline

disgusted
distinction
distinguished
dominant
duplicate
economic
efficiency
eighth
elaborate
eligible

MECHANICS

embarrass
emergency
employee
encouraging
environment
equipped
essential
evidently
exaggerate
exceedingly

excellent
excessive
excitable
exercise
existence
expense
extraordinary
fascinating
fatal
favorably

fictitious
financier
flourish
fraternity
frequent
further
glimpse
glorious
grabbed
gracious

graduating
grammar
gross
gymnasium
happiness
hasten
heavily
hindrance
humorous
hungrily

hypocrisy
hypocrite
icy
ignorance
imagination
immediately
immense
incidentally
indicate
indispensable

inevitable
innocence
inquiry
insurance
intelligence
interfere
interpretation
interrupt
investigation
judgment

knowledge
leisure
lengthen
lieutenant
likelihood
liveliness
loneliness
magazine
maneuver
marriage

marvelous
mechanical
medieval
merchandise
minimum
mortgage
multitude
muscle
mutual
narrative

naturally
necessary
negligible
niece
noticeable
obligation
obstacle
occasionally
occurrence
offense

official
omit
operation
opportunity
oppose
optimism
orchestra
organization
originally
paid

paradise
parallel
particularly
peasant
peculiar
percentage
performance
personal
personality
perspiration

persuade
petition
philosopher
picnic
planning
pleasant
policies
politician
possess
possibility

practically
precede
precisely
preferred
prejudice
preparation
pressure
primitive
privilege
probably

procedure
proceed
professor
proportion
psychology
publicity
pursuit
qualities
quantities
readily

reasonably
receipt
recognize
recommendation
referring
regretting
reign
relieve
remembrance
removal

renewal
repetition
representative
requirement
residence
resistance
responsibility
restaurant
rhythm
ridiculous

sacrifice
satire
satisfied
scarcely
scheme
scholarship
scissors
senate
sensibility
separate

sergeant
several
shepherd
sheriff
similar
skis
solemn
sophomore
source
specific

sponsor
straighten
substantial
substitute
subtle
succeed
successful
sufficient
summary
superior

suppress
surprise
survey
suspense
suspicion
temperament
tendency
thorough
transferring
tremendous

truly
unanimous
unfortunately
unnecessary
urgent
useful
using
vacancies
vacuum
varies

MECHANICS

30 CORRECTING COMMON ERRORS

Key Language Skills Review

This chapter reviews key skills and concepts that pose special problems for writers.

- Sentence Fragments and Run-on Sentences
- Subject-Verb and Pronoun-Antecedent Agreement
- Verb Forms
- Clear Pronoun Reference
- Comparison of Modifiers
- Dangling and Misplaced Modifiers
- Capitalization
- Punctuation—Commas, Quotation Marks, Apostrophes, Semicolons, and Colons
- Spelling
- Standard Usage

Most of the exercises in this chapter follow the same format as the exercises found throughout the grammar, usage, and mechanics sections. You will notice, however, that two sets of review exercises are presented in standardized test formats. These exercises are designed to provide you with practice not only in solving usage and mechanics problems but also in dealing with these kinds of problems on such tests.

EXERCISE 1 **Identifying Sentences and Revising Sentence Fragments**

Identify each numbered word group in the following paragraph as either a fragment (*F*) or a sentence (*S*). Then, make each fragment part of a complete sentence either by adding words to it or by combining it with another fragment or sentence in the paragraph. Change the punctuation and capitalization as necessary.

EXAMPLES   [1] I discovered that the jacket was made of linen. [2] When I got home.
1. *S*
2. *F—When I got home, I discovered that the jacket was made of linen.*

[1] Before you spend your money on that expensive shirt. [2] Read the label carefully! [3] Because some clothes must be sent to the dry cleaner. [4] They will cost you extra money. [5] A lot of money in the long run. [6] Other clothes must be washed by hand. [7] Requiring extra time and care for their upkeep. [8] If you are looking for quality clothes. [9] That are both attractive and inexpensive to own. [10] It pays to read the label.

EXERCISE 2 **Revising Run-on Sentences**

Each of the following numbered items is a run-on sentence. Revise each run-on, using the method given in brackets after it. Be sure to change punctuation and capitalization as necessary.

EXAMPLE   1. Today's world offers many kinds of popular entertainment earlier Americans relied mainly on music and dancing. [*comma and coordinating conjunction*]
1. *Today's world offers many kinds of popular entertainment, but earlier Americans relied mainly on music and dancing.*

1. Just imagine your life without TV, audio and video recordings, and movies surely you would spend your time differently than you do now. [*two sentences*]
2. In a world without recorded music, a musician could often attract a crowd even today, good musicians can make a living on the streets of a large city. [*semicolon*]

3. Music was important to the early settlers, they often made their own instruments. [*comma and coordinating conjunction*]
4. Many settlers owned fiddles, dulcimers, flutes, and guitars music could be a part of everyday life. [*semicolon and conjunctive adverb*]
5. Long before the settlers arrived, there was already plenty of music in North America American Indians prized music and song. [*semicolon*]
6. The Seneca used rattles similar to maracas the Maidu played flutes and whistles. [*comma and coordinating conjunction*]
7. Northern Plains Indians used the hand drum musicians today incorporate such Native American instruments into popular music. [*two sentences*]
8. The banjo is widely regarded as a traditional American musical instrument, the banjo originated in Africa. [*semicolon and conjunctive adverb*]
9. West Africans made banjolike instruments out of gourds for strings, they used dried animal gut. [*semicolon*]
10. Early banjos had no frets and only four strings frets are the ridges positioned at intervals on the necks of banjos and guitars. [*two sentences*]

▷ EXERCISE 3   **Revising Sentence Fragments and Run-on Sentences**

Most of the following groups of words are either run-on sentences or sentence fragments. Identify and correct each sentence fragment and run-on sentence. If the group of words is already a complete sentence, write C.

EXAMPLE   1. The area where I live used to be a prehistoric sea, sometimes my friends and I find fossilized sharks' teeth.

1. *The area where I live used to be a prehistoric sea, and sometimes my friends and I find fossilized sharks' teeth.*

1. Walking slowly over the rocky terrain.
2. A strange rock caught our attention Jackie broke it open.
3. Inside it were rows and rows of brilliant amethyst crystals, we gasped at our discovery.

4. Is one of the best places in the world for prospectors.
5. Gold lies hidden in the West, many people still seek their fortune there.
6. When rainfall, a landslide, or some other act of nature alters the landscape.
7. Can find gold, silver, platinum, and other precious metals.
8. Although most commonly used for jewelry, gold is necessary for several industries and has numerous other uses.
9. You can grow your own crystals, some grow quite quickly.
10. With a kit from a hobby shop only two blocks away from my house in Phoenix.

▶ EXERCISE 4 **Choosing Verbs That Agree in Number with Their Subjects**

For each of the following sentences, choose the correct form of the verb in parentheses.

EXAMPLE **1.** One of the customs most readily shared among cultures (*is, are*) games.
1. *is*

1. Almost everybody (*has, have*) played games that originated in faraway places.
2. Few of these games (*is, are*) difficult to play.
3. Pictures of people playing with yo-yos (*appears, appear*) on ancient Greek pottery.
4. (*Was, Were*) the first people who played lacrosse American Indians?
5. Arctic peoples, Africans, the Maori of New Zealand, and others as well (*plays, play*) cat's cradle.
6. Somewhere, somebody in one of the world's cultures probably (*is, are*) spinning a top right now.
7. Not all card games (*uses, use*) a standard deck of cards.
8. Most of these games (*requires, require*) at least two players.
9. Several ancient African games still (*enjoys, enjoy*) popularity.
10. None of these Chinese tangrams (*turns, turn*) out to be easy.

CORRECTING COMMON ERRORS

 EXERCISE 5   **Proofreading a Paragraph for Subject-Verb Agreement**

Identify the ten errors in subject-verb agreement in the following paragraph. Then, change each incorrect verb to agree with its subject.

EXAMPLE   [1] Many a building design don't meet the needs of people with disabilities.
     1. *don't—doesn't*

[1] Ordinary houses or an average building sometimes present problems for people with disabilities. [2] For example, a person using a wheelchair or crutches often have difficulty maneuvering in narrow halls. [3] Narrow doorways and a small hall makes access difficult for anyone using a wheelchair or a walker. [4] Moreover, inadequate shower access or high counters needlessly poses problems for people with wheelchairs. [5] One builder and solver of these problems are Craig Johnson. [6] Johnson, with a team of advisors and decorators, seek to make life easier for people with various disabilities. [7] Johnson recognizes that easy access and freedom from barriers is becoming both an issue for our aging population and a growing business opportunity. [8] Creating designs and making modifications for people with disabilities helps others, too. [9] For instance, doesn't most people find that levers are easier to operate than doorknobs are? [10] Also, neither a handrail nor a ramp give anyone any difficulty; in fact, both can come in handy to everyone.

EXERCISE 6   **Identifying Antecedents and Writing Pronouns**

Each of the following sentences contains a blank where a pronoun should be. Identify the antecedent for each missing pronoun. Then, complete each sentence by inserting a pronoun that agrees with that antecedent.

EXAMPLE   **1.** At about the age of fifteen, Janet Collins followed ____ dream to the Ballet Russe de Monte Carlo.
     1. *Janet Collins—her*

1. Until Janet Collins, nobody of African heritage had ever made ____ debut on the stage of the Metropolitan Opera House.

2. While waiting to audition, she saw other ballerinas on a winding staircase doing ____ warm-up exercises.
3. Everyone who saw Janet at her audition clapped ____ hands.
4. Yet, because of Collins's color, Mr. Massine, the choreographer, could not hire her for ____ production.
5. Collins continued practicing, and in the end ____ was rewarded.
6. The Metropolitan Opera opened ____ doors to the prima ballerina.
7. Rudolph Bing admired her adagio dancing so much that ____ gave her many opportunities to leap and jump.
8. Two of her roles were in *Carmen* and *Aida*, and ____ helped to make her famous.
9. To be successful, a ballerina must discipline ____ .
10. Either Ms. Lawton or Ms. Vicks will show the class ____ autographed picture of Collins.

▶ EXERCISE 7 **Proofreading Sentences for Pronoun-Antecedent Agreement**

Proofread the following sentences for pronouns that do not agree with their antecedents. Give the correct form of each incorrect pronoun. If a sentence is correct, write C.

EXAMPLE **1.** From the earliest times, people all over the world have decorated himself or herself.
1. *themselves*

1. Whether for war, religious rituals, or beauty, cosmetics have always had its place in human society.
2. In ancient Egypt, both men and women used various kinds of cosmetics to make himself or herself more attractive.
3. In addition, nearly all Egyptians painted their eyelids with green paste to prevent sunburn.
4. One of the Egyptian kings was even buried with rouge and lip color in their tomb.
5. Ancient cosmetics were usually made from natural ingredients, some of which were poisonous to its users.
6. Arsenic and mercury were two of the most dangerous, and it ruined many lives.

7. The Roman man or woman who used a depilatory of arsenic was slowly killing themselves.
8. Similarly, in Queen Elizabeth's time, the English girl or woman who used a skin whitener containing mercury risked having their teeth fall out.
9. Since before the time of Cosmis, who sold makeup during the reign of Julius Caesar, to the present, enterprising people have made their fortunes by providing products that help others meet their cultures' standards of beauty.
10. Surely, Galen, a famous man of science in ancient Rome, would be pleased to find that today's cold cream is based on the same formula they invented.

▶ EXERCISE 8   **Writing Correct Verb Forms**

Fill in the blank in each sentence with the correct past or past participle form of the verb in italics.

EXAMPLE   **1.** *do* Have you ____ any research on Cajun culture?
         1. *done*

1. *blow*   Yesterday, a hurricane ____ through Louisiana, where most Cajuns live.
2. *begin*   The Cajun culture ____ after French immigrants to Acadia, Canada, traveled south.
3. *come*   While in Canada, these immigrants ____ to be known as Acadians.
4. *take*   In Louisiana, the name *Acadian* ____ on a different pronunciation, *Cajun.*
5. *choose*   The Cajuns ____ to befriend the Choctaws, as well as settlers from Germany and Spain.
6. *put*   Cajun cooks ____ to their own use what they learned from the Choctaws about native plants and animals.
7. *eat*   They ____ seafood seasoned with the Choctaw's filé made of powdered sassafras leaves.
8. *drink*   They ____ coffee flavored with chicory.
9. *raise*   German settlers in the bayou country ____ the beef and pork that the Cajuns used in their tasty dishes.
10. *bring*   The Cajuns were also delighted with okra, which was called *gumbo* by the Bantu, who had ____ it with them from Africa.

▶ EXERCISE 9 **Identifying Correct Forms of Irregular Verbs**

For each of the following sentences, choose the correct form of the verb in parentheses.

EXAMPLE **1.** For many years, teams of scientists have (*took, taken*) the opportunity to study the Antarctic Peninsula during the summer.
1. *taken*

1. They (*went, gone*) there to study the delicate balance of the ecosystem.
2. These scientists (*knew, knowed*) that worldwide weather patterns are influenced by events in Antarctica.
3. Before the twentieth century, few people (*choosed, chose*) to brave the frigid voyage to the Antarctic.
4. However, new means of transportation have (*brought, brung*) more people, especially scientists, to Antarctica.
5. Now, countries as diverse as Brazil, England, and Russia have (*began, begun*) exploring what's beneath Antarctica's ice and snow.
6. No one knows how long Antarctica's waters have (*ran, run*) red with krill, tiny creatures at the bottom of the food chain.
7. Many times, the Ross Ice Shelf has (*shook, shaken*) as a huge iceberg known as B9 has crashed into it.
8. An oil rig could have (*fell, fallen*) if struck by a massive, roving iceberg.
9. If that had happened, a huge oil spill would likely have (*did, done*) major damage to the ecosystem.
10. In Antarctica, the nations of the world have been (*gave, given*) a chance to work together in peace.

▶ EXERCISE 10 **Proofreading Sentences for Correct Verb Forms**

Most of the following sentences contain an incorrect verb form. If a sentence is correct, write *C*. If the form of a verb is wrong, write the correct form.

EXAMPLE **1.** His horse weared a braided bridle.
1. *wore*

1. Luis Ortega has been describe as the greatest rawhide braider in history.

2. For years, collectors and cowhands alike have spoke of him with respectful awe.
3. Ortega was lucky to have had a fine teacher; many braiders do not teach their craft because students have stole their secrets.
4. However, even after a generous American Indian taught Ortega to braid, it taked young Luis many years of practice to perfect his skill.
5. Ortega was not one who shrinked from hard work.
6. Once a *vaquero* himself, he throwed many a lasso in his younger days.
7. However, since the 1930s, Ortega has wore the title of professional braider.
8. Ortega not only mastered the traditional craft, but striked out on his own by adding color to braiding.
9. Unlike whips, which have stinged many a runaway steer, a *riata* (or *reata*) is a type of lariat used for roping.
10. Pity the cowhand whose heart must have sunk as a steer ran off with his treasured Ortega *riata*!

▶ EXERCISE 11　**Identifying Correct Forms of Pronouns**

Choose the correct pronoun in parentheses in each of the following sentences. Then, tell whether the pronoun is used as a *subject,* a *predicate nominative,* a *direct object,* an *indirect object,* an *object of a preposition,* or an *appositive.*

EXAMPLE　**1.** Mr. Kwan and (*we, us*) members of the recycling club picked up all the litter along the highway last Saturday.
　　　　　1. *we—subject*

1. Do you know (*who, whom*) safely disposes of old batteries?
2. The two Earth Club members who collect items for recycling are James and (*she, her*).
3. (*Who, Whom*) threw these cans in the garbage?
4. Save all recyclable material for (*we, us*) club members.
5. Give the cochairpersons, Lisa and (*she, her*), all the cans you have collected.
6. Ask (*whoever, whomever*) you know in the neighborhood for old newspapers.
7. (*Who, Whom*) could the next recycling team leader be?
8. To (*whom, who*) do we give this cardboard?

9. The city gave Mr. Kwan, (*who, whom*) everyone in the school respects, an award.
10. (*Whom, Who*) have you invited to the award ceremony?

▶ EXERCISE 12   **Correcting Errors in the Use of Pronouns**

Correct each error in the use of pronouns in the following sentences. If a sentence is correct, write *C*.

EXAMPLE   **1.** When you take medication for your allergies, be sure to read them carefully.
         1. *When you take medication for your allergies, be sure to read the directions carefully.*

1. Annie said that she must have sneezed two dozen times today and that it was really bothering her.
2. Annie asked Heather several questions about her allergy medication.
3. Heather has more problems with allergies than I.
4. Pollen, molds, and animal dander are widespread in our environment; that is why they are three of the most common causes of allergies.
5. Different plants release pollen at different times of the year, which is why people have discomfort at various times.
6. Annie has more summer allergies than me.
7. To take a pollen count, they place a glass slide coated with oil outside for twenty-four hours.
8. The slide is then placed under a microscope, and the grains of pollen sticking to it are counted.
9. When it rains, the pollen count drops.
10. In the news reports, they often give the pollen count.

▶ EXERCISE 13   **Using Comparative and Superlative Forms**

Fill in the blank in each sentence with the correct comparative or superlative form of the word in italics.

EXAMPLE   **1.** *well*   Carl can do CPR ＿＿＿ than I can.
         1. *better*

1. *few*   Bicyclists who wear helmets have ＿＿＿ serious injuries from accidents than bicyclists who do not wear helmets.

2. *many* Our family follows _____ safety procedures than we used to follow.

3. *bad* Some of the _____ accidents are most likely to happen in the home.

4. *much* Is the kitchen or the bathroom the _____ likely room in which to have an accident?

5. *well* Emergency crews can spot luminous house numbers _____ than numbers that do not glow in the dark.

6. *bad* A grease fire will become _____ if you put water on it.

7. *good* Do you know the _____ way to extinguish an electrical fire?

8. *many* Smoke detectors are found in _____ homes than ever before.

9. *much* In many small fires, smoke causes _____ of the damage.

10. *good* Of course, the _____ safety tip of all is to prevent fires from starting in the first place.

▶ EXERCISE 14 **Proofreading Sentences for Correct Comparative and Superlative Forms**

Correct each error in the use of comparative and superlative forms in the following sentences. If no modifiers need to be corrected in a sentence, write *C*.

EXAMPLE **1.** Most oftenest, I plan my day in the morning.
         1. *Most often*

1. One of the importantest skills is the ability to set priorities.
2. You can establish your priorities more easily if you know your goals.
3. Owning a good car, having a rewarding job, and owning a house are three of the most commonest goals people share.
4. You, however, may want a pilot's license, a medical degree, an eighteen-wheeler, or just a comfortabler bed.
5. Whatever your goal, you will be much more likelier to achieve it if you plan your time carefully.
6. Look at even the most small unit of your time.
7. Can you think of any ways that you could use your time more better than you do?

8. Try every day to work on your most highest priority.
9. Try more hard to stick to your schedule.
10. With a plan, you can meet your goals quicklier than you could without one.

▶ EXERCISE 15 **Revising Sentences to Correct Double Negatives**

Revise each of the following sentences to correct the double negative it contains.

EXAMPLE **1.** The jurors couldn't say nothing about the trial.
1. *The jurors could say nothing about the trial.*
or
1. *The jurors couldn't say anything about the trial.*

1. Those machines don't take no dollar bills.
2. My grandfather doesn't hardly let anything bother him.
3. Don't never accept a ride from a stranger!
4. Why didn't no one take the message when Mom called?
5. Never use none of those microwave oven pans in a regular oven.
6. The movie hadn't scarcely started when the power went off.
7. I can't see nothing from here.
8. There aren't none of those tamales left now.
9. Don't let nobody tell you that you can't win!
10. Neither cold nor heat nor nothing else discouraged them.

▶ EXERCISE 16 **Revising Sentences by Eliminating Misplaced Modifiers**

Revise the following sentences to correct errors in the use of modifiers. You may need to rearrange or add words to make the meaning clear.

EXAMPLE **1.** Cold and overcast, the tour group left the city.
1. *The tour group left the cold and overcast city.*

1. I watched the hawk swoop down and grab its prey with my binoculars.
2. He is such a hard-working student that he did every bit of his homework when he even got the flu.

3. Running through town, soft moonlight fell on the freight train.
4. You should take rides from people only you know.
5. A kingfisher sat alertly on the fence post that had been hunting by the creek.
6. I figured out the answer studying the problem.
7. Bulky and dusty, we moved all of the boxes out of the attic.
8. Filled with wildflowers she'd picked, Amy put the vase on her desk.
9. Suddenly, the bats swarmed out of the cave that we had awakened.
10. A package sat on the doorstep with my name on it.

▶ EXERCISE 17 **Revising Sentences by Eliminating Dangling Modifiers**

Most of the following sentences contain dangling modifiers. If a sentence is correct, write *C*. If a sentence is incorrect, revise it to eliminate the dangling modifier.

EXAMPLE **1.** Following the path, a tiny cottage came into view.
  1. *As we were following the path, a tiny cottage came into view.*

1. Rounding third base, the coach and the fans cheered and applauded.
2. To manage your time better, making a schedule will help.
3. Modified to allow space for an additional bedroom, the final plan did not include closets.
4. While studying for exams, a storm knocked out my electricity.
5. Before beginning your library research, a specific topic must be chosen.
6. Right in the middle of making a copy of my report, the out-of-paper message flashed.
7. Tired from the long hike, our camp was a welcome sight.
8. After hanging the new plants, the room appeared larger.
9. To save money, a realistic budget is necessary.
10. While we watched the children play, our problems seemed small.

▶ EXERCISE 18 **Correcting Errors in Standard Usage**

Correct each error in the use of standard English in the following sentences.

EXAMPLE **1.** I ain't going to the movies on Saturday.
1. *am not*

1. Please bring this note to Ms. Nichols in the gym.
2. Who else was late to the party beside Ronnie and Ed?
3. My science project took alot of time last weekend.
4. Oh, no! I can't find my raincoat anywheres.
5. Common elements include oxygen, hydrogen, iron, and etc.
6. The weather can effect people's moods.
7. Starting next year, each student will wear an uniform.
8. Look out! You almost busted my CD player!
9. Gradually, our dog excepted the new kitten.
10. The little steam engine pulled all the faster it could.

▶ EXERCISE 19 **Correcting Errors in Standard Usage**

Revise the sentences in the following paragraph to correct all errors in the use of standard English.

1. Artists which study colors know that color, value, and contrast form the foundation of a good painting.
2. Many artists would not even begin no painting without they first planned how they'd use these elements.
3. One of the basics that nearly all artists learn is where color is divided into warm colors and cool colors.
4. Like you might of guessed, red is a warmer color then blue, while green is cooler than orange.
5. The darkness, or value, of a color can indicate that objects differ some in distance from the viewer.
6. For example, a dark color may be used to indicate that something is a long ways off.
7. Contrast is when two very different colors are placed besides each other.
8. Contrasting values help to show detail, as does the contrast among this here white page and black type.
9. For them artists that work only in black and white, contrast and value are major concerns.
10. Many people feel that the affect of a painting can depend more on color then on other elements.

Grammar and Usage Test: Section 1

DIRECTIONS   In the following sentences, either part or all of each sentence is underlined. Using the rules of standard written English, choose the answer that most clearly expresses the meaning of the sentence. If there is no error, choose *A*. Indicate your response by shading in the appropriate oval on your answer sheet.

EXAMPLE

1. In 1990, restoration began on the Sphinx <u>and it is an ancient Egyptian statue.</u>
    (A) and it is an ancient Egyptian statue
    (B) because it is an ancient Egyptian statue
    (C) , an ancient Egyptian statue
    (D) , being an ancient Egyptian statue
    (E) when it was an ancient Egyptian statue

SAMPLE ANSWER   1. Ⓐ Ⓑ  Ⓓ Ⓔ

1. <u>The magnificent glass pyramids at the Louvre, which were designed by the American architect I. M. Pei.</u>
    (A) The magnificent glass pyramids at the Louvre, which were designed by the American architect I. M. Pei.
    (B) Being designed by the American architect I. M. Pei, the magnificent glass pyramids at the Louvre.
    (C) The American architect I. M. Pei, who designed the magnificent glass pyramids at the Louvre.
    (D) The American architect I. M. Pei designed the magnificent glass pyramids at the Louvre.
    (E) I. M. Pei, an American architect, designing the magnificent glass pyramids at the Louvre.

2. Have you read <u>about the tornado that damaged so many homes in today's paper?</u>
    (A) about the tornado that damaged so many homes in today's paper
    (B) in today's paper about the tornado that damaged so many homes
    (C) about the tornado in today's paper that damaged so many homes
    (D) about the destructive tornado in today's paper
    (E) today about the destructive tornado in the paper

3. Most people believe that the Loch Ness monster is just a <u>myth, sightings of the monster continue to be reported.</u>
    (A) myth, sightings of the monster continue to be reported
    (B) myth, and people report still seeing the monster
    (C) myth. Sightings of the monster continue to be reported
    (D) myth; sightings of the monster continue to be reported
    (E) myth; however, sightings of the monster continue to be reported

4. Tamara told Jenny <u>that she probably made an A</u>.
   - (A) that she probably made an A
   - (B) that an A was probably what she made
   - (C) that she thought Jenny probably made an A
   - (D) about her making an A probably
   - (E) that her grade was probably an A

5. To fully appreciate many of Gary Soto's stories, <u>some knowledge of Mexican American culture is necessary</u>.
   - (A) some knowledge of Mexican American culture is necessary
   - (B) the reader needs some knowledge of Mexican American culture
   - (C) you must learn all about Mexican American culture
   - (D) knows something about Mexican American culture
   - (E) the necessity is to know something about Mexican American culture

6. <u>In this article, it says that the Chinese were using paper money by the thirteenth century</u>.
   - (A) In this article, it says that the Chinese were using paper money by the thirteenth century
   - (B) According to this article, it says the Chinese were using paper money by the thirteenth century
   - (C) By the thirteenth century, the Chinese in this article were using paper money
   - (D) In this article, they say that the Chinese were using paper money by the thirteenth century
   - (E) According to this article, the Chinese were using paper money by the thirteenth century

7. <u>The capital of Liberia, Monrovia, which was named by freed slaves in honor of President James Monroe</u>.
   - (A) The capital of Liberia, Monrovia, which was named by freed slaves in honor of President James Monroe
   - (B) Monrovia, the capital of Liberia, named by freed slaves in honor of President James Monroe
   - (C) Named by freed slaves, Monrovia, the capital of Liberia, in honor of President James Monroe
   - (D) In honor of President James Monroe, freed slaves named the capital of Liberia Monrovia
   - (E) In honor of President James Monroe, freed slaves who named Monrovia the capital of Liberia

8. I bought a collar <u>for my kitten that has a reflective tag and a breakaway buckle</u>.
   - (A) for my kitten that has a reflective tag and a breakaway buckle
   - (B) for my kitten with a reflective tag and a breakaway buckle
   - (C) that has a reflective tag and a breakaway buckle for my kitten
   - (D) for my kitten having a reflective tag and a breakaway buckle
   - (E) for my kitten, and it has a reflective tag and a breakaway buckle

CORRECTING COMMON ERRORS

9. Henry Ford wanted to make his cars affordable to everyone; that is why he developed an efficient assembly-line method for manufacturing them.

   (A) Henry Ford wanted to make his cars affordable to everyone; that is why he developed an efficient assembly-line method for manufacturing them.
   (B) Henry Ford wanted to make his cars affordable to everyone so that he could develop an efficient assembly-line method for manufacturing them.
   (C) Henry Ford wanted to make his cars affordable to everyone because he developed an efficient assembly-line method for manufacturing them.
   (D) Henry Ford developed an efficient assembly-line method for manufacturing his cars because he wanted to make them affordable to everyone.
   (E) To develop an efficient assembly-line method for manu-facturing his cars, Henry Ford wanted to make them affordable to everyone.

10. Having seen that people in some countries were denied basic civil rights, my uncle's appreciation for the Bill of Rights grew.

   (A) Having seen that people in some countries were denied basic civil rights, my uncle's appreciation for the Bill of Rights grew.
   (B) My uncle, having seen the Bill of Rights, knew that people in some countries were denied basic civil rights.
   (C) When basic civil rights are denied people in some countries, my uncle's appreciation for the Bill of Rights grows.
   (D) My uncle's appreciation for people denied basic civil rights in some countries grew as he read the Bill of Rights.
   (E) My uncle's appreciation for the Bill of Rights grew after he had seen that people in some countries were denied basic civil rights.

Grammar and Usage Test: Section 2

DIRECTIONS   Read the paragraph below. For each numbered blank, select the word or group of words that best completes the sentence. Indicate your response by shading in the appropriate oval on your answer sheet.

EXAMPLE

More powerful than optical microscopes, electron microscopes __(1)__ researchers to study extremely small objects.

   1. (A) enabled
      (B) are enabling
      (C) will enable
      (D) enable
      (E) enables

SAMPLE ANSWER   1.

An electron microscope, using a beam of electrons, __(1)__ a magnified image. Unlike an optical microscope, __(2)__ instrument does not depend on __(3)__ light rays. Instead, an electron lens __(4)__ a system of electromagnetic coils that focus the electron beam. The electrons __(5)__, of course, aren't visible to the naked eye. Rather, __(6)__ are directed at a specimen to form __(7)__ image on a photographic plate. The wavelength of an electron beam is __(8)__ than the wavelength of light. Therefore, __(9)__ magnification is possible with an electron microscope __(10)__ optical microscope.

1. (A) create
   (B) is creating
   (C) creates
   (D) will create
   (E) will have created

2. (A) this here
   (B) this
   (C) these
   (D) these kind of
   (E) that there

3. (A) any
   (B) not one
   (C) no
   (D) hardly any
   (E) barely some

4. (A) use
   (B) has used
   (C) will use
   (D) uses
   (E) had been using

5. (A) themself
   (B) themselves
   (C) theirself
   (D) theirselves
   (E) itself

6. (A) them
   (B) it
   (C) these
   (D) this
   (E) they

7. (A) its
   (B) their
   (C) they're
   (D) its'
   (E) it's

8. (A) short
   (B) shorter
   (C) more short
   (D) more shorter
   (E) shortest

9. (A) good
   (B) gooder
   (C) better
   (D) more better
   (E) more good

10. (A) then with an
    (B) then with a
    (C) than with an
    (D) than with a
    (E) then a

▶ EXERCISE 20 **Correcting the Capitalization of Words and Phrases**

Correct the capitalization of the following words and phrases by either changing lowercase letters to capitals or changing capitals to lowercase letters.

EXAMPLE **1.** Hank's poem "Waiting for morning in july"
1. *Hank's poem "Waiting for Morning in July"*

1. geometry I, latin, and civics
2. *national geographic* magazine
3. the god of abraham, isaac, and jacob
4. an Island in the gulf of mexico
5. liberty bell
6. great depression
7. readings from "the scarlet ibis"
8. internal revenue service forms
9. mother's day
10. an episode of *party of five*
11. Grandfather Ben and my Cousin
12. Hiroshige's painting *The Moon Beyond The Leaves*
13. an italian custom
14. bill of rights
15. a passage from the koran
16. Is that an okidata® printer?
17. dr. and mrs. Dorset
18. a congressional medal of honor recipient
19. chief joseph
20. *King Of The Wind*

▶ EXERCISE 21 **Identifying and Correcting Errors in Capitalization**

Each of the following sentences contains errors in capitalization. Correct each error by changing capital letters to lowercase letters or lowercase letters to capitals.

EXAMPLE **1.** Often, i feel like a World traveler in my hometown.
1. *I, world*

1. When I ride the bus down central avenue, I can hear people speaking spanish, hindi, japanese, and some languages I don't even recognize.
2. On independence day, my Mother and I drove our old ford thunderbird to Taylor park.

3. Near there we saw mr. Narazaki and Ms. white eagle talking.
4. They were in front of the Lincoln building, where the federal bureau of investigation has offices.
5. On that same Saturday, we also saw several muslim women wearing long robes and veils in front of hill medical center next to the Park.
6. After the band played John philip Sousa's "the Stars And Stripes Forever," people stood beside a statue of the Greek deity Athena and gave readings from the declaration of independence and the bible.
7. Later, mayor Mendoza read a fax from the president of the united states, gave a speech, and awarded Medals to several people for their public service.
8. As soon as the big dipper was clearly visible, the fireworks started, and I thought, "This is definitely the greatest place on Earth!"
9. Next year, I will take United States history II at West creek high school.
10. I am going to look in my new history book for a list of all the peoples that make up our country, from the inupiats of alaska to the hawaiians of hilo bay.

▶ EXERCISE 22   **Using Commas Correctly**

Add or delete commas to punctuate each of the following sentences correctly.

EXAMPLE   **1.** A first-aid kit should contain adhesive tape scissors antiseptic and a variety of bandages.
          1. *A first-aid kit should contain adhesive tape, scissors, antiseptic, and a variety of bandages.*

1. Yes I have a screwdriver and some screws and wood glue.
2. On the balcony of a second-floor apartment a large macaw sat watching us.
3. We moved on October 15 and our new address is 5311 East Baker Street, Deerfield Illinois, 60015.
4. All you need to bring are a change of clothes shoes and socks and a toothbrush and toothpaste.
5. Phobos is I believe one of the moons around Mars Mrs. Farris.

6. Fire damaged a number of houses yet no one was injured not even any pets.
7. Because acrylic a type of water-based paint dries rapidly you must work quickly with it.
8. Birds sang frogs jumped and children played on that hot sunny day.
9. Malfunctioning dangerously the robot moved jerkily toward the table picked up a dish dropped it on the floor and rolled out the door.
10. Easing up on the throttle she coasted in for a smooth landing.

▶ EXERCISE 23   **Using Commas Correctly**

Add or delete commas to punctuate each of the following sentences correctly.

EXAMPLE   **1.** They made beads out of small white seashells Ed.
          1. *They made beads out of small, white seashells, Ed.*

1. Deer thrived and sea life flourished and all manner of edible plants grew in the region, that is now California.
2. Up and down the coastline of California communities of American Indians have lived for centuries.
3. The Karok Pomo Yurok and Modoc are just four of the dozens of peoples living in this area.
4. Skilled in basketwork the Pomo became known for the decoration variety and intricate weaving of their baskets.
5. The Yurok developed an elaborate monetary system which they used in fixing a price on every privilege or offense.
6. While many peoples favored dentalium shells as currency they also exchanged other items in trade.
7. Yurok marriages were arranged with care for marriage was an important public and historic alliance.
8. Yes Helen, the Gabrielino hunted with a stick similar to the boomerang the famous Australian weapon.
9. Traditionally, the Coast Miwok peoples were each represented by a male chief, and a female chief and a female ceremonial leader called a *maien*.
10. Kintpuash who was also called Captain Jack was the Modoc leader, who escaped capture on November 29 1872.

▶ EXERCISE 24 **Proofreading for Correct Use of Semicolons and Colons**

Add or delete semicolons and colons to correct the punctuation in the following sentences.

EXAMPLE   **1.** The party starts at 7 30, we will need to leave our house by 7 00.

             1. *The party starts at 7:30; we will need to leave our house by 7:00.*

1. John is bringing the drinks, ice, and cups, and Wanda is bringing the plates, knives, and forks.
2. During our party on the Fourth of July last year, a huge storm forced everyone inside, then, lightning knocked the power out.
3. Don't forget to pick up: Carlos, Kam, Lisa, and Mary at 7 15 sharp.
4. We have invited exchange students from Dublin, Ireland, Paris, France, and Tokyo, Japan.
5. The dance committee still needs to get the following equipment a CD player, two outdoor speakers, and a microphone.

▶ EXERCISE 25 **Using Punctuation Correctly in Sentences**

Add end marks, commas, semicolons, and colons to correct the punctuation in the following sentences.

EXAMPLE   **1.** In almost every corner of the world dogs do useful work

             1. *In almost every corner of the world, dogs do useful work.*

1. Herding flocks collies and briards and other varieties of sheepdogs are on the job wherever there are sheep.
2. Did you know that German shepherds which make good guard dogs can also herd sheep
3. Dogs guard our homes dogs herd sheep and dogs hunt game.
4. Sled dogs include the following Samoyeds, huskies, Alaskan malamutes, and a few other strong breeds with thick fur.
5. Partners with police the world over bloodhounds are feared by criminals and praised by the parents of lost children whom these dogs have found.

6. The basenji comes from Africa and is in fact called the Congo dog many people share their homes with these animals whose ancestors date back to 3000 B C

7. Although Chihuahuas which take their name from the Mexican state of Chihuahua are tiny they fiercely take on any foe they don't back down even when facing a larger dog.

8. Chihuahuas ignore the good advice in Ecclesiastes 9 4

9. Those famous lines make an obvious point "A living dog is better than a dead lion."

10. My favorite neighbor Edward Nichols Jr bought his Pekingese on Wednesday February 7 1996.

EXERCISE 26 **Correcting Errors in the Use of Quotation Marks and Other Punctuation**

For each of the following sentences, correct any error in the use of quotation marks, commas, and end marks.

EXAMPLE **1.** The troop leader said that we should bring the 'barest essentials': a change of clothes, a toothbrush, and a comb.

1. *The troop leader said that we should bring the "barest essentials": a change of clothes, a toothbrush, and a comb.*

1. James seemed excited and said, "Did you see the news last night?

2. "Sorry, Emma" Becky began "but I'm late already."

3. When Coach Myers announced the tryouts this morning, she said, "that anyone could try out."

4. Ms. Waters asked us to read The Tell-Tale Heart and one other short story of our choice this weekend.

5. They are watching reruns of *The Magic School Bus;* this episode is Lost in the Solar System.

6. For tomorrow, read The Price of Freedom, the next chapter in your textbook.

7. My favorite regular feature in *Reader's Digest* is Humor in Uniform.

8. Why don't you title your poem "Words and Music"? Tom asked

9. The recent article Carbon Monoxide: The Silent Killer details the effects of this deadly gas.

10. Didn't you hear me yell Call 911! asked Erik.

▶ EXERCISE 27 **Punctuating and Capitalizing Quotations**

For each of the following sentences, correct any error in the use of quotation marks, commas, end marks, and capitalization.

EXAMPLE **1.** Larry told me that "you were sitting in the library."
　　　　　1. *Larry told me that you were sitting in the library.*

1. "I can't decide which selection to use for my project" sighed Fran.
2. Mary nodded and said "I haven't made up my mind either." "Are you going to choose a poem or a story"?
3. "I'm going to make a diorama of "Stopping by Woods on a Snowy Evening," interrupted Greg.
4. What if Ms. Hill says 'that you can't'? asked Mary.
5. Didn't she say "anything goes?" Greg answered.
6. "You're right." The instructions do read 'write a song, present a play, or draw a picture, added Mary.
7. You play the guitar, Fran pointed out. Maybe you could write a song."
8. Mary smiled and said, "great idea!
9. What I'd like to do is write extra verses for Woody Guthrie's song This Land Is Your Land, Fran said.
10. Or even," Mary added "make a video of it"!

▶ EXERCISE 28 **Using Apostrophes Correctly**

Add or delete apostrophes to punctuate the items correctly. If an item is correct as it is, write *C*.

EXAMPLE **1.** Weve got Matts tickets'.
　　　　　1. *We've got Matt's tickets.*

1. Dont use so many *sos*.
2. Its time for Janes report.
3. Ronnies and Eriks desks
4. Mom and Dads only car
5. PBSs most popular show
6. Who's your brother?
7. my sister's-in-laws cars
8. geeses caretaker
9. baby birds' beak
10. Kerrys and your project
11. anyone's guess
12. Russs' *Us* look like *Ns*.
13. Youre right!
14. foxes dens
15. The blame is theirs'.
16. Lets eat at six oclock.
17. my March of Dimes donation
18. Shell bring ours'.
19. There's still time.
20. Bobs dog

▶ EXERCISE 29 **Proofreading for Spelling Errors**

Correct each spelling error in the following sentences.

EXAMPLE   **1.** To succede, you must keep triing.
        1. *succeed; trying*

1. I cannot easily make dayly visits, even though I would surly like to.
2. The judge finaly conceeded that the other driver had been exceding the speed limit.
3. The members of the procession carryed one hundred twenty-five baskets of beautiful flowers.
4. The dessert heat and dryness stoped both armys.
5. My neighbor's childs are always getting into mischeif.
6. A word with two *es*, such as *deers,* has a long vowel sound.
7. The children truely enjoied hearing thier echoes bounce off the canyon walls.
8. The candidate siezed the opportunity to give a breif statement of his beleifs.
9. Leafs fluttered off the trees and down the desertted beachs during that 1st day of winter.
10. 5 years ago, both of my brother-in-laws were working two jobs.

▶ EXERCISE 30 **Proofreading for Words Often Confused**

For each of the following sentences, correct any error in word usage.

EXAMPLE   **1.** Do meteors ever brake the sound barrier?
        1. *Do meteors ever break the sound barrier?*

1. The roar of the plain's engine broke the quite of the night.
2. Its time to get you're suitcase packed.
3. I put my desert right here on the kitchen table, and now its gone.
4. As the mustangs made there way through the canyon, they unknowingly past a cougar hiding in the rocks.
5. Who was the warrior who lead the Zulus in there famous battle against the Boers?
6. Be careful, or you will brake that mirror into a million peaces.

7. Every knight choose his own way threw the forest.
8. First, the pigs got lose; than, we spent all afternoon trying too catch them.
9. He couldn't here us because he was too week from the fever.
10. Who's biography did you chose to read?

▶ EXERCISE 31   **Proofreading a Business Letter**

For each numbered item in the following business letter, correct any error in usage or mechanics. An item may contain more than one error. If an item is correct, write *C*.

EXAMPLE   [1] 813, east Maple street
           1. *813 East Maple Street*

---

    813 East Maple Street
[1] Belleville IL, 62223
[2] Febuary 12th, 1997

Customer Service
Super Sport Shoes
147 Central Avenue
[3] Woodinville WA, 98072

[4] Dear Sir or Madam,

[5] Thank you for your prompt response to my order (number 51238) for two pairs of shoes white joggers. [6] These shoes are the comfortablest ones I have ever worn.

[7] However, one of the pairs that I recieved are the wrong size. [8] This pair is to small and don't fit; consequently, I am returning it with this letter. [9] Please exchange these shoes for a pair of white joggers two sizes larger.

[10] Your's truly

Neville Walters

Neville Walters

Mechanics Test: Section 1

DIRECTIONS Each of the following sentences contains an underlined word or group of words. Choose the answer that shows the correct capitalization, punctuation, and spelling of the underlined part. If there is no error, choose answer E (Correct as is). Indicate your response by shading in the appropriate oval on your answer sheet.

EXAMPLE

1. Marla <u>asked, "did</u> you see the meteor shower last night?"
   - (A) asked, "Did
   - (B) asked "Did
   - (C) asked "did
   - (D) asked did you
   - (E) Correct as is

SAMPLE ANSWER 1. ● Ⓑ Ⓒ Ⓓ Ⓔ

1. We keep a variety of emergency equipment in the trunk of our <u>car, a first-aid</u> kit, jumper cables, a blanket, a flashlight, and road flares.
   - (A) car. A first-aid
   - (B) car: a first-aid
   - (C) car: A first-aid
   - (D) car: a 1st-aid
   - (E) Correct as is

2. Alvin <u>Ailey, who's choreography</u> thrilled audiences for years, formed the dance company that still bears his name.
   - (A) Ailey who's choreography
   - (B) Ailey whose choreography
   - (C) Ailey who's choreography,
   - (D) Ailey, whose choreography
   - (E) Correct as is

3. Jerome <u>said, "I cant believe</u> that Ben Franklin wanted the turkey to be the symbol for the United States!"
   - (A) said, "I can't believe
   - (B) said "I can't believe
   - (C) said, "I can't beleive
   - (D) said, 'I can't believe
   - (E) Correct as is

4. "Do <u>you," asked Kay 'Know</u> the story of Icarus?"
   - (A) you, asked Kay, "know
   - (B) you?" asked Kay. "Know
   - (C) you," asked Kay, "know
   - (D) you," asked Kay, 'know
   - (E) Correct as is

5. I often struggle to open my gym <u>locker; its</u> lock is probably rusty.
   - (A) locker, its
   - (B) locker; Its
   - (C) locker. It's
   - (D) locker: It's
   - (E) Correct as is

6. Please <u>bring too tomatos,</u> a head of lettuce, and some feta cheese from the market.
   - (A) bring: two tomatoes,
   - (B) bring 2 tomatoes
   - (C) bring two tomatoes,
   - (D) bring to tomatoes,
   - (E) Correct as is

7. "Did Principal Reeves really say, 'We need *less* <u>discipline?"</u> asked Cassandra.
   - (A) discipline,'"
   - (B) discipline'?"
   - (C) discipline?'
   - (D) discipline'"?
   - (E) Correct as is

8. Grandfather enjoyed the <u>childrens storys</u> about their visit to the wildlife sanctuary.
   - (A) childrens story's
   - (B) childrens' stories
   - (C) childrens stories
   - (D) children's stories
   - (E) Correct as is

9. The Leonards <u>visited: Rome, Italy,</u> Athens, Greece; and Istanbul, Turkey, on their vacation.
   - (A) visited Rome, Italy;
   - (B) visited: Rome, Italy;
   - (C) visited, Rome, Italy;
   - (D) visited Rome; Italy;
   - (E) Correct as is

10. Did <u>aunt Susan,</u> bring the coleslaw?
    - (A) aunt Susan
    - (B) aunt, Susan,
    - (C) Aunt Susan
    - (D) Aunt, Susan,
    - (E) Correct as is

Mechanics Test: Section 2

DIRECTIONS   Each numbered item below contains an underlined group of words. Choose the answer that shows the correct capitalization, punctuation, and spelling of the underlined part. If there is no error, choose answer E (Correct as is). Indicate your response by shading in the appropriate oval on your answer sheet.

EXAMPLE

[1]   200 north Vine Street
    (A)   200 North Vine street
    (B)   200 North Vine Street
    (C)   Two Hundred North Vine Street
    (D)   200, North Vine Street
    (E)   Correct as is

SAMPLE ANSWER   1. (A) ● (C) (D) (E)

---

    200 North Vine Street
    Austin, TX 78741
[1] May, 5 1997

    Athena Wilson
    Worldwide Travel, Inc.
    4135-A Anderson Avenue
[2] San Antonio, Tex. 78249

[3] Dear Ms. Wilson:

[4] Thank you for you're prompt response to my request for information about traveling to Australia. The color brochures describing the [5] different, Australian tours were especially helpful. My family and I are interested in the "Natural Wonders" [6] package, that includes day trips to [7] the great Barrier reef. [8] Well also want to schedule a three-day stay in Sydney. How much will the entire package [9] cost, for three adults and one child?

[10] Yours truly

Naomi Baskin

Naomi Baskin

1. (A) May 5 1997
    (B) May Fifth 1997
    (C) May 5th 1997
    (D) May 5, 1997
    (E) Correct as is

2. (A) San Antonio, Tex. 78249
    (B) San Antonio Texas 78249
    (C) San Antonio, TX 78249
    (D) San Antonio TX 78249
    (E) Correct as is

3. (A) Dear Ms. Wilson,
    (B) Dear ms. Wilson:
    (C) Dear Ms Wilson,
    (D) Dear Ms. Wilson;
    (E) Correct as is

4. (A) Thank you for youre
    (B) Thank you for youre'
    (C) Thank you for your
    (D) Thank you for your'
    (E) Correct as is

5. (A) different Australian
    (B) different australian
    (C) different, Australian,
    (D) different, australian,
    (E) Correct as is

6. (A) package that includes
    (B) package that, includes
    (C) package: that includes
    (D) package that includes:
    (E) Correct as is

7. (A) the Great Barrier Reef
    (B) the great Barrier Reef
    (C) the Great Barrier reef
    (D) The great Barrier reef
    (E) Correct as is

8. (A) Well, also
    (B) We'll, also,
    (C) We'll also
    (D) We'll, also
    (E) Correct as is

9. (A) cost for 3
    (B) cost? For three
    (C) cost: for three
    (D) cost for three
    (E) Correct as is

10. (A) Yours' truly,
    (B) Yours truly:
    (C) Your's truly,
    (D) Yours truly,
    (E) Correct as is

CORRECTING COMMON ERRORS

PART THREE

ADMIT
ONE
253002
253002
INDIANA TICKET

RESOURCES

31 Speaking

32 Listening and Viewing

33 The Library/Media Center

34 The Dictionary

35 Vocabulary

36 Letters and Forms

37 Reading, Studying, and Test Taking

APPENDIX OF DIAGRAMING

GLOSSARY OF TERMS

GLOSSARY

31 SPEAKING

Skills and Strategies

To communicate most effectively, you should consider

- your purpose in speaking
- the topic you are speaking about
- the audience you are speaking to

The Communication Cycle

Communication is a process. You communicate your feelings or ideas, and the person you are communicating to then responds. This response is called *feedback.*

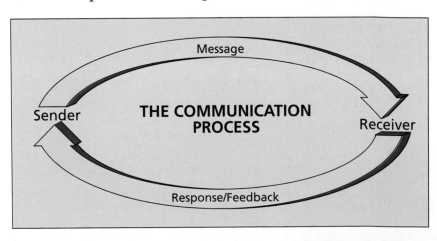

Message

Sender

**THE COMMUNICATION
PROCESS**

Receiver

Response/Feedback

Nonverbal Communication

In addition to verbal signals (words), you can communicate meaning with nonverbal signals.

NONVERBAL COMMUNICATION	
NONVERBAL SIGNALS	EXAMPLES
Gestures	thumbs up (approval, encouragement), shrugging (uncertainty), nodding head (agreement), shaking head (disagreement)
Facial expressions	smiling, raising an eyebrow, smirking, frowning, grimacing, pouting, grinning (meanings vary depending on context)
Body language	turning away (rejection), stroking the chin (puzzlement), crossing arms on chest (reluctance, uncertainty)
Sounds	laughing, groaning, giggling (meanings vary depending on context)

Speaking Informally

Impromptu Speaking

An *impromptu speech* is one you make on the spur of the moment, with no time for developing or preparing your ideas. Remember the following pointers.

1. *Consider your purpose.* Impromptu speeches are often informative (telling what you know about a subject) or persuasive (giving your opinion or trying to convince your listeners).
2. *Consider your topic.* Cover the main ideas and add details to support or explain your main points.
3. *Consider your audience.* Think about the time and place of the speaking occasion, and remember the interests of your audience.

Communicating Effectively

In many social situations, you need to speak politely and clearly in order to communicate effectively.

Speaking on the Telephone

1. Call people when it's appropriate for them.
2. Identify yourself and state the reason for your call.
3. Be polite and patient.
4. Keep your call to an appropriate length.

Giving Instructions or Directions

1. Divide the information into clear, logical steps.
2. Give the steps in order.
3. Check to be sure your listeners understand.

Making Social Introductions

1. Take the initiative; introduce yourself if no one else does.
2. When introducing others, identify them by name.
3. It is customary to address first
   - a person of higher status
   - an older person before a younger person
   - the person you know best

Speaking Formally

Preparing a Speech

Formal speaking is done at a specific time and place. Your speech may inform, persuade, or entertain.

PURPOSE	DESCRIPTION OF SPEECH	EXAMPLES OF SPEECH TITLES
To inform	gives facts *or* explains how to do something	Life Cycle of the Frog How to Solve Cryptograms

(continued)

PURPOSE	DESCRIPTION OF SPEECH	EXAMPLES OF SPEECH TITLES
To persuade	attempts to change an opinion *or* attempts to get listeners to act	Why Voting Makes a Difference Why Our Town Should Sponsor a Bicycle Safety Campaign
To entertain	relates an amusing story or incident	How *Not* to Spend Your Summer Vacation

Selecting a Topic

If you can choose the topic for your speech, you will probably base your decision on the following questions.

- *What is your overall purpose in speaking?* Do you want to inform, persuade, or entertain your listeners?
- *What is the occasion for the speech?* Will the topic you have chosen fit the occasion?
- *How much time will you have?* Have you limited your speech topic to a manageable length?

Analyzing Your Audience

To give an effective speech, you must also consider your audience's needs and interests.

AUDIENCE CONSIDERATIONS		
QUESTIONS ABOUT AUDIENCE	EVALUATION	YOUR SPEECH WILL NEED
What does the audience already know about this subject?	very little	to provide background or details to better inform your listeners
	a little	to include some background details
	a lot	to focus on interesting aspects or issues

(continued)

AUDIENCE CONSIDERATIONS *(continued)*		
QUESTIONS ABOUT AUDIENCE	EVALUATION	YOUR SPEECH WILL NEED
How interested will the audience be in this subject?	very interested	to maintain their interest
	somewhat interested	to focus on aspects that most interest your listeners
	uninterested	to focus on persuading your listeners that this topic is important

Organizing Speech Notes and Materials

The method most often used to give a speech is called *extemporaneous speaking.* When you organize your notes for an extemporaneous speech, you usually prepare a complete outline of your main points. Then you prepare note cards that you can refer to when you are giving your speech.

Here are suggestions for making note cards.

1. Put one key idea (and possibly an example or detail) per card.
2. Make a special note card for a quotation or a series of dates or statistics that you plan to read word for word.
3. Make a special note card to indicate when to show a visual, such as a chart, diagram, or model.
4. Number your completed cards to help keep them in order.

Speaking Expressively

Practice speaking expressively by using your voice well and using effective nonverbal signals.

1. *Stand confidently.* Look alert and interested and use natural gestures.
2. *Speak clearly.* Speak loudly enough so the back row can hear every word. Pronounce your words slowly and carefully.

3. *Make direct eye contact with your audience.*
4. *Use variety in speaking.* Vocal variety helps emphasize your message.
   - *Volume:* Your voice should be loud enough to be heard, but strengthen or soften your tone for emphasis.
   - *Pitch:* Use the rise and fall of your voice to emphasize various ideas.
   - *Stress:* Emphasize important words.
   - *Rate:* Speak at a comfortable, relaxed pace.

Giving Your Speech

Feeling nervous before giving a speech is normal. It's important not to let the nervousness you feel about giving a speech distract you so much that you forget what you're doing. The following suggestions will help.

1. *Be prepared.* Organize and practice with your note cards and visuals.
2. *Practice your speech.* Rehearse as if you're giving the actual presentation.
3. *Focus on your purpose.* Remember what you want to accomplish. Think how your speech will affect your audience instead of focusing on yourself.

Special Types of Formal Speaking Situations

Formal speaking situations are those that have a set time and place. You therefore have time to plan what you wish to say.

Making Announcements

The purpose of an announcement is to give information. Follow these suggestions to make effective announcements.

1. When you are writing your announcement, include all the necessary facts and add interesting details that will motivate your listeners.
2. When you are giving your announcement, first get your audience's attention. Then announce your message slowly, clearly, and carefully.

Making an Introduction to a Presentation

An introduction is often given before a speaker's presentation or before a short performance. An introduction gets the audience's attention. It also gives the audience important information about the speaker, the players, the subject, the dramatic work, or the author of the work being presented. For a shortened work, the introduction fills in details that the audience might need to know before the presentation begins.

Group Discussions

Establishing a Purpose

Group discussions or cooperative learning groups work best when the group has a specific purpose to accomplish. This purpose may be

- to share ideas and cooperate in group learning
- to suggest solutions for solving a problem
- to make an evaluation, decision, or recommendation

To establish the purpose for the group, decide on time limits and what the group needs to accomplish.

Assigning Roles for a Discussion

Each participant in a group discussion takes a role with specific responsibilities. Sometimes a group selects a chairperson who will help keep the discussion moving along smoothly. Another group member may be chosen to be secretary or reporter, with the responsibility of taking notes during the discussion.

Frequently, a group establishes an *agenda,* or outline of the order of topics to follow in the discussion. Setting the agenda is often the responsibility of the chairperson, but the agenda may sometimes be agreed upon by all the members.

A Chairperson's Responsibilities

1. Announce the topic and establish the agenda.
2. Follow the agenda.
3. Encourage each member to participate.
4. Avoid disagreements.

A Secretary's or Reporter's Responsibilities

1. Note significant information.
2. Prepare a final report.

A Participant's Responsibilities

1. Take part in the discussion.
2. Cooperate and be polite.

Using Parliamentary Procedure

Groups sometimes use a plan of action called *parliamentary procedure* to keep meetings running smoothly.

RULES OF PARLIAMENTARY PROCEDURE

The meeting follows a step-by-step agenda.

1. The chairperson calls the meeting to order.
2. The secretary reports details of the last meeting.
3. The treasurer makes a report.
4. Unresolved issues or actions are discussed.
5. New issues or proposed actions are discussed.
6. The chairperson ends the meeting.

The meeting has specific procedures for discussion.

1. Anyone wishing to speak must raise his or her hand until recognized by the chairperson.
2. To introduce a motion, say "I move that . . ."
3. To support the motion or suggestion, another participant must say "I second the motion." If no one seconds it, the motion is dropped.
4. If a motion is seconded, it is discussed by the group.
5. After discussion, the group votes on the motion. The chairperson usually votes only in case of a tie.

RESOURCES

Oral Interpretation

Oral interpretation is like an acting performance. You use vocal techniques, facial expressions, body language, and gestures to indicate the meaning of the literary work you are interpreting.

Adapting Material

When you adapt material for an oral interpretation, you usually have a specific purpose, audience, and occasion in mind. Every situation has its own requirements. Be sure you have thought about factors such as the length of time for your presentation and your audience's interests. Most oral readings do not require any props or costumes. Instead, the audience is usually expected to imagine such details.

You will often need to make an abbreviated version, or *cutting,* of a work of fiction or nonfiction, a long poem, or a play. Here are suggestions for making a cutting.

1. Follow the story line in time order.
2. Delete dialogue tags such as *he said angrily.* Instead, use these clues to tell you how to interpret the character's words.
3. Take out passages that don't contribute to the intended overall impression of your oral interpretation.

Presenting an Oral Interpretation

You may need to write an introduction to your interpretation to set the scene, tell something about the author, or give some necessary details about what has already taken place in the story.

☞ REFERENCE NOTE: For more about writing an introduction for a presentation, see page 902.

To be effective in presenting an oral interpretation, you will need to prepare a *reading script.* A reading script is usually typed (double-spaced) and can be marked to assist you in your interpretive reading. For example, you might

underline words for emphasis, or mark a slash (/) to indicate a pause.

Once you have developed a reading script, rehearse
several different ways until you have chosen the most
effective manner of interpreting the passage.

Use your voice in a manner that suits your presentation. Be sure to pronounce your words carefully. You can
use your body and your voice to show that you are por-
traying different characters. Use body language and gestures to emphasize your meaning or to reveal traits of the
major characters in the story as you act out what they say.

 COMPUTER NOTE: Consider using your word processor's bold,
italic, and underline styling to emphasize words in your script.

 EXERCISE 1 **Exploring Telephone Speaking
Situations**

In each of the following situations, explain how you might
handle the problem. What would you say to be polite but
clear?

1. You are visiting at a friend's house and the phone
   rings while your friend is not immediately available.
   How would you answer the phone and greet the
   caller?
2. You left something (such as a school book or gym
   bag) on the bus. You have the number to dial direct
   to the bus company's lost-and-found department.
   What would you say to the bus company employee
   who answers the phone?

 EXERCISE 2 **Giving Instructions**

Draw a grid with six squares to a side. (You will have a
grid of thirty-six boxes.) Color in any five squares. Write a
set of instructions so that someone can reproduce your
exact arrangement without looking at your drawing.

RESOURCES

▶ EXERCISE 3   **Making Social Introductions**

In each of the following situations, explain what you might say in making a social introduction.

1. You are going to the first meeting of a club to plan for the recycling of materials at your school. Only one other person is there when you arrive. Introduce yourself.
2. You have an appointment with Mr. Yumita at the Big Box Company. (He has donated some cardboard to be used for posters at your school.) Introduce yourself to the receptionist and explain whom you want to see.
3. You are introducing your mother (or father, or other relative) to your principal.

▶ EXERCISE 4   **Preparing and Giving a Speech**

Choose a topic for a short, three- to five-minute speech to give to your English class. Consider your audience and purpose when choosing your speech topic. Next, prepare note cards for your speech. Include one visual, such as a chart, diagram, time line, or drawing. Prepare a separate note card to indicate at what point in your speech you should pause to explain and incorporate this visual. Finally, deliver your speech, using effective vocal variety and appropriate nonverbal expressions.

▶ EXERCISE 5   **Making an Announcement**

Write an announcement for one of the following events. Supply specific details wherever they are needed.

1. A bake sale will be held by the Parents Club with the proceeds going toward new magazine racks for the library.
2. A pep rally will be held after school as the team (choose a sport) leaves to play an evening game. All students are invited.
3. This year's school pictures will be taken next week. Students need to bring money to pay for a package of pictures. Students who do not want to buy pictures will be photographed free for the yearbook.

▶ EXERCISE 6   **Introducing a Speaker**

Prepare and deliver in class an introduction for your state or national representative or senator, your mayor, your county commissioner, a school board member, or a famous person from history.

▶ EXERCISE 7   **Analyzing a Public Meeting**

Attend a public meeting such as a school board or city council meeting. Report to the class about the manner in which the meeting was conducted. Be able to answer each of the following questions.

1. What business was transacted?
2. What motions were presented?
3. What was the nature of the discussion? (For example, was it friendly, heated, or apathetic?)
4. How did the members of the group as a whole participate in the discussion?

▶ EXERCISE 8   **Presenting an Oral Interpretation**

Select a portion of a short story or a section of a novel that contains a scene for one or two characters. Prepare a script for a five-minute oral interpretation to present to your classmates. Write a brief introduction telling the title and author of the selection. Give enough background information so that your audience can understand the meaning of the scene.

RESOURCES

32 LISTENING AND VIEWING

Strategies for Listening and Viewing

Hearing and listening are not the same thing. Hearing is the detection of sounds. Listening, however, is an active process. It requires you to think as well as hear. Viewing involves both watching and listening. With practice, you can learn to be a more effective listener and a critical viewer.

Listening with a Purpose

One way to become a more effective listener is to keep your purpose in mind as you listen. You hear things differently depending on what you are listening for. Common purposes for listening are

- for enjoyment or entertainment
- to gain information
- to understand information or an explanation
- to evaluate or form an opinion

Listening for Information

Listening for Details

When you listen for information, you are listening for details that answer the basic *5W-How?* questions: *Who? What? When? Where? Why?* and *How?*

For example, when you are asked to take messages on the telephone, you will need to get important details from the caller, such as

- the caller's name
- who the call is for
- the caller's message
- the caller's telephone number

Listening to Instructions

Instructions are usually made up of a series of steps. When you listen to instructions, be sure you understand everything you are required to do.

1. *Listen for the order of steps.* Listen for words that tell you when each step ends and the next one begins, such as *first, second, next, then,* and *last.*
2. *Identify the number of steps in the process.* Take notes if the instructions are long or complicated.
3. *Visualize each step.* Imagine yourself actually performing each step. Try to get a mental image of what you should be doing at every step in the process.
4. *Review the steps.* When the speaker is finished, be sure you understand the process from beginning to end.

Listening and Responding

When you are listening to someone speak, you are taking part in the communication cycle. People who are speaking usually respond to you as a listener, depending on how well it appears you are paying attention.

RESOURCES

Here's how to listen and respond politely.

1. *Respect the speaker.* Be tolerant of individual differences such as the speaker's accent.
2. *Don't interrupt.* Wait until the speaker finishes.
3. *Pay attention.* Don't distract others.
4. *Keep an open mind.* Try to understand the speaker's point of view.
5. *Don't judge too soon.* Listen to the speaker's entire message before you make judgments.
6. *Ask appropriate questions in an audible voice.* Summarize or paraphrase the speaker's point to help the speaker answer the question.
7. *Use effective body language.* Show the speaker you understand the message.

Using the LQ2R Method

The LQ2R study method is especially helpful when you are listening to a speaker who is giving information.

L *Listen* carefully to material as it is being presented.

Q *Question* yourself as you listen. Mentally or in your notes, make a list of questions that occur to you.

R *Recite* in your own words the information as it is being presented. Summarize the material in your mind.

R *Relisten* as the speaker concludes the presentation. Major points may be reemphasized.

Conducting an Interview

An *interview* is a special listening situation that usually takes place between two people, an interviewer and the person being interviewed (called the *interviewee*).

Here's how you can be an effective interviewer.

Before the Interview

- Decide what information you really want.
- Make a list of questions.
- Make an appointment and be prompt.

RESOURCES

During the Interview

- Be polite. Do not rush the interviewee.
- When you ask a question, listen to the answer.
- Ask permission if you plan to quote the interviewee directly.
- Respect the interviewee's opinion. You can ask him or her to explain an opinion, but be polite.
- Conclude by thanking the interviewee.

After the Interview

- Review your notes to be sure they are clear.
- Write a summary of your impressions while you still remember the interview clearly.

 COMPUTER NOTE: You can input your notes into the computer and view them while writing your report.

Critical Listening

You can't remember every word a speaker says. But if you listen critically, you'll be able to find the parts of the speaker's message that are most important.

GUIDELINES FOR LISTENING CRITICALLY	
Find main ideas.	What are the most important points? Listen for clue words a speaker might use, such as *major, main, most important,* or similar words.
Identify significant details.	What dates, names, or facts does the speaker use to support the main points of the speech? What kinds of examples or explanations are used to support the main ideas?
Distinguish between facts and opinions.	A fact is a statement that can be proved to be true. An opinion is a belief or a judgment about something. It cannot be proved to be true.

(continued)

GUIDELINES FOR LISTENING CRITICALLY *(continued)*	
Identify the order of organization.	What kind of order is the speaker using to arrange his or her presentation—time sequence, spatial order, order of importance?
Note comparisons and contrasts.	Are some details compared or contrasted with others?
Understand cause and effect.	Do some events that the speaker refers to relate to or affect others?
Predict outcomes and draw conclusions.	What can you reasonably conclude from the facts and evidence you have gathered from the speech?
Listen to detect bias.	Is the speaker biased, or prejudiced, toward one point of view?

 REFERENCE NOTE: For more information about interpreting and analyzing information, see pages 950–954.

Taking Lecture Notes

When you listen to a speaker, don't rely entirely on your memory. Be sure to take good notes to help you remember information. You can take notes by simply writing words or phrases the speaker says. Other methods you can use for note taking include *paraphrasing* and *summarizing*.

Paraphrasing. When you *paraphrase* material, you express the ideas of others in your own words. As you listen, translate complex terms that the speaker is using into your own words and write your paraphrase in your study notes. If the speaker uses a complicated example, think of one that seems more familiar. Use your own knowledge or experience to help you translate the speaker's ideas.

Summarizing. When you *summarize,* you condense material by restating it in fewer words. As you listen to the speaker, sum up the major points of the lecture and record them in your notes.

Advertising and Mass Media

The *mass media* are forms of communication (television, radio, movies, newspapers and magazines) that reach a large audience daily. The mass media are sources of both entertainment and information. The media make money by selling a portion of their broadcast time or publication space to advertisers. Advertisers try to get your attention and persuade you to buy various products.

Knowing about persuasive techniques used by advertisers will help you evaluate methods used to influence you.

PERSUASIVE TECHNIQUES USED IN THE MEDIA	
Bandwagon	Those who use this technique urge you to "jump on the bandwagon" by suggesting that you should do or believe something because everyone (or everyone admirable or worthwhile) does or believes it. ■ "Don't you want to fit in? Buy the latest styles in clothing from The In Crowd store." ■ "The Furioso Deluxe outsells all other cars in its class by a six-to-one margin."
Testimonial	Experts or famous people sometimes give a personal "testimony" about a product or idea. However, the person paid to offer the testimonial may not really know much about that particular product or idea. ■ "I'm a glamorous movie star, and I use this brand of motor oil. I think you should, too." ■ "I'm a university professor specializing in environmental studies, and I use these biodegradable garbage bags."
"Plain folks"	Ordinary people (or actors playing ordinary people) are often used to persuade others. People tend to believe others who seem to be similar to themselves. ■ "Hey, I'm just an average guy, but I know quality when I see it. That's why I always buy this brand of aftershave."

RESOURCES

PERSUASIVE TECHNIQUES USED IN THE MEDIA *(continued)*	
Emotional appeals	This technique appeals to your emotions rather than to your ability to reason. ■ "How can you be certain that your loved ones and valuables are always safe? By installing Federal Security alarms, of course!"

Critical Viewing

If you're like most people, you watch television for a variety of reasons. When you watch situation comedies, dramas, action shows, and science fiction, your main purpose, probably, is to be entertained. Entertainment is also one aim of good literature. In fact, TV shows and literary works have more in common than you might think. Because literary works and television shows share certain features, you can apply the evaluative skills you've developed for literary works to analyze television shows.

Here are some elements literature and TV shows share, together with questions that can help you evaluate those elements in TV shows.

EVALUATING TELEVISION PROGRAMS	
Element	**Key Questions**
Character/characterization	What are the main characters' traits and personalities? Are characters developed? How?
Motivation	What motivates the main characters? Do all the characters' actions have motivations?
Plot/story line	Is the plot predictable? Are plot developments plausible, or unbelievable?
Theme	Is there a theme? If so, is it significant, or is it trivial?

The Sights and Sounds of TV

Although television and literature have elements in common, there are of course dramatic differences between these media. The most notable difference is that TV is a visual and aural (sound) medium. A good TV show capitalizes on visuals and sounds through the use of *setting, dialogue,* and *sound effects.*

Setting.   Think for a moment about how much information you receive from a show's **setting.** Even if you are not explicitly told what a show's setting is, you can watch for clues to information such as the season or time of day.
    Note the kinds of details supplied by setting:

- the location of most of the show's action (home, hospital, spaceship)
- the time period, or era
- the characters' clothes and hairstyles
- the kinds of cars driven
- the kinds of homes lived in (apartments or farmhouses; modest or luxurious) and the kinds of furnishings

Then, ask yourself these questions:

- Is the setting appropriate to the show's plot and characters? That is, does it promote the plot and allow for character development?
- What aspects of everyday life are not shown?
- What does the setting suggest about the characters and their lives?
- If the show is a sitcom, action show, or drama, is the setting realistic?
- If the show is science fiction or fantasy, is the setting believable, yet different from everyday reality?

Dialogue and Sound Effects.   If setting sends information to your eyes, the TV soundtrack sends a wealth of information to your ears. To evaluate a TV show's sounds, ask yourself:

- Is the **dialogue** interesting? Is it appropriate to the characters and the plot?

RESOURCES

- How are accents or dialects used to characterize the people in the show?
- Is music used in the show? If so, in what ways is it used—to create a mood or to signal danger?
- If there is a laugh track, what is its effect on you?
- Why do some shows have laugh tracks?
- What other **sound effects** do you notice? (Examples are car, train, or plane noises, explosions, and animal sounds.) What effects do they have on you? Do they improve the show or detract from it?

Television Versus Reality

Television's vivid visual and sound effects sometimes make us forget that the world TV creates is not the real world. TV shows can be highly realistic in some ways, yet unrealistic in others. For example, a show focusing on police work may show the complex relationships between characters. At the same time, it may romanticize police work by not depicting its less sensational aspects.

TV shows also present unrealistic pictures when they show **stereotypes**—fixed character portrayals that assume that all individuals of a particular group are the same. Typical TV examples include the brainy kid who is socially awkward and wears thick glasses or the detective who can solve any crime. Think about what groups of people TV tends to stereotype. Watch for ways in which clothes, dialects, facial expressions, gestures, and behavior create stereotypes.

RESOURCES

Review

▶ EXERCISE 1   **Listening to Instructions**

Read your class a list of instructions that explain how to do something, and allow your classmates a chance to ask questions. Then, call on them to repeat your instructions.

▶EXERCISE 2　**Listening Critically**

Listen to a short speech presented by your teacher in class. Take brief notes. Then, answer these questions.

1. What are the main ideas expressed in the speech?
2. What details support the main points in the speech?
3. Identify one fact and one opinion mentioned in the speech. What reasons support the opinion?
4. What is the order of the speech's organization?
5. Draw a conclusion about the ideas presented in the speech. Did you find the speech convincing? Explain.

▶EXERCISE 3　**Analyzing Persuasive Techniques**

Identify the persuasive technique used in each of the following numbered items.

1. "Being a quarterback like me is a tough job. You've got to stay one step ahead of your opponents at all times. That's why I support the president's foreign policy. He's keeping America on top."
2. "Join the automotive revolution. Drive the car everyone is raving about!"
3. "Does your hairstyle make you look and feel unattractive? Then get a whole new outlook on life with a new makeover from our beauty experts."
4. "As a working mother, I support Ann Smith for mayor. She understands the needs of parents."

▶EXERCISE 4　**Analyzing Television Entertainment**

Review in your mind the TV entertainment shows you watch. Then, think about a TV program that involves a situation you're familiar with, such as a group of people your age. Use your own experience to analyze how realistic the show's depictions are. Should TV shows always try to be realistic? Explain.

▶EXERCISE 5　**Evaluating Television Shows**

Decide which you think are the best two or three shows on TV today, and try to pinpoint what makes them good. Then, evaluate them according to the chart on page 914. Share your evaluation with a small group of students.

RESOURCES

33 THE LIBRARY/ MEDIA CENTER

Finding and Using Information

Libraries classify and arrange books by a classification system such as the Dewey decimal system or the Library of Congress system. By using one of these, a library can give a number and letter code—a *call number*—to each book. This call number tells how the book has been classified and where it has been placed on the shelves.

Classifying and Arranging Information

Many school libraries use the *Dewey decimal system.* This system assigns a number to nonfiction books according to ten general subject areas. Books of fiction are grouped alphabetically by the authors' last names. Works of fiction by the same author are arranged alphabetically by the first important word of the title.

The *Library of Congress* system uses code letters to identify subject categories. The first letter of the call number tells the book's general category (such as History or Literature). The second letter tells the subcategory. Call numbers include these letter codes and are followed by numbers that identify specific books within a category.

Online Catalog and Card Catalog

Libraries use online catalogs and card catalogs to provide the title, author, call numbers, and publication facts about the books in their holdings. An *online catalog* is a computerized version of the card catalog. To search for a book, type in an author's name, a title, or a subject. The computer will retrieve the information you request.

AUTHOR:	Highwater, Jamake.
TITLE:	Anpao: an American Indian odyssey/ Jamake Highwater; pictures by Fritz Scholder.
PUBLISHED:	Philadelphia: Lippincott, c1977.
DESCRIPTION:	256 p.: ill.; 24 cm
NOTES:	Bibliography: p. 253–254. Summary: Traditional tales from North American Indian tribes woven into one story that relates the adventures of one boy as he grows to manhood.
SUBJECTS:	Indians of North America—Legends
OTHER AUTHORS:	Scholder, Fritz, 1937–
ISBN:	0397317506
OCLC NUMBER:	3034645

A *card catalog* is a cabinet of drawers filled with alphabetically arranged cards. These cards list books by title, author, and subject. For each book in the library, there are at least two cards—a *title card* and an *author card*. If the book is nonfiction, there is a third card—a *subject card*. You can tell what type of card it is by what is printed on its top line. Occasionally, you may also find *"See"* or *"See also" cards* that advise you where to look for additional information.

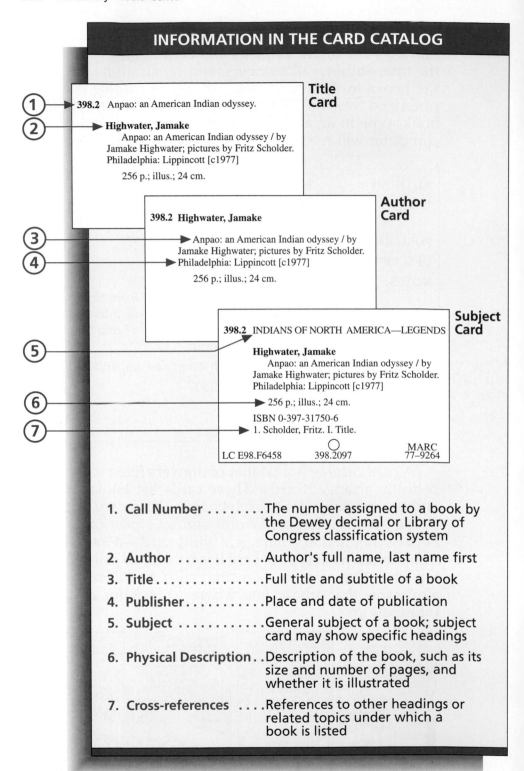

INFORMATION IN THE CARD CATALOG

Title Card

① → **398.2** Anpao: an American Indian odyssey.

② → **Highwater, Jamake**
  Anpao: an American Indian odyssey / by
Jamake Highwater; pictures by Fritz Scholder.
Philadelphia: Lippincott [c1977]

  256 p.; illus.; 24 cm.

Author Card

398.2 Highwater, Jamake

③ → Anpao: an American Indian odyssey / by
Jamake Highwater; pictures by Fritz Scholder.
④ → Philadelphia: Lippincott [c1977]

  256 p.; illus.; 24 cm.

Subject Card

398.2 INDIANS OF NORTH AMERICA—LEGENDS

  Highwater, Jamake
  Anpao: an American Indian odyssey / by
⑤ → Jamake Highwater; pictures by Fritz Scholder.
Philadelphia: Lippincott [c1977]

⑥ → 256 p.; illus.; 24 cm.

  ISBN 0-397-31750-6
⑦ → 1. Scholder, Fritz. I. Title.

  LC E98.F6458   398.2097   MARC
77–9264

1. **Call Number** . . . . The number assigned to a book by the Dewey decimal or Library of Congress classification system

2. **Author** . . . . Author's full name, last name first

3. **Title** . . . . Full title and subtitle of a book

4. **Publisher** . . . . Place and date of publication

5. **Subject** . . . . General subject of a book; subject card may show specific headings

6. **Physical Description** . . Description of the book, such as its size and number of pages, and whether it is illustrated

7. **Cross-references** . . . . References to other headings or related topics under which a book is listed

RESOURCES

Using Reference Materials

The *Readers' Guide*

To find a magazine article, use the *Readers' Guide to Periodical Literature*. The *Readers' Guide* indexes articles, poems, and stories from more than one hundred magazines.

Entries may contain abbreviations. Use the key at the front of the *Readers' Guide* to find the meanings of these abbreviations.

As the sample entry shows, magazine articles are listed alphabetically by author and by subject. The headings are in boldface type.

CAMPBELL, LAWRENCE, 1914–
Objects on parade. il *Art in America*
v84 p90–1 + Ja '96

CAMPBELL TAGGART, INC.
How Eagle became extinct. R. A. Melcher.
il *Business Week* p68–9 Mr 4 '96

CAMPING
See also
Backpacking
Camps

    Equipment
See also
Sleeping bags

CAMPING ETIQUETTE
Close quarters. C. Neasel. il *Backpacker*
v23 p28 + D '95

CAMPS
How to find the best novice programs
[tennis camps and resorts] R. Cox. il
Tennis v31 p64–5 Ja '96

(1) **Author entry**

(2) **Title of article**

(3) **Date of magazine**

(4) **Author of article**

(5) **Page reference**

(6) **Subject cross-reference**

(7) **Subject entry**

(8) **Name of magazine**

(9) **Volume number of magazine**

RESOURCES

Special Information Sources

The ***vertical file*** is a set of file drawers containing up-to-date materials such as pamphlets, newspaper clippings, and pictures.

Microforms are photographically reduced articles from newspapers and magazines. The two most common kinds of microforms are *microfilm* and *microfiche*. Special machines enlarge the images and project them onto a screen.

Electronic Information Sources

Libraries also have computerized information services that link them to *online databases.* These databases store all types of information on the computer. Some libraries have CD-ROM indexes to publications such as the MAS FullTEXT and the *Social Issues Resources Series* (SIRS). Searching for a subject index on a CD-ROM is easy when you identify *keywords* for your topic. You can print out the information that you find or *download* the information onto a disk. Other libraries are linked to the *Internet,* an international network of computers. As with the CD-ROM indexes, you search for a specific topic by typing a keyword or phrase and printing out the information that you find.

The following excerpt is a partial example of MAS Full-TEXT as it would appear on a computer screen, using the keywords *backpacking* and *mountains.*

1. Subject:	YELLOWSTONE National Park—Description and travel	
Title:	A natural history of the Yellowstone tourist. By O'Gara, Geoffrey	
Source:	(Sierra, Mar/Apr96, Vol. 81 Issue 2, p54, 8p, 9c, 4bw) (0161–7362)	
	** FullTEXT Available on CD-ROM**	
2. Subject:	PINALENO Mountains (Ariz.)—Description and travel	
Title:	A Pinaleno mountain odyssey. By St. John, Julie L.; Noebels, Peter	
Source:	(Arizona Highways, Feb96, Vol. 72 Issue 2, p14, 8p, 11c) (0004–1521)	

Reference Sources

There are many types of reference sources that you can use to find specific kinds of information.

REFERENCE SOURCES	
TYPE	CONTENT DESCRIPTION
ENCYCLOPEDIAS *Collier's Encyclopedia, The New Encyclopaedia Britannica, The World Book Multimedia Encyclopedia*™	■ multiple volumes ■ articles arranged alphabetically by subject ■ best source for general information
GENERAL BIOGRAPHICAL REFERENCES *Dictionary of American Biography, World Biographical Index on CD-ROM*	■ information about birth, nationality, and major accomplishments of prominent people
SPECIAL BIOGRAPHICAL REFERENCES *Contemporary Authors*® *on CD-ROM, Mexican American Biographies*	■ information about people noted for accomplishments in a specific field or for membership in a specific group
ATLASES *Atlas of World Cultures, National Geographic Atlas of the World*	■ maps and geographical information
ALMANACS *Information Please Almanac: Atlas & Yearbook*	■ up-to-date information about current events, facts, statistics, and dates
BOOKS OF QUOTATIONS Bartlett's *Familiar Quotations, The Oxford Dictionary of Quotations*	■ famous quotations indexed or grouped by subject ■ information about author, source, and date

(continued)

REFERENCE SOURCES *(continued)*	
TYPE	CONTENT DESCRIPTION
BOOKS OF SYNONYMS *Roget's International Thesaurus, Webster's New Dictionary of Synonyms*	■ lists of exact or more interesting words to express ideas
LITERARY REFERENCES *Gale Literary Index CD-ROM, Granger's Index to Poetry*	■ information about various works of literature

Review

▶ EXERCISE 1 **Finding Information Using the Card Catalog**

Using the card catalog or online catalog in your library, find the following information. If the information cannot be found, write "not in our library."

1. List a book title by each of the following authors.
   a. F. Scott Fitzgerald **b.** Alice Walker
2. Find a book on each subject below. List a title, author, call number, and publication date for each.
   a. Recycling **b.** Sign Language
3. List the title and the author of a book about:
   a. Amelia Earhart **b.** Pancho Villa
4. If your library has a CD-ROM database, search for the following topics. Then, print the records.
   a. Adolescents **b.** Classical Music

▶ EXERCISE 2 **Interpreting *Readers' Guide* Entries**

Use the excerpt from the *Readers' Guide* on page 921 to find the following information.

1. Identify two subject entries and two magazine titles.
2. What two headings could you use to find more information about camping?
3. Write the title of the article by C. Neasel, the name and date of the magazine, and its page numbers.
4. What entry has a "See also" reference?

34 THE DICTIONARY

Types and Contents

Types of Dictionaries

There are several different types of dictionaries that vary in the kinds of information they provide and the arrangement of their contents.

TYPES OF DICTIONARIES		
EXAMPLE	NUMBER OF ENTRIES	NUMBER OF PAGES
Webster's Third New International Dictionary, Unabridged (Unabridged)	460,000	2,662
Random House College Dictionary (Abridged or College)	173,000	1,565
Funk and Wagnall's Standard Dictionary (Paperback)	82,000	1,014

A SAMPLE ENTRY

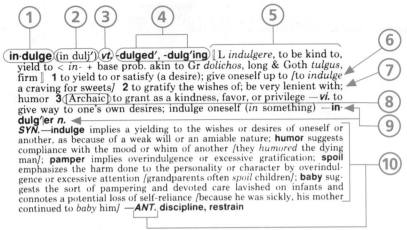

① **in·dulge** ② (in dulj′) ③ *vt.* ④ **-dulged′, -dulg′ing** ⑤ ⟦ L *indulgere*, to be kind to, yield to < *in-* + base prob. akin to Gr *dolichos*, long & Goth *tulgus*, firm ⟧ **1** to yield to or satisfy (a desire); give oneself up to *[to indulge a craving for sweets]* **2** to gratify the wishes of; be very lenient with; humor **3** ⟨Archaic⟩ to grant as a kindness, favor, or privilege —*vi.* to give way to one's own desires; indulge oneself (*in* something) —**in·dulg′er** *n.*

SYN.—**indulge** implies a yielding to the wishes or desires of oneself or another, as because of a weak will or an amiable nature; **humor** suggests compliance with the mood or whim of another *[they humored the dying man]*; **pamper** implies overindulgence or excessive gratification; **spoil** emphasizes the harm done to the personality or character by overindulgence or excessive attention *[grandparents often spoil children]*; **baby** suggests the sort of pampering and devoted care lavished on infants and connotes a potential loss of self-reliance *[because he was sickly, his mother continued to baby him]* —**ANT.** discipline, restrain

⑥ ⑦ ⑧ ⑨ ⑩

1. **Entry word.** The entry word shows how the word is spelled and how it is divided into syllables. The entry word may also show capitalization and alternate spellings.
2. **Pronunciation.** The pronunciation is shown by the use of accent marks and either phonetic respellings or diacritical marks. A pronunciation key explains the meaning of diacritical marks or phonetic symbols.
3. **Part-of-speech labels.** These labels (usually in abbreviated form) indicate how the entry word should be used in a sentence. Some words may be used as more than one part of speech. In this case, a part-of-speech label is given in front of each numbered (or lettered) series of definitions.
4. **Other forms.** These may show spellings of plural forms of nouns, tenses of verbs, or the comparison forms of adjectives and adverbs.
5. **Etymology.** The etymology is the origin and history of a word. It tells how the word (or its parts) came into English.
6. **Examples.** Phrases or sentences may demonstrate how the defined word is used.
7. **Definitions.** If there is more than one meaning, definitions are numbered or lettered.

8. **Special usage labels.** These labels identify words that have special meaning or are used in special ways in certain situations.
9. **Related word forms.** These are various forms of the entry word, usually created by adding suffixes or prefixes.
10. **Synonyms and antonyms.** Sometimes synonyms or antonyms appear at the end of some word entries.

Review

▶ EXERCISE 1 **Practicing Pronunciation**

How does your dictionary indicate the pronunciation of each of the following words? Copy each word carefully, showing syllables, accent(s), and sounds. Practice saying the words aloud.

EXAMPLE **1.** hindrance
1. *hin´drəns*

1. appropriate (used as an adjective)
2. appropriate (used as a verb)
3. address (used as a noun)
4. separate (used as a verb)
5. precedent (used as an adjective)

▶ EXERCISE 2 **Finding Parts of Speech**

Look up the following words in a dictionary. Give all the parts of speech listed for each word and an example of how the word is used as each part of speech.

EXAMPLE **1.** kind
1. *noun—this <u>kind</u> of paper*
adjective—a <u>kind</u> person

1. base
2. plate
3. court
4. forward
5. material

RESOURCES

▶ EXERCISE 3   **Dividing Words into Syllables**

Divide the following words into syllables. Check your work in a dictionary.

1. forevermore
2. impractical
3. old-fashioned

4. preliminary
5. recognize

▶ EXERCISE 4   **Identifying the Usage Labels of Words**

If your college or unabridged dictionary lists special usage labels for entry words, look up the following words and write the usage label given for the word or for any of its meanings.

1. pep
2. dude
3. crisp
4. leader
5. cantina

6. boondocks
7. gumshoe
8. Plutonic
9. brass
10. ballyhoo

▶ EXERCISE 5   **Finding Synonyms for Words**

Write all the synonyms you can think of for each of the following words. Then, use a thesaurus or dictionary to check your list and to add to it.

1. freedom
2. laughable
3. shrewd

4. rough
5. loud

35 VOCABULARY

Learning and Using New Words

One of the best ways to learn new words is to discover them when reading books. You can also increase your vocabulary by figuring out the meanings of unfamiliar words in context. That is, when you read a passage that contains an unfamiliar term, you can sometimes discover its meaning by looking at how it's used in the sentence or paragraph. Other ways of increasing your vocabulary include studying the meanings of common word parts and learning how they're combined to form new words.

Add to Your Word Bank

One good way to increase your vocabulary is to create a word bank. Start saving words. When you come across new words in your classes or in your readings, write these new words in your notebook along with their definitions. Check your dictionary to see if you have understood the meaning of each word.

Using Context Clues

Sometimes you can figure out the meaning of an unfamiliar word by examining the context in which it's used. The *context* of a word includes the words that surround the word and the circumstances in which the word is used. Sometimes clues that help define an unfamiliar word can be found in the sentence in which the word appears.

The following chart shows examples of some of the common types of context clues.

HOW TO USE CONTEXT CLUES	
TYPE OF CLUE	EXPLANATION
Definitions and Restatements	Look for words that define the term or restate it in other words. ■ The judge seemed *impartial,* not favoring one side in the case over the other.
Examples	Look for examples used in context that reveal the meaning of an unfamiliar word. ■ Many *sovereigns* attended the exhibit, including the queen of England and the king of Denmark.
Synonyms	Look for clues that indicate an unfamiliar word is similar in meaning to a familiar word or phrase. ■ Rico, like his overjoyed teammates, was *exultant* about the team's victory.
Antonyms	Look for clues that indicate an unfamiliar word is opposite in meaning to a familiar word or phrase. ■ Instead of being stormy, the weather turned *balmy* in the afternoon.
Cause and Effect	Look for clues that indicate an unfamiliar word is related to the cause or is the result of an action, feeling, or idea. ■ Because his pet lizard was lost, Mark felt *dejected.*

RESOURCES

Determining Meanings from the General Context

Writers don't include obvious context clues in every sentence or in every paragraph. Sometimes you have to read an entire passage to understand the meaning of a word. However, you can draw on prior knowledge and experience to determine the meaning of unfamiliar terms.

Choosing the Right Word

Many English words have more than one meaning. Therefore, when you're looking for the meaning of a word, look at *all* the definitions given. Keep in mind the context in which you read or heard the word. Then, try the various definitions in that context until you find the one that fits best.

English contains many *synonyms*—words that have the same general meaning but also have subtle shades of difference between them. Choosing the right synonym is very important when you are trying to write clearly and effectively. Make sure that you understand the exact context in which the word is being used.

 COMPUTER NOTE: Create your own vocabulary file on a computer. You can add new words to the end of the file and use the Sort command to arrange the additional words alphabetically.

Using Word Parts

English words can be classified into two types: those that cannot be divided into parts, and those that can. Words that cannot be divided, like *sharp, break,* and *ground,* are called **base words.** Words that can be divided, like *unbelievable, rejection,* and *prepare,* are made up of **word parts.**

The three types of word parts are roots, prefixes, and suffixes. Knowing the meanings of roots, prefixes, and suffixes can help you determine the meanings of many unfamiliar words.

RESOURCES

Roots

The *root* is the foundation a word is built on. It carries the word's core meaning, and it is the part to which prefixes and suffixes are added.

COMMONLY USED ROOTS		
ROOTS	MEANINGS	EXAMPLES
GREEK		
–bibli–, –biblio–	book	bibliography, bibliophile
–chron–	time	chronological, synchronize
–dem–	people	democracy, epidemic
–graph–	write, writing	autograph, geography
–log(ue)–, –logy–	study, word	logic, mythology
–micr–	small	microbe, microscope
–phil–	love	audiophile, philharmonic
–phon–	sound	phonograph, euphony
–sym–, –syn–	with, together	symphony, synchronize
LATIN		
–aud–, –audit–	hear	audible, auditorium
–bene–	well, good	benefit, benevolent
–cis–	cut	incision, concise
–cogn–	know	recognize, cognition
–duc–, –duct–	lead	educate, conductor
–fid–	belief, faith	fidelity, infidel
–gen–	birth, kind, origin	generate, generic, generous
–ject–	throw	projectile, reject
–loqu–, –loc–	talk, speech	eloquent, locution
–magn–	large	magnitude, magnify
–mal–	bad	malady, dismal
–mit–, –miss–	send	remit, emissary
–ped–	foot	pedal, quadruped
–pend–, –pens–	hang, weigh	pendant, suspense
–port–	carry, bear	export, important
–tract–	pull, draw	tractor, extract
–vis–, –vid–	see	visible, videotape

Prefixes

A *prefix* is a word part that is added before a root. The word that is created from a prefix and a root combines the meanings of both its parts.

COMMONLY USED PREFIXES		
PREFIXES	MEANINGS	EXAMPLES
GREEK		
anti–	against, opposing	antipathy, antithesis
dia–	through, across, between	diagonal, diameter
hemi–	half	hemisphere, hemicycle
syn–, sym–, syl–, sys–	together, with	synchronize, sympathy, syllable, system
LATIN AND FRENCH		
bi–	two	bimonthly, bisect
co–, col–, com–, con–, cor–	with, together	coexist, collide, compare, convene, correspond
de–	away, from, off, down	defect, desert, decline
in–, im–	in, into, within	induct, impose
inter–	between, among	intercede, international
non–	not	nonsense, noncooperative
post–	after, following	postpone, postscript
pre–	before	prevent, predisposed
re–	back, backward, again	revoke, recede, recur
sub–, suf–, sum–, sup–, sus–	under, beneath	subjugate, suffuse, summon, suppose, suspect
trans–	across, beyond	transmission, transfer
OLD ENGLISH		
mis–	badly, not, wrongly	misfire, misspell
over–	above, excessive	oversee, overdo
un–	not, reverse of	untrue, unfold

Suffixes

A *suffix* is a word part that is added after a root. Often, adding or changing a suffix will change both a word's meaning and its part of speech, as in *please/pleasure*.

COMMONLY USED SUFFIXES		
SUFFIXES	MEANINGS	EXAMPLES
GREEK, LATIN, AND FRENCH		
NOUNS		
–ance, –ancy	act, quality	acceptance, hesitancy
–ity	state, condition	possibility, ability
–ment	result, action	disappointment
–tion	action, condition	selection, relation
ADJECTIVES		
–able	able, likely	capable, changeable
–ible	able, likely	flexible, possible
–ous	characterized by	religious, furious
ADJECTIVES OR NOUNS		
–ant, –ent	actor, showing	servant, confident
–ite	formed, showing	composite, favorite
VERBS		
–ate	become, cause	populate, activate
–fy	make, cause	identify, glorify
–ize	make, cause to be	sterilize, motorize
OLD ENGLISH		
NOUNS		
–dom	state, condition	freedom, wisdom
–hood	state, condition	childhood, falsehood
–ness	quality, state	softness, shortness
ADJECTIVES		
–en	made of, like	wooden, golden
–ish	suggesting, like	smallish, childish
VERBS		
–en	cause to be	deepen, darken

 REFERENCE NOTE: For guidelines on spelling when adding suffixes, see pages 840–844.

Review

▶ EXERCISE 1   **Using Context Clues to Find the Definition**

Using context clues in each of the following sentences, choose the letter of the definition that best fits the meaning of each italicized word.

> **a.** well-qualified   **e.** sentimental
> **b.** fictional   **f.** ordinary
> **c.** able to float   **g.** primitive
> **d.** beautiful   **h.** weak

1. The critic's statement that the artist's work is *unsophisticated* refers to the fact that his style is very simple, even crude.
2. The lively conversations of the fascinating guests made up for the rather *mediocre* dinner.
3. Lamont draws only *mythical* creatures, like unicorns and dragons.
4. The prime minister seemed to be *feckless,* as he constantly acted ineffectively and complained that he felt powerless to change what was happening in his government.
5. We learned in our safety class that if someone falls from a boat, you should throw the person a life vest or another *buoyant* object.

▶ EXERCISE 2   **Choosing Correct Definitions for Words in Context**

Using a dictionary, find the definition that best fits each italicized word.

1. Both candidates appeared to tire in the last *hectic* days of the campaign.
2. The dictator's courts made a *farce* of justice.
3. Quan Li's friends often *impose* on her generosity.
4. Harry never thinks of the *orthodox* solution to a problem.
5. The ruthless leader's civilized manners were only a *veneer.*

▶ EXERCISE 3 **Using Roots to Determine Meanings**

Using the list of commonly used roots on page 932, identify the root or roots in each of the following words. Then, guess the meaning of each word. Check your answers in a dictionary.

EXAMPLE **1. malcontent**
         1. *–mal– (bad);* malcontent *means "dissatisfied"*

1. audiovisual
2. autograph
3. bibliographer
4. vision
5. tractable

6. auditions
7. mission
8. chronology
9. cognizant
10. portable

▶ EXERCISE 4 **Identifying Words with Prefixes**

Give an example of a word containing each of the following prefixes. (Do not use any of the words given as examples or exercises in this chapter.) Then, tell what each word means.

EXAMPLE **1. un–**
         1. *unbending—not bending; stiff or stubborn*

1. de–
2. post–
3. pre–
4. re–
5. inter–

6. dia–
7. non–
8. sub–
9. mis–
10. co–

 EXERCISE 5 **Identifying Suffixes and Defining Words**

Identify the suffix in each word and guess what the word means. Check your answers in a dictionary.

EXAMPLE **1. theorize**
         1. *-ize (to make or cause to be)* = *to make a theory*

1. magnify
2. transmissible
3. parenthood

4. capability
5. porous

36 LETTERS AND FORMS

Style and Contents

You will find it useful to learn how to write clear, concise, and effective letters for a variety of purposes. There is an accepted set of procedures and a style to follow to give your writing a professional look. You will also find that there are a few general procedures you should follow in completing printed forms.

The Appearance of a Business Letter

- Use plain, unlined $8\frac{1}{2}''$ x $11''$ paper.
- Type your letter if possible (single-spaced, leaving an extra line between paragraphs). Otherwise, neatly write the letter by hand, using black or blue ink. Avoid cross-outs, smudges, erasures, and inkblots. Check for typing errors and misspellings.
- Center your letter on the page with equal margins on the sides and at the top and bottom.
- Use only one side of the paper. If your letter won't fit on one page, leave a one-inch margin at the bottom of the first page and carry over at least two lines onto the second page.

Writing Business Letters

The Parts of a Business Letter

The six parts of a business letter are

    (1) the heading
    (2) the inside address
    (3) the salutation
    (4) the body
    (5) the closing
    (6) the signature

These six parts are usually arranged on the page in one of two styles. When you use the *block form,* begin every part of the letter at the left margin and don't indent any paragraphs. However, if you use the *modified block form,* place the heading, the closing, and your signature to the right of the center of the page. Put all the other parts of the letter at the left margin and indent the paragraphs.

Block Style

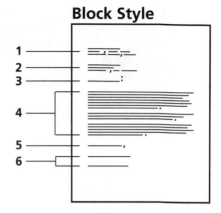

Modified Block Style

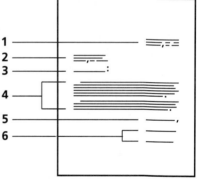

The Heading.   The heading usually has three lines:

- your street address
- your city, state, and ZIP Code
- the date the letter was written

The Inside Address. The inside address gives the name and address of the person you are writing. If you're directing your letter to someone by name, use a courtesy title (such as *Mr., Ms., Mrs.,* or *Miss*) or a professional title (such as *Dr.* or *Professor*) in front of the person's name. After you write the person's name, include the person's business title, if you know what it is.

The Salutation.   The salutation is your greeting. If you are writing to a specific person, begin with *Dear*, followed by a courtesy title or a professional title and the person's name.

If you don't have the name of a specific person, use a general salutation, such as *Dear Sir or Madam* or *Ladies and Gentlemen*. Or you can use a department or a position title, with or without the word *Dear*.

The Body.   The body, or main part, of your letter contains your message. If the body of your letter contains more than one paragraph, leave a blank line between paragraphs.

The Closing.   The closing should end your letter courteously. There are several closings that are often used in business letters, such as *Yours truly, Sincerely,* or *Sincerely yours.*

The Signature.   Your signature should be handwritten in ink, directly below the closing and above your typed or printed name. For a business letter, always sign your full name. When making a signature, do not use a title (such as *Mr., Ms., Dr.,* and so on).

GUIDELINES FOR THE CONTENTS OF A BUSINESS LETTER

Business letters that get results follow a few simple guidelines.

- *Use a polite, respectful, professional tone.* A courteous letter is more effective than a rude or angry one.

- *Use formal, standard English.* Avoid slang, contractions, and most abbreviations. Informal language that might be acceptable in a telephone conversation or personal letter is often inappropriate in a business letter.

- *Explain the purpose of your letter quickly and clearly.* Be polite, but get to the point.

- *Include all necessary information.* Be sure your reader can understand why you wrote and what you are asking.

RESOURCES

Types of Business Letters

Request or Order Letters

In a *request letter,* you're asking for something. Perhaps you want information about a product you're thinking about buying or a place you're planning to visit. Or maybe you want someone to do something for you—speak to your class, sponsor a charity walkathon, or provide space for a school event.

An *order letter* is a special kind of request letter that asks for something specific, such as a free brochure advertised in a magazine. An order letter may be used to order an item in a catalog or magazine when you don't have a printed order form.

Bethlehem High School
700 Delaware Avenue
Delmar, NY 12054
October 12, 1998

Ms. Ellen Phillips, Staff Writer
The Albany Times Mirror
News Plaza, Box 1000
Albany, NY 12212

Dear Ms. Phillips:

    I would like to invite you to be one of our speakers at the Bethlehem High School Career Day. This year's event will be held on December 16, from 9:00 A.M. to 4:00 P.M.

    Please let me know if you would be interested in speaking to an audience of about fifty students for a fifteen-minute talk about your career in journalism. We can schedule your talk at your convenience.

    I look forward to hearing from you soon.

                 Yours truly,

                 Jennifer Savage

                 Jennifer Savage,
                 Student Coordinator
                 Career Day '98

When you are writing a request or order letter, remember the following points.

1. Clearly state your request.
2. If you're asking someone to send you information, enclose a self-addressed, stamped envelope.
3. If you're asking someone to do something for you, make your request well in advance.
4. If you're ordering something, include all important information. Give the size, color, brand name, or any other specific information. If there are costs involved, add the amount correctly.

Complaint or Adjustment Letters

The purpose of a *complaint* or an *adjustment letter* is to report an error or to state that you have not received services or products that you have reason to expect.

Here is the body of a sample adjustment letter.

> On January 2, 1998, I ordered a plaid shirt from your catalog: Item #3121HH, size 38 medium, described as "a washable wool/polyester blend." The shirt cost $27, plus $1.50 shipping and handling, for a total of $28.50.
>
> However, the first time I washed the shirt, the side seam split apart. I followed the washing directions on the label carefully.
>
> I am returning the shirt. Please send a replacement shirt or a refund. Thank you for your attention to this matter.

When you are writing a complaint or an adjustment letter, remember these points.

1. Be prompt about registering your complaint.
2. Be sure to mention specifics. Necessary details might include
   - why you are unhappy with the product or service
   - how you were affected (lost time, money, or convenience)
   - what solution you want to correct the problem
3. Keep the tone of your letter calm and courteous.

RESOURCES

Appreciation or Commendation Letters

In an *appreciation* or *commendation letter,* you express your appreciation for a person, a group, an organization, or a product or service. Be specific about why you are pleased. For example, you may have appreciated the fine service you received at a restaurant.

Here is the body of a sample appreciation letter.

> I am writing to let you know how much I enjoyed your museum's recent exhibition on contemporary African American artists. My high school's art class was impressed and inspired by what we saw. I particularly enjoyed the paintings by Jacob Lawrence.
>
> I hope you will continue to present such exceptional shows. I plan to revisit your gallery whenever I can.

 COMPUTER NOTE: Remember to save your work every ten to fifteen minutes. Turn on automatic Save if you have it.

Writing Informal or Personal Letters

There are times when a letter is the most appropriate form of communication for personal messages. Thank-you letters, invitations, or regret letters are less formal than business letters. Use the modified block form, but do not include an inside address.

Thank-you letters. These are informal letters of appreciation that you send to tell someone that you appreciate his or her taking time, trouble, or expense on your behalf. Mention why the gift is special to you.

Invitations. An informal invitation should contain specific information about the occasion, the time and place, and any other special details your guest might need to know (such as that everyone is expected to bring a gift, wear a costume, or bring a snack to share).

Letters of Regret. Send a letter of regret if you have been invited somewhere and are unable to go. A written reply is especially appropriate if you were sent a written invitation with the letters *R.S.V.P.* (in French, an abbreviation for "please reply").

Personal letters are usually neatly handwritten rather than typed. You can use almost any matching white or solid-colored stationery.

Addressing an Envelope

Place your complete return address in the top left-hand corner of the envelope. Center the name and address of the person to whom you are writing on the envelope. For a business letter, the addressee's name and address should exactly match the inside address. Use the two-letter state code on the envelope rather than writing out the state name.

Completing Printed Forms

Printed forms vary, but there are certain standard techniques that will help you fill out any form accurately and completely.

Read all of the instructions carefully. Be sure you know what to do before you begin writing.

Type or write neatly, using a pen or pencil as directed. Unless you are specifically instructed to use pencil, type or print your information on the form in either blue or black ballpoint pen.

Proofread your completed form. Make sure you have given all the information that has been requested on the form. Check for errors and correct them neatly.

RESOURCES

Review

 EXERCISE 1   **Arranging the Parts of a Business Letter**

Practice arranging the parts of the following business letter. Use one style, either the block form or the modified block form, to place the parts of this outlined letter correctly on the page. Remember to use the correct punctuation marks.

1. *Heading* (Use your own address and today's date.)
2. *Inside Address* (You are writing to Ms. Sandra Alvarez, who is the manager of the Alvarez Gallery at 14 Hartford Road in Austin, Texas 78703.)
3. *Salutation* (Use *Dear Ms. Alvarez:* as your salutation.)
4. *Body* (To indicate the body of your letter, draw twelve lines divided into three paragraphs. Show indentations if appropriate to your format.)
5. *Closing* (Use *Yours truly,* as your closing.)
6. *Signature* (Use your own name.)

EXERCISE 2   **Writing a Request Letter**

You are working on a science project or social studies report. Write a request letter to a scientist, a specialist, or a public figure (such as your state representative or senator), requesting information about your topic. Use your own return address and today's date. Make up any other information you need to write your letter.

EXERCISE 3   **Writing a Complaint or Adjustment Letter**

Practice writing a letter of adjustment or complaint. Write to a mail-order company, complaining that you have received the wrong merchandise. Be specific about the error the company made in filling the order. You are returning the merchandise; tell the company what adjustment you expect them to make. Use your own return address but make up any other information you need to write the letter.

> EXERCISE 4 **Writing a Letter of Appreciation or Commendation**

Choose one of the following situations to practice writing a letter of appreciation or commendation. Use your own return address and today's date, but make up any other information you need to write the letter.

1. Write a letter to the manager of a local business, expressing your satisfaction with a product you purchased there or with the service you received from one of the employees.
2. Write a letter to a newspaper or magazine editor, commending a recent article that you think was particularly interesting, important, or well written. Tell why this article made an impact on you.
3. Write a letter to a member of your community, thanking him or her for efforts that will improve the community. Be specific about what this person did and what it meant to you.

> EXERCISE 5 **Writing a Thank-You Letter**

Write a thank-you letter to someone you know. Express your appreciation for a specific comment, gift, or action.

> EXERCISE 6 **Addressing Business Envelopes**

Draw rectangular outlines to represent three envelopes. Address each envelope, using the following information. Use your own return address.

1. Address a business envelope to Zachary Keller, who lives at 847 North Fountain Avenue in Springfield, Ohio (ZIP Code 45504–5203).
2. Address an envelope to Wilma Robinson. Mrs. Robinson is the Director of Tribal Development for the Choctaw Nation of Oklahoma, located in Durant, Oklahoma (ZIP Code 74702–1210).
3. Address an envelope to the customer service department of the Gardener's Friend Nursery, located at 27 Corte Madera Lane in Mill Valley, California (ZIP Code 94941–0249).

RESOURCES

37 READING, STUDYING, AND TEST TAKING

Using Skills and Strategies

Do you understand what you read in school? Do you use your time efficiently when you study? If you answered no to either of these questions, don't be discouraged. By organizing your time and using certain reading strategies, you can improve your study habits and become a better reader.

Planning a Study Routine

You need to organize a realistic study schedule and stick to it. Here are some suggestions.

1. *Know your assignments.* Record on an assignment planner or a calendar the assignments you have and when they are due. Make sure you understand what you're supposed to do for each assignment.
2. *Make a plan.* Break larger assignments into smaller steps. Schedule time to finish each step.
3. *Concentrate when you study.* Select a time and a place to study. Focus your attention only on your assignment. Avoid distractions.

Strengthening Reading and Study Skills

Reading and Understanding

You are more likely to keep alert and to remember what you read if you read with a purpose. Three common purposes for reading are

- to find specific details
- to find main ideas
- to understand and remember

Adjust your rate of reading to suit your purpose.

READING RATES ACCORDING TO PURPOSE		
READING RATE	PURPOSE	EXAMPLE
Scanning	Reading for specific details	Hunting for the name of the town that is used as the setting for a short story
Skimming	Reading for main points	Reviewing chapter headings, subheadings, and time lines in your history textbook the night before a test
Reading for mastery	Reading to understand and remember	Taking notes and outlining a section in your science textbook before you begin your homework

Writing to Learn

Your writing can be a valuable method to help you in the process of learning. Writing is an act of discovery that will allow you to focus your thoughts, respond to ideas, record your observations, and plan your work.

Although there are many different types of writing, here are some suggestions of ways that writing can help you explore your ideas.

TYPE OF WRITING	PURPOSE	EXAMPLE
Freewriting	To help you focus your thoughts	Writing for three minutes before beginning an essay to explain the meaning of a poem
Autobiographies	To help you examine and express the meaning of important events in your life	Writing about an incident that taught you a valuable lesson
Diaries	To help you recall your impressions and express your feelings	Writing about your reactions to issues raised in your classes
Journals and Learning Logs	To help you record your observations, descriptions, solutions, and questions	Writing about solutions for solving word problems in math
	To help you present a problem, analyze it, and propose a solution	Writing about the way you will approach a term paper for your history class

Using Word-Processing Tools for Writing

A word processor or a word-processing program for a computer can help you plan, draft, and edit your writing. These tools can make every step of the writing process easier.

Prewriting. With a little practice, you can type quickly using word-processing tools. You can rewrite your notes or ideas without having to retype them.

Writing First Drafts. You can write, revise, and re-arrange your ideas as often as you want. Then, use the printer to produce a hard copy, or printout.

Evaluating. Word-processing tools can let you try out different versions of your work. Save your original document and make an electronic copy. Type your changes in the copy. If you don't like the changes, you still have the original.

Revising. Type your final changes in the original document. Then, you can print a clean copy without retyping the unchanged portions.

Proofreading. Some word-processing tools can check for errors in spelling and grammar, but they can't find misused words such as the homonyms *to, two,* and *too.*

Publishing. Print one or more copies of your final work. You may wish to share your writing with others.

 COMPUTER NOTE: Use your word-processing program's Border and Box tools to set off text and to create eye-catching pages.

Using the SQ3R Reading Method

An educational psychologist, Francis Robinson, developed a method of study called SQ3R. The SQ3R reading method is made up of five simple steps.

S *Survey* the entire study assignment. Look at the headings, the material in boldface and italics, the charts, outlines, and summaries.
Q *Question* yourself. What should you know after completing your reading? Make a list of questions to be answered.
R *Read* the material section by section. Think of answers to your questions as you read.
R *Recite* in your own words answers to each question.
R *Review* the material by rereading quickly, looking over the questions, and recalling the answers.

Using the SQ3R method, you can turn routine assignments into interesting and active reading sessions. [Remember: When you respond actively to what you are reading, you are much more likely to recall what you have read.]

☞ REFERENCE NOTE: For study techniques to help with listening skills, see page 910.

RESOURCES

Interpreting and Analyzing What You Read

Every essay, article, or textbook chapter that you read follows an organizational pattern in which the ideas are related to one another. Interpreting and analyzing these relationships will help you think critically about what you read.

Stated Main Idea. When you read to find the main idea, you are trying to identify the most important point that the writer wants to make. Sometimes the main idea is stated, meaning that the author clearly expresses the major point. If the main idea is stated, it can usually be found in one specific sentence.

Implied Main Idea. Sometimes, however, the main idea is not stated directly but is implied, or suggested, instead. In this case, you have to figure out the main idea by analyzing the meaning of the details you are given and deciding what overall meaning these details combine to express.

HOW TO FIND THE MAIN IDEA

- Skim the passage. (What topic do the sentences have in common?)
- Identify the general topic. (What's the passage about?)
- Identify what the passage says about the topic. (What's the message of the passage as a whole?)
- Sum up the meaning of the passage in one clear sentence.
- Check back over the passage. (If you have correctly identified the main idea, all of the other details that are included in the passage will support this one main idea.)

 REFERENCE NOTE: For additional information on finding the main idea, whether stated or implied, see pages 68–70 and pages 76–77.

Reading to Find Relationships Among Details

To understand the meaning of a reading passage, you'll need to learn to recognize details and understand how they are related to the main idea and to each other.

FINDING RELATIONSHIPS AMONG DETAILS	
Identify specific details.	What details answer specific questions such as *Who? What? When? Where? Why?* and *How? (5W-How?* questions)?
Distinguish between fact and opinion.	What information can be proved true or false? What statements express a personal belief or attitude?
Identify similarities and differences.	Are there any details that are shown to be similar to or different from one another?
Understand cause and effect.	Is there any event that happened before and had an impact or effect on another?
Identify an order of organization.	In what kind of order are the details arranged—chronological order, spatial order, order of importance, or some other organizing pattern?

Reading Passage

Jade Snow Wong is a Chinese American woman who was able to start a flourishing pottery business because she refused to lose faith in herself and in her work. Born in 1922 in San Francisco, Jade Snow Wong attended San Francisco Junior College and Mills College, graduating in 1942. After working as a secretary during World War II, she began her pottery manufacturing business in 1946.

At first, Ms. Wong had difficulty finding a market for her pottery. Because her pottery was made from crude clay and was shaped much like the pots used by Chinese peasants, many people in the Chinese American community didn't appreciate it.

Sample Analysis

DETAIL: Where was Ms. Wong's home?
ANSWER: *She lived in the San Francisco area.*

FACT: When did Ms. Wong start her pottery business?
ANSWER: *1946*

OPINION: What did some Chinese Americans think of Ms. Wong's pottery?
ANSWER: *They scorned her work.*

SIMILARITY: How was Ms. Wong's work like that of Chinese peasants?

RESOURCES

If they weren't interested in her pots, who would be?

But Ms. Wong did not give up. She received good advice from another Chinese artist. The artist explained to Ms. Wong his opinion that good art is rarely popular with the majority of people. He thought Ms. Wong would have to be persistent about finding and cultivating an audience for her work. She took this advice and continued to produce and promote her pottery.

In time, Jade Snow Wong found her audience. San Franciscans outside the Chinese American community loved her traditional Chinese pottery for its simplicity and understated beauty. Soon her pottery business was thriving and her work became highly regarded. Ms. Wong's pottery has since been awarded regional and national prizes, and many of her pieces have been added to museum collections. Jade Snow Wong's faith in her work was richly rewarded.

ANSWER: *It was shaped similarly and made from similar materials.*

CAUSE AND EFFECT: What was the effect of the Chinese artist's advice?
ANSWER: *Ms. Wong decided to continue to search for a receptive audience for her work.*

ORDER: How are the details arranged in this passage?
ANSWER: *The details in the passage are arranged in chronological order.*

Applying Reasoning Skills to Your Reading

It's important to gather evidence and facts from your reading, evaluate this information, and interpret it. When you are drawing *conclusions,* you come to decisions by reasoning from clearly expressed facts and evidence.

When you are making *inferences,* you come to decisions by reasoning from evidence that is only hinted at or implied.

For example, based on your analysis of the reading passage on pages 951–952, you might make the following conclusions or inferences about the character of Jade Snow Wong.

RESOURCES

Ms. Wong does not give up easily. (Evidence: She refused to give up on her pottery when she ran into early difficulties.)

Ms. Wong has confidence in herself and in her art. (Evidence: She was determined to find an appreciative audience for her art even though her type of pottery had not yet been popularly appreciated.)

A *valid conclusion* is one that is firmly grounded in facts, evidence, or logic. But an *invalid conclusion* is one that isn't really reasonable or logical based on the evidence. For example, it is invalid to conclude that Ms. Wong's success is due primarily to luck. This conclusion is not consistent with facts in the reading passage, such as Ms. Wong's persistence and devotion to her work.

When you draw conclusions and make inferences, you are doing what a detective does to solve a mystery.

HOW TO DRAW CONCLUSIONS OR MAKE INFERENCES	
Gather all the evidence.	What facts or details have you learned about the subject?
Evaluate the evidence.	Do you know enough to add things up without jumping to conclusions or assuming things that you can't prove?
Make appropriate connections.	What can you reasonably conclude or infer from the evidence you have gathered and evaluated?

Reading Graphics and Illustrations

Many of your textbooks and many newspaper and magazine articles include visuals such as diagrams, maps, graphs, and illustrations. These graphics make information clearer and more understandable.

Detailed information presented in paragraph form is often difficult to read and to remember, while graphs or diagrams are often much easier to understand. Graphics and illustrations help you understand the relationships between one set of facts and another. For example, the bar graph below shows how many hours a week different age groups watch television.

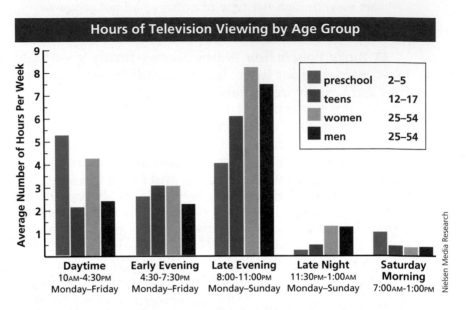

Hours of Television Viewing by Age Group

From this graph you can quickly see relationships between various age groups and the hours they spend watching television.

Suppose you were a motion picture producer who wanted to advertise a new movie written for audiences between the ages of twelve and seventeen years old. By looking at the graph, you could see that the best time to run your advertisement would be during the late evening hours, 8:00 P.M. to 11:00 P.M., Monday through Sunday. As the graph shows, this is the time that most teens watch television.

Should you run your advertisement in the daytime between 10:00 A.M. and 4:30 P.M.? As the graph illustrates, your movie's intended audience only watches approximately two hours of television during this time period. Why? As you might infer, this is the time that teens between the ages of twelve and seventeen are in school.

Graphs such as the one shown, therefore, help you make decisions more easily because you can actually see complex relationships between items of data.

Applying Study and Reading Strategies

Study and reading strategies are ways of organizing and handling information. There are a variety of strategies, but some of the most common are

- taking notes
- classifying
- organizing information visually
- outlining
- paraphrasing
- summarizing
- memorizing

Taking Notes

Careful note taking while reading or listening to a lecture helps you organize information for studying, taking tests, and writing research papers.

HOW TO TAKE STUDY NOTES	
Recognize and record main points.	Set off main points as headings in your notes. ■ In a lecture, listen for key words and phrases used by the speaker, such as *major* or *most important.* These words, as well as similar verbal clues, may indicate key points that you should take note of. ■ In a textbook, watch for chapter headings, subheadings, lists, charts, or time lines. These often give reliable clues to help you identify main ideas.
Summarize.	Don't record every detail. Summarize or abbreviate, using single words or phrases to record key ideas. Indent supporting points.
Note important examples.	You might make note of a few vivid examples used to support a major idea. These details can help you remember main points.

Look at the following example. These are study notes that a careful student might make about the Reading Passage on pages 951–952. The student who made these notes identified the main points in the passage and then listed these main points in groups. Notice that each of the groups of main points has a heading that identifies the key idea.

Jade Snow Wong

Biography

- Chinese American
- born in 1922 in San Francisco
- attended San Francisco Junior College
- graduated from Mills College in 1942
- secretary during World War II
- began pottery business in 1946

Art

- her pottery not accepted at first
- considered too crude, like peasant pots

Perseverance

- received good advice (good art rarely
  popular with majority)
- continued producing pottery

Success

- pottery sold outside her native community
- people loved Chinese simplicity,
  understated beauty
- business soon thriving, work highly regarded
- awarded regional and national prizes
- pottery placed in museums

Classifying

Classification is a method of organizing by arranging items into categories. You use classification when you make an outline, deciding which ideas fit together under a certain heading. When you group things, you identify relationships among them.

EXAMPLE   What do the following items have in common?
grapefruit, lemons, bananas, pears

ANSWER   They are all fruits with yellow-colored peels.

You also use classifying when you identify patterns. For example, look at the relationship between the following sequence of numbers.

What's the next number in the series?

1   5   10   16   23   _____?_____

ANSWER   To the first number, *1, 4* is added to produce the second number, *5.* To the second number, *5* is added; *6* is added to the third; and *7* to the fourth. Therefore, *8* should be added to the fifth number, *23,* to produce the next number in the series, which should be *31.*

Organizing Information Visually

Mapping, diagraming, and charting are techniques that allow you to organize new information so that it is visually presented. This makes the ideas easier to understand.

For example, the passage that follows compares and contrasts two sports.

> If you are familiar with baseball, you'll find some aspects of the British sport of cricket to be similar. In both sports, there is a large playing field with one team at bat and the opposing team in the field. In baseball, the object of the game is to hit the ball and run around all four bases. In cricket, the object is to score runs

between the two wickets and to prevent the opposing team from knocking the wicket down with the ball.

In each sport there are two teams. There are nine members per team in baseball, eleven in cricket. In each sport there are innings. In baseball, there are usually nine innings with three outs per team, while in cricket there are usually two innings with ten outs for each team.

It would be very difficult to read this passage and try to explain or remember all the details. However, you can organize the information visually in a chart like the one below. This method allows you to place items that relate to one another side by side and helps to make the information in the paragraph easier to remember. Other methods, such as mapping or diagraming, can also be used.

BASEBALL	CRICKET
large playing field	same
1 team at bat, 1 in field	same
four bases	two wickets
object: hit ball, score runs	same; plus prevent opponents from knocking wicket down with ball
9 players each team	11 players each team
9 innings, 3 outs per team	2 innings, 10 outs per team

Outlining

An *outline* can help you organize ideas and information. When you write an outline, you record important information and ideas. You also group these ideas in an organized pattern that shows their order and their relationship to one another.

FORMAL OUTLINE FORM

I. Main Point
  A. Supporting Point
    1. Detail
      a. Information
        or detail

If you are taking lecture notes, however, you might want to use informal outline form. This method helps you organize information quickly. (See the sample notes on page 956.)

INFORMAL OUTLINE FORM
Main Idea
Supporting detail
Supporting detail
Supporting detail

Paraphrasing

A *paraphrase* is a restatement of someone else's ideas in your own words. Paraphrasing is a good way to check your understanding of what you read. A written paraphrase is often approximately the same length as the original.

As you read materials that are difficult to understand, paraphrase by putting them into your own words. Your paraphrase might include dialect or slang expressions, if these are more familiar to you.

In language arts classes, you may be asked to paraphrase a short passage or a poem. Here is an example.

Bribe
by Pat Mora

I hear Indian women
   chanting, chanting
I see them long ago bribing
the desert with turquoise threads,
in the silent morning coolness,
kneeling, digging, burying
their offering in the Land
   chanting, chanting
     Guide my hands, Mother,
     to weave singing birds
     flowers rocking in the wind, to trap
     them on my cloth with a web of thin threads.

Secretly I scratch a hole in the desert
by my home. I bury a ballpoint pen
and lined yellowing paper. Like the Indians
I ask the Land to smile on me, to croon
softly, to help me catch her music with words.

RESOURCES

As an example, here is a possible paraphrase of the poem.

> The speaker in the poem is remembering Indian women's ritual songs. These women were offering turquoise threads to the desert. The ritual was performed early in the morning. On their knees, these women would bury the threads in the ground. They sang as they gave the threads to the Land. In their song they asked the Land, calling it Mother, to give its beauty to their cloth in exchange for the threads. They wanted to capture the birds and flowers in their weaving.
>
> Remembering this, the speaker buries his or her own pen and paper. The speaker makes this offering, asking in a song for the Land to allow its music to be captured in the speaker's poetry.

Use the following guidelines to help you when you write a paraphrase.

HOW TO PARAPHRASE

1. Read or listen carefully before you begin.
2. Be sure you understand what the material means. Look up any unfamiliar words.
3. Identify the main idea of the selection. Keep it in mind while you write your paraphrase.
4. Identify the speaker in fictional material. (Is the poet or author speaking, or is it a narrator or a character?)
5. Write your paraphrase in your own words, using complete sentences and traditional paragraph form.
6. Check to be sure that your paraphrase expresses the same ideas as the original.

You will use paraphrasing when you write research reports. To avoid *plagiarism,* remember that you must cite your sources when you use someone else's ideas.

☞ REFERENCE NOTE: For more about paraphrasing in research reports, see pages 385–386.

Summarizing

A *summary* is a restatement in condensed form of the main points of a passage. A summary (sometimes called a *précis*) is a useful way to record the most important points of the material you are studying. Writing a summary makes you think critically about what you read because, in writing the summary, you must analyze the material. You decide what is most important and should be included in the summary or what can be left out.

HOW TO SUMMARIZE

1. Review the material and identify the main ideas.
2. Reread the passage and look for supporting details.
3. Write a sentence in your own words about each main idea. Try to write one sentence for each major point in the original.
4. Use your numbered list of sentences to write your summary in paragraph form. Use transitional words between the ideas to show how the ideas are related.
5. Evaluate and revise your summary, checking to see if your summary covers the most important points. Make sure that the information is clearly expressed and that your readers can follow your ideas.

Here is a sample summary of the article on pages 364–366.

Humans have involuntary defensive reactions that help fight severe chilling of the body. One reaction is called "blood shunting." Human nerves respond effectively to cold. When the body senses dangerous loss of heat, it reacts quickly. The body constricts blood vessels and maintains blood flow only to the essential central organs. At the same time, the body greatly lessens the flow of blood to the outer portions of the body. Blood shunting interests medical researchers because it is apparently an evolutionary holdover that has contributed to helping some people survive exposure to low temperatures by using less energy.

Memorizing

To memorize and remember what you have learned, you should practice in frequent, short, focused sessions. You are more likely to retain information if you follow these guidelines.

HOW TO MEMORIZE	
Condense the information, if possible.	If you're studying a chapter, the information can often be summarized or condensed.
Rehearse the material in several different ways.	Use several different senses. Write or copy the material so you can see it as well as touch it. Say it out loud so you can hear it.
Play memory games.	Make a word out of the initials of key terms, or try other ways to make them memorable.

Improving Test-Taking Skills

Preparing for Different Kinds of Tests

One of the most important factors in doing well on a test is your attitude. Most people feel nervous before a big test. However, those who do well have learned to channel their nervous energy in ways that help them.

HOW TO PREPARE FOR A TEST
Analyze your attitude. Make sure you have studied thoroughly. Decide early what you most need to do, and then prepare to the best of your ability.
Focus on the positive. Be confident. If you have studied for the test, you know you have prepared. During the test, focus only on reading and answering the questions.
Make a commitment. Be determined to keep trying. Know that you can find the right method for improving your study effectiveness.

The two basic types of test questions are objective and essay questions. There are strategies you can learn that will help you prepare for each of these types of test questions.

Objective Tests

Objective tests may contain many forms of questions: multiple-choice, true/false, matching, reasoning or logic, analogy, or short-answer questions. Even though they appear in different forms, objective questions usually have only one correct answer. You will need to prepare by identifying and reviewing the specific information that will be included in the test. Look over the study skills listed earlier in this chapter. Almost all of them will help you prepare for objective limited-response tests.

HOW TO STUDY FOR OBJECTIVE TESTS

1. Look through the study questions in your textbook. Be sure you know the answers. Review your class notes to identify important terms or facts that you should know.
2. Review the information in more than one form. For example, you may be responsible for knowing a number of important terms. List these terms. Then test yourself on how well you can define each one without looking at your book or notes.
3. Practice and repeat factual information. Use flashcards, or ask someone to read definitions to you to see if you can remember the correct terms. Identify names of important people, places, events, ideas, or dates. Note which items you have difficulty with, and go over these items again.
4. If possible, review all the terms once more, shortly before the actual test.

RESOURCES

For some types of objective tests, you may have to adapt your study strategies a little. For example, if your test will include labeling diagrams or a map, test yourself by labeling a practice version of the diagram or map that you may be asked to label for the actual test. If problem solving of some sort will be included, do practice problems and then check your answers with the book.

Taking Different Kinds of Objective Tests

When you begin to take an objective test, quickly scan the test to see how many test items there are. This will help you decide how to budget your time as you go along. For each type of objective test, you can use specific, effective strategies.

Multiple-Choice Questions. This type of test question asks you to select a correct answer from among a number of choices.

EXAMPLE **1.** After working as a secretary during World War II, in 1946 Jade Snow Wong
    Ⓐ started a pottery manufacturing business.
    B enrolled at Mills College.
    C was awarded prizes for her pottery.
    D started a family.

HOW TO ANSWER MULTIPLE-CHOICE QUESTIONS	
Read the initial statement carefully.	■ Make sure you understand this statement before examining the choices. ■ Look for qualifiers such as *not* or *always* because these limit the answers.
Read all the answers before making a choice.	■ Narrow the choices by eliminating incorrect answers. Some are clearly wrong, while others are somewhat related to the correct answer. ■ Seek the most correct choice. Sometimes the correct answer includes two or more choices (such as "Both A and B" or "All of the above").

True/False Questions. This type of test question asks you to determine whether a given statement is true or false.

EXAMPLE **1.** T Ⓕ Women aged twenty-five to fifty-four always watch more hours of television than any other age group.

HOW TO ANSWER TRUE/FALSE QUESTIONS	
Read the statement carefully.	■ If any part of the statement is false, the whole statement is false.
Check for qualifiers.	■ Words such as *always* or *never* qualify or limit a statement. ■ A statement is true only if it is entirely and always true.

Matching Questions.   In matching questions, two lists are placed near each other so that you may match items on one list with those on the other.

Directions: Write the letter of the item described in the right-hand column into the blank space preceding the matching numbered item in the left-hand column.

<u>D</u> **1.** ten   **A** number of players on a cricket team
<u>C</u> **2.** nine   **B** number of cricket wickets
<u>A</u> **3.** eleven   **C** number of players on a baseball team
<u>B</u> **4.** two   **D** number of outs per inning in cricket

HOW TO ANSWER MATCHING QUESTIONS	
Read the directions carefully.	Sometimes answers may be used more than once.
Scan the columns, and match items you know first.	You can gain more time to evaluate items you are less sure about.
Complete the matching process.	Make your best guess on remaining items.

Reasoning or Logic Questions.   Some questions may test your reasoning abilities more than your knowledge of a specific subject. These questions often ask you to identify the relationship between several items (usually words, pictures, or numbers), or they may ask you to predict what the next item in a series would be.

Reasoning questions might ask you to identify a pattern in a number sequence (for example: 2, 4, 8, 16—these are powers of the number 2). Or you might be asked to predict the next item in a sequence of drawings.

RESOURCES

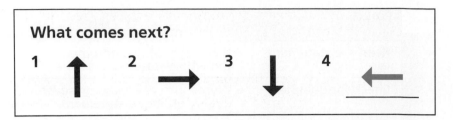

What comes next?

1   2   3   4

In this sequence of drawings, the arrows are moving in a clockwise sequence, so the next arrow would be pointing left.

HOW TO ANSWER REASONING OR LOGIC QUESTIONS	
Be sure you understand the instructions.	Reasoning or logic questions are usually multiple-choice. Sometimes, however, you may need to write a word or phrase, write out a number sequence, or draw a picture for your answer.
Analyze the relationship implied in the question.	Look at the question carefully to gather information about the relationship of the items.
Draw reasonable conclusions.	Evaluate the relationship of the items to decide your answer.

Analogy Questions. Analogy questions are special types of reasoning and logic questions. Analogy questions ask you to analyze the relationship between one pair of words and to identify or to supply a second pair of words that has the same relationship.

Analogy questions usually appear on standardized tests in multiple-choice form.

EXAMPLE **1.** Directions: Select the appropriate pair of words to complete the analogy.

HAND : ARM :: _____
A toe : finger
B foot : leg
C teeth : eyes
D bowl : spoon

Sometimes, however, analogies are written as fill-in-the-blank questions, and you may need to give the missing item.

EXAMPLE **2.** Directions: Complete the following analogy.

HAMMER : NAIL :: stapler : _____*staple*_____

HOW TO ANSWER ANALOGY QUESTIONS	
Analyze the first pair of words.	Identify the relationship between the first two items. (In Example 1 on page 966, the relationship between a hand and an arm is a part to a whole. A hand is one of the parts of a whole arm.) See the Analogy Chart below.
Express the analogy in sentence or question form.	The first example on page 966 could be read as "A *hand* has the same relationship to an *arm* as . . . (what other pair of items among the choices given?)."
Find the best available choice to complete the analogy.	■ If multiple choices are given, select the pair of words that has the same type of relationship between them as the first pair given in the question. ■ If you are supposed to fill in the blank to complete the analogy, you are often given one word of the second pair of items and you are expected to supply the final word. (In Example 2, above, a *hammer* is a tool that is used with a *nail*. With a *stapler*, you would use a *staple*.)

RESOURCES

ANALOGY CHART		
TYPE	EXAMPLE	SOLUTION
Synonyms	DRY : ARID : : horrid : ghastly	*Dry* is similar in meaning to *arid,* just as *horrid* is similar in meaning to *ghastly.*

(continued)

ANALOGY CHART *(continued)*		
TYPE	EXAMPLE	SOLUTION
Antonyms	ETHICAL : IMMORAL : : compassionate : cruel	*Ethical* behavior is the opposite of *immoral* behavior, just as *compassionate* behavior is the opposite of *cruel* behavior.
Cause	ACCIDENT : SADNESS : : gift : joy	An *accident* causes *sadness*, just as a *gift* causes *joy*.
Effect	SORROW : WAR : : happiness : peace	*Sorrow* is the effect of *war*, just as *happiness* is the effect of *peace*.
Part to whole	CHAPTER : BOOK : : act : play	A *chapter* is part of a *book*, just as an *act* is part of a *play*.
Whole to part	POEM : STANZAS : : play : acts	A *poem* consists of *stanzas*, just as a *play* consists of *acts*.
Classification	SPIDER : ARACHNID : : frog : amphibian	A *spider* is part of the *arachnid* class, just as a *frog* is part of the *amphibian* class.
Characteristic	LIONS : CARNIVOROUS : : cows : herbivorous	*Lions* are always *carnivorous* (meat eaters), just as *cows* are always *herbivorous* (plant eaters).
Degree	CHUCKLE : LAUGH : : whimper : cry	A *chuckle* is a little *laugh*, just as a *whimper* is a little *cry*.
Use	BOW : VIOLIN : : keyboard : computer	A *bow* is used to play the *violin*, just as a *keyboard* is used to operate a *computer*.

(continued)

RESOURCES

ANALOGY CHART *(continued)*		
TYPE	EXAMPLE	SOLUTION
Measure	THERMOMETER : TEMPERATURE : : clock : time	A *thermometer* is used to measure *temperature*, just as a *clock* is used to measure *time*.
Action to performer	STONECUTTING : MASON : : sewing : tailor	*Stonecutting* is performed by a *mason*, just as *sewing* is done by a *tailor*.
Performer to action	DOCTOR : HEAL : : pilot : fly	A *doctor* performs actions to *heal*, just as a *pilot* performs actions to *fly*.
Place	NEW ORLEANS : LOUISIANA : : Louisiana : United States	*New Orleans* is located in *Louisiana*, just as *Louisiana* is located in the *United States*.

Short-Answer Questions. Short-answer questions require you to demonstrate your knowledge in short, precise answers. These are similar to other objective questions because they usually have only one correct answer. However, you do not choose an answer. You have to write the response yourself.

Some short-answer questions (such as a map or diagram that you are supposed to label, or fill-in-the-blank questions) can be answered with one or a few words. Another type of short-answer question requires a full response, usually one or two sentences in length. These questions, like the example below, may have more than one part.

EXAMPLE   What type of art did Jade Snow Wong create, and what group of people were her major customers?

ANSWER   *Jade Snow Wong created pottery that was influenced by her Chinese American heritage. She discovered an audience for her pottery by selling her artworks to an admiring American public.*

HOW TO RESPOND TO SHORT-ANSWER QUESTIONS	
Read the question carefully.	Some questions have more than one part, and you will have to include an answer to each part to receive full credit.
Plan your answer.	Briefly, decide what you need to include in the answer.
Be as specific as possible in your answers.	Give a full, exact answer.
Budget your time.	Begin by answering first those questions you are certain about. Return later to the questions you are less sure about.

Essay Tests

Essay tests require you to think critically about material you have learned and to express your understanding of that material in an organized way. You will be expected to write at least a full paragraph, perhaps several paragraphs. The length of essay answers may vary, but you will need to cover the major points asked for in the question.

HOW TO STUDY FOR ESSAY TESTS
1. Read your textbook carefully.
2. Make an outline, identifying main points and important details.
3. Make a practice set of possible questions, and practice writing out the answers.
4. Evaluate and revise your practice answers, checking your notes and textbook for accuracy and the composition section of this book for help in writing.

Taking Essay Tests

When you begin an essay test, quickly scan the questions. Determine how many answers you are expected to write.

If you can choose from several items, decide which one or ones you think you can answer best. Then, plan how much time to spend on each answer, and stay on this schedule.

Read the question carefully. There may be several parts to the answer.

Pay attention to important terms in the question. Essay questions on tests usually ask you to perform specific tasks. Each of these tasks is expressed with a verb. You can prepare for essay tests by becoming familiar with the key verbs and the tasks that you will need to accomplish in a good essay response.

ESSAY TEST QUESTIONS		
KEY VERB	**TASK**	**SAMPLE QUESTION**
argue	Take a viewpoint on an issue and give reasons to support this opinion.	Argue whether or not the school year should be extended to twelve months.
analyze	Take something apart to see how each part works.	Analyze the relationships in an ecosystem.
compare	Point out likenesses.	Compare Martin Luther King, Jr., and Mohandas K. Gandhi as civil rights leaders.
contrast	Point out differences.	Contrast the description of Mme. Loisel's personality at the beginning and at the end of "The Necklace."
define (or identify)	Give specific details that make something unique.	Define the term *federalism* as it applies to the foundations of the U.S. Constitution.
demonstrate (also show, illustrate, or present)	Provide examples to support a point.	Demonstrate that Romeo's major flaw is his haste.

(continued)

RESOURCES

ESSAY TEST QUESTIONS *(continued)*		
KEY VERB	TASK	SAMPLE QUESTION
describe (in the sense of presenting explicit details)	Give a picture in words.	Describe the insane behavior that reveals the madness of the main character in Poe's "The Tell-Tale Heart."
describe (in the sense of giving details in a list; other words may include develop, list, outline, or trace)	Give a complete series of steps in order or a complete list of details about a subject.	Describe the events leading up to Romeo's meeting with Juliet in the balcony scene of *Romeo and Juliet.*
discuss	Examine in detail.	Discuss the term *separation of powers.*
explain (or interpret)	Give reasons or make the meaning clear.	Explain the development of the two-party political system.
summarize	Give a brief overview of the main points.	Summarize the "greenhouse effect."

Take a moment to use prewriting strategies. After considering the key verbs in the question, you can make notes or an outline to help you decide what you want to say. Write notes or a rough outline on scratch paper.

Evaluate and revise as you write. You may not be able to redraft your whole essay, but you can edit your essay to strengthen it.

QUALITIES OF A GOOD ESSAY ANSWER

- The essay is well organized.
- The main ideas and supporting points are clearly presented.
- The sentences are complete and well written.
- There are no distracting errors in spelling, punctuation, or grammar.

Review

▶ EXERCISE 1 **Choosing an Appropriate Reading Rate**

Identify the reading rate that best fits each of the given situations.

1. There will be a 100-question multiple-choice test next week on a chapter that you have not yet read in your history textbook.
2. You are playing a new board game, and you can't remember the rule about how you are supposed to make a particular move.
3. You have been assigned to read the novel *Shane* for your English class.
4. You have ten minutes to review your notes before a test.
5. You want to find, in your biology textbook, the name of the man who discovered the existence of recessive and dominant genes.

▶ EXERCISE 2 **Applying the SQ3R Reading Method**

Use the SQ3R method explained on page 949 while reading a newspaper article or a chapter that you need to read for a class. List at least five questions about your reading. Then, write a brief answer to each question.

▶ EXERCISE 3 **Reading: Analyzing Details in a Passage**

Answer the following questions about the reading passage on pages 951–952.

1. Give two facts or details about Jade Snow Wong (other than those already noted in the Sample Analysis).
2. What aspects of Ms. Wong's pottery making caused the Chinese American community to disregard her early work?
3. What was the Chinese artist's opinion about the path Ms. Wong might have to take for her art to be appreciated?

RESOURCES

4. In regard to Ms. Wong's pottery, how was the opinion of the Chinese American community different from the opinion of San Franciscans outside that community?

5. Give two facts that indicate that Ms. Wong's pottery making has been successful.

> EXERCISE 4 **Reading: Drawing Conclusions and Making Inferences**

Using the reading passage on pages 951–952, identify the evidence or reasoning you might use to make the following inferences or draw the following conclusions.

1. Even though Ms. Wong was frustrated at first, she was encouraged after talking to the Chinese artist.
2. Ms. Wong listened to the advice of the Chinese artist.
3. When a person faces an obstacle, he or she should not lose heart.

> EXERCISE 5 **Reading: Interpreting Graphic Information**

A. Using the graph on page 954, answer the following questions.

1. How many hours a week does the average teen between the ages of twelve and seventeen watch daytime television?
2. How much difference is there between the amount of late evening television watched by men of twenty-five to fifty-four and the amount watched by preschool children?
3. In what time slot does overall television viewing drop to its lowest level?
4. In what time slot is overall viewing at its highest?
5. Which group views more television than any other group?

B. Make inferences from the graph, considering factors such as school hours, bedtimes, working hours, and time spent at home.

6. What is a possible reason for the difference between the number of late evening viewing hours for an adult and for a preschool child?

7. Why might women of twenty-five to fifty-four view more television in the late evening?
8. Give a possible explanation for the fact that daytime and Saturday morning is when preschoolers lead in number of viewing hours.

▶ EXERCISE 6   **Analyzing Your Note-Taking Method**

For one day, take notes in all of your classes by using the techniques suggested on page 955. Write a paragraph, comparing and contrasting your usual method and this new method. Which works better? Why?

▶ EXERCISE 7   **Identifying Classifications**

For each of the following groups, identify the category.

1. Spain, France, Germany, Denmark, Italy
2. heavy sweaters, woolen caps, down-filled coats, padded boots
3. 2, 8, 10, 14, 22, 100
4. ouch, oh, rats, gee, wow
5. monkeys, dogs, whales, mice, bats

▶ EXERCISE 8   **Reading: Applying Visual Organization**

After reading the paragraph below, draw a visually organized representation of its contents. Use your graphic to answer the numbered questions.

How do we get rain? The cycle of water follows five steps. First, the water is drawn from the environment by means of evaporation. While we usually think of water as coming from the ocean, it may also be drawn from rivers, lakes, and even trees. Second, warm masses of air and winds transport the water, which is now a vapor, across the earth. Third, when warm air meets colder air, the water turns from a vapor back into a liquid. Now clouds are formed. Fourth, the small drops become larger and raindrops are formed. Fifth, as the raindrops become too heavy, they fall. This precipitation is what we call rain.

RESOURCES

1. Besides the ocean, where does water come from during evaporation?
2. What happens during the second step of this process?
3. What happens to the vapor when warm air meets cold air?
4. What happens when raindrops become too heavy?

EXERCISE 9   **Reading: Paraphrasing a Poem**

Read the following short poem by Dorothy Parker. Then, write a paraphrase of the poem.

> ### One Perfect Rose
> by Dorothy Parker
>
> A single flow'r he sent me, since we met.
>   All tenderly his messenger he chose;
> Deep-hearted, pure, with scented dew still wet—
>   One perfect rose.
>
> I knew the language of the floweret;
>   "My fragile leaves," it said, "his heart enclose."
> Love long has taken for his amulet
>   One perfect rose.
>
> Why is it no one ever sent me yet
>   One perfect limousine, do you suppose?
> Ah no, it's always just my luck to get
>   One perfect rose.

EXERCISE 10   **Completing Analogies**

Consider the first relationship; then write the word that best indicates the second relationship so that it parallels the first. There may be more than one correct answer. (See pages 966–969.)

1. BASS : LOW : :
   soprano : _____
2. INTRODUCTION : CONCLUSION : :
   sunrise : _____
3. SUN : LIGHT : :
   eclipse : _____
4. ICE : COOLNESS : :
   fire : _____
5. HAND : FINGER : :
   tree : _____
6. RIB : SKELETAL SYSTEM : :
   bicep : _____

7. PANTHER : FELINE : :
   wolf : _____

8. HERMIT : SECLUDED : :
   scholar : _____

9. GIRL : WOMAN : :
   boy : _____

10. NEWARK : NEW JERSEY : :
    Nashville : _____

▶ EXERCISE 11   **Analyzing Essay Questions**

Identify the key verb(s) that states the specific task in each of the following essay questions. (See pages 971–972.) State briefly what you would need to do to answer the question.

1. Compare the scoring systems used in three different sports.
2. Show how the use of a first-person narrator helps create the controversial tone in the Toni Cade Bambara short story "My Delicate Heart Condition."
3. While many people consider comic books a waste of time, others claim that they are valuable in making less able readers more interested in reading, that they represent a legitimate popular art form, and that a collection can be a worthwhile economic investment. Argue your personal opinion about the value of comics, using specific examples.
4. List the commands in the BASIC programming language that will tell the computer to print your name on the screen five times.
5. Both "Loveliest of Trees" and "I Wandered Lonely as a Cloud" express delight in nature. Compare and contrast the two speakers' attitudes toward nature.
6. Trace the changes in the U.S. Constitution that affect the selection of the president.
7. Analyze the economic conditions that helped cause the Civil War. Include at least three factors.
8. Summarize the steps involved in making a bill become a law.
9. Compare the military abilities of General Custer and of Chief Sitting Bull.
10. There have been cockroaches since the days of the dinosaurs. Describe some of the characteristics that make this insect such a good survivor.

RESOURCES

DIAGRAMING SENTENCES

A *sentence diagram* is a picture of how the parts of a sentence fit together and how the words in a sentence are related.

Subjects and Verbs (pages 502–510)

The sentence diagram begins with a horizontal line intersected by a short vertical line, which divides the complete subject from the complete predicate.

EXAMPLE   Fish swim.

Fish	swim

Understood Subjects (page 513)

EXAMPLE   Wait!

(you)	Wait

Nouns of Direct Address (page 513)

EXAMPLE   Sit, **Fido.**

Fido

(you)	Sit

Sentences Beginning with *There* or *Here* (page 511)

EXAMPLE **There** is a fly in my soup.

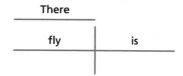

Compound Subjects (page 514)

EXAMPLE **Carmen** and **Basil** were fishing.

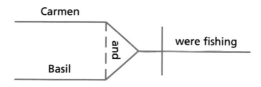

Compound Verbs (page 515)

EXAMPLE They **stopped** and **ate**.

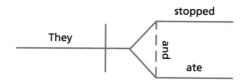

This is how a compound verb is diagramed when the helping verb is not repeated.

EXAMPLE They are **sitting** and **reading**.

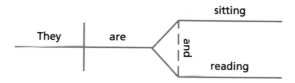

Compound Subjects and Compound Verbs (page 516)

EXAMPLE **Coaches** and **players jumped** and **cheered**.

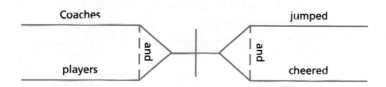

Sometimes parts of a compound subject or a compound verb will be joined by correlative conjunctions. Correlatives are diagramed like this:

EXAMPLE **Both** Bob **and** Teri can **not only** draw **but also** paint.

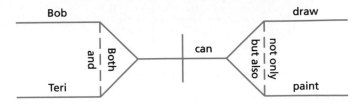

Adjectives and Adverbs (pages 472–475 and 485–489)

Both adjectives and adverbs are written on slanted lines connected to the words they modify.

EXAMPLE **That old** clock has **never** worked.

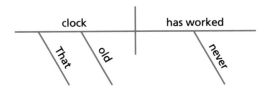

When an adverb modifies an adjective or an adverb, it is placed on a line connected to the word it modifies.

EXAMPLE This **specially** designed glass **very** seldom breaks.

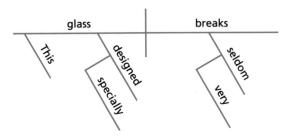

Notice the position of the modifiers in the example at the top of the next page.

EXAMPLE **Soon** Anne and **her** sister will graduate and will move.

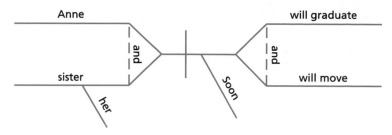

Her modifies only one part of the compound subject: *sister. Soon* modifies both parts of the compound verb: *will graduate* and *will move.*

When a conjunction joins two modifiers, it is diagramed like this:

EXAMPLE The **English** and **Australian** athletes worked **long** and **very hard.**

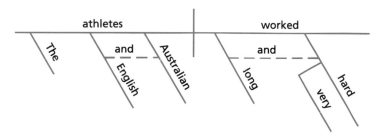

Subject Complements (page 519)

The subject complement is placed on the horizontal line with the subject and verb. It comes after the verb. A line *slanting toward the subject* separates the subject complement from the verb.

Predicate Nominatives (page 519)

EXAMPLE Cathedrals are **large churches.**

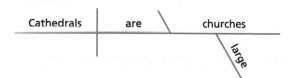

Predicate Adjectives (page 519)

EXAMPLE   Cathedrals are **large.**

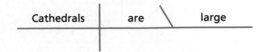

Compound Subject Complements (page 519)

EXAMPLE   My friend is **small** and **quiet.**

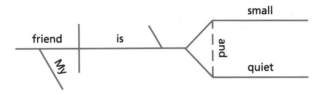

Objects (pages 522–524)

Direct Objects (page 522)

EXAMPLE   We like **music.**

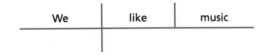

Notice that a vertical line separates the direct object from the verb.

Compound Direct Objects (page 524)

EXAMPLE   We like **plays** and **movies.**

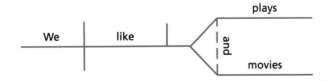

Indirect Objects (pages 523–524)

The indirect object is diagramed on a horizontal line beneath the verb.

EXAMPLE   Pete bought **Mario** a sandwich.

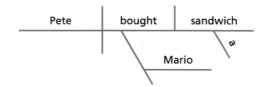

Compound Indirect Objects (page 524)

EXAMPLE   LaTonya gave her **family** and **friends** free tickets.

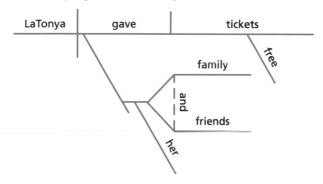

Phrases (pages 532–559)

Prepositional Phrases (pages 533–538)

The preposition is placed on a line slanting down from the word the phrase modifies. The object of the preposition is placed on a horizontal line connected to the slanting line.

EXAMPLES   **By chance,** a peasant uncovered a wall **of ancient Pompeii.** [adverb phrase modifying the verb; adjective phrase modifying the direct object]

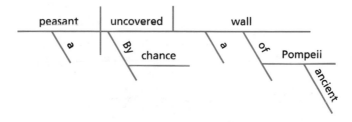

Our team practices late **in the afternoon.** [adverb
phrase modifying an adverb]

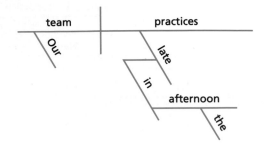

They drove **through the Maine woods** and **into
southern Canada.** [two phrases modifying the same
word]

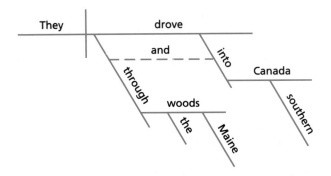

Mom taught the computer game **to my father, my
uncles, and me.** [compound object of preposition]

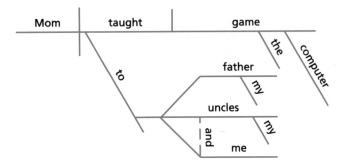

Follow the signs **to Highway 3 in Laconia.** [phrase modifying the object of another preposition]

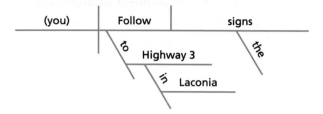

Participles and Participial Phrases (pages 541–545)

EXAMPLES   I found him **crying.**

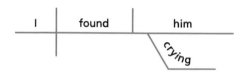

Wagging its tail, the large dog leaped at me.

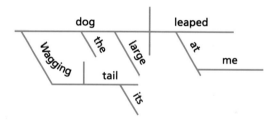

Gerunds and Gerund Phrases (pages 546–549)

EXAMPLES   **Walking** is healthful exercise. [gerund used as subject]

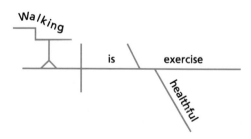

Being tired of the constant cold is a good reason for **taking a vacation in the winter.** [gerund phrases used as subject and as object of preposition]

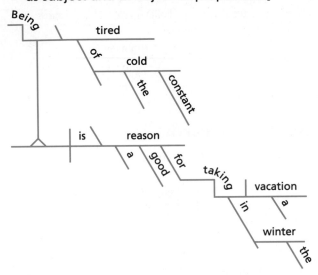

Infinitives and Infinitive Phrases (pages 550–552)

EXAMPLES   **To leave** would be rude. [infinitive used as subject]

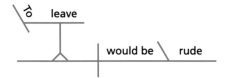

To join the Air Force is her longtime ambition. [infinitive phrase used as subject]

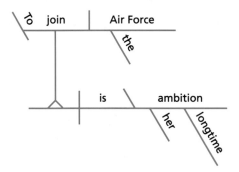

   Infinitives and infinitive phrases used as modifiers are diagramed like prepositional phrases.

EXAMPLES   I am leaving early **to get the tickets.** [infinitive phrase used as adverb]

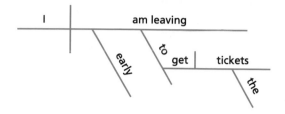

   Our brother helped us **play the game.** [infinitive phrase with subject, *us,* and *to* used as direct object, omitted]

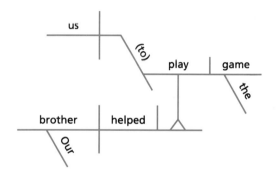

Appositives and Appositive Phrases (pages 556–557)

Place the appositive in parentheses after the word it identifies or explains.

EXAMPLES   My brother **Josh** is a drummer in the band.

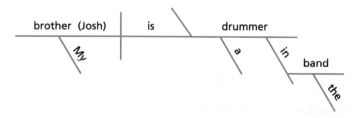

The next show, **a musical comedy about high school,** was written by Mike Williams, **a talented young playwright.**

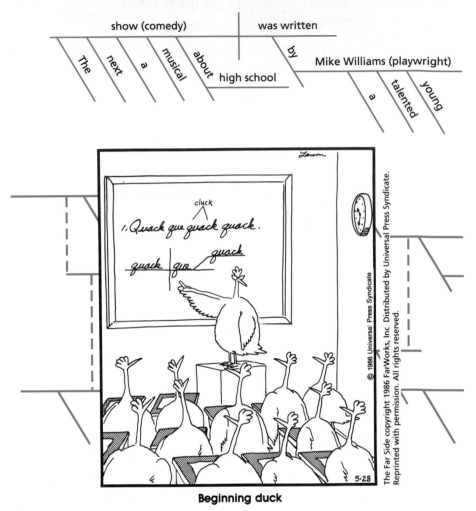

Beginning duck

Subordinate Clauses (pages 565–575)

Adjective Clauses (pages 567–568)

An adjective clause is joined to the word it modifies by a broken line leading from the relative pronoun to the modified word.

EXAMPLES   The restaurant **that we like best** serves excellent seafood.

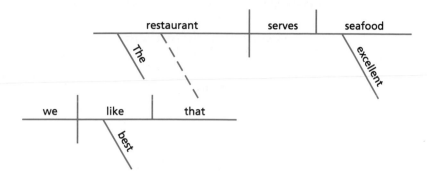

He is the teacher **from whom I take lessons.**

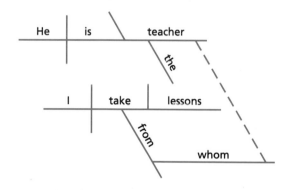

Adverb Clauses (pages 570–571)

Place the subordinating conjunction that introduces the adverb clause on a broken line leading from the verb in the adverb clause to the word the clause modifies.

EXAMPLE   **If you visit Texas,** you should see the Alamo.

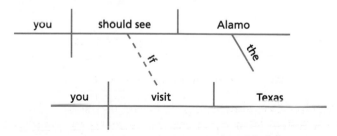

Noun Clauses (pages 574–575)

Noun clauses often begin with introductory words such as *that, what, who,* or *which.* These introductory words may have a function within the dependent clause, or they may simply connect the clause to the rest of the sentence. How a noun clause is diagramed depends upon its use in the sentence. It also depends on whether or not the introductory word has a specific function in the noun clause.

EXAMPLES **What you eat affects your health.** [The noun clause is used as the subject of the independent clause. The introductory word *what* functions as the direct object of the noun clause.]

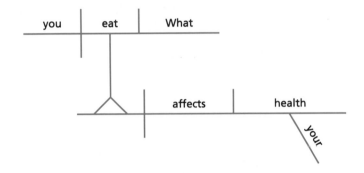

We strongly suspected that the cat was the thief. [The noun clause is the direct object of the independent clause. The introductory word *that* does not have a specific function within the noun clause.]

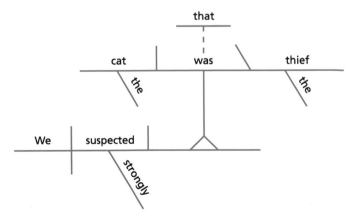

Sometimes the introductory word in a subordinate clause may be omitted. In the example at the bottom of the previous page, the word *that* can be left out: *We strongly suspected the cat was the thief.* To diagram this new sentence, simply omit the word *that* and the solid and broken lines under it from the diagram above. The rest of the diagram stays the same.

Sentences Classified According to Structure (pages 577–578)

Simple Sentences (page 577)

EXAMPLE   George Vancouver was exploring the Northwest.

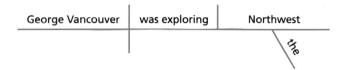

Compound Sentences (pages 577–578)

EXAMPLE   James Baldwin wrote many articles for magazines, but he is probably more famous for his novels.

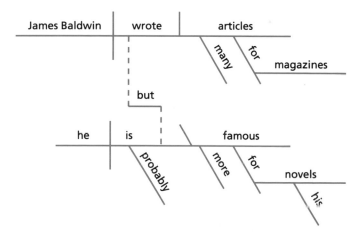

NOTE: If the compound sentence has a semicolon and no conjunction, place a straight broken line between the two verbs.

EXAMPLE   Baldwin was a distinguished essayist; his nonfiction works include *Notes of a Native Son.*

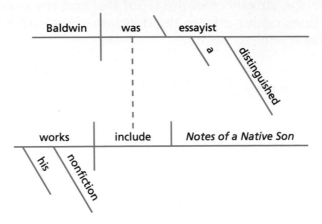

Complex Sentences (page 578)

EXAMPLE   Jaime Escalante always believed that his students could make high scores on the math achievement test.

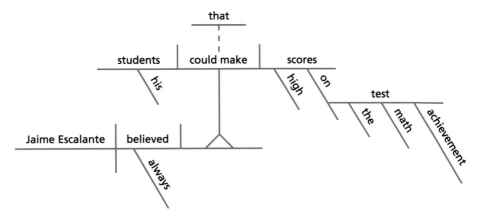

Compound-Complex Sentences (page 578)

EXAMPLE   Before her plane mysteriously disappeared in 1937,
Amelia Earhart had already forged the way for women
in aviation, and she was later recognized for her
achievements.

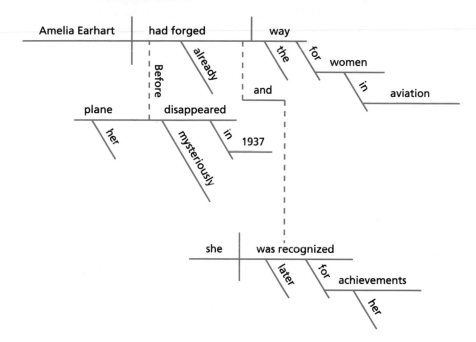

Glossary of Terms

Abstract noun An abstract noun names an idea, a feeling, a quality, or a characteristic. (See page 466.)

Action verb An action verb is a verb that expresses physical or mental activity. (See page 477.)

Active voice A verb in the active voice expresses an action done *by* its subject. (See page 633.)

Adjective An adjective is a word used to modify a noun or a pronoun. (See page 472.)

Adjective clause An adjective clause is a subordinate clause used as an adjective to modify a noun or a pronoun. (See page 567.)

Adjective phrase An adjective phrase is a prepositional phrase used as an adjective. (See page 535.)

Adverb An adverb is a word used to modify a verb, an adjective, or another adverb. (See page 485.)

Adverb clause An adverb clause is a subordinate clause that modifies a verb, an adjective, or an adverb. (See page 570.)

Adverb phrase An adverb phrase is a prepositional phrase used as an adverb to tell *when, where, how, why,* or *to what extent.* (See page 537.)

Agreement Agreement refers to the correspondence, or match, between grammatical forms. (See Chapter 18.)

Aim An aim is one of the four basic purposes, or reasons, for writing. (See page 7.)

Antecedent An antecedent is a word to which a pronoun refers. The antecedent usually comes before the pronoun and gives the pronoun its meaning. (See page 469.)

Antonym An antonym is a word that is opposite in meaning to another word. (See page 930.)

Appositive An appositive is a noun or a pronoun placed beside another noun or pronoun to identify or explain it. (See page 556.)

Appositive phrase An appositive phrase is made up of an appositive and its modifiers. (See page 556.)

Article *A, an,* and *the* are the most frequently used adjectives and are called articles. (See page 474.)

Audience An audience is the person(s) who reads or listens to what a writer or speaker says. (See pages 36 and 899.)

B

Base form The base form, or infinitive, is one of the four principal, or basic, parts of a verb. (See page 618.)

Body The body of a composition is one or more paragraphs that state and develop the composition's main points. (See page 124.)

Brainstorming Brainstorming is a technique for finding ideas by using free association. In brainstorming, a writer records every idea about a subject that comes to mind without stopping to evaluate any of the ideas. (See page 25.)

Business letter A business letter is a formal letter in which a writer might request or order something, complain about or seek the correction of a problem, or express appreciation for someone or something. (See page 937.)

C

Call number A call number is a number and letter code a library assigns to a book. The call number tells how the book has been classified and tells where it has been placed on the shelves. (See page 918.)

Chronological order Chronological order is a way of arranging ideas in a paragraph or composition by ordering them according to the time they happened. (See page 79.)

Classification Classification is a strategy of development in which a writer classifies a subject as it relates to other subjects in a group. (See page 94.)

Clause A clause is a group of words that contains a verb and its subject and is used as part of a sentence. (See page 564.)

Cliché A cliché is an overused, worn-out figure of speech. (See page 460.)

Clincher sentence A clincher sentence is the concluding sentence of a paragraph that pulls all the details together by restating or summarizing the main idea. (See page 75.)

Clustering Clustering is a visual technique for finding writing ideas and gathering information. The writer breaks a large subject into its smaller parts, creating a visual map of his or her thoughts. (See page 27.)

Coherence Coherence, in a paragraph or composition, is a quality achieved when all the ideas are clearly arranged and connected. (See pages 79 and 124.)

Collective noun A collective noun is a noun that is singular in form but names a *group* of persons or things. (See page 602.)

Colloquialism A colloquialism is an informal expression, many times a figure of speech, that is not meant to be taken literally. (See page 452.)

Comma splice A comma splice is a run-on sentence in which there is only a comma to separate complete sentences. (See page 415.)

Common noun A common noun names any one of a group of persons, places, or things and is not capitalized. (See pages 465 and 721.)

Comparative degree Comparative degree is the form a modifier takes when comparing two things. (See page 680.)

Complement A complement is a word or group of words that completes the meaning of a predicate. (See page 517.)

Complex sentence A complex sentence has one independent clause and at least one subordinate clause. (See page 578.)

Compound-complex sentence A compound-complex sentence contains two or more independent clauses and at least one subordinate clause. (See page 578.)

Compound noun A compound noun consists of two or more words used together as a single noun. (See page 467.)

Compound sentence A compound sentence has two or more independent clauses but no subordinate clauses. (See page 577.)

Compound subject A compound subject consists of two or more subjects that are joined by a conjunction and have the same verb. (See pages 514 and 597.)

Compound verb A compound verb consists of two or more verbs that are joined by a conjunction and have the same subject. (See page 515.)

Conclusion (1) A conclusion reinforces a main idea and brings a composition to a definite close. (See page 126.) **(2)** A conclusion is a decision or determination reached by reasoning from clearly expressed facts and evidence found in a reading passage or other materials. (See page 952.)

Concrete noun A concrete noun names an object that can be perceived by the senses. (See page 466.)

Conjunction A conjunction is a word used to join words or groups of words. (See page 493.)

Connotation The connotation of a word is a word's meanings suggested by or associated with that word. (See page 457.)

Context The context of a word includes the surrounding words and the way the word is used. (See page 930.)

Contraction A contraction is a shortened form of a word, a figure, or a group of words. Apostrophes in contractions indicate where letters or numerals have been omitted. (See pages 602 and 818.)

Creative writing Creative writing is writing that aims at creating literature: stories, poems, songs, and plays. (See page 7.)

Dangling modifier A dangling modifier is a modifying word, phrase, or clause that does not clearly and sensibly modify a word or a group of words in a sentence. (See page 686.)

Declarative sentence A declarative sentence makes a statement and is followed by a period. (See page 527.)

Denotation The denotation of a word is its direct, plainly expressed meaning—the meaning a dictionary lists. (See page 456.)

Description Description is a strategy of development in which a writer uses sensory details to describe something. (See pages 90 and 171.)

Dialect A dialect is a distinct version or variety of a language used by a particular group of people. (See page 442.)

Dialogue Dialogue is the "talk," or conversation, in a story. (See page 221.)

Direct object A direct object is a noun or pronoun that receives the action of the verb or shows the result of the action. It answers the question "Whom?" or "What?" after an action verb. (See page 522.)

Direct quotation A direct quotation is a reproduction of a person's exact words and is enclosed in quotation marks. (See pages 384 and 792.)

Direct reference A direct reference connects ideas in a paragraph or composition by referring to a noun or pronoun used earlier. (See pages 83 and 124.)

Double negative A double negative is the use of two negative words when one is sufficient. (See page 711.)

Early plan An early plan, sometimes called an **informal** or **rough outline,** is a writer's rough plan for a composition in which he or she groups and orders information. (See page 115.)

Emotional appeal An emotional appeal is a strategy used to support a writer's opinion and to persuade an audience by appealing to readers' feelings. (See page 298.)

End marks End marks are punctuation marks (periods, question marks, exclamation points) used to indicate the purpose of a sentence. (See page 741.)

Essay test An essay test is a test that requires a student to think critically about material learned and to express his or her understanding of that material in writing in an organized way. (See page 970.)

Essential clause/Essential phrase An essential (or **restrictive**) clause or phrase is one that is necessary to the meaning of a sentence. Commas are not used. (See page 567.)

Ethnic dialect An ethnic dialect is a distinct version of a language used by people who share the same cultural heritage. (See page 449.)

Euphemism A euphemism is an agreeable term that is substituted for a more direct, less pleasant-sounding one. (See page 458.)

Evaluating Evaluating is the stage in the writing process in which a writer goes over a draft, making judgments about its strengths and weaknesses in content, organization, and style. (See pages 6 and 21.)

Evaluation Evaluation is a strategy of development in which a writer makes judgments about a subject in an attempt to determine its value. (See page 97.)

Example An example is a specific instance, or illustration, of a general idea. (See page 73.)

Exclamatory sentence An exclamatory sentence expresses strong feeling and is followed by an exclamation point. (See page 528.)

Exposition *See* Informative writing.

Expressive writing Expressive writing is writing that aims at expressing a writer's feelings and thoughts. (See page 7.)

Extemporaneous speaking Extemporaneous speaking is a common method for giving a speech in which a speaker delivers a rehearsed but not memorized speech. (See page 900.)

Fact A fact is something that can be checked and proved to be true by concrete information. (See pages 72 and 291.)

Feedback Feedback is the reaction of a receiver to the message given by a sender during the communication process. (See page 896.)

Figure of speech Figures of speech are words that have meaning other than their literal ones. (See page 196.)

5W-How? questions The *5W-How?* questions—*Who? What? Where? When? Why? How?*—are questions a writer uses to collect information about a subject. (See page 29.)

Formal outline A formal outline is a highly structured, clearly labeled writing plan. It has a set pattern, using letters and numbers to label main headings and subheadings. (See pages 116 and 387.)

Freewriting Freewriting is a technique for finding ideas in which a writer writes whatever pops into his or her head without regard to form. (See page 24.)

Fused sentence A fused sentence is a run-on sentence in which there is no punctuation separating the run-together sentences. (See page 415.)

Gerund A gerund is a verb form ending in *–ing* that is used as a noun. (See page 546.)

Gerund phrase A gerund phrase contains a gerund and its modifiers or complements. (See page 548.)

Homonyms Homonyms are words that are spelled differently and mean different things, but are pronounced alike. (See page 850.)

"How-to" process writing "How-to" process writing is a form of writing in which a writer explains how to do something. (See page 254.)

Idiom An idiom is a phrase that means something different from the literal meaning of the words. (See page 455.)

Imperative sentence An imperative sentence gives a command or makes a request and is followed by either a period or an exclamation point. (See page 527.)

Impromptu speech An impromptu speech is a short speech made on the spur of the moment, with little or no time for development or preparation of ideas. (See page 897.)

Independent clause An independent (or **main**) clause is a group of words that contains a verb and its subject and expresses a complete thought. It can stand by itself. (See page 564.)

Indirect object An indirect object is a noun or pronoun that precedes a direct object and usually tells *to whom* or *for whom* (or *to what* or *for what*) the action of the verb is done. (See page 523.)

Indirect quotation An indirect quotation is a rewording or paraphrasing of something a person has said. (See page 792.)

Inference An inference is a decision or determination reached by reasoning from evidence that is hinted at or implied in a reading passage or other materials. (See page 952.)

Infinitive An infinitive is a verb form, usually preceded by *to*, that can be used as a noun, an adjective, or an adverb. (See page 550.)

Infinitive phrase An infinitive phrase consists of an infinitive together with its modifiers and complements. (See page 551.)

Informative writing Informative writing is writing that aims at conveying information or explaining something. (See page 7.)

Interjection An interjection is a word used to express emotion. It has no grammatical relation to the rest of the sentence. (See page 495.)

Interrogative sentence An interrogative sentence asks a question and is followed by a question mark. (See page 527.)

Interview An interview is a special listening situation with the specific purpose of gathering information. (See page 910.)

Intransitive verb An intransitive verb expresses action (or tells something about the subject) without passing the action from a doer to a receiver. (See page 478.)

Introduction An introduction begins a composition and should catch the reader's interest, set the composition's tone, and present the thesis statement. (See page 120.)

Invalid conclusion An invalid conclusion is a conclusion that isn't really reasonable or logical based on the available evidence. (See page 953.)

Irregular verb An irregular verb is a verb that forms its past and past participle in some other way than by adding *–d* or *–ed*. (See page 620.)

Jargon Jargon consists of words and phrases that have special meanings for particular groups of people. (See page 456.)

Linking verb A linking verb serves as a link between its subject and another word. (See page 480.)

Literary analysis A literary analysis is a form of writing in which a writer analyzes the elements, or parts, of a work such as a poem, a play, a novel, or a short story. (See Chapter 9.)

Loaded words Loaded words are words intended to provoke strong feeling, either positive or negative. (See page 457.)

Logical appeal A logical appeal is a strategy used to support a writer's opinion and to persuade an audience by appealing to reason. (See page 297.)

Logical order Logical order is a way of arranging details in a paragraph or composition according to what makes logical sense, such as grouping related ideas together. (See page 81.)

M

Main idea A main idea is the idea around which a paragraph or composition is organized. (See page 68.)

Mass media The mass media are forms of communication (television, radio, movies, newspapers, and magazines) that reach a large audience daily. (See page 913.)

Metaphor A metaphor is a figure of speech that directly compares two things without using the words *like* or *as*. A metaphor says that something *is* something else. (See page 196.)

Misplaced modifier A misplaced modifier is a word, phrase, or clause that sounds awkward because it modifies the wrong word or group of words. (See page 689.)

Mood Mood is the emotional effect of a story or poem. (See page 334.)

N

Narration Narration is a strategy of development in which a writer relates events or actions over a period of time, usually arranging ideas and information in chronological order. (See page 91.)

Nominative case Nominative case is the case a noun or pronoun takes as the subject of a sentence. Predicate nominatives also take this case. (See page 651.)

Nonessential clause/Nonessential phrase A nonessential (or **nonrestrictive**) clause or phrase adds information that is not necessary to the main idea in the sentence. It is set off by commas. (See page 750.)

Nonverbal communication Nonverbal communication is communicating a message without the use of verbal signals (words). (See page 897.)

Noun A noun is a word used to name a person, place, thing, or idea. (See page 465.)

Noun clause A noun clause is a subordinate clause used as a noun. (See page 574.)

Noun of direct address A noun of direct address identifies the person spoken to or addressed in a sentence. (See page 513.)

Number Number is the form of a word that indicates whether the word is singular or plural. (See page 589.)

O

Object An object is a complement that does not refer to the subject. (See page 522.)

Objective case Objective case is the case a noun or pronoun takes when used as a direct object, indirect object, and object of a preposition. (See page 654.)

Objective test An objective test is one that may contain multiple-choice, true/false, matching, reasoning or logic, analogy, or short-answer questions. It requires a student to give a specific, limited response. (See page 963.)

Object of a preposition The noun or pronoun that ends a prepositional phrase is the object of the preposition that begins the phrase. (See page 533.)

Opinion An opinion is a belief or attitude. Opinions vary from person to person. (See page 291.)

Oral interpretation Oral interpretation is an expressive presentation of a literary work to an audience, using vocal techniques, facial expressions, body language, and gestures. (See page 904.)

Order of importance Order of importance is a way of arranging details in a paragraph or composition according to the details' level of importance. Details can be arranged from least to most important or from most to least important. (See page 80.)

Parallel structure Parallel structure is the use of the same form or part of speech to express equal, or parallel, ideas in a sentence. (See page 432.)

Paraphrase A paraphrase is a restatement of someone's ideas in different words. (See pages 385 and 959.)

Parenthetical expression A parenthetical expression is a side remark that adds information or relates ideas. (See page 759.)

Parenthetical note A parenthetical note, or **citation,** is a form of documentation that places source information in parentheses at the end of a sentence in which someone else's word or ideas are used. (See page 390.)

Parliamentary procedure Parliamentary procedure is a plan for following a priority of actions that groups sometimes use to keep meetings running smoothly. (See page 903.)

Participial phrase A participial phrase is a phrase containing a participle and any complements or modifiers it may have. (See page 544.)

Participle A participle is a verb form that can be used as an adjective. (See page 541.)

Passive voice A verb in the passive voice expresses an action done *to* its subject. (See page 633.)

Personal letter A personal letter is an informal letter in which a writer might thank someone for something, invite someone to a particular event or occasion, or reply to an invitation. (See page 942.)

Personal narrative A personal narrative is a form of writing in which an author explores and shares the meaning of a personal experience. (See Chapter 4.)

Personification Personification is a writing technique in which human characteristics are given to nonhuman things. (See page 197.)

Persuasive essay A persuasive essay is a form of writing in which a writer supports an opinion and tries to persuade an audience. (See Chapter 8.)

Persuasive writing Persuasive writing is writing that aims at persuading people to change their minds about something or to act in a certain way. (See page 7.)

Phrase A phrase is a group of related words that is used as a single part of speech and does not contain both a predicate and its subject. (See page 532.)

Plagiarism Plagiarism is using someone else's words or ideas without giving credit for them. (See pages 377 and 384.)

Plot The plot is the series of events in a story that follow each other and cause each other to happen. (See pages 217 and 334.)

Point of view Point of view is the vantage point, or position, from which a writer tells a story. (See pages 213 and 335.)

Possessive case Possessive case is the case taken by a noun or pronoun when used to show ownership or relationship. (See pages 650 and 807.)

Predicate The predicate is the part of a sentence that says something about the subject. (See page 502.)

Predicate adjective A predicate adjective is an adjective in the predicate that modifies the subject of the sentence. (See page 519.)

Predicate nominative A predicate nominative is a noun or pronoun in the predicate that explains or identifies the subject of the sentence. (See page 519.)

Prefix A prefix is a word part that is added before a word root. (See page 933.)

Preposition A preposition is a word used to show the relationship of a noun or a pronoun to some other word in a sentence. (See page 491.)

Prepositional phrase A prepositional phrase is a group of words beginning with a preposition and ending with a noun or a pronoun. (See page 533.)

Prewriting Prewriting is the first stage in the writing process. In this stage, a writer thinks and plans, figures out what to write about, collects ideas and details, and makes a plan for presenting ideas. (See pages 6 and 22.)

Principal parts of a verb The principal parts of a verb are a verb's forms: the *base form*, the *present participle*, the *past*, and the *past participle*. The principal parts are used to form the verb tenses. (See page 618.)

Process explanation A process explanation is a form of writing in which a writer explains how something works or occurs. (See page 254.)

Pronoun A pronoun is a word used in place of a noun or more than one noun. (See page 469.)

Proofreading Proofreading is the stage of the writing process in which a writer carefully reads a revised draft to correct mistakes in grammar, usage, and mechanics. (See pages 6 and 56.)

Proper adjective A proper adjective is a modifier formed from a proper noun. (See page 721.)

Proper noun A proper noun names a particular person, place, or thing and is always capitalized. (See pages 465 and 721.)

Publishing Publishing is the last stage of the writing process. In this stage, a writer makes a final, clean copy of a paper and shares it with an audience. (See pages 6 and 58.)

Purpose Purpose is the reason for writing or speaking: to express yourself; to be creative; to entertain; to explain, inform, or explore; or to persuade. (See pages 36 and 898.)

R

Regional dialect A regional dialect is a distinct version of a language used by people in or from a particular geographical area. (See page 448.)

Regular verb A regular verb is a verb that forms its past and past participle by adding *-d* or *-ed* to the infinitive. (See page 618.)

Relative pronoun A relative pronoun (*who, whom, whose, which, that*) is a pronoun that relates an adjective clause to the word that the clause modifies. (See page 567.)

Research report A research report is a form of writing in which a writer presents factual information that he or she has discovered through exploration and research. (See Chapter 10.)

Revising Revising is the stage of the writing process in which a writer goes over a draft, making changes in its content, organization, and style in order to improve it. (See pages 6 and 51.)

Root A root is the base a word is built on. It carries the word's core meaning. (See page 932.)

Run-on sentence A run-on sentence is two or more complete sentences run together as one. (See page 415.)

S

Sensory details Sensory details are precise bits of information that a writer observes, or collects, through any of the five senses— sight, hearing, smell, touch, taste. (See pages 71 and 178.)

Sentence A sentence is a group of words that contains a subject and a verb and expresses a complete thought. (See pages 406 and 501.)

Sentence fragment A sentence fragment is a piece of a sentence that does not express a complete thought. (See pages 406 and 501.)

Setting The setting is where and when a story takes place. It may provide background for understanding characters and events, create the conflict, or create the mood in a story. (See pages 215 and 334.)

Simile A simile is a figure of speech that compares two basically unlike things, using the words *like* or *as*. (See page 196.)

Simple sentence A simple sentence has one independent clause and no subordinate clauses. It may have a compound subject, a compound verb, and any number of phrases. (See page 577.)

Slang Slang is a form of informal language that is made up of newly coined words or of old words used in unconventional ways. (See page 453.)

Source card A source card is an index card on which bibliographical information about a source is recorded. (See page 378.)

Spatial order Spatial order is a way of arranging details in a paragraph or composition by ordering them according to how they are spaced— nearest to farthest, left to right, and so on. (See page 80.)

Statistic A statistic is a fact that is based on numbers. (See page 72.)

Story map A story map is a written plan of the essential elements of a story. (See page 218.)

Stringy sentence A stringy sentence is a sentence that has too many independent clauses. Usually, the clauses are strung together with coordinating conjunctions like *and* or *but*. (See page 433.)

Subject The subject is the part of a sentence that names the person or thing spoken about in the rest of the sentence. (See page 502.)

Subject complement A subject complement is a noun, pronoun, or adjective that follows a linking verb. (See page 519.)

Subordinate clause A subordinate (or **dependent**) clause is a group of words that contains a verb and its subject but does not express a complete thought and cannot stand alone. (See page 565.)

Subordinating conjunction A subordinating conjunction is a conjunction used to introduce an adverb clause. (See page 571.)

Suffix A suffix is a word part that is added after a word root. (See page 934.)

Summary A summary is a restatement, in condensed form, of the main points of a passage. (See pages 385 and 961.)

Superlative degree Superlative degree is the form a modifier takes when comparing more than two things. (See page 680.)

Supporting sentences Supporting sentences give specific details or information to support a main idea. (See page 71.)

Syllable A syllable is a word part that can be pronounced by itself. (See page 837.)

Synonym A synonym is a word that has a meaning similar to but not exactly the same as another word. (See page 931.)

Synthesis Synthesis is a critical thinking skill that involves putting together parts into a unified whole. (See page 46.)

Tense Tense is the time expressed by a verb. Every verb has six tenses: *present, present perfect, past, past perfect, future,* and *future perfect.* (See page 629.)

Theme A theme is the underlying meaning or message a writer wants to communicate in a piece of writing to his or her readers. (See pages 211 and 335.)

Thesis statement A thesis statement is a sentence or two in a composition that announces a writer's limited topic and his or her main, or unifying, idea about that topic. (See page 111.)

Time line A time line is a visual arrangement of information in chronological order. (See page 44.)

Tired word A tired word is a word that has lost its freshness and force. It has been used so often and so carelessly that it has become worn-out and almost meaningless. (See page 459.)

Tone Tone is the feeling or attitude a writer conveys about a topic. (See page 120.)

Topic sentence A topic sentence is the sentence that expresses the main idea of a paragraph. (See page 69.)

Transitional expressions Transitional expressions are words and phrases that connect ideas in a paragraph or composition by showing how ideas and details are related. (See pages 84 and 124.)

Transitive verb A transitive verb is an action verb that expresses an action directed toward a person or thing named in a sentence. (See page 478.)

U

Understood subject The understood subject is the unstated subject *you* in a request or a command. (See page 513.)

Unity Unity, in a paragraph or composition, is a quality achieved when all the sentences or paragraphs work together as a unit to express or support one main idea. (See pages 76 and 124.)

V

Valid conclusion A valid conclusion is a conclusion that is firmly grounded in facts, evidence, or logic. (See page 953.)

Verb A verb is a word used to express an action or a state of being. (See page 477.)

Verbals Verbals (participles, gerunds, and infinitives) are formed from verbs. Like verbs, they may be modified by adverbs and may have complements. However, verbals are used as other parts of speech. (See page 541.)

Verb phrase A verb phrase consists of a main verb preceded by at least one **helping verb** (also called an **auxiliary verb**). (See page 482.)

Visualizing Visualizing is a way of thinking of details for writing in which a writer makes images of something in his or her "mind's eye." (See page 34.)

W

"What if?" questions Asking "What if?" questions is a creative thinking technique that can help a writer draw upon imagination to explore ideas for writing. (See page 33.)

Word bank A word bank is a writer's storehouse of words that he or she can use in writing. (See page 178.)

Works Cited The Works Cited page is a list of all the print and nonprint sources used in a research report; the term **bibliography** means that only print sources were used. (See page 392.)

Writer's journal A writer's journal is a written record of a person's experiences and observations, feelings and opinions, ideas and questions. (See page 23.)

Writing Writing is the stage in the writing process in which a writer puts his or her ideas into words in some form, organizing them by following a plan for presenting the ideas. (See pages 6 and 45.)

Writing process The writing process is the series of stages or steps that a writer goes through to develop ideas and to communicate them clearly in a piece of writing. (See pages 6 and 20.)

Glossary

This glossary is a short dictionary of words found in the professional writing models in this textbook. The words are defined according to their meanings in the context of the writing models.

Pronunciation Key

Symbol	Key Words	Symbol	Key Words
a	asp, fat, parrot	b	bed, table, dub, ebb
ā	ape, date, play, break, fail	d	dip, beadle, had, dodder
ä	ah, car, father, cot	f	fall, after, off, phone
e	elf, ten, berry	g	get, haggle, dog
ē	even, meet, money, flea, grieve	h	he, ahead, hotel
		j	joy, agile, badge
i	is, hit, mirror	k	kill, tackle, bake, coat, quick
ī	ice, bite, high, sky	l	let, yellow, ball
ō	open, tone, go, boat	m	met, camel, trim, summer
ô	all, horn, law, oar	n	not, flannel, ton
o͞o	look, pull, moor, wolf	p	put, apple, tap
o͞o	ooze, tool, crew, rule	r	red, port, dear, purr
yo͞o	use, cute, few	s	sell, castle, pass, nice
yo͞o	cure, globule	t	top, cattle, hat
oi	oil, point, toy	v	vat, hovel, have
ou	out, crowd, plow	w	will, always, swear, quick
u	up, cut, color, flood	y	yet, onion, yard
₩r	urn, fur, deter, irk	z	zebra, dazzle, haze, rise
ə	a in ago	ch	chin, catcher, arch, nature
	e in agent	sh	she, cushion, dash, machine
	i in sanity	th	thin, nothing, truth
	o in comply	th	then, father, lathe
	u in focus	zh	azure, leisure, beige
ər	perhaps, murder	ŋ	ring, anger, drink

Abbreviation Key

adj. adjective
adv. adverb
n. noun
pl. plural

prep. preposition
vi. intransitive verb
vt. transitive verb

A

ad·dled [ad″ld] *adj.* Being confused or muddled.

ap·pre·hen·sion [ap′rē hen′shən] *n.* An uneasy feeling about the future; dread.

ar·bi·trar·y [är′bə trer′ē] *adj.* Acting on one's own thoughts or whims and not by the rules.

ar·cane [är kān′] *adj.* Known by only a few.

a·troc·i·ty [ə träs′ə tē] *n.* Monstrousness; brutality; cruelty.

a·twit·ter [ə twit′ər] *adj.* Trembling or fluttering with excitement or eagerness.

B

bat·ter·y [bat′ər ē] *n.* A group of soldiers who operate artillery.

Bee·tho·ven [bā′tō′vən], **Lud·wig van** [lōōt′viH vän] *n.* (1770–1827) A German composer and pianist who gradually became deaf during his career. He wrote the Ninth Symphony when he was completely deaf.

bi·o·ta [bī ōt′ə] *n.* Plant and animal life, usually of a particular region.

boor·ish [bōōr′ish] *adj.* Rude.

Brahms [brämz], **Jo·han·nes** [yō hän′əs] *n.* (1833–1897) A German composer who wrote symphonies during the Romantic period.

bro·me·li·ad [brō mē′lē ad′] *n.* A plant in the pineapple family with stiff leaves and colorful flowers.

bun·ting [bun′tiŋ] *n.* A small brightly colored type of sparrow.

C

ca·per [kā′pər] *vi.* To jump around playfully.

ca·tas·tro·phe [kə tas′trə fē] *n.* A sudden and great disaster.

Chuang-tzu [jōō äŋ dzōō′] *n.* A 4th-century B.C. Chinese philosopher, who is considered the most important early interpreter of Taoism. His book *Chuang-tzu* is seen as being even more significant and comprehensive than the *Tao-te Ching,* a book by Lao-tzu, the first major figure of **Taoism.**

clam·ber [klam′bər] *vi.* To climb with effort.

cog·ni·tive [käg′nə tiv] *adj.* That which is perceiving, remembering, and judging.

com·mod·i·ty [kə mäd′ə tē] *n.* Something that is valuable or useful.

con·ceive [kən sēv′] *vi.* To become pregnant.

con·straint [kən strānt′] *n.* A restriction.

con·trived [kən trīvd′] *adj.* Too obviously planned.

cul·mi·nate [kul′mə nāt′] *vi.* To reach its climax (in); to result (in).

cur·mudg·eon [kər muj′ən] *n.* A surly, bad-tempered fellow.

D

de·mure [di myōōr′] *adj.* Being modest or shy.

de·plete [dē plēt′] *vt.* To gradually empty of resources or strength.

des·e·cra·tion [des′i krā′shən] *n.* The act of corrupting something that is respected or sacred.

dex·ter·i·ty [deks ter′ə tē] *n.* The ability to use one's hands skillfully.

di·lute [di lōōt′] *vt.* To change or weaken by mixing with something else.

dis·charge [dis chärj′] *n.* Release; emission.

dis·joint·ed [dis joint′id] *adj.* Not connected.

dis·par·ag·ing [di spar′ij iŋ′] *adj.* Showing disregard or disrespect.

dis·si·pa·tor [dis'ə pā'tər] *n.* Something able to disperse or spread out something.

doc·u·dra·ma [däk'yoo drä'mə] *n.* A TV drama based on historical events or actual people.

dull·ard [dul'ərd] *n.* A slow-witted or boring person.

E

ec·cen·tric [ək sen'trik] *adj.* Having the axle of a wheel off center.

e·mer·i·tus [ē mer'i təs] *adj.* Being retired from a job but continuing to hold the rank or title earned in that job.

en·thrall [en thrôl'] *vi.* To fascinate; enchant.

er·rat·ic [er rat'ik] *adj.* Irregular; constantly changing.

ex·trem·i·ty [ek strem'ə tē] *n.* An arm, hand, leg, or foot.

F

fa·cade [fə säd'] *n.* A false appearance or front.

fe·al·ty [fē'əl tē'] *n.* The quality or state of remaining faithful.

fiend·ish·ly [fēn'dish lē] *adv.* Done in a wicked or cruel way.

fur·tive [fur'tiv] *adj.* Done in a secretive or sneaky way.

fu·tile [fyoot''l] *adj.* Hopeless and worthless.

G

gene pool [jēn pool] *n.* All the genes of a species which determine its characteristics.

Gen·tile [jen'tīl'] *n.* A person who is not Jewish; often a person who is Christian.

gross [grōs] *vt.* To earn a total amount of money before any deductions, as in income.

gryph·on [grif'ən] *n.* The British spelling of **griffin**—a mythical character with a body and hind legs like a lion but head, wings, and claws like an eagle.

H

hal·yard [hal'yərd] *n.* A rope for raising or lowering a sail or flag.

ham·mock [ham'ək] *n.* A fertile mound with hardwood trees.

hei·nous [hā'nəs] *adj.* Terribly wicked.

her·biv·o·rous [hər biv'ər əs] *adj.* Feeding mostly or entirely on plants.

hie [hī] *vt.* To hurry.

hump·back chub [hump'bak chub'] *n.* An endangered species of freshwater fish found in the Green and Colorado rivers.

hy·po·thal·a·mus [hī'pō thal'ə məs] *n.* A part of the brain that regulates many body functions including temperature.

I

il·lu·mine [i loo'mən] *vt.* To light up.

im·pas·si·ble [im pas'ə bəl] *adj.* Unfeeling.

in·con·gru·ous [in käŋ'groo əs] *adj.* Not conforming to what is right or normal.

in·dus·tri·ous [in dus'trē əs] *adj.* Characterized by steady, hard work.

in·fer [in fur'] *vt.* To conclude or know something by reasoning.

in·her·ent [in hir'ənt] *adj.* Inborn; characteristic of.

in·quis·i·tive [in kwiz'ə tiv] *adj.* Asking many questions.

in·un·date [in'ən dāt'] *vt.* To cover with an overflowing of water; flood.

krait [krīt] *n.* A type of Asian snake.

Liszt [list], **Franz** [fränts] *n.*
(1811–1886) A Hungarian composer and pianist who invented the solo recital.

lit·ter [lit′ər] *n.* The young born at one time to an animal that has more than one baby at a time.

lout [lout] *n.* A rude, stupid person.

lu·di·crous [loo′di krəs] *adj.* Ridiculous.

lu·nar mod·ule [loo′nər mäj′yool′] *n.* A detachable section of a spacecraft, used to carry astronauts from the main spacecraft to the moon and back.

ma·lac·ca [mə lak′ə] *n.* A type of lightweight walking stick.

me·tab·o·lism [mə tab′ə liz′əm] *n.* The chemical and physical processes that go on inside a body or cell to keep it alive.

nay·say·er [nā′sā′ər] *n.* One who opposes, denies, or is skeptical about something.

op·pos·able [ə pō′zə bəl] *adj.* That which can be positioned opposite something else, such as a thumb to the fingers.

or·a·tor [ôr′ət ər] *n.* A skilled public speaker.

out·flank [out′flank′] *vt.* To outsmart.

par·a·pet [par′ə pet′] *n.* A low wall built to protect troops from frontal enemy fire.

peat [pēt] *n.* A block of decaying, moisture-absorbing plant material used as a fuel.

phys·i·ol·o·gist [fiz′ē äl′ə jist] *n.* An expert in the study of the functions and processes of the body that are necessary for continuing life.

plum·met [plum′it] *vi.* To drop or fall quickly.

poach·er [pōch′ər] *n.* A person who hunts animals illegally.

pom·pa·dour [päm′pə dôr′] *n.* A hairstyle in which the hair is brushed straight up from the forehead for a puffy look.

pom·pon [päm′pän′] *n.* A variety of the chrysanthemum that has a small, round flower.

prone [prōn] *adj.* Having a natural inclination for something.

pro·phet·ic [prō fet′ik] *adj.* Predicting future events.

Proust [proost], **Mar·cel** [mär sel′] *n.* (1871–1922) A French writer who is considered one of the greatest novelists in the twentieth century; known for writing in the first-person point of view and for his work *Remembrance of Things Past.*

pungency [pun′jən sē] *n.* A biting or penetrating quality.

qua·drille [kwə dril′] *n.* A French square dance.

ram·page [ram pāj′] *n.* An occurrence of wild, violent behavior.

ram·part [ram′pärt′] *n.* A wall of earth surrounding a fort or castle for defense against attack.

rank *adj.* Having a strong or offensive odor; rancid.

rap·tur·ous [rap′chər əs] *adj.* Filled with joy; ecstatic.

rear [rir] *vt.* To bring up or raise an animal or a child.

rec·la·ma·tion [rek′lə mā′shən] *n.* Rescue or recovery, especially of a desert or wasteland.

re·frain [ri frān′] *n.* A verse or chorus of a song.

rem·i·nis·cence [rem′ə nis′əns] *n.* A past incident remembered.

res·o·nant [rez′ə nənt] *adj.* Resounding; intensifying sound through vibration.

re·sus·ci·ta·tion [ri sus′ə tā′shən] *n.* The act of bringing someone back to life or consciousness.

ret·i·nue [ret″n yōō′] *n.* A group of followers or servants for a person of importance or high rank.

re·ver·ber·ate [ri vʉr′bə rāt′] *vt.* To reflect or echo.

rhet·o·ric [ret′ər ik] *n.* **(1)** Verbal communication. **(2)** Showy language lacking clear ideas or sincere emotion.

row [rou] *n.* A loud commotion or quarrel.

ru·di·ment [rōō′də mənt] *n.* A basic rule of a subject.

S ▼

sac·ri·lege [sak′rə lij] *n.* The act of showing disrespect to something that is respected or sacred.

sam·ba [säm′bə] *n.* A ballroom dance that originated in Brazil and has African influences.

Schu·bert [shōō′ bərt], **Franz** [fränts] *n.* (1797–1828) An Austrian composer who lived in poverty and whose music was not appreciated until after his death.

scrap·ple [skrap′əl] *n.* A mixture of cornmeal and pork scraps that is boiled and allowed to set, then sliced and fried.

sed·i·ment [sed′ə mənt] *n.* Matter deposited by water, wind, or glaciers.

sen·sor [sen′sər] *n.* A device used to measure physical changes and transmit its measurements.

sere [sir] *adj.* Dry; withered.

shunt [shunt] *vt.* To flow in a different, diverted pathway than originally taken.

slew [slōō] *n.* A colloquial word for a large number or amount.

spec·u·la·tive [spek′yōō lāt′iv] *adj.* Characteristic of risky business transactions that offer the chance of quick and large profit; uncertain.

splayed [splād] *adj.* Spread out.

stern *n.* The back part of something, usually a ship or boat.

sto·ic [stō′ik] *adj.* Seemingly unaffected by pain, grief, or pleasure; calm or unemotional.

strife [strīf] *n.* Conflict or struggling.

sub·ject [səb jekt′] *vt.* To expose to.

T ▼

tan·a·ger [tan′ə jər] *n.* A small songbird; the male bird is brightly colored.

Tao·ism [dou′iz′əm] *n.* A philosophy and system of religion based on the teachings of Lao-tzu, a 6th-century B.C. Chinese philosopher; advocates simplicity and selflessness.

Tchai·kov·sky [chī kôf′skē] **Pe·ter** [pēt′ər] **Il·ich** [il′yich] *n.* (1840–1893) A Russian Romantic composer who wrote *The Sleeping Beauty.*

ten·sile [ten′sil] *adj.* Of, experiencing, or applying tension.

teth·er [te'*th*ər] *vt.* To restrict or limit the movement of something as with a rope or chain.

thwart·ing [*th*wôrt'iŋ] *adj.* Frustrating.

tor·rent [tôr'ənt] *n.* A flood or rushing flow.

tra·jec·to·ry [tra jek'tə rē] *n.* The curved path of an object moving swiftly through space.

tri·fec·ta [trī fek'tə] *n.* A bet in which one wins by picking the first three finishers of a race in the correct order.

un·a·mi·a·bly [un ā'mē ə blē] *adv.* Done in an unfriendly way.

un·wont·ed [un wän'tid] *adj.* Not common or habitual; unusual.

V

ven·om [ven'əm] *n.* A poison secreted by some snakes, spiders, and insects.

ver·i·si·mil·i·tude [ver'ə si mil'ə tōōd] *n.* The quality of seeming real or true.

ves·tige [ves'tij] *n.* A part of the body, usually an internal organ, that was more fully developed in an earlier stage of development of the species.

vig·i·lant [vij'ə lənt] *adj.* Consistently watchful.

vi·gnette [vin yet'] *n.* A short scene.

vil·i·fy [vil'ə fī] *vt.* To defame or malign.

W

whee·dle [hwēd''l] *vt.* To persuade someone by coaxing.

whip·lash [hwip'lash] *n.* The striking part of a whip.

wisp *n.* Something that is thin, slight, or faint.

Z

zo·ol·o·gist [zō äl'ə jist] *n.* An expert in the study of animals.

Index

A

A, an, 474, 697
A lot, 698
Abbreviations, punctuating, 742–43
Accept, except, 697
Acronym, possessive and, 814
Action verb, 477, 522
Active voice
    defined, 633
    in persuasive essay, 313
Adjective, 472–75
    articles, 474
    capitalizing, 721–27
    commas and, 747
    comparison of, 675
    defined, 472
    distinguished from pronouns, 473
    nouns used as, 473
    placement in sentence, 474–75
    proper, 721
Adjective clause
    and combining sentences, 430
    defined, 567
    essential and nonessential, 567
    relative pronoun, 567–68
Adjective phrase, 535–36
    defined, 535
    distinguished from adjective, 535
Adjustment letters, 941
Adverb, 485–89
    comparison of, 675
    conjunctive, 416, 428, 772
    defined, 485
    distinguished from preposition, 492
    forms of, 488–89
    modifying adjectives, 486
    modifying other adverbs, 488
    modifying verbs, 485
    placement in sentence, 485
Adverb clause, 412, 570–71
    and combining sentences, 430
    comma after introductory adverb
        clause, 571
    defined, 570
    punctuating, 430
    subordinating conjunction, 430,
        571–72

Adverb phrase, 537–38
Advertising
    and mass media, 913–14
    and persuasion, 318–19
Advice, advise, 850
Affect, effect, 697, 850
Affixes. *See* Prefixes; Suffixes.
Agenda, in group discussions, 902
Agreement, number, 590–91, 592
Agreement, pronoun-antecedent,
        608–10, 669
    antecedent as masculine or
        feminine, 609
    antecedent of personal pronoun as
        another kind of pronoun, 609
    antecedents joined by *and*, 610
    antecedents joined by *or* or *nor*,
        609–10
    each, either, neither, one, everyone,
        etc., 609
    his or *her* construction, 609
    number and gender, 608–10
Agreement, subject-verb, 590–605
    collective nouns, 602–603
    and combining sentences, 427
    compound subject, 597–98
    don't and *doesn't*, 602
    each, either, neither, etc., 594
    every or *many a*, 605
    indefinite pronouns, 594
    nouns plural in form with singular
        meaning, 605
    number, 590–91, 592
    plural subjects, 590
    predicate nominative, mistaken
        agreement with, 603
    in questions, 603
    sentences beginning with *here* and
        there, 603–604
    several, few, both, many, 594
    singular subjects, 590
    some, all, most, any, none, 594–95
    subject following verb, 603–604
    subjects joined by *and*, 598
    subjects joined by *or* or *nor*, 598
    titles, 604
    words stating amount, 604
Aims for writing
    creative, 7, 20

expressive, 7, 20
informative, 7, 20
persuasive, 7, 20
Ain't, 697
Airborne Again!, 43
All– (prefix), 827
All ready, already, 850
All right, 850
All the farther, all the faster, 698
All together, altogether, 850
Almanacs, 923
Always Coming Home, 80
American Childhood, An, 168–69, 197–98
Among, between, 698–99
An, a, 474, 697
Analogy questions, in tests, 966–69
And etc., 698
Anecdote, in introduction, 121
Angle, Paul M., 16–18
Antecedent
agreement with pronoun, 608–10
defined, 469–70
inexact reference to, 669–70
Antonyms
in dictionaries, 927
and vocabulary, 930
Anywheres, 698
"Apocalypse, How?," 121, 126
Apostrophe, 807–21, 823
with contractions, 818–19
to form plural possessives, 808
to form singular possessives, 807
indefinite pronouns, 812
individual possession, 815
personal pronouns, unnecessary
for, 811
plurals of letters, numbers,
symbols, words used as words,
820–21, 847
possessive case, 807–15
to show omitted letters or
numbers, 818
Appositive, 556–57
defined, 410, 556
pronoun as, 665–66
punctuating with commas, 557,
757
Appositive phrase, 409, 410, 556–57
and combining sentences, 425
defined, 410, 556
punctuating with commas, 557,
757
as sentence fragment, 410

Appreciation letters, 942
"Are Road Bikes Dead?," 128
Arias, Ron, 796
Arrangement of information,
library/media center, 918–19
Arranging ideas, 40
Arranging information, 40–41
Article
definite, 474
indefinite, 474, 697
As, like, 704–705
As if, like, 705
As though, like, 705
At, 698
Atlases, 923
Attacking the person, 300
Audience, 38–39
describing a mechanism, 173–74
literary analysis, 343
personal narrative, 143
persuasive essay, 295
process paper, 258
research paper, 372
short story, 211–12
speech preparation, 899–900
writing process, 36–39
Author card, 919
Auxiliary verb. *See* Helping verb.

Babbitt, 90
Background information, in
introduction, 122
Bad, comparison of, 677
Bambara, Toni Cade, 215
Bandwagon, as persuasive technique
of mass media, 913
Barrio Boy, 64–66, 68
Base form, 618–19
Be, forms of, 480
Beadle, Muriel, 81
Begin, principal parts, 621
Beside, besides, 698
Between, among, 698–99
Bibliography, in research paper, 392
Biographical references, 923
Biographical sketch, 246–47
Bird Feeder Book, The, 73
"Birds, The," 77
Blow, principal parts, 621

Blue Jay's Dance, The, 134–37
Body (of piece of writing)
    business letter, 939
    coherence of, 124
    in composition, 124
    direct references in, 124
    transitional expressions in, 124
    unity of, 124
Book report, 404–405
Bosveld, Jane, 121, 126
Bozzi, Vincent, 106–108
Brainstorming, writing process, 25–26
Brake, break, 851
Break, principal parts, 621
"Bribe," 959
Bring, principal parts, 621
Bring, take, 699
Brooks, Gwendolyn, 16–18
Buck, Pearl S., 79
Burns, Ken, 41
Burns, Ric, 41
Burst, principal parts, 621
Business letters
    adjustment letters, 941
    appearance of, 937
    appreciation letters, 942
    body, 939
    closing, 939
    commendation letters, 942
    complaint letters, 941
    contents of, 939
    heading, 938
    inside address, 938
    order letters, 940–41
    parts of, 938–39
    request letters, 940–41
    salutation, 939
    signature, 939
    types of, 940–42
Bust, busted, 699

of first word in line of poetry, 719
of geographical names, 722–23
of government bodies, 725
of historical events, periods, 726
of hyphenated number, 723
of institutions, 726
of interjection *O*, 720
of names consisting of more than
    one word, 721
of names of holy celebrations, holy
    writings, 732–33
of names of people, 722
of names of religions and their
    followers, 732–33
of names of ships, monuments,
    awards, planets, 727
of nationalities, races, peoples, 727
of organizations, 725
of pronoun *I*, 720
of proper adjectives, 721–27
of proper nouns, 721–27
of school subjects, 729
of special events, 726
of specific deities, 732–33
summary style sheet, 737–38
of teams, 725
of titles of books, periodicals,
    poems, stories, historical
    documents, 731–32
of titles of movies, television
    programs, works of art, musical
    compositions, 731–32
of titles of persons, 731
of words showing family
    relationship, 731
Card catalog, 919–20
    author card, 919
    online catalog, 919
    See and *See also* cards, 919
    subject card, 919
    summary of information, 920
    title card, 919
Carroll, Lewis, 250–52
Case forms
    defined, 649
    nominative case, 651–53
    objective case, 654–58
    personal pronouns, 650
    possessive case, 807–15
Cat, The: History, Biology, and Behavior, 81
Cause and effect
    essay, 278–80
    false, 300
    in narration, 92
    and vocabulary, 930

Call to action, in conclusion, 128
"Calling Arthur Murray," 304–305
Calvino, Italo, 204–206
"Canal Street," 196
Capital, capitol, 851
Capitalization, 719–33
    of brand names, 727
    of businesses, 725
    of calendar items, 726
    direct quotation, 793
    of first word in every sentence, 719

Caxton, William, 444
CD-ROMs, 378, 922
–cede, –ceed, –sede, spelling rule for, 839
Characters
  literary analysis, 335
  short story, 215, 220–21
Chart, in arranging ideas, 43–44
Choose, chose, 851
Choose, principal parts, 621
Chronological order
  in composition, 115
  in a paragraph, 79
  in personal narrative, 149
Circular reasoning, 299–300
Civil War, The: An Illustrated History, 41
Classification
  comparing and contrasting, 96
  in composition, 115
  defining, 95–96
  in developing paragraph, 94–96
  dividing, 94–95
  literary analysis, 356
  strategy of, 89
  as study skill, 957
Classification system, in library/media center, 918–19
Classified ad, 199
Clause. *See also* Independent clause; Subordinate clause.
  adjective clause, 430, 567–68
  adverb clause, 412, 570–71
  defined, 411, 564
  essential (restrictive), 751
  independent, 564
  nonessential (nonrestrictive), 750
  noun clause, 430–31, 574–75
  punctuating, 565
  subordinate, 437, 564
Cliché, 460
Climax, literary analysis, 334
Clincher sentence, in a paragraph, 75
Closing, in a business letter, 939
Clustering, writing process, 27–28
Coarse, course, 851
Cohen, Daniel, 70, 91–92, 123
Coherence
  chronological order, 79
  in composition, 124
  connections between ideas, 83–84
  direct references, 83–84
  logical order of ideas, 81
  order of ideas, 79–81

order of importance, 80–81
  in a paragraph, 79–86
  spatial order, 80
  transitional expressions, 84–86
  transitions, 83
"Cold Facts About Human Survival, The," 364–66
College dictionaries, 925
Collier, Eugenia W., 440
Colloquialism, defined, 452
Colon, 779–80
  and appositives, 779
  in conventional situations, 780
  with direct quotation, 794
  before list of items, 779
  before long, formal statement or quotation, 780
  in reference to biblical chapter and verse, 780
  after salutation in business letter, 780
  between titles and subtitles, 780
  in writing time, 780
Combining sentences, 421–31
  with adjective clause, 430
  with adverb clause, 430
  agreement of subject and verb, 427
  with appositive phrases, 425
  with complex sentence, 430–31
  with compound sentence, 428–29
  with compound subject or verb, 426–27
  inserting groups of words, 424–25
  inserting words, 422
  with noun clause, 430–31
  with participial phrases, 424–25
  with prepositional phrases, 424
Come, principal parts, 621
Comma splice, 415
Commas, 745–62
  adjectives preceding noun, 747
  with appositive and appositive phrase, 557, 757
  and compound noun, 747
  and compound sentence, 428
  with compound subject, 514
  in conventional situations, 761
  and direct address, 758
  with direct quotation, 793
  and elements that interrupt sentence, 757
  and independent clauses, 749
  and introductory elements, 755–56
  and items in a series, 746–47

and items in dates and addresses, 761

after letter salutations and closings, 761

after name followed by abbreviation, 761

with nonessential clause, 567, 750–51

with nonessential phrase, 750–51

and parenthetical expressions, 759–60

unnecessary use, 762

Commendation letters, 942

Communication, nonverbal, 897

Communication cycle, 896

Community resources, for research paper, 377

Comparative degree of comparison, 680–84

Comparing and contrasting, in classification, 96

Comparison and contrast frameworks
block method, 348–49
point-by-point method, 348–49

Comparison of modifiers, 675–84
clear comparisons, 683–84
comparative degree, 680–84
double comparisons, 683
irregular, 677
other and *else*, 682
regular, 675–76
superlative degree, 680–84

Comparisons, 179–80

Complaint letters, 941

Complement, compliment, 852–53

Complements, 517–24
defined, 517
never part of prepositional phrase, 518
subject complement, 519

Complete predicate, 503

Complete subject, 503–504

Complex sentence
and combining sentences, 430–31
defined, 578

Composition, 110–29
body, 124–25
coherence, 124
conclusion, 126–29
direct references, 124–25
early plan, 115–16
formal outline, 116–19
framework for, 129
grouping information, 115

introduction, 120–23
ordering information, 115–16
reflecting, 131
thesis statement, 111–12
transitional expressions, 124–25
unity, 124

Compound-complex sentence, defined, 578

Compound noun
commas and, 747
defined, 467
plurals, 846

Compound number, hyphen with, 827

Compound preposition, 492

Compound sentence
and combining sentences, 428–29
conjunctive adverb, 416
coordinating conjunction, 429
defined, 428, 577
punctuating, 416, 428, 429, 749

Compound subject
agreement, 597–98
and combining sentences, 426–27
defined, 514, 597

Compound verb
and combining sentences, 426–27
defined, 515

Compound word
hyphens and, 826
possessive and, 814

Computer software, 91. *See also* Word processor.
bibliography list and, 396
border and box tools, 949
character tracking, 221
collaborative prewriting or drafting, 257
creating vocabulary file, 931
Cut and Paste commands, 313
desktop publishing, 61
graphics, 185
for notes and report writing, 911
spell-checking program, 353
tables, 147
for thesaurus, 126

Computers, for research paper, 370

Conclusion
call to action, 128
in composition, 126–29
final comment, 128
final idea, 127
main idea, 126
refer to introduction, 129

summary, 127
techniques for writing, 126–29
Concrete nouns, defined, 466
Conflict
  external, 217
  internal, 217
  literary analysis, 334
Conjunction
  with compound subject, 514
  with compound verb, 515
  coordinating, 416, 426, 428, 429, 493
  correlative, 493–94
  defined, 493
  subordinating, 430, 571–72
Conjunctive adverb
  and compound sentence, 428
  examples of, 772
  punctuating, 416
Connections between ideas. *See*
    Direct references; Transitional
    expressions.
Connotation, 456–57
Consul, council, councilor, counsel,
    counselor, 853
Context clues, 930–31
Contractions, 818–19
  agreement and, 602, 604
  confused with possessive
    pronoun, 811, 819
Coordinating conjunction
  and compound sentence, 428, 429
  and compound subjects or verbs, 426
  defined, 493
  and revising run-on sentence, 416
  use of comma within compound
    sentence, 416
Corliss, Richard, 98
Cormier, Robert, 454
Correlative conjunction, 493–94
Could of, 701
Council, councilor, consul, counsel,
    counselor, 853
Course, coarse, 851
Creative writing, 208, 359. *See also*
    Short story.
  free verse, 200–201
  paragraph, 102–103
  reflecting, 103
Critical listening, 911–12
Critical thinking
  analyzing your audience, 38–39
  arranging details, 261–62
  arranging information, 40–41
  evaluating details, 183
  evaluating dialogue, 235

evaluating topics for personal
    narrative, 141
evaluating your reasoning,
    299–301
short story analysis, 336
synthesizing ideas, 46–47
synthesizing ideas and
    information, 388–89
viewing, 914–16
Cross-reference cards, 919
Cutting, in oral interpretation, 904

Dahl, Roald, 77
Dangling modifiers, defined, 686
Dark Side of the Moon, 324–26
Dashes
  for abrupt break in thought, 829
  for parenthetical elements, 829
  for unfinished statement or
    question, 829
Data, in persuasive essay, 297–98
Database, 922
"Death of a Tree, The," 408
Declarative sentence
  defined, 527
  punctuating, 741, 742
Defining, in classification, 95–96
Definition. *See also* Meaning of a word.
  in dictionaries, 926
  and vocabulary, 930
Demonstrative pronoun, 471
Denotation, 456–57
Dependent clause. *See* Subordinate
    clause.
Description
  comparisons, 179
  details, 177–86
  in developing paragraph, 90
  evaluating and revising, 191–93
  imagery and, 167–71
  and mass media, 199
  of mechanism, 172–95
  objective, 173, 186
  prewriting, 172–85
  proofreading and publishing, 194
  reflecting, 194
  strategy of, 89
  subjective, 175, 196–98
  writing your first draft, 186–90
Desert, dessert, 853
Desktop publishing, 61. *See also*
    Computer software.

Details, 177–86
    arrangement of, in process paper,
      261–62
    chart of, 148
    events, 145–46
    examples, 73
    facts, 72–73
    listening for, 909
    and literary analysis, 344–45
    meaning of experience, 150
    organizing, 149, 182
    in a paragraph, 71–73
    people, 146
    in personal narrative, 145–50
    places, 147
    recalling, 145
    recognizing relationships among,
      950–52
    sensory, 71–72
    statistics, 72–73
    thoughts and feelings, 147
Development of a paragraph, 89–98
Dewey decimal system, fiction and
    nonfiction, 918
Diagraming sentences, 978–93
Dialect
    American English, 448–49
    and English language origins, 442
    ethnic, 449
    regional, 448–49
Dialogue
    evaluating in short story, 235
    in fictional literature and TV, 916
    in personal narrative, 146
    punctuating, 239
    short story, 221
"Dialogue on Film: Bill Moyers," 122
Dictionaries, 925–27
    as an aid to spelling, 837
    antonyms, 927
    college, 925
    definitions, 926
    entry word, 926
    etymology, 926
    examples, 926
    part-of-speech labels, 926
    pronunciation, 926
    related, 927
    synonyms, 927
    types of, 925–27
    unabridged, 925
    usage labels, 927
    word forms, 926
Dillard, Annie, 92, 168–69, 196, 197–98
Direct address, commas and, 758

Direct object
    compound, 524
    defined, 522
    never in prepositional phrases, 522
    pronoun, objective case, 654
Direct quotation
    in note taking, 384
    in research paper, 397
Direct references
    and coherence, 83–84
    in composition, 124–25
Discover, invent, 701
Discussions. *See* Group discussions.
Dive, principal parts, 621
Dividing, in classification, 94–95
Do, principal parts, 621
Documenting sources in a research
    paper, 390–91
Doesn't, don't, 602, 701
Double comparison, 683
Double negative, 711–12
Double subject, 704
Douglas, Marjory Stoneman, 69
Drafting, 948
    computer software for, 257
Drink, principal parts, 621
Drive, principal parts, 621
Du Maurier, Daphne, 77
Durbin, Richard, 321
Durrell, Gerald, 96

E

Each, either, neither, one, everyone, etc.,
    594, 609
Early plan
    in composition, 115–16
    for research paper, 383
Eat, principal parts, 621
Ebert, Roger, 360–61
Effect, affect, 697, 850
Ehrlich, Anne, 76
Ehrlich, Paul, 76
ei, ie, spelling rule for, 839
"El Mago," 796
El Mahdy, Christine, 96
–elect, 827
Elements that interrupt sentence,
    commas and, 757–60
Ellison, Ralph, 350
Else and *other*, in comparisons, 682
Emotional appeal, 298–99
    as persuasive technique of mass
      media, 914

Encyclopedia of Monsters, The, 70, 91–92
Encyclopedias, 923
End marks, 741–43
    exclamation point, 741–42
    period, 741
    question mark, 741
Ending, literary analysis, 334
English language
    American English, 446
    Anglo-Saxon, 443
    Black English, 449
    cliché, 460
    colloquialism, 452–53
    connotation, 456–57
    denotation, 456–57
    dialects of, 448–49
    euphemism, 458–59
    formal compared with informal, 451
    Hispanic English, 449
    history of, 441–47
    idiom, 455
    informal, 452–54
    jargon, 456
    loaded word, 457
    London English, 444–45
    meaning of a word, 455–60
    Middle English, 443–44
    Modern English, 444–46
    nonstandard English, 450, 697
    Old English, 443
    origins, 442
    regional dialects, 448–49
    slang, 453–54
    standard English, 449–51, 697
    tired words, 459
    varieties of, 448–54
    vocabulary growth, 447
    world use, 447
Entry word, in dictionaries, 926
Envelope, addressing, 943
Erdrich, Louise, 134–37
Erikson, Kai, 93
Essay. *See* Informative writing; Persuasive essay.
Essay tests, 970–72
    essay test questions, 971–72
    qualities of good answer, 972
    study methods, 970
Essential clause or phrase, commas and, 567, 751
Etc., 698
Ethnic dialects, 449
Etymology, in dictionaries, 926

Euphemism, 458–59
Evaluating and revising
    in developing paragraph, 97–98
    guidelines for, 54
    literary analysis, 350–51
    of objective description, 191–92
    peer evaluation, 49–50
    personal narrative, 157
    persuasive essay, 310–11
    process paper, 273
    research paper, 397–98
    short story, 233–34
    strategy of, 89, 97
    subjective description, 198
    writing process, 6, 21, 49–54
Everglades, The: River of Grass, 69
Every or *many a,* 605
Everything in Its Path, 93
Everywheres, 698
Evidence, in persuasion, 297–98
Ex– (prefix), 827
Examples
    defined, 73
    in dictionaries, 926
    in introduction, 121
    in a paragraph, 73
    and vocabulary, 930
Except, accept, 697
Exclamation point, 741–42
    with direct quotation, 793
Exclamatory sentence, 528, 741–42
Explaining, purposes of, 254
Expletive, 511
Exposition. *See also* Literary analysis; Process paper; Research paper.
    informative essay, 130–31
    informative paragraph, 100–101
    informative writing, 248–83
Expressive writing, 99–100
Extemporaneous speech, 900
Extinction, 76

Facts
    defined, 72
    in introduction, 121
    in a paragraph, 72–73
    in persuasion, 297
Factual details, 177
Fall, principal parts, 621
Feedback, 896
Feldman, David, 72–73

Fewer, less, 701
Fiction, arrangement of, 919
Fictional literature and TV, 914–16
  and reality, 916
"fifteen," 11
Figures. *See* Graphics.
Figures of speech, 196–98
Final comment, in conclusion, 128
Final idea, in conclusion, 127
Fincher, Jack, 36–37
First-person point of view, 143, 175,
  196, 213–14, 335
5W-How? questions, 29, 242, 909
*Flood Is Called Right Tonic for Grand
    Canyon,* 242–43
Focused freewriting, 24
Focused listening, writing process, 32
Focused prewriting, 172
Focused reading, writing process, 31
Folsom, Marcia, 179, 186–87
Folsom, Michael, 179, 186–87
Footnotes, 391
"For Goodness Sake?," 122
Formal English, 451
Formal outline
  in composition, 116–19
  defined, 116
  writer's model, 117–19
Formal speaking
  making an introduction to a
    presentation, 902
  making announcements, 901
  speech preparation, 898–900
Formally, formerly, 854
Forms, completing, 943
Fractions used as adjectives, 827
Fragment. *See* Sentence fragment.
Frazier, Ian, 196
Free verse poems, 200–201
Freewriting, writing process, 24
Freeze, principal parts, 621
French
  prefixes, 933
  suffixes, 934
Frost, Robert, 165
Fused sentence, 415
Future perfect tense, 630
Future tense, 630

Galarza, Ernesto, 64–66, 68
Gender, agreement in, 608–10
General context, and vocabulary, 931

Generalization, hasty, 300–301
Gerund
  defined, 546
  distinguished from present
    participle, 547
Gerund phrase, 548–49
  defined, 548
  possessive noun or pronoun with, 549
Give
  conjugation in passive voice,
    634–35
  principal parts, 621
Glancy, Diane, 200
Gleiberman, Owen, 324–26
Gliatto, Tom, 125, 127
Go, principal parts, 621
Good, comparison of, 677
Good, well, 701
Grammar, in objective description,
  191
Graphics
  describing a mechanism, 185
  reading and study skills, 953–54
"Great American Symbol, A," 321
Greek
  loan words, 847
  prefixes, 933
  roots, 932
  suffixes, 934
Greene, Bob, 75
Group discussions
  agenda, 902
  assigning roles, 902–903
  parliamentary procedure, 903
  purpose, 902
Grouping information, in
  composition, 115
Grow, principal parts, 621
"Guiltless Snacks," 121

Had of, 701
Had ought, hadn't ought, 704
Hajdu, David, 264–69
"Happy Man's Shirt, The," 204–206
Hardly, scarcely, 712
He, she, they as double subject, 704
Heading, in a business letter, 938
Hear, here, 854
Helping verb, 482, 515
His or her, 609
History and personal narratives,
  163–64

How to Shoot an Amateur Naturalist, 96
"How to Shoot Your Own Video,"
264–69
"How-to" process, 255
"How-to" video, 282–83
Humorous skit, 245–46
Hyphen, 826–27
with compound numbers, 827
with compound words, 826
with fractions used as adjectives,
827
with prefixes, 827
with suffix *–elect*, 827
for word division at end of line,
826

I

"I felt freedom in my bones," 36–37
I-Search paper, 402–403
Ideas for writing. *See also* Main idea.
arrangement of, 40–44
synthesis of, 46–47
Idioms, 455
ie, ei, spelling rule for, 839
Illustrations. *See also* Graphics.
describing a mechanism, 185
reading and study skills, 953–54
Imagery, 167
Imperative sentence
defined, 527
punctuating, 742
subject of, 274
Imponderables, 72–73
Impromptu speech, 897
Incomplete construction, pronoun in,
668–69
Indefinite article, 697
Indefinite pronoun
examples of, 471
possessive case, 812
Independent clause
commas and, 749
and complex sentence, 430
defined, 411, 564
punctuating, 565
and semicolon, 770–773
Indirect object
compound, 524
defined, 523
pronoun, objective case, 655
Indirect question, 741
Indirect quotation, 792

Inference, 952
Infinitive
defined, 550
distinguished from prepositional
phrase, 550
with *to* omitted, 552
Infinitive phrase, 551–52
Informal English
colloquialisms, 452
formal English compared with,
451
slang, 453–54
Informal speaking
communicating effectively, 898
impromptu speech, 897
instruction, 898
social introductions, 898
telephone, 898
Information
arrangement of, in library/media
center, 918–19
classification of, in library/media
center, 918–19
interpretation for study, 950–52
listening for, 909–14
Information sources
community resources, 377
database, 922
evaluating, 377–78
library resources, 376
microforms, 922
reference books, 923–24
for research paper, 376–81
vertical file, 921
World Wide Web and online
services, 377
Informative writing. *See also* Process
paper.
essay, 130–31
paragraph, 100–101
reflecting, 276
Inside, 705
Inside address, in a business letter, 938
Instructions
giving, 898
listening to, 909
Interjection, 495
Internet, 378, 922
Interrogative pronoun, 471
Interrogative sentence
defined, 527–28
punctuating, 741, 742
Interview, listening methods, 910–11
Intransitive verb, 478
Introduction

anecdote, 121
background information, 122
in composition, 120–23
and conclusion, 129
example, 121
facts, 121
quotation, 122
readers' interest, 120
techniques for writing, 120–23
thesis, 120, 123
tone, 120
Introductory elements, commas and,
    755–56
Invent, discover, 701
Invitations, 942–43
Irregular comparison of modifiers, 677
Irregular verbs
    defined, 620
    list of, 621
"It Pays to Advertise," 319
Italics (underlining), 789–90
    for foreign words, 790
    for titles of books, plays, films,
        etc., 789–90
    for titles of long poems and
        musical compositions, 790
    for words, letters, and figures, 790
Items in a series
    and commas, 746–47
    and semicolons, 774
Its, it's, 854
It's me, 653

Jargon, 456
Journal, writer's, 23
Journal writing, 161–62

Kantor, MacKinlay, 330–33
Key language skills, review of, 864–93
Kind, sort, type, 704
Know, principal parts, 621
Kooser, Ted, 102
Kornbluth, Jesse, 43

Language. *See* English language.
Latin
    loan words, 847

prefixes, 933
roots, 932
suffixes, 934
Lay, lie, 637–38
Le Guin, Ursula K., 80
Lead, in news story, 242
Lead, led, 854
Learn, teach, 704
Leave, let, 704
Lee, Andrea, 71–72
"Left Face," 106–108
Less, fewer, 701
Letter to editor, 316–17
Letters. *See* Business letters; Personal
    letters.
Lewis, Sinclair, 90
Library/media center
    arrangement of information, 918–19
    card catalog, 919–20
    classification of information, 918–19
    Dewey decimal system, 918
    information sources, 921–24
    Library of Congress system, 918
    reference materials, 921–23
Library of Congress system, 918
Library resources, for research paper,
    376
Lie, lay, 637–38
"Light Bulb," 186–87
Like
    as, 704–705
    as if, as though, 705
Limiting a topic, 370–71
Linking verb, 480, 519
Listening
    conducting an interview, 910–11
    critical listening, 911–12
    for details, 909
    focused, 32
    for information, 909–11
    to instructions, 909
    LQ2R study method, 910
    note taking, 912
    politely, 909–10
    purposeful listening, 908
Literary analysis, 330–55
    audience, 343
    basic elements of story, 334–35
    body, 346
    characters, 335
    choosing story elements for
        analysis, 342
    classification, 356
    climax, 334

collecting and organizing details,
344–45
comparing and contrasting
elements, 339
conclusion, 346
conflict, 334
development of, 340–43
ending, 334
evaluating and revising, 350–51
fictional literature and TV, 914–16
framework of, 348–49
identifying main idea, 342
individual elements, 338
introduction, 346
mood, 334
organizing details, 345
personal response, 330–33
plot, 334
point of view, 335
prewriting, 338–45
proofreading, 353
proofreading and publishing, 353–54
publishing, 354
purpose of, 328–29, 343
reading, 330–33
reading closely, 340–41
reflecting, 354
setting, 334
structure of, 338–39
theme, 335
tone, 343
writer's model, 346–47
writing a first draft, 346–49
Literature, reference books, 924
"Living Like Weasels," 196
Loaded words, 457
"Lobster-Quadrille, The," 250–52
Logical appeals
evidence, 297–98
reasons, 297
sources of reasons and evidence, 298
Logical order, 81
London, Jack, 83–84
Looping, 24
Loose, lose, 854
LQ2R study method, 910
–ly, –ness, spelling rule for, 840–41

M

Macaulay, David, 174
*Macmillan Book of How Things Work,
The*, 179, 186–87
Main clause. *See* Independent clause.

Main idea
in conclusion, 126
identifying, 950
of a paragraph, 68
and paragraph unity, 76–77
Making Connections/Writing Across
the Curriculum
Advertising and Persuasion,
318–19
A Biographical Sketch, 246–47
Creative Writing, Free Verse,
200–201
Description and Mass Media, 199
Desktop Publishing, 61
The "How-to" Video, 282–83
A Humorous Skit, 245–46
Informing Through Evaluation
Book Report, 404–405
Writing a Review, 359–61
Narratives Across the Curriculum,
History, 163–64
Narratives in Literature, Poetry, 165
Persuasion Across the Curriculum,
Social Studies, 320–21
Sentence Craft, 440
Sentences in Poetry, 419–420
Speaking and Listening, Research
and Nonprint Media, 405
Write an Advertisement, 461
Writing Across the Curriculum,
Creative Writing, 359
Writing Across the Curriculum,
Science, 281–82
Writing an Informative Essay,
130–31
Writing Paragraphs for Different
Purposes, 99–103
"Man Who Had No Eyes, A," 330–33
Manuscript form, guidelines for, 59
Many, comparison of, 677
"Marigolds," 440
Martin, Scott, 128
Martina, 70
Mass media
and advertising, 913–14
description and, 199
persuasive techniques in, 913–14
Matching questions, in tests, 965
Maxson, Peter Flagg, 316
McCaffrey, Anne, 197
Meaning of a word
cliché, 460
connotation, 456–57
denotation, 456–57
dictionary definition, 926

euphemisms, 458–59
idiom, 455
jargon, 456
loaded word, 457
tired word, 459
and vocabulary, 930
Memorizing, as study skill, 962
Metaphor, 196
Microforms, 922
Might of, 701
Miller, Annetta, 39
Misplaced modifiers, 689–91
MLA format for source credit, 390–91
Modifiers. *See also* Adjective; Adverb.
    comparative degree, 680–84
    comparison, 675–84
    dangling, 686–88
    defined, 472
    forms of, 675
    irregular comparison, 677
    misplaced, 689–91
    regular comparison, 675–76
    single-word, 437
    superlative degree, 680–84
Mood, literary analysis, 334
Mora, Pat, 959
Moral, morale, 855
Mori, Toshio, 222–29
"Mother," 71–72
"Moustache, The," 454
Moving text, computer software for, 313
Much, comparison of, 677
Multiple-choice questions, in tests, 964
Mummies, Myth and Magic, 96
"Mushrooming Meters," 316
Must of, 701

Narration. *See also* Personal narrative;
    Short story.
    in developing paragraph, 91–92
    explaining a process, 92
    explaining cause and effect, 92–93
    strategy of, 89
    telling a story, 91–92
Navratilova, Martina, 70
Nerilka's Story, 197
–ness, –ly, spelling rule for, 840–41
News story, 242–44
No, nothing, none, 712
Nominative case. *See also* Predicate
    nominative; Subject.
    predicate nominative, 653

subject of verb, 651
Nonessential clause or phrase,
    commas and, 567, 750–51
Nonfiction, classification of, 918
Nonprint media and research, 405
Nonrestrictive clause or phrase. *See*
    Nonessential clause or phrase.
Nonstandard English, 450, 697
Nonverbal communication, 897
Norris, Helen, 450
Note cards, for research paper, 383–86
    in speech preparation, 900
Note taking
    direct quotation, 384
    listening skills, 912
    paraphrase note, 385
    paraphrasing, 912
    as reading and study skill, 955–56
    for research paper, 383–86
    summarizing, 912
    summary note, 385
Nothing, no, none, 712
Noun
    abstract, 466
    as adjective, 473
    capitalizing, 721–27
    collective, 602–603
    common, 465–66, 721
    compound, 467
    concrete, 466
    defined, 465
    of direct address, 513
    plurals, forming, 844–47
    proper, 465–66, 721
Noun clause
    in complex sentences, 430–31
    defined, 574
    introductory word, 575
Nowheres, 698
Number. *See also* Plurals.
    agreement in, 589, 590–91, 592,
        608–10
    defined, 589
    plural, 589
    singular, 589
Numbers
    hyphen with compound numbers,
        827
    spelling rules for, 849

Object of preposition
    compound, 658

defined, 533–34
pronoun, objective case, 657–58
Object of verb
defined, 522
direct, 522, 524, 654
indirect, 523, 524, 655
pronoun, objective case, 654–55
transitive verbs, 478
Objective case
for direct object of verb, 654
for indirect object of verb, 655
for object of preposition, 657–58
Objective description, 173, 186
Objective tests, 963–70
analogy questions, 966–69
matching questions, 965
multiple-choice questions, 964
reasoning or logic questions, 965–66
short-answer questions, 969–70
study methods, 963
true/false questions, 964–65
Observation, 179–80
Of, 705
Off, 705
"Old Demon, The," 79
"One Perfect Rose," 976
Online catalog, 919
Online database, 922
Online services, 378
Opinion
emotional appeals to support,
298–99
logical appeals to support, 297–98
support of, in persuasive essay,
297–99
Oral interpretation
adapting material, 904
cutting, 904
presenting, 904–905
reading script, 904–905
Order letter, 940–41
Order of ideas
chronological order, 79
logical order, 81
order of importance, 80–81
spatial order, 80
Order of importance, 80–81, 115
Ordering information, in
composition, 115–16
Organization, of details, 182
Other and *else*, in comparisons, 682
Ought to of, 701
Outline
in composition, 116–19
defined, 116

in research paper, 386–87
in speech preparation, 900
as study skill, 958–59
topic, 116
writer's model, 117–19
Outside, 705

Panati, Charles, 42
Panati's Browser's Book of Beginnings,
42
Paperback dictionaries, 925
Paragraph, 68–98
classification, 94–96
clincher sentence, 75
coherence, 79–86
creative, 102–103
description, 90
development of, 89–98
evaluation, 97–98
to express yourself, 99–100
informative, 100–101
main idea, 68, 76–77
narration, 91–93
persuasive, 101–102
sequence of events, 77
supporting sentences, 71–73
topic sentence, 69–70, 76
unity, 76–77
Parallel structure, 432–33
Paraphrasing
in note taking, 385, 912
as study skill, 959–60
Parentheses
to enclose material added to
sentence, 831
punctuating within, 831
Parenthetical citations, 390–91
Parenthetical expressions
commas and, 759–60
dashes and, 829
Parker, Dorothy, 976
Parliamentary procedure, rules of,
903
Part-of-speech labels, 926
Participial phrase
and combining sentences, 424–25
defined, 544
Participle
defined, 541
distinguished from verb phrase,
542

past participle, 542
present participle, 541–42
Parts of speech
adjectives, 472–75
adverbs, 485–89
conjunctions, 493–94
determined by use, 496
interjections, 495
nouns, 465–67
prepositions, 491–92
pronouns, 469–71
summary chart, 499
verbs, 477–83
Passed, past, 855
Passive voice
defined, 633
use of, 635
Past participle, 542
Past perfect tense, 630
Past tense, 630
Peace, piece, 855
Peer evaluation
guidelines, 50
writing process, 49–50
Period
after abbreviation, 742
at end of sentence, 741, 742
inside quotation marks, 794
Personal attacks, 300
Personal letters
invitations, 942–43
regrets, 943
thank-you letters, 942
Personal narrative, 139–59
across the curriculum, 163–64
audience, 143
basic elements, 151
body, 151
choosing a topic, 139
chronological order of details, 149
conclusion, 151
dialogue, 146
evaluating and revising, 157
framework, 154–56
gathering details, 145–50
and history, 163–64
introduction, 151
in literature, 165
meaning of experience, 150
and poetry, 165
prewriting steps, 139–50
proofreading and publishing,
159
purpose, 143
reflecting, 159

structure of, 151
symbols for revising and
proofreading, 60
tone, 143–44
writer's model, 154–55
writing a first draft, 151–56
Personal pronoun
case forms, 650
examples of, 470
in personal narratives, 144
possessive, 473
Personification, 197
Persuasive essay, 291–315
active voice in, 313
audience, 295
basic elements, 303
choosing a topic, 291–93
evaluating and revising, 310–13
framework of, 306–309
prewriting steps, 291–301
proofreading and publishing,
314
purpose, 295
supporting your opinion, 297–301
tone, 295
writer's model, 307–308
writing a first draft, 303–309
Persuasive writing
across the curriculum, 320–21
and advertising, 318–19
and mass media, 913–14
methods of, 290
paragraph, 101–102
reflecting, 314
and social studies, 320–21
Phrase
adjective, 535–36
adverb, 537–38
appositive, 409, 410, 425, 556–57
defined, 409, 532
gerund, 548–49
infinitive, 551–52
participial, 424–25, 544–45
placement in sentence, 410
prepositional, 409, 410, 424,
533–38
and varying sentence beginnings,
437
verb, 482
verbal, 409, 541–56
Phrase fragment, 409
Piano Lesson, The, 286–88
Picture This
action verbs, 479
active voice, 637

adverb clause, 574
agreement, pronoun-antecedent, 611
capitalization, 724–25
end marks, 745
hyphens, dashes, and parentheses, 833–34
italics (underlining), 791–92
possessive case, 817–18
subject, 512–13
usage, 707
verbals and verbal phrases, 555–56
who, whom, 664–65
Pictures. *See* Imagery.
Piece, peace, 855
Plagiarism, in research paper, 377, 384, 960
Plain, plane, 856
"Plain folks," as persuasive technique of mass media, 913
Plan, early
in composition, 115–16
for research paper, 383
Plot
conflict, 217–18
literary analysis, 334
short story, 217–18
Plurals
compound nouns, 846
forming, 820, 844–47
Latin and Greek loan words, 847
of letters, 820–21
nouns, irregular, 846
nouns, regular, 844
nouns ending in *f* or *fe*, 845
nouns ending in *o*, 845
nouns ending in *s, x, z, ch, sh*, 844
nouns ending in *y*, 845
numerals, letters, symbols, words used as words, 847
Poems, free verse, 200–201
Poetry
and personal narratives, 165
sentences, 419
Point of view
first-person, 143, 175, 196, 213–14
literary analysis, 335
second-person, 174
short story, 213–14
third-person, 173–74, 213–14
third-person omniscient, 213
"Poison," 77
"Portable Phonograph, The," 86

Portfolio, 58, 103, 131, 159, 162, 194, 198, 240, 244, 276, 280, 314, 317, 354, 358, 400, 403
Positive degree of comparison, 680–84
Possessive case, 807–15
acronyms, 814
compound words, 814
indefinite pronouns, 812
individual possession, 815
joint possession, 814
organizations and businesses, 814
personal pronouns, 811
plural noun, 808
singular noun, 807
Possessive pronoun
confused with contraction, 811, 819
personal, 473
Précis, 961
Predicate, 502–16. *See also* Verb.
complete, 503
defined, 502
simple, 505–506
Predicate adjective, 519
Predicate nominative
defined, 519, 653
pronoun, nominative case, 653
Prefixes
French, 933
Greek, 933
hyphens and, 827
Latin, 933
Old English, 933
spelling rule for, 840
Preiss, Byron, 278–79
Preposition
compound, 492
defined, 491
distinguished from adverbs, 492
examples of, 491–92
object of, 533–34
Prepositional phrase, 533–38
adjective phrase, 535–36
adverb phrase, 537–38
and combining sentences, 424
comma after series of phrases, 755
defined, 410, 533
indirect object distinguished from, 524
as sentence fragment, 409, 410
subject follows verb in, 509
Present participle, 541–42
Present perfect tense, 630
Present tense, 629

Prewriting, 948
  computer software for, 257
  description, 172–85
  literary analysis, 338–45
  personal narrative, 139–50
  persuasive essay, 291–301
  process paper, 255–62
  research paper, 369–87
  short story, 209–19
  subjective description, 198
  writing process, 6, 21, 22–44
Principal, principle, 856
Principal parts of verbs, defined, 618
Process explanation, in narration, 92.
      See also Cause and effect.
Process paper, 255–77
  audience, 258
  basic elements, 264–69
  body, 264
  choosing a "how-to" process, 255–56
  conclusion, 264
  definitions, 260
  evaluating and revising, 273–74
  framework, 270–72
  gathering information, 260–61
  introduction, 264
  materials, 260
  proofreading and publishing, 276
  purpose, 258
  steps, 260
  tone, 258
  writer's model, 270–71
  writing a first draft, 264–72
Progressive forms of verbs, 630–31
Pronoun
  agreement with antecedent,
      608–10, 669
  antecedents, 469–70
  as appositive, 665–66
  case form, 649–58
  defined, 469
  demonstrative, 471
  distinguished from adjectives, 473
  in incomplete construction, 668–69
  indefinite, 471
  inexact pronoun reference, 669
  interrogative, 471
  in nominative case, 651–53
  in objective case, 654–58
  in personal narratives, 144
  personal pronouns, 144, 470
  possessive, confused with
      contractions, 811, 819
  possessive personal, 473
  reference to antecedents, 669

  reflexive, 471
  relative, 471
  after *than* and *as* in incomplete
      construction, 668–69
  unnecessary, double subject, 704
  usage, 648–70
  who, whom, 662–63
Pronoun-antecedent agreement. *See*
      Agreement, pronoun-antecedent.
Pronouns, tone and, 175
Pronunciation, in dictionaries, 926
Proofreading and publishing, 56–60
  desktop publishing, 61
  guidelines for proofreading, 57
  guidelines for publishing, 59
  literary analysis, 353–54
  of objective description, 194
  personal narrative, 159
  persuasive essay, 314
  process paper, 276
  subjective description, 198
  symbols for revising and
      proofreading, 60
  and writing process, 6, 21
Proper adjective
  defined, 721
  rule for capitalizing, 721–27
Proto-Indo-European language, 442
Publishing. *See* Proofreading and
      publishing.
Punctuation
  apostrophes, 807–21, 823
  colons, 779–80
  commas, 745–62
  dashes, 829
  end marks, 741–43
  hyphens, 826–27
  italics (underlining), 789–90
  parentheses, 831
  and possessive case, 807–15
  quotation marks, 792–99
  semicolons, 770–74
  titles, 381, 780
Purpose
  describing a mechanism, 173
  literary analysis, 343
  personal narrative, 143
  persuasive essay, 295
  process paper, 258
  research paper, 372
  short story, 211
  writing process, 36–38
Purposeful listening, 908
Purposes for writing
  creative, 7, 20

expressive, 7, 20
informative, 7, 20
persuasive, 7, 20
Put, principal parts, 621

Question mark, 741
Questions. *See also* Tests.
   5W-How? questions, 22, 23, 29,
      242, 909
   for research paper, 374–75
   "What if?" questions, 33–34
   writing process, 29
Quiet, quite, 856
Quotation marks, 792–99
   and dialogue, 795–96
   to enclose direct quotation,
      792–93
   in literary analysis, 353
   in long passage, 798
   in multiple paragraphs, 797–98
   with other marks of punctuation,
      794
   quotation within a quotation, 798
   single quotation marks, 798
   for titles of articles, short stories,
      etc., 799
Quotations
   in introduction, 122
   in note taking, 384
   reference books, 923
   in research paper, 397

Raise, rise, 641
"Raymond's Run," 215
Readers' Guide to Periodical Literature,
   921
Readers' interest, in introduction, 120
Reading
   focused, 31
   graphics and illustrations, 953–54
Reading script, in oral interpretation,
   904–905
Reading skills, 947–62
   conclusions, 952–53
   finding relationships among
      details, 950–52
   identifying main idea, 950

inferences, 952–53
interpreting and analyzing
   information, 950–52
invalid conclusion, 953
note taking, 955–56
reasoning, 952–53
strategies, 955–62
valid conclusion, 953
Reality, television and, 916
Reasoning
   circular, 299–300
   evaluating, 299–301
Reasoning or logic questions, in tests,
   965–66
Rebound, 75
Recall, 180
Reference books. *See also* Information
   sources.
   almanacs, 923
   atlases, 923
   biographical references, 923
   dictionaries, 925–27
   encyclopedias, 923
   literature, 924
   quotations, 923
   *Readers' Guide to Periodical
      Literature*, 921
   synonyms, 924
   thesaurus, 924
Reflecting, 58
   composition, 131
   informative essay, 276
   literary analysis, 354
   on objective description, 194
   paragraph, 103
   personal narrative, 159
   persuasion, 314
   research paper, 400
Reflexive pronoun, 471
Regional dialects, 448–49
Regrets (letters), 943
Regular comparison of modifiers
   multiple-syllable modifier, 676
   one-syllable modifier, 675
   two-syllable modifier, 676
Regular verb, defined, 618
Relative pronoun, 471, 567–68
Report—From part one, 16–18
Request letters, 940–41
Research and nonprint media, 405
Research paper, 369–401
   audience, 372
   basic elements of, 388
   choosing a topic, 369–71
   direct quotations, 384, 397

early plan, 383
evaluating and revising, 397–98
evaluating information sources,
    377–78
footnotes, 391
giving credit to sources, 390–96
I-Search report, 402–403
information sources, 376–81
limiting the topic, 370
locating information sources,
    376–77
note cards, 378, 383–86
outline, 386–87
paraphrase note, 385
parenthetical citations, 390–91
plagiarism, 377
prewriting, 369–87
proofreading and publishing, 400
purpose, 372
reflecting, 400
research questions, 374–75
revising, 397–98
source cards, 378–81
sources in the body of the paper,
    390–91
suitability of topic, 371
summary note, 385
taking notes, 383–86
tone, 373
works cited, 392
writer's model, 392–96
writing a first draft, 388–96
Research questions, for research
    paper, 374–75
Restatements, and vocabulary, 930
Restrictive clause or phrase. *See*
    Essential clause or phrase.
Review writing, 359–61
Revising
    content, 51
    guidelines for, 54
    literary analysis, 350–51
    of object description, 192–93
    organization, 51
    personal narrative, 157
    persuasive essay, 310–13
    process paper, 273–74
    research paper, 397–98
    short story, 233–34
    style, 51
    symbols for revising and
        proofreading, 60
    techniques of adding, cutting,
        replacing, reordering, 52

writing process, 6, 21, 49–54
Ride, principal parts, 621
Ring, principal parts, 621
Rise, raise, 641
Roots
    Greek, 932
    Latin, 932
Run, principal parts, 621
Run-on sentence
    comma splice, 415
    defined, 415
    fused sentence, 415
    revising, 416–17
    revising with compound sentence,
        416
"Runaway, The," 165

S

"Saints in the Neighborhood," 98
Salutation, in a business letter, 939
Scarcely, hardly, 712
Science, 281–82
Second-person point of view, 174
"Secret World of Pandas, The,"
    278–79
–sede, –cede, –ceed, spelling rule for, 839
See, principal parts, 621
Self– (prefix), 827
Self-evaluation, writing process, 49
Semicolon, 770–74
    and compound sentence, 428
    within compound sentence, 416
    with conjunctive adverbs, 416
    between independent clauses
        joined by conjunctive adverbs
        or transitional expressions, 772
    between independent clauses
        joined by coordinating
        conjunction when clauses
        contain commas, 773
    between independent clauses not
        joined by *and*, etc., 770–71
    between items in a series
        containing commas, 774
"Sense and Sensibility," 125, 127
Senses, use in writing process, 30
Sensory details, 178
    defined, 71
    and linking verbs, 521
    in a paragraph, 71–72
Sentence
    adjective placement in, 474–75

beginnings, varying, 436–37
classified by purpose, 527–28
classified by structure, 577–78
clincher, 75
combining, 421–31
complex, 578
compound, 416, 577–78
compound-complex, 578
declarative, 527
defined, 406, 501
diagraming, 978–93
exclamatory, 528
fragment, 406–14
imperative, 527
interrogative, 527–28
kinds of, 527–28
in poetry, 419
punctuating, 741–43
run-on, 415–17
simple, 577
stringy, 433–34
supporting, 71–73
topic, 69–70, 76
wordy, 435
Sentence fragment, 406–14
appositive phrase, 410
defined, 406, 501
phrase fragment, 409–10
prepositional phrase, 410
series of items, 413–14
subordinate clause fragment, 411–14
verbal phrase, 409
Sentence parts
complements, 517–24
objects, 522–24
predicate, 502–16
subject, 502–16
Sentence structure, 577–78
Sentence style, 432–37
beginnings, varying, 436–37
parallel structure, 432–33
stringy sentences, 433–34
wordy sentence, 435
Sequence of events, and paragraph
unity, 77
Series of items
punctuating, 746–47, 774
as sentence fragment, 413–14
Set, sit, 639–40
Setting
of fictional literature and TV, 915
literary analysis, 334
short story, 215–16
Several, few, both, many, 594
Shake, principal parts, 621

She, he, they, 704
Shone, shown, 857
Short-answer questions, in tests, 969–70
Short story, 209–41
analyzing, 221–29
audience, 211–12
basic elements, 220–21
characters, 215, 220–21
conflict, 217, 334
creating interest, 220
dialogue, 221, 239
ending, 221
evaluating and revising, 233–34
framework, 229–32
literary analysis, 338–45
mood, 334
narrator, 213
plot, 217–18
point of view, 213–14
prewriting steps, 209–19
proofreading, 239
proofreading and publishing, 239–40
publishing, 240
purpose, 211
reflecting, 240
setting, 215–16
story ideas, 209–10
story map, 218–19
story plan, 211–19
theme, 211
tone, 212
writer's model, 230–32
writing a first draft, 220–32
Should of, 701
Shown, shone, 857
Shrink, principal parts, 621
Signature, in a business letter, 939
Silko, Leslie Marmon, 419
Simile, 196
Simple predicate, 505–506
Simple sentence, defined, 577
Simple subject, defined, 504
"Singing Well, The," 450
Single-word modifier, and varying
sentence beginnings, 437
Sink, principal parts, 621
Sit, set, 639–40
"Six Rows of Pompons, The," 222–29
Sketch, biographical, 246–47
Skit, humorous, 245–46
"Skunk Dreams," from *The Blue Jay's
Dance,* 134–37
Slang, 453–54
So, 429
Social introductions, 898

Social studies and persuasion, 320–21
Software. *See* Computer software.
Some
    all, most, any, none, 594–95
    somewhat, 708
Somewheres, 698
Sort, kind, type, 704
Sound effects, in TV, 916
Source cards, for research paper,
    378–81
Spatial order, 80, 115
Speak, principal parts, 621
Speaking
    communication cycle, 896
    formal, 898–902
    group discussions, 902–903
    impromptu speech, 897
    informal, 897–98
    nonverbal communication, 897
    oral interpretation, 904–905
    speech delivery, 901
    speech preparation, 898–99
    techniques for speaking
        expressively, 900–901
Speech
    extemporaneous, 900
    impromptu, 897
Speech delivery, 901
Speech preparation
    audience, 899–900
    note cards, 900
    organizing notes and materials, 900
    outline, 900
    selecting a topic, 899
    speaking expressively, 900–901
Spell-checking program, 353
Spelling
    –cede, –ceed, and *–sede,* 839
    dictionary as an aid, 837
    final consonants and suffix, 843
    final *e* before suffix, 841–42
    good habits, 836–38
    ie and *ei,* 839
    learning word list, 861 63
    –ness, –ly, 840–41
    numbers, 849
    plurals of nouns, 844–47
    prefixes, 840
    pronunciation as an aid, 836
    rules for, 839–49
    spelling notebook as an aid, 838
    studying as an aid, 836
    suffixes, 840–43
    syllables as an aid, 837

words commonly misspelled, list
    of, 860–61
words ending in *y* and suffix, 842
words often confused, 850–59
writing as an aid, 836
SQ3R study method, 949
St. John, Marie, 41–42, 163–64
Stafford, William, 11
"Stand and Deliver," 360–61
Standard American English, 449–51
Standard English, 449–51, 697
Starr, Roger, 152–53
Stationary, stationery, 857
Statistics
    defined, 72
    in a paragraph, 72–73
    in persuasion, 297
Steal, principal parts, 621
Stereotypes, 916
Sting, principal parts, 621
Stokes, Donald, 73
Stokes, Lillian, 73
Story map, 218–19
Storytelling, 91–92
Strategies for writing
    classification, 89, 94–96
    description 89, 90
    evaluation 89, 97–98
    narration 89, 91–93
"Streetcars on Penn Avenue," 168–69
Strike, principal parts, 621
Stringy sentence, 433–34
Study skills, 947–62
    analyzing graphics and
        illustrations, 953–54
    classification, 957
    conclusions, 952–53
    identifying main idea, 950
    inferences, 952–53
    interpreting and analyzing
        information, 950–52
    LQ2R study method, 910
    memorizing, 962
    methods, 955–62
    note taking, 955–56
    organizing information visually,
        957–58
    outlining, 958–59
    paraphrasing, 959–60
    reading and understanding, 947
    reasoning skills, 952–53
    recognizing relationships among
        details, 950–52
    routine, 946

SQ3R method, 949
summarizing, 961
writing to learn, 947–49
Style, sentence structure, 432–37
Subject, 502–16
  agreement with verb, 590–605
  complete, 503, 504
  compound, 514
  defined, 502
  double, 704
  how to find, 508–10
  never in prepositional phrase, 509
  pronoun, nominative case, 651
  in questions, 510–11
  in sentences beginning with *There,*
    511–13
  simple, distinguished from
    complete, 504–505
  understood, 513
Subject card, 919
Subject complement, 519
Subjective description, 175, 196–98
Subject-verb agreement. *See*
    Agreement, subject-verb.
Subordinate clause
  adjective clause, 567–68
  adverb clause, 412, 570–71
  and complex sentence, 430
  defined, 564
  noun clause, 574–75
  placement of, 565
  as sentence fragment, 411–14
  uses of, 567–75
  and varying sentence beginnings, 437
  who, whom in, 662–63
Subordinating conjunctions, 571–72
Subtitles, punctuating, 780
Suffixes
  drop final *e,* 841
  and final consonants, 843
  Greek, Latin, and French, 934
  hyphens and, 827
  keep final *e,* 841–42
  –ness or *–ly,* 840–41
  Old English, 934
  words ending in *y,* 842
Summary
  in conclusion, 127
  in note taking, 385, 912
  as study skill, 961
Superlative degree of comparison,
    680–84
Supporting sentences, in a
    paragraph, 71–73
Supporting your opinion
  emotional appeals, 298–99

logical appeals, 297–98
  for persuasive essay, 297–301
Swear, principal parts, 621
Swift, E. M., 304–305
Swim, principal parts, 621
Syllables
  as an aid to spelling, 837
  defined, 837
  and dividing words at end of line,
    826
Symbols for revising and
    proofreading, 60
Synonyms
  in dictionaries, 927
  reference books, 924
  and vocabulary, 930
Syntax. *See* Sentence structure.
Synthesis, defined, 46
Synthesizing ideas, 46–47

Tables, 147
Take, bring, 699
Take, principal parts, 621
Taking notes. *See* Note taking.
"Tale of the Rodent," 152–53
Teach, learn, 704
Teale, Edwin Way, 408
Tear, principal parts, 621
Technical writing, 172–95
Telephone communication, 898
Television. *See* Fictional literature and
    TV.
Tense
  conjugation of *give,* 629–31
  consistency of, 631
  defined, 629–30
Testimonial, as persuasive technique
    of mass media, 913
Tests, 962–72
  analogy questions, 966–69
  essay test questions, 971–72
  essay tests, 970–72
  matching questions, 965
  multiple-choice questions, 964
  objective tests, 963–70
  preparing for, 962
  reasoning or logic questions, 965–66
  short-answer questions, 969–70
  true/false questions, 964–65
Than, then, 708, 857
Thank-you letters, 942
That, which, who, 709
The, 474

Their, there, they're, 857
Them, 708
Theme, literary analysis, 335
Thesaurus, 126, 178
Thesis statement, 111–12, 120, 123
They, she, he, 704
Thinking. *See* Critical thinking.
Third-person point of view, 173,
 213–14, 335
This here, that there, 708
Threw, through, 858
Throw, principal parts, 621
Time line, 44
"Time We Climbed Snake Mountain,
 The," 419
Tired words, 459
Title card, 919
Titles
 agreement, subject-verb, 604
 punctuating, 381, 780
To, too, two, 858
"To Build a Fire," 83–84
Tone
 describing a mechanism, 173–74
 introduction, 120
 literary analysis, 343
 personal narrative, 143–44
 persuasive essay, 295
 process paper, 258
 research paper, 373
 short story, 212
Topic
 evaluating in personal narrative, 141
 for persuasive essay, 291–93
 for research paper, 369–71
Topic sentence
 importance of, 69–70
 location of, 69
 in a paragraph, 69–70
 and unity, 76
Transitional expressions
 and coherence, 84–86
 in composition, 124–25
 defined, 83, 84
 examples of, 773
Transitive verb, 478
True/false questions, in tests, 964–65
"Trust Your Material," 127
Type, kind, sort, 704

Unabridged dictionaries, 925
Underlining (italics). *See* Italics
 (underlining).

Understood subject, 513
Unity
 in composition, 124
 in a paragraph, 76–77
Unless, without, 709
Usage. *See also* Agreement; English
 language; Modifiers; Pronoun;
 Verb.
 common problems, 696–709
 double negative, 711–12
Usage labels, in dictionaries, 927

Van Tilburg Clark, Walter, 86
Variety in sentences, varying
 sentence structure, 274, 436–37
Vecsey, George, 70
Verb, 477–83
 action, 477, 522
 active voice, 633–35
 agreement with subject, 590–605
 compound, 515
 conjugation, 629–30
 defined, 477
 helping, 482, 515
 intransitive, 478
 irregular, 620–22
 lie, lay, 637–38
 linking, 480, 519
 passive voice, 633–35
 principal parts, 618–31
 progressive forms, 630–31
 regular, 618–19
 rise, raise, 641
 simple predicate, 505–506
 sit, set, 639–40
 tense, 629–31
 transitive, 478
Verb phrases, 482–83
Verbal phrase, 541–56
 defined, 409
 gerund phrase, 548–49
 infinitive phrase, 551–52
 participial phrase, 544–45
 as sentence fragment, 409
Verbals, 541–56
 defined, 409
 gerund, 546–47
 infinitive, 550
 participle, 541–42
 past participle, 542
 present participle, 541–42

Vertical file, 921
"Victims, The," 123
Viewing, critical, 914–16
Visualizing, writing process, 34–35
Vocabulary
    antonyms, 930
    cause and effect, 930
    choosing the right word, 931
    context clues, 930–31
    definitions, 930
    examples, 930
    general context, 931
    prefixes, 933
    restatements, 930
    roots, 932
    suffixes, 934
    synonyms, 930
    word bank, 929
    word parts, 931–34
Voice
    active and passive, 633
    natural writing, 38

W

Waist, waste, 858
Ward, Geoffrey C., 41
Way, ways, 708
Way Things Work, The, 174
Weak, week, 859
Wear, principal parts, 621
Weather, whether, 859
Webbing, 27
Well, comparison of, 677
Well, good, 701
"What if?" questions
    visualization and, 34–35
    writing process, 33–34
When, where, 708
Which, that, who, 709
Who, whom, 662–65
Who's, whose, 859
Wilson, August, 286–88
Without, unless, 709
"Without Title," 200
Wolkomir, Richard, 364–66
"Woods Were Tossing With Jewels,
    The," 41–42, 163–64
Word bank, 178, 929
Word forms, in dictionaries, 926, 927
Word parts
    prefixes, 933
    roots, 932
    suffixes, 934
    and vocabulary, 931–34
Word processor, reading and study
    skills, 948–49. *See also* Computer
    software.
Words
    choosing the right word, 931
    commonly misspelled, list of,
        860–61
    compound, 826
    hyphenated, 826
    often confused (spelling), 850–59
    one-syllable, 826
    rules for dividing at end of line,
        826
    spelling words, 861–63
Wordy sentence, 435
"Work and What It's Worth," 39
Workplace skills
    business letters, 937–42
    classified ad, 199
    technical writing, 172–95
Works Cited, in research paper, 392
World Wide Web, 377
Wornom, Howard, 122
Would of, 701
Write, principal parts, 621
Writers at Work, 350
Writer's journal, 23
Writer's model, of objective
    description, 188–89
Writing, reading and study skills,
    947–49
Writing a first draft
    describing a mechanism, 186–90
    literary analysis, 346–49
    personal narrative, 151–56
    persuasive essay, 303–309
    process paper, 264–72
    research paper, 388–96
    short story, 220–32
    writing process, 21, 45–47
Writing Across the Curriculum,
    281–82, 359
Writing and science, 281–82
Writing Application
    adjectives, 476
    agreement, subject-verb, 596–97
    apostrophes, 815–16
    capitalization, 734–35
    colons, 782–83
    commas, 765
    comparative and superlative
        degrees of modifiers, 684–85
    linking verbs, 521
    prepositional phrase, 540–41

quotation marks, 796–97
standard English, 713–15
variety of sentence structure,
    580–81
verb tense, 631–32
Writing Life, The, 92
Writing process. *See also* Evaluating
    and revising; Prewriting;
    Proofreading and publishing;
    Revising; Writing a first draft.
arranging ideas, 40–44
asking questions, 29
audience, 36–39
brainstorming, 25–26
charts, 43–44
clustering, 27–28
evaluating and revising, 6, 21,
    49–54
finding ideas for writing, 22–35
5W-How? questions, 29
focused freewriting, 24
focused listening, 32
focused reading, 31
freewriting, 24
looping, 24
peer evaluation, 49–50
prewriting, 6, 21, 22–44
proofreading and publishing, 6,
    21, 56–60
purpose, 20, 36–38
reflecting, 58
self-evaluation, 49

stages, 20–21
using five senses, 30
visualizing, 34–35
webbing, 27
"What if?" questions, 33–34
writer's journal, 23
writing a first draft, 6, 21, 45–47
Writing Workshop
cause-and-effect essay, 278–80
definitions, 356–58
I-Search report, 402–403
journal, 161–62
letter to editor, 316–17
news story, 242–44
subjective description, 196–98

Xueyu, Gao, 278–79

Your, you're, 859

Zinsser, William, 127

Acknowledgments

For permission to reprint copyrighted material, grateful acknowledgment is made to the following sources:

Aladdin Paperbacks, an imprint of Simon & Schuster: From *Airborne Again! The Triumph and Struggle of Michael Jordan* by Jesse Kornbluth. Copyright © 1995, 1996 by Jesse Kornbluth.

Andrews and McMeel: From "Stand and Deliver" from *Roger Ebert's Movie Home Companion 1990 Edition* by Roger Ebert. Copyright © 1990 by Roger Ebert. All rights reserved.

Ronald Arias: From "El Mago" by Ronald Arias from *El Grito: A Journal of Contemporary Mexican-American Thought,* Spring 1970.

Arte Público Press: "Bribe" from *Chants* by Pat Mora. Copyright © 1985 by Pat Mora. Published by Arte Público Press, University of Houston, 1985.

Associated Press: From "Flood Is Called Right Tonic for Grand Canyon" from *The New York Times,* National Edition, April 14, 1996. Copyright © 1996 by Associated Press.

R. Bemis Publishing, Ltd: From *The Everglades: River of Grass* by Marjory Stoneman Douglas. Copyright 1947 by Marjory Stoneman Douglas.

Bicycling Magazine: From "Are Road Bikes Dead?" by Scott Martin from *Bicycling,* vol. XXXI, no. 5, June 1990. Copyright © 1990 by Bicycling magazine.

Broadside Press: From *Report From Part One* by Gwendolyn Brooks. Copyright © 1972 by Gwendolyn Brooks Blakely.

The Caxton Printers, Ltd.: "The Six Rows of Pompons" from *Yokohama, California* by Toshio Mori. Published by The Caxton Printers, Ltd., Caldwell, Idaho.

Clarion Books/Houghton Mifflin Company: From "The Victims" from *Masters of Horror* by Daniel Cohen.

Copyright © 1984 by Daniel Cohen. All rights reserved.

Daniel Cohen and Henry Morrison, Inc.: From "Bigfoot" and "Jackalope" from *Encyclopedia of Monsters* by Daniel Cohen. Copyright © 1982 by Daniel Cohen.

Eugenia Collier: From "Marigolds" by Eugenia Collier from *Negro Digest,* November 1969. Copyright © 1969 by Eugenia Collier.

Estate of Roald Dahl and the Watkins/Loomis Agency: From "Poison" from *Someone Like You* by Roald Dahl. Copyright 1950 by Roald Dahl.

Discover Magazine: From "Humpback Poets" from "Whale Watch" by Mark Kemp from *Discover,* July 1989. Copyright © 1989 by Mark Kemp.

Doubleday, a division of Bantam Doubleday Dell Publishing Group, Inc.: From "The Birds" from *Kiss Me Again Stranger* by Daphne du Maurier. Copyright 1952 by Daphne du Maurier.

Dutton Signet, a division of Penguin Books USA Inc.: From *The Piano Lesson* by August Wilson. Copyright © 1988, 1990 by August Wilson.

EBSCO Publishing: From "Yellowstone National Park" to "Pinaleno Mountains (Ariz.)" from *(MAS FullTEXT Select) CD-ROM database.*

Entertainment Weekly: From "Dark Side of the Moon" by Owen Gleiberman (movie review of *Apollo 13*) from *Entertainment Weekly,* June 30, 1995. Copyright © 1995 by Time Inc.

Charlotte St. John Evans: From "The Woods Were Tossing with Jewels" by Marie St. John, edited by Charlotte St. John.

Facts On File, Inc.: From *Marching Toward Freedom: Blacks in the Civil War 1861–1865* by James M. McPherson. Copyright © 1965, 1967, 1991 by James M. McPherson.

Simon & Schuster Books for Young Readers, an imprint of Simon & Schuster Children's Publishing Division: From "Light Bulb" from *The Macmillan Book of How Things Work* by Michael Folsom and Marcia Folsom. Text copyright © 1987 by Michael Folsom and Marcia Folsom.

Sports Illustrated: From "Calling Arthur Murray" by F. M. Swift from *Sports Illustrated*, April 24, 1995, p. 72. Copyright © 1995 by Time Inc. All rights reserved.

The Estate of William Stafford: "Fifteen" from *Stories That Could Be True* by William Stafford. Copyright © 1977 by William Stafford. Published by HarperCollins.

Thames & Hudson Ltd.: From "What is a mummy?" from *Mummies, Myth and Magic in Ancient Egypt* by Christine El Mahdy. Copyright © 1989 by Thames & Hudson Ltd.

Rosemary Thurber: From "The Scotty Who Knew Too Much" from *Fables for Our Time* by James Thurber. Copyright © 1940 by James Thurber, copyright © 1968 by Helen Thurber. Published by HarperCollins Publishers, Inc.

Time Inc. From "Saints in the Neighborhood" by Richard Corliss (movie review of *Anne Frank Remembered*) from *Time*, March 4, 1996, p. 62. Copyright © 1996 by Time Inc.

University of Connecticut Library, Storrs: From "The Death of a Tree" from *Dune Boy* by Edwin Way Teale. Copyright 1943, © 1971 by Edwin Way Teale. All rights reserved.

University of Notre Dame Press: From *Barrio Boy* by Ernesto Galarza. Copyright © 1971 by University of Notre Dame Press.

USA Today: From "Ray Charles: His career milestones" from *USA Today*, September 25, 1990. Copyright © 1990 by USA Today.

Viking Penguin, a division of Penguin Books USA Inc.: From "Ralph Ellison" by Alfred Chester and Vilma Howard from *Writers at Work: The Paris Review Interviews*, Second Series, edited by George A. Plimpton, introduced by Van Wyck Brook. Copyright © 1963 by The Paris Review. From *Rebound: The Odyssey of Michael Jordan* by Bob Greene. Copyright © 1995 by John Deadline Enterprises, Inc. From "One Perfect Rose" from *The Portable Dorothy Parker*, introduction by Brendan Gill. Copyright 1929 and renewed © 1957 by Dorothy Parker.

The H. W. Wilson Company: From "Campbell, Lawrence, 1914" to "Camps" from *Readers' Guide to Periodical Literature*, vol. 96, no. 2, April 1996. Copyright © 1996 by The H. W. Wilson Company.

Jon Winokur: Quotes by Bernard Malamud, Toni Morrison, Dorothy Parker, and Ezra Pound from *Writers on Writing*, selected and compiled by Jon Winokur. Copyright © 1986, 1990 by Jon Winokur.

Richard Wolkomir: From "The Cold Facts About Human Survival" by Richard Wolkomir from *National Wildlife* Magazine, Dec. 1990/Jan. 1991. Copyright © 1991 by Richard Wolkomir.

World Book, Inc.: From "Camera" by Lawrence R. White from *The World Book Encyclopedia*. Copyright © 1996 World Book, Inc.

The Wylie Agency, Inc.: "The Time We Climbed Snake Mountain" by Leslie Marmon Silko. Copyright © 1981 by Leslie Marmon Silko.

William K. Zinsser: From "Trust Your Material" from *On Writing Well*, Third Edition by William Zinsser. Copyright © 1976, 1980, 1985, 1988 by William K. Zinsser.

PHOTO CREDITS

Abbreviations used: (t)top, (c)center, (b)bottom, (l)left, (r)right, (bkgd) background.

COVER: Postcard of *The Washington Capitol Building*, taken by David Noble, is used on the cover courtesy of Capsco, Inc.; Ralph J. Brunke Photograph.

TABLE OF CONTENTS: Page vi, Bill Tague/The Contemporary Forum; vii(t,c,b), Joe and Kathy Heinre/Stockworks; ix(br), A. Eurard/Viesti Associates, Inc.; x(t), Barry Seidman/The Stock Market; xii(t), Culver Pictures; xiv(tr), R. Batzdorff/Universal/Shooting Star; xv(r), Schuster/SuperStock; xvii(tr), Shostal Associates/SuperStock; xvii(cl), Manley Features/Shostal/SuperStock; xxi(br), Mike Powell/Allsport; xxii(b), Bob Daemmrich/The Image Works; xxv(b), Antonin Novy/Wide World Photos; xxvi(c), Eric Brissaud/Gamma Liaison; xxvii(br), Bob Daemmrich/The Image Works; xxxii(b), Joseph A. DiChello, Jr.; xxxv(t), Jeffrey W. Myers/Nawrocki Stock Photo; xxxvi(cr), Kevin R. Morris/Tony Stone Images; xxxvi(bl), Bob Aldman/Magnum Photos.

INTRODUCTION: Pages 2–3, David Joel/Tony Stone Images/Chicago, Inc.; 4, Mike Valeri/FPG International; 5, Ron Chapple/FPG International; 6, Joseph A. DiChello, Jr.; 7, Robert Frerck/Tony Stone Images/Chicago, Inc.; 12, Dave Stoecklein/The Stock Market.

CHAPTER 1: Page 17, Bill Tague/The Contemporary Forum; 25, Henry T. Kaiser/The Picture Cube; 26(cl), John Launois/Black Star; 26(cr), SuperStock; 27, Jeffry W. Myers/Nawrocki Stock Photo; 29, David R. Frazier Photolibrary; 32(l), Everett Collection, Inc.; 32(tr), Sygma; 32(tl), Kevin R. Morris/Tony Stone Images; 32(br), Eric Robert/Sygma; 32(bc), Larry Busacca/Retna Ltd.; 32(t), Les Stone/Sygma; 32(c), Victor Malaf/Archive Newsphotos; 34, HRW Photo by John Langford; 35, H. McManners/Ace/Nawrocki Stock Photo; 37, 42, The Bettmann Archive; 43, SuperStock; 47(bl), Farrell Grehan/FPG International; 47(bc), Mary Kate Denny/PhotoEdit; 47(br), Suzanne L. Murphy/FPG International; 48, Nawrocki Stock Photo; 50, T. Rosenthal/SuperStock; 51, Costa Manos/Magnum Photos, Inc.; 55, Mark M. Walker/The Picture Cube.

CHAPTER 2: Pages 62–63, Joe and Kathy Heinre/Stock Works; 70, David R. Frazier Photolibrary; 72, Culver Pictures; 73, Calvin Larsen/Photo Researchers, Inc.; 75, Barry Gossage/NBA/Allsport USA; 78, Rick Friedman/Black Star; 86, Four by Five/SuperStock; 87, C. May/SuperStock; 88(t), Nathan Bilow/Allsport USA; 88(b), R. Walker/H. Armstrong Roberts; 92, Charles Krebs/Allstock/Tony Stone Images; 95(cl)(c), Manfred Cage/Peter Arnold, Inc.; 95(cr), R. Knauft/Biology Media/Photo Researchers, Inc.; 100, Peter Gregg/Imagery; 101, Steve Elmore/Tony Stone Images/Chicago, Inc.

CHAPTER 3: Page 110(bl), Tony Freeman/PhotoEdit; 110(br), Tony Stone Images/Chicago, Inc.; 114, HBJ Photo by Bob Daemmrich; 119(tl,cl), CNRI/Science Photo Library/Photo Researchers, Inc.; 122, Everett Collection; 125, Clive Coote/Columbia/TriStar/Archive Photos; 126, Photolabs/Royal Observatory, Edinburgh; 128, Brian Yarvin/Peter Arnold, Inc.

CHAPTER 4: Pages 132–133, Viesti Associates; 139(l)(cl), HRW Photo by Ken Lax; 139(cr), HRW Photo by Russell Dian; 139(r), HRW Photo Research Library; 142(l), Tony Freeman/PhotoEdit; 142(r), Myrleen Ferguson/PhotoEdit; 146, Laura Dwight/Peter Arnold, Inc.; 147, George Mars Cassidy/The Picture Cube; 151, Runk/Schoenberger/Grant Heilman Photography; 155, Shoes courtesy of RunTex, Austin, Texas/HRW Photo by John Langford; 164, Lewis H. Ellsworth/SuperStock.

CHAPTER 5: Page 172(l) Greim/The Stock Shop; 172(r), Tony Freeman/PhotoEdit; 173, Peter Menzel; 175(r), Claude Charlier/The Stock Market; 175(l), 176(t), Tony Freeman/PhotoEdit; 177, Runk/Schoenberger/Grant Heilman; 179, Barry Seidman/The Stock Market; 180, Kevin Syma/David R. Frazier Photolibrary; 183, David Lawrence/The Stock Market; 184, Ron Wyatt/Sportschrome, Inc.; 199(l), Frink/Waterhouse/H. Armstrong Roberts; 199(r), Harry Ausloos/ Animals, Animals; 201, Les Campbell/Positive Images.

CHAPTER 6: Page 209(l), Photofest; 209(b), Overseas Film Group/Shooting Star, 209(r), Hollywood Pictures/Shooting Star; 213, Culver Pictures; 214, Joseph A. DiChello, Jr.; 216(l), Linda Dufurrena/Grant Heilman; 216(c), SuperStock; 216(inset), David R. Frazier Photolibrary; 216(r), Marc Muench/David Muench Photography, Inc.; 217, Shooting Star; 238(l), Michael Brohm/Nawrocki Stock Photo; 238(c), Reed Kaestner/Nawrocki Stock Photo; 238(r), W. J. Scott/H. Armstrong Roberts; 245(l)(r), Photoworld/FPG International; 245(c), FPG International; 246, HRW Photo by Daniel Schaefer; 247, Eddie Sanderson/Shooting Star.

CHAPTER 7: Pages 250, 251, 252, Culver Pictures; 255, Vandystadt/Allsport USA; 257, Tony Freeman/PhotoEdit; 259, Joe McDonald/Animals, Animals; 265, Courtesy of Columbia Pictures; 267, HRW Photo by Daniel Schaefer; 268, Lance Schriner; 271, Jerry Howard/Positive Images; 279, Jeffrey Sylvester/FPG International; 283, HRW Photo by Eric Beggs.

CHAPTER 8: Page 293, Mel Digiacomo/The Image Bank; 294(l), HRW Photo by Daniel Shaefer; 294(r), Andy Sacks/Tony Stone Images; 296, HRW Photo by Emily Werbow; 298, Lance Schriner; 301, HRW Photo by Rodney Jones; 305, Gay Eklanger Davis/Doré Studios; 308, Tony Freeman/PhotoEdit; 310, Frank Wolf; 315(l),

ILLUSTRATION CREDITS

Brian Battles—xxviii, xxxiii, 30, 66, 97, 116, 408, 435, 527, 574, 623, 652, 820, 925

Kate Beetle—204, 207, 253

Kim Behm—13, 108, 327, 349, 367

Linda Blackwell—19, 127, 150, 194, 274, 310, 329, 397

Mary Lynn Blasutta—233

Keith Bowden—vi, 17, 47, 70, 161, 214, 217, 245, 255, 280, 293, 366, 442, 449, 503, 545, 569, 596, 601, 754, 764, 771, 809

Rondi Collette—139

Chris Ellison—169

Richard Erickson—xiii, xvii, 248, 249, 288, 289, 332, 445, 679, 801

Janice Fried—355

Tom Gianni—181

John Hanley—xxvi, 220, 279, 319, 438, 643, 703, 710, 713, 775

Tom Herzberg—331

Linda Kelen—33, 46, 73, 121, 193, 282, 303, 312, 316, 407, 453, 455, 460, 645, 711

Susan B. Kemnitz—74, 147, 231, 232

Judy Love—xi, 84, 222, 223, 224, 227, 661

Yoshi Miyake—78, 106, 165, 189, 359, 591, 700–701, 844

Richard Murdock—251, 253

Precision Graphics—625

Preface, Inc.,—125, 176, 180, 760, 954

Linda Reilly—64, 65, 197

Jack Scott—286, 497

Steve Shock—107, 324, 325, 357, 848

Chuck Solway—170, 190

Sam Thiewes—91

Troy Thomas—134–135, 136

Nancy Tucker—69, 81, 112, 153

Bob Voigts—187

Jim Williams—205, 206